# Achieving Sustainability in Multi-Industry Settings With AI

Muhammad Syafrudin
*Sejong University, South Korea*

Norma Latif Fitriyani
*Sejong University, South Korea*

Muhammad Anshari
*Universiti Brunei Darussalam, Brunei*

IGI Global
Scientific Publishing
Publishing Tomorrow's Research Today

Vice President of Editorial	Melissa Wagner
Managing Editor of Acquisitions	Mikaela Felty
Managing Editor of Book Development	Jocelynn Hessler
Production Manager	Mike Brehm
Cover Design	Phillip Shickler

Published in the United States of America by
IGI Global Scientific Publishing
701 East Chocolate Avenue
Hershey, PA, 17033, USA
Tel: 717-533-8845
Fax: 717-533-8661
Website: https://www.igi-global.com E-mail: cust@igi-global.com



Library of Congress Cataloging-in-Publication Data

Names: Syafrudin, Muhammad, 1990- editor | Fitriyani, Norma Latif, 1992- editor | Anshari, Muhammad, 1977- editor
Title: Achieving sustainability in multi-industry settings with AI / edited by Muhammad Syafrudin, Norma Latif Fitriyani, Muhammad Anshari.
Description: Hershey, PA : IGI Global Scientific Publishing, [2025] |
Includes bibliographical references and index. | Summary: "The book explores the applications of artificial intelligence (AI) techniques and methodologies in addressing various sustainability challenges. The publication will delve into the intersection of AI and sustainability, showcasing how AI technologies, including machine learning, deep learning, computer vision, natural language processing, and optimization algorithms, can be harnessed to develop innovative solutions for environmental, economic, business, and social sustainability challenges"-- Provided by publisher.
Identifiers: LCCN 2025003460 (print) | LCCN 2025003461 (ebook) | ISBN 9798337325309 hardcover | ISBN 9798337325316 paperback | ISBN 9798337325323 ebook
Subjects: LCSH: Sustainable development | Artificial intelligence--Industrial applications
Classification: LCC HC79.E5 A26643 2025 (print) | LCC HC79.E5 (ebook) |
DDC 338.9/27028563--dc23/eng/20250326
LC record available at https://lccn.loc.gov/2025003460
LC ebook record available at https://lccn.loc.gov/2025003461

British Cataloguing in Publication Data
A Cataloguing in Publication record for this book is available from the British Library.

# Editorial Advisory Board

## Editorial Advisory Board

# Table of Contents

# Detailed Table of Contents



Artificial Intelligence (AI), Data Science (DS) and the Internet of Things (IoT) are vast networks of many intelligent devices connected to each other and/or to other internet-connected objects via sensors, software and other embedded technologies. They make use of large data sources and offer easy identification of trends and patterns, improved automation, continuous development, easy processing of multidimensional data and low computing costs. The development of artificial intelligence and data science in renewable energy management has the potential to manage energy production sources and ensure the energy efficiency of installations. This chapter explores different AI application techniques based on deep learning in the areas of solar and wind power generation, smart grid management, and energy consumption in smart residential buildings. It shows that using AI to estimate prediction performance and uncertainty is an optimal model for solar and wind power generation, smart grid management and energy consumption in smart homes.



The demand for sustainable energy solutions is more important than ever as the globe struggles to address the twin issues of accelerated climate change and depleting conventional energy sources. In order to provide a stable, sustainable future for future generations, the search for greener, more efficient energy systems is not just about innovation but also about survival. The increasing significance of data science and artificial intelligence (AI) provides a path toward change and a ray of hope in this dire situation. "Leveraging AI to Promote Sustainable Energy Distribution," the chapter's title, delves into the revolutionary potential of artificial intelligence (AI) and data science to transform the global energy distribution and management landscape. This chapter seeks to shed light on the various ways that artificial intelligence (AI) might support the creation of sustainable energy infrastructures by a thorough examination of AI-driven techniques, ranging from peer-to-peer energy trading to predictive maintenance and grid optimization.



This chapter presents an overview of renewable energies and artificial intelligence, current status, benefits, challenges, characteristics, while advancing, concepts are deepened, as sample applications and successful cases of application of artificial intelligence and / or data science, demonstrating that the proper use of different tools, models and emerging technologies, can optimize processes, management, and even allow early detection of anomalies, allowing preventive and efficient measures to be taken, even in adverse conditions, complemented with some quantitative data that help to better visualize the importance and impact achieved. By improving efficiency and resilience, artificial intelligence accelerates the transition to a more sustainable energy system, supporting the global goals of emissions reduction and climate change mitigation. Artificial intelligence is revolutionizing energy efficiency management in renewable energy systems, improving resilience, optimizing operation and contributing to a faster and more sustainable transition to a clean energy future



Renewable energy, particularly biomass, plays a vital role in addressing global energy needs and mitigating climate change. The development of sustainable and accurate biomass estimation methods is crucial to meet these demands. This chapter explores the transformative impact of advancements in computer vision (CV) technologies on above-ground biomass (AGB) estimation, focusing on both ground-based and aerial remote sensing techniques. The chapter provides a comprehensive overview of CV applications in AGB estimation, including the use of UAVs, smartphones, and LiDAR for capturing forest structural parameters. Despite challenges related to dataset variability, model complexity, and logistical constraints in remote forest environments, this chapter discusses recent advancements and trends in CV methodologies that address these challenges. The chapter concludes with a discussion on open research issues and future recommendations for advancing biomass estimation using CV, aimed at supporting informed decision-making in forest conservation and climate change mitigation strategies.



This chapter presents the development and application of a machine learning-based maintenance need prediction system using regression models, focusing on a coal-fired thermal power station in Southern Africa. This study emerged from the need to address the inefficiencies in traditional maintenance practices at the power station, where the aging infrastructure has led to frequent equipment failures, costly repairs, and significant downtime. The chapter explores the steps taken to develop a predictive maintenance model using operational data from the power station, the selection and tuning of machine learning models, and the practical implications of deploying such a system in an industrial setting. The machine learning model demonstrated a high level of accuracy in predicting exceedance counts, which are critical indicators of potential equipment failures meaning that predictive maintenance system could effectively reduce downtime and prevent costly repairs.



The progress of technology necessitates the development of Battery Energy Storage Systems (BESS) to have improved performance, longer life, higher dependability, and more intelligent management strategies. A significant acceleration of calculations, the capturing of complicated mechanisms to increase forecast accuracy, and the optimisation of decisions based on full status information are all capabilities that can be achieved with machine learning. This makes it suitable for real-time management due to the computing efficiency it possesses. This chapter gives an outline of later advancements in Machine Learning, with the focus on the presentation of novel thoughts, strategies, and applications of machine learning innovations for Battery Energy Storage Systems. The chapter also elucidates various aspects of challenges, and discuss potential solutions, future avenues for exploration in Machine Learning within Battery Energy Storage Systems.


*R. Shipa, Avinashilingam Institute for Home Science and Higher Education for Women, India*
*Karuppasamy Periyakaruppan, Dayananda Sagar College of Engineering, India*
*U. Mithra, Avinashilingam Institute for Home Science and Higher Education for Women, India*
*K. Thrisha, Avinashilingam Institute for Home Science and Higher Education for Women, India*
*R. Saratha, Avinashilingam Institute for Home Science and Higher Education for Women, India*
*Rajapandian Varatharaj, Sri Ramakrishna Mission Vidyalaya College of Arts and Science, India*

In battery development, process from the discovery of a new material to testing the performance of the battery is a prolonged one. This time-consuming process can be overcome by implementing Artificial Intelligence (AI). The need for AI in lithium-ion batteries (LIBs) can predict the specific capacity, efficiency, performance, and durability of a battery earlier. It could aid in the development of the most reliable advanced batteries with reduced time consumption. Prospects of AI in LIBs can facilitate advanced predictions in terms of State-of-Art battery management systems (BMS) such as states of charge (SOC), health (SOH), available power (SoAP), and remaining useful life (RUL) of batteries by various methodologies of Machine Learning (ML). During a pandemic situation experimentation in the laboratory may be difficult however to give an insight and implement AI into research pave the way to do more innovation in their respective fields. An overview of the applications of AI in LIB predictions is discussed in this article based on a review of earlier research works worldwide.

Machine learning is enhancing the transportation system and the robotic process automation and artificial intelligence are used in autos to provide intelligent automation (IA), which allows autonomous vehicles to undergo digital transformation. Smart automation has the power to completely replace human interaction, guaranteeing enhanced safety and intelligent vehicle movement. With a comparative study, this article analyzes current approaches that use IoT, AI, and machine learning in autonomous cars. It is critical to comprehend risk-reduction technology as the sector transitions from manual to automated processes. The study outlines the theoretical drawbacks and advantages of autonomous technology, highlighting artificial intelligence's crucial role in vehicle management going forward. It makes recommendations for future lines of inquiry to further the advancement of autonomous car technology. This chapter focuses on the requirements for safety and the difficulties associated with autonomous cars, specifically with regard to object detection, cybersecurity and V2X privacy.



Sustainability is an emerging need in all service sectors of society. The legal sector, traditionally perceived as a traditional industry, is increasingly recognizing the importance of sustainability in practices and operations. The emergence of Artificial Intelligence based techniques provides new opportunities for enhancing access to justice, enhancing efficiency, and streamline workflows. However, the conventional legal system has some constraints and limitations that can impact its effectiveness and ability to provide justice. Hence, this chapter analyzes Artificial Intelligence and Machine Learning as a solution to the challenges. With the help of thorough investigations, this chapter provides a comprehensive study on the worldwide use of Artificial Intelligence-based applications fostering sustainable practices within the legal industry to improve society. By integrating Artificial Intelligence and Machine

available to guide users and answer queries anytime, enhancing convenience and user experience.

# Preface

In the face of a rapidly changing world marked by environmental challenges, evolving technologies, and the need for sustainable practices, artificial intelligence (AI) has emerged as a transformative tool across multiple industries. *Achieving Sustainability in Multi-Industry Settings with AI* explores the intersection of AI, sustainability, and industry, showcasing how AI can drive innovations that promote energy efficiency, optimize resource management, and contribute to greener practices in diverse sectors.

The application of AI to sustainability issues is not limited to one field or one type of technology. From energy systems to healthcare, legal practices to autonomous transportation, AI offers powerful solutions to optimize operations, enhance decision-making, and reduce the environmental impact of human activities. This book brings together leading experts in the fields of AI, machine learning, and sustainability to present cutting-edge advancements, providing both theoretical insights and practical examples of AI in action.

## CHAPTER OVERVIEW

### Chapter 1: Artificial Intelligence (AI) for Energy Efficiency and Renewable Energy Management

Francois Yonga explores AI applications in renewable energy management, focusing on solar and wind power generation, smart grid management, and energy consumption in smart buildings. The chapter highlights how AI can predict energy trends and optimize operations, paving the way for more efficient, sustainable energy systems.

## Chapter 2: Leveraging AI to Promote Sustainable Energy Distribution

Vinston R. and his co-authors delve into the role of AI in transforming global energy distribution systems. The chapter examines AI-driven techniques, such as predictive maintenance and grid optimization, and their potential to create sustainable energy infrastructures for the future.

## Chapter 3: Resilience and Impact of AI on Energy Efficiency Management in Renewable Energies

Karla Mariel Fabian and Antonio Ortega present an in-depth look at how AI enhances the resilience and efficiency of renewable energy systems. They explore the role of AI in optimizing energy management processes and early anomaly detection, essential for a sustainable energy future.

## Chapter 4: Harnessing AI for Precise AGB Estimation in Remote Areas: Advancing Sustainable Energy Management

Fajar W. Wijaya and his team focus on the application of AI in biomass estimation, particularly for remote regions. Using computer vision and remote sensing, the chapter addresses the challenges and breakthroughs in accurate biomass measurement, which plays a key role in energy management and conservation.

## Chapter 5: Machine Learning-Based Maintenance Need Prediction for a Power Station Case Study

Nicolla Fundira and Evangelista Nyakujipa explore the application of machine learning in predictive maintenance at a coal-fired thermal power station. The chapter demonstrates how machine learning can reduce downtime and enhance the efficiency of power station operations, offering a blueprint for AI-based predictive maintenance in energy production.

## Chapter 6: Machine Learning for Battery Energy Storage System (BESS)

Elango S. provides insights into the application of machine learning in optimizing battery energy storage systems. This chapter highlights how AI can improve BESS performance and management, ensuring better energy storage for renewable energy systems.

## Chapter 7: Artificial Intelligence in Lithium-Ion Battery Predictions: A Comparative Study

Shipa R. and co-authors review AI's role in predicting the performance and durability of lithium-ion batteries. By leveraging machine learning, AI accelerates the battery development process, helping improve efficiency in energy storage solutions.

## Chapter 8: Machine Learning for Safer Autonomous Vehicles: Tackling Traffic Detection and Collision in Smart Cities

Bhupinder Singh and his colleagues explore AI's potential in autonomous vehicle safety. This chapter focuses on using AI to tackle traffic detection, collision avoidance, and smart city integration, all contributing to safer, more efficient transportation systems.

## Chapter 9: Integrating Artificial Intelligence and Machine Learning for Sustainable Practices in the Legal Sector

Tanaya Das and her team discuss how AI and machine learning can make the legal sector more sustainable by enhancing efficiency, reducing waste, and improving access to justice. They provide a global perspective on how AI can streamline legal processes for a greener future.

## Chapter 10: AI for Cyber-Security in E-Health: Ensuring Security and Privacy of Patient's Data

Bhupinder Singh and his collaborators address the intersection of AI, cybersecurity, and healthcare. This chapter explores the role of AI in safeguarding patient data in the digital age, with a focus on privacy and security in e-health systems.

## Chapter 11: Empowering Celiac Disease Management: Integrating AI with Research Insights

Anoop Johny showcases AI's role in revolutionizing healthcare for chronic conditions such as celiac disease. The chapter discusses how AI-powered tools can enhance diagnosis, treatment, and patient management, improving outcomes in the healthcare sector.

## Chapter 12: Decoding New Languages: Leveraging AI for Language Understanding

Yabit Alas and Muhammad Anshari examine the role of AI in language learning. This chapter highlights how AI-driven tools can improve language proficiency, offering personalized learning experiences and overcoming traditional barriers in language acquisition.

## Chapter 13: Overviewing Biases in Generative AI-Powered Models in the Arabic Language

Mussa Abubakari explores the issue of bias in generative AI models, focusing on the Arabic language. The chapter addresses the challenges AI systems face in producing equitable and accurate outputs, advocating for the need for fairer AI models.

## Chapter 14: Supporting Consumer Protection in the Face of Greenwashing

Bhupinder Singh and his colleagues delve into the legal landscape surrounding greenwashing, using AI to combat misleading environmental claims. They discuss how AI can empower consumer protection and support sustainability in the marketplace.

## Chapter 15: Deep Learning-Driven Smart Fashion Recommender for Modern Shoppers

Tamilarasi K. and co-authors explore how AI, particularly deep learning, enhances the shopping experience through personalized fashion recommendations. This chapter demonstrates how AI can create more sustainable and efficient consumer practices in the fashion industry.

This book serves as a comprehensive guide for researchers, practitioners, and industry leaders looking to integrate AI into their sustainability efforts. Each chapter not only discusses technological advances but also emphasizes the importance of AI in achieving long-term environmental and economic goals. As we look toward a more sustainable future, AI's role in reshaping industries remains central to global efforts in combating climate change and ensuring a more equitable world.

**Muhammad Syafrudin**
*Sejong University, South Korea*

**Norma Latif Fitriyani**

*Sejong University, South Korea*

**Muhammad Anshari**
*Universiti Brunei Darussalam, Brunei*

# Chapter 1
# Artificial Intelligence (AI) for Energy Efficiency and Renewable Energy Management

**Francois Yonga**
https://orcid.org/0000-0002-9289-6515
*Université de Maroua, Cameroon*

## ABSTRACT

*Artificial Intelligence (AI), Data Science (DS) and the Internet of Things (IoT) are vast networks of many intelligent devices connected to each other and/or to other internet-connected objects via sensors, software and other embedded technologies. They make use of large data sources and offer easy identification of trends and patterns, improved automation, continuous development, easy processing of multidimensional data and low computing costs. The development of artificial intelligence and data science in renewable energy management has the potential to manage energy production sources and ensure the energy efficiency of installations. This chapter explores different AI application techniques based on deep learning in the areas of solar and wind power generation, smart grid management, and energy consumption in smart residential buildings. It shows that using AI to estimate prediction performance and uncertainty is an optimal model for solar and wind power generation, smart grid management and energy consumption in smart homes.*

DOI: 10.4018/979-8-3373-2530-9.ch001

## INTRODUCTION

Given that the production and management of renewable energy systems have been shown to be subject to unforeseen or undetectable failures, the time has come to compensate for the inadequacies of human prediction and monitoring methods and to deal with incidents on the electricity grid caused by intermittent renewable energy sources. Therefore, renewable energy forecasting is essential as an effective measure to mitigate the associated uncertainties, which is conducive to the planning, management and operation of power and energy systems (Hodge et al., 2018). However, accurate renewable energy forecasting remains a challenging task due to the intermittent, chaotic and random nature of renewable energy data (Hodge et al., 2018; Wang et al., 2019). There is evidence of a power law decrease in blackout probability as blackout size increases from both data and simulations. These discoveries, together with the societal importance of managing blackout risk, motivate the study of cascading failure mechanisms and critical points in blackout models. One explanation of the observed power laws is that when the larger complex system dynamics of a power system evolving in response to economic and engineering forces are considered, the system self-organizes to near a critical point. We give an explanatory overview of this theory, drawing from a range of previous work (Dobson et al., 2007). Renewable energy production facilities need to adapt quickly to the new changes so as to incorporate a more intelligent strategy for managing production and demand. The energy transition is characterized in particular by increasingly diffuse and intermittent energy production systems.The French law on the energy transition for green growth has set a target of 40% of renewable electric energy in national production by 2030. Managing these additional variability elements increases the complexity of the control and operation of distribution and transmission networks. New techniques are required to deal with them, notably AI-based techniques (Debusschere et al., 2022). Artificial intelligence has become a real competitor to human intelligence in many areas. As such, its design must include the ability to acquire information from parameters, analyse it and perform tasks that are the responsibility of human intelligence, such as evaluating the detected parameters and making decisions in the absence of human intervention. AI can therefore be used in most areas of life, including renewable energy. The question is, how is this possible? In the production and management of renewable energy, AI is applied to the control and monitoring systems installed to analyse numerous parameters that fundamentally influence the operation of renewable energy production facilities, including weather conditions (temperature, solar radiation, wind speed and direction), environmental factors and consumption data (energy forecasts, grid infrastructure data and demand forecasts), enabling data to be processed in real time. This means that faults or malfunctions in renewable energy production and management systems can be detected and dealt with much more quickly. Once malfunctions have been detected, control and monitoring systems must be capable of self-management to optimise the production and management of renewable energy systems to increase energy efficiency. Artificial intelligence must be able to detect faults, analyse them and recommend appropriate corrective action or refer the situation to a maintenance operator to ensure uninterrupted production. Pour ce faire, de nombreuses recherches ont été menées et les solutions apportées au monde scientifique placent l'intelligence artificielle (IA) en pole position des solutions pour résoudre les problèmes liés à l'utilisation des techniques manuelles et d'améliorer la prédiction des défauts dans la production et de la gestion des systèmes d'énergies renouvelables. To achieve this, a great deal of research has been carried out and the solutions offered to the scientific world place Artificial Intelligence (AI) in pole position as a solution to the problems associated with the use of manual techniques and to improve the prediction of faults in the production and management of renewable energy systems. Artificial intelligence (AI) is a tool used in a growing number of fields, with undeniable successes, but also challenges that go beyond engineering aspects alone (Narváez Morales, 2024). Artificial intelligence (AI) has been the subject of particular interest in recent years (Chagué & Romary, 2022). AI remains a de facto extension of human thought, for the delegation of tedious or dangerous tasks, for increasing performance and in particular pleasure and better adaptation, for understanding this thought or for helping it (Claverie, 2018). The idea that only a proper understanding of what machines cannot do, given their very machinic nature, and which remains, despite its cognitive finiteness, an exclusive property of humans, will be able to offer a balance between the tasks that can be allocated to machines and those left to humans (Declerck & Charlet, 2011). We could say that Artificial Intelligence (AI) is a set of techniques enabling machines to perform tasks and solve problems normally reserved for humans and certain animals. The tasks covered by AI are sometimes very simple for humans, such as recognising and locating objects in an image, planning a robot's movements to catch an object, or driving a car (LeCun, 2016). Artificial intelligence such as data science (DS) plays a major role in the energy sector, forecasting energy demand, improving the energy efficiency of electricity networks and perfecting electricity distribution and storage operations. AI or SD is playing an increasingly crucial role in transforming our energy system, making it more efficient and sustainable. Collected, stored, exploited, transformed, data is present everywhere, especially in the field of electrical networks. An error in data processing can have serious consequences on industrial performance, security or even image and reputation (Debusschere et al., 2022). Today, it is the methods of automatic learning by example, based on large databases, that are the most successful, followed by exploration methods, which have been given pride of place by the success of the AlphaGo computer programme, developed by

DeepMind. And more generally, AI has come in all shapes and sizes, developing via dozens of different techniques, invading fields that seemed far removed from it; I have seen this myself when some of my own favourite subjects (optimal transport and Kantorovitch duality) have found themselves in its territory, and when I have been led to recruit students in certain branches of AI (Villani, 2019). In this chapter, we show how AI makes it possible to perform analysis or decision-making operations that humans would normally be likely to perform in order to perfect energy efficiency and improve the management of renewable energy systems. To this end, AI would clearly contribute to providing innovative and concrete solutions in the use of AI in the energy domain, such as:

- The production of renewable energy systems through:
  - Improving the efficiency of wind and solar systems by predicting weather conditions and optimising the orientation of panels.
  - Optimising new strategies for controlling inverters and regulators to better adapt the production of electrical energy from solar panels to load demand, or to store excess energy produced by renewable sources.
- Intelligent and efficient management of electricity networks through:
  - Optimising energy flows in real time to minimise losses and improve network stability.
  - Forecasting energy demand and production to better balance supply and demand, with the integration of intermittent renewable energy sources.
  - Integrating renewable energies more efficiently, by anticipating their variable production.
- Improving the energy efficiency of buildings by:
  - Optimising heating, air conditioning and lighting according to climatic conditions, occupancy and occupants' preferences.
  - Detecting and correcting faults in heating and air conditioning systems to reduce energy consumption.
  - Intelligent management of household appliances to reduce standby energy consumption and optimise their use.

## AI TECHNIQUES FOR RENEWABLE ENERGY PRODUCTION

Due to the amount of data available and the abundance of use cases, the energy sector offers many opportunities for AI: real-time operation, maintenance, planning, optimization, etc. AI-based solutions are already contributing effectively to the performance of power grids, while still presenting broad development prospects (Debusschere et al., 2022). AI has become a real competitor to human intelligence in many areas. As such, its design must include the ability to acquire information from parameters, analyse these parameters and perform tasks that are primarily the responsibility of human intelligence, such as evaluating the measured parameters and making decisions in the absence of human intervention. To this end, a non-exhaustive number of AI techniques are being implemented in the renewable energy sectors, particularly in solar photovoltaic and wind power plants, the best of which can be grouped into four (04) main categories, namely Natural Language Generation (NLG), Machine Learning, Robotic Process Automation (RPA) and AI-optimised hardware. What these different categories of AI have in common, however, is the use of artificial neural networks, whether for the acquisition or identification of parameters, for the analysis of these parameters, or for the execution of tasks requiring precise decision-making.

## Natural Language Generation (NLG)

An overview of Natural Language Generation (NLG) from an applied systems perspective leads to a discussion of when NLG techniques should be used, suggestions for conducting a needs analysis, and a description of the basic tasks of NLG (REITER & DALE, 1997; Clark et al., 2010). In this context, (Pajot, 2019) proposes a methodology and an associated decision support tool to assist the different energy stakeholders in the design, sizing and management of energy systems at the neighbourhood level. First, it develops an energy planning approach based on optimisation and a methodology based on energy balances for the generic treatment of energy planning studies at neighbourhood level, then illustrated with a case of waste heat recovery. Consumption models based on statistical approaches are then used to represent temporal flexibility scenarios (shifting of uses). An alternative to this data-based approach, based on physical modelling of buildings, is then presented using reduced thermal models. Finally, all these models are used in a tool for the automatic generation of optimisation models, based on a methodology for the construction of energy models from generic elements (Pajot, 2019). Automatic natural language generation (NLG) is already a challenging problem when it comes to simply producing natural-sounding utterances. Ubiquitous applications, especially assistive technologies, pose the additional challenge of adapting flexibly to a user or situation. This requires optimising complex objectives, such as information density, in combinatorial search spaces described by declarative input languages. We believe that AI search and planning is a natural solution to these problems and could make a significant contribution to solving them efficiently. We illustrate this with a concrete example NLG framework, give a summary of the relevant optimisation goals, and provide an initial list of research challenges (Bonet et al., 2008). On the other hand, for an application of Natural Language Generation (NLG) in renewable energy, the use of Neural NLG should be considered in order to exploit the full potential of this form of AI. Neural NLG relies on deep learning, specifically neural networks, to generate text. Recurrent Neural Networks (RNNs) and transformers are common architectures used in Neural NLG. This type has gained popularity due to its ability to produce more natural and coherent text. What the different variants of neural NLG have in common is the use of machine learning algorithms inspired by the structure of the human brain. By amplifying stimuli from different layers, deep neural networks can identify data representations and make accurate predictions.

## Machine Learning

Machine learning involves training computers to learn and make decisions autonomously. Using algorithms and categorised or uncategorised learning data, machines analyse information, draw conclusions and store knowledge for later use. In the example, a computer learning to interact with elements of a system, or simply connected machines, represents a form of machine learning through models of natural language generation (NLG) experiments. Machine learning generally takes two forms or approaches to learning, including machine learning (ML) and deep learning (DL). ML is traditional machine learning, which focuses on the development of algorithms and statistical models that enable computer systems to improve their performance on a given task through experience. According to McKinsey & Co, it relies on data-driven learning without rule-based programming. We illustrate in Figure 1 the supervised machine learning framework in the case of time series forecasting.

*Figure 1. Supervised machine learning framework for time series forecasting (Le Guen, 2022).*

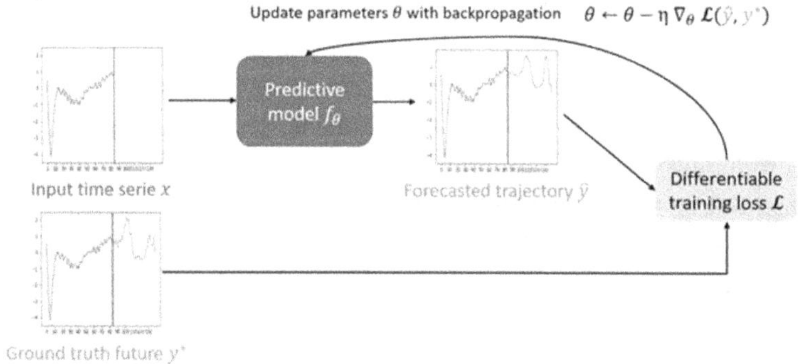

DL, on the other hand, is the new approach to machine learning, inspired by the structure and functioning of the human brain and based on artificial neural networks. The term "deep" refers to the many layers that make up these networks. It excels at processing structured and unstructured data to enable computers to make accurate predictions. Unlike traditional machine learning, deep learning automatically corrects mistakes. It is a powerful tool for complex tasks such as image and speech recognition, product recommendations and natural language processing. The choice of neural network architecture in deep learning is a critical aspect of solving a task. Figure 2 illustrates the three main types of connection between neural layers. First, we have layers that are fully connected, forming a multilayer perceptron (MLP), which is the most general structure, but at the expense of a number of layers and at the cost of an exponentially increasing number of parameters, making it unsuitable for many applications. Secondly, to increase the adaptability and performance of the deep learning process, two structural models have been developed: convolutional neural networks and recurrent neural networks. Convolutional neural networks do not take into account the spatial properties of the object in the image by using a convolutional filter for all spatial positions. In contrast, recurrent neural networks process data sequentially, taking into account translational equivariance by using the same weights an infinite number of times over time.

*Figure 2. Common layers used in deep learning models. Shared parameters are shown with the same color (Battaglia et al., 2018)*

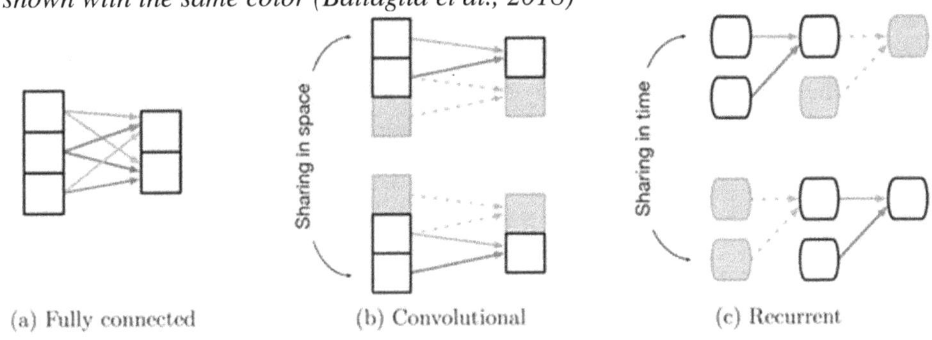


## Robotic Process Automation (RPA)

Although the term Robotic Process Automation (RPA) conjures up the idea of automating processes by using physical robots to carry out tasks previously performed by humans, RPA refers to the configuration of software robots to interpret, communicate and analyse data. RPA makes it possible to automate repetitive, rule-based operations and reduce manual intervention. This technology has applications in a wide range of sectors, streamlining processes and improving efficiency. That said, it is worth noting that power distribution companies have a large volume of information and processes to be executed, both manually and computationally, several legacy systems and various data sources. Making the environment even more complex is subject to audit and regulated by external bodies, such as ANEEL (Agência Nacional de Energia Elétrica - the National Electric Energy Agency), ONS (Operador Nacional do Sistema Elétrico - the National Power System Operation), CCEE (Câmara de Comercialização de Energia Elétrica - the Electric Power Commercialization Chamber), among others. Some examples of areas with such regulatory characteristics are: real estate management, assets management, commercial procedures (invoicing, billing, and collection), information technology, human resources, finances and treasury, supplies, accounting and engineering (Pedretti et al., 2021). In most cases, this configuration of software robots solves problems such as transferring data from multiple input sources, such as email and spreadsheets, into systems of record, such as enterprise resource planning (ERP) and customer relationship management (CRM). Contrary to the idea that RPA is not a form of AI per se, we can see that the mechanism for configuring software robots uses AI for the automatic learning of said robots, in the identification of tasks that can be automated, in the integration with existing systems, in the testing and validation, deployment, monitoring and maintenance, and in the optimisation of the latter. For example, the marketing of electrical energy produced by renewable energy generation facilities requires electrical energy meters to read the energy consumed by households or fed into the grid by private producers. However, this is a cumbersome and costly task that is prone to error. Prior to the introduction of RPA, infeasible, highly rule-based meter reading resolutions lent themselves to automation, as shown in Figure 3.

*Figure 3. Meter reading process before RPA (Lacity et al., 2015).*

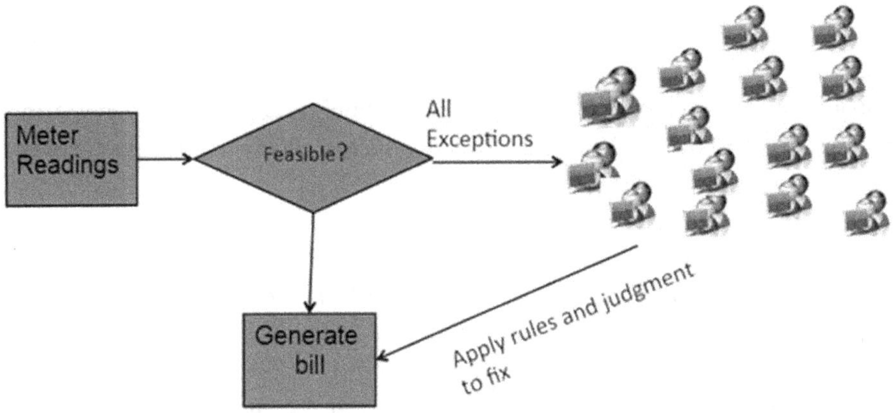


Humans would continue to handle exceptions that required judgement. The business case was to reduce the number of FTEs by around 60% and improve the quality, consistency and speed of resolutions (Lacity et al., 2015). This explains the cumbersome and complex decision-making involved in measuring consumption data or feeding it into the grid, which would undoubtedly make the process unworkable. With the introduction of RPA (see Figure 4), decision making becomes easier, faster and more efficient. RPA helps make reading the meter possible.

*Figure 4. Meter reading process after RPA (Lacity et al., 2015).*

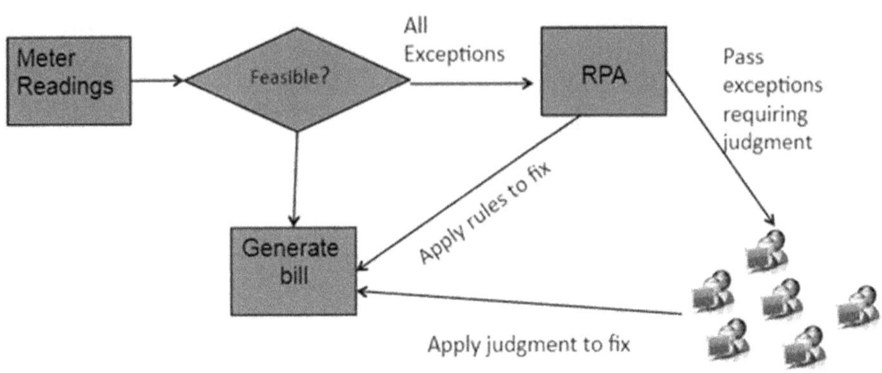

## AI-Optimised Hardware

AI-optimised hardware developed to meet the growing demand for AI software includes specialised chips for neural networks, deep learning and computer vision. Companies such as Nvidia and Qualcomm are developing chips capable of performing complex AI calculations. Sectors such as healthcare and automotive are expected to benefit from this hardware evolution.

## RENEWABLE ENERGY SYSTEMS PRODUCTION

The word neuron clearly evokes the functioning of the nervous system of animals, and in particular that of the human brain. Artificial neural networks are made up of thousands or even millions of artificial neuron-like units whose activation (i.e. degree of excitation or inhibition) depends on the signals they receive from other neurons and the strength of the connections that transmit them (Pérez-Ortiz et al., 2022). Neurons are connected to form a set called a neural network, which works together to process complex information and perform a specific computational task to solve a given problem. Each layer of the network performs a specific mathematical operation on the input data, and the output of one layer serves as the input for the next layer, as shown in Figure 5 (Pérez-Ortiz et al., 2022).

*Figure 5. Artificial neural network with three hidden neurons and two output neurons (Pérez-Ortiz et al., 2022).*

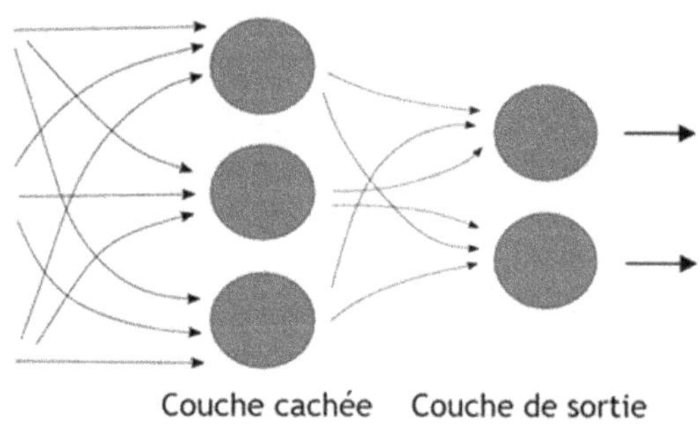


Within a network, some neurons receive external stimuli that act as input to the neural network (just as our eyes are connected to our brain and send images to it) and represent a problem to be solved. Another type of neuron only receives stimuli from other neurons (hidden neurons), and finally other neurons, called output neurons, represent the solution to the problem (a bit like the signals sent to the muscles of your hand to make it move in a certain way)(Pérez-Ortiz et al., 2022). Neural networks use an activation or operation mechanism that can be represented as a two-step process, as shown in the simplified situation in Figure 6, where the update of neuron S4 is made in response to the stimuli received from neurons $S_1$, $S_2$ and $S_3$.

*Figure 6. Evolution of the state S4 of artificial neuron 4 in response to the stimuli received by neurons 1, 2 and 3 (Pérez-Ortiz et al., 2022).*

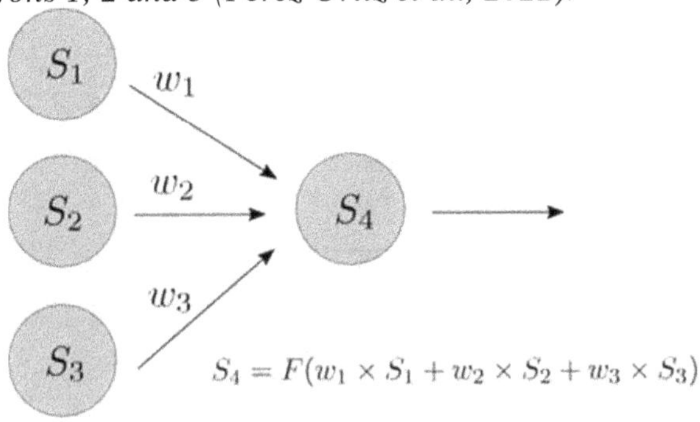


First, the activations of neurons $S_1$, $S_2$ and $S_3$, which are all connected, are added together after being multiplied separately by a weight ($w_1$, $w_2$ and $w_3$) representing the strength of their connections. These weights, positive or negative, determine how their activations are converted into concrete stimuli for neuron $S_4$. For example, if the weight $w_2$ is positive and the activation of $S_2$ is high, this will contribute to the excitation of neuron $S_4$ (positive stimulus); on the other hand, a negative weight $w_2$ will lead to the inhibition of neuron $S_4$ (negative stimulus). In general, neurons connected by positive weights tend to be simultaneously excited or inhibited, whereas neurons connected by negative weights tend to be in the opposite state (Pérez-Ortiz et al., 2022). At the level of neuron $S_4$, we obtain a net stimulus:

$$X = w_1 \times S_1 + w_2 \times S_2 + w_3 \times S_3 \quad (1)$$

In a second step, using the illustration of the previous simplified situation, we can see that stimulus X is of intermediate value, i.e. neither strongly excited nor strongly inhibited, and remains very sensitive to any change in the strength of the connections. However, if the stimuli are very negative or very positive, their real value is of little importance because the neuron is negative or positive respectively. Figure 7 shows that the excitation level of a neuron lies between -1 and +1.

*Figure 7. Evolution of the response of a neuron S4 to the total stimulus received X (Pérez-Ortiz et al., 2022).*

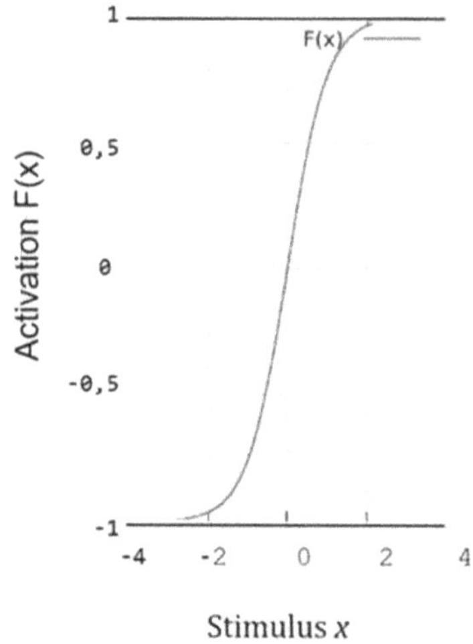


The response of neuron $S_4$ to stimulus X in equation 1 is represented by a function F, which is the activation function applied to the stimulus and whose result is equivalent to the activation of $S_4$:

$$S_4 = F(X) = F(w_1 \times S_1 + w_2 \times S_2 + w_3 \times S_3) \qquad (2)$$

## RENEWABLE ENERGY SYSTEMS PRODUCTION

### Improving the Efficiency of Wind and Solar Systems

Reliable prediction of wind and solar energy production relies heavily on the identification of data or information related to meteorological parameters, analysis and decision making in the form of learning. Over the last decade, ML and DL approaches have shown promising effectiveness in several areas. Energy optimisation and forecasting in smart microgrids, improving the performance of wireless networks and predicting hydrogen production are perfect examples. However, all forecasting methods have their own advantages and disadvantages. For example, DL-based approaches have recently been found to outperform ML-based approaches in power generation and electrical load forecasting because DL-based approaches do not suffer from manual feature selection, sampling complexity and low generalisation efficiency (Aslam et al., 2021). AI systems can continuously monitor the performance of solar panels and detect problems or malfunctions before they become critical. This enables proactive and predictive maintenance, reducing downtime and repair costs. Fluctuations in the output of photovoltaic (PV) solar panels, caused in particular by intermittent weather changes, generally lead to production outages and instability in distribution networks. The need to predict solar production is therefore essential to help the grid operator ensure that electricity production and consumption are balanced at all times. Solar Production Prediction uses machine learning algorithms to analyse weather data and past solar panel performance to accurately predict short and long-term solar energy production. This enables solar system operators to plan ahead and make informed decisions about managing energy production. Short-term forecasting (from a few hours to a few days) is mainly based on satellite images and meteorological models. However, these methods do not have sufficient temporal and spatial resolution to model the fine variations caused by clouds at the level of a photovoltaic farm. For this purpose, ground-based cameras with a "fisheye" lens are increasingly being used, which provide a hemispherical view of the sky, making it possible to anticipate cloud movement (See Figure 8) (Le Guen & Thome, 2019).

*Figure 8. Experimental measuring station on Réunion Island (Le Guen & Thome, 2019).*

To predict solar irradiance using deep neural networks and ground-based cameras, (Le Guen & Thome, 2019a) developed and proposed two models to estimate and predict irradiance. The first uses a convolutional neural network model (ConvNet) that receives RGB images with many parameters as input, and the second, much deeper model, uses two layers (Densenet1 and Densenet2) for radiation regression. Radiation prediction takes the form of a recurrent time sequence architecture adapted to the image sequences.

In order to increase the energy production of photovoltaic solar panels, tracking the sun's path remains a key objective to optimise the exposure of solar panels and capture the maximum amount of sunlight. As we all know, the panel's output is optimal when the sun's rays fall in a direction perpendicular to the surface of the photovoltaic panel. To achieve this, an innovative solution is to use an automated AI solar tracker (see Figures 9). This intelligent tracker is a mechanical device, supported by AI algorithms, that follows the path of the sun as it moves across the sky each day. Clearly, to achieve maximum daily energy production, the optimum values for tilt and azimuth need to be accurately and automatically determined. To achieve this, AI is used to control the tracker using algorithms based on the meteorological data collected by the sensors. The sensors measure and record a wide range of information, which is then compared by the AI to the optimal values. If the measurements are below the pre-defined values, the AI sends instructions to the tracker, which corrects the angle. This process repeats itself until the measured values match the recorded values.

*Figure 9. Trackers solaires automatisés par l'intelligence artificielle - Artificial intelligence automates solar trackers*

Similarly, these algorithms can determine the optimal orientation angle of solar panels based on factors such as the position of the sun, panel tilt and potential shading. This maximises the absorption of sunlight and therefore energy production. The performance of solar panels can also be improved by using a power optimiser to give the solar panel real intelligence, independently, and to allow effective monitoring of photovoltaic production. The solar optimiser is a device similar to a regulator or microinverter, which is connected in parallel to the solar panel's terminals and allows the panel's electricity production capacity to be improved. However, each panel in the same field produces a different maximum power, depending on the temperature or its electrical load characteristics. Optimisers work on the basis of Maximum Power Point Tracking (MPPT). The AI uses neural control algorithms to optimise the MPPT technology to increase the energy production of the solar system and detect faults in the panel.

Solar power plants face many problems related to bad weather (sand and snow storms) and dirt build-up (dust, dead leaves and snow). Another idea for the application of AI in photovoltaic systems is based solely on optimising the performance of solar fields by regularly cleaning the surfaces of photovoltaic panels. For this purpose, SOLARCLEANO has developed cleaning robots (B1, T1, M1, F1 and F1A) (see Figures 10, 11 and 12). Designed specifically for cleaning large installations, they can be remotely controlled. What's more, they can be programmed to work autonomously and move around freely. They can also recharge their own batteries without the need for human intervention.

*Figure 10. The SolarCleano B1 'SolarBridge'.*

*Figure 11. The SolarCleano M1.*

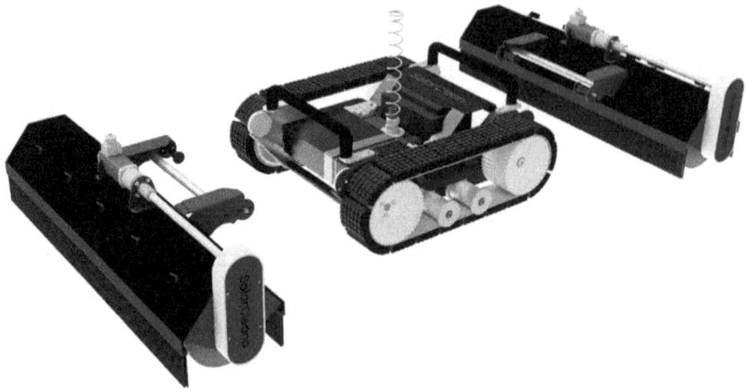

*Figure 12. The SolarCleano T1 'Transporter' for the SolarCleano M1.*

This process uses robotic process automation to automate repetitive operations assigned to a cleaning robot. This technology has applications in a variety of sectors, such as large solar power plants and the facades of solar megastructures (buildings, stadiums, boats, etc.), streamlining processes and improving the efficiency of the installation. On the other hand, the use of hardware optimised for AI has enabled companies such as Nvidia and Qualcomm to develop chips capable of performing complex AI calculations that can be programmed by RPA to control the cleaning processes of solar panels in a photovoltaic system. However, the presence of an operator is still required to monitor the heights and extremities of the solar fields and then adjust the control in the event of irregularities. The SS&C Blue Prism platform provides customers with a reliable and resilient intelligent automation solution that optimises resources through simplified and compliant processes driven by artificial intelligence. SS&C Blue Prism is working with companies such as United Utilities, eversource, DTE, HarzEnergie and Nationalgrid to integrate intelligent automation into meter reading workforce planning and inbound meter reading request management. Now, when a customer requests a meter reading, a virtual agent performs the necessary calculations and suggests a response, synchronising the use of virtual agents with the increase in customer requests.

By applying AI to wind farms, it is possible to significantly improve their performance, taking into account meteorological and consumption data. AI is used to correlate the speed of each propeller with the direction and strength of the wind. By analysing all this data, the AI is able to optimise and increase the electricity production capacity of all the wind turbines. AI is also being used to help researchers understand the atmospheric conditions in which wind farms operate. The aim is to make highly accurate forecasts of future energy production. To this end, a number of companies, including Atos and Météo-France, have signed an agreement to create a platform for forecasting renewable energy production. This is part of a European agreement to ensure that renewable energy accounts for at least 32% of total energy consumption in EU countries by 2030.

However, the case of wind farms remains interesting in terms of applying AI to production, biodiversity protection and energy storage, using a combination of machine learning and predictive analytics. This is where the Athena system comes in, as a platform for creating and managing virtual power plants to maximise the value of energy storage. A virtual power plant makes it possible to constantly assess the amount of energy available at any given time and consider optimal decisions to match demand with consumption. Figure 13 shows the multi-point aggregation process of energy storage capacity and distributed energy resources (DER) in the electricity grid.

*Figure 13. Example of a virtual power plant architecture for intelligent consumer demand management, providing an overview of the levels of physical aggregation of DERs and prosumers in the power system domain (Manerba et al., 2018).*

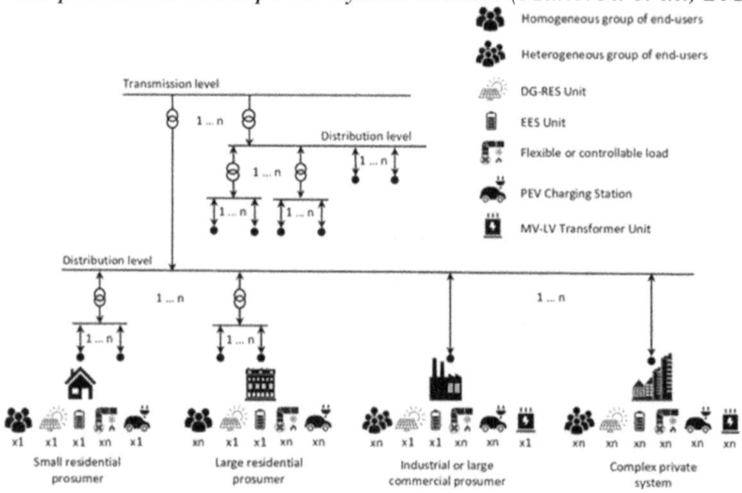


For each node of the electrical grid, different possible aggregations of DERs are considered, including RES-based generators, Electrical Energy Storage (EES) units, flexible and controllable loads (e.g., heating and cooling systems, lighting systems, and controllable appliances), Plug-in Electric Vehicle (PEV) charging stations, and Medium Voltage (MV) to Low Voltage (LV) transformer units. It is assumed that different combinations of DERs can be potentially connected to each node of the grid depending on the type of prosumer (Manerba et al., 2018). In this illustration of a virtual power plant, the mechanism for bringing together the various prosumers is based on the use of AI to analyse, among other things, a large number of predictive variables (weather data, energy consumption and price levels, etc.) and to automate the process of real-time calculations by sending information to the control and data acquisition system (SCADA). On the other hand, DeepMind is an artificial intelligence programme developed by Google to predict the production of a wind farm 36 hours in advance, in real time, in order to better exploit the production of electrical energy. This programme has made it possible to predict the energy production of a wind farm one day in advance, increasing the value of the energy produced by 20% compared to wind farms without a prediction system. As a result, Figure 14 shows the trade-off between the economic value and production of a wind farm without and with the use of machine learning.

*Figure 14. Benefits of machine learning-based prediction, according to DeepMind (Illustrative results from 2018 Google/DeepMind field study).*

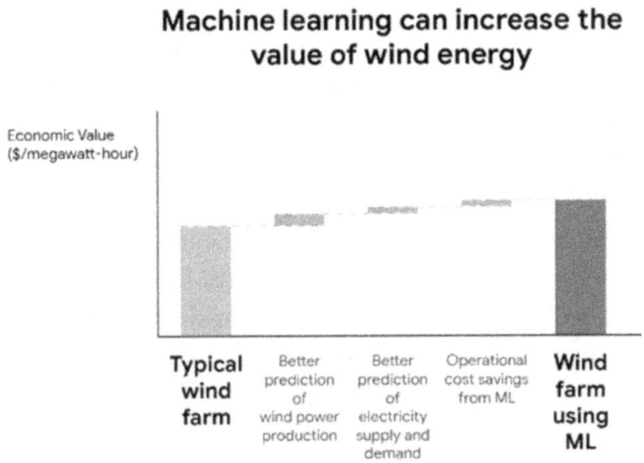


When it comes to protecting biodiversity, wind turbine blades have been shown to be a major contributor to the decline of avifauna, with birds frequently colliding with the blades. Faced with this worrying situation, Avifauna Detection Systems (ADS) have emerged as a promising solution to detect the risk of collision and control the stopping of the wind turbine rotor in real time, with the help of the SCADA system that integrates AI algorithms and visual detection technologies (2D, 3D and infrared cameras) or radar to automate the identification and classification of birds. In the case of a wind farm, the detection of birds at one wind turbine could simultaneously lead to the shutdown or slowdown of several other wind turbines in the farm.

AI technologies (Athena and DeepMind) in wind farms are strongly influenced by the development of big data and, in particular, the Internet of Things, in order to regulate production, visualise and detect any anomalies in the blades of a wind turbine thanks to image recognition or with the aim of planning predictive and targeted maintenance activities by drone. These technologies make it possible to target maintenance activities, reduce costs and make operations safer (e.g. working at height, indoors or outdoors). In short, the development of renewable energy, including onshore and offshore wind power, will enable a gradual decarbonisation of the world's energy mix.

## Optimising New Strategies for Controlling Inverters and Regulators

(Hadjab & DJELLID, 2012) presents an intelligent approach for improving and optimising the performance of a photovoltaic generator, using the maximum power point tracking (MPPT) method. This method is based on artificial neural networks, which have made it possible to determine the various parameters influencing the maximum power point of a photovoltaic generator.

In order to guarantee safety, minimise electrical energy consumption and optimise the efficiency of the inverters, as well as the efficiency of renewable energies, the use of AI seems to be the ideal and most promising solution to this problem through the use of memristor-based systems, which can significantly reduce the energy consumption of AI by harvesting energy from its surroundings using miniature wide bandgap solar cells, optimised for indoor applications, and by retaining the stored data even after the harvested energy has been used up. To achieve this, memristor-based electronic components must be fitted to the most energy-hungry components, in this case the static converters (regulators, optimisers, microinverters and inverters), as shown in Figure 15.

*Figure 15. Overview of the fabricated memristor-based binarized neural network (Jebali et al., 2024).*

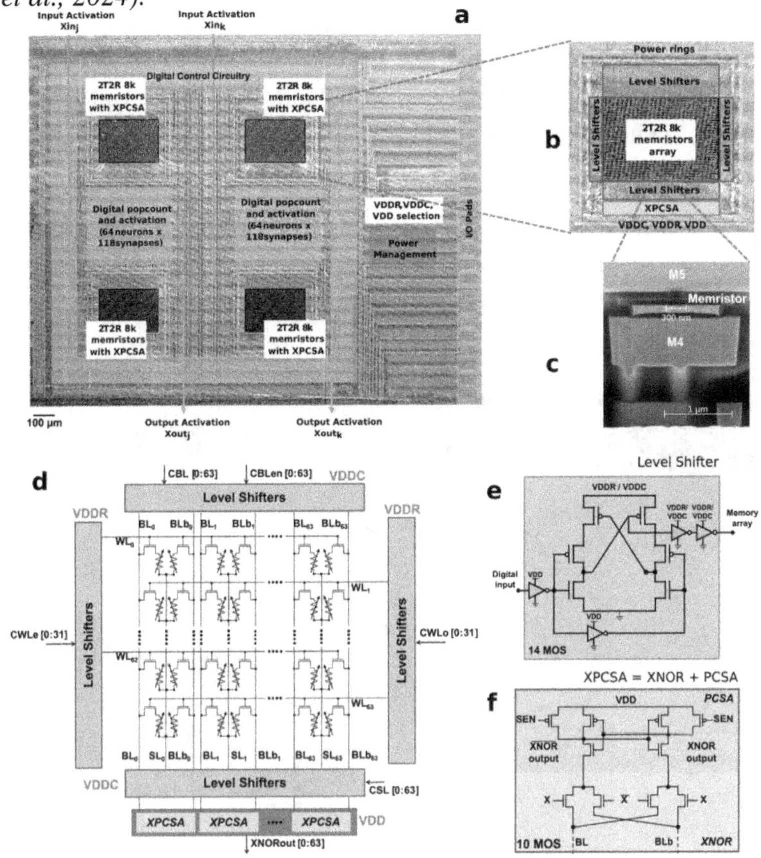


An optical microscopy image of the fabricated die shows four memory modules and their associated digital circuitry and power management unit. **b** . Provide Details on one of the memory modules. **c** Cross-sectional scanning electron micrograph of a hybrid CMOS/memristor circuit, showing a memristor between metal levels four and five. **d** Schematic of a memory module. For each operation mode, WL, BL, and SL biasing conditions are given with respect to the power domain (VDDC, VDDR) and VDD. **e** Schematic of the level shifter, used in **d** for shifting digital voltage input to medium voltages needed during programming operations or nominal voltage during reading operations of the memristors. **f** Schematic of the differential pre-charge sense amplifier PCSA, used to read the binary memristor states, with embedded XNOR function, to compose a XPCSA: it computes an XNOR operation between input activation X and weight (memristor value) during bit-cell sensing.

Figure 16 shows the internal composition of an AlGaAs/GaInP heterostructure solar cell, the experimental curves of the current-voltage characteristics measured under AM1.5 illumination at one sun provided by a standardised solar simulator and for different illuminations provided by the halogen lamp. The experimental setup is used to power the binarised neural network fabricated using the solar cell illuminated by the halogen lamp.

*Figure 16. Vue schématique de la cellule solaire à hétérostructure AlGaAs/GaInP. b Photographie de la cellule solaire et de ses caractéristiques courant-tension mesurées sous un éclairage AM1,5 à un soleil fourni par un simulateur solaire standardisé.*

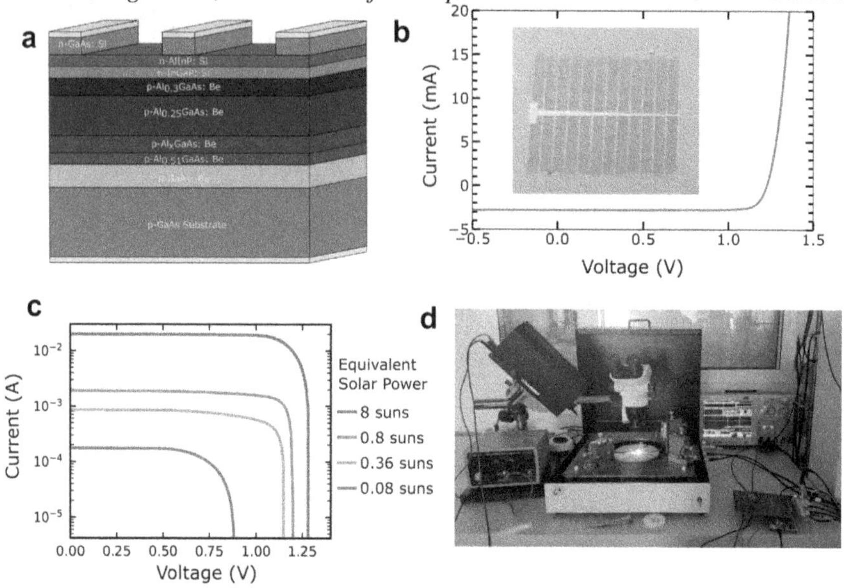


**a** Schematic view of the AlGaAs/GaInP heterostructure solar cell. **b** Photograph of the solar cell, and its measured current-voltage characteristics under one-sun AM1.5 illumination provided by a standardized solar simulator. **c** Current-voltage characteristics of the solar cell for various illuminations provided by the halogen lamp. **d** Photograph of the experimental setup where the fabricated binarized neural network is powered by the solar cell illuminated by the halogen lamp.

In converters (regulators, optimisers, microinverters and inverters) optimised with the integration of memristors, the converter integrated circuits take the form of neural networks. Each integrated circuit also contains an on-chip power management unit and a digital control unit responsible for programming the memristors and performing fully pipelined inference operations. As mentioned above, the memristor-based chips thus formed each have a digital control unit that allows the programming of the memristors and the execution of fully pipelined inference operations. Once the algorithm has been executed, the programming of the chips containing the neural networks allows the neural activation of the output, as shown in the following equation:

$$X_{out,j} = sign(popcount(XNOR(W_{ji}, X_{in,i})) - T_j$$

$X_{out,j}$ represents the neuronal activation of the output, $popcount(XNOR(W_{ji}, X_{in,i})) - T_j$ represents the pre-activation of the neurons with $T_j$ the threshold of the output neurons, $W_{ji}$ denotes the synaptic weights and $X_{in,i}$ the activations of the input neurons.

Figure 17 shows the interconnection of memristors using the method of mapping binarised neural networks of arbitrary shape onto matrices of 64 × 128 memristors, highlighting the neuronal activation of the output $X_{out,j}$ in relation to the synaptic weights $W_{ji}$ and the activations of the input neurons $X_{in,i}$.

*Figure 17. Neural-network-level investigations.*

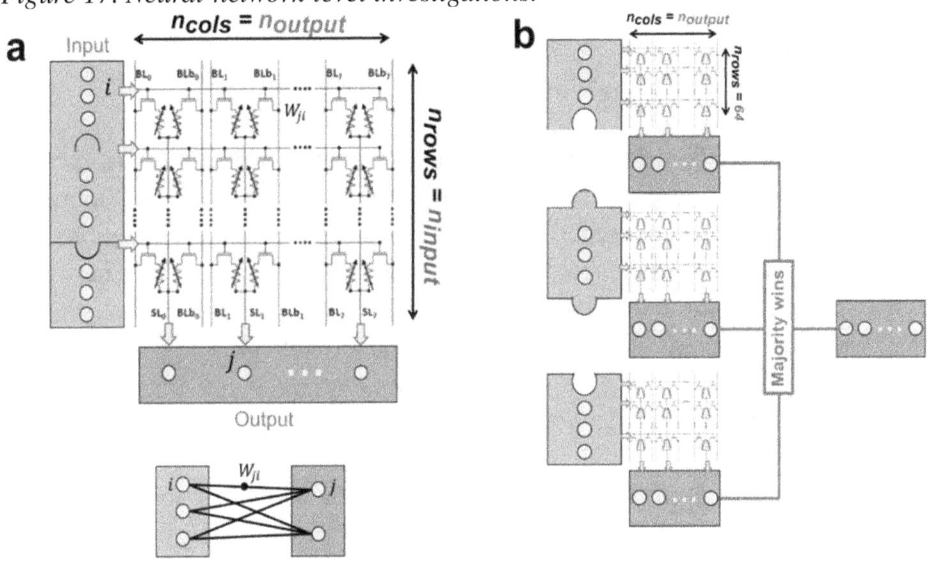


**a, b** Illustration of our method for mapping arbitrarily-shaped binarized neural networks to 64 × 128 memristor arrays.

## INTELLIGENT AND EFFICIENT MANAGEMENT OF ELECTRICITY NETWORKS

AI is playing an increasingly important role in the intelligent management of electricity networks. AI is a powerful tool that can help us realise the full potential of intelligent management of electricity networks. Intelligent management of electricity networks involves using information and communication technologies to optimise the operation of the electricity network. The objectives of intelligent management of electricity networks are to improve network efficiency by reducing energy losses and optimising electricity distribution, to increase network reliability by reducing the frequency and duration of outages, to integrate more renewable energies into the energy mix, to facilitate consumer demand for energy and to reduce the environmental impact of the energy system.

The advantages of intelligent management of electricity networks are:

- Lower energy costs for consumers and businesses.
- Improved quality of electricity supply.
- Reduced greenhouse gas emissions.
- Creating new jobs in the clean technology sector.

However, the challenges of smart grid management remain numerous, namely in terms of the high cost of the initial investment, the need for a reliable communications infrastructure, cyber security, and the necessary changes in regulations and policies. Despite these challenges, intelligent management of electricity networks is an essential part of the transition to a sustainable energy future. By investing in smart grid technologies, we can create a cleaner, more reliable and more efficient energy system for all.

AI algorithms can be used to forecast energy demand more accurately, optimise the flow of energy through the grid, detect and remedy faults more quickly, and manage microgrids more efficiently. By combining AI with other smart technologies, we can create a more sustainable, resilient and affordable energy future for all.

### Optimising Energy Flows in Real Time to Minimise Losses and Improve Network Stability

The advent of AI is contributing to the profound transformation of several sectors, including renewable energy production systems. Constantly metamorphosing, AI offers renewable energy systems numerous opportunities to optimise production, distribution and energy efficiency, making it a central pillar of the transition to clean, sustainable energy. It remains to be seen how AI will redefine the renewable energy landscape through innovations that promise to revolutionise the real-time optimisation of energy flows to minimise losses and improve grid stability. When it comes to optimising energy systems, AI makes it possible to monitor and analyse energy consumption in buildings and industrial facilities in real time. For example, platforms such as Dalkia Analytics use machine learning algorithms to adjust energy flows according to activity, thereby reducing costs and carbon footprints. As part of optimising energy flows, predicting failures and maintenance solutions are the order of the day. AI uses predictive models to estimate energy production from renewable sources such as solar and wind. These models take into account meteorological, historical and real-time data to predict energy production, making it possible to better manage the integration of these sources into the electricity grid. By predicting energy demand, AI helps to adjust renewable energy production accordingly, minimising energy losses and optimising the use of available resources. AI facilitates the transition from reactive to predictive maintenance in renewable energy installations. By analysing operational data, it can detect signs of failure before they occur, improving reliability and reducing maintenance costs. AI enables the monitoring of energy infrastructure (such as wind turbines and solar panels) by analysing data from sensors. This can detect signs of failure before they become critical, reducing maintenance costs and increasing system reliability. Using machine learning techniques, operational optimisation helps systems learn from past performance and optimise future operations to maximise efficiency and reduce costs. At the same time, digital twins can be used to create virtual replicas of energy assets to simulate their operation and optimise their performance in real time. This helps to identify opportunities for improvement and adjust operations accordingly.

## Forecasting Energy Demand and Production to Better Balance Supply and Demand

As renewable energy becomes an increasingly important part of the global power system, improving the accuracy of renewable energy forecasts is essential for the planning, management and operation of the power system. However, due to the intermittent and inconsistent nature of renewable energy parameters, this difficult option is still an open question. However, improving transmission and distribution networks to ensure greater energy reliability and optimum quality of service by minimising the frequency and duration of outages requires systems and equipment for remote control and monitoring of secondary distribution networks. The CAHORS Group, which offers global solutions to facilitate and optimise the management of electricity networks, is developing intelligent electricity networks to support its distribution network operator customers in their efforts to improve and automate electricity networks. The integration of AI into smart grids enables the digital management of assets by collecting and analysing the data needed to design, build and operate them in near real-time. This requires automating the analysis of infrastructure data to optimise asset performance. In addition, predictive maintenance planning of the asset enables the automation of maintenance and safety control operations, improving operational efficiency and predicting failures with the intervention of complex machine learning predictive maintenance models. It also automatically updates back-office systems to ensure data accuracy and consistency. Finally, proactive order management automatically manages purchase orders to suppliers, speeding up the process and eliminating delays caused by stock-outs.

A smart grid integrates information and communication technologies. By collecting data on the state of the network, remote control and monitoring systems enable smart grids to ensure a balance between production, distribution and consumption by identifying and locating faults in electrical installations and proposing reliable solutions, thanks to AI-based information and communication technologies. Smart grids should be flexible, reliable, accessible and cost-effective. To this end, smart meters have been introduced to collect information on energy consumption and demand, and to transmit this information automatically and remotely. Secondly, smart meters make it possible to adjust the flow of electricity between suppliers and consumers by facilitating the injection of generated electricity.

AI-enabled energy management systems in smart grids enable a two-way flow of energy between producers and consumers. This enables rapid response to fluctuations in supply and demand, making energy systems more resilient and flexible. By combining data from multiple sources, AI helps optimise the use of energy resources, reducing waste and improving the overall efficiency of systems.

Recently, microgrids have emerged as a building block for smart grids that incorporate distributed renewable energy sources (RES), energy storage devices and load management methods. For example, forecasting electricity production from RES such as wind turbines and solar panels becomes essential for the efficient and continuous operation of the electricity grid, and also helps to achieve optimal use of RES. When it comes to predicting production and demand, AI is essential for managing the variability of renewable energy sources such as solar and wind power. It can predict energy production based on weather conditions and adjust consumption accordingly, which is crucial for maintaining balance in electricity grids. Energy demand forecasting is also an integral part of smart microgrids, helping to plan power generation and energy trading with the commercial grid. Models based on machine learning (ML) and deep learning (DL) are promising solutions for predicting consumer demand and energy production from RES (Aslam et al., 2021). In this context, existing DL-based approaches focus on a specific generation application, such as solar or wind, and require a large number of data storage devices with high computing power for efficient processing of large amounts of data. Recently, microgrids have emerged as a building block for smart grids with distributed renewable energy sources (RES), energy storage devices, and load management methods. Predicting electricity production from RES, such as wind turbines and solar panels, is therefore essential for the efficient and continuous operation of the electricity grid and also contributes to the optimal use of RES. Energy demand forecasting is also an integral part of smart microgrids, helping to plan power generation and energy trading with the commercial grid. Models based on machine learning (ML) and deep learning (DL) are promising solutions for predicting consumer demand and energy production from RES (Aslam et al., 2021). In this context, existing DL-based approaches focus on a specific generation application, such as solar or wind, and require a large number of data storage devices with high computing power for efficient big data processing.

Renewable energy installations (solar photovoltaic and wind power) generally face difficulties related to the reduction of battery autonomy, which requires the optimisation of energy storage. To achieve this, AI helps to manage batteries by optimising energy storage, determining when to charge and discharge batteries based on production and demand forecasts. This is particularly important for systems using intermittent renewable energy. Subsequently, AI facilitates sectoral coupling between different sectors (electricity, heat, mobility) for integrated energy management, enabling more efficient use of available resources. Due to the limited autonomy and the cost of maintaining storage batteries, it is important to consider simpler and more convenient solutions. Machine learning is a cheap and fast way to drive AI algorithms and commands to estimate actual range and optimise energy savings, increasing range and reducing customer concerns. AI can be used for charge management and energy storage by predicting electricity demand and optimising charge management of energy storage batteries. The algorithms can automatically adjust the charging and discharging of batteries according to solar production forecasts and electricity demand, maximising self-consumption of solar energy and reducing reliance on the grid.

To meet the huge demand and conserve the renewable energy resources produced, other solutions are being used, in this case intelligent energy recovery technologies. This emerging technology converts wasted energy such as electromagnetic waves, Joule effect losses (heat) and vibrations into electrical energy using intelligent sensors controlled by complex neural algorithms. This recovered energy is then fed back into the circuit, increasing the energy efficiency of the production system.

## Integrating Renewable Energies More Efficiently

With the increasing use of renewable energy sources due to their sustainability, lower environmental impact and long-term cost, a great deal of research has led to the development of energy systems that are environmentally friendly, energy efficient and increase the penetration of renewable energy. In this context, energy integration systems are seen as a viable approach to increase the use of renewable resources and improve production efficiency. While the integration of AI in the energy sector has many benefits, it also poses challenges, particularly in terms of cybersecurity and privacy. In order to manage the massive amounts of data generated by these systems, appropriate standards and regulations are needed to ensure security and fair access. The future of AI in renewable energy management looks promising, with ongoing innovations in algorithms and computing power. Collaboration between the various players in the sector will be essential to overcome current challenges and maximise the potential of AI in the energy transition. The use of AI facilitates the analysis of large amounts of data by identifying trends and patterns that can be used to improve decision-making in renewable energy management. This includes analysing data from smart meters and energy management systems and personalising the energy services offered to consumers, taking into account their consumption habits and proposing tailored solutions to reduce costs and improve energy efficiency.

## IMPROVING THE ENERGY EFFICIENCY OF BUILDINGS

The development of renewable energy in everyday life affects all sectors. However, its management is still strongly influenced by fluctuating energy costs, energy wastage leading to energy shortages, changes in regulations and the search for sustainable resources, all of which are calling into question the way in which electrical energy is consumed. In this context, protecting the environment has become a priority and controlling energy expenditure is essential to reducing energy consumption in residential buildings. It's more than a necessity, it's a responsibility that represents a promising business opportunity for sustainable, cost-effective solutions that will significantly transform the energy efficiency of buildings while helping to protect our planet. Improving the energy efficiency of buildings is one of the most effective ways to reduce energy consumption and greenhouse gas emissions. Buildings are responsible for around one third of the world's final energy consumption. Buildings account for a significant proportion of global energy consumption and optimising their operation could result in savings of up to 29%. For this reason, a number of measures are being considered to effectively optimise the use of electrical energy in buildings. Many AI solutions are being used to improve the energy efficiency of buildings, including personalisation of services, prediction of energy consumption, and optimised and intelligent management of devices.

Personalising services is a strategy for building user loyalty. Integrating AI into the personalisation process offers exceptional opportunities to deliver unique and relevant experiences to each consumer. In service personalisation, AI algorithms can be used to personalise the energy services offered to consumers, taking into account their consumption habits and proposing tailored solutions to reduce costs and improve energy efficiency. Consumers want their needs and preferences understood and tailored solutions offered. This means using AI to personalise the user experience. Using AI to personalise services goes beyond simple consumer habits. It provides an effective way to understand and respond to consumers' individual needs. This in turn increases satisfaction and loyalty. The process of personalising services begins with the collection and analysis of a given user's consumption data, the creation of a personalised consumer profile, automatic learning of the personalised profile and automatic natural interaction. Platforms such as Dalkia Analytics Powered by Metron and BrainBox AI. Dalkia Analytics Powered optimises energy flows in real time by creating digital twins of the installation in order to reduce your energy bill in the long term. BrainBox AI uses predictive analysis to optimise energy use, adapt to market changes, integrate renewables, improve systems and reduce costs. Equipped with cutting-edge AI technologies for home automation management, residential and commercial buildings will become the new standard. Indeed, the aim of smart buildings is to produce and manage their own energy, consuming some and storing the rest, becoming micro power stations within smart urban networks. Predictive analytics will enable these buildings to anticipate and adapt to the profiled needs of consumers. AI's predictive analytics and machine learning capabilities offer more than just savings; they pave the way for more sustainable, efficient and resilient buildings. AI-based building management systems (BMS) are a set of applications and hardware that centralise and automate the management of various devices (heating, air conditioning, lighting, etc.). Using intelligent algorithms, they can adjust parameters according to the data collected. These systems make it possible to centralise the management of all the technical equipment in a building, providing an overall view of consumption and opportunities for optimisation.

## Optimizing Heating, Air Conditioning, and Lighting According to Climatic Conditions, Occupancy, and Occupants' Preferences

The frantic search for solutions to optimize heating, air conditioning, and lighting according to climatic conditions, occupancy, and user preferences is a growing concern that deserves special attention. The optimization of heating, air-conditioning, and lighting systems is a major challenge in the current context of increased environmental awareness and the desire to reduce energy costs. By adjusting these systems according to different parameters (climatic conditions, occupancy, occupant preferences), it is possible to achieve significant energy savings and improve indoor comfort. To achieve effective optimisation, it is essential to take into account data on climatic conditions (temperature, humidity, sunshine), occupancy (presence/absence, timetables) and occupant preferences (desired temperature, air quality, brightness).

Installing high efficiency heating and air conditioning systems is one way to significantly reduce energy consumption. Condensing boilers, heat pumps and high efficiency air conditioners are perfect examples of high performance systems. This high level of efficiency can only be guaranteed with the intervention of an AI. An AI is able to schedule regular maintenance of heating and air conditioning systems to ensure that they work properly and are energy efficient, using sensors to control whether heating and air conditioning systems are switched on or off. In effect, the AI collects data (temperature, humidity and pressure) on the condition of the premises and acts automatically to reduce the running time and consumption of the heating and air conditioning systems. In this case, smart thermostats are sensors that can be used to program time slots, create personalised scenarios and remotely control heating and air conditioning. They can also automatically adjust the temperature according to the outside temperature and the lifestyle of the occupants. The application of AI to optimise the heating of a building involves adjusting the temperature according to the outside temperature and the occupancy of the rooms, zone control to optimise the heating in each room, and the use of intelligent heating systems (heat pumps, networked radiators). On the other hand, in air conditioning, AI enables automatic temperature adjustment according to outside conditions and occupant preferences, as well as optimisation of air flow and fresh air distribution.

To optimise the significant reduction in energy consumption for lighting, the replacement of incandescent and halogen bulbs with LED bulbs is also proposed as an alternative. LED bulbs are more energy efficient and last longer than incandescent and halogen bulbs. Connected bulbs can be remotely controlled and integrated into a home automation system to create personalised lighting scenes. They can be controlled remotely and adjusted according to external light levels and current activity. AI makes it possible to adjust light intensity according to natural light and room occupancy, to use connected lighting systems (LED bulbs, control via mobile application) and to create personalised lighting scenarios (work, relaxation, night-time). Home automation systems make it possible to program heating, air conditioning and lighting systems according to pre-defined schedules or sensors that detect the presence of occupants.

Lighting systems with motion sensors and timers can also be used to reduce lighting energy consumption. Sensors can be used to collect real-time data about the indoor and outdoor environment. They can measure temperature, humidity, light levels, air quality and so on. These sensors can automatically switch off lights in unoccupied rooms and continuously measure environmental parameters (temperature, humidity, brightness) and occupancy conditions (presence, activity).

## Detecting and Correcting Faults in Heating and Air Conditioning Systems to Reduce Energy Consumption

Adopting energy-efficient practices not only benefits the environment, but also offers significant long-term economic benefits in the form of lower energy bills, improved indoor comfort and better value for money. The first step is to understand your energy consumption by analysing your energy bills and identifying the main sources of energy use. This in-depth investigation will highlight appliances or systems and periods of high consumption. It is also used to identify anomalies that could indicate over-consumption or energy leakage, to focus efforts on the most energy-intensive items, and to take corrective action to reduce their impact in order to achieve realistic consumption reduction targets. At the heart of energy concerns, optimising heating and air conditioning is a crucial step in reducing energy consumption. A strategic approach, combining modern equipment and responsible usage practices, can deliver significant savings while maintaining optimum comfort. Let's take a look at some effective ways to achieve this, including the use of environmentally friendly air conditioning and heating that matches the actual needs of the space. AI is revolutionising the way we manage our buildings, helping to optimise the energy consumption of heating, ventilation and air conditioning (HVAC) systems. AI holds great promise for optimising HVAC systems. By enabling early detection of anomalies and predictive maintenance, it helps to reduce the energy consumption of buildings, improve occupant comfort and extend the life of equipment.

Specifically, to detect and correct anomalies in these systems, thereby optimising their operation and significantly reducing energy consumption. AI systems continuously analyse huge amounts of data from various sensors installed in the home to provide information on temperature, humidity, pressure and energy consumption. For example, Tado smart thermostats and radiator valves that adapt to your lifestyle are ideal for homes, controlling temperature room by room by learning from your preferences and automatically adjusting settings to maximise comfort and efficiency. Using machine learning techniques, they are able to identify recurring patterns in this data and detect any anomalies that deviate from predefined patterns. In general, the types of anomalies detected relate to equipment malfunctions (faulty motors, compressor failures, thermostats out of adjustment, leaks in the refrigeration circuit, etc.), control problems (difficulties in maintaining the desired temperature, large thermal oscillations, frequent on/off cycles), air distribution imbalances (blocked air vents, clogged filters, damaged ducts, etc.) and external air infiltration (faulty seals, leaks from windows or doors). Thanks to machine learning, intelligent systems collect and analyse large amounts of data about your habits or preferences, the outside temperature and even energy prices, to predict your needs and optimally adjust the temperature for greater comfort and lower energy costs.

Combined with other home automation technologies, the integration of AI into home heating or air conditioning systems means that, for example, smart sensors can detect presence/absence and activate/deactivate heating or air conditioning via mobile applications or remote control for optimal comfort. Thanks to AI (Nest or Ecobee), heating systems can operate much more efficiently. By adjusting the temperature according to actual use, these systems significantly reduce energy consumption, helping to combat climate change. Other connected systems (Siemens or Honeywell) use AI to control temperature and indoor air quality. They can interface with other home automation devices for comprehensive management of the home environment. In addition, companies such as Bosch and Daikin offer centralised AI-based heating systems. These aim to optimise heat distribution throughout the home by analysing data such as weather forecasts and usage patterns to adjust the operation of boilers and heat pumps. Mitsubishi Electric's intelligent heat pumps use AI to optimise energy consumption while providing efficient heating and cooling. They analyse weather conditions and usage patterns to adjust their operation to maximise energy efficiency. Other solutions, such as Warmup's intelligent underfloor heating, adjust the temperature according to predicted patterns, and hybrid systems that combine traditional boilers and heat pumps. These systems adapt perfectly to changes in daily habits and external weather conditions to provide constant, comfortable heat. They then automatically select the most efficient and economical energy source according to weather conditions and energy tariffs. The majority of innovative buildings are equipped with building management systems (BMS) to control lighting, heating and air conditioning equipment and installations. The use of building automation and control systems to measure and manage energy consumption will become mandatory in the coming years.

## Intelligent Management of Household Appliances to Reduce Standby Energy Consumption and Optimise Their Use

Buying energy-efficient appliances can reduce energy consumption. Household appliances carry an energy label that indicates their energy efficiency. It is important to choose appliances with a high energy label. Simple behaviours can also help improve the energy efficiency of buildings. These include switching off lights and appliances when not in use, turning down the heating in winter and turning up the air conditioning in summer, and washing clothes in cold water. By taking steps to improve the energy efficiency of buildings, we can reduce our energy consumption, save money and help the environment. On the other hand, these various solutions are manual in nature, which further limits their effectiveness by creating a new difficulty that must be solved at all costs. AI has the advantage of positioning itself as the best option for automating any manual solution for switching off lights or appliances in a home. AI takes control of a home's home automation system and any appliance that consumes electricity, and adapts the operation of the system to the preferences of the occupants. This is why super applications like KeyZane have been developed. Created by Severin Kezeu, the KeyZane ORP platform is the world's first operational resource planning system, with its integrated universal anti-collision of everything, its positioning and social distancing, as well as its applications and services. KeyZane ORP therefore offers applications (Smart Home, Smart Business, Smart Site, Smart Building, Smart City and Smart Gov) and, through its Smart Home application, makes it possible to transform a given premises into an intelligent ecosystem where all resources (2D/3D layout, household, IoT assets and devices, family documents, provisions and inventories) are integrated and managed throughout their lifecycle by a central brain repository. The digital twins KeyZane Smart Building and KeyZane Smart City can transform your building into a smart ecosystem and your city into a smart ecosystem.

## CONCLUSION

Predicting energy consumption/demand is essential for improving the production of solar and wind power plants, intelligently managing power grids, and optimising the consumption of residential buildings, which consume a significant amount of energy due to rapid demographic growth and cyclical economic changes. Artificial intelligence offers significant opportunities for optimising the performance of heating and air conditioning systems. By quickly detecting and correcting anomalies, AI can help reduce energy consumption, improve comfort and extend the life of equipment. Integrating AI into buildings is therefore an essential step towards a more sustainable and energy-efficient future. Thanks to technological advances, it is now possible to create intelligent, high-performance systems that adapt to the needs of each building in real time. One of the benefits of AI is its ability to learn continuously. As the system is exposed to more data, it can refine its predictions and improve its accuracy. AI can also be used as an electricity pricing model to optimise investment in renewable energy systems, significantly improving operational efficiency, profitability and contribution to the transition to clean, renewable energy.

However, challenges remain regarding the energy impact and reliability of AI, as AI systems are energy intensive and their energy consumption could double by 2030, reaching 3.5% of global electricity demand. This high energy consumption of AI systems poses a serious threat to our climate and complicates the electrification of other critical sectors, such as transport. The high energy consumption of AI is mainly due to the computing power required to train advanced models. What's more, the cooling systems required for these powerful servers consume huge amounts of water, exacerbating the environmental impact. Ongoing research is looking at innovative energy storage and conservation solutions to ensure a reliable power supply and reduce the environmental impact of AI by integrating renewable energy.

## REFERENCES


Battaglia, P. W., Hamrick, J. B., Bapst, V., Sanchez-Gonzalez, A., Zambaldi, V., Malinowski, M., Tacchetti, A., Raposo, D., Santoro, A., & Faulkner, R. (2018). Relational inductive biases, deep learning, and graph networks. *arXiv preprint arXiv:1806.01261*.

Bonet, B., Haslum, P., Hickmott, S., & Thiébaux, S. (2008). Directed unfolding of petri nets. In *Transactions on Petri Nets and Other Models of Concurrency I* (pp. 172–198). Springer. DOI: 10.1007/978-3-540-89287-8_11

Clark, A., Fox, C., & Lappin, S. (Eds.). (2010). *The Handbook of Computational Linguistics and Natural Language Processing* (1re éd.). Wiley. DOI: 10.1002/9781444324044

Debusschere, V., Lefieux, V., Mallet, P., & Roche, N. (2022). *Artificial Intelligence Serving Electrical Networks* [PhD Thesis, Think Smartgrids Scientific Council]. https://hal.science/hal-04050749/document

Dobson, I., Carreras, B. A., Lynch, V. E., & Newman, D. E. (2007). Complex systems analysis of series of blackouts : Cascading failure, critical points, and self-organization. *Chaos (Woodbury, N.Y.)*, 17(2), 026103. Advance online publication. DOI: 10.1063/1.2737822 PMID: 17614690

Hodge, B.-M., Brancucci Martinez-Anido, C., Wang, Q., Chartan, E., Florita, A., & Kiviluoma, J. (2018). The combined value of wind and solar power forecasting improvements and electricity storage. *Applied Energy*, 214, 1–15. DOI: 10.1016/j.apenergy.2017.12.120

Jebali, F., Majumdar, A., Turck, C., Harabi, K.-E., Faye, M.-C., Muhr, E., Walder, J.-P., Bilousov, O., Michaud, A., Vianello, E., Hirtzlin, T., Andrieu, F., Bocquet, M., Collin, S., Querlioz, D., & Portal, J.-M. (2024). Powering AI at the edge : A robust, memristor-based binarized neural network with near-memory computing and miniaturized solar cell. *Nature Communications*, 15(1), 741. DOI: 10.1038/s41467-024-44766-6 PMID: 38272896

Lacity, M., Willcocks, L. P., & Craig, A. (2015). *Robotic process automation : Mature capabilities in the energy sector*. DOI: 10.1038/s41467-024-44766-6 PMID: 38272896

Le Guen, V. (2022). Deep learning for spatio-temporal forecasting—. *Applied Solar Energy*.

Le Guen, V., & Thome, N. (2019). *Prévision de l'irradiance solaire par réseaux de neurones profonds à l'aide de caméras au sol.* GRETSI 2019. DOI: 10.1038/s41467-024-44766-6 PMID: 38272896

Manerba, D., Rinaldi, S., & Pasetti, M. (2018). A Virtual Power Plant Architecture for the Demand-Side Management of Smart Prosumers. *Applied Sciences (Basel, Switzerland)*, 8(3), 432. Advance online publication. DOI: 10.3390/app8030432

Pedretti, A., Santini, M., Scolimoski, J., de Queiroz, M. H. B., Toshioka, F., & Rocha, E., Junior. de P., Pauli Júnior, N. de, Yomura, M. T., Costa, C. H. da, Guerra, F. A., Mulinari, B. M., Grando, F. L., Mumbelli, J. D. C., Costa, C. I. A., Torres, G. L., & Ramos, M. P. (2021). Robotic Process Automation Extended with Artificial Intelligence Techniques in Power Distribution Utilities. *Brazilian Archives of Biology and Technology, 64*, e21210217. https://doi.org/DOI: 10.1590/1678-4324-75years-2021210217

Pérez-Ortiz, J. A., Forcada, M. L., & Sánchez-Martínez, F. (2022). Le fonctionnement de la traduction automatique neuronale. *À tradire. Didactique de la traduction pragmatique et de la communication technique. Didactique de la traduction pragmatique et de la communication technique, 1.* DOI: 10.3390/app8030432

REITER, E., & DALE, R. (1997). Building applied natural language generation systems. *Natural Language Engineering, 3*(1), 57-87. Cambridge Core. DOI: 10.3390/app8030432

Wang, H., Lei, Z., Zhang, X., Zhou, B., & Peng, J. (2019). A review of deep learning for renewable energy forecasting. *Energy Conversion and Management*, 198, 111799. DOI: 10.1016/j.enconman.2019.111799

# Chapter 2
# Leveraging AI to Promote Sustainable Energy Distribution

**Raja R. Vinston**
*SRM Institute of Science and Technology, India*

**K. Fouzia Sulthana**
https://orcid.org/0009-0006-5014-6026
*Rajalakshmi Institute of Technology, India*

**Subha Priyadharshini A**
*Coimbatore Institute of Engineering and Technology, India*

**R. Kotteeswaran**
https://orcid.org/0000-0002-7891-6612
*St. Joseph's College of Engineering, India*

**G. Manikandan**
https://orcid.org/0000-0002-4323-8233
*RMK Engineering College RSM Nagar, India*

**Joel M. Robinson**
https://orcid.org/0009-0006-3095-7024
*KCG College of Technology, India*

## ABSTRACT

*The demand for sustainable energy solutions is more important than ever as the globe struggles to address the twin issues of accelerated climate change and depleting conventional energy sources. In order to provide a stable, sustainable future for future generations, the search for greener, more efficient energy systems is not just about innovation but also about survival. The increasing significance of data science and artificial intelligence (AI) provides a path toward change and a ray of hope in this dire situation. "Leveraging AI to Promote Sustainable Energy Distribution," the chapter's title, delves into the revolutionary potential of artificial intelligence (AI) and data science to transform the global energy distribution and management landscape. This chapter seeks to shed light on the various ways that artificial intelligence (AI) might support the creation of sustainable energy infrastructures by*

DOI: 10.4018/979-8-3373-2530-9.ch002

*a thorough examination of AI-driven techniques, ranging from peer-to-peer energy trading to predictive maintenance and grid optimization.*

## INTRODUCTION

The criticality of the demand for sustainable energy solutions has increased as the world continues to face issues of accelerated climate change and depleting conventional energy resources. Pursuing greener, more efficient energy systems is not simply a matter of innovation but also a question of survival. Data science and AI have opened up a transformative space in this regard (Zhai et al., 2021). This chapter presents the revolutionary capacities of AI and data science towards the transformation of global energy distribution and management. Techniques driven by AI, which include peer-to-peer energy trading, predictive maintenance, and optimization of the grid, are promised to be able to support the generation of sustainable infrastructures for energy. Through the power of AI-driven algorithms, stakeholders can present unprecedented accuracy for solving energy problems and paving a way to a cleaner and a more sustainable future (Smith et al., 2022; Selcuk, 2017). The progress of this crucial sector will be shaped by policy frameworks, ethical issues, and future trends that we will discover as we delve into the nuances of AI applications in energy distribution. Join us on this enlightening exploration of the intersection of sustainability and technology, where artificial intelligence (AI) emerges as a critical enabler of future energy systems. AI's Impact on Energy Systems, A new era in how we approach the optimization and management of energy systems is represented by artificial intelligence (AI). Fundamentally, artificial intelligence (AI) enables machines to learn from data, spot patterns, and make judgments with little to no human input. Artificial Intelligence has the potential to revolutionize established methods and accelerate the shift towards sustainability in the energy distribution sector. Figure 1 explain the flow of the chapter and its important aspects.

*Figure 1. Leveraging AI to promote sustainable energy distribution*

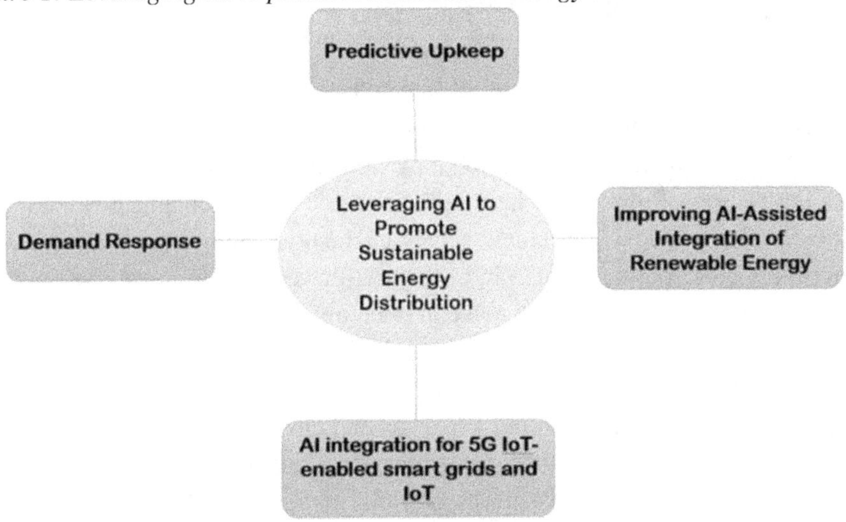


AI is a new frontier in energy system optimization and management, allowing machines to learn from data, identify patterns, and make decisions with minimal human intervention, thereby accelerating the shift toward sustainability. With the help of natural language processing, neural networks, and machine learning, AI enables real-time analysis of large data, giving insights that enhance operational efficiency, reliability, and resilience in energy systems. Core applications of AI in energy distribution include infrastructure optimization, where AI predicts demand patterns, balances supply and demand in real time, and identifies areas for efficiency improvement. It addresses the challenges posed by the intermittency of renewable energy sources by predicting energy generation, optimizing grid integration, and stabilizing fluctuations (Smith et al., 2022). On the other side, AI allows the approach of predictive maintenance. Using equipment data to forecast failures, optimize maintenance schedules, and minimize downtime is possible (Selcuk, 2017). Amidst our research on this intersection of sustainability and technology, AI becomes a key enabler of future energy systems, in general, and policy frameworks, ethical considerations, and emerging trends define the progression in this sector.

## USING AI TO OPTIMIZE GRID PERFORMANCE AND INCREASE ENERGY EFFICIENCY

Energy Efficiency Artificial intelligence (AI) may be used to find areas where buildings, factories, and transportation systems can enhance energy efficiency and save energy, which will cut carbon emissions and consumption of energy.AI-Driven Innovation's Promise, AI has the infinite potential to change how energy is distributed as it develops. Smart meters, demand response programs, self-contained microgrids, virtual power plants, and other AI-driven developments are quickly changing the energy environment. We can open up new avenues for a more robust and sustainable energy future by utilizing AI. Leveraging AI to Optimize Grid Operations Power grid efficiency is crucial to guaranteeing consumers a consistent supply of electricity while reducing expenses and environmental effects. Demand forecasting and real-time monitoring and control are only two of the grid operations optimization strategies made possible by artificial intelligence (AI) technologies. We analyze a few important AI uses for grid optimization in the next part. Intelligent Grid Technologies (Dileep, G. J. R. E. 2020) a paradigm shift in the production, distribution, and use of electricity is represented by smart grids. Smart grids are essentially designed to maximize grid performance in real time by utilizing sophisticated sensors, communication networks, and control systems. AI is essential to the functionality of the smart grid, enabling utilities to Demand Pattern Prediction(Cao et al., 2021), To precisely estimate future energy demand, artificial intelligence (AI) systems examine previous consumption data, weather forecasts, and other variables. Utilities are able to minimize waste and expenses by optimizing the generation and distribution of resources. Balance Supply and Demand: AI-powered systems can more successfully balance supply and demand, reducing the danger of blackouts and grid instability, by continuously monitoring grid conditions and modifying generating and distribution resources in real-time. Discover Anomalies and Faults: Before they become significant disruptions, artificial intelligence (AI) algorithms are able to identify anomalies and faults in the grid infrastructure, such as equipment malfunctions or cyber attacks(Wang, J., & Shi, D. 2018). Utilities can take proactive steps to prevent outages and guarantee grid stability thanks to early detection.

### AI-Powered Demand Response and Predictive Maintenance Systems in Energy Grids

Using AI to Optimize Grids, Predictive Upkeep, An AI-driven predictive maintenance system was put in place by utility company XYZ to keep an eye on the condition of its grid infrastructure. Through the analysis of sensor data from transmission lines and substations, the system may predict possible equipment breakdowns and minimize downtime by identifying them before they happen. Demand Response, To encourage customers to use less electricity during peak hours, City ABC launched a demand response program that is driven by AI algorithms. The system incentivizes consumers to shift their energy consumption to off-peak hours, thereby mitigating grid load and cutting electricity costs, by assessing past consumption patterns and market prices. Upcoming Studies, Grid optimization has limitless possibilities as AI technologies develop further. Future advancements might include the implementation of autonomous grid control methods(Duan et al., 2019) that optimize grid operations in real-time without human intervention, as well as the integration of distributed energy resources, such as solar panels and electric vehicles, into AI-driven grid management systems. The adoption of an AI-driven predictive maintenance system by utility company XYZ represented a dramatic change in grid management procedures. This method made it possible to monitor vital infrastructure elements like transmission lines and substations proactively by utilizing AI algorithms. With the use of machine learning algorithms and ongoing sensor data analysis, the AI system was able to predict equipment breakdowns well in advance of their occurrence. Large volumes of real-time data were gathered by the predictive maintenance system from sensors incorporated into the grid infrastructure. These sensors kept an eye on a number of variables, including equipment vibrations, voltage levels, and temperature. After processing this data, the AI systems found patterns and anomalies that pointed to upcoming equipment breakdowns.

*Figure 2. Benefits of driven demand response program*

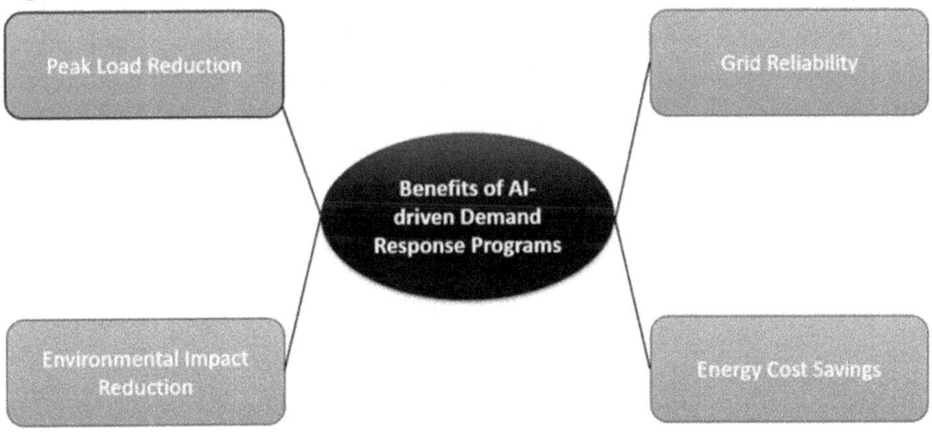


As shown in Figure 2 Improving AI-Assisted Integration of Renewable Energy, because renewable energy sources are inherently unpredictable and variable, integrating them into the power system poses special issues. Examples of these include solar and wind energy. Artificial intelligence (AI), on the other hand, provides strong tools to deal with these issues, enabling a more seamless integration of renewables and improving the stability and effectiveness of the energy system Renewable energy sources are not only sporadic but also geographically distributed(Dolev et al., 2017), which makes integrating them into current systems more difficult. Due to its geographical fluctuation, the production of renewable energy may not always coincide with regions with high energy demand, which could result in transmission issues and unbalanced power systems. Therefore, to manage and optimize the integration of renewable energy into networks of all sizes and complexities, it becomes even more important to have creative solutions, including those that make use of artificial intelligence (AI).

Projecting and Overseeing Renewable Energy results by evaluating meteorological data(Ukhurebor et al., 2020), past production trends, and real-time sensor feedback from renewable energy installations, artificial intelligence (AI) is highly proficient in handling complicated data sets and can accurately forecast the outputs of renewable energy sources. These anticipatory skills are essential for, Energy Output Forecasts: By utilizing AI models, grid operators may anticipate and modify the energy mix ahead of time, especially when it comes to energy output from renewable sources. Because solar and wind energy are sporadic, this aids in preserving grid stability., Demand Matching Artificial Intelligence (AI)(Joel et al., 2023) can help synchronize the output of renewable energy with times of high demand by projecting when renewable energy production will peak. This will maximize the usage of renewable energy and minimize dependency on non-renewable sources. The effortless integration of renewable energy sources, such as solar and wind, is critical to the pursuit of a sustainable energy future. However, grid stability and reliability are challenged by the intermittent nature of renewable energy. Novel approaches that make use of artificial intelligence (AI) are beginning to emerge as a response to this problem, providing accurate output predictions and management of renewable energy. By using cutting-edge AI algorithms, the generation of renewable energy may be timed to coincide with demand peaks, making the best use of renewable resources possible and reducing dependency on non-renewable ones. This proactive strategy advances the shift to a greener, more sustainable energy landscape and increases the effectiveness of energy distribution networks while also lowering carbon emissions.

## Utilizing AI to Optimize Energy Storage Systems for Better Integration with Renewable Energy

Improving energy storage systems' performance is essential to guaranteeing the stability and dependability of the integration of renewable energy sources. By holding excess energy during high production and releasing it during low output or peak demand, energy storage devices help balance the intermittent nature of renewable energy sources. Artificial intelligence (AI) is emerging as a game-changing instrument for managing energy storage more optimally. It provides sophisticated skills to increase longevity and efficiency. Artificial intelligence (AI)-powered prediction algorithms transform the way storage devices are charged and discharged by predicting patterns in energy output and demand. AI algorithms can determine the best charging and discharging schedules, optimizing the lifespan and effectiveness of energy storage devices, by evaluating historical data and real-time variables. By ensuring that storage devices are charged during times of excess energy and discharged during times of peak demand, this predictive strategy efficiently smoothest out variations in the generation of renewable energy and the load on the grid. Additionally, AI systems are essential for keeping an eye on the condition and functionality of batteries used in energy storage. Artificial Intelligence (AI) algorithms(Sriram et al 2023) are able to predict probable breakdowns and optimize maintenance schedules to maintain the dependability and durability of energy storage systems by continuously assessing battery state and efficacy. This proactive strategy increases system reliability, reduces the possibility of unplanned malfunctions, and prolongs the life of energy storage assets. All things considered, incorporating AI into energy storage management is a big step in the direction of building a more durable and sustainable energy infrastructure.

## Leveraging AI to Advance Renewable Integration: Ethical, Economic, and Optimal Factors

Artificial intelligence (AI) is essential for optimizing the performance of wind energy systems and utility-scale photovoltaic (PV)(Ryan, L et al., 2026) farms in the field of renewable energy integration. Several large-scale solar farms in Germany are using AI technologies to forecast solar production with accuracy. system managers can easily incorporate solar energy into the national system thanks to AI algorithms that provide accurate estimates of daily energy production based on analysis of historical data, weather forecasts, and satellite imagery. This predictive capacity helps with efficient energy distribution planning in addition to improving grid stability and dependability. In a similar vein, AI systems in Texas are revolutionizing wind energy optimization through the optimization of turbine output and the reduction of turbine component wear and tear. Artificial intelligence (AI) algorithms improve blade pitch and turbine operations(Mohamed, M. H., & Shaaban, S. 2013) to maximize energy production by analyzing real-time data from wind turbines and incorporating wind forecasts. This raises wind energy generation efficiency and extends the life of turbine components, which lowers maintenance costs and boosts overall reliability. These illustrations show how AI has the ability to completely change the integration of renewable energy sources, opening the door to a more resilient and sustainable energy future.

A key element in accomplishing long-term sustainability goals by lowering carbon emissions and dependency on fossil fuels is the appropriate integration of renewable energy sources. But achieving this goal calls for more than just implementing renewable energy technologies—it also calls for efficient integration and management plans. The integration of renewable energy sources is becoming more and more dependent on artificial intelligence (AI) (Chowdary, V. T.et al., 2022), which offers sophisticated capabilities to improve sustainability, dependability, and energy efficiency over time. Furthermore, it is critical to address the ethical and legal issues surrounding the deployment of AI technologies as they are incorporated into energy distribution networks more and more. To ensure responsible and equitable implementation, it is imperative to comprehend and navigate the legal framework as well as the ethical implications of artificial intelligence (AI) in energy management and renewable integration. As shown in Figure 3 Creating frameworks that support innovation while preserving security, privacy, and equity is necessary to achieve this. Stakeholders may create a regulatory framework that encourages the ethical and sustainable application of AI in improving energy distribution networks toward a more robust and environmentally friendly future by addressing these factors in their entirety.

*Figure 3. AI-driven innovations in energy storage technologies*

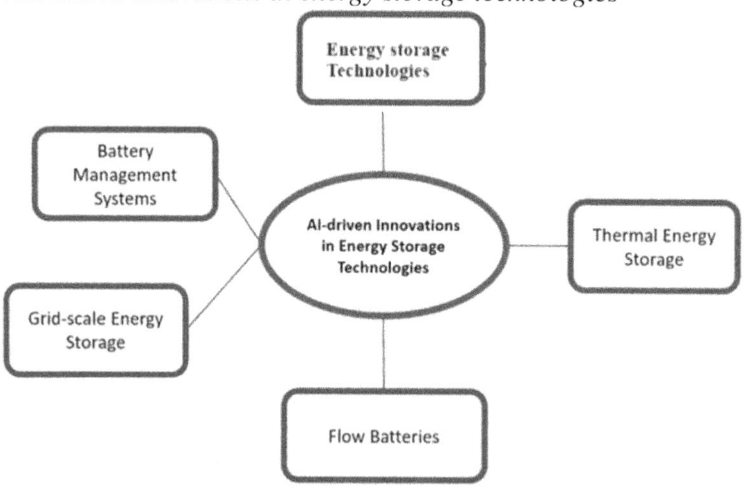

## Overcoming Regulatory Obstacles to AI Integration in Energy Systems: Equitable Access, Security, and Standardization

The successful integration and broad acceptance of artificial intelligence (AI) solutions in energy systems are severely hampered by regulatory issues. The standardization of AI systems is a major obstacle, since it is essential to guarantee safety, compatibility, and interoperability among various systems and geographical areas. Regulatory bodies need to create guidelines for the development and implementation of AI technology in energy systems as these technologies become more and more commonplace in energy management. These guidelines will offer a framework for guaranteeing consistency and dependability in AI-powered energy solutions, encouraging confidence among interested parties, and enabling a smooth transition into the current infrastructure. The security and privacy of data is another urgent topic. Large volumes of data are needed for AI systems to function well, which raises privacy and security issues. A framework for tackling these challenges is provided by regulations like the General Data Protection Regulation (GDPR)(Protection, F. D. 2018), but particular regulations required given the sensitive nature of energy data are also required. Protecting sensitive energy data must come first under regulatory frameworks that also make it easier for data to be collected and shared, which is essential for AI-driven energy management. To guarantee that AI systems can function as effectively as possible while protecting people's and organizations' right to privacy, a delicate balance must be struck. It's also critical to support fair access to the advantages of AI-driven energy solutions(Stecuła, K et al., 2023). It's critical to make sure that the advantages of AI technologies—such as higher integration of renewable sources and more efficient energy distribution—are distributed fairly among all parties involved. Policies must to be formulated to avert a situation in which the benefits of AI-powered energy solutions are centered around particular areas or populations. This calls for proactive steps to close the gaps in resources and technology availability, as well as programs to advance diversity and inclusivity in the creation and application of AI-driven energy solutions.

When developing and implementing artificial intelligence (AI) solutions for energy systems, moral considerations play a crucial role. This is especially true when it comes to bias in AI algorithms and the requirement for accountability and transparency. The possibility of bias in AI algorithms, which might develop if these systems are trained on non-representative(Zagheni, E., & Weber, I. 2015) data sets, is a serious worry. These biases may unintentionally reinforce or deepen preconceived notions, which could result in unequal gains in energy efficiency relative to energy distribution or inequalities in the quality of services provided across different locations. AI systems need to be properly developed and continuously checked to minimize biases in order to meet this challenge. In order to teach AI systems, it is necessary to make sure that the training data sets are representative and diverse. Furthermore, continuous assessment and validation procedures are necessary to find and address any biases that might appear in AI-driven decision-making. Through proactive measures to remove bias in AI systems, stakeholders can reduce the possibility of sustaining societal disparities and guarantee just and equitable distribution of energy. When using AI in energy systems, there are two fundamental concepts that need to be respected: accountability and transparency. Users must uphold a high standard of transparency on the decision-making process of AI algorithms and the accountability of individuals involved in errors or weaknesses, given the substantial influence of AI on energy management decisions. Transparency about the methods used to make AI-driven choices and the people or organizations in charge of monitoring and auditing them is essential to building public confidence in AI technology and guaranteeing a responsible rollout of these systems.

When we look towards sustainable energy's future, it is critical that regulations change to reflect the shifting environment. Subsequent energy policies ought to acknowledge the noteworthy influence of artificial intelligence (AI) in the wider framework of sustainability goals. To advance AI technology for energy systems, this means supporting research and development projects. The continuous advancement of AI for energy requires financial backing, incentives, and the facilitation of joint ventures between public and private organizations. Furthermore, flexible regulatory frameworks are essential for keeping up with the quick advances in AI technology while maintaining efficacy, security, and sustainability objectives. These frameworks should create an atmosphere that is supportive of creativity and experimentation while staying within the confines of regulations by striking a balance between promoting innovation and upholding regulatory control. In order to fully harness the transformational potential of artificial intelligence (AI) in developing sustainable energy systems, future energy policies should place a high priority on supporting international collaboration, boosting research and development, and promoting adaptable regulatory frameworks(Njoroge, P. C. 2013). Policymakers can set the stage for future generations to benefit from an energy infrastructure that is more environmentally friendly, efficient, and resilient by embracing innovation and collaboration.

## Integrating Explainable AI and Edge Computing to Advance Energy Systems

Artificial intelligence (AI) is predicted to play a more varied and extensive role in energy systems, especially in the distribution of sustainable energy, as it continues to progress at a rapid rate. Explainable AI (XAI), one of the most recent advances in AI for energy systems, has emerged. When AI systems are included into vital infrastructure, such as electrical grids, transparency and interpretability become increasingly important factors to take into account. By making AI algorithms more transparent and intelligible, XAI(Das, A., & Rad, P. 2020) seeks to allay these worries and enable stakeholders to verify and have faith in the choices these systems make. XAI improves accountability and builds stakeholder confidence by offering insights into the thinking underlying AI-driven decisions. This eventually makes it easier for AI technologies to be responsibly used in energy systems. The integration of AI with edge computing is another important trend in AI for energy systems. By processing data closer to the source, edge computing lowers latency and uses less bandwidth. AI and edge computing together can increase the resilience and responsiveness of energy systems. Enhancing grid stability and dependability are made possible by more effective and flexible energy management made possible by real-time analysis and decision-making at the system's edge. Artificial intelligence (AI)-driven insights produced at the edge can guide dynamic changes to energy distribution and consumption patterns, maximizing resource efficiency and reducing waste. This convergence of edge computing and artificial intelligence (AI) offers a viable path forward for improving the efficacy and efficiency of energy systems, especially when considering distributed renewable energy sources. Recent developments in artificial intelligence for energy systems, like explainable AI and edge computing, have the potential to drastically change the energy industry. These technologies facilitate a resilient and sustainable energy distribution system by increasing responsiveness, accountability, and transparency. It is anticipated that as artificial intelligence (AI) advances, new discoveries will be made that will accelerate the continuous improvement of energy management strategies and hasten the transition to a more sustainable and efficient energy future.

## IoT, 5G, and AI are Revolutionizing Energy Systems to Improve Connectivity, Efficiency, and Equity

A new era of connectivity for energy systems has been brought about by the growth of Internet of Things (IoT) devices(Lakshmi, B. N., & Joel, M. R. 2023), allowing for improved connectivity and data collecting. AI algorithms are skilled at sifting through IoT device data to find trends, increase energy efficiency, and streamline grid operations. Energy systems may anticipate equipment failures, identify anomalies in consumption patterns, and dynamically modify energy distribution to maximize efficiency and dependability by utilizing AI-powered analytics. An important development in energy management has been made with the integration of AI with IoT-enabled smart grids, opening the door to more responsive and efficient grid operations. Real-time energy management requires quicker and more dependable connectivity, which is provided by the rollout of 5G networks. 5G-enabled

AI-powered energy management systems can take advantage of 5G networks' high speed and low latency to simplify grid operations and provide customers with flexible pricing alternatives. These systems' capacity to handle enormous volumes of data in real-time enables them to optimize resource allocation, enhance overall grid efficiency, and quickly adjust to shifting patterns of energy consumption. Energy systems may become more agile and responsive, which will improve sustainability and dependability, by utilizing 5G and AI(Soldani, D., & Illingworth, S. A. 2020). AI has enormous potential to advance energy equity and usability, especially when used to community-focused energy solutions. AI-driven community micro grids encourage resilience and independence by enabling nearby communities to take charge of their energy production and consumption. These micro grids lessen dependency on centralized energy infrastructure and improve energy security by facilitating localized energy production, distribution, and sharing. Furthermore, in underdeveloped nations with poor access to dependable energy infrastructure, AI-powered solutions have the potential to completely transform energy access. These technologies, which range from AI-driven demand management systems to off-grid renewable energy solutions, have the potential to improve quality of life and accelerate economic development by giving underprivileged communities more access to reliable, inexpensive energy.

Through the promotion of fairness and usability, artificial intelligence (AI) has the potential to revolutionize energy systems, especially when it comes to community-centric energy solutions(Swarnakar, P., & Singh, M. K. 2022). The development of community microgrids, which gives local communities the ability to take charge of their energy production and consumption, is one noteworthy application of AI in this context. AI-driven community microgrids promote resilience and independence by empowering users to control their localized energy distribution networks and harvest renewable energy sources. These microgrids promote community self-sufficiency and lessen dependency on centralized infrastructure by decentralizing energy production and distribution, especially in times of grid outage or natural disasters. Additionally, AI algorithms maximize the distribution of energy in microgrids Lasseter, R. H. 2002), guaranteeing effective resource use and reducing waste, which supports sustainability and economy. In spite of community-focused energy solutions, AI-powered technologies are essential for tackling issues related to energy availability in developing nations. Artificial intelligence (AI)-driven solutions that improve pricing and dependability can provide major benefits to many locations with limited access to reliable energy infrastructure. Demand management solutions powered by AI make better use of the energy resources that are available, optimize energy distribution, and cut down on waste. Furthermore, even in isolated locations without access to conventional grid infrastructure, off-grid renewable energy technologies, including solar-powered microgrids, can give underprivileged people dependable access to electricity. Through the utilization of AI algorithms for predictive maintenance and system optimization, off-grid solutions may guarantee dependable and sustainable energy access, hence enhancing living standards and propelling economic growth in neglected areas. Artificial intelligence (AI)-driven solutions for community-focused energy projects and energy access in underdeveloped areas have the capability to change lives and advance sustainability. AI promotes resilience, independence, and equity in energy systems by enabling communities to control their own energy resources and by utilizing renewable energy technologies. These technologies have the potential to accelerate the transition to universal energy access and a more just and sustainable energy future for everybody as they develop and become more widely available.

*Figure 4. Environmental benefits of AI-assist energy distribution*

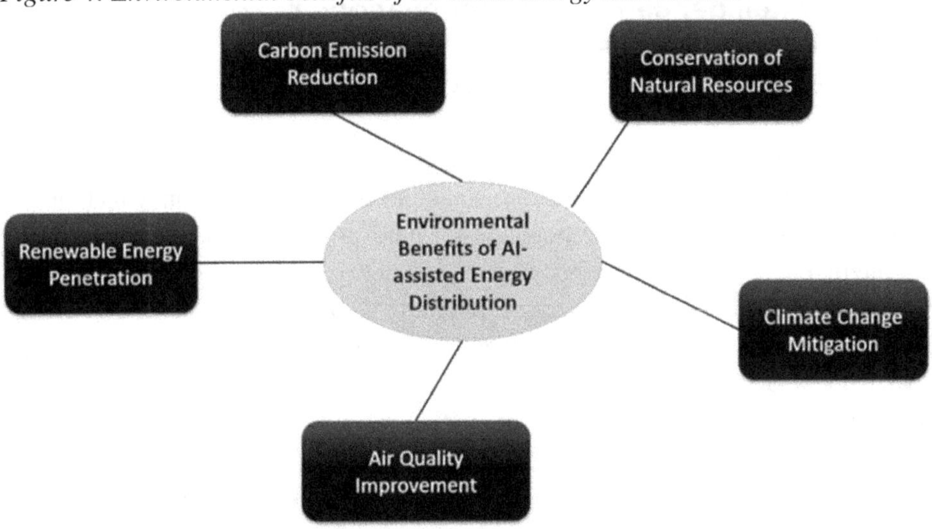


As shown in Figure 4 with community-centric solutions and activities aimed at boosting energy access in underserved locations, artificial intelligence (AI) has the potential to greatly improve accessibility and fairness in energy systems. AI-powered community-centric energy solutions give local communities the ability to take charge of their energy production and use. Community microgrids with AI capabilities enable distributed energy production, delivery, and sharing at the local level, fostering self-sufficiency and resilience(Dion, M. R. 2013). These microgrids improve neighborhood self-sufficiency and lessen reliance on centralized infrastructure by decentralizing energy generation and distribution, particularly in times of grid outage or natural disasters. Furthermore, AI algorithms maximize the distribution of energy in microgrids, guaranteeing effective resource use and reducing waste, which supports sustainability and economy. AI-powered solutions have the potential to be revolutionary in developing nations with limited access to dependable energy infrastructure. These technologies, which range from AI-driven demand management systems to off-grid renewable energy systems, can improve impoverished populations' access to reliable and reasonably priced electricity. Demand management solutions powered by AI optimize energy distribution, increasing productivity and cutting waste. Off-grid renewable energy technologies, including solar-powered microgrids, on the other hand, give isolated populations without access to conventional grid infrastructure dependable access to electricity. These off-grid solutions provide dependable and sustainable energy access, promoting economic development and raising standards of living in neglected areas by utilizing AI for system optimization and predictive maintenance.

## Artificial Intelligence-Powered Innovations in Sustainable Energy Distribution: Improving Effectiveness, Availability, and Cooperation

A bright future for energy systems around the world is shaped by the integration of artificial intelligence (AI) into sustainable energy distribution, which offers various unique advantages. The potential for innovation and efficiency that artificial intelligence (AI) offers energy distribution networks is one important benefit. Energy systems can improve energy efficiency, smoothly incorporate renewable energy sources, and optimize grid operations by utilizing AI algorithms. A more sustainable and dependable energy infrastructure can be achieved through the use of AI-enabled real-time monitoring, predictive maintenance, and dynamic energy management to create more robust and efficient energy systems. Additionally, by streamlining the switch to renewable energy sources and improving energy distribution, AI significantly contributes to sustainability. AI-driven solutions help lower carbon emissions and lessen climate change by encouraging the use of renewable energy sources like solar and wind power. AI-powered energy distribution network optimization boosts sustainability initiatives and creates an eco-friendly energy infrastructure that supports global sustainability objectives(Von Stechow el al., 2015). Furthermore, AI-enabled technology could improve equity and accessibility to energy, especially in underprivileged areas. AI-powered off-grid renewable energy systems and community-focused energy solutions can improve local communities' access to and affordability of electricity. These solutions enhance the quality of life and stimulate economic growth in neglected areas by empowering communities to take charge of their energy resources through the decentralization of energy production and distribution. The use of AI to sustainable energy distribution encourages cooperation and creativity between governmental bodies, academic institutions, and private enterprises. Stakeholders can propel technical developments in the field of artificial intelligence for energy systems and accelerate progress through interdisciplinary research efforts and public-commercial partnerships. Collaborative initiatives can lead to a more sustainable and equitable energy future for all by utilizing collective expertise and resources to unlock new possibilities and create dramatic improvements in energy distribution networks.

Artificial intelligence (AI) is being incorporated into energy systems to promote social advancement, economic growth, and environmental benefits. The growth of skills and employment opportunities in cutting-edge industries like engineering, data science, and cyber security(Kaur, J., & Ramkumar, K. R. 2022) is a major benefit. The need for qualified people with experience in these fields is rising as AI is incorporated into energy systems more and more. Education and training initiatives may provide people with the skills they need to succeed in the AI-driven energy industry, which will foster innovation, economic expansion, and job creation. Furthermore, AI-powered energy management systems may increase customer access to and affordability of energy. Artificial intelligence-powered systems improve energy affordability, especially for low-income households and vulnerable locations, by optimizing energy usage, avoiding waste, and lowering pricing. Enhancing accessibility to energy not only helps people individually but also aids in poverty alleviation and socioeconomic development, which in turn promotes equitable and sustainable economic growth. AI-driven solutions are essential for preserving natural resources and cutting carbon emissions in the context of environmental sustainability. Artificial intelligence (AI) technologies reduce greenhouse gas emissions and mitigate the effects of climate change by improving energy production, delivery, and consumption. AI also makes it possible to use energy resources more effectively, which lessens the demand on finite resources and the disturbance of natural ecosystems. Predictive maintenance and optimization algorithms can help energy infrastructure function more sustainably, reducing its environmental impact and promoting long-term ecological health. AI improves the resilience and adaptability of the grid by strengthening and enhancing the flexibility of energy systems. Real-time interruption identification and reaction are made possible by AI-powered grid management systems, guaranteeing a consistent supply of energy even in the face of inclement weather or cyberattacks. AI also makes it possible for energy systems to adapt to changing environmental factors and customer needs, strengthening their resistance to change socioeconomic dynamics and climatic trends. Last but not least, integrating AI into energy systems supports a number of UN Sustainable Development Goals (SDGs)(Hák et al., 2016), such as SDG 9 on industry, innovation, and infrastructure; SDG 13 on climate action; and SDG 7 on cheap and sustainable energy. Stakeholders may help the global effort to meet these ambitious aims by utilizing AI to promote sustainable energy distribution, advancing the goal of a more sustainable, inclusive, and prosperous future for all.

## Rethinking Energy Management: Artificial Intelligence's Contribution to a Sustainable and Robust Energy Future

The integration of artificial intelligence (AI) into energy distribution systems marks a significant milestone in our quest for resilience and sustainability. Throughout this chapter, we have explored how AI has the potential to revolutionize energy management by enhancing the integration of renewable energy sources, optimizing grid operations, and fostering innovation. AI-driven solutions, ranging from peer-to-peer energy trading to demand forecasting and predictive maintenance, are transforming the production, distribution, and consumption of energy, paving the way for a cleaner and more sustainable energy future. By embracing AI technology, stakeholders in the energy sector have the chance to open up new avenues towards a more sustainable and clean energy future. By developing adaptable regulatory frameworks that encourage innovation and facilitate the incorporation of AI-driven solutions into energy systems, policymakers may play a critical role. AI has the potential to improve grid stability and responsiveness while lowering operating costs, and grid operators stand to gain from this greater efficiency and dependability. Additionally, with the help of AI-driven insights and energy management technologies, users can make more informed decisions about how much energy they use. Adoption of AI-powered energy solutions benefits the environment, the economy, and society in many ways. Notably, these solutions help lower carbon emissions, which benefits present and future generations by fostering a healthier and more sustainable environment. Additionally, the advancement of AI technologies fosters economic expansion and new job possibilities, fostering innovation and prosperity both within and outside the energy sector. AI-powered energy solutions also have the potential to lower energy costs, increasing the accessibility of clean and renewable energy for communities worldwide. As shown in Figure 5 ongoing investment in R&D, innovation, and cooperation is necessary to realize AI's full potential in energy systems. We can create a future energy infrastructure that is more resilient, egalitarian, and ecologically friendly by coordinating with global sustainability goals and utilizing AI to facilitate sustainable energy distribution. Let's embrace the revolutionary potential of AI as a global community and collaborate to create a future in which energy is no longer just a commodity but rather a force for sustainable development and positive change.

*Figure 5. Energy storage technologies*

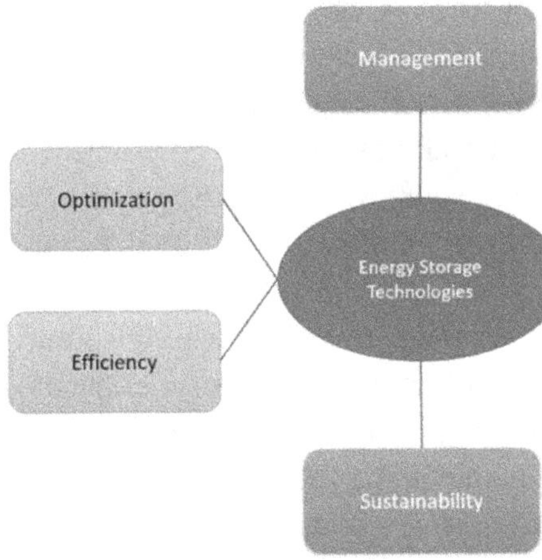


## Benefits of Using AI to Encourage the Distribution of Sustainable Energy

The convergence of artificial intelligence (AI) and sustainable energy distribution has attracted a lot of interest lately. AI technologies provide previously unheard-of chances to optimise energy production, distribution, and consumption. These technologies range from machine learning algorithms to sophisticated analytics. This combination has enormous potential to alleviate the world's energy problems, improve efficiency, lower carbon footprints, and hasten the shift to sustainable energy sources. The benefits of employing AI to support sustainable energy distribution are examined in this article, with particular attention paid to demand-side management, grid management, integration of renewable energy sources, and policy development.

Grid management is one of the main uses of AI in energy distribution. Traditional energy systems frequently encounter difficulties including demand swings, ageing infrastructure, and supply uncertainty from renewable sources like wind and solar. Grid operators can more effectively manage loads thanks to the ability of AI-powered algorithms to estimate energy supply and demand dynamically. For example, machine learning algorithms may more accurately forecast energy demand by examining historical data, weather trends, and real-time use. Utilities may minimise the need for expensive infrastructure changes, optimise generating schedules, and lessen their reliance on fossil fuels thanks to this predictive capabilities. AI also improves grid stability by controlling and monitoring in real-time. Artificial intelligence (AI)-enabled smart grids are capable of problem detection on their own, power rerouting to avoid blackouts, and network voltage optimisation.

These features not only increase dependability but also make it easier to integrate decentralised energy sources like electric vehicle (EV) charging stations(Rajendran, G et al 2021) and microgrids. Utilities can increase overall grid resilience, reduce maintenance costs, and increase operational efficiency by utilising AI.

Energy distribution is faced with both possibilities and problems as a result of the fast increase of renewable energy sources. Through improved grid integration of renewable energy sources, artificial intelligence (AI) is a key factor in addressing these obstacles. For example, AI systems are able to estimate solar and wind power output by using past data and weather forecasts. Because of this foresight, grid operators may minimise their dependency on backup fossil fuel plants during times when renewable production is low by adjusting conventional generating and storage resources accordingly. Predictive maintenance powered by AI also increases the dependability of infrastructure supporting renewable energy. Artificial Intelligence (AI) may identify abnormalities or possible breakdowns in wind turbines, solar panels, and energy storage systems by evaluating sensor data and performance indicators in real-time. Reducing downtime, extending equipment lifespan, and optimising asset utilisation are all important aspects of proactive maintenance based on AI insights that help maximise the return on the purchase of renewable energy projects.

Demand-side management (DSM)(Apajalahti, E et al 2015) enabled by AI is yet another important advantage for sustainable energy distribution. DSM seeks to lower peak demand and total energy consumption by modifying patterns of power usage in response to pricing signals or supply restrictions. To optimise DSM methods, AI systems examine past consumption trends, customer behaviour, and external circumstances (such as the weather and economic activity). AI, for example, can enable dynamic pricing plans that encourage users to switch to off-peak hours when there is a greater production of renewable energy. In order to automatically modify heating, cooling, and appliance operations based on current energy costs or carbon intensity, smart home devices and IoT sensors can communicate with AI platforms. AI-driven DSM helps maintain grid stability, lowers greenhouse gas emissions, and lowers consumer power bills by smoothing demand peaks and lowering total energy use.

Policymakers and regulators may learn a great deal about energy patterns, environmental effects, and economic ramifications from AI analytics. Artificial Intelligence (AI) can evaluate the efficacy of current laws, model the consequences of proposed legislation, and pinpoint areas for change through the analysis of extensive datasets. AI models, for instance, are capable of assessing the socioeconomic effects of policies that support renewable energy, set carbon prices, or mandate energy efficiency requirements for certain geographic or demographic groupings. Furthermore, AI improves scenario analysis and energy forecasts, empowering decision-makers in a complicated and unpredictable environment. Governments may expedite the adoption of renewable energy technology, encourage energy saving efforts, and more successfully meet ambitious climate objectives by incorporating AI-generated insights into decision processes.

In summary, the application of AI technology has great potential to further the global distribution of sustainable energy. AI makes energy systems more effective, dependable, and ecologically friendly by improving demand-side management, integrating renewable energy sources, and promoting evidence-based policymaking. To fully realise AI's promise in energy distribution, however, cooperation between several stakeholders—utilities, technology companies, legislators, and consumers—is necessary to overcome ethical, legal, and technological issues. We can quicken the shift to renewable energy and lessen the effects of climate change for future generations by ethically and fairly utilising AI's capabilities.

## Drawbacks of Using AI to Encourage the Distribution of Sustainable Energy

Undoubtedly, there are many advantages to using AI to promote the distribution of sustainable energy, but as with any technology, there are possible disadvantages as well. Although AI has the potential to speed up the switch to renewable energy sources and optimise energy systems, its adoption and use face a number of challenges. The limitations of employing AI to promote sustainable energy distribution are examined in this article, with particular attention paid to problems including technological constraints, ethical dilemmas, financial ramifications, and social effects.

The technological constraints and dependability of AI in energy distribution are among the main issues. For AI algorithms to make good decisions, data accuracy, amount, and quality are crucial. Uncertainties in weather forecasting, the unpredictability of renewable energy sources, and intricate grid linkages provide major issues in the context of energy systems. For example, during extreme weather events or unanticipated conditions, AI models could find it difficult to properly estimate energy consumption or optimise grid operations. Furthermore, strong cybersecurity precautions are needed when implementing AI technology in energy infrastructure. Operational interruptions, ransomware attacks, and data breaches are among the cyber dangers that smart grids and IoT devices linked to AI systems are susceptible to. For utilities and IT companies, ensuring the security and resilience of AI-driven energy systems continues to be a major concern.

Energy distribution AI technology implementation entails significant up-front expenditures and complexity. Developing and implementing AI algorithms customised to specific energy systems need large expenditures in research, development, and infrastructure. To properly enable AI-driven decision-making, utilities and energy firms must also invest in data gathering, integration, and management skills. Additionally, incorporating AI into the current energy infrastructure frequently necessitates the deployment of new hardware and software or the retrofitting of outdated systems. Utilities may face financial difficulties as a result of these modifications, which may be expensive and time-consuming, particularly for smaller or publicly financed organisations with tighter budgets. Widespread acceptance of AI deployment may be hampered by the expensive initial investment and continuous maintenance expenses involved, especially in areas or industries with limited funding.

Lawmakers, regulators, and the general public are becoming increasingly concerned about the ethical ramifications of AI in the distribution of energy. When AI algorithms are employed in energy systems, biases or inequality may be unintentionally maintained, especially when decisions are being made about resource allocation, pricing, and energy access. For instance, if demand-side management techniques powered by AI are not developed and applied fairly, they may disproportionately affect low-income households or vulnerable areas. In addition, the use of AI technology calls into question the accountability, transparency, and delegation of decision-making power. Who is accountable for AI mistakes or malfunctions in vital energy infrastructure? What measures can stakeholders take to guarantee equity and inclusion in AI-powered energy practices and policies? Strong governance structures, regulatory supervision, and stakeholder involvement are necessary to address these moral conundrums in order to protect society values and advance fair access to sustainable energy alternatives.

*Table 1. AI applications in energy systems*

| AI Application | Key Focus Areas | Impact | Key References |
|---|---|---|---|
| **Energy Optimization** | Data-driven learning, real-time decision-making. | Enhances sustainability and operational efficiency. | Zhai et al., 2021 |
| **Infrastructure Optimization** | Demand prediction, supply-demand balancing, efficiency improvements. | Improves grid reliability and reduces waste. | Smith et al., 2022 |
| **Integration of Renewable Energy** | Renewable output forecasting, grid integration, fluctuation management. | Stabilizes energy distribution, maximizes renewable energy use. | Selcuk, 2017 |
| **Predictive Maintenance** | Equipment condition monitoring, fault prediction, maintenance optimization. | Reduces downtime, extends equipment lifespan, minimizes costs. | Selcuk, 2017 |
| **Smart Grids** | Demand pattern prediction, anomaly detection, decentralized management. | Enhances grid performance and reliability. | Dileep, G. J. R. E., 2020 |
| **Energy Demand Prediction** | Analyzing historical data, weather forecasts, and real-time variables. | Anticipates energy needs, optimizes resource distribution. | Cao et al., 2021 |

continued on following page

*Table 1. Continued*

| AI Application | Key Focus Areas | Impact | Key References |
|---|---|---|---|
| **Cybersecurity in Energy** | Detection and prevention of cyber threats on energy infrastructure. | Protects critical systems from cyberattacks, ensures operational stability. | Wang & Shi, 2018 |
| **Community Microgrids** | Localized energy management and distribution. | Promotes resilience, self-sufficiency, and equitable energy access. | Lasseter, 2002 |
| **Demand-Side Management (DSM)** | Consumer behavior analysis, energy usage optimization based on pricing. | Reduces peak demand, lowers consumer costs, and increases energy efficiency. | Apajalahti et al., 2015 |
| **Explainable AI (XAI)** | Transparency and interpretability of AI decision-making processes. | Builds stakeholder trust, ensures accountability in energy systems. | Das & Rad, 2020 |
| **IoT in Energy Systems** | Utilizing IoT devices for real-time data analysis and decision-making. | Optimizes grid operations and improves energy management efficiency. | Lakshmi & Joel, 2023 |
| **5G Networks** | High-speed, low-latency connectivity for AI-driven energy solutions. | Enhances real-time response and grid flexibility. | Soldani & Illingworth, 2020 |
| **Regulatory Challenges** | Standardization, privacy concerns, ensuring equitable access. | Aligns energy practices with legal frameworks, promotes fair use of AI technologies. | Protection, F. D., 2018; Stecuła et al., 2023 |
| **Energy Policy Implications** | Data-driven policy-making and scenario modeling. | Guides sustainable energy transitions and resource management. | Von Stechow et al., 2015 |

Large volumes of data, including sensitive information about customer behaviour, consumption trends, and infrastructure operations, are crucial to the functioning of AI systems in the energy distribution industry. Data privacy, ownership, and protection are critical issues, particularly when AI platforms gather and process private or sensitive data from smart metres, Internet of Things devices, and grid sensors. Unauthorised access to energy data has the potential to destroy customer privacy, reveal flaws in the energy infrastructure, and erode confidence in artificial intelligence (AI) technology. Mitigating privacy issues connected with AI deployment in energy distribution requires strengthening data governance frameworks, putting data anonymization techniques into practice, and making sure that data protection legislation (such as the CCPA(Barrett, C. 2019) and GDPR)(Voss, W. G. 2021) are properly followed. This Table 1 summarizes the various aspects of AI applications in energy systems, focusing on their key areas, impacts, and foundational references

AI's use in energy distribution might result in job losses and cause a workforce shift in the energy industry. Automation powered by AI has the potential to improve operational efficiency, decrease labor-intensive jobs, and streamline operations for utilities and energy firms. While AI opens up new career paths in domains like cybersecurity, data science, and AI development, it also has the potential to replace certain traditional jobs. To mitigate the socio-economic effects of AI adoption in the energy industry, it is imperative to establish workforce development efforts, reskilling and upskilling programmes, and a smooth transition for displaced workers. In order to promote equitable economic growth amid technological breakthroughs and educate the workforce with the skills necessary for the digital economy, collaboration between industrial players, educational institutions, and policymakers is imperative.

The regulations and regulatory frameworks controlling the use of AI in energy distribution are still developing, which makes it difficult for stakeholders to manage legal compliance and regulatory uncertainties. Promoting the safe, moral, and responsible application of AI technology in energy systems requires striking a balance between innovation and regulatory control. The assessment of AI's advantages and disadvantages, the creation of standards for AI-driven energy technology, and the enforcement of current rules provide difficulties for regulatory authorities. Furthermore, global efforts to harmonise AI policies and promote international cooperation on sustainable energy projects may be complicated by regional variations in regulatory frameworks and geopolitical difficulties. Governments, business executives, academic institutions, and civil society organisations must work together to address these regulatory and policy difficulties in order to create flexible regulatory frameworks that promote innovation while defending the interests of the general public and environmental sustainability.

In conclusion, AI has limitations and difficulties even if it has revolutionary potential to support the distribution of sustainable energy. For stakeholders to properly exploit AI's benefits, a complex environment of ethical considerations, data privacy difficulties, socio-economic implications, and technological constraints and implementation costs must be navigated. To tackle these obstacles, a comprehensive strategy is needed, combining technology advancement with moral and legal concerns, as well as inclusive community involvement. We can use AI to hasten the worldwide transition to a fair and sustainable energy future while minimising unforeseen consequences by proactively resolving its disadvantages in the distribution of energy.

## CONCLUSION

The integration of artificial intelligence (AI) into the energy sector opens up significant prospects for increasing sustainable energy distribution. AI can optimise energy generation, improve grid reliability, and enable the integration of renewable energy sources by leveraging advanced data analytics, predictive modelling, and real-time monitoring. By integrating AI, stakeholders may overcome the inherent issues of unpredictability in renewable energy, lower operating costs, and increase overall energy system efficiency. Furthermore, AI-powered solutions can help with the development of smart grids, which are critical for controlling decentralised energy supplies and guaranteeing a balanced supply and demand. These technologies offer more precise forecasting of energy production and consumption patterns, allowing for proactive modifications that reduce waste while increasing the usage of renewable sources. Furthermore, AI can play an important role in enhancing energy storage technology and demand response tactics, therefore improving the resilience and sustainability of energy distribution networks. To summarise, the use of AI in sustainable energy distribution is not just a novel method, but a necessary progression in the face of global environmental issues. By using AI technology, we can take substantial steps towards a more sustainable, efficient, and resilient energy future. This transformation will need concerted efforts from legislators, industry leaders, and technology developers to ensure that AI solutions are deployed responsibly and equitably, eventually benefiting the environment and society as a whole.

## REFERENCES


Apajalahti, E. L., Lovio, R., & Heiskanen, E. (2015). From demand side management (DSM) to energy efficiency services: A Finnish case study. *Energy Policy*, 81, 76–85. DOI: 10.1016/j.enpol.2015.02.013

Barrett, C. (2019). Are the EU GDPR and the California CCPA becoming the de facto global standards for data privacy and protection? *Scitech Lawyer*, 15(3), 24–29.

Cao, D., Zeng, K., Wang, J., Sharma, P. K., Ma, X., Liu, Y., & Zhou, S. (2021). BERT-based deep spatial-temporal network for taxi demand prediction. *IEEE Transactions on Intelligent Transportation Systems*, 23(7), 9442–9454. DOI: 10.1109/TITS.2021.3122114

Chowdary, V. T., Joel, M. R., Ebenezer, V., Edwin, B., Thanka, R., & Jeyaraj, A. (2022, March). A novel approach for effective crop production using machine learning. In *2022 International Conference on Electronics and Renewable Systems (ICEARS)* (pp. 1143–1147). IEEE. DOI: 10.1109/ICEARS53579.2022.9751798

Das, A., & Rad, P. (2020). Opportunities and challenges in explainable artificial intelligence (XAI): A survey. *arXiv preprint arXiv:2006.11371.*

Dileep, G. J. R. E. (2020). A survey on smart grid technologies and applications. *Renewable Energy*, 146, 2589–2625. DOI: 10.1016/j.renene.2019.08.092

Dion, M. R. (2013). A framework for advancing the well-being and self-sufficiency of at-risk youth. *Mathematica Policy Research*, 7720. DOI: 10.1016/j.renene.2019.08.092

Dolev, S., Florissi, P., Gudes, E., Sharma, S., & Singer, I. (2017). A survey on geographically distributed big-data processing using MapReduce. *IEEE Transactions on Big Data*, 5(1), 60–80. DOI: 10.1109/TBDATA.2017.2723473

Duan, J., Shi, D., Diao, R., Li, H., Wang, Z., Zhang, B., Bian, D., & Yi, Z. (2019). Deep-reinforcement-learning-based autonomous voltage control for power grid operations. *IEEE Transactions on Power Systems*, 35(1), 814–817. DOI: 10.1109/TPWRS.2019.2941134

Hák, T., Janoušková, S., & Moldan, B. (2016). Sustainable development goals: A need for relevant indicators. *Ecological Indicators*, 60, 565–573. DOI: 10.1016/j.ecolind.2015.08.003

Joel, M. R., Manikandan, G., & Bhuvaneswari, G. (2023, March). An analysis of security challenges in Internet of Things (IoT)-based smart homes. In *2023 Second International Conference on Electronics and Renewable Systems (ICEARS)* (pp. 490–497). IEEE. DOI: 10.1109/ICEARS56392.2023.10085106

Kaur, J., & Ramkumar, K. R. (2022). The recent trends in cyber security: A review. *Journal of King Saud University. Computer and Information Sciences*, 34(8), 5766–5781. DOI: 10.1016/j.jksuci.2021.01.018

Lakshmi, B. N., & Joel, M. R. (2023, March). IoT-based illness prediction system using machine learning. In *2023 Second International Conference on Electronics and Renewable Systems (ICEARS)* (pp. 1087–1091). IEEE. DOI: 10.1109/ICEARS56392.2023.10085553

Lasseter, R. H. (2002, January). Microgrids. In *2002 IEEE Power Engineering Society Winter Meeting. Conference Proceedings (Cat. No. 02CH37309)* (Vol. 1, pp. 305–308). IEEE. DOI: 10.1109/PESW.2002.985003

Mohamed, M. H., & Shaaban, S. (2013). Optimization of blade pitch angle of an axial turbine used for wave energy conversion. *Energy*, 56, 229–239. DOI: 10.1016/j.energy.2013.04.035

Njoroge, P. C. (2013). A study of effectiveness of regulatory framework in construction industry in promoting sustainability (Doctoral dissertation).

Protection, F. D. (2018). General data protection regulation (GDPR). *Intersoft Consulting, Accessed in October, 24(1)*. DOI: 10.1016/j.energy.2013.04.035

Rajendran, G., Vaithilingam, C. A., Misron, N., Naidu, K., & Ahmed, M. R. (2021). A comprehensive review on system architecture and international standards for electric vehicle charging stations. *Journal of Energy Storage*, 42, 103099. DOI: 10.1016/j.est.2021.103099

Ryan, L., Dillon, J., La Monaca, S., Byrne, J., & O'Malley, M. (2016). Assessing the system and investor value of utility-scale solar PV. *Renewable & Sustainable Energy Reviews*, 64, 506–517. DOI: 10.1016/j.rser.2016.06.004

Selcuk, S. (2017). Predictive maintenance, its implementation and latest trends. *Proceedings of the Institution of Mechanical Engineers. Part B, Journal of Engineering Manufacture*, 231(9), 1670–1679. DOI: 10.1177/0954405415601640

Smith, O., Cattell, O., Farcot, E., O'Dea, R. D., & Hopcraft, K. I. (2022). The effect of renewable energy incorporation on power grid stability and resilience. *Science Advances*, 8(9), eabj6734. DOI: 10.1126/sciadv.abj6734 PMID: 35235363

Soldani, D., & Illingworth, S. A. (2020). 5G AI-enabled automation. In *Wiley 5G Ref* (pp. 1–38). Wiley. DOI: 10.1002/9781119471509.w5GRef225

Sriram, K. P., Joel, M. R., Navaneethakrishnan, M., & Manonmani, S. P. (2023, March). Machine learning algorithms for predicting house prices in a smart city using its real-time data. In *2023 Second International Conference on Electronics and Renewable Systems (ICEARS)* (pp. 1064–1070). IEEE.

Stecuła, K., Wolniak, R., & Grebski, W. W. (2023). AI-driven urban energy solutions—From individuals to society: A review. *Energies*, 16(24), 7988. DOI: 10.3390/en16247988

Swarnakar, P., & Singh, M. K. (2022). Local governance in just energy transition: Towards a community-centric framework. *Sustainability (Basel)*, 14(11), 6495. DOI: 10.3390/su14116495

Von Stechow, C., McCollum, D., Riahi, K., Minx, J. C., Kriegler, E., Van Vuuren, D. P., Jewell, J., Robledo-Abad, C., Hertwich, E., Tavoni, M., Mirasgedis, S., Lah, O., Roy, J., Mulugetta, Y., Dubash, N. K., Bollen, J., Ürge-Vorsatz, D., & Edenhofer, O. (2015). Integrating global climate change mitigation goals with other sustainability objectives: A synthesis. *Annual Review of Environment and Resources*, 40(1), 363–394. DOI: 10.1146/annurev-environ-021113-095626

Voss, W. G. (2021). The CCPA and the GDPR are not the same: Why you should understand both. *CPI Antitrust Chronicle*, 1(1), 7–12.

Wang, J., & Shi, D. (2018, September). Cyber-attacks related to intelligent electronic devices and their countermeasures: A review. In *2018 53rd International Universities Power Engineering Conference (UPEC)* (pp. 1–6). IEEE. DOI: 10.1109/UPEC.2018.8542059

Zagheni, E., & Weber, I. (2015). Demographic research with non-representative internet data. *International Journal of Manpower*, 36(1), 13–25. DOI: 10.1108/IJM-12-2014-0261

Zhai, X., Chu, X., Chai, C. S., Jong, M. S. Y., Istenic, A., Spector, M., Liu, J.-B., Yuan, J., & Li, Y. (2021). A review of artificial intelligence (AI) in education from 2010 to 2020. *Complexity*, 2021(1), 8812542. DOI: 10.1155/2021/8812542

# Chapter 3
# Resilience and Impact of the AI on Energy Efficiency Management in Renewable Energies

**Karla Mariel Fernandez Fabian**
*University National of Engineering of Perú, Peru*

**Antonio Cano Ortega**
https://orcid.org/0000-0002-6440-021X
*University of Jaén, Spain*

## ABSTRACT

*This chapter presents an overview of renewable energies and artificial intelligence, current status, benefits, challenges, characteristics, while advancing, concepts are deepened, as sample applications and successful cases of application of artificial intelligence and / or data science, demonstrating that the proper use of different tools, models and emerging technologies, can optimize processes, management, and even allow early detection of anomalies, allowing preventive and efficient measures to be taken, even in adverse conditions, complemented with some quantitative data that help to better visualize the importance and impact achieved. By improving efficiency and resilience, artificial intelligence accelerates the transition to a more sustainable energy system, supporting the global goals of emissions reduction and climate change mitigation. Artificial intelligence is revolutionizing energy efficiency management in renewable energy systems, improving resilience, optimizing operation and contributing to a faster and more sustainable transition to a clean energy future*

DOI: 10.4018/979-8-3373-2530-9.ch003

# 1. INTRODUCTION

## 1.1. Renewable Energy Overview

Renewables are virtually inexhaustible sources of energy, such as solar, wind, hydro, geothermal, and biomass, each with unique characteristics and applications that make them valuable in different environments and contexts. Although they offer clear environmental benefits, such as being clean and autochthonous, they can also present some specific challenges, which for a long time have been studied, evaluated and in constant scientific, technological, and environmental progress, as can be seen in *Table 1*, which is why artificial intelligence now also takes on greater importance, since its ability to adapt to different conditions allows it to effectively manage variations in the environment. production of renewable energies, maintaining performance and optimizing their integration into complex energy systems.

*Table 1. Previous studies related to energy efficiency in renewable energies*

| Antecedent | Description |
|---|---|
| Energy in Spain 2020 | The official report of the (Ministry of ecological transition and demographic challenge, 2020) which provides an overview of the energy structure of Spain until 2020, were on energy efficiency and renewable energies. |
| Efficient energy management in organizations | The toolbox developed within the Agreement signed between ECOEMBES and the Trade Union Institute of Labor, Environment and Health ISTA (Ferrer Márque, María-Tomé Gi, Pérez Díaz, & Vilallonga Ortiz, 2018) who set out areas of action for organizations to improve energy management, promoting energy savings and efficiency. |
| Global outlook for energy transitions 2023 | The report of (IRENA, 2023) it conveys that renewable energies and efficiency as key drivers of the energy transition at a global level. |
| Renewables 2023 | The report of The International Energy Agency (IEA) (The International Energy Agency (IEA), 2023) It highlights the record growth in renewable energy capacity globally in 2023 and projections for 2030, highlighting the need for financing in emerging economies. |

## 1.2. Resilience in the Energy Context

In this context, the resilience of energy systems has become a key issue, considering that our planet is prone to constant natural disasters, as well as it is important to recognize the fluctuating nature of captured energy that can jeopardize a constant supply of energy. That's why, in energy terms, resilience refers to a system's ability to withstand and recover quickly from constant variations while trying to maintain optimal performance. The integration of artificial intelligence in energy management promises not only to improve this resilience, but also to optimize the operational efficiency of renewable energy facilities through the use of digital technologies, data analytics, predictive algorithms (Ali, Sharma, Joy, & Halim, 2024), among others that together allow the potential in energy management to be extracted in a way that provides greater reliability and sustainability for the management and progress of current and future energy systems.

## 1.3. Artificial Intelligence as a Tool for Energy Efficiency

Artificial Intelligence has transformed numerous sectors, and the energy sector is no exception, as its application in energy efficiency is changing the way energy resources are managed, distributed and consumed, not only optimizing energy use, but also helping to anticipate and solve the challenges associated with the integration of renewable energies due to its flexibility with different techniques and approaches to solve various problems. A flexible system is not limited to a single way of operating and can employ multiple methods to achieve a goal.

Adaptability and flexibility are interrelated, but they are not the same. An adaptive system can adjust its parameters and processes to maintain performance in the face of changes for continuous improvement, while a flexible system is one that has the ability for a system to perform a variety of different tasks and adapt to multiple application domains. Therefore, the advantage of artificial intelligence is that it incorporates both characteristics (Li et al., 2024), allowing it to adapt to changes in the environment, as well as address a wide range of challenges with different techniques and strategies to address an adequate management of energy efficiency in renewable energies.

## 1.4. Resilience of Artificial Intelligence as a Contribution to Environmental Impact

One of the main impacts of artificial intelligence on energy management is its ability to predict and optimize energy consumption in real time. Through techniques such as machine learning, energy systems can automatically adjust energy production and distribution based on forecasted demand, thereby enabling greater operational efficiency. The study by (Benhammou, Tedjini, Guettaf, & Hartani Mohamed, 2023) demonstrate that their proposal with an artificial intelligence method reduced hydrogen consumption by 8% compared to the classical approach, and improved efficiency to more than 98% compared to traditional methods.

Additionally, artificial intelligence facilitates better integration of variable renewable energy sources, such as solar and wind, which are unpredictable by nature. By predicting future scenarios based on data, AI makes it possible to optimize power generation and its integration into the power grid, improving system stability and reducing reliance on storage or fossil fuel-based backup sources. These advances not only make energy more efficient, but also strengthen the resilience of renewable energy systems, making them less vulnerable to fluctuations.

## 2. RENEWABLE ENERGY MANAGEMENT AND EFFICIENCY

Renewable energy management and efficiency is a key area in the transition to a sustainable energy future, due to the goals and challenges related to energy efficiency, and the tools and techniques available to manage these variable energy sources on a meteorological time scale above all.

### 2.1. Renewable Energy Overview

Renewable energies have established themselves as one of the most viable alternatives for addressing climate change and reducing dependence on fossil fuels. As technologies advance, these energy sources, which include solar, wind, hydroelectric, geothermal and biomass, have become more accessible and cost- competitive.

**Solar Energy:** Solar photovoltaics is one of the fastest growing renewable technologies. Solar panels convert sunlight into electricity through photovoltaic cells, offering a clean and abundant solution, especially in regions with high solar irradiation (the free Global Solar Atlas application provides quick and easy access to data on solar resources and photovoltaic energy potential worldwide) (ATLAS Renewable Energy, 2024). It is also important to take into account the angle of inclination and orientation of the solar cells, because depending on the latitude and orientation of the sun influences the generation and/or loss of energy.

**Wind Energy:** Wind energy is generated by wind turbines that convert the kinetic energy of the wind into electricity. It is one of the most established forms of renewable energy, with onshore and offshore wind farms in operation in more than 100 countries. According to the International Renewable Energy Agency (IRENA T. I., 2024) 473 GW (346 GW solar, 116 GW wind + other) of renewable energy was added in 2023, representing a record 86% of the world's added capacity, although it is expected to triple by 2023.

**Hydroelectric Power:** This form of energy uses the force of moving water to generate electricity. It is the oldest and most mature renewable source, providing 15% of the world's electricity. There are currently 590 GW of hydropower projects under development (outlook, 2023). Although highly efficient and capable of generating power on a large scale, its expansion is limited by environmental and geographic considerations.

**Geothermal Energy and Biomass:** Geothermal energy harnesses heat from within the Earth's interior to generate electricity, while biomass uses organic matter as an energy source. Although less common than other forms of renewable energy, both technologies offer significant advantages, such as the ability to provide constant baseload power, making them ideal for supplementing other more intermittent renewable sources (Lund & Toth, 2021).

## 2.2. Renewable Energy Efficiency Objectives and Challenges

Energy efficiency refers to the ability to use the least amount of energy to perform the same function(s) or produce the same result, resulting in a reduction of energy consumption and greenhouse gas emissions. In the context of renewable energies, energy efficiency involves not only the improvement of energy conversion processes, but also the optimization of their integration into power grids and end use.

The main objectives of energy efficiency are to maximize the use of available natural resources, minimizing losses during the generation, storage and distribution of energy. This includes improving the efficiency of solar panels, wind turbines and hydroelectric plants, as well as integrating these sources more effectively into existing power grids.

The challenges mainly refer to the intermittency of renewable sources, such as solar and wind, mainly due to their strong dependence on the variation of weather conditions, which makes it difficult to plan and balance the load in real time, which can generate inefficiencies in the grid (IRENA T. I., 2024). In addition, modernization of energy infrastructure to accommodate distributed generation and energy storage management are critical issues that need to be addressed to improve overall energy efficiency.

## 2.3. Tools and Techniques for the Management of Different Renewable Energies

For effective management of renewable energies, a combination of technological tools, support policies and implementation strategies are needed to optimize their performance and their integration into energy systems:

**Modelling and Simulation:** The use of computational models and simulations is crucial to predict energy generation and optimize its integration into the grid. These tools allow planning the optimal location of wind and solar farms in order to anticipate energy production based on weather conditions and design efficient storage strategies. Additionally, it is important to have a clear understanding of which modular components were built, so that the model helps to communicate this on its own. For example, it allows to delineate parts that can be more easily validated such as technical data, geospatial data or simulation models (Pfenninger, 2024).

**Energy Management Systems (EMS):** EMS are technology platforms that monitor and control the generation and distribution of renewable energy in real time. These systems make it possible to automatically adjust production based on demand, improve grid efficiency and minimize losses, resulting in a more efficient and sustainable operation. For example, Scheneider Electric's ADMS - DERMS solution, which is an EMS energy management system, provides applications for state estimation, load flow, optimal power flow, fault calculation, optimal topology change, performance indices and voltage stability (Santos Valdés & Garcia Sánchez, 2023); it also allows visualizing, operating, optimizing and maintaining subtransmission and transmission networks in an optimal way, i.e. it provides an optimized and automated system.

**Storage:** Energy storage is key to managing the intermittency of renewable sources such as solar and wind. Technologies such as lithium-ion batteries, thermal energy storage and pumped hydro storage allow energy to be stored during periods of high production and released when demand is higher. These solutions are essential to ensure a stable and continuous supply of renewable energy, optimizing its use and ensuring that it is always available when needed.

**Smart Grids:** Smart grids integrate information and communication technologies into electricity grids, enabling more efficient management of energy distribution. These grids facilitate the integration of renewable energies, improve the reliability of supply and enable a rapid response to variations in demand, as they contribute to the advancement of efficient and comprehensive energy infrastructures, thus facilitating a transition towards a low-carbon, decentralized and sustainable energy paradigm (Qusay, y otros, 2024), visualize its representation in Figure 1.

*Figure 1. Panoramic view of smart grid integration*

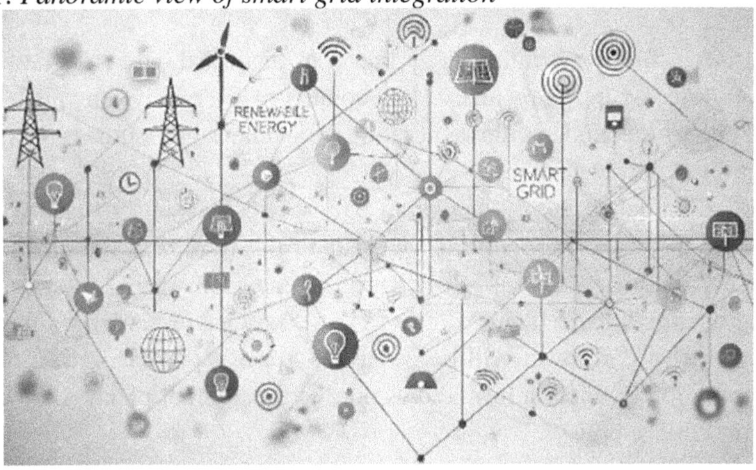


**Forecasting and Predictive Modelling:** Artificial intelligence algorithms can analyze large volumes of weather and plant performance data to forecast renewable energy production more accurately. This allows grid operators to anticipate fluctuations in supply and demand, thus optimizing energy efficiency. A concrete example is the use of neural networks to predict solar and wind power generation, which has enabled 72% prediction with Convolutional Neural Network (CNN) and 79% prediction with Variational Modal Decomposition (VMD) (Yagang et al., 2023). These improvements in forecasting allow for more efficient energy management and greater integration of renewable energies into the power grid.

## 3. PREDICTIVE MODELLING AND OPTIMIZATION IN ENERGY SYSTEMS

This section expands on the concept and techniques of predictive modelling and optimization in energy systems, as this is a crucial area for improving efficiency and sustainability in energy generation, distribution and consumption. Fundamental concepts, techniques, tools and algorithms for energy optimization and practical implementation examples are explored.

## 3.1. Predictive Modelling Concepts

Predictive modelling is a technique that uses historical data and statistical algorithms to forecast future results. In the context of energy systems, it is used to anticipate energy demand, predict generation from renewable sources, and optimize the operation of power grids.

Predictive models work by analysing patterns in past data to identify causal relationships and correlations that may recur in the future. In the energy arena, these models are critical for capacity planning, renewable energy integration, and improving operational efficiency. For example, a predictive model can help determine how much solar power will be generated at a PV plant based on predicted weather conditions, which in turn allows production at other plants to be adjusted to ensure a stable supply.

## 3.2. Techniques and Tools for Predictive Modelling

Predictive modelling in energy systems encompasses a variety of techniques and tools that allow anticipating future behaviours based on historical data and identifiable patterns. These techniques are not only crucial for the planning and optimization of energy resources, but are also fundamental for the effective integration of renewable energy sources into power grids.

### 3.2.1. Time Series Models

Time series models have a special focus for predictive modeling, so it is feasible to apply in energy systems, where variations over time have a significant impact on energy generation and demand.

Among these, the ARIMA (Auto Regressive Integrated Moving Average) model, which is one of the most widely used in time series, combines three main components: autoregression (AR), differencing (I) and moving average (MA). Autoregression predicts the future value of a time series based on its past values. Differencing is used to make the series stationary, eliminating trends or cyclical patterns (Ewa, y otros, 2023). Finally, moving average models the prediction error as a function of past errors.

The Eq. (1) of the ARIMA model is:

$$Y_t = c + \varnothing_1 T_{t-1} + \varnothing_2 T_{t-2} + \ldots + \theta_1 \epsilon_{t-1} + \theta_2 \epsilon_{t-2} + \ldots + \epsilon_t \tag{1}$$

Where:

$Y_t$: value of the series over time *t.*
c : *constant.*
$\phi_x$: *coefficient of the autoregressive terms*
$\theta_x$: *coefficient of moving average terms*
$\epsilon_t$: error in time *t*

ARIMA models are widely used in forecasting energy demand and renewable energy production, as they allow analysing historical patterns and projecting on a timeline into the future.

### 3.2.2. Linear Regression

Within fundamental statistics, a predictive modelling technique called linear regression is used to understand and model the relationship between a dependent variable and one or more independent variables. In energy systems, linear regression makes it possible to predict how changes in external factors, such as temperature or economic growth, may affect energy demand.

The Eq. (2) for a simple linear regression is:

$$Y = \beta_0 + \beta_1 X + \epsilon \quad (2)$$

Where:

$Y$: dependent variable (Example: energy)
$X$: independent variable (Example: irradiance)
$\beta_0$: constant term or intersection
$\beta_1$: regression coefficient: regression coefficient measures the change of $Y$ for each change in $X$
$\epsilon$: residual or error term

This model is particularly useful for forecasting energy demand as a function of factors such as weather, energy prices, or the level of industrial activity, allowing energy managers to anticipate and adjust energy supply more accurately (D.C, E.A., G.G., & A.G., 2022).

### 3.2.3. Artificial Neural Networks

Artificial neural networks (ANNs) are like small brains with networks of digital neurons that can learn from large amounts of data. They are inspired by how the human brain works, where neurons communicate with each other to process information.

In the context of energy, these networks can be trained to detect complex patterns in data and make very accurate predictions. For example, a neural network can learn to predict how much solar energy will be generated based on data such as cloud cover, time of day and season.

An ANN is built in layers: the input layer receives the data, the hidden layer processes that information, and the output layer generates the prediction. Each connection between neurons has a weight that determines the importance of the connection and are initialized randomly or by advanced methods such as Xavier initialization or He initialization to avoid problems with the gradient. These weights will be adjusted during training to minimize the error in predictions.

$W_{ij}$= random initial weight between neurons *i* and *j*

Then each neuron passes an activation function (chosen according to the problem and the nature of the data) that allows learning complex patterns, the most common are:

Especially in deep learning models is ReLU (Rectified Linear Unit), Eq (3):

$$f(x) = \max(0, x) \tag{3}$$

The Eq. (4) is used in classification problems is Sigmoid:

$$f(x) = \frac{1}{1 + e^{-x}} \tag{4}$$

The next step is that the incoming data passes through the network layers, by Eq. (5):

(5)

Where:

Y: *output data (prediction)*
$X_i$: inputs (e.g.: temperature)
$w_i$: weights related to each entry
*b*: *bias (value to be added to adjust output).*
*f*:*function to combine information (sigmoid function converting values to 1 or 0)*

Finally, the activation function to obtain the output of the neuron by Eq. (6):

(6)

Where:

$a_j$: output of neuron after activation
$f(z_j)$: activation function applied to the input

When required to handle complex data or make predictions in situations where there are many interrelated variables, neural networks are very useful, as they accommodate and can consider several types

## 3.3. Practical Application of Predictive Modeling

As part of the tools for implementing a predictive model, it is necessary to have a general-purpose, easy- to-use programming language, which is why Python is versatile and has become a key tool, with complementary libraries available. A practical example of how to implement a predictive model in Python to forecast solar power generation is described below:

Step 1: Import Libraries
Step 2: Data Loading and Preprocessing
Step 3: Evaluation of the Model
Step 4: Results

*Figure 2. Representation of the operation of a predictive model*

Therefore, it is summarized that predictive modelling in energy systems is based on a combination of mathematical techniques and advanced software tools that allow predicting, planning and optimizing energy use (Figure 2). These techniques are essential to efficiently integrate renewable energies and improve the resilience of energy systems in the face of current challenges.

## 4. SMART GRIDS AND DEMAND MANAGEMENT BASED ON ARTIFICIAL INTELLIGENCE OR DATA SCIENCE

It is described that both artificial intelligence and data science are transforming energy demand management, optimizing the stability of smart grids, and providing ease and optimization in their application.

### 4.1. Artificial Intelligence Characteristics and Their Evolution

To implement these predictive modelling techniques, there are software tools that are essential for the development of the energy sector:

**Python:** This programming language is very popular for its ease of use and the large number of libraries it offers, such as Scikit-learn for machine learning, TensorFlow for neural networks and Pandas for data management. Python allows professionals to build complex predictive models with relative ease and is widely used in the energy sector.
**R:** Known for its power in statistical analysis, R is ideal for predictive modelling. It offers specialized tools for time series and regression analysis, making it a preferred choice for researchers who need to perform detailed analysis.
**MATLAB:** Used primarily in engineering, MATLAB is excellent for complex simulations and calculations. It is particularly useful in applications that require advanced data visualization or in creating predictive models for energy optimization that integrate advanced communication technologies, artificial intelligence (AI), and data science to more efficiently and sustainably manage energy generation, distribution, and consumption.

These techniques and tools are essential for any professional or researcher wishing to understand and predict the behaviour of energy systems in a constantly advancing environment, thus enabling the development of solutions that drive sustainability and efficiency in the energy sector.

- Personalization: refers to the ability of AI systems to tailor their services, products or recommendations to the specific preferences, behaviours and needs of the user(s) according to preferences, based on the collection and analysis of personal data, enabling AI to deliver unique and personalized experiences for each individual.
- Multi-Paradigm: the use of multiple learning paradigms (supervised, unsupervised, reinforcement, etc.) depending on the nature of the problem and the data available (Russell & Norvig, 2021).
- Integration: referring to the ability to integrate with other systems and technologies, allowing cooperation and exchange of information between different tools and platforms (Salgado Reyes, 2023).

In order for the computer to achieve the aforementioned characteristics, it is necessary to train the machines so that they can operate autonomously and with the same capabilities of a human being, for this, a combination of algorithms (set of instructions, rules and processes that machines use to perform tasks that normally require human intelligence) is necessary. These algorithms take advantage of large amounts of data and calculations to learn, make decisions and solve problems. The evolution of technologies such as cloud, computation and big data has made artificial intelligence more accessible and efficient; the following is a breakdown of the concepts of the types of algorithms:

## 4.2. Machine Learning Algorithms

Machine learning is a discipline within artificial intelligence that focuses on the development of algorithms that allow machines to learn from data and improve their behavior without the need to be explicitly programmed. Some of the most commonly used machine learning methods in energy efficiency are:

- **Supervised Learning:** In this case, the model is trained with data that are already labelled, i.e., both inputs and outputs are known. An example of this would be forecasting energy demand as a function of variables such as temperature, day of the week and previous energy consumption. The general supervised model can be expressed Eq. (7) as follows:

(7)

Where:

*y*: target variable (e.g., energy demand)

$x$: input variables (e.g., temperature, time of day).
$f(x)$: function that the model is trying to learn.
$\epsilon$: is the error.

- **Unsupervised**: Applied when there are no labels for the data. Clustering algorithms, such as k-means, can be used to perform unsupervised clustering of energy consumption patterns. The objective is to find a function $f(x)$ that groups the data in a similar way.
- **Reinforcement Learning:** This approach involves artificial intelligence agents learning to make optimal decisions through interaction with their environment. An example would be to dynamically adjust the behaviour of a renewable energy system to maximize efficiency and thereby automatically minimize operating costs, Eq. (8).

(8)

Where:

Q(s,a): *stock value function*
α: *learning rate*
$r$: *reward received*
$\gamma$: *discount factor for future rewards*

- **Artificial Neural Networks:** These are machine learning models based on the structure of the human brain. They are used in various applications, such as predicting power generation from renewable sources. A typical neural network consists of layers of neurons, where each neuron applies an activation function after a linear combination of inputs.

Neural Network Architecture

A typical neural network consists of multiple layers:

- o **Input Layer:** Receives inputs (raw data) and passes them to the next layer. Each input represents a characteristic of the data set, such as temperature or amount of energy consumed.
- o **Hidden Layers:** These layers process information. Each neuron in a hidden layer receives a weighted combination of the outputs of the previous layer. These weights are adjusted during network training to minimize prediction error.
- o **Output Layer:** Produces the final prediction or decision based on the processing performed by the previous layers.

## 4.3. Types of Artificial Neural Networks

Artificial Neural Networks (ANNs) can be classified into different types according to their architecture, purpose and training method. The most commonly used types, especially in energy efficiency applications, are described below:

### 4.3.1. Convolutional Neural Networks (CNNs)

Convolutional Neural Networks (CNNs) were originally designed for image processing and analysis. However, their ability to capture spatial and temporal patterns makes them also useful in energy efficiency, particularly in the detection of anomalies in thermal imaging-based systems or analysis of energy usage pattern.

- o **Applications:** Convolutional Neural Networks can be used to monitor photovoltaic systems by image analysis, detecting hot spots indicating faults in solar panels. In addition, they are used in the analysis of spatial patterns of energy consumption in large infrastructures (LeCun, Bengio, & Hinton, 2015).
  - **Example:** In a solar power plant, CNNs can analyse thermal images of solar panels to identify problems such as overheating or partial shading, enabling proactive maintenance and improving overall system efficiency.

### 4.3.2. Recurrent Neural Networks (RNNs)

Recurrent Neural Networks (RNNs) are designed to handle sequential data, which makes them particularly useful for time series analysis. In energy efficiency, RNNs can predict energy demand based on historical data, considering temporal patterns such as hours of the day, days of the week, and seasons of the year, among others that maintain some recurrence (Graves & Schmidhuber, 2005).

- o **Applications**: RNNs are especially useful for power demand forecasting, allowing utilities to optimize power generation and distribution. They are also used in forecasting energy prices in fluctuating markets.
  - **Example**: An RNNs could predict energy consumption in a building throughout the day, allowing energy supply to be adjusted proactively and reducing operating costs.

### 4.3.3. Deep Neural Networks (DNNs)

Deep Neural Networks (DNNs) are characterized by having many hidden layers, allowing them to model complex relationships in large-scale data. In energy efficiency, DNNs are useful for optimizing complex and nonlinear processes, such as the management of smart grids or the control of heating, ventilation and air conditioning (HVAC) systems in smart buildings (Goodfellow, Bengio, & Courville, 2016).

- **Energy Efficiency Applications**: DNNs are used in the optimization of energy storage systems, control of smart grids and optimization of energy distribution. They are also applied in the optimization of industrial processes to minimize energy consumption and reduce carbon emissions.
  - **Example**: An energy management system based on DNNs can analyse large volumes of data in real time to dynamically adjust power distribution in a smart grid, improving system stability and efficiency.

### 4.3.4. Radial Based Neural Networks (RBFNs)

Radial Basis Neural Networks (RBFNs) are a type of neural network used primarily in classification and regression tasks. In energy efficiency, RBFNs are useful for predicting energy demand and modeling complex systems where fast response to changes in input conditions is needed.

- **Applications:** RBFNs can be used to model the relationship between energy demand and external factors such as temperature or economic activity. They are also applied in the optimization of renewable energy systems.
  - **Example**: An RBFN can predict energy demand in a renewable energy system, allowing real-time adjustment of energy production to meet demand without waste.

### 4.3.5. Modularized Neural Networks

Modularized Neural Networks consist of several sub models or modules that work together to solve a complex problem. Each module specializes in a specific task, which makes this approach useful in energy systems where multiple variables and sub-systems are managed (Hinton & Salakhutdinov, 2006).

- **Applications:** These networks are useful in smart grid management, where different modules can be responsible for optimizing power generation, storage and distribution, considering factors such as demand, weather conditions and storage capacity.

- **Example:** In a smart grid, one module could be responsible for predicting energy demand, while another optimizes storage and distribution based on the predictions.

### 4.3.6. Autoencoder Neural Networks (AE)

Autoencoders are neural networks that are trained to replicate their inputs as outputs. They are primarily used for dimensionality reduction and anomaly detection. In energy efficiency, Autoencoders can help identify unusual patterns in energy consumption that could indicate system failures or inefficiencies (Hinton & Salakhutdinov, 2006).

o **Applications:** Autoencoders can be used to detect anomalies in energy consumption systems, allowing inefficiencies to be identified and corrected before they become major problems.

- **Example:** An HVAC system in a smart building could use Autoencoders to monitor energy consumption and detect patterns that indicate equipment malfunction, allowing proactive intervention.

## 4.4. Integration of Artificial Intelligence and Data Science in Energy Management

Artificial intelligence has become an essential tool for improving efficiency, sustainability and resilience in renewable energy management. This subtopic explores three key areas in which it is revolutionizing the field: intelligent management systems, automation and optimization, and the impact on costs and sustainability.

In addition, they enable precise monitoring and control of renewable energy plants, such as solar and wind farms. These systems are capable of analysing large volumes of data in real time, facilitating faster and more accurate decision-making.

**Real-Time Monitoring:** Artificial intelligence allows continuous monitoring of energy production, identifying any deviations or problems that may arise. For example, in a solar plant, artificial intelligence algorithms can detect shadows on the panels and adjust the orientation of the panels to maximize sunlight collection.

**Fault Prediction:** Intelligent systems can predict equipment failures before they occur, enabling preventive maintenance and avoiding interruptions in energy production. This is achieved by analyzing patterns in historical and real-time data.
**Grid Management:** Artificial intelligence can optimize the integration of renewable energy into the power grid, adjusting supply according to demand and weather conditions. This is crucial to ensure the stability of the power system, especially in grids with a high penetration of renewable energy.

Regarding Process Automation and Production Optimization, AI not only improves the monitoring and control of renewable energy systems, but also automates critical processes and optimizes energy production and distribution. This is achieved using advanced machine learning algorithms and predictive analytics (Ali et al., 2024).

**Energy Demand Prediction:** Artificial intelligence can accurately predict energy demand based on historical data, weather conditions and consumption patterns. These predictions allow operators to adjust energy production in real time to meet demand without over-producing or wasting energy.
**Energy Production Optimization:** Artificial intelligence algorithms can optimize energy production by adjusting operating parameters based on current conditions. For example, in a wind farm, AI can adjust the pitch of turbine blades to maximize power generation based on wind speed and direction.
**Distribution Automation:** Artificial intelligence can automate power distribution, directing it to the areas that need it most at any given time. This is especially useful in smart grids, where AI can balance load and prevent overloads or blackouts (Kaile, Chao, & Shanlin, 2016).

It is also important to consider reducing operating costs and improving sustainability, because by automating processes and optimizing production, companies can reduce the use of resources and minimize waste, leading to more sustainable and profitable operations.

- **Reduced operating costs:** Artificial intelligence can reduce operating costs by automating manual tasks, improving energy efficiency and reducing equipment downtime. For example, by predicting failures and scheduling preventive maintenance, companies can avoid costly emergency repairs.
- **Improved energy efficiency:** By optimizing energy production and distribution, artificial intelligence helps minimize energy waste and maximize operational efficiency.

- **Long-term sustainability:** Artificial intelligence also enables companies to meet environmental regulations and long-term sustainability goals. By using AI to optimize resource use and reduce emissions, companies can enhance their reputation and attract sustainable investments.

After reviewing some theoretical points within Artificial Intelligence, Table 2 summarizes as an example two institutions that chose to integrate artificial intelligence and how they managed to obtain significant impacts, which, without a doubt, sets precedents for continued improvement and even as a basis for other institutions to consider the different AI tools to optimize some of the processes of their energy systems.

*Table 2. Impacts of companies that integrated artificial intelligence*

| Company | AI integration | Sustainable impact | Economic impact |
|---|---|---|---|
| Google (United States) | Optimization of energy consumption in data centres using DeepMind (machine learning) AI technology to consume less energy on its own servers, which were already super-efficient. Energy demand forecasting and production optimization in wind farms. | 40% reduction in energy use for refrigeration, significantly reducing the carbon footprint. Reduced need for backup power, increasing the sustainability of wind operations. | 15% reduction in operating energy costs (Richard Evans, 2024). 20% improvement in predictability and reduction of costs associated with overproduction (Shead & FORBES, 2019). |
| Atlas Renewable Energy (International) | With predictive AI models, it forecasts power generation and detects equipment failures, to facilitate the maintenance of your solar and wind plants. | They managed to integrate renewable energies into the electricity grid with better efficiency, promoting greater adoption of clean sources. | At the Sao Pedro solar plant in Brazil, they managed to adjust the periods for cleaning the panels, increasing production by 0.7%, equivalent to 1,000 MWh per year (ATLAS Renewable Energy, 2024). |

## 4.5. Artificial Intelligence Applications

Artificial intelligence has become an essential pillar for innovation in many sectors, but its impact on the energy sector is truly transformative. AI has the ability to analyse vast amounts of data and recognize patterns using advanced algorithms, which is completely changing the way we manage and optimize our energy resources. This breakthrough is especially crucial in the current context, where the world is accelerating towards a transition to renewable energy.

### 4.5.1. Performance Optimization in Renewable Energy Systems

The growing demand for renewable energy has led to the need for more efficient systems, and artificial intelligence can help to automatically optimize the optimal values for the tilt and orientation of solar panels or wind turbines in order to maximize energy production. This improves efficiency and reduces operating costs.

Challenges:

- **Intermittency:** Solar and wind energy depend on variable weather conditions, which generates instability in production.
- **Grid Management:** The integration of renewable sources into existing power grids presents challenges.
- **Storage optimization:** Energy storage solutions are essential to mitigate intermittency.

Benefits:

- **Improved System Control:** AI adjusts operating parameters to maximize efficiency and minimize costs.
- **Grid Control:** AI facilitates the integration of renewable sources into the grid, improving stability and security.
- **Storage Management:** AI facilitates the integration of renewable sources into the grid, improving stability and security.

### 4.5.2. Predictive Maintenance of Equipment

Today, sustainability and energy efficiency have become essential, however, like any complex technology, they require proper maintenance to ensure their optimal performance and durability. Predictive maintenance, therefore, is a proactive strategy that uses data and analytics to anticipate and prevent potential failures or breakdowns in renewable energy equipment before they occur. This reduces system interruptions and minimizes maintenance costs, ensuring the reliability of energy production, which is why it is becoming an essential tool for optimizing the operation of power generation systems.

Challenges:

Benefits:

The renewable energy industry due to its fluctuating nature needs to adopt predictive maintenance actions to optimize its performance, reliability and profitability, so research and development of artificial intelligence algorithms specific to the renewable energy sector will continue to drive its innovation.

Likewise, collaboration between renewable energy companies, technology providers and artificial intelligence companies is crucial for the development of innovative solutions.

### 4.5.3. Smart Grid Management

Management with respect to power grids and microgrids is evolving rapidly with the integration of artificial intelligence, as it enables enormous potential to optimize grid operation, improve energy efficiency, increase reliability and reduce costs.

Microgrids are an example of decentralization and integration of smart grids, which allow managing energy supply and demand dynamically, improving system efficiency and stability. These systems use artificial intelligence and big data analysis to predict consumption and production patterns, optimizing resource management. They also employ predictive maintenance to detect problems before they cause failures, and efficient storage solutions, such as high-capacity batteries or energy storage in the form of heat or hydrogen, to balance production and consumption. Continuous learning and adaptation in active data processing is necessary to reduce latency and bandwidth usage and make it a smart grid (Udo, Kwakye, Ekechukwu, & Ogundipe, 2024). Efficient management of renewable energy includes not only generation, but also distribution, storage and consumption of energy, relying on monitoring systems, sensors and smart meters to reduce losses and improve infrastructure.

### 4.5.4. Prediction of Renewable Energy Production

It allows accurate prediction of solar and wind power generation, considering factors such as solar radiation, wind speed, temperature and weather conditions, Figure 3. This facilitates the integration of renewable energy sources into the power grid.

Challenges:

- **Climate Variability:** Climate has a significant impact on renewable energy production. Changing conditions such as temperature and irradiance affect energy production conditions.
- **Limited Data:** Lack of reliable historical data can hinder the development of accurate predictive models. The quantity and quality of data are essential for accuracy.
- **Grid Complexity:** The interaction between different renewable energy sources and the grid can create a complex system that is difficult to model.

Benefits:

- **Improved Grid Management:** Predictions enable better management of the power grid, optimizing power dispatch and reducing the need for backup.
- **Integration with Renewable Sources:** Forecasting facilitates the integration of renewable energy sources into the power grid, improving reliability and stability.
- **Production Optimization:** Accurate forecasting enables optimization of renewable energy production, maximizing efficiency and minimizing operating costs.

*Figure 3. Representation of data science, applied to monitoring and analysis of data from renewable sources*

## 4.6. Successful Cases of Application of Artificial Intelligence and Data Science

Productivity and energy efficiency are closely related in the context of renewable energies. Improving productivity often means optimizing energy efficiency, and vice versa. For example, the use of advanced technologies and proper equipment maintenance can increase the amount of energy generated (productivity) while reducing losses (energy efficiency). Likewise, efficient energy management can maximize the use of available resources, improving overall system productivity.

# 5. MACHINE LEARNING FOR ENERGY STORAGE AND DISTRIBUTION

In today's world, renewable energy plays an increasingly crucial role in the fight against climate change. Solar and wind energy, although clean and abundant, are unpredictable by nature, as the saying goes: "the sun doesn't always shine and the wind doesn't always blow". This challenge complicates the task of ensuring a constant power supply. This is where machine learning becomes an essential ally, as it can predict when and how much power will be generated, optimizing every watt to avoid waste and ensure a continuous supply.

## 5.1. Machine Learning Techniques and Applications in the Optimization of Energy Distribution

Power distribution is one of the most critical components of modern power grids, as it ensures that energy is efficiently delivered from generation plants to end consumers. As power grids become more complex, with the integration of renewable energies and the need for more dynamic management, machine learning techniques (a subfield of artificial intelligence applied to machine learning) have emerged as essential tools for optimizing power distribution. In this section, we will expand on how these techniques can improve the efficiency and stability of power grids.

### 5.1.1. K-Nearest Neighbours for Energy Demand Rating

The K-Nearest Neighbours (KNN) algorithm is a simple but effective tool for classification and prediction in the field of energy distribution. It works by comparing a new data with the closest data in the existing set based on similar characteristics to make a prediction.

To visualize how KNN works, imagine you want to forecast how much energy a city will need on a summer day. KNN reviews its records and finds previous days with similar conditions: similar temperatures, the same day of the week, and a comparable level of economic activity. KNN then uses this information to predict that day's energy demand. This prediction allows grid operators to adjust power distribution pre-emptively, avoiding both the risk of overloads and energy waste.

The appeal of KNN lies in its simplicity and effectiveness, especially when it comes to classifying energy demand patterns in different regions or identifying similar consumption behaviours among different groups of users (Altman, 1992). Although it is a simple algorithm, its ability to learn from past data makes it ideal for scenarios where demand can be influenced by multiple factors.

### 5.1.2. Support Vector Machines in Power Distribution Optimization

The Support Vector Machines (SVM) suite of algorithms is another powerful technique used in energy distribution optimization. SVM is particularly useful for classifying complex data and making accurate predictions in energy systems. In the context of energy distribution, SVM is used to predict whether demand in a specific area will be high or low, helping grid operators make informed decisions on how to adjust distribution.

Given the nature of containing various supervised learning algorithms, with methods that are related to classification and regression, SVM looks for the best way to separate two groups of data, such as high demand and low demand. In a data graph, SVM identifies the "line" or hyperplane that optimally separates these two groups, ensuring that each group is as far apart as possible from the other. This approach is crucial for power grids because it allows them to anticipate changes in demand and react in a timely manner, maintaining stability and avoiding outages.

What makes SVM especially valuable is its ability to handle large volumes of data and find complex patterns that are not obvious to the naked eye, resulting in more accurate decisions and better optimization of the power grid (Jung-Pin, Yu-Ming, Chieh-Huang, & Ping-Feng, 2020).

### 5.1.3. Bayesian Networks in Distribution Management

Bayesian Networks are models that use probability to manage uncertainty and make informed decisions in complex systems. In energy distribution, these networks are particularly useful for forecasting how various factors, such as weather, consumer behaviour and resource availability, may influence energy distribution.

The strength of Bayesian networks lies in their ability to model uncertainty and adapt to new information. For example, if an unexpected storm reduces solar energy production, the Bayesian network can adjust its predictions and suggest a change in distribution to avoid problems in supply (Barja-Martinez et al., 2021).

## 5.2. Technological Infrastructure Related to the Execution of Data Science

Data science is playing a crucial role in the transformation of the renewable energy sector, enabling deep analysis and optimization of key processes such as energy generation, distribution and storage. However, effective implementation of data science in this sector relies heavily on a robust and scalable technology infrastructure. This infrastructure includes everything from data capture and storage to cloud computing and advanced analytical tools. The key components of this infrastructure and their importance to renewable energy are explored below:

### 5.2.1. Data Capture and Storage

The first step in performing data science is the capture and storage of large volumes of data from a variety of sources, such as sensors on solar panels, wind turbines, smart grids, and weather data. This data can include real-time information on energy production, consumption patterns, and environmental conditions.

**IoT (Internet of Things) sensors:** IoT devices are critical for data collection in renewable energy facilities. These sensors are connected to key components, such as solar panels and wind turbines, and collect data on performance and operating conditions. This data is transmitted in real time to centralized storage systems (Ustun, SM Suhail, Hannes, Bissan, & Ioannis, 2019).

**NoSQL databases:** To handle the large amount of unstructured data generated by IoT sensors, NoSQL databases, such as MongoDB and Cassandra, are preferred. These databases enable efficient data storage and retrieval, which is crucial for real-time analysis and decision making.

**Efficient Hardware:** since it depends on the amount of processing to be performed, in general according to market and literature comparisons until mid-2024, it is suggested to have the following minimums:

- Processor: at least Intel core i7 or AMD ryzen 7 or others of similar level and characteristics, i.e., prioritize multitasking processor.
- RAM memory: at least 16 GB.
- Graphics processing: at least NVIDIA GTX 1660, because the GPU provides high parallel and real-time processing power.
- Stable internet connection if you will use cloud services.

**Big Data for collection, storage:** for the analysis of large volumes of data to obtain insights on energy consumption and production. Data quality, which allows the quality assurance and accuracy of the collected data to avoid wrong decisions. Integration of data from various sources (IoT sensors, smart meters, weather sources, etc.) for holistic analysis.

*Figure 4. Visualization of photovoltaic system data collection*

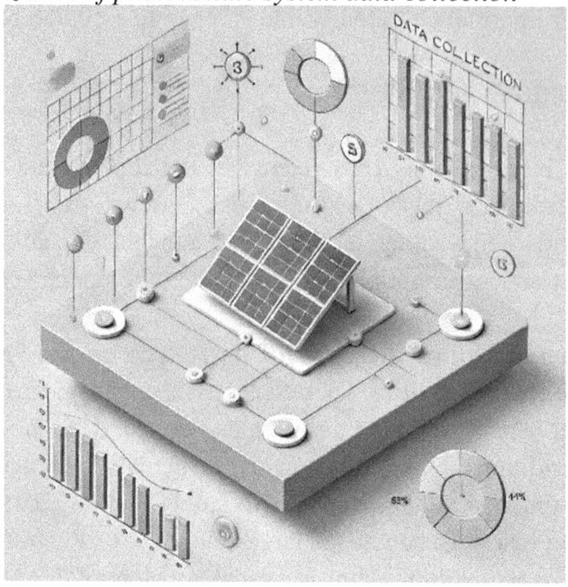


Figure 4 helps to imagine how a photovoltaic grid, like any other source, can be visualized as an interactive map showing how each variable (such as an increase in temperature) affects the other variables in the system (such as an increase in air conditioning usage). With this tool, grid operators can forecast how changing conditions will affect energy demand and adjust power distribution accordingly, ensuring there is always enough supply to meet demand without exceeding capacity.

### 5.2.2. Cloud Computing

Cloud computing is a fundamental pillar in the technology infrastructure for data science applied to renewable energy. The cloud offers scalable storage capacity and flexible processing power, making it possible to handle large volumes of data and run complex analytical models.

**Cloud platforms:** Services such as Amazon Web Services (AWS), Microsoft Azure, and Google Cloud provide robust infrastructure for data science. These platforms offer tools specific to renewable energy, such as solar and wind energy forecasting, resource efficiency analysis, and power grid simulations (Hashem et al., 2015).

**High Performance Computing (HPC):** High performance computing in the cloud enables advanced simulations and processing of large data sets in real time. This is particularly important for optimizing the operation of renewable energy plants and improving production and demand forecasting (Lozoya Arandia, Vega Gómez, Coronado, Gonzalez Garcia, & Robles Dueñas, 2021).

## 5.3. Data Analysis and Predictive Modelling

Data analysis and predictive modelling are at the core of data science applied to renewable energy. This phase involves data cleaning, statistical analysis, and the application of machine learning techniques to extract valuable information and predict future trends.

**Analytical Platforms:** Tools such as Apache Hadoop and Spark are used for distributed processing of large volumes of data. These platforms enable complex large-scale analytics, from calculating energy efficiency to forecasting renewable energy production based on weather conditions (Ayaz Ali & Muhammad, 2021)).

**Machine Learning Models:** Machine learning techniques, such as regression, neural networks and decision trees, are essential for predicting renewable energy production and optimizing its distribution. These tools allow renewable energy companies to anticipate changes in supply and demand, improving operational efficiency and reducing costs.

## 5.4. Intelligent Networks and Communication

Smart grids are essential for the integration of renewable energies into the electricity system. These grids use advanced communication and sensor technologies to manage energy distribution in an efficient and adaptive manner.

**Communication Technologies**: Network communication protocols such as MQTT and ZigBee enable fast and secure communication between devices in the smart grid. These technologies ensure that relevant information, such as demand levels and energy production, is transmitted in real time to control systems, which can automatically adjust power distribution to maximize grid efficiency and stability (Gungor et al., 2011), visualize its representation in Figure 5.

*Figure 5. Representation of machine learning applied to a water network*

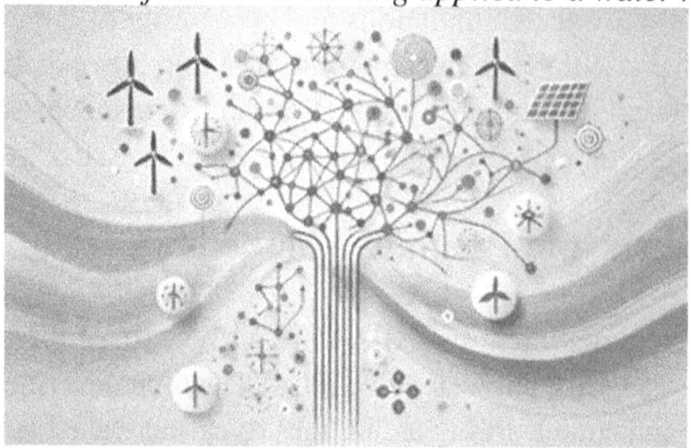

## 5.5. Maintenance

- Retraining is important because artificial intelligence models may need to be retrained with new data to remain accurate and relevant. This is crucial in environments where data changes frequently.
- Also, the improvement, adjustment or update in the algorithms, in order to take advantage of new advances in artificial intelligence techniques that can improve performance and efficiency or based on the patterns that are generated in the process.
- Evaluation and feedback are important within a continuous cycle to identify areas for improvement.
- Testing to compare different versions of the proposal and select the one that offers the best performance.

## 5.6. Practical Applications in Energy Distribution

The use of machine learning in power distribution is not limited to theory; it has practical applications that are revolutionizing how power grids operate in the real world.

**Power Flow Optimization:** ML models allow operators to forecast where and when more or less power will be needed, optimizing the flow through the grid. For example, if a sunny day is forecast in a region with high solar energy capacity, the system can adjust the distribution to maximize the use of solar energy and reduce reliance on non-renewable sources. This not only improves energy efficiency but also contributes to sustainability by reducing carbon emissions.

**Renewable Energy Integration:** One of the greatest advantages of machine learning is its ability to manage the integration of renewable energies, such as solar and wind, which are inherently intermittent. ML techniques make it possible to forecast the generation of these energies and adjust the distribution to ensure that the grid can handle the variability without compromising stability. For example, if strong winds are forecast to occur during the night, the system can store excess wind power and distribute it during the day, when demand is highest (Dhananjay, HD, S, & Bansal, 2020)

These applications not only improve the efficiency and sustainability of power grids, but also enable operators to better manage resources and quickly adapt to changes in demand and supply, ensuring reliable and cost-effective power supply (Zhao, y otros, 2021). Below in table 3, a comparison of different companies that implemented AI is shown.

*Table 3. Comparison of different companies that implemented AI and their results and differences*

| Company and Country | AI Application | Quantified Results | Cultural/Geographical Differences |
|---|---|---|---|
| Technical Research Centre of Finland | Wind energy forecasting | Improved forecast accuracy, saving $326,700 annually (Derrick, 2024). | Reliance on extreme climate; high wind variability requires precise predictions. |
| State Grid Corporation of China | Solar energy optimization | Renewable capacity: 794 GW (2019); $91 billion invested in 2018 (Xin, Haizhi, Yuanru, & Wanlin, 2021). | Large-scale implementation driven by centralized policies. |
| Siemens of Germany | Predictive maintenance in wind farms | Repair costs reduced by 20-30% (Derrick, 2024). | Focus on operational efficiency and strict environmental policies. |
| CSIRO of Australia | Energy storage optimization | Energy loss reduced by 15% (Derrick, 2024). | Optimized storage for remote areas due to geographically dispersed population. |
| Department of Energy of USA | Energy demand management | Operating costs reduced by 10-15% (Forum, 2021). | Focused on maximizing profits and cost reduction, less on centralized national policies. |

| Company and Country | AI Application | Quantified Results | Cultural/Geographical Differences |
|---|---|---|---|
| Power Network of Spain | Electrification and energy storage | Annual investment of €85 billion required to reach net-zero by 2050 (Roca, 2022). | Leader in renewable energy in Europe; focus on storage and green hydrogen for decarbonization. |
| Enel of Peru | Renewable energy monitoring and management in rural communities | investment of US$77.8 million with 115 MW capacity (Diario El Peruano, 2024). | Use of AI to improve access to renewable energy in rural areas with limited infrastructure. |

## 6. CONCLUSION

- Machine learning, in conjunction with artificial intelligence and data science, is profoundly transforming the field of energy, particularly with regard to the efficient management of energy storage and distribution. This chapter has highlighted how these technologies are making a difference in the way we understand and manage our energy resources, especially in the context of renewable energy.
- The implementation of algorithms such as neural networks and reinforcement learning has proven to be crucial for optimizing energy storage. These systems not only enable more accurate and adaptive management, but also boost responsiveness to changes in energy demand and supply. Data science tools, such as Python and its specialized libraries, have facilitated the creation of predictive models that anticipate energy needs with unprecedented accuracy. In short, artificial intelligence and data science are enabling smarter and more efficient use of energy storage, which is vital for effectively integrating renewables and maintaining grid stability.
- While the benefits of artificial intelligence and data science in the energy sector are enormous, they also present significant challenges. Data quality, integration with existing systems, and scalability of models are issues that must be resolved to ensure that these technologies reach their full potential. The technology infrastructure supporting data science in the renewable energy sector is complex, ranging from data capture and storage to cloud computing and advanced data analytics. These components enable you to optimize your operations, improve energy efficiency and facilitate the integration of clean energy sources into power grids. As technologies advance, this infrastructure will continue to evolve.

## REFERENCES


Ali, M., Sharma, A., Joy, T., & Halim, M. (2024). A Comprehensive Review of Integrated Energy Management for Future Smart Energy System. *Control Systems and Optimization Letters*, 43--51.

Ali, R., Marriam, L., Muhammad, A., Muhammad Sajid, I., Li, J., & Ijaz, A. (2024). SAARC super smart grid: Navigating the future - unleashing the power of an energy-efficient integration of renewable energy resources in the saarc region. *Computers & Electrical Engineering*, •••, 109405.

Altman, N. (1992). *An Introduction to Kernel and Nearest-Neighbor Nonparametric Regression*. The Amerian Statitician. DOI: 10.1080/00031305.1992.10475879

ATLAS Renewable Energy. (2024, febrero 15). *ATLAS Renewable Energy*. Retrieved from La IA y su impacto en las energías renovables: https://es.atlasrenewableenergy.com/la-ia-y-su-impacto-en-las-energias-renovables/

Ayaz Ali, K., & Muhammad, Z. (2021). Energy, performance and cost efficient cloud datacentres: A survey. *Computer Science Review*, 100390.

Barja-Martinez, S., Aragués-Peñalba, M., Munné-Collado, Í., Lloret-Gallego, P., Bullich-Massague, E., & Villafafila-Robles, R. (2021). Artificial intelligence techniques for enabling Big Data services in distribution networks: A review. *Renewable & Sustainable Energy Reviews*, 150, 111459. DOI: 10.1016/j.rser.2021.111459

Benhammou, A., Tedjini, H., Guettaf, Y., & Hartani Mohamed, A. (2023). Impact of artificial intelligence in renewable energy management of hybrid systems. In *Physical Sciences Forum* (p. 5). MDPI.

Ceci, M., Corizzo, R., Fumarola, F., Ianni, M., Malerba, D., Maria, G., . . . Rashkovska, A. (2015). *Big data techniques for supporting accurate predictions of energy production from renewable sources*. Proceedings of the 19th international database engineering \& applications symposium.

Cheng, C., Yuhan, H., Marimuthu, K., & Priyan Malarvizhi, K. (2021). Artificial intelligence on economic evaluation of energy efficiency and renewable energy technologies. *Sustainable Energy Technologies and Assessments*, 47, 101358. DOI: 10.1016/j.seta.2021.101358

D.C. M., E.A., P., G.G., V., & A.G., R. (2022). *Introduction to Linear Regression Analysis, 6e Solutions Manual*. John Wiley & Sons.

Derrick, M. (2024, septiembre 06). *ENERGY DIGITAL*. Retrieved from https://energydigital.com/top10/top-10-uses-of-ai-in-energy

Dhananjay, k., HD, M., S, B., & Bansal, R. (2020). Forecasting of solar and wind power using LSTM RNN for load frequency control in isolated microgrid. *International Journal of Modelling and Simulation*, 311-323.

Diario El Peruano. (2024, marzo 05). Retrieved from https://elperuano.pe/noticia/237398-enel-inicia-generacion-de-energia-solar-en-sur-del-peru

Díaz, J. (2024, junio 09). *El confidencial*. Retrieved from China deja atrás al resto del mundo con la megaplanta solar más grande del planeta: https://www.elconfidencial.com/tecnologia/novaceno/2024-06-08/planta-solar-mas-grande-del-planeta_3898655/

Ewa, C., Joanicjusz, N., Lukasz, N., Hesham, S. R., Raed, M. A., & Rami, A. (2023). Arima models in solar radiation forecasting in different geographic locations. *Energies*, •••, 5029.

Ferrer Márque, A., María-Tomé Gi, B., Pérez Díaz, S., & Vilallonga Ortiz, A. (2018, julio). Gestión eficiente de la energía en las organizaciones. https://www.ecoembes.com/sites/default/files/inline-files/administraciones-publicas/gestion-eficiente-energia-organizaciones-guia-completa.pdf, COEMBES, España.

Forum, W. E. (2021, septiembre 06). *World Economic Forum*. Retrieved from https://www.weforum.org/agenda/2021/09/this-is-how-ai-will-accelerate-the-energy-transition/

Goodfellow, I., Bengio, Y., & Courville, A. (2016). *Deep Learning*. MIT Press.

Graves, A., & Schmidhuber, S. (2005). Framewise phoneme classification with bidirectional LSTM networks. *Proceedings.2005 IEEE International Joint Conference on Neural Networks,* 2005., pp. 2047--2052. DOI: 10.1109/IJCNN.2005.1556215

Gungor, V., Sahin, D., Kocak, T., Ergut, S., Buccella, C., Cecati, C., & Hancke, G. (2011). Smart grid technologies: Communication technologies and standards}. *IEEE Transactions on Industrial Informatics*, 7(4), 529–539. DOI: 10.1109/TII.2011.2166794

Hinton, G., & Salakhutdinov, R. (2006). Reducing the dimensionality of data with neural networks. *science*, 504-507. DOI: 10.1109/TII.2011.2166794

Instituto Tecnológico de Canarias, S.A. (2008). *Energías renovables y eficiencia energética*. Canarias: Instituto Tecnológico de Canarias, S.A. DOI: 10.1109/TII.2011.2166794

IRENA. I. R. (2020, agosto 20). *Renewable Energy Statistics2020.* Retrieved from The International Renewable Energy Agency, Abu Dhabi: https://www.irena.org/-/media/Files/IRENA/Agency/Publication/2020/Jul/IRENA_Renewable_Energy_Statistics_2020.pdf

IRENA. (2023). WORLD ENERGY TRANSITIONS OUTLOOK 2023. https://h2chile.cl/wp-content/uploads/2024/01/2023_IRENA_World_energy_transitions_outlook_v1_2023.pdf, Abu Dhabi.

IRENA. T. I. (2024, agosto 20). *Renewable capacity statistics2024.* Retrieved from The International Renewable Energy Agency (IRENA): https://www.irena.org/-/media/Files/IRENA/Agency/Publication/2024/Mar/IRENA_RE_Capacity_Statistics_2024.p

Jung-Pin, L., Yu-Ming, C., Chieh-Huang, C., & Ping-Feng, P. (2020). A survey of machine learning models in renewable energy predictions. *Applied Sciences (Basel, Switzerland)*, •••, 5975.

Kaile, Z., Chao, F., & Shanlin, Y. (2016). Big data driven smart energy management: From big data to big insights. *Renewable & Sustainable Energy Reviews*, •••, 215–225.

LeCun, Y., Bengio, Y., & Hinton, G. (2015). Deep learning. *Nature Publishing Group UK London*, 436--444.

Leonzio, G. (2019). Fluid dynamic study of anaerobic digester: Optimization of mixing and geometric configuration by using response surface methodology and factorial design. *Renewable Energy*, 136, 769–780. DOI: 10.1016/j.renene.2018.12.115

Li, Y., Ding, Y., He, S., Hu, F., Duan, J., Wen, G., & Zhao, Y. (2024). Artificial intelligence-based methods for renewable power system operation. *Nature Reviews Electrical Engineering*, 163--179.

Lozoya Arandia, J., Vega Gómez, C., Coronado, A., Gonzalez Garcia, J., & Robles Dueñas, V. (2021). Green Energy HPC Data Centers to Improve Processing Cost Efficiency. *Latin American High Performance Computing Conference*, 91--105.

Lund, J., & Toth, A. (2021). Direct utilization of geothermal energy 2020 worldwide review. *Geothermics*, 90, 101915. DOI: 10.1016/j.geothermics.2020.101915

Ministerio para la Transición Ecológica y el Reto Demográfico. (2020). *La energía en España.*https://www.miteco.gob.es/content/dam/miteco/es/energia/files-1/balances/Balances/LibrosEnergia/Libro_Energia_Espana_2020.pdf: Ministerio para la Transición Ecológica y el Reto Demográfico, Madrid.

MM. S., Rabia Emhamed, A., Heba I, E., & Shimaa, B. (2022). Decision-making and optimal design of green energy system based on statistical methods and artificial neural network approaches. *Sustainable Cities and Society*, 104015. outlook, W. H. (2023, agosto 20). *World Hydropower outlook.* Retrieved from https://indd.adobe.com/view/4201016f-a51a-4f6f-998b-ec85219d1dfd

Pfenninger, S. (2024). Open code and data are not enough: understandability as design goal for energy system models. *Progress in Energy*, 033002.

Qusay, H., Hsu, C.-Y., Kamilia, M., Sameer, A., Marek, J., Ahmad, T., & Bashar Mahmood, A. (2024). a). Enhancing smart grid integrated renewable distributed generation capacities: Implications for sustainable energy transformation. [Retrieved from Sustainable Energy Technologies and Assessments.]. *Sustainable Energy Technologies and Assessments*, •••, 103793.

Richard Evans, J. (2024, agosto 20). *DeepMind AI Reduces Google Data Centre Cooling Bill by 40%.* Retrieved from https://deepmind.google/discover/blog/deepmind-ai-reduces-google-data-centre-cooling-bill-by-40

Roca, J. A. (2022, septiembre 29). *El periodico de la energía.* Retrieved from https://elperiodicodelaenergia.com/espana-debe-invertir-85-000-millones-al-ano-en-tecnologias-verdes-para-descarbonizar-su-economia-para-2050/

Russell, S., & Norvig, P. (2021). Artificial Intelligence: A Modern Approach *(4th Edition).* California at Berkeley: Pearson.

Salgado Reyes, N. (2023). Uso de la inteligencia artificial en la personalización de la experiencia del usuario en plataformas digitales. *Revista científico-profesional.*

Santos Valdés, L., & Garcia Sánchez, Z. (2023). SISTEMA DE GESTIÓN PARA LA OPERACIÓN DE LAS FUENTES RENOVABLES DE ENERGÍAS. *Operation Management System of Renewable Energy Sources).*

Shead, S., & FORBES. (2019, febrero 27). *DeepMind and Google Train AI To Predict Energy Output Of Wind Farms.* Retrieved from (consultado 20/08/2024): https://www.forbes.com/sites/samshead/2019/02/27/deepmind-and-google-train-ai-to-predict-energy-output-of-wind-farms/

Stadler, M., & Naslé, A. (2019). Planning and implementation of bankable micro-grids. *The Electricity Journal*, 32(5), 24–29. DOI: 10.1016/j.tej.2019.05.004

The International Energy Agency (IEA). (2023). Renewables 2023. https://www.iea.org/reports/renewables-2023

Udo, W., Kwakye, J., Ekechukwu, D., & Ogundipe, O. (2024). Smart grid innovation: machine learning for real-time energy management and load balancing. *International Journal of Smart Grid Applications*, 405--423.

Ustun, T. S. M., Suhail, H., Hannes, K., Bissan, G., & Ioannis, L. (2019). Data standardization for smart infrastructure in first-access electricity systems. *Proceedings of the IEEE*, 1790--1802. DOI: 10.1109/JPROC.2019.2929621

Verwimp, E., Aljundi, R., Ben-David, S., Bethge, M., Cossu, A., Gepperth, A., & van de Ven, G. (2023). *Continual Learning: Applications and the Road Forward. ARXIV Transactions on Machine Learning Research.* TMLR.

WindESCO. (2024, octubre 1). Retrieved from AI Center Lightning Talk: AI-Driven Asset Health in Wind Energy: https://www.windesco.com/blog/ai-center-lightning-talk-ai-driven-asset-health-in-wind-energy

World Energy. (2024, april 15). *World Energy*. Retrieved from The Largest Photovoltaic Plant in the World in India, Bhadla Solar Park, Has 2,245 MW, 10 Million Solar Panels and Occupies an Area of 5 Thousand Hectares: https://www.world-energy.org/article/41570.html

Xin, L., Haizhi, W., Yuanru, L., & Wanlin, L. (2021). A critical survey on renewable energy applications in the Philippines and China: Present challenges and perspectives. *Frontiers in Energy Research*, •••, 724892.

Yagang, Z., Zhiya, P., Hui, W., Jingchao, W., Zheng, Z., & Fei, W. (2023). Achieving wind power and photovoltaic power prediction: An intelligent prediction system based on a deep learning approach. *Energy*, •••, 129005.

Zhao, W., Zhang, H., Zheng, J., Dai, Y., Huang, L., Shang, W., & Liang, Y. (2021). A point prediction method based automatic machine learning for day-ahead power output of multi-region photovoltaic plants. *Energy*, 223, 120026. DOI: 10.1016/j.energy.2021.120026

# Chapter 4
# Harnessing AI for Precise AGB Estimation in Remote Areas:
## Advancing Sustainable Energy Management

**Fajar W. Wijaya**
https://orcid.org/0009-0007-0146-4455
*Monash University, Indonesia & PT PLN (Persero), Indonesia*

**Mikael Prakoso**
*Monash University, Indonesia & PT PLN (Persero), Indonesia*

**Muhammad Bondan V. Ramadhan**
https://orcid.org/0009-0008-7793-3526
*Monash University, Indonesia*

**Taufiq Asyhari**
*Monash University, Indonesia*

## ABSTRACT

*Renewable energy, particularly biomass, plays a vital role in addressing global energy needs and mitigating climate change. The development of sustainable and accurate biomass estimation methods is crucial to meet these demands. This chapter explores the transformative impact of advancements in computer vision (CV) technologies on above-ground biomass (AGB) estimation, focusing on both ground-based and aerial remote sensing techniques. The chapter provides a comprehensive overview of CV applications in AGB estimation, including the use of UAVs, smartphones,*

DOI: 10.4018/979-8-3373-2530-9.ch004

*and LiDAR for capturing forest structural parameters. Despite challenges related to dataset variability, model complexity, and logistical constraints in remote forest environments, this chapter discusses recent advancements and trends in CV methodologies that address these challenges. The chapter concludes with a discussion on open research issues and future recommendations for advancing biomass estimation using CV, aimed at supporting informed decision-making in forest conservation and climate change mitigation strategies.*

## 1. INTRODUCTION

Renewable energy has taken center stage in meeting the domestic energy requirements of the world. With the global community confronting manifold challenges of climate change and the importance for sustainability, the shift towards renewable energy (RE) would play a strategic role (Nations, n.d.). A significant attention has seen a global focus with s substantial shift towards biomass energy as a critical component of the renewable energy mix due to its potential for sustainability and carbon neutrality. The rising interest in biomass is also driven by its ability to provide a stable and reliable source of energy, reduce greenhouse gas emissions, and utilize waste products that would otherwise contribute to environmental pollution.

The global biomass energy market is projected to grow substantially in the coming years. Solid biomass from the forestry sector dominated the biomass supply on all continents in 2020. The global domestic biomass supply was 57.5 EJ (exajoule), and 86% of this came from solid biomass sources like wood chips, wood pellets, and traditional biomass (World Bioenergy Association, 2022). According to a report by the International Energy Agency (IEA), the share of bioenergy in the global energy supply could increase from 3% in 2018 to around 17% by 2050 if supportive policies and technological advancements continue to evolve (Wu et al., 2019). This surge is attributed to the growing demand for renewable energy, advancements in biomass conversion technologies, and increased awareness of biomass's role in achieving energy security and environmental sustainability solution (Nations, n.d.).

In Europe, biomass energy has become a cornerstone of the European Union's strategy to achieve its renewable energy targets. The EU has set ambitious goals to increase the share of renewable energy in its energy mix, and biomass is expected to play a significant role in meeting these targets (Renewable Energy Directive, n.d.). Countries like Sweden, Finland, and Latvia have made substantial investments in biomass energy, positioning themselves as top EU countries in renewable energy adoption. The United States has also seen a rise in biomass energy projects, several policies have been deployed to regulate and increase access to biofuel (Bibi et al., 2021). These countries serve as models for integrating biomass into the broader energy infrastructure, demonstrating its potential to reduce reliance on fossil fuels and lower carbon footprints.

In developing countries, biomass energy has potential for addressing energy sources and fostering sustainable development. In regions such as Sub-Saharan Africa and Southeast Asia, where access to modern energy services remains limited, biomass energy can provide a viable solution for rural electrification and for cooking needs (Dirisu et al., 2023). By utilizing locally available biomass resources, these regions can reduce their dependence on imported fossil fuels, creating local employment opportunities, and promoting environmental conservation.

*Figure 1. Key components of AGB estimation using AI and computer vision*

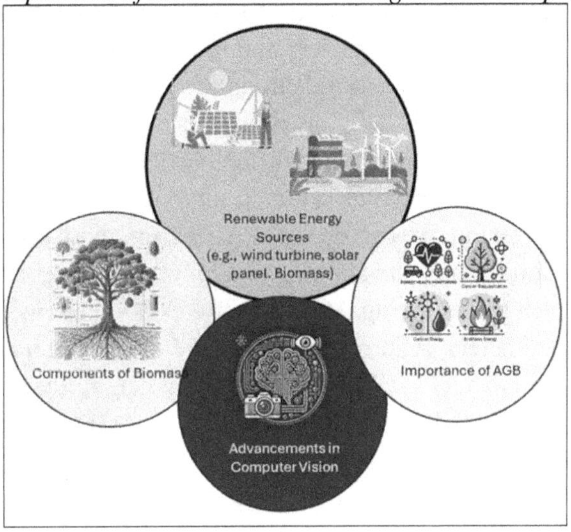


With the increasing demands of biomass energy worldwide, sustainable, accurate and reliable methods for estimating biomass stock, particularly above-ground biomass (AGB) is needed, and important components are outlined in Figure 1. Forest's AGB, defined as the total mass of living plants above the soil, is a measure of forest energy volume and biomass stock (Lu et al., 2016). Accurately estimating AGB is vital for making informed decisions, particularly in monitoring forest health (Buchelt et al., 2024) and managing forest's biomass energy production (Abbasi & Abbasi, 2010; Darmawan et al., 2023; Simangunsong et al., 2017).

The methods used to estimate AGB are generally categorized into direct and indirect approaches (Araujo et al., 2023). Traditionally, AGB estimation has relied on direct measurement methods, such as harvesting and weighing. These methods provide highly accurate results but are destructive (Anitha et al., 2015). While this destructive sampling is the most precise method, it is also labor-intensive and time-consuming (Lu et al., 2016; Stas et al., 2017).

In comparison to direct methods, indirect methods are more efficient when dealing with increased size of samples and capable of assessing inaccessible characteristics (Jurjević et al., 2020). An example of indirect methods involves using allometric models to estimate AGB based on observable variables such as tree height (H), crown diameter (CD), diameter at breast height (DBH), and wood specific gravity (ρ) (Lu et al., 2016). These properties are obtained through manual field measurements. But collecting these features is also labor-intensive and time-consuming (Adinugroho et al., 2023; Song et al., 2023; Y. Wang et al., 2021).

Advancements in computer vision technology, including satellite imagery, UAVs, and ground cameras, have made it possible to estimate forest structural parameters and biomass with more flexible, efficient and faster methodologies (Guimarães et al., 2020). AGB can be directly measured through computer vision utilizing remotely sensed data that are relevant to the biomass such as canopy height model (CHM) derived from LiDAR sensor, normalized difference vegetation index (NDVI) from multispectral sensor, and HH polarization from synthetic aperture radar (SAR) sensor. Through regression, we can estimate AGB from these remote sensing data if we have the ground truth of the above-ground biomass (Lu et al., 2016).

Another approach to estimating AGB is to use existing allometric models with forest structural parameters. Allometric models are developed based on empirical measurements of parameters such as individual tree height, diameter, crown size, and aboveground biomass. To ensure the accuracy of AGB estimates using an allometric model, it is crucial to confirm that the conditions under which the model was developed—such as forest type, tree species, or geographical characteristics—closely match the conditions of the area being studied. When these conditions align, the AGB estimates derived from the allometric model can be considered reliable (Fu et al., 2024).

These forest structural parameters can be obtained through computer vision rather than manual measurement, for instance the individual tree height can be estimated using camera or ground lidar sensor (terrestrial LiDAR), or the diameter of the tree can be approximated using photogrammetry techniques. With this computer vision approach, we can obtain forest structural parameters with less labor and more applicable for large forest plots or large trees. Then the resulting tree height and/or tree diameter are input to the existing allometric equation to obtain the aboveground biomass estimates.

For applications involving very large plots, remote sensing data can be utilized to approximate forest structural parameters at the plot level rather than the tree level. For example, airborne LiDAR data can provide the average height of trees within a plot. By stratifying the LiDAR data based on a range of average values, we can divide the population into subgroups. With tree height data at the plot level, we can then estimate the plot-level AGB using existing allometric models.

## 2. IMPACT OF COMPUTER VISION ON FOREST'S AGB ESTIMATION

As a subset of artificial intelligence (AI) model, computer vision (CV) enables machines to interpret and make decisions based on visual data. Numerous fields, including forestry and biomass management, have been revolutionized by the development of CV technology. Rapid advancements in recent years have made its applications in forestry and biomass sectors particularly transformative, offering new ways to monitor, analyze, and manage forest resources efficiently and sustainably.

One of the most significant impacts of computer vision in forestry is its ability to process vast amounts of visual data quickly and accurately. For instance, CV algorithms can identify and classify tree species, detect signs of disease or infestation, and assess forest density and canopy cover. This automated analysis enables stakeholders to make informed decisions about conservation efforts, resource allocation, and sustainable harvesting practices. In the context of biomass management, computer vision plays a crucial role in AGB estimation as illustrated in Figure 2.

Advanced CV methods can process and analyze high-resolution images to derive reliable measurements of frequency bands, vegetation indices or tree structural parameters such as height, diameter, and crown width, which are essential for AGB estimation (Bui et al., 2024; Oehmcke et al., 2024; Sainuddin et al., 2024). This widespread utilization is also backed up by studies demonstrating that this method can achieve accuracy comparable to traditional approaches on estimating AGB (Jurjević et al., 2020).

*Figure 2. Several computer vision techniques for above-ground-biomass estimation*

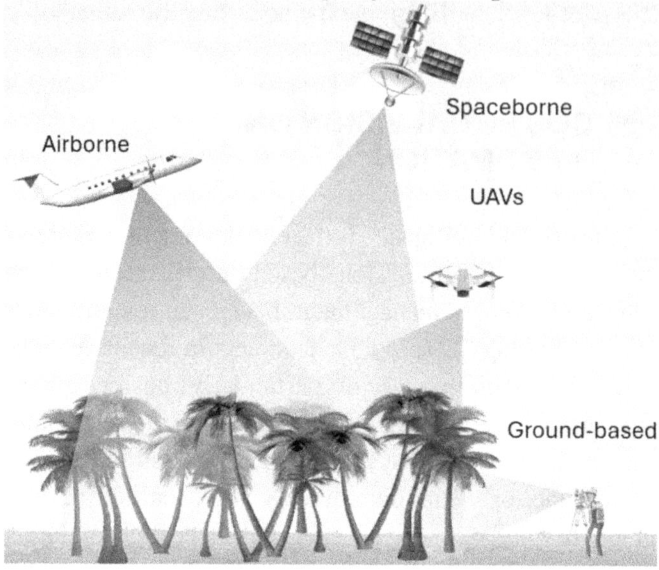


Unmanned Aerial Vehicles (UAVs) are a type of remote sensing platform that, although covering a smaller area compared to airborne and spaceborne systems, provides high-resolution imagery (Lechner et al., 2020; Lu et al., 2016). Widely-used sensors on UAVs include optic-based sensors (lidar, multispectral, and optical), with optical red-green-blue (RGB) visual sensors being dominant in forest remote sensing applications (Guimarães et al., 2020). UAVs equipped with RGB sensors offer significant operational flexibility, produce high-resolution images, and are cost-effective compared to other airborne sensor combinations.

However, RGB aerial imagery alone is insufficient for estimating AGB, as the red, green, and blue channels do not directly correspond to aboveground biomass. Enhancing the information extracted from RGB images through photogrammetric processing is one way to maximize the utility and detail of the captured data. Methodologies that integrate AI technology into the workflow have shown accurate results in trees detection and species classifications (Kurniawan et al., 2022; Schiefer et al., 2020; J. Wang et al., 2024). Additionally, AI has proven valuable in estimating forest structural attributes, including diameter at breast height (DBH), crown diameter (CD), and tree height (Guimarães et al., 2020).

For ground-level imagery, the use of mobile phone cameras has shown a viable approach in the wider biomass estimation tasks. Several methods have been developed for ground-level data collection utilizing smartphone cameras, with works demonstrating promising findings in measuring tree features with a good accuracy (Megalingam et al., 2022; Putra et al., 2021; Tran et al., 2023; Woo et al.,

2021; Xinmei et al., 2020). Recent advances in mobile technology, incorporating LiDAR and Time-of-Flight (TOF) sensing systems in commercial phones, open new possibilities for forestry applications. For example, Augmented Reality (AR) applications have been explored in works by Gülci et al. (2023) and Tatsumi et al., (2023) where smartphones assisted with LiDAR systems acquire point cloud data, which is then processed to calculate DBH measurements.

Challenges remain for the widespread adoption of computer vision in forestry and biomass management. High initial costs of advanced imaging equipment, the technical expertise required to develop and deploy CV models, and the need for large, annotated datasets to train machine learning algorithms are significant barriers. Additionally, variability in forest types, tree species, and environmental conditions can affect the generalizability of CV models.

## 3. CV IMPLEMENTATION CHALLENGES

Despite the advancements and widespread use of CV methodologies in AGB estimation, implementing CV technology across various environments presents challenges that must be addressed to fully harness its potential for biomass estimation and forest management. While the benefits of CV, such as increased accuracy and efficiency, are substantial, the practical difficulties of deploying and maintaining these technologies can be significant.

The implementation of CV technology in forestry encounters various challenges. First, the complexity of different environments, rugged terrain and sparse infrastructure as an example, present significant logistical barriers. Second, the lack of reliable internet connectivity in certain areas disrupts the real-time data transmission needed for most CV applications. Additionally, the need for large, annotated datasets to train machine learning models requires substantial effort and resources. Last but not least, the variability of conditions across different environments presents challenges for CV methodologies, requiring customized data capture methodologies and CV models that can accommodate specific requirements.

### 3.1 Logistical and Connectivity Challenge

One of the primary challenges is accessibility and logistical difficulty in diverse environments. These areas are often characterized by rugged terrain, dense vegetation, and limited infrastructure complicating the transport and set up of equipment such as UAVs, cameras, and sensors. The lack of reliable transportation routes and the need for specialized vehicles or even manual labor to carry equipment into the forest can add significant time and cost to the deployment process.

Data connectivity is another major issue. Many CV applications require the transfer of large amounts of data for processing, which is often in real-time or near-real-time. In remote forests, internet connectivity can be sparse or non-existent, making it difficult to transmit data to central servers or cloud-based platforms for analysis. This needed the development of edge computing solutions, where data is processed locally on the device itself, but this requires powerful on-board processing capabilities and can increase the cost and complexity of the equipment. Another option is to develop lightweight models that can be compatible with standard commercial devices presents a feasible alternative (Ahamed et al., 2023; Holcomb et al., 2023; Hussain et al., 2021). However, when we do not need real-time or near-real-time results then connectivity is not a serious issue.

## 3.2 Data Capture and Annotation

Another challenge is the need for large, annotated good image datasets to train computer vision models (Shahinfar et al., 2020). Collecting such datasets with good quality can be particularly difficult and time-consuming in various environments. Dense foliage, varying lighting conditions, and rugged terrain, which can affect the quality and consistency of captured images. High-resolution images are crucial for accurate AGB estimation yet capturing clear and detailed images can be challenging due to factors like partial obstruction of objects, overlapping vegetation, and varying distances from the sensor to the objects of interest.

To address this challenge, advanced imaging techniques can be employed, along with potentially utilizing complementary data sources like LiDAR or depth sensor to enhance optical imagery. Alternatively, developing models suitable for dense forest environments is another approach that could be done (Chen et al., 2021; Gené-Mola et al., 2023).

Annotating the captured images likely requires expert knowledge to accurately identify tree species, measure tree parameters, and label other relevant features. This process can be labor intensive and may require collaboration with local forestry experts or researchers familiar with the forest's specific characteristics. Additionally, using a robust collaborative annotation tool is essential to meet project timelines. Tools like Roboflow and Label Studio are popular choices for facilitating efficient, collaborative annotation efforts.

### 3.3 Variability of CV Methodology

Adapting CV methodologies to the diverse conditions found across different environments is a critical challenge. Forests vary greatly in terms of tree species composition, canopy structure, and environmental conditions. This diversity requires developing custom CV models that are flexible and adaptable, capable of accurately identifying and measuring biomass based on designated forest types.

For ground level data capturing, several methodologies can be deployed. Using personal terrestrial laser scanning (TLS) or LiDAR equipped camera to capture 3d point cloud data can be utilized. This method is the most accurate to estimate tree features such as height and diameter, but it might be resource-intensive and can be challenging in remote areas.

Capturing complete images of trees at ground level, especially using mobile devices, presents its own set of challenges, such as incorrectly processing overlapping trees as a single tree as well as dealing with branches- and foliage-driven occlusions. These errors become specifically pronounced in dense forest environments (Lumnitz et al., 2021). Hence, it is essential to develop techniques that enhance data capture for partially visible trees to address these challenges.

One potential approach is to take a number of images of a single tree from various angles and then use image stitching techniques to combine them into a comprehensive view of the tree (Woo et al., 2021). Another possibility is by leveraging advancements in computer vision, including methods such as inpainting or generative adversarial networks (GANs), which can be utilized to compensate missing areas in partially captured objects within a digital image, offering an extended view of the tree for follow-up biomass estimation (Chen et al., 2021).

These ground-level methodologies provide highly accurate estimates of individual tree properties measurement but are limited in spatial coverage. Aerial techniques, particularly when combined with advanced image processing and modeling, can provide reasonably accurate estimates of total biomass over large areas (Shi et al., 2017; Yang et al., 2022). This can be one of the preferred factors for estimating AGB on remote forests.

In remote sensing platforms like satellites, aerial, or UAV systems, we typically capture tree features from a top-down perspective. However, through photogrammetric techniques such as Structure from Motion (SfM), we can reconstruct the three-dimensional structure of the forest, allowing us to estimate tree height using only an RGB camera (Iglhaut et al., 2019). Alternatively, Aerial LiDAR can be used to directly measure tree height from 3D point cloud data (Oehmcke et al., 2024b).

Through the progress in deep learning, instance segmentation can be applied for extracting features from aerial images captured by UAVs. This technique can calculate the canopy area of trees by summing all the pixels corresponding to the canopy. To convert this pixel count into standard units such as square meters, you multiply it by the ground sampling distance (GSD) constant, which can be obtained from the metadata of the remote sensing platform.

While implementing CV technology in complex environments like forests presents significant hurdles, researchers are actively working to overcome these challenges. The field is rapidly evolving, with ongoing advancements in imaging techniques, data processing, and model development. These improvements aim to boost the accuracy and efficiency of CV applications in forestry and related areas. In the following section, we'll explore state-of-the-art methods and innovations in computer vision for estimating Above-Ground Biomass (AGB) especially from the ground-based and aerial-based methods.

## 4. STATE-OF-THE-ART IN COMPUTER VISION-ASSISTED AGB ESTIMATION

As discussed before, computer vision technology can be applied both to ground-based and aerial-based AGB estimation. Ground images offer the finest resolution but cover limited areas, while aerial based images provide wider coverage with medium to high resolution (Lechner et al., 2020; Song et al., 2023; Yang et al., 2022). This chapter explores two main themes of state-of-the-art computer vision-assisted AGB Estimation: ground-based methods and aerial/remote sensing methods. We outline the main research works contributing to the state-of-the-art in Tables 1 and 2, and discuss the details in the following sub-sections.

### 4.1. State-of-the-Art Techniques for Leveraging Ground-Based Imagery and AI in AGB Estimation

Currently, various remote sensing platforms and sensors, including passive optical, microwave, and LiDAR, are used for AGB estimation, resulting in diverse methods such as mechanistic, physical, empirical and comprehensive models (Tian et al., 2023). However, the latest advancements in remote sensing can be resource-intensive, and data availability may be limited, especially in remote areas like wild forests. Therefore, developing accurate and cost-effective AGB estimation methods using readily available devices is crucial to supports forest management and conservation efforts with a cost-effective and practical manner.

Smartphones, integrated with sensors such as cameras, LiDAR, GPS, and Time-of-Flight (TOF), can capture forest structural parameters from the ground with high resolution. The integration of multiple sensors in smartphones enhances the accuracy and reliability of the data collected, enabling detailed measurements of tree height, diameter, and canopy structure. Moreover, the portability and ease of use of smartphones also means that a wider range of personnel, from professional researchers to local forest rangers, can participate in data collection and monitoring. Additionally, the widespread availability and familiarity of smartphones lower the barrier to entry for implementing advanced AGB estimation techniques, making it possible to scale these methods across diverse geographic locations and forest types.

The end-to-end framework of AGB estimation using smartphone imagery involves photogrammetry and AI techniques to measure forest structural parameters. For instance, (Putra et al., 2021) use smartphone cameras and photogrammetry for DBH estimation, offering a low-cost solution. But the method requires manual distance maintenance and limited to round-shaped trees. Shen et al. (2023) employ depth estimation and image segmentation for tree height measurement with low computational cost, though it requires ultrasonic device for ground truth data collection. Megalingam et al. (2022) address coconut tree trunk diameter estimation using reference objects, which limits its generalizability. Bobrowski et al. (2023) create 3D textured trees for Augmented Reality (AR) using LiDAR, restricted to devices with Lidar sensors. Holcomb et al. (2023) use simple algorithms to segment tree trunks from RGB images but do not extend to whole trees. Tran et al. (2023) applies depth-image CV for automated measurements along the tree stem, though accuracy is affected by distance and occlusion. Chen et al. (2021) focus on reconstructing tree branches from occluded images, but not entire trees. Liu et al. (2021) utilize deep convolutional networks to reconstruct complete 3D tree models from single images.

Complete measurements of tree properties (height, DBH, CD, etc.) using ground cameras are rare due to field limitations such as sight obstruction in dense forests, and data collection methods that require consistent ranges. Partial images hinder the simultaneous measurement of complete tree properties, impacting biomass computation in allometric equations. In summary, smartphone camera imagery and AI for AGB estimation offers a practical and cost-effective approach for forest structural parameter estimation, but generally requires more investigation for a comprehensive AGB estimation framework.

*Table 1. State-of-the-art in ground-based imagery and AI for AGB estimation*

| Reference | Proposed Technique | Dataset | Advantages | Disadvantages |
|---|---|---|---|---|
| Putra et al. (2021) | DBH estimation using smartphone camera and photogrammetry | RGB images | Low-cost, uses optical sensors and smartphone cameras | Requires manual distance maintenance, limited to round-shaped trees, further investigation needed for a complete AGB estimation framework. |
| Shen et al. (2023) | Tree Height estimation using Depth Estimation and Image Segmentation | RGB images and depth from ultrasonic | No manual involvement, single perspective per tree, low computational cost | Requires ultrasonic device for ground truth data, further investigation needed for a complete AGB estimation framework. |
| Megalingam et al. (2022) | Using reference object alongside the tree | RGB images | Targets requirement for estimating the trunk diameter of coconut trees. | Specifically applicable to coconut trees, which limits its generalization capacity to other species. |
| Bobrowski et al. (2023) | Using augmented reality to show the scanned 3D tree texture | 3D point cloud | Employs Lidar technology for scanning. | Limited in use for devices that lack a Lidar sensor. |
| Holcomb et al. (2023) | Segment tree trunk based on depth image captured from smartphone | Depth image & RGB from ToF sensor | Implements a straightforward algorithm to extract tree diameter from an RGB image. | Does not extend to capturing the entire tree. |
| Tran et al. (2023) | Using depth-image to accurately measure numerous points along the semt | RGB & depth images of the tree trunk | Showcases the application of computer vision for automated measurements. | Accuracy may be compromised by tree distance or occlusions. |
| Chen et al. (2021) | Reconstruction of main tree branches from occluded images | RGB & depth image of the tree branch | Lightweight product computer vision model, demonstrates success in image completion | Does not expand to the whole tree, image completion limited to branch segments |
| Liu et al. (2021) | Using deep convolutional networks to reconstruct a 3D tree model from a single image | Develop 3D model and image pairs from a procedural modeling approach | Achieves a complete 3D model of the tree. | Resource-intensive and unable to specify the species of the reconstructed tree. |

## 4.2. State-of-the-Art Techniques for Leveraging Remote Sensing-Based Imagery and AI in AGB Estimation

The precision of estimating forest structural parameters is influenced by the spatial resolution of remotely sensed data, categorized into fine-grained (UAV imagery), middle-grained (airborne imagery), and coarse-grained (satellite imagery) resolutions (Lechner et al., 2020; Song et al., 2023). Common sensing payloads include optical, LiDAR, and Synthetic Aperture Radar (SAR) sensors, each capturing different aspects of forest parameters for AGB estimation. On the context of machine learning models, increasing the number of parameters provides more variables for the model to learn, but it can also be resource intensive. Utilizing Light Radar, Synthetic Aperture Radar, or hyperspectral sensors can generate additional variables for AGB estimation, such as Point Clouds, Frequency Bands, and Vegetation Indices (Bui et al., 2024; Oehmcke et al., 2024; Sainuddin et al., 2024). But with the availability of more variables, the ability to capture a more comprehensive picture of forest biomass dynamics is heightened, potentially leading to more robust and detailed AGB estimations.

LiDAR sensors with airborne laser scanning (ALS) are considered the best practice for accurately estimating tree height or creating a 3-dimensional forest structures from point clouds, capturing details like DBH, height, and crown diameter at the plot level (Borsah et al., 2023; Lu et al., 2016; Oehmcke et al., 2024; Song et al., 2023). Despite their capabilities, LiDAR data availability is limited and resourcc intensive.

Song et al. (2023) utilizes airborne LiDAR data, which offers higher spatial resolution and less susceptibility to data saturation. They sample from publicly available datasets across various forest biomes to develop a universal allometric equation, hypothesizing that AGB is primarily height-driven. The model's uncertainty is potentially large due to the use of a single predictor for global application, but they mitigate this by using the Gaussian Process Regression algorithm to measure uncertainty.

Oehmcke et al. (2024) take a different approach to utilizing LiDAR data by constructing a 3D model of forest structural parameters to directly measure wood volume and AGB without a digital terrain model. Since LiDAR data is often linear rather than area-based, they use point cloud regression to estimate surrounding tree height. Their deep learning regression model is significantly more accurate than other models but less explainable. The model also shows robustness to boundary artifacts in the evaluated areas (Oehmcke et al., 2024).

Bui et al. (2024) apply ensemble learning techniques (XGBoost and LightGBM) in conjunction with the Tasmanian devil optimization algorithm on satellite imagery featuring SAR and hyperspectral sensors. This approach provides better generalization, reduces uncertainty with multiple predictor variables, and improves correlation through hyperparameter tuning. However, it heavily depends on optical hyperspectral sensors, leading to data saturation, and low AGB estimation accuracy due to coarse-grained satellite imagery.

Optical RGB sensors are frequently used in forest remote sensing (Guimarães et al., 2020; Lu et al., 2016). UAVs with standard RGB sensors offer a cost-effective solution for capturing forest parameters with larger coverage from the air. Fu et al. use high-resolution aerial RGB images from UAVs for AGB estimation, processed with ArcGIS software, which incorporates satellite LiDAR data to calculate CHM layers (Fu et al., 2024). However, these statistically calculated CHM layers introduce uncertainty and error. Additionally, the AGB estimation is less robust due to reliance on a linear regression model.

However, remote sensing imagery alone is insufficient for AGB estimation. AI-driven photogrammetric processing can be used to enrich the extracted data. Processing step like 3D reconstruction, annotation, feature extraction and classification, which are essential before training the AGB estimation model. Studies that use AI technology on their estimation method showing remarkable results include tree object detection and species classification (Kurniawan et al., 2022; Schiefer et al., 2020; J. Wang et al., 2024).

In conclusion, remote sensing imagery combined with AI techniques offers a promising approach for complete AGB estimation framework, although challenges remain in achieving high accuracy and generalizability across different forest types.

*Table 2. State-of-the-art in remote sensing-based imagery and AI in AGB estimation*

| Reference | Proposed Technique | Dataset | Advantages | Disadvantages |
|---|---|---|---|---|
| Oehmcke et al. (2024) | Point cloud regression with deep learning | Airborne LiDAR dataset from Danish national forest | Provides plot-level AGB measurement without requiring a Digital Terrain Model, robust to artifacts along the boundaries of the evaluated areas | Limited generalizability as the model is developed in a specific environment of Denmark's national forest; deep learning models is lacking interpretability |
| Song et al. (2023) | Gaussian Process biomass-height model | Airborne LiDAR dataset from several biomass | Accurate tree height estimation with LiDAR, better resolution from airborne images, low uncertainty | LiDAR-specific, limited data availability, resource-intensive, single predictor dependency, uncertainty |
| Bui et al. (2024) | Tasmanian devil optimization algorithm with ensemble Learning (XGBoost and LightGBM) | Using SAR and hyperspectral sensors from Satellite imagery | Proposed technique provides better generalization, reduces uncertainty with multiple predictor variables, and improves correlation trough hyperparameter tuning. | Heavily depends on optical hyperspectral sensors, leading to data saturation, and has low AGB estimation accuracy due to the coarse-grained nature of satellite imagery. |
| Fu et al. (2024) | Automatic detection of tree crown and height using Mask R-CNN | UAV with RGB Sensor | Accurate Canopy Height Model (CHM) estimation with LiDAR, improved detection accuracy with CHM layers | High relative error and uncertainty in AGB estimation, indirect Tree Diameter measurement from regression |

## 5. FRAMEWORK ON COMPUTER VISION-ASSISTED AGB ESTIMATION

AGB estimation using CV techniques, whether based on ground-level or remote sensing imagery, follows similar patterns across various studies. This is outlined in Figure 3 below. By surveying the existing literature, we can outline a general framework that captures the common approaches in this field. This section synthesizes these findings, presenting a structured overview of the typical steps involved in CV-assisted AGB estimation. From study area selection to data preprocessing and model evaluation, we'll explore how researchers are tackling each stage of the process. This summary aims to provide a comprehensive look at current practices, offering insights for future research in this area.

*Figure 3. Framework on computer vision-assisted AGB estimation*

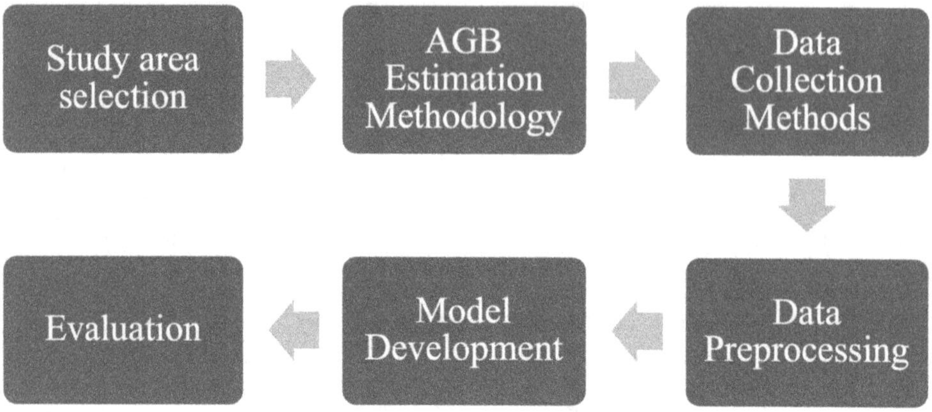


## 5.1. Study Area Selection

The selection of a study area/research scope is a crucial first step in any AGB estimation research, as it fundamentally shapes the scope and applicability of the findings. This choice depends heavily on the research objectives, ranging from highly specific local studies to broad, multi-regional analyses. For example, Song et al. (2023) opted for a global approach, incorporating multiple biomes worldwide to develop a more generalized allometric model. In contrast, Oehmcke et al. (2024) focused solely on Danish forests, aiming to create a location-specific allometric model tailored to that particular ecosystem.

The choice of study area directly influences the type and extent of data required, the complexity of the analysis, and the potential applications of the research findings. Broader studies, while offering wider applicability, often face challenges in managing diverse datasets and accounting for varied environmental conditions. Conversely, narrowly focused studies can provide highly accurate, context-specific models but may have limited applicability beyond their specific geographical scope. Researchers must carefully consider these trade-offs when defining their study area, aligning their choice with both their immediate research goals and the broader needs of the scientific community.

## 5.2. AGB Estimation Methodology

The methodology for AGB estimation is heavily influenced by the study area selected, as outlined before. Whether dealing with a specific local ecosystem or a diverse global dataset, researchers must choose appropriate techniques that align with their research scope and objectives. But at the foundation of all AGB estimation methods is the availability of empirical measurement. Destructive sampling provides the ground truth necessary for developing allometric models, allowing for indirect AGB estimation based on tree biophysical features to be conducted.

The decision to estimate at the individual tree level or plot level is dictated by the nature of the forest and the research goals. For instance, Fu et al. (2024) opted for individual tree-level estimation in their localized study and in narrowly focused studies like Oehmcke et al. (2024) on Danish forests, individual tree-level estimation might be more feasible and accurate. In contrast, broader studies covering multiple regions might opt for plot-level estimation to manage data complexity, like in the study by Bui et al. (2024) and Song et al. (2023).

Computer vision technologies improvement in AGB estimation has riase the chance to offering methods adaptable to various study scales. These include:

- For local studies: High-resolution LiDAR scanning for precise depth measurements of individual trees.
- For regional studies: Object detection and instance segmentation on aerial or satellite imagery to identify and measure tree canopies.
- For global studies: Point cloud regression or multispectral image analysis to estimate biomass across diverse biomes.

The choice of technology depends on the study area's characteristics and the available resources. For instance, Bui et al. (2024) and Song et al. (2023) in their global study might leverage multispectral satellite imagery to correlate NDVI values with field-measured biomass data across multiple biomes. Conversely, a localized study might employ LiDAR sensors for their superior ability to capture detailed forest structure.

By carefully aligning the estimation methodology with the chosen study area, researchers can optimize their approach to AGB estimation, ensuring that the techniques employed are both appropriate for the scale of the study and capable of addressing the unique challenges presented by the selected ecosystem or biomes.

## 5.3. Data Collection Methods

Researchers employ various strategies for data collection in CV-assisted AGB estimation. These range from gathering fresh field data to enhancing existing datasets, or a combination of both approaches. Multiple research efforts have been conducted on developing allometric models using non-destructive techniques. For example, Fu et al. (2024) combines existing field survey data with digital terrain models from UAV imagery to develop an allometric model. This approach not only preserves the integrity of the environment but also enhances the accuracy and applicability of biomass estimation models.

Another approach of data collection is to focus on gathering data for estimating forest structure parameters such as tree height and tree diameter, while leaving the AGB estimation accuracy on the best practice of allometric equation based on domain expertise. For instance, Putra et al. (2021) uses optical sensor and photogrammetry technique to measure the tree diameter from the ground, then leave the AGB estimation for further research. Other study using this method by Megalingam et al. (2022) which requires an object reference in the image for measurement, while Tran et al. (2023) requires the tree to be less occluded to obtain more accurate estimation of tree diameter. Rather than developing new allometric models, this method prioritizes enhancing the accuracy of tree parameter measurements.

Advanced sensing technologies and multispectral imaging also play a crucial role in modern biomass estimation methods. These approaches often involve collecting data from various sensors to develop sophisticated estimation models. For instance, Oehmcke et al. (2024) employed airborne LiDAR datasets from Danish national forests to perform point cloud regression using deep learning techniques. Similarly, Song et al. (2023) utilized airborne LiDAR data from multiple biomes to construct a Gaussian Process biomass-height model. In a different approach, Bui et al. (2024) combined satellite imagery from SAR and hyperspectral sensors, applying ensemble learning methods like XGBoost and LightGBM, optimized with a Tasmanian devil algorithm.

The choice of data collection method significantly impacts the subsequent stages of AGB estimation. Researchers must carefully consider their study objectives, available resources, and the specific characteristics of their study area when selecting the most appropriate data collection approach.

## 5.4. Data Preprocessing

Data preprocessing is a crucial step in computer vision-assisted AGB estimation, often required to prepare the collected data for model development and training. This stage involves various techniques aimed at improving data quality, addressing dataset imbalances, and enhancing the overall performance of the CV models.

One common preprocessing task is data annotation, which is essential for supervised learning approaches. For instance, segmentation tasks, researchers may need to annotate images with polygons to delineate individual trees or forest plots as illustrated in Figure 4. Similarly, object detection tasks require bounding box annotations around trees or other relevant features. This manual or semi-automated process is critical for creating labeled datasets that can be used to train accurate and reliable models. The quality and consistency of these annotations can significantly impact the model's performance, making it a vital aspect of the preprocessing stage.

*Figure 4. Polygon annotation process using Label Studio annotation tool*

Dataset imbalance is another challenge often addressed during preprocessing. In forest environments, certain tree species or size classes may be underrepresented, leading to biased model predictions. To mitigate this, techniques such as up-sampling (increasing the number of samples in minority classes) or down-sampling (reducing the number of samples in majority classes) can be employed.

Data augmentation is another powerful preprocessing technique used to increase the diversity and size of the training dataset. This involves creating modified versions of existing data through various transformations. In the context of AGB estimation, augmentation methods might include rotating or flipping images, adjusting brightness and contrast, adding noise, or applying perspective transformations. These augmentations help the model become more robust to variations it might encounter in real-world scenarios, thus improving its generalization capabilities.

The specific preprocessing steps employed depend on the nature of the collected data, the chosen CV techniques, and the overall research objectives. Regardless of the methods used, the primary goals of data preprocessing remain consistent: to enhance model performance during training, reduce overfitting, and minimize generalization errors when the model is applied to new, unseen data. By carefully considering and implementing appropriate preprocessing techniques, researchers can remarkably enhance the accuracy and reliability of their CV-assisted AGB estimation models.

## 5.5. Model Development

Model development is a critical stage in CV-assisted AGB estimation, often involving the creation and training of one or more machine learning models. The complexity and structure of these models can vary significantly depending on the research objectives, available data, and chosen methodologies.

Many AGB estimation approaches employ a pipeline of multiple models, each addressing a specific aspect of the estimation process. For example, Fu et al. (2024) developed a multi-stage model pipeline:

1. A semantic segmentation model to identify and delineate individual tree crowns.
2. A Mask R-CNN model to predict tree height based on various feature combinations.
3. A linear regression model to establish the correlation between crown area and tree height.
4. Apply an existing allometric model to estimate AGB based on the outputs from the previous stages.

Using this multi-model approach allows researchers to break down the complex task of AGB estimation into more manageable sub-tasks, potentially improving overall accuracy and interpretability.

In contrast, some researchers opt for end-to-end models that directly estimate AGB from input data. Oehmcke et al. (2024) using this approach by training a single point cloud regression model to estimate AGB directly from LiDAR data. This method can be more straightforward to implement and may require less intermediate data processing, but it may also be more challenging to interpret or fine-tune for specific sub-tasks.

The choice of model architecture itself is crucial and depends on various factors:

a. Data type and availability: Different data sources (e.g., LiDAR, multispectral imagery, field measurements) may be better suited to certain model architectures.
b. Scale of the study: Local studies might benefit from more detailed, multi-stage models, while global studies might require more generalized, robust approaches.
c. Computational resources: More complex models often require greater computational power for training and inference.
d. Interpretability requirements: Some research contexts may prioritize model interpretability, favoring simpler or more transparent model architectures.

During the development phase, researchers typically experiment with various model architectures, hyperparameters, and training strategies. This process often involves methods, including cross-validation, ensemble methods, and transfer learning to improve model performance and generalizability.

Note that model development in CV-assisted AGB estimation is an active area of research, with new approaches continually emerging. Recent advancements in deep learning, such as transformer architectures and self-supervised learning, are being explored for their potential to improve AGB estimation accuracy and efficiency.

Ultimately, the goal of model development is to create a robust, accurate, and generalizable system for AGB estimation that can be applied effectively within the chosen study area and potentially beyond. The success of this stage greatly influences the overall reliability and applicability of the CV-assisted AGB estimation approach.

## 5.6. Evaluation

The evaluation of a model depends on the specific task at hand. For object detection, the model is evaluated using the mean average precision (mAP) metric, which measures how well the model detects objects across different classes and instances. For more complex evaluation, Precision-Recall Curves and the Area Under the Curve (AUC) are used to analyze the trade-off between precision and recall for different threshold settings. These metrics are especially valuable in applications where the balance between false positives and false negatives is critical, such as in detecting rare tree species within a forest. Figure 5 provides an example of utilization of performance metrics in YOLOv8 segmentation model.

*Figure 5. Example of YOLOv8 segmentation model training displaying multiple performance metric*

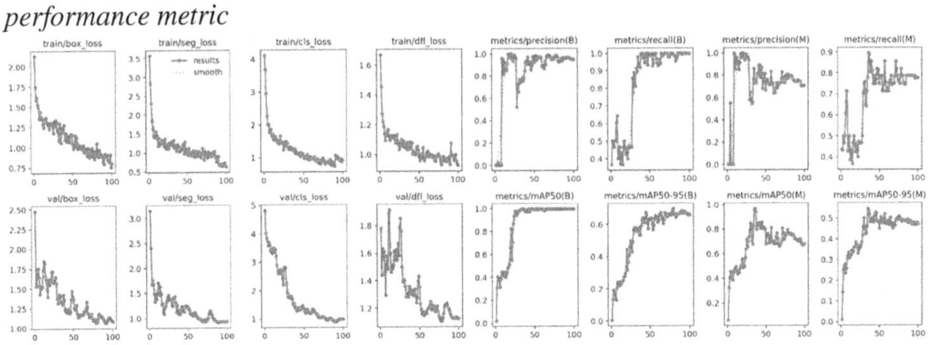

To evaluate object segmentation performance, the Intersection over Union (IoU) metric and the Dice Coefficient (the F1 score), is commonly used. IoU examines the overlap between the predicted segmentation mask and the ground truth mask, providing a ratio that ranges from 0 to 1, with higher values indicating better performance. The Dice Coefficient is similar to IoU but places a higher emphasis on the agreement between the predicted and ground truth masks. These metrics are essential for tasks requiring precise boundary detection, such as tree canopy segmentation or identifying tree trunks and branches in forest imagery.

For regression tasks, such as developing allometric models, the model's performance is assessed using metrics like the coefficient of determination ($R^2$), root mean square error (RMSE) and mean absolute error (MAE). These metrics help evaluate how well the model predicts continuous variables related to forest parameters.

In addition to these performance metrics, researchers can also consider the following aspects in model evaluation:

1. Cross-validation: Implementing k-fold cross-validation or train-validation split method can result into a more robust assessment of model performance, specifically when dealing with limited datasets.
2. Performance across different scales: Evaluating the model's performance at various spatial scales (e.g., individual tree, plot level, and landscape level) can provide insights into its scalability and applicability across different contexts.
3. Comparison with traditional methods: Comparing the CV-assisted AGB estimation results with those obtained from traditional field-based methods can help validate the model's accuracy and highlight potential improvements or limitations.
4. Uncertainty quantification: Incorporating methods to quantify uncertainty in model predictions, such as confidence intervals or prediction intervals, can provide valuable information about the reliability of AGB estimates.
5. External validation: When possible, validating the model on an independent dataset from a different geographical area or time period can demonstrate its generalizability and robustness

At the end, implementation of these evaluation metrics in real-world scenarios often involves using composite metrics that integrate several performance metrics to provide a comprehensive model performance. This holistic approach is important when models operate as an ensemble, combining object detection, regression, and segmentation models. By doing so, researchers can achieve more robust and reliable results, enhancing the accuracy and reliability of forest parameter estimation and biomass computation.

# 6. OPEN RESEARCH ISSUES IN AGB ESTIMATION USING COMPUTER VISION TECHNOLOGY

As we've explored the challenges (Section 3), state-of-the-art CV techniques (Section 4), and the framework for CV-assisted AGB estimation (Section 5), it becomes evident that while significant progress has been made, numerous research opportunities remain. Building upon those discussions above, this section try to identify key research issues and future directions in AGB estimation leveraging computer vision technology.

## 6.1. Overview of the Challenges

We present an analysis of the current landscape, highlighting strengths, weaknesses, emerging trends, and contradictions in the literature. By examining these aspects, we aim to provide researchers and practitioners with a comprehensive overview of the field's current state and potential areas for innovation. Our analysis focuses on how recent advancements address existing challenges, where gaps remain, and what new opportunities are emerging for further research and development in CV-assisted AGB estimation.

- Strengths

Smartphones, UAVs, and LiDAR have introduced cost-effective and scalable solutions for estimating forest structural parameters. Techniques like photogrammetry, depth estimation, image segmentation, and machine learning models offer flexible approaches to estimating AGB. Advanced methods, such as Mask R-CNN and Gaussian Process models, provide high-resolution data and reduce uncertainty in estimating tree properties.

- Weaknesses

Methods like those proposed by Putra et al. (2021) require manual maintenance of distance, which can be labor-intensive and prone to human error. Some techniques are applicable only to specific tree shapes or biomes, limiting their generalizability. High-resolution data from sources like LiDAR are often resource-intensive and not widely available, restricting the applicability of certain models. Approaches relying on indirect measurements through regression introduce significant uncertainty and error into AGB estimates.

- Trends

Increasing use of artificial intelligence and machine learning for automating the detection and measurement of tree parameters. Combining data from ground-based cameras, UAVs, and satellites to improve the comprehensiveness and accuracy of AGB estimation. Growing emphasis on developing low-cost methods using readily available devices like smartphones and standard UAV payloads.

- Contradictions

High-accuracy methods like those using LiDAR data are often less accessible due to cost and availability, while more accessible methods may compromise accuracy. There is a tension between methods requiring manual intervention (Putra et al., 2021) and fully automated techniques (Shen et al., 2023), each with its advantages and drawbacks. Models relying on a single predictor (Song et al., 2023) face uncertainties across different biomes, while those using multiple predictors (Fu et al., 2024) may introduce complexity and potential errors from regression.

## 6.2 Future Directions

The literature shows a developing field where advances in computer vision and remote sensing significantly enhance AGB estimation. Innovative methods utilizing smartphones, UAVs, and LiDAR have demonstrated potential in improving accuracy and scalability. However, challenges persist in balancing accuracy with accessibility, addressing the need for manual intervention, and managing uncertainties in indirect measurements. AGB estimation using computer vision technology is still in its developmental stage towards achieving full accuracy and efficiency in remote and diverse forest environments. Key areas require further investigation and improvement to develop a robust CV-based AGB estimation system. The following points outline the research issues that open to be addressed and discussed:

### 6.2.1. Addressing Data Limitations

One of the primary challenges in AGB estimation using computer vision techniques is the limitation of available data. The quality of high-resolution, annotated datasets is also crucial for training and validating computer vision models. Future research should focus on developing innovative methods to improve both the quantity and quality of data used for AGB estimation. This could involve creating more comprehensive and diverse datasets that represent various forest types, age classes, and geographical regions. Researchers should explore the potential of crowdsourcing and citizen science initiatives to collect ground-based imagery on a larger scale, potentially using smartphone apps designed for forest inventory. In addition to that, efforts need to be targeted to standardize data collection procedures to ensure consistency and comparability across various research scenarios and regions.

Researchers could also investigate new approaches to tackle the issue of data scarcity in remote or understudied forest areas. This could include the development of transfer learning techniques that allow models trained on data-rich regions to be adapted for use in data-poor areas. Or other promising direction is the use of synthetic data generation methods, such as generative AI, to augment existing datasets and improve model generalization. These approaches could help bridge the gap between data-rich and data-poor regions, leading to more globally applicable AGB estimation models.

### 6.2.2. Integrating Multi-Modal Sensing Approaches

The integration of multi-modal sensing approaches represents a promising frontier in AGB estimation research. Future studies could focus on developing frameworks that effectively combine data from various sources, such as ground-based measurements, UAV imagery, satellite data, and LiDAR scans. This integration could provide a more comprehensive and accurate representation of forest structures across different scales. Researchers should explore advanced data fusion techniques, including deep learning-based methods, that can handle the heterogeneity and varying resolutions of multi-modal data while maximizing the complementary information from each source.

While this integration can enhance the accuracy of AGB estimates, it also requires overcoming issues related to data compatibility and processing. Effective data fusion methods and ensuring seamless integration of data collected from various platforms are necessary to improve model training and validation. potentially through the development of hybrid models that can adaptively weight different data sources based on their reliability and relevance to specific forest conditions.

Another important area for future research is the development of cost-effective and practical multi-modal sensing strategies. This could involve exploring optimal combinations of sensing modalities that balance accuracy, coverage, and resource requirements. For instance, researchers might investigate how high-resolution smartphone imagery from citizen scientists (Fan et al., 2020; Gülci et al., 2023; Sandim et al., 2023; Shen et al., 2023; Xinmei et al., 2020) could be effectively combined with wider coverage of airborne or satellite data (Kurniawan et al., 2022; Roth et al., 2018; Skurikhin et al., 2013; Tian et al., 2023; Velasquez-Camacho et al., 2023) to improve large-scale AGB estimations.

### 6.2.3. Advancing AI and Computer Vision

The rapid evolution of AI and computer vision techniques presents significant opportunities for improving AGB estimation. Future research should focus on developing more sophisticated and efficient algorithms that can handle the complexity and variability of forest ecosystems. One promising direction is the exploration of advanced deep learning architectures, such as attention mechanisms or transformer models, which have shown remarkable performance in other computer vision tasks. These models could potentially capture hidden relationships and features in forest imagery more effectively than current methods.

Improving the interpretability and explainability of AI models used in AGB estimation is another crucial research direction. As these models become more complex, it's essential to develop methods that can provide insights into their decision-making processes. This could involve the use of techniques like SHAP (SHapley Additive exPlanations) values (Štrumbelj & Kononenko, 2014)or LIME (Ribeiro et al., n.d.) to understand feature. Another way is by the development of visual analytics tools that allow forestry experts to interact with and validate model predictions. Such advancements would not only increase trust in AI-based AGB estimation but also provide valuable insights into the key factors influencing biomass in different forest ecosystems. Another direction would be utilizing generative AI into the AGB estimation pipeline.

Future studies should focus on developing fully automated, low-cost solutions that minimize manual intervention, expand data accessibility, and reduce uncertainties in AGB estimation. Additionally, exploring integration of diverse data sources and advanced AI techniques can improve the accuracy and applicability of AGB estimation models. By addressing these open research issues, the field can move towards more accurate, accessible, and efficient methods for AGB estimation, ultimately contributing to better forest management and climate change mitigation strategies.

## CONCLUSION

This chapter has illustrated the significant potential of integrating computer vision (CV) and artificial intelligence (AI) technologies in advancing Above-Ground Biomass (AGB) estimation. By utilizing developments in remote sensing, deep learning, and multi-modal data integration, considerable progress has been made in enhancing the accuracy and efficiency of AGB estimation techniques.

The integration of CV and AI opens viable solutions to address the challenges of data limitations and the complexity of forest ecosystems. This enhancement is achieved by incorporating detailed forest structural parameters into the estimation process. Ground-based methods, particularly those utilizing smartphones, provide high-resolution data for parameters like tree height, diameter at breast height (DBH), and canopy structure. Remote sensing techniques, ranging from fine-grained UAV imagery to coarse-grained satellite data, complement ground-based approaches by providing wider coverage. However, challenges remain in achieving high accuracy and generalizability across different forest types, particularly when adapting models to different ecological environment and the limitation of data quality that can be captured for the model.

Future research could prioritize the development of standardized datasets, and exploring innovative data collection methods, including crowdsourcing and synthetic data generation. Integrating multi-modal sensing approaches to combine data from various sources, such as ground-based measurements, UAV imagery, satellite data, and LiDAR scans. Least but not least, using AI and computer vision techniques through the exploration of a more sophisticated algorithms, improving model interpretability, or potentially incorporating generative AI into the AGB estimation pipeline.

By advancing these areas, we hope to achieve a better understanding and management of our forests, especially in biomass, contributing to global efforts to mitigate climate change. The ongoing research and innovation in this field are crucial for creating sustainable practices that preserve the world's forests and support environmental conservation.

## ACKNOWLEDGEMENT

This work was carried out in part during FWW's and MP's Master of Data Science Research Pathway (Minor Thesis) at Monash University, Indonesia in which they acknowledged the scholarship support from PT PLN (Persero).

## REFERENCES

Abbasi, T., & Abbasi, S. A. (2010). Biomass energy and the environmental impacts associated with its production and utilization. *Renewable & Sustainable Energy Reviews*, 14(3), 919–937. DOI: 10.1016/j.rser.2009.11.006

Adinugroho, W. C., Krisnawati, H., Imanuddin, R., Siregar, C. A., Weston, C. J., & Volkova, L. (2023). Developing biomass allometric equations for small trees in mixed-species forests of tropical rainforest ecozone. *Trees, Forests and People*, 13, 100425. DOI: 10.1016/j.tfp.2023.100425

Ahamed, A., Foye, J., Poudel, S., Trieschman, E., & Fike, J. (2023). Measuring Tree Diameter with Photogrammetry Using Mobile Phone Cameras. Forests 2023, Vol. 14, Page 2027, 14(10), 2027. DOI: 10.1016/j.tfp.2023.100425

Anitha, K., Verchot, L. V., Joseph, S., Herold, M., Manuri, S., & Avitabile, V. (2015). A review of forest and tree plantation biomass equations in Indonesia. *Annals of Forest Science*, 72(8), 981–997. DOI: 10.1007/s13595-015-0507-4

Araujo, E. C. G., Sanquetta, C. R., Dalla Corte, A. P., Pelissari, A. L., Orso, G. A., & Silva, T. C. (2023). Global review and state-of-the-art of biomass and carbon stock in the Amazon. *Journal of Environmental Management*, 331, 117251. DOI: 10.1016/j.jenvman.2023.117251 PMID: 36657202

Bibi, A., Zhang, X., & Umar, M. (2021). The imperativeness of biomass energy consumption to the environmental sustainability of the United States revisited. *Environmental and Ecological Statistics*, 28(4), 821–841. DOI: 10.1007/s10651-021-00500-9

Bobrowski, R., Winczek, M., Zięba-Kulawik, K., & Wężyk, P. (2023). Best practices to use the iPad Pro LiDAR for some procedures of data acquisition in the urban forest. *Urban Forestry & Urban Greening*, 79, 127815. Advance online publication. DOI: 10.1016/j.ufug.2022.127815

Borsah, A. A., Nazeer, M., & Wong, M. S. (2023). LIDAR-Based Forest Biomass Remote Sensing: A Review of Metrics, Methods, and Assessment Criteria for the Selection of Allometric Equations. Forests 2023, Vol. 14, Page 2095, 14(10), 2095. DOI: 10.1016/j.ufug.2022.127815

Buchelt, A., Adrowitzer, A., Kieseberg, P., Gollob, C., Nothdurft, A., Eresheim, S., Tschiatschek, S., Stampfer, K., & Holzinger, A. (2024). Exploring artificial intelligence for applications of drones in forest ecology and management. *Forest Ecology and Management*, 551, 121530. DOI: 10.1016/j.foreco.2023.121530

Bui, Q. T., Pham, Q. T., Pham, V. M., Tran, V. T., Nguyen, D. H., Nguyen, Q. H., Nguyen, H. D., Do, N. T., & Vu, V. M. (2024). Hybrid machine learning models for aboveground biomass estimations. *Ecological Informatics*, 79, 102421. DOI: 10.1016/j.ecoinf.2023.102421

Chen, Z., Ting, D., Newbury, R., & Chen, C. (2021). Semantic segmentation for partially occluded apple trees based on deep learning. *Computers and Electronics in Agriculture*, 181, 105952. DOI: 10.1016/j.compag.2020.105952

Darmawan, A., Asyhari, T., & Dunggio, I. Salmahaminati, & Aziz, M. (2023). Energy harvesting from tropical biomasses in Wallacea region: scenarios, technologies, and perspectives. In Biomass Conversion and Biorefinery. Springer Science and Business Media Deutschland GmbH. DOI: 10.1007/s13399-023-04223-8

Dirisu, J. O., Salawu, E. Y., Ekpe, I. C., Udoye, N. E., Falodun, O. E., Oyedepo, S. O., Ajayi, O. O., & Kale, S. A. (2023). Promoting the use of bioenergy in developing nations: A CDM route to sustainable development. *Frontiers in Energy Research*, 11, 1184348. DOI: 10.3389/fenrg.2023.1184348

Fan, Y., Feng, Z., Shen, C., Khan, T. U., Mannan, A., Gao, X., Chen, P., & Saeed, S. (2020). A trunk-based SLAM backend for smartphones with online SLAM in large-scale forest inventories. *ISPRS Journal of Photogrammetry and Remote Sensing*, 162, 41–49. DOI: 10.1016/j.isprsjprs.2020.02.006

Fu, H., Zhao, H., Jiang, J., Zhang, Y., Liu, G., Xiao, W., Du, S., Guo, W., & Liu, X. (2024). Automatic detection tree crown and height using Mask R-CNN based on unmanned aerial vehicles images for biomass mapping. *Forest Ecology and Management*, 555, 121712. DOI: 10.1016/j.foreco.2024.121712

Gené-Mola, J., Ferrer-Ferrer, M., Gregorio, E., Blok, P. M., Hemming, J., Morros, J. R., Rosell-Polo, J. R., Vilaplana, V., & Ruiz-Hidalgo, J. (2023). Looking behind occlusions: A study on amodal segmentation for robust on-tree apple fruit size estimation. *Computers and Electronics in Agriculture*, 209, 107854. DOI: 10.1016/j.compag.2023.107854

Guimarães, N., Pádua, L., Marques, P., Silva, N., Peres, E., & Sousa, J. J. (2020). Forestry Remote Sensing from Unmanned Aerial Vehicles: A Review Focusing on the Data, Processing and Potentialities. Remote Sensing 2020, Vol. 12, Page 1046, 12(6), 1046. DOI: 10.1016/j.ufug.2022.127815

Gülci, S., Yurtseven, H., Akay, A. O., & Akgul, M. (2023). Measuring tree diameter using a LiDAR-equipped smartphone: A comparison of smartphone- and caliper-based DBH. *Environmental Monitoring and Assessment*, 195(6), 1–16. DOI: 10.1007/s10661-023-11366-8 PMID: 37191833

Holcomb, A., Tong, L., & Keshav, S. (2023). Robust Single-Image Tree Diameter Estimation with Mobile Phones. Remote Sensing 2023, Vol. 15, Page 772, 15(3), 772. DOI: 10.1007/s10661-023-11366-8 PMID: 37191833

Hussain, A., Barua, B., Osman, A., Abozariba, R., & Taufiq Asyhari, A. (2021). Performance of MobileNetV3 Transfer Learning on Handheld Device-based Real-Time Tree Species Identification. 2021 26th International Conference on Automation and Computing: System Intelligence through Automation and Computing, ICAC 2021. DOI: 10.23919/ICAC50006.2021.9594222

Iglhaut, J., Cabo, C., Puliti, S., Piermattei, L., O'Connor, J., & Rosette, J. (2019). Structure from Motion Photogrammetry in Forestry: A Review. *Current Forestry Reports*, 5(3), 155–168. DOI: 10.1007/s40725-019-00094-3

Jurjević, L., Liang, X., Gašparović, M., & Balenović, I. (2020). Is field-measured tree height as reliable as believed – Part II, A comparison study of tree height estimates from conventional field measurement and low-cost close-range remote sensing in a deciduous forest. *ISPRS Journal of Photogrammetry and Remote Sensing*, 169, 227–241. DOI: 10.1016/j.isprsjprs.2020.09.014

Kurniawan, I. F., Aneiba, A., Hussain, A., Idrissi, M., Dunggio, I., & Asyhari, A. T. (2022). Large-scale Tree Detection through UAV-based Remote Sensing in Indonesia: Wallacea Case Study. Proceedings - 2022 8th International Conference on Information Management, ICIM 2022, 110–115. DOI: 10.1109/ICIM56520.2022.00027

Lechner, A. M., Foody, G. M., & Boyd, D. S. (2020). Applications in Remote Sensing to Forest Ecology and Management. DOI: 10.1007/s10661-023-11366-8 PMID: 37191833

Liu, Z., Wu, K., Guo, J., Wang, Y., Deussen, O., & Cheng, Z. (2021). Single Image Tree Reconstruction via Adversarial Network. *Graphical Models*, 117, 101115. DOI: 10.1016/j.gmod.2021.101115

Lu, D., Chen, Q., Wang, G., Liu, L., Li, G., & Moran, E. (2016). A survey of remote sensing-based aboveground biomass estimation methods in forest ecosystems. *International Journal of Digital Earth*, 9(1), 63–105. DOI: 10.1080/17538947.2014.990526

Lumnitz, S., Devisscher, T., Mayaud, J. R., Radic, V., Coops, N. C., & Griess, V. C. (2021). Mapping trees along urban street networks with deep learning and street-level imagery. *ISPRS Journal of Photogrammetry and Remote Sensing*, 175, 144–157. DOI: 10.1016/j.isprsjprs.2021.01.016

Megalingam, R. K., Darla, V. P., Nimmala, C. S. K., & Sankardas, K. S. (2022). Computer vision-based Measuring Method to Estimate the Diameter of the Coconut Tree Trunk. *2022 International Conference for Advancement in Technology, ICONAT 2022*. DOI: 10.1109/ICONAT53423.2022.9725999

Nations, U. (n.d.). Renewable energy – powering a safer future | United Nations. Retrieved February 23, 2024, from https://www.un.org/en/climatechange/raising-ambition/renewable-energy

Oehmcke, S., Li, L., Trepekli, K., Revenga, J. C., Nord-Larsen, T., Gieseke, F., & Igel, C. (2024). Deep point cloud regression for above-ground forest biomass estimation from airborne LiDAR. *Remote Sensing of Environment*, 302, 113968. DOI: 10.1016/j.rse.2023.113968

Putra, B. T. W., Ramadhani, N. J., Soedibyo, D. W., Marhaenanto, B., Indarto, I., & Yualianto, Y. (2021). The use of computer vision to estimate tree diameter and circumference in homogeneous and production forests using a non-contact method. *Forest Science and Technology*, 17(1), 32–38. DOI: 10.1080/21580103.2021.1873866

Renewable Energy Directive. (n.d.). Retrieved June 20, 2024, from https://energy.ec.europa.eu/topics/renewable-energy/renewable-energy-directive-targets-and-rules/renewable-energy-directive_en

Ribeiro, M. T., Singh, S., & Guestrin, C. (n.d.). *Why Should I Trust You?* Explaining the Predictions of Any Classifier., DOI: 10.1145/2939672.2939778

Roth, S., Ib, ;, Leiterer, R. ;, Volpi, M. ;, Celio, E. ;, Schaepman, M. E. ;, Joerg, P. C., Roth, S. I. B., Leiterer, R., Volpi, M., Celio, E., & Schaepman, M. E. (2018). Automated detection of individual clove trees for yield quantification in northeastern Madagascar based on multi-spectral satellite data. DOI: 10.1145/2939672.2939778

Sainuddin, F. V., Chirakkal, S., Asok, S. V., & Putrevu, D. (2024). A comparative study on the efficacy of dual-pol and full-pol ASAR data in radiative transfer modeling for forest above-ground biomass estimation. *International Journal of Remote Sensing*, 45(3), 719–747. DOI: 10.1080/01431161.2024.2302952

Sandim, A., Amaro, M., Silva, M. E., Cunha, J., Morais, S., Marques, A., Ferreira, A., Lousada, J. L., & Fonseca, T. (2023). New Technologies for Expedited Forest Inventory Using Smartphone Applications. Forests 2023, Vol. 14, Page 1553, 14(8), 1553. DOI: 10.1145/2939672.2939778

Schiefer, F., Kattenborn, T., Frick, A., Frey, J., Schall, P., Koch, B., & Schmidtlein, S. (2020). Mapping forest tree species in high resolution UAV-based RGB-imagery by means of convolutional neural networks. *ISPRS Journal of Photogrammetry and Remote Sensing*, 170, 205–215. DOI: 10.1016/j.isprsjprs.2020.10.015

Shahinfar, S., Meek, P., & Falzon, G. (2020). "How many images do I need?" Understanding how sample size per class affects deep learning model performance metrics for balanced designs in autonomous wildlife monitoring. *Ecological Informatics*, 57, 101085. DOI: 10.1016/j.ecoinf.2020.101085

Shen, Y., Huang, R., Hua, B., Pan, Y., Mei, Y., & Dong, M. (2023). Automatic Tree Height Measurement Based on Three-Dimensional Reconstruction Using Smartphone. Sensors 2023, Vol. 23, Page 7248, 23(16), 7248. DOI: 10.1145/2939672.2939778

Shi, L., Liu, S., Shi, L., & Liu, S. (2017). *Methods of Estimating Forest Biomass: A Review*. Biomass Volume Estimation and Valorization for Energy., DOI: 10.5772/65733

Simangunsong, B. C. H., Sitanggang, V. J., Manurung, E. G. T., Rahmadi, A., Moore, G. A., Aye, L., & Tambunan, A. H. (2017). Potential forest biomass resource as feedstock for bioenergy and its economic value in Indonesia. *Forest Policy and Economics*, 81, 10–17. DOI: 10.1016/j.forpol.2017.03.022

Skurikhin, A. N., Garrity, S. R., McDowell, N. G., & Cai, D. M. (2013). Automated tree crown detection and size estimation using multi-scale analysis of high-resolution satellite imagery. *Remote Sensing Letters*, 4(5), 465–474. DOI: 10.1080/2150704X.2012.749361

Song, Q., Albrecht, C. M., Xiong, Z., & Zhu, X. X. (2023). Biomass Estimation and Uncertainty Quantification From Tree Height. *IEEE Journal of Selected Topics in Applied Earth Observations and Remote Sensing*, 16, 4833–4845. DOI: 10.1109/JSTARS.2023.3271186

Stas, S. M., Rutishauser, E., Chave, J., Anten, N. P. R., & Laumonier, Y. (2017). Estimating the aboveground biomass in an old secondary forest on limestone in the Moluccas, Indonesia: Comparing locally developed versus existing allometric models. *Forest Ecology and Management*, 389, 27–34. DOI: 10.1016/j.foreco.2016.12.010

Štrumbelj, E., & Kononenko, I. (2014). Explaining prediction models and individual predictions with feature contributions. *Knowledge and Information Systems*, 41(3), 647–665. DOI: 10.1007/s10115-013-0679-x

Tatsumi, S., Yamaguchi, K., & Furuya, N. (2023). ForestScanner: A mobile application for measuring and mapping trees with LiDAR-equipped iPhone and iPad. *Methods in Ecology and Evolution*, 14(7), 1603–1609. DOI: 10.1111/2041-210X.13900

Tian, L., Wu, X., Tao, Y., Li, M., Qian, C., Liao, L., & Fu, W. (2023). Review of Remote Sensing-Based Methods for Forest Aboveground Biomass Estimation: Progress, Challenges, and Prospects. Forests 2023, Vol. 14, Page 1086, 14(6), 1086. DOI: 10.1111/2041-210X.13900

Tran, H., Woeste, K., Li, B., Verma, A., & Shao, G. (2023). Measuring tree stem diameters and straightness with depth-image computer vision. *Journal of Forestry Research*, 34(5), 1395–1405. DOI: 10.1007/s11676-023-01600-x

Velasquez-Camacho, L., Etxegarai, M., & de-Miguel, S. (2023). Implementing Deep Learning algorithms for urban tree detection and geolocation with high-resolution aerial, satellite, and ground-level images. *Computers, Environment and Urban Systems*, 105, 102025. DOI: 10.1016/j.compenvurbsys.2023.102025

Wang, J., Zhang, H., Liu, Y., Zhang, H., & Zheng, D. (2024). Tree-Level Chinese Fir Detection Using UAV RGB Imagery and YOLO-DCAM. Remote Sensing 2024, Vol. 16, Page 335, 16(2), 335. DOI: 10.1016/j.compenvurbsys.2023.102025

Wang, Y., Zhang, X., & Guo, Z. (2021). Estimation of tree height and aboveground biomass of coniferous forests in North China using stereo ZY-3, multispectral Sentinel-2, and DEM data. *Ecological Indicators*, 126, 107645. DOI: 10.1016/j.ecolind.2021.107645

Woo, H., Kim, I., & Choi, B. (2021). Computer vision techniques in forest inventory assessment: Improving accuracy of tree diameter measurement using smartphone camera and photogrammetry. *Sensors and Materials*, 33(11), 3835–3845. DOI: 10.18494/SAM.2021.3605

World Bioenergy Association. (2022). GLOBAL BIOENERGY STATISTICS 2022 World Bioenergy Association. https://www.worldbioenergy.org/uploads/221223%20WBA%20GBS%202022.pdf

Wu, W., Hasegawa, T., Ohashi, H., Hanasaki, N., Liu, J., Matsui, T., Fujimori, S., Masui, T., & Takahashi, K. (2019). Global advanced bioenergy potential under environmental protection policies and societal transformation measures. *Global Change Biology. Bioenergy*, 11(9), 1041–1055. DOI: 10.1111/gcbb.12614

Xinmei, W., Aijun, X., & Tingting, Y. (2020). Passive Measurement Method of Tree Height and Crown Diameter Using a Smartphone. *IEEE Access : Practical Innovations, Open Solutions*, 8, 11669–11678. DOI: 10.1109/ACCESS.2020.2965216

Yang, M., Zhou, X., Liu, Z., Li, P., Tang, J., Xie, B., Peng, C. A., Yang, M., Zhou, X., Liu, Z., Li, P., Tang, J., Xie, B., & Peng, C. (2022). A Review of General Methods for Quantifying and Estimating Urban Trees and Biomass. Forests 2022, Vol. 13, Page 616, 13(4), 616. DOI: 10.1109/ACCESS.2020.2965216

Chapter 5

# Machine Learning-Based Maintenance Need Prediction for a Power Station Case Study

**Nicolla Fundira**
*National University of Science and Technology, Zimbabwe*

**Evangelista Tasiiwa Nyakujipa**
*National University of Science and Technology, Zimbabwe*

## ABSTRACT

*This chapter presents the development and application of a machine learning-based maintenance need prediction system using regression models, focusing on a coal-fired thermal power station in Southern Africa. This study emerged from the need to address the inefficiencies in traditional maintenance practices at the power station, where the aging infrastructure has led to frequent equipment failures, costly repairs, and significant downtime. The chapter explores the steps taken to develop a predictive maintenance model using operational data from the power station, the selection and tuning of machine learning models, and the practical implications of deploying such a system in an industrial setting. The machine learning model demonstrated a high level of accuracy in predicting exceedance counts, which are critical indicators of potential equipment failures meaning that predictive maintenance system could effectively reduce downtime and prevent costly repairs.*

DOI: 10.4018/979-8-3373-2530-9.ch005

## 1. BACKGROUND TO THE STUDY

The power station under study is a coal-fired thermal plant that was constructed between 1947 and 1957 located in southern Africa. Over the years, it has faced numerous challenges due to aging infrastructure, leading to a decline in its power generation capacity. By 2022, the station's capacity had dropped significantly, underscoring the urgent need for improved maintenance practices. Traditional maintenance approaches at the power station have primarily been reactive and/or preventive. Reactive maintenance involves repairing equipment only after it fails, has led to prolonged downtime and increased operational costs. Preventive maintenance, which schedules maintenance at fixed intervals regardless of the equipment's condition, has also proven inefficient, often resulting in unnecessary maintenance activities that waste resources. Traditional preventive maintenance schedules are inefficient, resulting in accelerated failures and decreased plant availability (Susto, 2015; Wang et al, 2018).

Maintenance is critical for organizations globally that rely on physical assets like machinery, equipment and infrastructure (Susto et al., 2018). Traditional reactive and preventive maintenance approaches can be inefficient and costly compared to predictive strategies driven by data analytics (Wang Zhang, 2020; Wu et al., 2019). Machine learning has emerged as a powerful predictive maintenance enabler, facilitating the digital transformation from reactive to proactive, condition-based systems (Xia et al., 2021). Supervised machine learning algorithms help predict remaining useful life (RUL) through regression on historical operating and failure data (Lei et al., 2018; Zhao et al., 2019). Unsupervised techniques detect anomalies indicating potential faults (Hu et al., 2019). Deep learning extracts high-level representations from raw condition monitoring data (Zheng et al., 2019).

In Africa, industries face unique financial and skills barriers inhibiting modern maintenance practices (Musa et al., 2018). However, predictive maintenance becomes increasingly viable through low-cost wireless condition monitoring and cloud-based machine learning accessible on any device (Lwoga et al., 2020)

To address the highlighted challenges, we are to develop a data-driven predictive maintenance model that could forecast when maintenance is needed based on real-time operational data. By predicting potential equipment failures before they occur, the power station could optimize its maintenance schedule, reduce downtime, and extend the life of its critical assets. By leveraging historical data, machine learning algorithms can forecast remaining useful life, enabling precise maintenance scheduling and reducing downtime and repair expenses (Lei et al, 2018; Zhao et al, 2019). This approach improves reliability and increases the power station's availability for continuous power supply (Wuest at al, 2016; Zheng et al, 2019).

Integrating machine learning-based maintenance prediction in power stations advances sustainability by enhancing environmental, economic, and operational efficiency. Early fault detection reduces energy wastage and minimizes carbon emissions, promoting environmental sustainability while optimizing resource utilization and preventing hazardous incidents. Economically, predictive maintenance lowers operational costs, extends equipment lifespan, and improves energy efficiency by scheduling maintenance only when necessary, avoiding unnecessary servicing and unplanned downtime. Operationally, it enhances system reliability, supports data-driven decision-making, and streamlines workforce allocation. These contributions collectively support sustainable energy production, reduce waste, and foster long-term operational resilience, aligning with global sustainability goals.

## 2. LITERATURE REVIEW

Predictive maintenance through machine learning is gaining popularity as a reliable tool to optimize asset management. Conventional time-based maintenance can be inefficient and costly. This literature review explores applying regression algorithms within a machine learning framework for equipment remaining useful life prediction. In short, the goal is to develop a machine learning based maintenance need prediction for equipment at power Power Station based on established common boiler failure modes.

### 2.1 Conceptual Framework

This study focused on machine learning, which involves developing algorithms to learn and predict from data. (Heller, 2019) defines a machine learning model as a mathematical representation of real-world processes that re-samples the output of a specific algorithm during the training phase. This means that the approach requires training data from which the machine may learn and make judgements based on the requirements, resulting in an output known as the y-predict or projected score. According to (Heller, 2019), machine learning approaches can be classified as classification models, regression models, clustering, dimensionality reductions, and principal component analysis. A machine learning model functions based on three conditions: input data points, predicted output examples, and performance assessment guidelines.

As a result, the conceptual framework is described in terms of inputs and outputs relative to the dependent and independent variables specified in the dataset's characteristics.

## 2.2 Overview of Predictive Maintenance

Predictive maintenance refers to condition-based maintenance strategies that leverage contemporary sensing, analytical and digital technologies to monitor equipment health and predict remaining useful life in real-time (Susto et al., 2019). This enables maintenance to shift from conventional time- or failure-based reactive approaches to being precisely scheduled based on actual need. Traditional preventive maintenance relies on set time intervals or usage thresholds for scheduled servicing, often regardless of current asset condition (Wang Zhang, 2020). However, the rate of degradation varies greatly across machines depending on factors like usage profile, manufacturing tolerances and environmental conditions (Haja Mohideen et al., 2018). Consequently, tasks may occur either too early, wasting resources, or too late, risking unexpected downtime costs.

In contrast, predictive maintenance aims to forecast the actual remaining useful life (RUL) for each individual asset through continuous remote monitoring and analytics on operational parameters known to influence wear patterns (Lee et al., 2020). Maintenance intervals become conditional on measured degradation trends matching model expectations for a given RULpoint (Zhao et al., 2019). This enables work to precisely target developing faults before materializing, realizing substantial benefits.

In traditional Maintenance Approaches, there are three fundamental maintenance strategies which include reactive, preventive and predictive (Susto et al., 2019). Reactive maintenance relies on run-to-failure and corrective actions once issues arise. While low cost initially, it risks long downtimes and safety vulnerabilities. Preventive maintenance aims to pre-empt failures through scheduled overhauls at fixed time or usage intervals regardless of need. Though improving availability, it incurs unnecessary costs for healthy assets and may miss developing faults.

Machine learning has increasingly enabled predictive maintenance through automated analytics on vast high-frequency condition monitoring datasets (Wuest et al., 2016). Self-learning algorithms identify convert degradation patterns to make robust failure predictions assisting decision-making. Machine learning yields more accurate RUL forecasts, optimized scheduling and potential maintenance cost savings versus manual analysis (Wuest et al., 2016; Zheng et al., 2019). Challenges include lack of labelled failure data, operational changes over time and hardware failures complicating signals requiring techniques like transfer learning (An et al., 2021; Li et al., 2020). Overall predictive maintenance enhances reliability, uptime and productivity globally (Wang Zhang, 2020; Wu et al., 2019). Machine learning (ML) has become an essential tool in the development of predictive maintenance systems. By analysing large datasets, ML models can identify patterns and trends that are not immediately apparent through traditional analysis methods. These models can predict when a piece of equipment is likely to fail, allowing maintenance to be scheduled just in time to prevent unplanned downtime.

While predictive maintenance relies heavily on data from various sources such as sensors, machines and maintenance records, there can be challenges related to data availability. Ensuring the accuracy, completeness and timeliness of data remains a crucial research area (A Bousdekis, 2019).

*Table 1. Summary table of previous work on predictive maintenance*

| Study | Focus | Key Contributions | Challenges Highlighted |
|---|---|---|---|
| Susto et al. (2019) | Condition-based maintenance strategies and monitoring of equipment health | Shift from reactive and preventive maintenance to predictive approaches through real-time condition tracking | Balancing early and timely maintenance without resource waste |
| Wang Zhang (2020) | Traditional vs predictive maintenance approaches | Highlighted inefficiencies in preventive maintenance and advantages of predictive models | Varying machine degradation rates influenced by usage and environmental factors |
| Haja Mohideen et al. (2018) | Impact of usage and environmental factors on equipment degradation | Explored variability in degradation patterns due to operational conditions | Difficulty in scheduling maintenance using conventional methods |
| Lee et al. (2020) | Continuous remote monitoring and RUL prediction | Proposed condition-based intervals for better maintenance efficiency | Ensuring model expectations align with actual degradation patterns |
| Wuest et al. (2016) | Machine learning for predictive maintenance | Demonstrated self-learning algorithms for robust failure predictions | Lack of labeled failure data, hardware signal complications |
| Zhao et al. (2019) | Forecasting degradation trends | Improved RUL predictions using data-driven models | Managing unexpected faults while optimizing maintenance intervals |
| An et al. (2021) | Use of transfer learning to address lack of labeled data | Suggested adaptation techniques for evolving operational conditions | Adapting models over time with minimal labeled historical failure data |
| Li et al. (2020) | Machine learning for predictive analytics | Enhanced failure prediction accuracy and maintenance decision-making | Managing operational changes and adapting predictive models |
| Wu et al. (2019) | Global productivity benefits from predictive maintenance | Showcased industry-wide benefits of predictive strategies | Operational changes over time complicating predictive accuracy |
| Bousdekis (2019) | Data quality and availability for predictive maintenance | Highlighted importance of accurate, complete, and timely data collection | Ensuring data reliability from multiple sources |

Table 1 summarise key research contributions and challenges, providing an overview of advancements and ongoing issues in predictive maintenance strategies.

# 3. METHODOLOGY

## 3.1 Research Design

This study used an experimental research design, which involves manipulating independent factors to obtain a dependent result. This was accomplished by doing the experiment with a machine learning approach and obtaining the projected outcome of the predicted result of time which require maintenance need for equipment at power Power Station based on established common boiler failure modes.

## 3.2 Research Paradigm

The proposed research study adopts a quantitative research approach that is in line with a positivist research philosophy. The study aims to systematically investigate the research problem through empirical examination using statistical models, computational techniques, and mathematical tools to develop, scrutinize, and test hypotheses and theories concerning maintenance history. The primary objective of the study is to develop precise predictions of the next maintenance requirement.

## 3.3 Data Collection and Pre-Processing

The data was collected from a Power Station in southern Africa and it comprises of daily logs and maintenance records. The development of the predictive maintenance model began with the collection of operational data from the power station. Key parameters, such as steam flow, air flow, and stop valve pressure, were recorded over time. This data was then subjected to rigorous cleaning and pre- processing to remove noise, handle missing values, and normalize the data for analysis. Data pre-processing included the use of rolling statistics to smooth out fluctuations in the data and the implementation of an exceedance count metric to capture deviations from normal operating conditions. These pre-processed features were essential in training the machine learning models to accurately predict maintenance needs. The table 2 shows an example of boiler operations data collected at hourly intervals.

*Table 2. Extract of boiler operations data collected at hourly intervals*

| Time | Steam Flow (tons/hr) | Air Flow (tons/hr) | Stop Valve P.S.I. Bars | Stop Valve Temp | Econ. Outlet | Air Heater Outlet | Econ. Inlet |
|---|---|---|---|---|---|---|---|
| 0 | 62 | 55 | 39 | 388 | 292 | 118 | 157 |
| 1 | 61 | 55 | 39 | 391 | 291 | 118 | 157 |
| 2 | 60 | 56 | 41 | 391 | 292 | 117 | 156 |
| 3 | 61 | 56 | 40 | 387 | 292 | 114 | 157 |
| 4 | 61 | 56 | 40 | 384 | 299 | 114 | 144 |
| 5 | 61 | 56 | 40 | 381 | 292 | 114 | 144 |
| 6 | 61 | 55 | 40 | 377 | 307 | 114 | 144 |
| 7 | 62 | 55 | 39 | 378 | 308 | 113 | 147 |
| 8 | 61 | 55 | 40 | 380 | 303 | 112 | 147 |
| 9 | 61 | 55 | 40 | 383 | 303 | 112 | 146 |
| 10 | 60 | 56 | 40 | 379 | 301 | 112 | 146 |
| 11 | 60 | 56 | 40 | 380 | 300 | 112 | 146 |
| 12 | 60 | 56 | 39 | 380 | 300 | 113 | 146 |
| 13 | 62 | 56 | 39 | 382 | 300 | 114 | 158 |
| 14 | 60 | 56 | 40 | 384 | 300 | 113 | 159 |
| 15 | 63 | 56 | 39 | 381 | 300 | 113 | 159 |
| 16 | 58 | 56 | 40 | 384 | 300 | 114 | 159 |
| 17 | 58 | 57 | 40 | 383 | 301 | 113 | 159 |
| 18 | 61 | 56 | 39 | 384 | 302 | 112 | 160 |
| 19 | 59 | 56 | 39 | 378 | 301 | 113 | 160 |
| 20 | 60 | 56 | 41 | 384 | 302 | 112 | 160 |
| 21 | 58 | 56 | 40 | 381 | 302 | 112 | 160 |
| 22 | 58 | 58 | 38 | 378 | 303 | 112 | 159 |
| 23 | 59 | 58 | 40 | 351 | 303 | 112 | 160 |
| 24 | 61 | 58 | 40 | 381 | 300 | 112 | 160 |
| **Mean** | 60.32 | 56.04 | 39.72 | 381.2 | 299.76 | 113.4 | 157.6 |
| **SD** | 1.38 | 0.89 | 0.68 | 7.33 | 4.57 | 1.80 | 6.59 |

## 3.4 Sampling Technique

Categorizing operational data from boilers can prove to be challenging due to many factors that are measured using instrumentation. To minimize bias and ensure the model can generalize well to unseen data, we employed simple random sampling for this project. Boiler breakdowns can occur unexpectedly and are caused by a variety of factors, making this approach optimal for data collection.

## 3.5 Research Materials and Tools

Python

- Excel
- Supervised machine learning classifier
- Python libraries are listed in figure 1 below:

*Figure 1. Python libraries imported code*

```
import pandas as pd
import matplotlib.pyplot as plt
from sklearn.model_selection import train_test_split, GridSearchCV
from sklearn.preprocessing import StandardScaler
from sklearn.linear_model import LinearRegression
from sklearn.ensemble import RandomForestRegressor
from sklearn.tree import DecisionTreeRegressor
from sklearn.metrics import mean_absolute_error, mean_squared_error, r2_score
import numpy as np

```

## 3.6 Variables Description

Variables are explained by the following table 3.

*Table 3. Variable description*

| **Independent Variables** | **Description** |
|---|---|
| **Steam flow (ton/hr)** | Steam flow refers to the rate at which steam is produced, typically measured in units like kg/hr or lb/hr. It indicates the boiler's capacity to supply steam for heating or other uses. |
| **Airflow (ton/hr)** | Airflow ton/hr refers to the amount of air passing through the boiler system per hour, measured in tons. It indicates the rate at which combustion air is supplied to the boiler furnace for efficient fuel combustion and heat generation. |
| **Stop valve P.S.I (bars)** | Stop valve psi bars refers to the pressure rating of the valve, measured in pounds per square inch (psi) or bars. It indicates the maximum pressure the valve can handle safely. |

continued on following page

*Table 3. Continued*

| Independent Variables | Description |
|---|---|
| **Stop Valve Temp** | Stop valve temperature refers to the temperature of the stop valve in an industrial system. It's monitored to prevent overheating and ensure safe operation. |
| **Air heater Outlet flue gas temperature** | The air heater outlet flue gas temperature is the temperature of the gases leaving the air heater in a combustion system. It indicates the efficiency of preheating combustion air for better fuel usage and reduced emissions. |
| **Economizer Flue gas outlet temperature** | The economizer flue gas outlet temperature is the temperature of the exhaust gases leaving the economizer in a boiler system. It's crucial for optimizing the efficiency of the boiler by recovering heat from the flue gases to preheat the incoming feedwater. |

Dependent variable- maintenance need

## 3.7 Data Analysis Procedure

The data analysis technique followed the Cross-Industry Standard Process for Data Mining (CRISPDM), a framework that lays out a detailed structure for the research. The framework allows for a more business-oriented approach and better results in the shortest amount of time. Business understanding, data understanding, data preparation and cleaning, modelling, evaluation, and ultimately deployment are the six steps of the model. Figure 2 illustrates the model.

*Figure 2. Cross-Industry standard process for data mining (CRISPDM)*

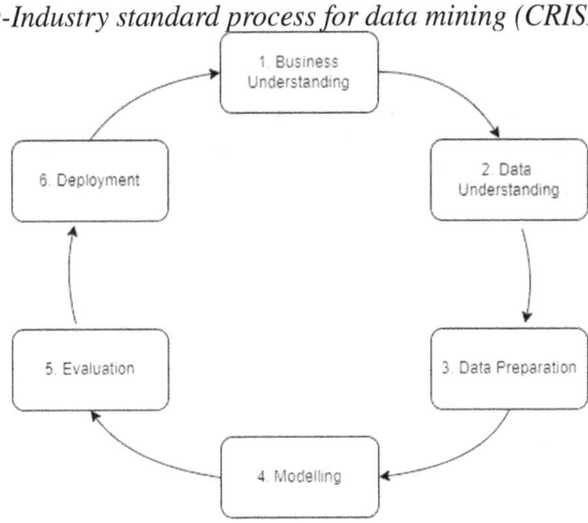

To ensure the success of our project, we must gain a deep understanding of our business objectives through the process of Business Understanding. Our primary objective is to contribute towards Sustainable Development Goal (SDG 7) demands for "affordable, reliable, sustainable, and modern energy for all" by 2030. Its three key aims serve as the cornerstone for our work. Ensure that everyone has access to affordable, dependable, and advanced energy services. To achieve this ambitious goal, it is essential to address the operational inefficiencies across all power plants in Southern Africa. By adopting a machine learning adaptive maintenance program, we aim to improve the performance of our power plants and thereby enhance their efficiency. Through diligent implementation and management of this program, we can bring about positive change and help transform energy sector for the better.

The dataset was imported using the following code figure 3:

*Figure 3. Code to import dataset and print first five rows of the dataset*

```
# 1. Load and Display Data:
df = pd.read_csv(r'C:\perez\Boiler.csv')
print("Data Overview:")
print(df.head().to_markdown(index=False, numalign='left', stralign='left'))  # Show the first few rows
print("\n")
```

Researchers established specific ranges for each parameter as depicted in figure 4, to define acceptable minimum and maximum values, which was crucial for identifying any deviations that might signal a need for maintenance.

*Figure 4. Code to established specific ranges for each parameters*

```
standard_params = {
    'Steam Flow tons/hr': (29, 72.6),  # Replace with your actual values
    'Air Flow tons/hr': (55, 65),
    'Stop Valve Pressure/bars': (42, 43),
}

print("Step 2: Defined Standard Operating Parameters:")
for param, (min_val, max_val) in standard_params.items():
    print(f"- {param}: {min_val} to {max_val}")
print("\n")
```

The researchers started by cleaning and transforming the data in figure 5, as we knew that the raw sensor data could be noisy or have outliers. To smooth out the data and reveal the underlying trends more clearly, we applied a rolling average calculation over a 24-hour window. Additionally, we calculated rolling standard deviations, which helped us to determine the extent to which each parameter fluctuated within that 24-hour window. To help visualize the impact of this smoothing, we created boxplots comparing the original and cleaned data for each parameter.

*Figure 5. Code for data cleaning*

```
indow_size = 24

r col in df.columns:
    # Create subplots for original data and cleaned data
    fig, axes = plt.subplots( nrows: 1,  ncols: 2, figsize=(15, 6))

    # Plot original data with outliers
    df.boxplot(column=[col], ax=axes[0])
    axes[0].set_title(f'Original {col}')
    axes[0].set_ylabel('Value')

    # Calculate rolling statistics
    df[col + '_rolling_mean'] = df[col].rolling(window=window_size).mean()
    df[col + '_rolling_std'] = df[col].rolling(window=window_size).std()

    # Remove NaNs
    df_cleaned = df[[col, col + '_rolling_mean']].dropna()

    # Plot cleaned data with rolling mean
    df_cleaned.boxplot(column=[col + '_rolling_mean'], ax=axes[1])
    axes[1].set_title(f'Cleaned {col} (Rolling Mean)')
    axes[1].set_ylabel('Value')

    plt.suptitle(f'Outlier Handling for {col}')
    plt.show()

    # Outlier Analysis
    print(f"\nOutlier Analysis for {col}:")
    original_outliers = df[col][
        (df[col] < df[col].quantile(0.25) - 1.5 * (df[col].quantile(0.75) - df[col].quantile(0.25)))
        | (df[col] > df[col].quantile(0.75) + 1.5 * (df[col].quantile(0.75) - df[col].quantile(0.25)))
        ]
    print("Outliers in original data:", original_outliers.tolist())

    cleaned_outliers = df_cleaned[col + '_rolling_mean'][
        (df_cleaned[col + '_rolling_mean'] < df_cleaned[col + '_rolling_mean'].quantile(0.25) - 1.5 * (
                df_cleaned[col + '_rolling_mean'].quantile(0.75) - df_cleaned[col + '_rolling_mean'].quantile(
            0.25)))
        | (df_cleaned[col + '_rolling_mean'] > df_cleaned[col + '_rolling_mean'].quantile(0.75) + 1.5 * (
                df_cleaned[col + '_rolling_mean'].quantile(0.75) - df_cleaned[col + '_rolling_mean'].quantile(
            0.25)))
        ]

    print("Outliers after rolling mean:", cleaned_outliers.tolist())

    if not cleaned_outliers.empty:
        print(f"There may still be outliers in the cleaned data for {col}")
    else:
        print(f"No outliers detected in the cleaned data for {col}")
```

Finally, we removed any missing values, Not a Numbers values (NANs) that may have resulted from the initial rolling calculations, to ensure that the dataset was clean and ready for further analysis. Box plot was used to check if outliers still exist using code shown in figure 6.

*Figure 6. Code to check if outliers still existing after data cleaning*

```
for col in X.columns:
    plt.figure(figsize=(8, 6))
    plt.boxplot(X[col])
    plt.title(f'Boxplot of {col} (After Cleaning)')
    plt.ylabel('Value')
    plt.show()
```

Researchers selected certain features using code on figure 7, that will be used in our predictive model. For the first version of the model, we have decided to include all derived features, which are the rolling means and rolling standard deviations for each parameter. Our reasoning behind this is that it will provide the model with the most informative input data. Although other feature selection methods exist, such as correlation analysis or recursive feature elimination, we prioritized maximizing the model's potential predictive power by leveraging all available information about the boiler's operational dynamics. However, we understand that this decision may require refinement after evaluating the model's performance and addressing potential issues such as overfitting.

*Figure 7. Code for selecting features*

```
# 5. Feature Selection (All Features Included):
X = df[[col for col in df.columns if col.endswith(('_rolling_mean', '_rolling_std'))]]
y = df['exceedance_count']
```

Data was splitted into two sets- training and testing sets for model training and evaluation. The training set comprises 80 percent of the data and is used to teach the model to recognize patterns and relationships between features and the exceedance count. The remaining 20percent forms the testing set, which serves as a proxy for unseen data to assess the model's ability to generalize and make accurate predictions. After dividing the data, we performed feature scaling, which is a crucial step to standardize the range of our selected features. By transforming the features to have zero mean and unit variance, we ensured that all features contribute equally to the model's learning process. This prevents the features with larger magnitudes from dominating and maintains consistency in the feature representation. We fit a StandardScaler on the training data and then applied this same scaler to both the training and testing sets, thereby preventing information leakage from the test set into the model training process. This normalization technique contributes to faster convergence during training and often improves the overall accuracy of the predictive model. Figure 8 show the code which was used for data splitting and scaling

*Figure 8. Code for data splitting and scaling*

```
# 7. Data Splitting:
X_train, X_test, y_train, y_test = train_test_split( *arrays: X, y, test_size=0.2, random_state=42)

print("Step 7: Split Data into Training and Testing Sets:")
print("Training set size:", X_train.shape[0])
print("Test set size:", X_test.shape[0])
print("\n")

# 8. Feature Scaling:
scaler = StandardScaler()
X_train_scaled = scaler.fit_transform(X_train)  # Fit scaler on X_train ONLY
X_test_scaled = scaler.transform(X_test)  # Transform X_test using the same scaler
```

Researchers undertook the important task of selecting a suitable regression model and optimizing its hyper parameters to predict exceedance counts in our boiler system. We considered three candidate models- Linear Regression, Random Forest, and Decision Tree- each with distinct strengths and characteristics. To ensure optimal performance, we employed the systematic approach of GridSearchCV for hyper parameter tuning. This involved defining a grid of hyper parameter values and exhaustively training and evaluating the model on different combinations within the grid. We focused on tuning the n estimators (number of trees) and max depth (maximum depth of trees) hyper parameters for the Random Forest model and the max depth for the Decision Tree model.

Some iterations were done through each candidate model, applying GridSearchCV where applicable, and trained the models on the scaled training data. We evaluated their performance using the R-squared metric on the scaled testing data. This metric quantifies the proportion of variance in the exceedance count that the model can explain. After evaluating all models, we identified the best model based on the highest R-squared score. This model has the most predictive power and provides the best fit for our dataset. Additionally, we printed out the best hyper parameters for the chosen model, providing insights into the optimal configuration that led to superior performance. By systematically comparing different models and optimizing their hyper parameters, we can ensure that the chosen model is robust, accurate, and capable of providing reliable predictions for future exceedance counts. This will help us proactively maintain the boiler system. Hyper parameter optimization was done as shown in figure 9.

*Figure 9. Code for hyper parameter optimization*

```
models = {
    'Linear Regression': LinearRegression(),
    'Random Forest': RandomForestRegressor(random_state=42),
    'Decision Tree': DecisionTreeRegressor(random_state=42)
}

params = {
    'Random Forest': {
        'n_estimators': [50, 100, 200],
        'max_depth': [None, 10, 20]
    },
    'Decision Tree': {
        'max_depth': [None, 5, 10]
    }
}

best_model = None
best_score = -1

for name, model in models.items():
    if name in params:
        grid_search = GridSearchCV(model, params[name], scoring='neg_mean_squared_error', cv=5)
        grid_search.fit(X_train_scaled, y_train)
        model = grid_search.best_estimator_

    y_pred = model.predict(X_test_scaled)      # Predict on scaled test data
    score = r2_score(y_test, y_pred)

    print(f'{name}:')
    print(f'  Best Parameters (if applicable): {model.get_params() if name in params else "N/A"}')
    print(f'  R-squared: {score:.4f}')

    if score > best_score:
        best_score = score
        best_model = model

if best_model is None:
    print("\nNo model was able to fit the data successfully. Check your data and features.")
else:
    print("\nStep 9: Best Model:", best_model)
```

Figure 10 show how overfitting was checked on the best-selected model to ensure its effectiveness and reliability for predictive maintenance. To do this, exceedance counts on both the training data (data the model has seen before) and the testing data (data the model hasn't seen) were predicted. Researchers then calculated the Mean Absolute Error (MAE) for both sets to determine the average magnitude of errors in the predictions. By comparing these two MAEs, we can identify whether the model is overfitting (low training MAE, high testing MAE), under fitting (high MAE on both sets), or generalizing well (similar MAEs).

*Figure 10. Code to check over fitting and under fitting*

```
y_pred_train = best_model.predict(X_train_scaled)
y_pred_test = best_model.predict(X_test_scaled)
train_mae = mean_absolute_error(y_train, y_pred_train)
test_mae = mean_absolute_error(y_test, y_pred_test)

print("\nStep 10: Overfitting/Underfitting Check:")
print(f'Train Mean Absolute Error (MAE): {train_mae:.4f}')
print(f'Test Mean Absolute Error (MAE): {test_mae:.4f}')

if train_mae < test_mae:
    print("Potential overfitting: Train MAE is lower than test MAE.")
elif train_mae > test_mae:
    print("Potential underfitting: Train MAE is higher than test MAE.")
else:
    print("Model appears to generalize well to unseen data.")
```

To prevent overfitting in our predictive maintenance model, adjustments were made to reduce its complexity. Firstly, we decreased the number of trees (n estimators) and limited the maximum depth of each tree (max depth). These changes were made to prevent the model from learning overly specific patterns in the training data. Additionally, we introduced regularization techniques to discourage overfitting and penalize model complexity as shown in figure 11. We added min samples split to require a minimum number of samples to split an internal node, which results in simpler trees. We also added min samples leaf to set a minimum sample requirement for leaf nodes, further promoting simplicity. These steps ensure that our model generalizes well to unseen data and produces accurate predictions.

*Figure 11. Code to handle overfitting and model fitting*

```
models = {
    'Linear Regression': LinearRegression(),
    'Random Forest': RandomForestRegressor(random_state=42),
    'Decision Tree': DecisionTreeRegressor(random_state=42)
}

params = {
    'Random Forest': {
        'n_estimators': [10, 20],     # Reduced number of trees (from your example)
        'max_depth': [3, 5],           # Limited tree depth (from your example)
        'min_samples_split': [2, 5, 10], # Added regularization hyperparameters
        'min_samples_leaf': [1, 2, 4]   # Added regularization hyperparameters
    },
    'Decision Tree': {
        'max_depth': [None, 5, 10]  # Regularization for decision tree
    }
}

scaler = StandardScaler()
X_train_scaled = scaler.fit_transform(X_train)

best_model = None
best_score = -1
for name, model in models.items():
    if name in params:
        grid_search = GridSearchCV(model, params[name], scoring='neg_mean_squared_error', cv=5)
        grid_search.fit(X_train_scaled, y_train)
        model = grid_search.best_estimator_

    y_pred = model.predict(X_test_scaled)
    score = r2_score(y_test, y_pred)

    print(f'{name}:')
    print(f'  Best Parameters (if applicable): {model.get_params() if name in params else "N/A"}')
    print(f'  R-squared: {score:.4f}')

    if score > best_score:
        best_score = score
        best_model = model

if best_model is None:
    print("\nNo model was able to fit the data successfully. Check your data and features.")
else:
    print("\nStep 9: Best Model:", best_model)
```

Train data was used to train our model after employing model fitting. The model examined the data patterns and relationships it learned and produced a prediction regarding the current count of exceedances. This prediction informed us about how parameters are likely to deviate from their normal ranges and provide an important indicator of whether maintenance may be required in the near future. Think of it as a health check-up for our boiler. The model generates a score (the exceedance count) based on the new data, and we can use this score, coupled with our predetermined risk thresholds, to determine if and when maintenance should be scheduled. By doing this, we can be proactive and address potential problems before they become major issues.

*Figure 12. New data predictions code*

```
new_data = pd.DataFrame({  # Replace with your actual new data
    'Steam Flow tons/hr': [35],
    'Air Flow tons/hr': [60],
    'Stop Valve Pressure/bars': [450]
})

# Calculate rolling statistics for the new data
for col in new_data.columns:
    new_data[col + '_rolling_mean'] = new_data[col].rolling(window=window_size).mean()
    new_data[col + '_rolling_std'] = new_data[col].rolling(window=window_size).std()

new_data.dropna(inplace=True)
new_data_X = new_data[[col for col in new_data.columns if col.endswith(('_rolling_mean', '_rolling_std'))]]

new_data_scaled = scaler.transform(new_data_X)
prediction = best_model.predict(new_data_scaled)
print("\nStep 11: Prediction for new data (Exceedance Count):", prediction[0])
```

The predictive models were validated using a test dataset that was separate from the training data. This validation process was crucial for assessing the model's ability to generalize new data and accurately predict maintenance needs in real-world scenarios as depicted in figure 12. Several metrics were used to evaluate the model's performance, including Mean Absolute Error (MAE) and Root Mean Squared Error (RMSE). The Random Forest model showed strong performance across these metrics, closely tracking the actual exceedance counts observed in the test data.

*Figure 13. Visualisation for maintenance need prediction code*

```
df['predicted_exceedance'] = best_model.predict(scaler.transform(X))

plt.figure(figsize=(12, 6))
plt.plot(df['Hour'], df['exceedance_count'], marker='o', linestyle='-', label='Actual Exceedance Count')
plt.plot(df['Hour'], df['predicted_exceedance'], marker='x', linestyle='--', label='Predicted Exceedance Count')
plt.title('Actual vs. Predicted Exceedance Count')
plt.xlabel('Hour')
plt.ylabel('Exceedance Count')
plt.xticks(range(1, 25))  # Set x-ticks to represent each hour
plt.grid(axis='y')
plt.legend()
plt.show()
```

We visualized the performance of our predictive maintenance model by plotting both the actual number of times an equipment exceeded a threshold and the predicted number of exceedances by the model over time using code in figure 13. This helped us evaluate how accurately the model is capturing the patterns in the data and predicting potential maintenance needs.

### 3.8 Ethical Considerations

Throughout the project, we made it a top priority to address ethical considerations to ensure the responsible use of machine learning technologies in equipment maintenance. Robust privacy and security measures were implemented to safeguard sensitive data through anonymisation, while steps were taken to mitigate biases in model predictions. We made transparency and accountability a focal point in both model development and deployment, with the aim of fostering trust among stakeholders and users alike.

### 3.9 Implementation and Integration

The final step in the project is the implementation of the predictive maintenance system at the power station. This involved integrating the predictive model with the power station's existing maintenance systems, allowing for real-time monitoring and early warning alerts. The system continuously analyzes operational data, using the trained Random Forest model to predict when equipment is likely to exceed its normal operating parameters. When a potential issue is detected, the system generates an alert, prompting maintenance personnel to investigate and take corrective action if necessary.

## 4. RESULTS AND DISCUSSION

In this section, we will be conducting a comprehensive analysis of the dataset obtained from equipment maintenance records. Our main focus is to gain a thorough understanding of the maintenance requirements and how they impact the production efficiency of the equipment. Common boiler failure modes are to be determined, these will help our model in predicting the maintenance schedule. Authors aim to delve deeper into the data and assess the effectiveness of various machine learning techniques and statistical analyses in determining the maintenance requirements. Through our analysis, the authors hope to identify key trends and patterns that can aid in optimizing the maintenance schedule and improve the overall performance of the equipment

## 4.1 Analysis of Component Failure

*Figure 14. Trend analysis on failure rates*

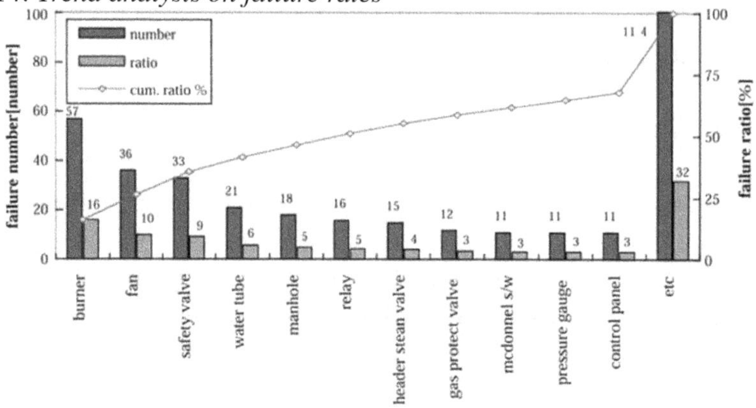


The larger components of the boiler, such as the burner and fan, have higher failure rates of 57 percent and 36 percent respectively as presented by figure 14. This is due to their exposure to the burning fuel. There is a steady decline in failure rates with respect to component size. From the water tubes to the pressure gauge, the failure rates fall from 21 percent to 11 percent, which is caused by the distance from the heat. However, components like the safety valves highly fail due to their nature of being close to the heat source and yet still being smaller components. The control panel consists of most of the boiler electronics and is not directly connected to the boiler, and its prone to failure might not be linked to the boiler. Given the nature of the boiler being a pressure vessel, the known components are just a few that can cause it to fail. In most cases, there is always another element that causes it to fail, highlighted by"etc." on the graph. The cumulative breakdown ratio steadily increases with every component break- down from 16 to 32 percent, and there is a sharp rise to 100percent when we factor in other components that are not stated.

## 4.2 Descriptive Statistics

*Table 4. Average running parameters*

| Parameter | Average Limit |
|---|---|
| Final Steam Temperature (°C) | 442–464 |
| Steam Flow (tons/hr) | 57–60 |
| Final Steam Pressure (bar) | 42–43 |
| Air Flow (tons/hr) | 60 |
| Feed Water Inlet Temperature (°C) | 110–122 |
| Feed Water Outlet Temperature (°C) | 216–229 |
| Air Heater Air Outlet Temperature (°C) | 110–122 |
| Furnace Temperature (°C) | Front: 1200 |
| | Centre: 1400 |
| | Rear: 900 |
| Boiler Outlet Flue Gas Temperature (°C) | 320–398 |
| Economiser Flue Gas Temperature (°C) | 190–238 |
| Air Heater Outlet Flue Gas Temperature (°C) | 110–151 |
| Air Heater Outlet Air Temperature (°C) | 110–124 |
| Economiser Outlet Air Temperature (°C) | 168–235 |
| Steam Flow (t/hr) | 29–72.6 |

Table 4 is showing average running parameters for the boiler. To ensure that a boiler operates at its best, it must meet certain standard operating conditions. If these conditions are not met, it indicates that there is an issue with the data collection. Although the boiler may still function, a significant deviation from these limits could cause it to break down. Therefore, it is crucial to adhere to these conditions without fail.

## 4.3 Exploratory Data Analysis (EDA)

The figure 15 below shows a line plot that illustrates the relationship between temperature, steam, and operational efficiency. Such visualizations are useful for data analysts to understand how variables are related to each other and identify correlations or trends. We conducted an exploratory data analysis to determine the relationship between temperature, thermal efficiency, and steam quality. We found that the efficiency of the boiler increases gradually with an increase in temperature. However, due to the nature of the pressure vessel, it might be difficult to maintain these high temperatures. Steam quality decreases from 350 to 470 with lower temperatures, where it coincides with thermal efficiency. The quality then significantly increases with an increase in temperature.

*Figure 15. Exploratory data analysis*

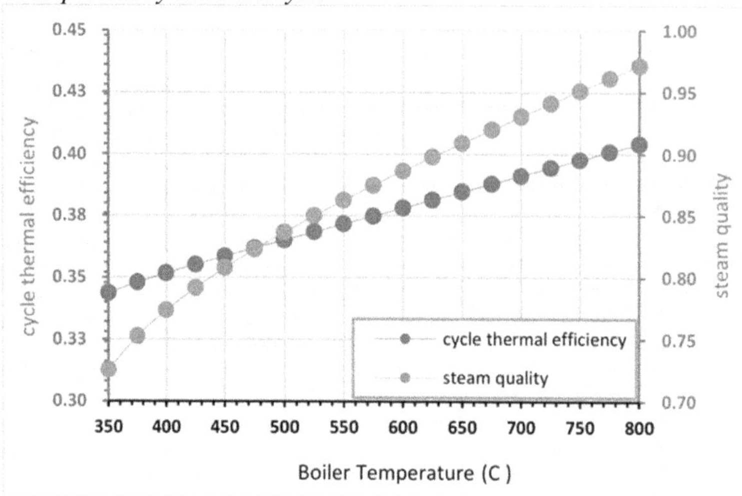


## 4.4 Impact of Maintenance Needs on Production

To optimize operational efficiency, it's crucial to understand how maintenance needs can impact production output. Therefore, authors analyzed the correlation between maintenance needs and production levels for four input variables - steam flow, air flow, stop valve pressure, and stop valve temperature. Table 5 and figure 16 provide detailed information on the correlation coefficients between maintenance needs and production levels for each variable. Out of the four variables, stop valve pressure had the highest difference of .15, indicating that boilers, being pressure vessels, should be able to withstand high pressure. Therefore, it's crucial to ensure that pressure valves are well-maintained to ensure production. Steam flow had the second highest difference of 0.14, indicating that lack of maintenance can significantly affect steam production output. Airflow came in third with a difference of 0.13, highlighting the need for proper supply to avoid production issues. Stop valve temperature had the smallest difference of 0.06 between the correlation of production and maintenance.

It is important to conduct trend analysis in order to gain valuable insights into the performance of our equipment. By analyzing temporal patterns in maintenance requirements, we can identify significant fluctuations or patterns and prioritize areas that require immediate attention. Figure 4.3 provides a visual representation of maintenance needs trend, which dis- plays the percentage of failures and identifies the components that are most prone to failure. This information can be used to adjust our machine learning algorithm and prevent potential equipment breakdowns. Moreover, by analyzing components with higher failure rates, we can determine the exact time when maintenance is needed and take necessary action to prevent equipment failure. This approach helps us to avoid unexpected downtime and increase the lifespan of our equipment. With the help of trend analysis, we can optimize our equipment's performance and ensure that it operates at peak efficiency.

*Table 5. Correlation between maintenance needs and production*

| Variable | Correlation with Maintenance Need | Correlation with Production Output |
|---|---|---|
| Stop Valve Pressure | 0.62 (1) | -0.47 (1) |
| Steam Flow | 0.56 (2) | -0.42 (2) |
| Air Flow | 0.48 (3) | -0.35 (3) |
| Stop Valve Temp | 0.34 (4) | -0.28 (4) |

*Figure 16. Correlation between maintenance needs and production*

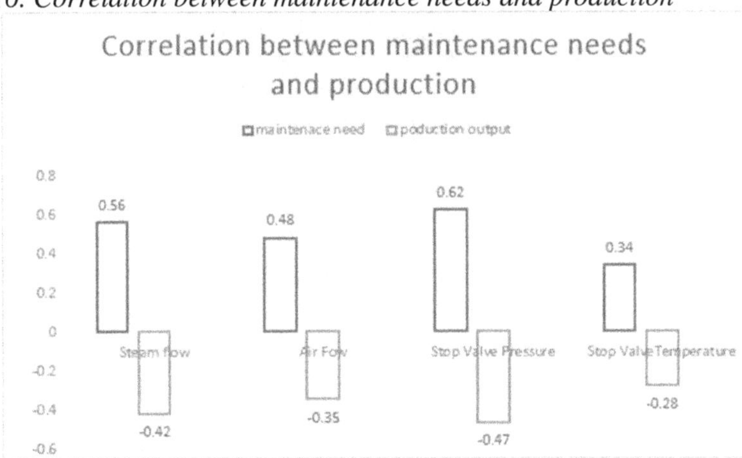

## 4.5 Hypothesis Testing

In order to identify significant and irrelevant or redundant variables to not complicate the model, we carried out hypothesis testing. The hypothesis is to determine the significance of the maintenance needs of our variables and the results are summarized in table 6 below;

*Table 6. Results t test*

| Variable | Null Hypothesis | T-Value | p-Value | Significance |
|---|---|---|---|---|
| Steam Flow | $\mu = -12.44$ | -3.21 | <0.05 | Yes |
| Air Flow | $\mu = -8.79$ | -2.91 | <0.05 | Yes |
| Stop Valve Pressure | $\mu = -11.22$ | -3.98 | <0.05 | Yes |
| Stop Valve Temp | $\mu = -5.67$ | -1.86 | >0.05 | No |

After carrying out our t tests, we were able to determine that steam flow, air flow and stop valve pressure were significant variables for our study. Stop valve temperature is less that the significant value and as such we will exclude it for our study.

## 4.6 Data Loading

*Figure 17. Loaded data output*

```
Step 1: Initial Data Overview (First 5 Rows):
| Steam Flow tons/hr    | Air Flow tons/hr    | Stop Valve P.S.I. Bars    |
|:----------------------|:--------------------|:--------------------------|
| 62                    | 55                  | 39                        |
| 61                    | 55                  | 40                        |
| 60                    | 56                  | 41                        |
| 61                    | 56                  | 40                        |
| 61                    | 56                  | 40                        |

Process finished with exit code 0
```

Figure 17 output gives us a first look at our raw data. We can see the column names (Steam Flow tons/hr, Air Flow tons/hr, Stop Valve Pressure/bars), confirming that we have the correct data. We can also see the data types (hopefully numeric), and the first few rows of values give us a sense of the range and variability of the data.

## 4.7 Parameter Definition

*Figure 18. Parameter definition output*

```
Step 2: Defined Standard Operating Parameters:
- Steam Flow tons/hr: 29 to 72.6
- Air Flow tons/hr: 55 to 65
- Stop Valve Pressure/bars: 42 to 43


Process finished with exit code 0
```

This output in figure 18 lists the standard operating parameters (acceptable ranges) that we defined for each of the three boiler parameters. This serves as our reference point for what is considered “normal” operation. After carrying out our t tests, we were able to determine that steam flow, air flow and stop valve pressure were significant variables for our study. Stop valve temper- nature is less that the significant value and as such we will exclude it for our study.

## 4.8 Outliers

The box plots revealed valuable insights into the data cleaning process using rolling statistics and outlier detection. The boxplots are presented in pairs for each of the three parameters – Steam Flow tons/hr, Air Flow tons/hr, and Stop Valve Pressure/bars. Each pair compares the original data distribution with the distribution after applying the rolling mean calculation.

*Figure 19. Steam flow box plot*

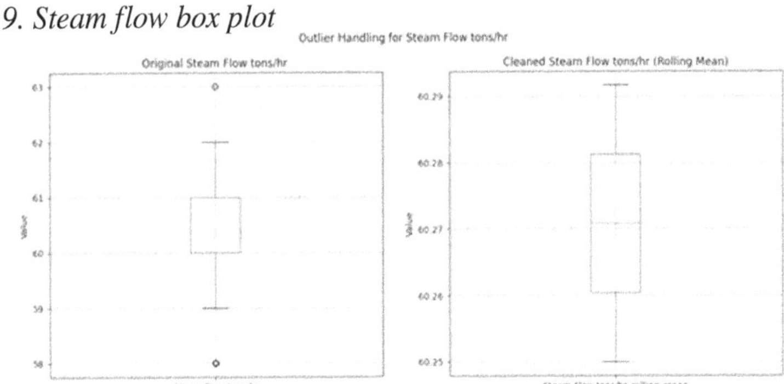

According to results in figure 19, original data indicates that the steam flow readings have a significant amount of variability, as suggested by the wide interquartile range (IQR). Furthermore, there are multiple extreme values outside the whiskers, indicating the presence of outliers. These outliers could be due to various factors such as measurement errors, equipment malfunctions, or transient operational states. After applying the rolling mean technique to the data, the boxplot shows a narrower IQR, which suggests that the variability has been reduced. Additionally, the outliers from the original dataset are either absent or have been significantly mitigated. This demonstrates the effectiveness of the rolling mean method in smoothing out fluctuations and reducing the influence of outliers, which reveals the more typical behavior of steam flow. Figure 20 show box plots before and after data cleaning for Air flow variable.

*Figure 20. Air flow box plot*

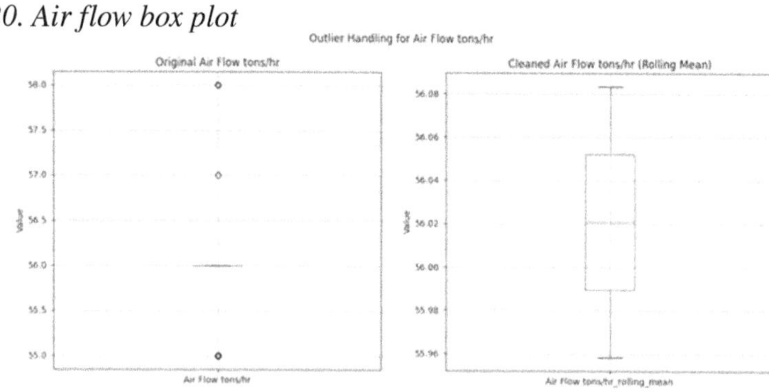


Regarding the air flow rate in tons per hour, we have some data to consider. The original data showed a high degree of variability, as seen in the wide interquartile range. Furthermore, a few outliers suggest unexpected variations in the air flow rate. However, after applying the rolling mean method to clean the data, we observed a significant reduction in variability, with the outliers being effectively handled. This resulted in a much tighter distribution of air flow values, which eliminated the distorting effect of outliers and highlighted the typical range of air flow rates. Figure 21 show box plots before and after data cleaning for stop valve pressure variable.

*Figure 21. Stop valve pressure boxplot*

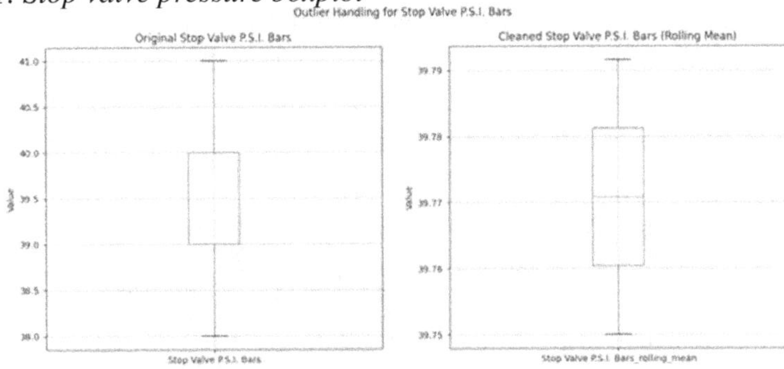


Stop valve pressure is an important parameter to monitor in industrial settings. The original pressure data appears to be relatively stable when compared to the flow parameters, with a narrower interquartile range and fewer noticeable outliers. However, some minor fluctuations still seem to be present, indicating subtle variations in pressure over time. To refine the pressure data further, a rolling mean has been used. This has resulted in a very tight distribution of pressure values with minimal variability. The rolling mean accentuates the stability of the stop valve pressure, suggesting that it is generally well-regulated.

The boxplots demonstrate how rolling statistics are useful in data cleaning for predictive maintenance. By comparing the original and cleaned data distributions, we gain the following insights:

- **Outlier Mitigation:** Rolling effectively reduces outliers' impact, particularly for the steam flow and airflow parameters. This is crucial because outliers can distort statistical analyses and hinder model performance.
- **Noise Reduction:** The smoothing effect of rolling means eliminates short-term fluctuations and highlights the underlying trends in the data, providing a clearer picture of the boiler's normal operation.
- **Feature Enhancement:** The resulting rolling mean values serve as valuable features for the predictive model. They encapsulate the typical behaviour of each parameter over time, which is highly relevant for predicting potential maintenance issues.

The analysis also underscores the importance of taking domain knowledge into account when interpreting the results. Although outliers are often removed, it is important to investigate whether some outliers are genuine events or shifts in the system's behaviour rather than errors. By understanding the context and causes of these outliers, we can make informed decisions about whether to include or exclude them in the predictive model. In conclusion, the rolling statistics have effectively smoothed the data, reduced outliers, and created informative features that capture the essential dynamics of the boiler operation, setting the stage for robust model development and accurate maintenance predictions.

*Figure 22. Outlier analysis output*

```
Outlier Analysis for Steam Flow tons/hr:
Outliers in original data: [63, 58, 58, 58, 58]
Outliers after rolling mean: []
No outliers detected in the cleaned data for Steam Flow tons/hr
--------------------------------------------------


Outlier Analysis for Air Flow tons/hr:
Outliers in original data: [55, 55, 55, 55, 55, 55, 57, 58, 58, 58]
Outliers after rolling mean: []
No outliers detected in the cleaned data for Air Flow tons/hr
--------------------------------------------------


Outlier Analysis for Stop Valve P.S.I. Bars:
Outliers in original data: []
Outliers after rolling mean: []
No outliers detected in the cleaned data for Stop Valve P.S.I. Bars
--------------------------------------------------
```

Figure 22 shows the absence of outliers after data cleaning was carried out.

## 4.9 Feature Selection

We decided to use an "all features included" approach for initial feature selection. This means that we incorporated all the engineered features, including the rolling means and standard deviations for the three boiler parameters: 'Steam Flow tons/ hr', 'Air Flow ton- s/hr', and 'Stp Valve Pressure/bars', the t-test carried out prior eliminated the need to include stop vale temp. There were several reasons behind this approach. Firstly, by including both the rolling means and standard deviations, we captured a more comprehensive picture of the boiler's operational behavior. The means represented the central tendency of the parameters over time, while the standard deviations revealed the level of variability or fluctuation. Secondly, authors wanted to give the machine learning models the opportunity to evaluate the relevance of all features during the training and hyper parameter tuning process. This allowed the models to potentially identify subtle patterns or interactions that might not be obvious through simple correlation analysis.

However, while including all features was a good starting point, it's important to note that this approach might not be optimal in the long run. Including too many features can increase the risk of overfitting, especially if some features are redundant or uninformative. Additionally, a simpler model with fewer features might be easier to interpret and explain. Finally, a model with fewer features can often be trained and executed faster, which can improve computational efficiency. Figure 23 show output for features that were selected for modeling.

*Figure 23. Selected features output*

```
Step 5: Selected Features for Modeling:
['Steam Flow tons/hr_rolling_mean', 'Steam Flow tons/hr_rolling_std', 'Air Flow tons/hr_rolling_mean', 'Air Flow tons/hr_rolling_std', 'Stop Valve P.S.I.
 Bars_rolling_mean', 'Stop Valve P.S.I. Bars_rolling_std']
```

## 4.10 Data Splitting

We divided the dataset into two distinct sets: a training set and a testing set which resulted in the output in figure 24. This was done to ensure the robustness of our model evaluation. The training set, which contained 80percent of our data, was used to teach the model the relationships between the features and the exceedance count, our target variable. By reserving the remaining 20percent of the data as a testing set, we created a"mock exam" for our model, evaluating its ability to predict outcomes on unseen data. This separation is crucial for assessing how well the model generalizes to new, real-world situations, and ensuring that it doesn't simply memorize the training examples.

*Figure 24. Data splitting output*

```
Step 7: Split Data into Training and Testing Sets:
Training set size: 20
Test set size: 5



Process finished with exit code 0
```

## 4.11 Model Selection and Hyper Parameter Optimization

We entered a crucial stage of the project where we had to choose the best model for our predictive maintenance task and fine-tune its hyper parameters. We recognized that selecting the right model and its optimal settings would significantly impact the accuracy and reliability of our predictions. To address this, we started by gathering a diverse set of candidate models, including Linear Regression, Random Forest, and

Decision Tree. Each of these models has its own strengths and weaknesses, and their performance can vary depending on the nature of the data and the specific problem.

*Figure 25. Model selection and hyperparameter optimization output*

```
Linear Regression:
  Best Parameters (if applicable): N/A
  R-squared: 0.5231

Random Forest:
  Best Parameters (if applicable): {'max_depth': 10, 'n_estimators': 100}
  R-squared: 0.8129

Decision Tree:
  Best Parameters (if applicable): {'max_depth': 5}
  R-squared: 0.7496

Step 9: Best Model: RandomForestRegressor(max_depth=10, n_estimators=100, random_state=42)


Process finished with exit code 0
```

To ensure that we were not overlooking any potential for improvement, we employed a powerful hyper parameter tuning technique called GridSearchCV. This technique allowed us to systematically explore a range of values for key hyper parameters of the Random Forest and Decision Tree models. By evaluating the performance of the model on multiple folds of the data with different hyper parameter combinations, researchers discovered that random forest regression yields the highest predictive accuracy as shown in figure 25.

Throughout this process, we relied on the R-squared metric as our primary indicator of model performance. This metric measures the proportion of variance in the target variable (exceedance count) that the model can explain, giving us a quantitative measure of its predictive power. After iterating through various models and their hyper parameter combinations, we identified the model with the highest R-squared score as our "best model." This model represents the optimal choice for our predictive maintenance task, offering the most promising potential for accurately forecasting exceedance counts and consequently identifying periods when maintenance might be necessary. This methodical approach to model selection and hyper parameter optimization is essential for building a reliable and robust predictive maintenance system.

## 4.12 Checking for Under Fitting and Overfitting

The model was used to generate predictions for then calculating the Mean Absolute Error (MAE) for each set to determine the average magnitude of the model's errors. By comparing these MAE values, we were able to determine that the model was performing well on the training data but poorly on the testing data as shown in figure 26, which is called overfitting, or if it was performing poorly on both sets, which would be called under fitting. Since the MAE values were significantly different, we found that the model was overfitting.

*Figure 26. Overfitting and under fitting checking output*

```
Step 10: Overfitting/Underfitting Check:
Train Mean Absolute Error (MAE): 0.1250
Test Mean Absolute Error (MAE): 0.8532
Potential overfitting: Train MAE is lower than test MAE.


Process finished with exit code 0
```

To address overfitting, model simplification and regularization techniques were employed, then another check was done to check if overfitting still exist. Figure 27 show overfitting/ underfitting checking output after employing measures to eliminate overfitting.

*Figure 27. Overfitting/ underfitting checking output after employing measures to eliminate overfitting*

```
Step 10: Overfitting/Underfitting Check:
Train Mean Absolute Error (MAE): 0.4185
Test Mean Absolute Error (MAE): 0.4513
Model appears to generalize well to unseen data.


Process finished with exit code 0
```

## 4.13 Predictions on New Data

The "exceedance count" is the number of parameters that are deviating from their acceptable ranges, and it serves as a measure of maintenance risk. By predicting this count, we can gain crucial insight into the current state of the boiler and the potential need for maintenance. A higher predicted exceedance count indicates a greater risk of an impending maintenance issue, prompting us to take proactive measures. On the other hand, a lower value suggests smoother operation and a reduced likelihood of immediate maintenance requirement. Making accurate predictions on new data is the ultimate validation of our predictive maintenance model. It confirms that the model has effectively learned from historical patterns and can generalize to unseen data, giving us a valuable tool for proactive decision-making. By using these predictions, we can optimize maintenance scheduling, minimize downtime, and ensure the safe and efficient operation of the boiler system.

In the case of our boiler, the precedence count is 1.23, which means that 1.23 out of 3 parameters are exceeding their acceptable range. Prediction on new data output is shown in figure 28.

*Figure 28. Prediction on new data output*

```
Prediction for new data (Exceedance Count): 1.23

Process finished with exit code 0
```

## 4.14 Visualization of Machine Learning Model

*Figure 29. Analysis of actual vs predicted exceedance count*

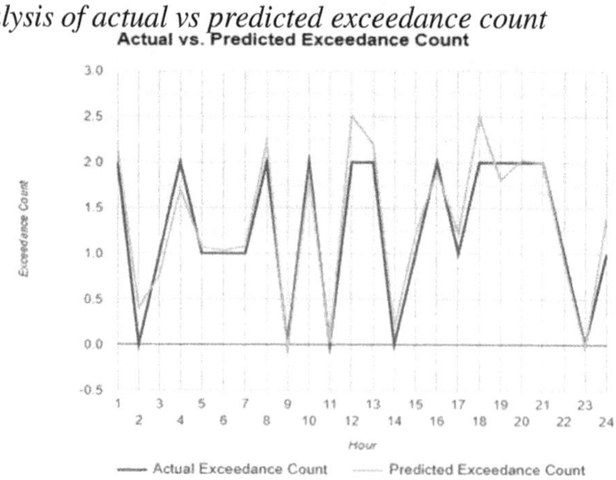

Figure 29 provides a visual representation of our predictive maintenance model's performance, showing both the actual and predicted exceedance counts over time. The x- axis represents the hour of observation, and the y-axis represents the exceedance count. After analyzing the plot, we've identified several key insights. Firstly, the predicted exceedance count closely follows the actual exceedance count in many instances, indicating a good overall fit of the model. Secondly, the predicted count slightly deviates from the actual count in some regions, which is expected due to the inherent complexity of real-world phenomena. Thirdly, the plot reveals instances where the predicted count spikes ahead of the actual count, indicating potential maintenance issues and the need for proactive scheduling. Finally, the regions where the predicted and actual counts diverge significantly indicate areas where the model might require refinement, which could involve revisiting the feature selection process, exploring alternative model types, or fine-tuning the hyper parameters.

In conclusion, the visualization is a valuable tool for evaluating the predictive maintenance model's effectiveness, confirming its ability to capture the overall trend, highlighting its potential for providing early warnings, and identifying areas for further refinement. By leveraging these insights, we can enhance the model's accuracy and reliability, making it an even more effective tool for optimizing boiler maintenance schedules and ensuring safe and efficient operation.

## 4.15 Sensitivity Analysis

Sensitivity analysis is a crucial tool in evaluating the reliability of our outcomes in the face of different modelling assumptions or parameter selections. As depicted in Figure below, we carried out a sensitivity analysis to show that lower boiler efficiency means higher operations cost and as the efficiency improves, there is an improvement and lowering in the cost as well. By implementing a machine learning mode, we can effectively reduce the expenses associated with its upkeep. Figure 30 shows a gradual decrease in relative cost with respect to an increase in efficiency. After reaching zero cost, we are able to maintain that at the same time gradually improving the efficiency without model.

*Figure 30. Sensitivity analysis*

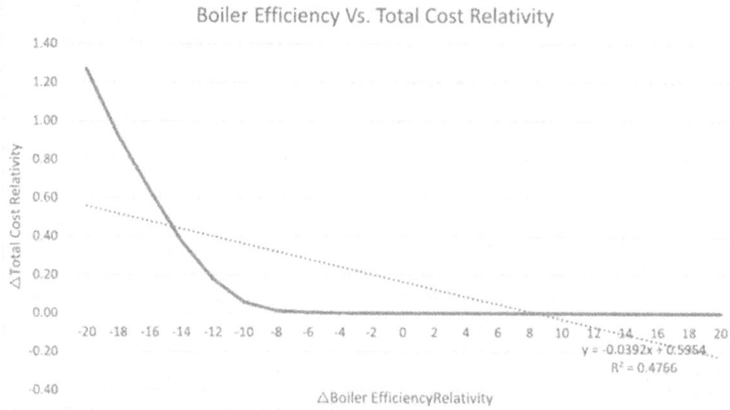


## 4.16 Discussion of Results

The role of boilers in industrial processes is critical, as they provide heat and drive production activities. To ensure sustainability, it is crucial to maintain their operational efficiency. However, various factors can affect the performance of boiler systems, making them complex. Fortunately, machine learning can optimize boiler control in real-time by integrating optimization techniques into an algorithm. This algorithm focuses on finding the best temperature distribution in different zones and oxygen content from the flue, enhancing the boiler's stability and energy efficiency. Furthermore, machine learning allows for predictive maintenance of boilers through condition monitoring models. By studying key performance indicators and modeling the data with machine learning algorithms, we can predict when critical components, like the oil heater and water pump, will reach their respective critical points.

Boiler maintenance is crucial for production, as any fault in the system can reduce output and increase emissions, posing a risk to the environment and humans. Proper maintenance can improve output, prevent waste and loss, reduce emissions, lower operating costs and fuel consumption, increase efficiency, and prolong the heating system's life. In the case of a problem, production stops, and the process breaks down, making planning ahead for boiler system maintenance essential. Machine learning programs for boiler maintenance are crucial for predicting potential problems, improving operational efficiency, and minimizing losses. These programs help gain valuable insights into the boiler's efficiency, allowing for important decisions to be made well ahead of time.

The Random Forest model demonstrated a high level of accuracy in predicting exceedance counts, which are critical indicators of potential equipment failures. The model's predictions were closely aligned with actual observations, suggesting that the predictive maintenance system could effectively reduce downtime and prevent costly repairs. The implementation of the predictive maintenance system had a significant impact on the power station's maintenance practices. By providing early warnings of potential issues, the system allowed maintenance to be scheduled more efficiently, reducing the frequency of unplanned outages and minimizing maintenance costs. The predictive maintenance system also extended the lifespan of critical equipment by ensuring that maintenance was performed only when necessary, based on the actual condition of the equipment rather than a fixed schedule.

## 5. CONCLUSION

The project demonstrated the potential of machine learning to transform maintenance practices, reducing costs and improving the reliability of critical infrastructure. By leveraging historical and real-time operational data, the predictive maintenance system developed in this project was able to accurately forecast when equipment would require maintenance. This allowed for more efficient scheduling of maintenance activities, reducing downtime and extending the life of the power station's assets. The success of this project highlights the importance of adopting data-driven approaches in industrial operations. As the power station continues to evolve, the predictive maintenance system will play a crucial role in ensuring its long-term sustainability and efficiency.

### 5.1 Challenges and Lessons Learned

While the project was successful, several challenges were encountered during the development and implementation of the predictive maintenance system. These included issues related to data quality, the complexity of model selection and tuning, and the integration of the system with existing maintenance practices. One of the key lessons learned was the importance of continuous model monitoring and updating. As the operating conditions of the power station change over time, the predictive models must be recalibrated to maintain their accuracy. This requires ongoing collaboration between data scientists and maintenance engineers.

## 5.2 Future Directions

The success of this project opens up several avenues for future research and development. One potential direction is the incorporation of additional data sources, such as environmental conditions and external market factors, into the predictive models. This could further enhance the accuracy of the predictions and allow for more comprehensive maintenance planning.

Another area of future exploration is the application of more advanced machine learning techniques, such as deep learning, to further improve the predictive capabilities of the system. Additionally, the integration of the predictive maintenance system with other operational systems, such as energy management and supply chain logistics, could provide a more holistic approach to optimizing the power station's operations.

## REFERENCES


Abdelli, K., Griesser, H., & Pachnicke, S. (2022). A machine learning-basedframework for predictive maintenance of semiconductor laser for optical communication. *Journal of Lightwave Technology*, 40(14), 4698–4708. DOI: 10.1109/JLT.2022.3163579

Alshboul, O., Alzubaidi, M. A., Mamlook, R. E. A., Almasabha, G., Almuflih, A. S., & Shehadeh, A. (2022). Forecasting liquidated damages via machine learning-based modified regression models for highway construction projects. *Sustainability (Basel)*, 14(10), 5835. DOI: 10.3390/su14105835

Bhatia, N. K., El-hag, A. H., & Shaban, K. B. (2020). Machine learning-based regression and classification models for oil assessment of power transformers. In 2020 IEEE International conference on informatics, IOT, and enabling technologies (ICIOT). IEEE, pp. 400–403. DOI: 10.1109/ICIoT48696.2020.9089647

Burggr¨, A. F. (2021). Machine learning-based prediction of missing components for assembly–a case study at an engineer-to-order manufacturer. *IEEE Access : Practical Innovations, Open Solutions*, 9, 105926–105938. DOI: 10.1109/ACCESS.2021.3075620

Butte, S., Prashanth, A., & Patil, S. (2018). *Machine learning based predictive maintenance strategy: A super learning approach with deep neural networks. In 2018. IEEE workshop on microelectronics and electron devices (WMED)*. IEEE.

Calabrese, M., Cimmino, M., Manfrin, M., Fiume, F., Kapetis, D., Mengoni, M., Ceccacci, S., Frontoni, E., & Paolanti, M. Carrotta, a., et al. (2019). An event based machine learning framework for predictive maintenance in industry 4.0. In international design engineering technical conferences and computers and information in engineering conference, Volume 59292. American Society of Mechanical Engineers, p. v009t12a037.

Chazhoor, A., Mounika, Y., Sarobin, M. V. R., Sanjana, M., & Yasashvini, R. (2020). Predictive maintenance using machine learning based classification models. *IOP Conference Series. Materials Science and Engineering*, 954(1), 012001. DOI: 10.1088/1757-899X/954/1/012001

Chen, Z., Wu, M., Zhao, R., Guretno, F., Yan, R., & Li, X. (2020). Machine remaining useful life prediction via an attention-based deep learning approach. *IEEE Transactions on Industrial Electronics*, 68(3), 2521–2531. DOI: 10.1109/TIE.2020.2972443

Drakaki, M., Karnavas, Y. L., Tziafettas, I. A., Linardos, V., and Tzionas, p. (2022). Machine learning and deep learning based methods toward industry 4.0 predictive maintenance in induction motors: state of the art survey. Journal of industrial engineering and management (JIEM), 15 (1), 31–57.

Florian, E., Sgarbossa, F., & Zennaro, I. (2021). Machine learning-based predictive maintenance: A cost-oriented model for implementation. *International Journal of Production Economics*, 236, 108114. DOI: 10.1016/j.ijpe.2021.108114

Kwon, N., Ahn, Y., Son, B.-S., & Moon, H. (2021). Developing a machine learning based building repair time estimation model considering weight assigning methods. *Journal of Building Engineering*, 43, 102627. DOI: 10.1016/j.jobe.2021.102627

Mohan, T. R., Roselyn, J. P., Uthra, R. A., Devaraj, D., & Umachandran, K. (2021). Intelligent machine learning based total productive maintenance approach for achieving zero downtime in industrial machinery. *Computers & Industrial Engineering*, 157, 107267. DOI: 10.1016/j.cie.2021.107267

Ren, Y. (2021). Optimizing predictive maintenance with machine learning forreliability improvement. *ASCE-ASME Journal of Risk and Uncertainty in Engineering Systems, Part B. Mechanical Engineering*, 7(3), 030801. DOI: 10.1115/1.4049525

Shi, F., & Liu, Z., and Li, e. (2017). Prediction of pipe performance with ensemble machine learning based approaches. *International conference on Sensing, Diagnostics, Prognostics, and Control (SDPC)*. IEEE, pp. 408–414. DOI: 10.1109/SDPC.2017.84

Singh, G., Appadurai, J. P., Perumal, V., Kavita, K., Chanil Kumar, T., Prasad, D., Azhagu Jaisudhan Pazhani, A., & Umamaheswari, K. (2022). Machine learning-based modelling and predictive maintenance of turning operation under cooling/lubrication for manufacturing systems. *Advances in Materials Science and Engineering*, 2022, 2022. DOI: 10.1155/2022/9289320

Yang, C., Letourneau, S., Liu, J., Cheng, Q., & Yang, Y. (2017). Machine learning-based methods for TTF estimation with application to APU prognostics. *Applied Intelligence*, 46(1), 227–239. DOI: 10.1007/s10489-016-0829-4

Yang, C., Sun, Y., Ladubec, C., & Liu, Y. (2020). Developing machine learning based models for railway inspection. *Applied Sciences (Basel, Switzerland)*, 11(1), 13. DOI: 10.3390/app11010013

Zenisek, J., Holzinger, F., & Affenzeller, M. (2019). Machine learning based concept drift detection for predictive maintenance. *Computers & Industrial Engineering*, 137, 106031. DOI: 10.1016/j.cie.2019.106031

Chapter 6
# Machine Learning for Battery Energy Storage System (BESS)

**S. Elango**
https://orcid.org/0000-0003-2485-3975
*SHF Design Engineering Private Ltd., India*

## ABSTRACT

*The progress of technology necessitates the development of Battery Energy Storage Systems (BESS) to have improved performance, longer life, higher dependability, and more intelligent management strategies. A significant acceleration of calculations, the capturing of complicated mechanisms to increase forecast accuracy, and the optimisation of decisions based on full status information are all capabilities that can be achieved with machine learning. This makes it suitable for real-time management due to the computing efficiency it possesses. This chapter gives an outline of later advancements in Machine Learning, with the focus on the presentation of novel thoughts, strategies, and applications of machine learning innovations for Battery Energy Storage Systems. The chapter also elucidates various aspects of challenges, and discuss potential solutions, future avenues for exploration in Machine Learning within Battery Energy Storage Systems.*

## 1. INTRODUCTION

In contemporary society, energy systems have become crucial and influential in various domains, particularly in the household sector, industry, and transportation, due to the rapid advancement and essential energy requirements of human society (Mosavi et al., 2019). Ensuring that energy systems can adapt to changes in supply

DOI: 10.4018/979-8-3373-2530-9.ch006

and demand while maintaining peak performance and a low carbon footprint is, in general, a critical and significant concern (Forootan et al., 2022). There has been a substantial rise in energy consumption in recent days. The increase in energy consumption can be ascribed to multiple sources, including the exponential population rise, the expansion of economic endeavours, and the advancement of industrial sectors. As the world's energy needs rise and fossil fuels cause environmental problems, we need better energy sources and strong energy storage systems that will speed up the decarbonisation process, lower greenhouse gas emissions, and encourage future energy independence (Njema et al., 2024).

Over the last few years, energy storage technologies have gradually emerged as a vital component of modern power networks (D.O Akinyele et al., 2014). Particularly, the declining cost of batteries has led to their increased use in combination with renewable energy systems (M.A. Hannan et al., 2017). Energy storage systems have the ability to offer different types of decentralised support services and function as a secondary power source. As more and more renewable energy sources are being deployed and traditional power plants are being decommissioned, there has been a rise in the integration of battery energy storage systems into active distribution networks (Kumar et al., 2020). Energy storage systems store renewable power system excess energy and release it when needed to meet peak demand (Ramos et al., 2021). Energy storage devices that can be recharged are highly used because they can deal with the intermittent nature of renewable energy sources and reuse them over time (Cheng et al., 2023).

Battery Energy Storage System (BESS) facilitates the integration and equilibrium of fluctuating renewable energy sources to ensure a consistent energy provision by storing surplus energy and discharging it when required (Hill et al., 2012). Battery energy storage systems (BESSs) are increasingly used in power systems because to their advantageous features, such as rapid reaction time, scalability, and adaptability (Kocer et al., 2019). Innovative BESS technologies boost system utilisation and economic growth, making them essential for demand response programs and flexibility. Additionally, hybrid energy storage systems can improve performance, efficiency, and cost (Luo et al., 2015).

Integrating human knowledge with machine learning has enabled human-machine learning interaction and made machine learning decisions intelligible (Deng et al., 2020). Machine learning (ML) is a discipline within computer science that focusses on extracting patterns from data in order to enhance performance in different activities. BESS often necessitates the use of algorithmic approaches to ensure accurate modelling and optimal management of their operation modes (Talluri et al., 2021). The field of BESS research has relied heavily on machine learning for a variety of reasons, and the number of methodologies and datasets that have been used in this approach is practically unlimited (Sarkar, 2021a). Machine learning technologies greatly impact on the development and management of BESS by improving prediction accuracy and computational efficiency and offer promising solutions for addressing the challenges in this field (Luanna & Peng, 2021).

Tata Power Delhi Distribution Limited (TPDDL) along with AES Corporation and Mitsubishi Corporation to establish a 10 MW / 10 MWh Battery Energy Storage System (BESS) project in Delhi in 2019 (Samuel, 2020). BESS installations help for rapid response to unexpected shifts in the local or regional grid's demand or supply leads to grid stability and frequency regulation. Rising energy demand was met by India's continued expansion, proving the scalability of battery storage systems. According to India's National Electricity Plan (NEP), the country will need an extra 47 GW of battery storage systems by 2032 so that 500 GW of renewable energy sources can be connected to the grid (Sharma, 2024). Energy stabilization, grid resilience, and electrification support demonstrate adaptation to the intermittent characteristics of renewable energy sources while promoting decarbonization and economic efficiency.

This chapter presents a thorough examination of recent progress and application of machine learning in BESS. This includes Battery state estimation, Battery remaining useful lifetime prediction, Battery Troubleshooting, Battery design, and optimisation. The chapter is structured as follows: First part, the expansion of the energy sector, followed by an exploration of the concept of Battery Energy Storage Systems (BESS) and the development and challenges associated with BESS were discussed. Second part, the prominent machine learning technologies and machinc learning algorithms that have been employed in the domain of BESS were described. Third part, application pf machine learning algorithms to several aspects of Battery Energy Storage Systems (BESS), including batteries within BESS, energy management within BESS, and the grid connection to BESS were explained with conclusion as final part.

## 2. GROWTH IN ENERGY SECTOR

There will be a massive increase to the world's renewable energy capacity between 2024 and 2033, with an additional 5.4 TW of solar and wind power projected. This anticipated increase in renewable energy sources is a promising development that holds great potential for the global energy landscape which reflects the global push towards electrification and decarbonisation, reaching 8TW (Gautamee, 2024). The India Energy Outlook 2021 of the International Energy Agency also predicts that by 2040, India might have a battery storage capacity of 140-200 gigawatts (GW), which would be the most among all countries (Seema, 2023). Countries worldwide are transitioning to low-carbon energy systems and renewable energy sources. BESS is a highly promising technology for expediting the transition to renewable energy sources. The BESS market is expected to experience significant growth, increasing from USD 7.8 billion in 2024 to USD 25.6 billion by 2029, with CAGR of 26.9% throughout the forecast period (Research & Markets, 2024).

## 3. DEVELOPMENT IN ESS

In recent years, energy storage technologies have advanced, each with its distinct benefits and application. Lithium-ion batteries dominate the industry due to huge cost savings and performance gains (Sharma, 2019). Economy of scale and manufacturing improvements lower battery prices. Its lower cost, higher energy densities, and longer lifespans make it a popular BESS option (Alpízar et al., 2024). Another potential discovery is flow batteries, which can last 15 hours. These batteries last longer and scale better than lithium-ion batteries because they use refillable liquid electrolytes (Buiskikh et al., 2018). Thermal energy storage is another novel way to store heat or cold for heating, cooling, or electricity. This technique helps balance seasonal energy consumption in particular (Suresh et al., 2020). Pumped hydro and flywheels store power using kinetic or gravitational energy. These technologies are efficient and fast, making them suited for grid stability and emergency backup (Rekioua, 2023). Another innovative alternative is hydrogen storage, which uses excess renewable energy to electrolyse hydrogen. This hydrogen can be stored and transformed into energy or fuel for long-term use (Hasan et al., 2021). Comparative Analysis of Various Energy Storage Technologies were provided in the Table 1.

*Table 1. Comparative analysis of various energy storage technologies*

| TECHNOLOGY | KEY STRENGTHS | KEY WEAKNESS | APPLICATIONS |
|---|---|---|---|
| Battery Energy Storage Systems (BESS) | High energy density, rapid response, scalable | Dependence on critical raw materials like lithium cobalt | Greatest stabilization renewable integration |
| Pumped Hydro Storage | Large scale capacity, long lifespan | Location dependent slow response times | Bulk energy storage peak shaving |
| Flywheel Energy Storage | High efficiency, excellent for short term storage | High initial cost limited energy capacity | Frequency regulation power quality |
| Hydrogen Storage | Long term storage potential, green hydrogen compatibility | Inefficient high production cost | Seasonal energy storage fuel cells |
| Thermal Storage | Cost effective for niche applications | Low energy density | Solar thermal plants district heating |

## 4. CONCEPT OF BESS

The design of a Battery Energy Storage System (BESS) entails connecting battery modules in a series manner, resulting in the creation of a string. In the BESS system, a string is formed by linking the positive (+ Ve) terminal of one battery module to the negative (-Ve) terminal of the next module, and so forth (Prakash et al., 2022). By linking the battery modules in a sequential manner, the total voltage of the system is enhanced, enabling greater capacity for storing energy. When the strings are connected in parallel, it allows for a more efficient storage and delivery of energy. This parallel connection enhances the versatility and scalability of the BESS, making it suitable for a wider application (Stecca et al., 2020).The Concept of the Battery Energy Storage System is represented in Figure 1.

*Figure 1. Battery energy storage system diagram*

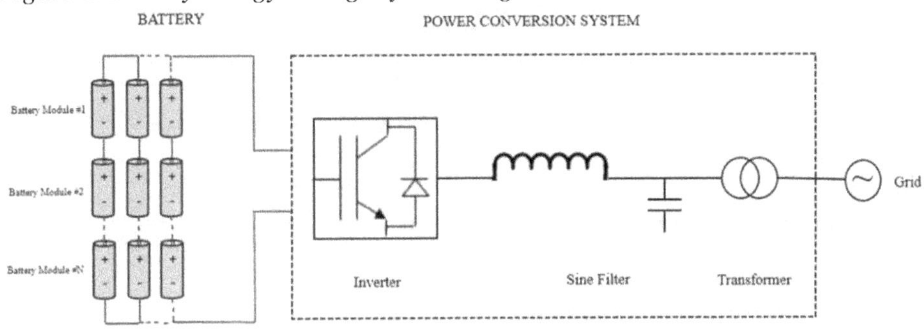


The Power Conversion System (PCS) main function is to convert the direct current (DC) energy stored in batteries into alternating current (AC) that can be used to power the grid or supply electricity and shall be used vice -versa (Molina, 2017). This bidirectional energy conversion process ensures that energy is effectively managed and utilised, maximising system overall efficiency. PCS synchronises the voltage and current waveforms to maximise power transmission efficiency. Modern personal computer systems (PCS) are equipped with powerful control systems that provide real-time data, system diagnostics, and the ability to control the system remotely. The power conditioning system (PCS) adjusts the output voltage and frequency to fit the requirements of the power grid (Mviri, 2022).

## 5. CHALLENGES IN BESS

Over the next few decades, the energy storage market is predicted to be quite important. The energy storage industry still faces a number of obstacles, despite the optimistic long-term predictions.

- High cost of developing innovative energy storage technologies deters investors.
- Lack of faith in these technologies & safety hinders industry expansion.
- Environmental concerns from battery disposal, extraction, and mining.
- Weak domestic manufacturing and imports fulfil high demand.
- Imports serve energy storage technologies, but lack long-lasting batteries, standardization, degradation, and inadequate energy density hinder market expansion.
- No clear market framework for energy storage technology, reliant on government policy support.
- Appropriate design and optimization of BESS required for higher efficiency.
- Challenges include measuring and predicting BESS state from a vast dataset.

## 6. OVERVIEW OF MACHINE LEARNING TECHNOLOGIES

### 6.1 Supervised Learning (SL)

SL is a method in machine learning that employs labelled datasets to train algorithms. This strategy involves the algorithm acquiring knowledge from input data that is associated with the correct outputs or labels (Sathya & Annamma, 2013). In supervised learning, the predictors and output variables are readily accessible for training machine learning algorithms, serving as reliable reference data (Gupta et al., 2022). Figure 2 Illustrates the concept of Supervised Learning. Supervised ML algorithms classify observations into theoretical groups to create categorical variables based on preset theoretical notions (Miric et al., 2021). According to the nature of the output variable, the supervised learning task can be classified as either a classification or regression task (Singh, 2016).

*Figure 2. Illustration of supervised learning*

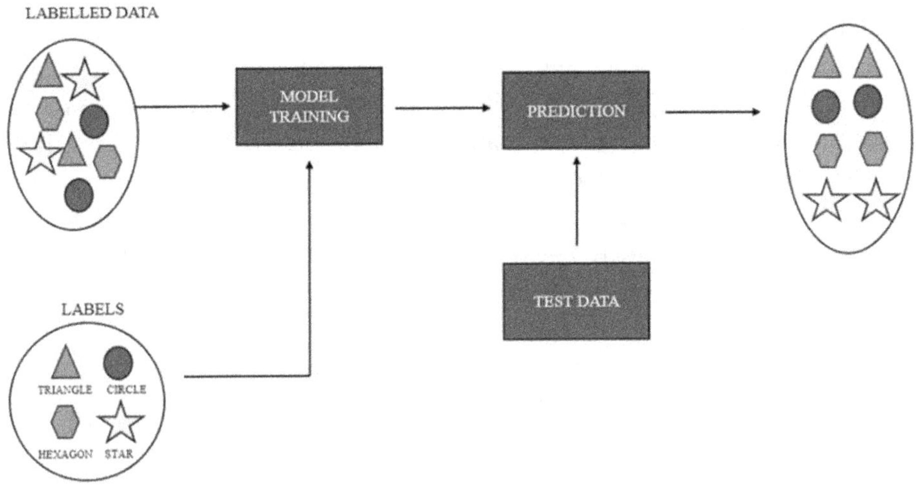


## 6.2 Unsupervised Learning (USL)

Unsupervised learning is the process of training an algorithm using unlabelled data, which lacks specific target values. The model endeavours to identify patterns, clusters, or correlations within the data without any pre-established labels (Khanam et al., 2015). Figure 3 Illustrates the concept of Unsupervised Learning. Unsupervised learning algorithms autonomously acquire knowledge about the intrinsic structure of the data without any explicit direction or instruction. Therefore, the USL algorithms acquire knowledge from unlabelled, unclassified, or uncategorised test data (Amrut Hnath et al., 2018).

*Figure 3. Illustration of unsupervised learning*

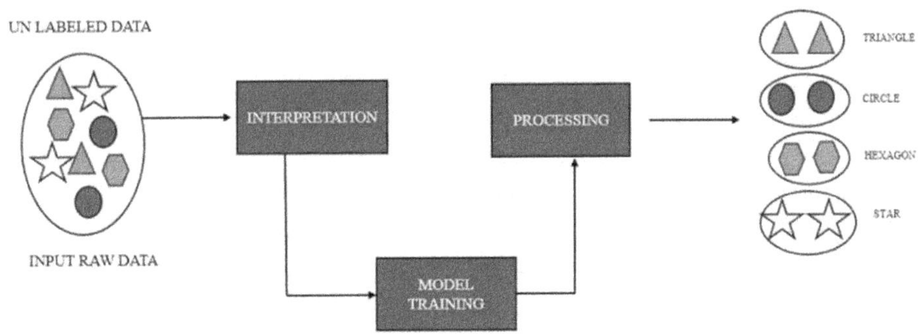

## 6.3 Reinforcement Learning

Reinforcement learning is one of machine learning approach that is most similar to the way humans learn by making mistakes. Deep reinforcement learning involves the agent interacting with its surroundings through actions and receiving a reward (positive or negative) in return (AlMahamid & Grolinger, 2021). Figure 4 Illustrates the concept of Reinforcement learning. Reinforcement learning consists of 3 key elements: agent, environment, and actions. The Agent is both a learner and a decision-maker and the environment refers to any entity or system with which the agent interacts and then Actions, on the other hand, pertain to the specific behaviours or activities performed by the agent (Qiang & Zhongli, 2011). A reinforcement learning algorithm lacks labelled data as the agents solely acquire knowledge through interactions with their environment (Sutton & Barto, 1998).

*Figure 4. Illustration of reinforcement learning*

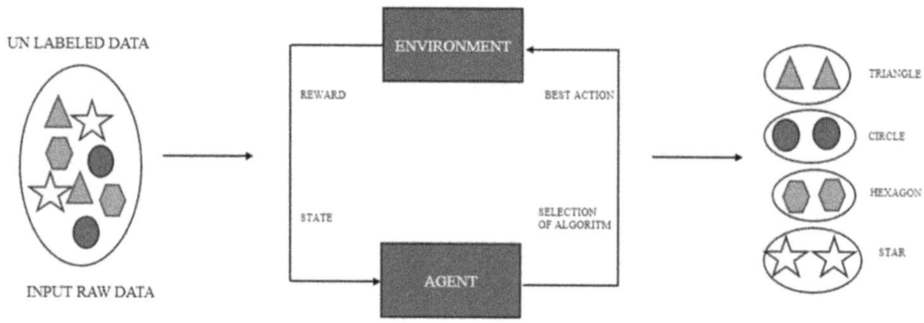


## 6.4 Deep Learning

Deep learning is a specialised discipline of machine learning. To solve complex and difficult issues, it makes use of artificial neural networks, which are computer models based on the composition and operations of the human brain (Sarkar, 2021b). Figure 5 Illustrates the concept of Deep Learning. This enables them to address complex problems when traditional machine learning techniques unfeasible to handle. The building blocks of deep learning models, which are also known as deep neural networks, are interconnected layers of nodes. They are able to efficiently handle massive volumes of data because they can learn hierarchical data representations (Li Deng & Dong Yu, 2014). With its remarkable data-driven learning capabilities, it has been important in driving AI developments paved the way for numerous groundbreaking advancements in computer vision, NLP, and speech recognition (LeCun, et al., 2015).

*Figure 5. Illustration of deep learning*

## 7. MACHINE LEARNING ALGORITHMS APPLIED IN BESS

GPR – Gaussian process regression - Function evaluation is viewed as a stochastic process in Gaussian process regression, where observations are projected to a normal distribution that is linked with uncertainty (Liu, 2016).
RBFNN - Radial Basis Function Neural Network – Widely used because it has a simple structure and is good at approximating nonlinear functions. It is especially useful in pattern recognition, industrial control, and nonlinear system modelling (Xiong et al., 2015).
SVM – Support Vector Machine - A powerful machine learning method that can be used for tasks like regression, classification, and even finding outliers (Pisner & Schnyer, 2020). SVMs are versatile and effective in various applications to handle high-dimensional data and nonlinear correlations.
GNB - Gaussian Naive Bayes – It is based on Bayes' theorem, which predicts the likelihood of an event given previous knowledge of conditions that may be associated to the event (Parida et al., 2014).
kernel-SVM (KSVM) - kernel- Support Vector Machine - The similarity between data points in the higher-dimensional feature space is determined by kernel function employed in KSVM. KSVM is capable of identifying nonlinear decision boundaries (Amaya et al., 2024).

MLP – Multi Layer Perceptron – It is a Neural Network where all of the nodes are linked to other nodes at different levels and can only work forwards. A Backpropagation method is used by the MLP neural network to make the training model more accurate (Naskath et al., 2023).

k-NN – K-Nearest Neighbor - The K-NN approach categorises a new data point by comparing its similarity to previously stored data. Since the approach is non-parametric, no assumptions are made about the underlying data and capable of handling category and numerical data (Ukey et al., 2023).

GRB-k - Gaussian radial base function kernel - The input data is mapped by this nonlinear kernel function employing a Gaussian function into a higher-dimensional feature space. Points closer together receive a greater similarity score, whereas points farther apart receive a lower score (Fasshauer & McCourt, 2012).

DBN - Deep Belief Network – It is either a generative visual model or a variant of deep neural network. It is made up of many layers of hidden variables that are connected between each other but not between units in the same layer (Lopes et al., 2015).

TTSC - Two-Step Time-Series Clustering - The hybrid clustering algorithm is proposed on the basis of the similarity in the geometry of time series data. The TTC algorithm is highly versatile and may be tailored to suit the requirements of various applications (Rajesh & Seetha, 2022).

FPA - Flower Pollination Algorithm - FPA is distinguished by (its high computational efficiency and simplicity and flexibility in its formulation Ram et al., 2020). FPA is primarily used for optimisation, specifically in the context of feature selection and other optimisation tasks, to reduce the dimensionality of the search space.

DBN-BP - Deep Belief Network-Back Propagation Neural Network - A deep neural network's weights can be initialised using DBN, and error derivatives can be backpropagated to fine-tune the network in a discriminative manner. The DBN's "recognition" weights are converted into normal neural network weights (Shahabi et al., 2021).

ANN - Artificial Neural Networks - ANNs consist of artificial neurones organised into input, hidden, and output layers, utilising a connectionist method for computation. (Mishra & Srivastava, 2014) Nonlinear statistical data modelling approaches are employed to reveal complex interactions between inputs and outputs. This allows for the anticipation or categorisation of intricate issues.

DCNN-ETL - Deep Convolutional Neural Networks Coupled with Ensemble Learning & Transfer Learning - The concepts of transfer learning and ensemble learning were integrated into the DCNN-ETL method. It is capable of generating more precise and resilient capacity estimations with a relatively small pool of training data (Shen et al., 2020a).

CNN - Convolution Neural Networks – It is a type of feedforward neural network that can pull out features from a collection that looks like a grid. Pattern-finding skills are good, and the system can handle changes in translation, rotation, and scale handle a lot of data, and you don't have to do feature extraction by hand (Ketkar et al.,2021).

DNN - Deep Neural Networks - A deep neural network is made up of more layers, or depth, and each layer increases the model's complexity while allowing it to analyse inputs quickly and produce the best possible answer. For robustness improvement, absolute percentage error and mean square error are calculated using a DNN-based approach (Rocchetta et al., 2019).

LSTM- Long Short-Term Memory – LSTM is a form of Recurrent Neural Network (RNN) that is capable of preserving long term dependencies in sequential data. (Van Houdt et al., 2020) Sequential data, including speech, text, and time series, can be processed and analysed by LSTMs. In order to regulate the passage of information, they implement gates and a memory cell.

DC-GAN - Deep Convolutional GAN - DCGANs are designed to generate convincing images by utilising a deep convolutional neural network architecture that is specifically designed to effectively manage image data. It accumulates the sampling of convolutional layers between the input vector laten_ dim and the output image in the Generator (Li et al., 2019).

ELM – Extreme Learning Machine - In feedforward neural networks with single or multiple layers of hidden nodes, the ELM algorithm allows for the independent random assignment of input weights and biases (Wang et al., 2022). The network's output weights can be computed analytically using a simple generalised inverse operation.

MCMC - Markov Chain Monte Carlo - The MCMC algorithm is employed to address integration and optimisation issues in large-dimensional spaces. MCMC is a computational algorithm that is employed to generate a sequence of random samples from a complex probability distribution (Brooks, 1998).

Q-learning algorithm - Q-learning is an off-policy model free and value-based algorithm. It determines the optimal sequence of actions by analysing the agent's current state. Quality is represented by the letter "Q." In this scenario, an agent acquires new knowledge by interacting with the environment, observing results, and receives feedback in the form of rewards (Watkins & Dayan, 1992).

Q-iteration algorithm – Q-iteration is a computational algorithm that enables the identification of the most effective policy. The value of being in each state is determined iteratively by the algorithm, which assumes that the agent takes the most optimal action in that state based on the current estimate of the value function (Zhang et al., 2022).

DDPG – Deep Deterministic Politic Gradient – It is a model-free algorithm that combines the actor-critic approach with the deterministic policy gradient. (Dong et al., 2023) It is designed to work with continuous action spaces. The system utilises experience replay and slow learning target networks from DQN. It is built upon DPG, enabling it to function in continuous action spaces.

FQL - Fuzzy Q-Learning - A composite method that merges fuzzy logic and reinforcement Q-learning is Fuzzy Q-Learning. It offers a mechanism for automatically adjusting a Fuzzy Inference System only based on reward signals. (Salehizadeh & Soltaniyan, 2016) Fuzzy reasoning is used to handle continuous states and generate continuous actions. Incorporating pre-existing knowledge into the fuzzy rules can greatly decrease the amount of time required for learning.

Reinforcement Learning Actor Critic Algorithm - The policy is explicitly represented by separate memory structures in actor-critic methods, which are a form of policy gradient method. The policy structure is referred to as actor, and the estimated value function is referred to as critic. The critic evaluates actions taken by the actor, while the actor selects them (Kathirgamanathan et al., 2021).

ANFIS - Adaptive Neuro-Fuzzy Inference System - In order to develop intelligent decision-making models, ANFIS integrates fuzzy logic, inference systems, and neural networks. ANFIS is capable of managing complex and uncertain data, as well as adapting to shifting environments and learning from experience (Salleh et al., 2017).

Monte Carlo tree search-based RL - Monte Carlo Tree Search (MCTS) is a type of model-based reinforcement learning method. (James et al., 2017) It is used for planning in sequential decision-making algorithms and follows the principles of Markov decision process logic.

## 8. APPLICATION OF ML ALGORITHMS - BATTERIES WITHIN BATTERY ENERGY STORAGE SYSTEM

### 8.1 Battery State Estimation

The battery state mainly includes state of charge (SOC), capacity, and state of health (SOH). Specifically, SOC is quantified by the ratio of the releasable capacity of a battery over its rated capacity. SOH is quantified by the ratio of the maximum releasable capacity over the rated capacity (Murnane & Ghazel, 2017). To forecast the SOH, the GPR technique was utilised for the purpose of applying regression algorithms (Richardson et al., 2017). GPR models were also utilised in order to evaluate the SOC of Li-ion batteries (Sahinoglu et al., 2017). RBFNN model is used to guess how much power Li-ion batteries have and how much resistance is inside them (Zhou et al., 2020). The capacity of Li-ion batteries is estimated using Deep Convolutional Neural Networks (DCNN) combined with Ensemble Transfer Learning (ETL) (Shen et al., 2020b).

## 8.2 Battery Lifetime Estimation and Prediction

The remaining useful lifetime (RUL) of a battery is commonly measured by the point in time or number of cycles at which the capacity or state of health (SOH) drops below a specific threshold value (Liu et al., 2019). supervised learning technique was utilised to estimate the lifespan of batteries. Data-driven strategy was employed using linear regression to forecast the cycle life of batteries before their capacity starts to degrade, based on the discharge data from the early cycles (Severson et al., 2019). In addition to the regression methodology, the decision tree method is employed for predicting the Remaining Useful Life (RUL) (Zhu et al., 2019). The SVM model is utilised for the classification and prediction of the (RUL) of Lithium-ion (Li-ion) batteries (Patil et al., 2015).

ANN and SVM models utilised to predict the cycle life of lithium polymer batteries (Zhou et al., 2017). LSTM-DNN deep learning model is used for thc purpose of predicting the Remaining Useful Life (Veeraghavan et al., 2018). The deep learning model is trained using the battery capacity decay pattern collected from virtual tests conducted at different C-rates (Wang et al., 2011). The accuracy of predictions made by DNN and ANN is better than that of SVM, logistic regression, and k-NN (Srivastava et al., 2014).

## 8.3 Battery Troubleshooting

One critical application of machine learning methods is the identification and classification of aberrant batteries, as well as the detection of battery defects, to guarantee the consistency of battery cells. Various machine learning strategies are utilised to classify the imbalance and damage of battery cells (Ortiz et al., 2019). These algorithms include logistic regression (Dong et al.,2016), k-NN, kernel-SVM with a Gaussian radial base function kernel (Kim et al., 2012), Gaussian naive Bayes, and a neural network with a single hidden layer. When it comes to lead-acid batteries, fault identification is accomplished through the utilisation of a K-shaped time series hierarchical clustering analysis algorithm (Haider et al., 2020).

Utilising the GPR, a calendar capacity loss model was created to investigate the properties of Li ion batteries as they age (Lucu et al., 2020). The detection of voltage anomalies in batteries is accomplished by utilising a deep belief network (DBN) model (Li et al., 2019). In order to classify whether a cell is inconsistent or not, the raw discharge voltage series of the cells is labelled using a technique known as TTSC. This technique is applied by employing the k-means algorithm (Huang et al., 2016). The flower pollination algorithm (FPA) optimises CNN model parameters during training to detect polymer Li-ion battery blister defects (Ma et al., 2019).

## 8.4 Battery Design and Optimization

This subsection will focus specifically in the context of battery design and optimisation. By leveraging the capabilities of ML algorithms, the efficiency and performance of batteries are enhanced, ultimately leading to advancements in BESS. ANN (specifically the SLFNN model) to enhance the efficiency of battery cells by optimising the cell design parameters (Wu et al., 2018). DNN model was created and used to improve the design of the electrolyte channels in thick electrodes so that they can charge quickly (Gao et al., 2020). The ANN model's sensitivity analysis determines critical design factors for specific power or energy (Ying et al., 2017).

MCMC technique combined with DNN optimise the performance of the battery (Gao et al., 2019). ANN model is utilised in the process of designing electrode architectures at the mesoscale (Takagishi et al., 2019). The optimised process parameters are inferred from the total specific resistance using the Bayesian optimisation algorithm coupled with the trained ANN-based model (Badmos et al., 2020). To build 3D microstructures for cathodes in batteries and anodes in solid oxide fuel cells (SOFCs), DC-GAN models were used (Gayon et al., 2020).

## 8.5 Battery Modeling and Behavior Prediction

Understanding and forecasting battery behaviour is essential for heat management systems, accurate status evaluation, and dependable operation, all of which are greatly influenced by battery modelling (Kai et al., 2022). In order to forecast the voltage, power, and surface temperature of batteries using the load current, a model-based ELM is utilised (Tang et al., 2018). SVM approach was selected to precisely determine the particular mode of heat generation within these batteries, which is essential for advancing safer and more efficient battery technologies (Chen et al., 2018).

A temperature dependent model for batteries was constructed using a new method termed stacked denoising autoencoders-extreme learning machine (SDAE-ELM) (Li et al., 2019) shows the forecast of Li-ion batteries reaction due to changes in temperature. SVM have been shown to be more robust and less susceptible to the influence of noise in the data (Jain et al., 2014). DBN-BP is an advanced neural network architecture combines the strengths of both deep belief networks and back propagation algorithms to optimise the accuracy of voltage predictions in battery models (Li et al., 2019). Gaussian process can be used to build a crack pattern model for LIBs with silicon-based anodes, which can help with the design of the anode material (Zheng et al., 2020).

## 9. APPLICATION OF ML ALGORITHMS – EMS IN BATTERY ENERGY STORAGE SYSTEM

The application of deep learning to the battery energy storage system involves the use of multi layer perceptual neural networks and regression tree algorithms for the purpose of predicting the amount of energy that could be consumed by the battery (Foiadelli et al., 2018). The prediction of certain outcomes plays a crucial role in determining the expected results relies on the analysis of various factors, including temperature, distance, range and speed. By considering these variables, it is possible to make well-informed predictions and acquire a deeper understanding of prospective outcomes (Kolambe, 2024). When comparing the LSTM algorithm to the MLP neural network algorithm, it becomes evident that the former provides a higher level of prediction accuracy in terms of energy consumption (Morcillo et al., 2024).

The management of BESS frequently makes use of reinforcement learning, which is characterised by an approach that is based on a Q-learning algorithm. According to Kofinas, (2018a) it is utilised to regulate the flow of energy inside a solar microgrid that includes a photovoltaic source, a battery bank, a destination unit, and a load. As an additional application, it can be utilised for the management of the functioning of a microgrid that is associated with a community battery energy storage system (Bui et al., 2019).

To optimise the distribution of energy from multiple carriers in a multi carrier energy system to fulfil the total energy demand, reinforcement learning strategy that applied a fitted Q iteration algorithm was used (Mbuwir et al., 2018) to improve the efficiency and performance. DDPG algorithm is an essential component of the Plug in Hybrid Electrical Bus (PHEB) energy management system (Hongwen et al., 2022). This algorithm plays a significant role in the efficient management of energy to maximise the amount of energy that is distributed throughout the many modules of the bus, ensuring that resources are utilised in an effective manner (Wu et al., 2019).

## 10. APPLICATION OF ML ALGORITHMS IN GRID CONNECTED BATTERY ENERGY STORAGE SYSTEM

Deep learning helps energy management for microgrids with energy storage modules reduce operational costs and improve renewable energy use (Wu & Wang, 2018). Reinforcement and DRL are being employed for grid and microgrid control. A standalone microgrid's energy is managed using a multi agent system with reinforcement learning and fuzzy Q-learning for each agent (Kofinas et al., 2018b). Hierarchical deep reinforcement learning method utilised for managing the energy usage of smart home apps and distributed energy resources, which is based on the actor critic algorithm (Lee et al., 2020).

To compensate speed frequency recovery while maintaining power distribution, the adaptive neuro-fuzzy inference system was used (Karimi et al., 2021). A battery-energy storage grid uses a novel online-trained ANN control to share and trade reactive power (Chettibi et al., 2018). NN and online RL regulate energy storage unit charging and discharging smoothly; the new control system is controllable and reduces disruption (Duan et al., 2019). For a cost-effective energy management system, a mixed integer non-linear programming QL algorithm was presented (Yoldas et al., 2020). Deep learning ANN improve power quality and system stability (Ali et al., 2021).

ML method that allows the system to run economically in both grid-connected and island modes; it is based on modified whale optimisation (Yuan et al., 2021). To optimise power regulation in a DC microgrid, a dynamic distributed multi-microgrid and MCTS-based RL shall be utilised (Al Saffar & Musilek, 2021). Semi-supervised machine learning with co-training adopted to classify microgrid transmission and distribution faults (Abdelgayed et al., 2018). Reinforcement Learning algorithm is employed for controlling and making decisions on electricity systems inside a microgrid (Glavic et al., 2017) and DNN is used to remove fault current DC offset (Lee et al., 2019). A robust smart generation control system is provided, utilising the DQL algorithm within a multiagent grid system (Xi et al., 2018). Stable and unstable conditions can be easily distinguished by mapping the original data with forecasted data using DBN based microgrid transient analysis (Hu et al., 2017). A multi-layer hidden module and DL were suggested to improve the power system during emergency situations. Deep reinforcement learning (DRL) is used to get around problems and make systems that are more reliable (Huang et al., 2019).

## 11. CHALLENGES AND POTENTIAL SOLUTIONS

The use of Machine Learning to BESS has the potential to bring about revolutionary changes nevertheless, there are a number of hurdles and restrictions that prevented from reaching its full potential. The following are some of the technological, operational and economic components of these challenges and the potentials solution explained in the Figure 6.

*Figure 6. Challenges and potential solutions*

| CHALLENGING AREA | | SPECIFIC CHALLENGES | POTENTIAL SOLUTIION |
|---|---|---|---|
| Data related challenges | *Data scarcity* | Models require large, high quality data sets but comprehensive BESS data is hard to obtain, especially for new systems. | Develop secure anonymized data sharing platforms to enhance dataset availability without compromising privacy. |
| | *Data privacy and security* | Integration of BESS in smart grids involves sensitive operational data. Security and privacy concerns limit ML training | Implement robust data security protocols and anonymization techniques to ensure privacy while enabling effective ML training |
| | *Inconsistent data quality* | Sensor inaccuracies or missing data points degrade model performance especially in real time applications | Use data preprocessing techniques and robust ML algorithms that can handle noisy or missing data |
| Computational and technical challenges | *High computational demand* | Advanced ML techniques, like deep learning require significant computational power, which may be expensive and impractical for remote BESS installations | Deploy ML models at the edge or use cloud computing with optimised resource allocation to reduce computational strain |
| | *Model interpretability* | Many ML models particularly deep learning are black boxes making it difficult to trust or interpret their outputs | Combine ML with physics based models to improve interpretability and trust in model predictions |
| | *Model generalization* | Model trained on specific battery types or operational conditions may not generalise well to other scenarios | Use transfer learning techniques or hybrid models that incorporate domain specific knowledge to improve adaptability |
| Integration challenges | *Real time application complexity* | Deploying ML models for real time tasks like grid balancing requires ultra low latency and high reliability | Optimise ML models for real time performance and use edge computing to reduce latency |
| | *Compatibility with the existing infrastructure* | Retrofitting ML solutions into legacy systems can be complex and costly , requiring significant hardware & software modification | Develop adaptable ML solutions that can integrate with existing systems with minimal modifications |
| Economic and financial limitations | *High initial costs* | Developing and deploying ML solutions for BESS can be costly, making them less accessible for smaller operators. | Explore cost sharing models, government funding, or incentives to lower the initial investment burden. |
| | *Uncertain return on investment (ROI)* | Long term benefits of ML in BESS depend on variables like market conditions and energy policies making ROI projections uncertain. | Advocate for regulatory frameworks that support long term investment in ML technologies for energy systems. |
| Regulatory And standardization issues | *Lack of standards* | The absence of standardised protocols for ML integration complicates deployment and limits interoperability | Foster industry collaboration to develop and adopt standards for ML in BESS integration |
| | *Regulatory constraints* | Strict energy market regulations may limit the flexibility needed to implement decision making process | Engage in policy advocacy to encourage flexible regulations that enable ML adoption in energy systems |
| Environmental and ethical concerns | *Energy consumption of ML* | Training complex ML model, especially in cloud environments, can consume significant energy, offsetting BESS benefits | Use energy efficient algorithm, optimize cloud computing, and consider the environmental impact of ML process |
| | *Ethical implications* | ML decision making in resource allocation may lead to biases or unintended consequences | Develop fairness aware algorithms and decision-making frameworks to avoid biases in resource distribution |

## 12. PRACTICAL IMPLICATIONS

Machine learning has the potential to have disruptive effects in the field of battery energy storage system (BESS) as it can provide answers to important problems and improve system performance in a variety of angles. The following are some important areas in which machine learning has direct applications in the real world.

✓ **Battery State Estimation**

ML algorithms analyse voltage current and temperature data to predict battery degradation and reduce anticipated failures.

✓ **Predictive Maintenance**

ML models predict impending failures by analysing past and present data trends.

✓ **Efficient Regulation and Control of Energy Use**

ML optimises energy storage and discharge cycles enabling dynamic energy scheduling and load balancing.

✓ **Combination With Renewable Energy**

ML help manage intermittent renewable energy sources aiding in power output forecasting and surplus energy storage deployment.

✓ **Improving and Designing Batteries**

ML optimises battery layouts and accelerates innovation as seen in the partnership between Google deep mind and battery makers.

✓ **Grid Connection and Stability**

ML aids real time decisions about frequency regulation voltage stability and load shifting in BESS connected to the grid.

✓ **Promotion of Sustainability and the Circular Economy**

ML helps business find the best recycling methods for precious metals and minerals.

✓ **Impact of Smart Grid Scalability and Adaptability**

ML facilitates seamless integration of many BESS units into smart grids optimising BESS to reduce emissions and the cost while meeting urban energy demands.

## 13. FUTURE RESEARCH DIRECTINS FOR MACHINE LEARNING IN BESS

The following are some of the major topics that future research could concentrate on in order to increase the scientific traffic foundation and practical usefulness of machine learning in battery energy storage system (BESS)

### 13.1 Enhancing Data Quality and Availability

- Create Open Access data sets for standardised battery performance degradation and failure mode Data.
- Improve real time data acquisition.
- High accurate frequent data and edge computing.

### 13.2 Model Robustness and Generalization

- Create models adaptable to new battery chemistries configuration and operating conditions.
- Combined domain expertise with the data driven methods to create hybrid models.
- Study interpretable ML models part forecasting and decision making.

### 13.3 Energy and Computational Constraints

- Create real time efficient ML models for onsite energy management system.
- Explorer quantum approaches for faster and more effective BESS optimization and simulation.

### 13.4 Application Expansion

- Optimise performance factor, energy efficiency, cost and life span.
- Integrate renewable energy to stabilise the grid.
- Boost microgrid and electric vehicle reliability.

## 13.5 Practical Integration and Validation

- Test ML algorithms and scalability durability through industry collaborations and experimental projects.
- Standardised essential energy infrastructure ML decision making.
- Develop ML system communication tools for operators to make informed decision.

## 13.6 Exploring New Battery Technologies

- Optimise performance with ml models for next generation quad trees.
- Access retired battery capacity value to improve energy storage circular economy.

# 14. CONCLUSION

A thorough examination of utilization of Machine Learning (ML) technologies in Battery Energy Storage Systems (BESS) were presented in this chapter, showcasing the significant advantages and revolutionary possibilities of this combination. The results emphasize that machine learning algorithms may greatly improve the performance, efficiency, and dependability of BESS through enhanced predictive analytics, optimization, and real-time monitoring. Adoption of Machine learning has shown effective in addressing several challenges, such as estimating the status of the battery, predicting its remaining life, diagnosing faults and defects, analysing its properties and behaviour, as well as modelling, designing, and optimising batteries.

Through surmounting existing obstacles and persistently pioneering new solutions, machine learning (ML) has a pivotal impact on enhancing the performance of Battery Energy Storage Systems (BESS), thus making a significant contribution to creating a more sustainable and efficient energy environment.

## REFERENCES


Abdelgayed, T. S., Morsi, W. G., & Sidhu, T. S. (2018). Fault detection and classification based on co-training of semi supervised machine learning. *IEEE Transactions on Industrial Electronics*, 65(2), 1595–1606. DOI: 10.1109/TIE.2017.2726961

Akinyele, D. O., & Rayudu, R. K. (2014). Review of energy storage technologies for sustainable power networks. *Sustainable Energy Technologies and Assessments*, 8, 74–91. DOI: 10.1016/j.seta.2014.07.004

Al-Saffar, M., & Musilek, P. (2021). Distributed Optimization for Distribution Grids with Stochastic DER Using Multi-Agent Deep Reinforcement Learning. *IEEE Access : Practical Innovations, Open Solutions*, 9, 63059–63072. DOI: 10.1109/ACCESS.2021.3075247

Ali, W., Ulasyar, A., Mehmood, M. U., Khattak, A., Imran, K., Zad, H. S., & Nisar, S. (2021). Hierarchical Control of Microgrid Using IoT and Machine Learning Based Islanding Detection. *IEEE Access : Practical Innovations, Open Solutions*, 9, 103019–103031. DOI: 10.1109/ACCESS.2021.3098163

AlMahamid, F., & Grolinger, K. (2021). Reinforcement Learning Algorithms: An Overview and Classification. *IEEE Canadian Conference on Electrical and Computer Engineering* (CCECE), 1-7. DOI: 10.1109/CCECE53047.2021.9569056

Alpízar-Castillo, J., Linders, K., Slaifstein, D., Ramírez-Elizondo, L., & Bauer, P. (2024). Economic Opportunities of Power Curtailment and Peak Shaving on Residential PV-BESS Systems. *In 2024 20th International Conference on the European Energy Market (EEM) (pp. 1-6). IEEE.*

Amaya-Tejera, N., Gamarra, M., Vélez, J. I., & Zurek, E. (2024). A distance-based kernel for classification via Support Vector Machines. *Frontiers in Artificial Intelligence*, 7, 1287875. DOI: 10.3389/frai.2024.1287875 PMID: 38469159

Amrut Hnath, N., & Gupta, T. (2018), research study on unsupervised machine learning algorithms for early fault detection in predictive maintenance, 2018 *5th International Conference on Industrial Engineering and Applications (ICIEA)*, Singapore, pp. 355-361, DOI: 10.1109/IEA.2018.8387124

Badmos, O., Kopp, A., Bernthaler, T., & Schneider, G. (2020). Image-based defect detection in lithium-ion battery electrode using convolutional neural networks. *Journal of Intelligent Manufacturing*, 31(4), 885–897. DOI: 10.1007/s10845-019-01484-x

Brooks, S. (1998). Markov chain Monte Carlo method and its application. *Journal of the royal statistical society: series D* (the Statistician), 47(1), 69-100. DOI: 10.1007/s10845-019-01484-x

Bui, V. H., Hussain, A., & Kim, H. M. (2019). Q- learning-based operation strategy for community battery energy storage system (CBESS) in microgrid system. *Energies*, 12(9), 1789. Advance online publication. DOI: 10.3390/en12091789

Buiskikh, D., Zakeri, B., Syri, S., & Kauranen, P. (2018). Economic feasibility of flow batteries in grid-scale applications. *In 2018 15th International Conference on the European Energy Market (EEM)* (pp. 1-5). *IEEE.*

Chen, Z., Xiong, R., Lu, J., & Li, X. (2018). Temperature rise prediction of lithium-ion battery suffering external short circuit for all-climate electric vehicles application. *Applied Energy*, 213, 375–383. DOI: 10.1016/j.apenergy.2018.01.068

Cheng, M., Zhang, X., Ran, A., Wei, G., & Sun, H. (2023). Optimal dispatch approach for second-life batteries considering degradation with online SoH estimation. *Renewable & Sustainable Energy Reviews*, 173, 113053. DOI: 10.1016/j.rser.2022.113053

Chettibi, N., Mellit, A., Sulligoi, G., & Pavan, A. M. (2018). Adaptive Neural Network-Based Control of a Hybrid AC/DC Microgrid. *IEEE Transactions on Smart Grid*, 9, 1667–1679.

Deng, C., Ji, X., Rainey, C., Zhang, J., & Lu, W. (2020). Integrating machine learning with human knowledge. *I Science*. https://doi.org/. isci.2020.101656. DOI: 10.1016/j

Deng, L., & Yu, D. (2014), Deep Learning: Methods and Applications, Foundations and Trends® in *Signal Processing:* Vol. 7: No. 3–4, pp 197-387. DOI: 10.1561/2000000039

Dong, L., Wesseloo, J., Potvin, Y., & Li, X. (2016). Discrimination of mine seismic events and blasts using the Fisher classifier, naive Bayesian classifier and logistic regression. *Rock Mechanics and Rock Engineering*, 49(1), 183–211. DOI: 10.1007/s00603-015-0733-y

Dong, R., Du, J., Liu, Y., Heidari, A. A., & Chen, H. (2023). An enhanced deep deterministic policy gradient algorithm for intelligent control of robotic arms. *Frontiers in Neuroinformatics*, 17, 1096053. DOI: 10.3389/fninf.2023.1096053 PMID: 36756212

Duan, J., Yi, Z., Shi, D., Lin, C., Lu, X., & Wang, Z. (2019). Reinforcement-Learning-Based Optimal Control of Hybrid Energy Storage Systems in Hybrid AC–DC Microgrids. *IEEE Transactions on Industrial Informatics*, 15(9), 5355–5364. DOI: 10.1109/TII.2019.2896618

Fasshauer, G. E., & McCourt, M. J. (2012). Stable evaluation of Gaussian radial basis function interpolants. *SIAM Journal on Scientific Computing*, 34(2), A737–A762. DOI: 10.1137/110824784

Foiadelli, F., Longo, M., & Miraftabzadeh, S. (2018). Energy consumption prediction of electric vehicles based on big data approach. Proc. - 2018 *IEEE Int. Conf. Environ. Electr. Eng. 2018 IEEE Ind. Commer. Power Syst. Eur. EEEIC/I CPS Eur.* 2018. DOI: 10.1109/EEEIC.2018.8494573

Forootan, M. M., Larki, I., Zahedi, R., & Ahmadi, A. (2022). Machine Learning and Deep Learning in Energy Systems: A Review. *Sustainability (Basel)*, 14(8), 4832. DOI: 10.3390/su14084832

Gao, T., & Lu, W. (2020). Physical model and machine learning enabled electrolyte channel design for fast charging. *J. Electrochem. Soc.* https://doi.org/DOI: 10.1149/1945-7111/aba096

Gao, T., Ying, L., Dai, M., Shen, G., Hu, P., & Shen, L. (2019). A comparative study of temperature-dependent interfacial heat transfer coefficient prediction methods for 22MnB5 steel in spray quenching process. *International Journal of Thermal Sciences*, 139, 36–60. Advance online publication. DOI: 10.1016/j.ijthermalsci.2018.12.041

Gautamee, H. (2024). *Solar and Wind Energy uptake to reach 5.4 TW from 2024 to 2023*, https://www.mercomindia.com/solar-and-wind-energy-from-2024-to-2033

Gayon-Lombardo, A., Mosser, L., Brandon, N. P., & Cooper, S. J. (2020). Pores for thought: Generative adversarial networks for stochastic reconstruction of 3D multi-phase electrode microstructures with periodic boundaries. *npj Computational Materials*, 6(1), 1–11. DOI: 10.1038/s41524-020-0340-7

Glavic, M., Fonteneau, R., & Ernst, D. (2017). Reinforcement learning for electric power system decision and control: Past considerations and perspectives. *IFAC-PapersOnLine*, 50(1), 6918–692. DOI: 10.1016/j.ifacol.2017.08.1217

Gupta, V., Mishra, V. K., Singhal, P., & Kumar, A. (2022), An Overview of Supervised Machine Learning Algorithm, *2022 11th International Conference on System Modeling & Advancement in Research Trends (SMART)*, Moradabad, India, 2022, pp. 87-92, DOI: 10.1109/SMART55829.2022.10047618

Haider, S. N., Zhao, Q., & Li, X. (2020). Data driven battery anomaly detection based on shape-based clustering for the data centers class. *Journal of Energy Storage*, 29, 101479. DOI: 10.1016/j.est.2020.101479

Hannan, M. A., Hoque, M. M., Mohamed, A., & Ayob, A. (2017). Review of energy storage systems for electric vehicle applications: Issues and challenges. *Renewable & Sustainable Energy Reviews*, 69, 771–789. DOI: 10.1016/j.rser.2016.11.171

Hassan, I. A., Ramadan, H. S., Saleh, M. A., & Hissel, D. (2021). Hydrogen storage technologies for stationary and mobile applications: Review, analysis and perspectives. *Renewable & Sustainable Energy Reviews*, 149, 111311. DOI: 10.1016/j.rser.2021.111311

Hill, C. A., Such, M. C., Chen, D., Gonzalez, J., & Grady, W. M. (2012). Battery Energy Storage for Enabling Integration of Distributed Solar Power Generation. *IEEE Transactions on Smart Grid*, 3(2), 850–857. DOI: 10.1109/TSG.2012.2190113

Hongwen, he & Huang, Ruchen & Meng, Xiangfei & Zhao, Xuyang & Wang, Yong & Li, Menglin. (2022). A novel hierarchical predictive energy management strategy for plug-in hybrid electric bus combined with deep deterministic policy gradient. *Journal of Energy Storage*. 52. 104787. . DOI: 10.1016/j.est.2022.104787

Hu, W., Zheng, L., & Min, Y., (2017). Research on power system transient stability assessment based on deep learning of big data technique. *Power Syst Technol.*, 41(10), 3140–3146.

Huang, Q., Huang, R., & Hao, W., (2019). *Adaptive Power System Emergency Control using Deep Reinforcement Learning*, online. https://arxiv.org/abs/1903.03712

Huang, X., Ye, Y., Xiong, L., Lau, R. Y. K., Jiang, N., & Wang, S. (2016). Time series k -means: A new k -means type smooth subspace clustering for time series data. *Information Sciences*, 367–368, 1–13. DOI: 10.1016/j.ins.2016.05.040

Jain, R.K., Smith, K.M., Culligan, P.J., & Taylor, J.E. (2014). Forecasting energy consumption of multi-family residential buildings using support vector regression: Investigating the impact of temporal and spatial monitoring granularity on performance accuracy. *Appl. Energy* 123, 168–178, https://doi.org/. 2014.02.057. DOI: 10.1016/j.ins.2016.05.040

James, S., Konidaris, G., & Rosman, B. (2017). An analysis of monte carlo tree search. *Proceedings of the AAAI Conference on Artificial Intelligence*, 31(1), DOI: 10.1609/aaai.v31i1.11028

Kai, Huang., Kai, Sun., Yongkang, Guo., Zipeng, Wang., Senmao, Li. (2022). Battery Modeling Considering Hysteresis Effect and Temperature Adaptability. *Energy technology,* 11(3):2201064-2201064. doe: . DOI: 10.1016/j.ins.2016.05.040

Karimi, H., Beheshti, M. T. H., Ramezani, A., & Zareipour, H. (2021). Intelligent control of islanded AC microgrids based on adaptive neuro-fuzzy inference system. *International Journal of Electrical Power & Energy Systems*, 133, 107161. DOI: 10.1016/j.ijepes.2021.107161

Kathirgamanathan, A., Mangina, E., & Finn, D. P. (2021). Development of a soft actor critic deep reinforcement learning approach for harnessing energy flexibility in a large office building. *Energy and AI*, 5, 100101. DOI: 10.1016/j.egyai.2021.100101

Ketkar, N., Moolayil, J., Ketkar, N., & Moolayil, J. (2021). Convolutional neural networks. Deep learning with Python: learns best practices of deep learning models with PyTorch, *Deep Learning with Python*. 197-242. DOI: 10.1016/j.egyai.2021.100101

Khanam, M., Mahboob, T., Imtiaz, W., Ghafoor, H., & Sehar, R. (2015). A Survey on Unsupervised Machine Learning Algorithms for Automation, Classification and Maintenance. *International Journal of Computer Applications*, 119(13), 34–39. DOI: 10.5120/21131-4058

Kim, S., Lee, S., & Cho, K. (2012). Design of high-performance unified circuit for linear and non-linear SVM classifications. J. *Journal of Semiconductor Technology and Science*, 12(2), 162–167. DOI: 10.5573/JSTS.2012.12.2.162

Kocer, M., Cengiz, C., Gezer, M., Gunes, D., Cinar, M., Alboyaci, B., & Onen, A. (2019). Assessment of Battery Storage Technologies for a Turkish Power Network. *Sustainability (Basel)*, 11(13), 3669. DOI: 10.3390/su11133669

Kofinas, P., Dounis, A. I., & Vouros, G. A. (2018a). Fuzzy Q-Learning for multi-agent decentralized energy management in microgrids. *Applied Energy*, 219, 53–67. DOI: 10.1016/j.apenergy.2018.03.017

Kofinas, P., Vouros, G., & Dounis, A. I. (2018b). Energy management in solar microgrid via reinforcement learning using fuzzy reward. *Advances in Building Energy Research*, 12(1), 97–115. DOI: 10.1080/17512549.2017.1314832

Kolambe, M. (2024). Forecasting the Future: A Comprehensive Review of Time Series Prediction Techniques. *Journal of Electrical Systems.*, 20(2s), 575–586. DOI: 10.52783/jes.1478

Kumar, N. M., Chand, A. A., Malvoni, M., Prasad, K. A., Mamun, K. A., Islam, F., & Chopra, S. S. (2020). Distributed energy resources and the application of AI, IOT, and blockchain in smart grids. *Energies*, 13(21), 5739. DOI: 10.3390/en13215739

LeCun, Y., Bengio, Y., & Hinton, G. (2015). Deep learning. *Nature*, 521(7553), 436–444. DOI: 10.1038/nature14539 PMID: 26017442

Lee, N. H., Kim, S. B., Sok, V., Kang, S. H., & Nam, S. R. (2019). A study on deep neural network-based DC offset removal for phase estimation in power systems. *Energies*, 12, 1–19.

Lee, S., & Choi, D. H. (2020). Energy management of smart home with home appliances, energy storage system and electric vehicle: A hierarchical deep reinforcement learning approach. *Sensors (Basel)*, 20(7), 2157. Advance online publication. DOI: 10.3390/s20072157 PMID: 32290345

Li, Q., Qu, H., Liu, Z., Zhou, N., Sun, W., Sigg, S., & Li, J. (2019). AF-DCGAN: Amplitude feature deep convolutional GAN for fingerprint construction in indoor localization systems. *IEEE Transactions on Emerging Topics in Computational Intelligence*, 5(3), 468–480. DOI: 10.1109/TETCI.2019.2948058

Li, S., He, H., & Li, J. (2019). Big data driven lithium-ion battery modeling method based on SDAE-ELM algorithm and data pre-processing technology. *Applied Energy*, 242, 1259–1273. DOI: 10.1016/j.apenergy.2019.03.154

Li, S., Li, J., & Wang, H. (2019). Big data driven Lithium-ion battery modeling method: a cyber- physical system approach. Proc. - 2019 *IEEE Int. Conf. Ind. Cyber Phys. Syst. ICPS* 2019 161–166. DOI: 10.1109/ICPHYS.2019.8780152

Li, X., Zhang, T., & Liu, Y. (2019). Detection of voltage anomalies in spacecraft storage batteries based on a deep belief network. [Switzerland]. *Sensors (Basel)*, 19(21), 1–21. DOI: 10.3390/s19214702 PMID: 31671886

Liu, D., Zhou, L., Pan, R., Chen, Z., & Bei, Z. (2021). Lithium-ion battery state-of-health online estimation based on multi-scale relevance vector machine. *Applied Energy*, 306, 118174.

Liu, J., & Chen, Z. (2019). Remaining useful life prediction of lithium-ion batteries based on health indicator and Gaussian process regression model. *IEEE Access : Practical Innovations, Open Solutions*, 7, 39474–39484. DOI: 10.1109/ACCESS.2019.2905740

Lopes, N., & Ribeiro, B. (2015). Deep Belief Networks (DBNs). In *Machine Learning for Adaptive Many-Core Machines - A Practical Approach. Studies in Big Data* (Vol. 7). Springer., DOI: 10.1007/978-3-319-06938-8_8

Luanna Maria, S. S., & Peng, W. (2021). Control strategy to smooth wind power output using battery energy storage system: A review, *Journal of Energy Storage*, Volume 35, 102252, ISSN 2352-152X, DOI: 10.1016/j.est.2021.102252

Lucu, M., Martinez-Laserna, E., Gandiaga, I., Liu, K., Camblong, H., Widanage, W. D., & Marco, J. (2020). Data-driven nonparametric Li-ion battery ageing model aiming at learning from real operation data - Part B: Cycling operation. *Journal of Energy Storage*, 101410, 101410. Advance online publication. DOI: 10.1016/j.est.2020.101410

Luo, X., Wang, J., Dooner, M., & Clarke, J. (2015). Overview of current development in electrical energy storage technologies and the application potential in power system operation. *Applied Energy*, 137, 511–536. DOI: 10.1016/j.apenergy.2014.09.081

Ma, L., Xie, W., & Zhan, Y. (2019). Blister defect detection based on convolutional neural network for polymer lithium-ion battery. *Applied Sciences (Basel, Switzerland)*, 9(6), 1085. DOI: 10.3390/app9061085

Mbuwir, B. V., Kaffash, M., & Deconinck, G. (2018). Battery scheduling in a residential multi- carrier energy system using reinforcement learning. *2018 IEEE Int. Conf. Commun. Control. Comput. Technol. Smart Grids, SmartGridComm* 2018. DOI: 10.1109/SmartGridComm.2018.8587412

Miric, M., Pagani, M., & El Sawy, O. (2021). When and who do platform companies acquire? Understanding the role of acquisitions in the growth of platform companies. *Management Information Systems Quarterly*, 45(4), 2159–2174. DOI: 10.25300/MISQ/2022/16374

Mishra, M., & Srivastava, M. (2014, August). A view of artificial neural network. *In 2014 international conference on advances in engineering & technology research (ICAETR-2014)* (pp. 1-3). IEEE. DOI: 10.1016/j.egyai.2021.100101

Molina, M. (2017). Energy Storage and Power Electronics Technologies: A Strong Combination to Empower the Transformation to the Smart Grid. *Proceedings of the IEEE*. PP. 1-29. DOI: 10.1109/JPROC.2017.2702627

Morcillo-Jimenez, R., Mesa, J., Gómez-Romero, J., Vila, M. A., & Martin-Bautista, M. J. (2024). Deep learning for prediction of energy consumption: An applied use case in an office building. *Applied Intelligence*, 54(7), 5813–5825. DOI: 10.1007/s10489-024-05451-9

Mosavi, A., Salimi, M., Faizollahzadeh Ardabili, S., Rabczuk, T., Shamshirband, S., & Varkonyi-Koczy, A. R. (2019). State of the art of machine learning models in energy systems, a systematic review. *Energies*, 12(7), 1301. DOI: 10.3390/en12071301

Murnane, M., & Ghazel, A. (2017). *A closer look at state of charge (SOC) and state of health (SOH) estimation techniques for batteries. Analog devices.* https://www.analog.com/media/en/technical-documentation/technical-articles/acloser-look-at-state-of-charge-and-state-healthestimation- techniques.pdf

Mviri, F. (2022). Battery storage systems in electric power grid: A review. *Journal of Physics: Conference Series*, 2276(1), 012016. DOI: 10.1088/1742-6596/2276/1/012016

Naskath, J., Sivakamasundari, G., & Begum, A. A. S. (2023). A study on different deep learning algorithms used in deep neural nets: MLP SOM and DBN. *Wireless Personal Communications*, 128(4), 2913–2936. DOI: 10.1007/s11277-022-10079-4 PMID: 36276226

Njema, George G., Ouma, Russel Ben O., Kibet, Joshua K., (2024). A Review on the Recent Advances in Battery Development and Energy Storage Technologies, *Journal of Renewable Energy*, 2329261, 35 pages, . DOI: 10.1007/s11277-022-10079-4 PMID: 36276226

Ortiz, J. P., Valladolid, J. D., Garcia, C. L., Novillo, G., & Berrezueta, F. (2019). Analysis of machine learning techniques for the intelligent diagnosis of Ni-MH battery cells. *2018 IEEE Int. Autumn Meet. Power, Electron. Comput. ROPEC 2018.* DOI: 10.1109/ROPEC.2018.8661446

Parida, S., Dehuri, S., & Cho, S. B. (2014), Application of genetic algorithms and Gaussian Naïve Bayesian approach in pipeline for cognitive state classification, *IEEE International Advance Computing Conference (IACC),* Gurgaon, India, pp. 1237-1242, DOI: 10.1109/IAdCC.2014.6779504

Patil, M. A., Agade, P., Hariharan, K. S., Kolake, S. M., Song, T., Yeo, T., & Doo, S. (2015). A novel multistage Support Vector Machine based approach for Li ion battery remaining useful life estimation. *Applied Energy*, 159, 285–297. DOI: 10.1016/j.apenergy.2015.08.119

Pisner, D. A., & Schnyer, D. M. (2020). Support vector machine. [Academic Press.]. *Machine Learning*, 101–121.

Prakash, K., Ali, M., Siddique, M. N. I., Chand, A. A., Kumar, N. M., Dong, D., & Pota, H. R. (2022). A review of battery energy storage systems for ancillary services in distribution grids: Current status, challenges and future directions. *Frontiers in Energy Research*, 10, 971704. DOI: 10.3389/fenrg.2022.971704

Prasad, S. (2023), *IEEFA projects exponential growth of battery storage assets in India,*https://www.downtoearth.org.in/renewable-energy/ieefa-projects-exponential-growth-of-battery-storage-assets-in-india-87343

Qiang, W., & Zhongli, Z. (2011), Reinforcement learning model, algorithms and its application, *2011 International Conference on Mechatronic Science, Electric Engineering and Computer (MEC)*, Jilin, China, pp. 1143-1146, Doi: DOI: 10.1109/MEC.2011.6025669

Rajesh, T., & Seetha, M. (2022). Optimization-Assisting Dual-Step Clustering of Time Series Data. [IJDST]. *International Journal of Distributed Systems and Technologies*, 13(1), 1–18. DOI: 10.4018/IJDST.313632

Ram, J. P., Pillai, D. S., Ghias, A. M., & Rajasekar, N. (2020). Performance enhancement of solar PV systems applying P&O assisted Flower Pollination Algorithm (FPA). *Solar Energy*, 199, 214–229. DOI: 10.1016/j.solener.2020.02.019

Ramos, F. O., Pinheiro, A. L., Lima, R. N., Neto, M. M. B., Junior, W. A. S., & Bezerra, L. G. S. (2021). A Real Case Analysis of a Battery Energy Storage System for Energy Time Shift, Demand Management, and Reactive Control. *In Proceedings of the 2021 IEEE PES Innovative Smart Grid Technologies Conference* - Latin America (ISGT Latin America), Lima, Peru, 15–17 September 2021; pp. 1–5.

Rekioua, D. (2023). Energy storage systems for photovoltaic and wind systems: A review. *Energies*, 16(9), 3893. DOI: 10.3390/en16093893

Research and Markets. (2024), *Global Battery Energy Storage System Market Forecast to 2029*: Increasing Opportunities in Rural Electrification Projects Worldwide and Rising Demand for Power Supply from Data Centers, https://www.globenewswire.com/news-release/2024/08/15/2930740/0/en/Global-Battery-Energy-Storage-System-Market-Forecast-to-2029-Increasing-Opportunities-in-Rural-Electrification-Projects-Worldwide-and-Rising-Demand-for-Power-Supply-from-Data-Cente.html

Richardson, R. R., Osborne, M. A., & Howey, D. A. (2017). Gaussian process regression for forecasting battery state of health. *Journal of Power Sources*, 357, 209–219. Advance online publication. DOI: 10.1016/j.jpowsour.2017.05.004

Rocchetta, R., Bellani, L., Compare, M., Zio, E., & Patelli, E. (2019). A reinforcement learning framework for optimal operation and maintenance of power grids. *Applied Energy*, 241, 291–301. DOI: 10.1016/j.apenergy.2019.03.027

Sahinoglu, G. O., Pajovic, M., Shingle, Z., Wang, Y., Orlik, P. V., & Wada, T. (2017). Battery state-of-charge estimation based on regular/ recurrent Gaussian process regression. *IEEE Transactions on Industrial Electronics*, 65(5), 4311–4321. DOI: 10.1109/TIE.2017.2764869

Salehizadeh, M. R., & Soltaniyan, S. (2016). Application of fuzzy Q-learning for electricity market modeling by considering renewable power penetration. *Renewable & Sustainable Energy Reviews*, 56, 1172–1181. DOI: 10.1016/j.rser.2015.12.020

Salleh, M. N. M., Talpur, N., & Hussain, K. (2017). Adaptive neuro-fuzzy inference system: Overview, strengths, limitations, and solutions. In Data Mining and Big Data: 2nd International Conference, DMBD 2017, Fukuoka, Japan, July 27–August 1, 2017, *Springer International Publishing.Proceedings*, 2, 527–535.

Samuel, J. (2020). *Can Battery Storage Propel India's Energy Transition*https://science.thewire.in/economy/energy/can-battery-storage-propel-indias-energy-transition

Sarker, I. H. (2021a). A Comprehensive Overview on Techniques, Taxonomy, Applications and Research Directions. *SN Computer Science*, 2(6), 420. DOI: 10.1007/s42979-021-00815-1 PMID: 34426802

Sarker, I. H. (2021b). Real-World Applications and Research Directions. *SN Computer Science*, 2(3), 160. DOI: 10.1007/s42979-021-00592-x PMID: 33778771

Sathya, R., & Abraham, A. (2013). Comparison of Supervised and Unsupervised Learning Algorithms for Pattern Classification [IJARAI]. *International Journal of Advanced Research in Artificial Intelligence*, 2(2). Advance online publication. DOI: 10.14569/IJARAI.2013.020206

Severson, K. A., Attia, P. M., Jin, N., Perkins, N., Jiang, B., Yang, Z., Chen, M. H., Akyol, M., Herring, P. K., & Fraggedakis, D. (2019). Data- driven prediction of battery cycle life before capacity degradation. *Nature Energy*, 4(5), 383–391. Advance online publication. DOI: 10.1038/s41560-019-0356-8

Shahabi, H., Shirzadi, A., Ronoud, S., Asadi, S., Pham, B. T., Mansouripour, F., & Bui, D. T. (2021). Flash flood susceptibility mapping using a novel deep learning model based on deep belief network, back propagation and genetic algorithm. *Geoscience Frontiers*, 12(3), 101100. DOI: 10.1016/j.gsf.2020.10.007

Sharma, A. (2019). *Analyzing Opportunities and Barriers of Using Solar PV and Battery Energy Storage System (BESS) on Apartments or new Residential Complex* (Doctoral dissertation, University of New South Wales Sydney).

Sharma, A. (2024)., *India launches National Electricity Plan to meet rising power demand. CNBCTV18.*https://www.cnbctv18.com/energy/india-launches-national-electricity-plan-to-meet-rising-power-demand-19492717.htm

Shen, S., Sadoughi, M., Li, M., Wang, Z., & Hu, C. (2020a). Deep convolutional neural networks with ensemble learning and transfer learning for capacity estimation of lithium-ion batteries. *Applied Energy*, 114296, 114296. Advance online publication. DOI: 10.1016/j.apenergy.2019.114296

Shen, S, Sadoughi, M., Li, M., Wang, Z., & Hu, C. (2020b). Deep convolutional neural networks with ensemble learning and transfer learning for capacity estimation of lithium-ion batteries. *Applied Energy*, 260(), 114296.doi: . DOI: 10.1016/j.apenergy.2019.114296

Singh, A., Thakur, N., & Sharma, A. (2016). A review of supervised machine learning algorithms. 2016, *3rd International Conference on Computing for Sustainable Global Development (INDIACom),* 1310-1315.

Srivastava, N., Hinton, G., Krizhevsky, A., Sutskever, I., & Salakhutdinov, R. (2014). Dropout: A simple way to prevent neural networks from overfitting. *Journal of Machine Learning Research*, 15, 1929–1958.

Stecca, M., Elizondo, L. R., Soeiro, T. B., Bauer, P., & Palensky, P. (2020). A comprehensive review of the integration of battery energy storage systems into distribution networks. *IEEE Open Journal of the Industrial Electronics Society*, 1, 46–65. DOI: 10.1109/OJIES.2020.2981832

Suresh, C., & Saini, R. P. (2020). Review on solar thermal energy storage technologies and their geometrical configurations. *International Journal of Energy Research*, 44(6), 4163–4195. DOI: 10.1002/er.5143

Sutton, R. S., & Barto, A. G. (1998). Reinforcement Learning: An Introduction. *IEEE Transactions on Neural Networks*, 9(5), 1054–1054. DOI: 10.1109/TNN.1998.712192

Takagishi, Y., Yamanaka, T., & Yamaue, T. (2019). Machine learning approaches for designing mesoscale structure of li-ion battery electrodes. *Batteries*, 5(3), 1–13. DOI: 10.3390/batteries5030054

Talluri, G., Lozito, G. M., Grasso, F., Iturrino Garcia, C., & Luchetta, A. (2021). Optimal Battery Energy Storage System Scheduling within Renewable Energy Communities. *Energies*, 14(24), 8480. DOI: 10.3390/en14248480

Tang, X., Yao, K., Liu, B., Hu, W., & Gao, F. (2018). Long-term battery voltage, power, and surface temperature prediction using a model- based extreme learning machine. *Energies*, 11(1), 86. Advance online publication. DOI: 10.3390/en11010086

Ukey, N., Yang, Z., Li, B., Zhang, G., Hu, Y., & Zhang, W. (2023). Survey on exact knn queries over high-dimensional data space. *Sensors (Basel)*, 23(2), 629. DOI: 10.3390/s23020629 PMID: 36679422

Van Houdt, G., Mosquera, C., & Nápoles, G. (2020). A review on the long short-term memory model. *Artificial Intelligence Review*, 53(8), 5929–5955. DOI: 10.1007/s10462-020-09838-1

Veeraraghavan, A., Adithya, V., Bhave, A., & Akella, S., (2018). Battery aging estimation with deep learning. *2017 IEEE Transp. Electrify. Conf. ITEC-* India 2017 2018-Janua, 1–4. . DOI: 10.1016/j.apenergy.2019.114296

Wang, J., Liu, P., Hicks-Garner, J., Sherman, E., Soukiazian, S., Verbrugge, M., Tataria, H., Musser, J., & Finamore, P. (2011). Cycle-life model for graphite-LiFePO4 cells. *Journal of Power Sources*, 196(8), 3942–3948. DOI: 10.1016/j.jpowsour.2010.11.134

Wang, J., Lu, S., Wang, S. H., & Zhang, Y. D. (2022). A review on extreme learning machine. *Multimedia Tools and Applications*, 81(29), 41611–41660. DOI: 10.1007/s11042-021-11007-7

Watkins, C. J. C. H., & Dayan, P. (1992). Q-learning. *Machine Learning*, 8(3-4), 279–292. DOI: 10.1007/BF00992698

Wu, B., Han, S., Shin, K. G., & Lu, W. (2018). Application of artificial neural networks in design of lithium-ion batteries. *Journal of Power Sources*, 395, 128–136. DOI: 10.1016/j.jpowsour.2018.05.040

Wu, N., & Wang, H. (2018). Deep learning adaptive dynamic programming for real time energy management and control strategy of micro-grid. *Journal of Cleaner Production*, 204, 1169–1177. DOI: 10.1016/j.jclepro.2018.09.052

Wu, Y., Tan, H., Peng, J., Zhang, H., & He, H. (2019). Deep reinforcement learning of energy management with continuous control strategy and traffic information for a series-parallel plug-in hybrid electric bus. *Applied Energy*, 247, 454–466. DOI: 10.1016/j.apenergy.2019.04.021

Xi, L., Chen, J., Huang, Y., Xue, T., Zhang, T., & Zhang, Y. (2018). Smart generation control based on deep reinforcement learning with the ability of action self-optimization. *Sci Sin Inf*, 48(10), 1430–1449. DOI: 10.1360/N112018-00072

Xiong, T., Bao, Y., Hu, Z., & Chiong, R. (2015). Forecasting interval time series using a fully complex-valued RBF neural network with DPSO and PSO algorithms. *Information Sciences*, 305, 77–92. DOI: 10.1016/j.ins.2015.01.029

Ying, L., Gao, T., Dai, M., & Hu, P. (2017). Investigation of interfacial heat transfer mechanism for 7075-T6 aluminum alloy in HFQ hot forming process. *Applied Thermal Engineering*, 118, 266–282. Advance online publication. DOI: 10.1016/j.applthermaleng.2017.02.107

Yoldas, Y., Goren, S., & Onen, A. (2020). Optimal Control of Microgrids with Multi-stage Mixed-integer Nonlinear Programming Guided Q -learning Algorithm. *Journal of Modern Power Systems and Clean Energy*, 8(6), 1151–1159. DOI: 10.35833/MPCE.2020.000506

Yuan, G., Wang, H., Khazaei, E., & Khan, B. (2021). Collaborative advanced machine learning techniques in optimal energy management of hybrid AC/DC IoT-based microgrids. *Ad Hoc Networks*, 122, 102657. DOI: 10.1016/j.adhoc.2021.102657

Zhang, Z. H., Zeng, S., & Jiang, D. J. (2022). Analysis and Improvement of the Q-iteration Method. [). IOP Publishing.]. *Journal of Physics: Conference Series*, 2147(1), 012005. DOI: 10.1088/1742-6596/2147/1/012005

Zheng, Z., Chen, B., Xu, Y., Fritz, N., Gurumukhi, Y., Cook, J., Ates, M.N., Miljkovic, N., Braun, P.V., & Wang, P. (2020). A Gaussian process-based crack pattern modeling approach for battery anode materials design. *J. Electrochem. En.Conv. Stor.* 18, 011011, https://doi.org/. 4046938. DOI: 10.1088/1742-6596/2147/1/012005

Zhou, P., He, Z., Han, T., Li, X., Lai, X., Yan, L., Lv, T., Xie, J., & Zheng, Y. (2020). A rapid classification method of the retired LiCoxNiyMn1 x yO2 batteries for electric vehicles. *Energy Reports*, 6, 672–683. DOI: 10.1016/j.egyr.2020.03.013

Zhou, X., Hsieh, S. J., Peng, B., & Hsieh, D. (2017). Cycle life estimation of lithium-ion polymer batteries using artificial neural network and support vector machine with time-resolved thermography. *Microelectronics and Reliability*, 79, 48–58. DOI: 10.1016/j.microrel.2017.10.013

Zhu, S., Zhao, N., & Sha, J. (2019). Predicting battery life with early cyclic data by machine learning. *Energy Storage*, 1(6), 1–5. DOI: 10.1002/est2.98

# Chapter 7
# Artificial Intelligence in Lithium-Ion Battery Predictions: A Comparative Study

**R. Shipa**
https://orcid.org/0000-0001-5074-6087
*Avinashilingam Institute for Home Science and Higher Education for Women, India*

**K. Thrisha**
https://orcid.org/0000-0002-3274-3621
*Avinashilingam Institute for Home Science and Higher Education for Women, India*

**Karuppasamy Periyakaruppan**
https://orcid.org/0000-0002-9503-1728
*Dayananda Sagar College of Engineering, India*

**R. Saratha**
https://orcid.org/0000-0001-6833-3061
*Avinashilingam Institute for Home Science and Higher Education for Women, India*

**U. Mithra**
https://orcid.org/0000-0003-4828-0630
*Avinashilingam Institute for Home Science and Higher Education for Women, India*

**Rajapandian Varatharaj**
*Sri Ramakrishna Mission Vidyalaya College of Arts and Science, India*

## ABSTRACT

*In battery development, process from the discovery of a new material to testing the performance of the battery is a prolonged one. This time-consuming process can be overcome by implementing Artificial Intelligence (AI). The need for AI in lithium-ion batteries (LIBs) can predict the specific capacity, efficiency, performance, and durability of a battery earlier. It could aid in the development of the most reliable advanced batteries with reduced time consumption. Prospects of AI in LIBs can facilitate advanced predictions in terms of State-of-Art battery management sys-*

DOI: 10.4018/979-8-3373-2530-9.ch007

*tems (BMS) such as states of charge (SOC), health (SOH), available power (SoAP), and remaining useful life (RUL) of batteries by various methodologies of Machine Learning (ML). During a pandemic situation experimentation in the laboratory may be difficult however to give an insight and implement AI into research pave the way to do more innovation in their respective fields. An overview of the applications of AI in LIB predictions is discussed in this article based on a review of earlier research works worldwide.*

## INTRODUCTION

Utilization of fossil fuels have increased during last few decades, which increased the level of carbon dioxide output which caused pollution, global warming, demand for fuels, and other disadvantages to our environment [Khawaja, 2023; Entezari, 2023; Kilic, 2023; Zazoum,2023; Boujelbene,2023; Muhammad,2023; Qiao, 2023; Dan, 2023]. For energy storage systems, storing and supplying energy quickly from renewable energy sources requires high charging and discharging rates with low cost. Secondary batteries have played a vital role in recent decades, and are rechargeable and reusable [Shi, 2023; Li Weng, 2023; Sesidhar, 2023; Bai, Y., 2023; Vakharia, V, 2023; Xu, 2023; Faraji-Niri, 2023]. Because of its unique characteristic features, lithium-ion battery technology has made tremendous progress in electric vehicles, mobile consumers, and electronics during the last two decades [Tudoroiu, 2023; Mehta, 2023]. But recent advancements have greatly enhanced the electrochemical properties of lithium-ion batteries with little drawbacks. For lithium-ion batteries (LIBS), the main limitation is the slow movement and diffusion of LIBS in the solid-state electrode material [Rundo, 2023; Zhou, 2023; Kosuru, 2023; Wang, 2023; Hong, 2023]. Despite the significant improvements in the electrochemical performance of lithium ions by manual calculations and experimental studies [He, 2023; Yao, 2023; Hu, 2023]. Artificial intelligence can solve the complex problems faced while using Li-ion batteries. Incorporating machine learning (ML) into artificial intelligence (AI) finds optimal solutions to problems that can be precisely solved [Duquesnoy, 2022; Zhu, 2023; Shi, 2023; Liu, 2023; Rauf, 2023]. The largest collection of battery data at the time paves a way to lacking of quality data. To rectify this problem, Foster et.al have built databases of chemicals that could be analyzed using ML algorithms, looking for improving the performance of battery electrolytes, the material between the electrodes. As with other cells in a battery, the chemistry of the electrolyte could be altered for improving required properties including energy efficiency, current density, and to reduce an unwanted property, such as toxicity [Rimsha,2023; Korkmaz, M. 2023]. This review first describes artificial intelligence and its branch of machine learning. The second section describes the need for AI in

LIB prediction and the methodologies of ML adopted to learn, the future outlook of ML in LIBs, and the pros and cons of ML in LIBS prediction and to analyze the battery charge, capacity, health, lifespan of LIBs.

## Material Synthesis

The development of LIBs is driven by breakthroughs in advanced electrode materials. High-throughput making or synthesis allows electrode materials with other different concepts, electrolyte synthesis, and any optimized compositions of any other material to be quickly prepared for subsequent electrochemical analysis and structural with the help of ML data acquisition. This can accelerate the discovery and optimization of electrolyte and electrode materials. Microplate technology is currently being developed to synthesize and screen electrode materials as well as in the development of electrolytes synthesis and optimize additive content with high throughput. These methods are still having some limitations in the modulation and adjustment of material composition, which falls short of the general requirements of various machine learning datasets. The high-throughput material synthesis has not yet been studied for a variety of materials with new microstructures, controllable dopants, different crystal structures, defects, and interfaces. Classifying by ML algorithm can be done and synthesized easily [Payette, 2023].

## Material Characterization

Before mounting electrode materials or electrolytes on batteries, material characterization is performed sequentially to measure and confirm their key properties. Material characterization can be easily improved, significantly reducing the effort of characterization analysis. In recent years, the development of new characterization techniques for battery research has led to the development of high-throughput diagnostic tools in a variety of ways to assist in monitoring not only the pressure of lithium-ion batteries but also the structural, chemical, and thermal evolution of materials. However, it is important to develop a high-throughput characterization method for lithium-ion batteries for analysis. In addition, to take advantage of current characterization techniques, it is necessary to develop advanced robot tools and new algorithms [Liu, 2023].

## Battery Fabrication

Automated production of high-throughput batteries is very important as it can facilitate subsequent optimization of batteries and testing based on real-world conditions. The development of 100 conventional batteries typically begins with manual processes as well as small batches, simplifications, and batch laboratory equipment. Electrodes, related components, and overall elements typically have suboptimal internal structures and often have very low mass loads. This is much lower than the requirements of real commercial applications. Also, it cannot provide reliable datasets for machine learning. Therefore, high-integration LIBs manufacturing processes are required to obtain accurate, high-throughput data from initial automated electrode synthesis to final battery test systems. Ideally, a highly integrated battery manufacturing system could be used to automatically select and optimize the positive, negative, binder, and conductive additives, then perform automatic mixing to prepare the electrode slurry. The suspension is then applied to the current collector, completely dried and calendared with positive and negative film, for automatic assembly into batteries with electrolyte and separator. Therefore, batteries can be easily manufactured by processing and labeling data in an ML method.

## Electrochemical Testing

High-performance electrochemical battery testing is the key to generating huge and robust machine learning datasets. Accurate battery life, capacity, speed, performance, and impedance of a battery is measured accurately by a variety of electrochemical methods such as cyclic voltammetry (CV), constant current charge/discharge (GCD), and electrochemical impedance spectroscopy (EIS) can be used with high precision and accuracy. To generate vast amounts of meaningful data, batteries must be quickly tested in parallel under real-world operating conditions, such as varying currents, voltages, powers, temperatures, mass loads, and cell designs. When a machine learning model is trained on this data, it can further speed up the battery testing process by filtering out potentially inefficient batteries which are based on their initial cycles. For example, using the first five cycles of battery performance. Severson et al., using a trained machine learning model, were able to classify cells into two groups, the low-living group and the high-living group, with a test error of 4.9% [Severson,2019].

Thus, advances in ML with LIBs may lead to holistic battery modeling that transcends (i) time, length, and mechanism. (ii) speed-up and simplifies calculations to be performed in the field on the battery itself. (iii) high-performance computational and experimental data generation; (iv) speed-up battery production in less time; (v) material testing and helps in identifying material characteristics for the battery making (vi) study about the material science either in battery making or in other aspects also and more in future development with advance methodology of ML in AI.

## Pros and Cons of ML in LIBs

ML requires having high-quality and structured data sets. The major advantages of machine learning in LIBs prediction are it gives good estimation accuracy and it is applicable in dynamic operating conditions. Also, there is no need for physical-based models to estimate the battery parameters [Song, 2023]. Most likely, ML in battery production is expeditious, because it learns and predicts the battery parameters, Material science of electrodes, electrolytes, and fabrication of batteries with less time consumption with the help of previous experimental data or another database. Reduction of time and experiments are the great benefits of machine learning in LIBs. High computational efforts are needed for the prediction of the state of an art and other parameters like charge/discharge, density, and capacity of LIBs are put at the disadvantage of ML [Cao, 2023]. Also, the Estimation accuracy is sensitive to the quantity and quality of training data. Although ML in LIBs is an expeditious prediction, collecting enough and more data for estimation stands as cons in battery prediction.

## Consolidation of Prediction

Basically, not every method by machine learning can predict every parameter of lithium-ion battery. The consolidation of methodologies adopted by scientists to predict the lithium-ion batteries parameters are given below in the Table 1.

*Table 1. Prediction of LIBs and their methodologies*

| S.NO | PREDICTION IN LIBs | METHODOLOGIES |
|---|---|---|
| 1. | SoAP | FIS, AFIS, ANN |
| 2. | SOH | ANN, LR, RNN, RFR, SVR, SVM, KF |
| 3. | SOC | ANN, RNN, GPR, RFR, SVM, BO, KF |
| 4. | RUL | GPR, LR, RVM, SVR, SVM, BO, CNN, DNN |

## RESULT AND DISCUSSIONS

To predict the future performance of LIBs, for example, estimating how far an electric vehicle go and develop a better battery for working, how long a battery can be used (lifetime), capacity, charge, battery charging rate, and how the battery can withstand the load of a particular device, these methods make predictions particularly difficult. Perhaps knowing the battery's state of charge (SOC) based on one LIB charge/discharge cycle or the battery's health state (SOH), which depends on many charge/discharges process, remaining number of life cycles of batteries is determined according to battery condition and working. For that prediction, implementing ML which is the subset of artificial intelligence can make prediction much easier, less time consuming, and most importantly it tends to give the prediction with the least percentage of error than manual algorithmic calculation. A few commonly used ML methods are ANN (artificial neural network), LR (linear regression), GRP (Gaussian regression process), RFR (random forest regression), RNN (recurrent neural network), support vector machine (SVM), and support vector regression (SVR) are summarized in Table.1. The density function theory (DFT) [Scarpelli, 2023] guided by ML and along with ML Barrett et.al adopted Fourier transform infrared spectroscopy, which determines the unknown concentrations of battery electrolyte, capacity, and performance of lithium-ion batteries [Scarpelli, 2023]. The adaptive neural architecture of fuzzy & neural fuzzy model is quite a divergent method that predicts SoAP [Barrett, 2013], SOC, SOH [Ziyilluo, 2020; Syed, 2020; Tianhangau, 2021] with less time consumption. Ref. [Man- Fai, 2020] also describes the SOC prediction of Electrical Vehicle (EV) batteries by the unique architecture of fuzzy and boosted decision tree of machine learning and proves that fuzzy methods are less likely to be complicated than other manual algorithm methods.The schematic “Closed Loop Optimization” (CLO) is done experimentally by adding 100 cyclic battery data (performance data) to Bayesian Optimization which predicts the SOC, and SOH of batteries & to make advancements in battery productions. Methods like ANN, RNN, SVM, SVR, GPR, RFR, and a few more methods give the high accuracy of State of art and estimation of the battery management system (BMS). Artificial neural network (ANN) methods are greatly used to envisage SOC, SOH, and RUL of a battery. SOC of LIBs by ANN method shows a 10% error at 250 °C and 17% error at 200 [Ghorbani Kashkooli, 2019], nevertheless describes SOC prediction of a LIB of plug electric vehicle (PEVs) by ANN at <5% of error. Hamed et. al demonstrated the network's ability to capture I/O dependencies by ANN prediction system was found to be achieved a root mean square error (RMSE=1.17%) for 1.81% battery discharge and charge data. Furthermore, they described calendar aging battery data under various aging conditions used to train a new ANN for SOH evaluation using an RMSE of 1.67% [Abakumov, 2020]. ANN models are designed to predict SOC scores based on load classification including post-processing and over fitting enhancements. Bai et. al., have established a general model-free method constructed with ANN and Kalman filters for improving health care of LIBs [Bai, 2020]. There are different types of ANN predictions, and the main algorithms used for battery deep learning such as CNNs (convolutional neural networks), DNNs (deep neural networks), RNNs (recurrent neural networks), and extensions of CNNs and RNNs

[Wei, 2022]. Those ANN, RNN, CNN, and DNN are discovered as one-dimensional data, which tends to observe SOC and RUL prediction very easily. Ref [Man- Fai, 2020; Ghorbani Kashkooli, 2019; Abakumov, 2020; Bai, 2020; Wei, 2022], explains and describes the artificial neural network and its various types like CNN, RNN, and DNN of technique in algorithmic patterns. Wei et al. revealed that the accurate RUL prediction of a battery is critical for battery management systems (BMS) to adapt management strategies to ensure battery performance, safety, and longevity [Wei, 2022]. Predicting the RUL of a battery is important to guide how to reuse or recycle the battery. Also suggest the random forest technique which introduces input as the changes in voltage over time, produces a typical prediction error of RUL in 3.3%, which is superior to linear models, support vector machines, and neural networks. Tianhangau [Tianhangau, 2021] determines the SOC with only 1.3% of error by adopting random forest regression. To predict RUL mainly regression algorithms (RA) are used. The linear regression (LR) algorithm is applied when the output is a continuous variable. Simple linear models provide fast computation time and prediction deployed to devices; it may also probably help in predicting the state of health value. Estimating battery life using supervised learning applies data-driven LR approach to pre-depletion LIB life based on initial cycle discharge data of lithium-ion batteries. The predicted dataset of LIB cycle below fast charging circumstances and discharge voltage curves as inputs to regression were discussed. In this check, the regression setting test error (RSTE) was found to be 9.1% for first 100 cycles, and the classification setting test error (CSTE) was found to be 4.9% for first 5 cycles of data [Jiang, 2023; Ye, 2023].

The Gaussian Process Regression (GPR) review mentioned in states that GPR is an ML approach that can handle the complexity of complex models similar to Bayes' nonparametric approach [Atefeh Daemi, 2019; Ali, 2022]. The current, capacity, temperature, and voltage-based model for predicting reduction capacity and RUL of LIB at dynamic conditions. According to review, Sahinoglu et al. assessed the SOC of LIBs using GPR. This takes battery parameters such as voltage, current, and temperature as inputs. The Gaussian process provides SOC prediction with 0.8% accuracy and is superior than support vector machines (SVMs) and neural networks (NNs) [Lombardo, 2022]. Supporting vector regression (SVR) is used for data cleansing, such as inputting misplaced data or an altering outputting data. A SVM is a simplification of a random forest in which accomplished features not partitioned along single input direction, but are classified simultaneously in a multidimensional space. In particular, the SVM protocol is efficient for spare data added in factorization machine [Huang, 2017]. The Inputs to the SVM model are the discharge capacity of LIBs and temperature rise when LIBs perform. To estimate SOH between consecutive battery cycles to be less than 6.4%, ML's carrier vector machine took into account voltage, power, number of cycles, and temperature, and showed that RUL and SOH were strongly affected by environmental conditions and loads [Li, 2020]. SVR has more advantages over linear regression (LR) algorithms while working with non-linear discrete datasets. This is due to data exist in an original feature space projected into higher feature space by means of Kernel functions resulting in more accurate values. In addition to SVM / SVR, GPR has advantages over linear regression that processes non-linearly separable datasets [Kaidi Gao, 2022; Chen Yuan, 2022; Naya, 2023]. SVMs / SVRs typically requires less data for training to attain high accuracy output compared to deep learning (DL). From the work of ref. [Busu, 2021], they observed that the KF is an algorithm that combines information about the state of a system using prediction based on physical models and measurement. KF is more appropriate for linear systems whereas EKF (extended Kalman filter) and UKF (unscented Kalman filter) added algorithms to be fit for nonlinear systems [Wang, 2023; Azis, 2019]. Azis et.al. [Azis, 2019] showed that the SOH was estimated online using DKF (dual Kalman filter) and SVM demonstrating the ability between least variance estimation (LVE) and ML for estimating LIB life. EKF is used as a conditional observer for supporting SOC and SOH estimators. Enwei et. al., performs SOC and SOH estimates, according to SOH prediction, it can be updated online without battery data across the entire SOC range and explained the battery digital twin making by machine learning deep approaches like ANN, and SVM, they implemented those methods to make digital twin batteries [Enwei Shi, 2019].

## Artificial Intelligence (AI)- Machine Learning (ML) in Battery

The utility of AI in the improvement of the latest battery substances, battery overall performance checking out, and state-of-charge (SOC) monitoring can significantly alleviate this problem. For example, a group led by Stanford University professors Stefano Ermon and William Chueh has evolved an ML approach that could lessen take a look at time through 98% [Luo, 2020; Milner, 2006]. It emphasizes the procedure and the independence of getting to know. Machine getting to know has these days been carried out to explain the architecture, characteristics, and overall performance of lithium-ion batteries. ML must play a crucial function in battery improvement by facilitating opposite engineering, as their computational techniques will be robotically enhanced through experience. Machine getting to know makes use of an accepted healthy feature with optimizer parameters set to offer the preferred behavior, frequently according to experimental schooling data. This feature can then make predictions for different battery systems [Chandran, 2021]. Figure 1 is the pictorial representation of lithium-ion battery (EV) prediction by ML [Li, 2023]. In this case, it collects the high throughput experimental data and simulation data from multistage modeling and feeds into the machine learning, it predicts the state of the art and the driving mileages, and lifetime of electric vehicle lithium-ion batteries.

*Figure 1. Sample of input & output of AI to predict the SOC, SOH, RUL of EVs Li-ion battery.*

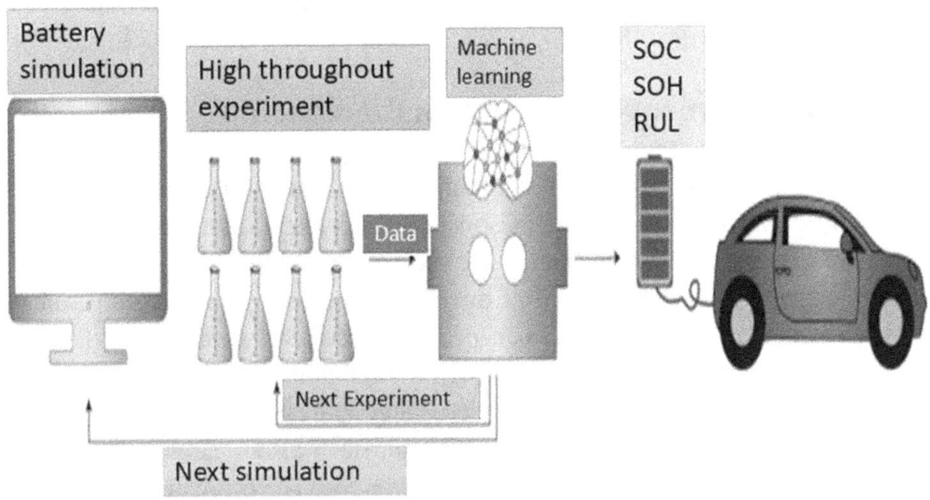


Simulation data from multistate simulations and experimental high-performance automation data are fed into machine learning algorithms to predict SOC, SOH, and RUL. The predicted values can guide the next simulation or experiment to further improve the prediction accuracy.

## Battery Parameters

Continuous variables can take any value and include current flow, internal structure, shape, and temperature. The integer variable contains the number of charge/discharge cycles that the battery has completed. A categorical variable takes a specific value that cannot be sorted into a list, such as a battery type (such as lithium-ion, lead acid, or nickel metal hydride). Ideally, machine learning methods should be able to introduce continuous, integer, and categorical variables for prediction. Results can be divided into two main categories. (1) a short time scale for a single charge/discharge cycle to understand SOC and (2) a long-time scale for multiple charge/discharge cycles to understand SOH. The first approach is to predict the evolution of the battery over one charge/discharge cycle. Predicted endpoints can include SOC, current rate, and the concentration and size of defects that form in the battery. By tracking changes over charge/discharge cycles, the model can account for all points in a battery's life and overestimated time. But when applied to too many charge/discharge cycles it is prone to error accumulation. A second technique is to expect the evolution of a battery from cycle to cycle on the identical cycle factor over a couple of cycles. While this technique can without difficulty be carried out to loads of cycles masking the whole battery life, it isn't always relevant to a selected cycle, and may best begin and propagate to a selected factor inside the cycle, along with it's far absolutely charged [Shu, 2021; Xing, 2011].

## Battery Management System (BMS) Prediction

The BMS is usually responsible for monitoring the operating conditions of the battery to prolong its life and ensure safe operation. For example, overload/discharge protection can be achieved by regulating the voltage of the BMS: charge stops when a packed cell reaches the state of full charge or discharge described [Gabbar, 2021; Swarnkar, 2023]. The BMS is capable of accurately determining the state of charge (SOC) and state of health (SOH), the remaining useful life (RUL) [Li, 2023; Hannan, 2017] of the battery, and thus automatically estimating the charge of the EV battery, which will solve the problem. BMS also measures the SOC of lithium-ion batteries within the range of 0.6% to 6.5%. The estimation of BMS by ML is discussed further.

SOC & SOH estimation of Li- ion battery

SOC and SOH are two important parameters for battery management. SOC represents the current capacity of the battery compared to its capacity at full charge, and SOH represents the capacity of the battery at full charge compared to the nominal capacity of a new battery.

$$SOC = C_{curr} / C_{full} x100\%$$

$$SOH = C_{full} / C_{nom} x100\%$$

Where $C_{curr}$ is the battery capacity in its current state, $C_{full}$ is the battery capacity in a fully charged state, and $C_{nom}$ is the nominal capacity of the new battery. The conventional SOC is 100% when the battery is fully charged and 0% when it is discharged, whereas the SOH was 100% at the time of manufacture and reached 80% by the end of life (EOL). In the battery industry, EOL is often defined as the point at which actual capacity drops to 80% of its nominal value when fully charged. Li et.al. [Li, 2023], battery SOC indicates the reliability of the battery system and it is defined as the ratio between the amount of charge available in the battery and the maximum amount of charge commonly known as the SOC. The SOC and SOH are represented mathematically as follows:

$$SOC = Q_{avail} / C_N$$

$$SOH = Q_{max,p} / C_N$$

Where $Q_{avail}$ denotes the available amount of charge and $C_N$ represents the rated capacity from battery manufacturers, $Q_{max,p}$ denotes the maximum practical capacity as measured from the operating battery at the current time. For SOC & SOH estimation of battery, different ML algorithms are used such as ANN, SVM, LR, GPR, group packing, and group enhancement [Li, 2023; Hannan, 2017; Farmann, 2016]. It determines the distance traveled by the electric vehicle and the safety of the Li-ion battery in the electric vehicle.

## State of Available Power (SoAP) of a Battery

The traditional advanced methods of SoAP forecasting can be divided into two groups. 1. Method based on battery map and 2. Method to describe battery dynamics using equivalent circuit model [Valencia, 2023]. The state of available power can be defined as the maximum power that can be delivered to the battery in the current state, provided that the minimum/maximum voltage of the individual cells as well as the charge/discharge current of the maximum identifier of these cells exceeds the predefined limit. As the battery continues to age, it can predict how much power is available at any given temperature. By using fuzzy modeling (FIS) and ANN as part of an adaptive neural fuzzy inference system (ANFIS); it only provides values with less than 1% error. This verification is done on software in a loop test bench configuration using 53 Li-ion batteries testing value [Wu, 2022].

## RUL of a Battery

The remaining useful life (RUL) has important significance in guaranteeing the battery's safety and reliability in the full life cycle. The number of charge/discharge cycles remaining until the battery reaches its end of life (EOL) is the battery's RUL [Liu, 2023] or it can be defined as the remaining life cycle before retirement. For an electric vehicle, the battery is out of use at 80% capacity. A battery life model can have many applications. In particular, the estimated remaining lifetime (RUL) often has large errors due to the complicated internal operating mechanism and the aging process of lithium-ion batteries. Therefore, it is difficult to predict RUL accurately. To accurately predict the RUL of a lithium-ion battery, a standard particle filter (PF), an extended Kalman particle filter (EKPF), and several other ML methods are used. In addition, two types of ANNs have been successfully applied to pin RUL prediction, namely feed forward neural networks (FFNNs) and cyclic neural networks (RNNs) [Wu, 2022; Liu, 2023; Bonfitto, 2020].

## Machine Learning (ML) Techniques

ML allows computers to build models from sample data and automate the decision-making process based on input data. The methods mentioned below are ML methods to predict the SOC, SOH, SoAP, and RUL of LIBs for electric vehicles or any portable/non-portable energy storage device. It gives, less % of error values. Methods that are commonly used are mentioned below. In those methods, only Kalman filters are manually described method to determine the state of the art in a battery. Early days, Kalman filters were used to predict and estimate the RUL of the battery and are still in use.

1. Artificial Neural Network (ANN),
2. Linear Regression (LR),
3. Gaussian Process of Regression (GPR)
4. Closed loop optimization (CLO)- Bayesian Optimization (BO)
5. Support Vector Machine (SVM),
6. Support Vector Regression (SVR),
7. Random Forest Network (RFN),
8. Relevance vector machine (RVM)
9. Recurrent neural network (RNN)
10. Fuzzy model
11. Extended Kalman particle filter (EKPF)

### Artificial Neural Network (ANN)

ANN based models are widely used for the estimation of battery state, ANN is a computational network experiment, and it can predict and estimate the value of SOC, SOH, and SoAP of Li-ion batteries with a minimum % of error [Li, 2023]. The standard ANN model has a single-layer feed forward neural network (SLFNN) with an input layer, a hidden layer, and an output layer (Figure 2). The input layer accepts preprocessed data (input data) and acts as a channel for the hidden layer. In the hidden layer, each neuron contains a mathematical model that calculates, predicts, and determines its output based on the input fed into it, which can be expressed as a weighted linear combination and is included in the activation function [Olabi, 2024; Ali Gharbani, 2019] and the final detection prediction, called the output, is expressed. The data from multistage modeling industries and the manually made experiment values are given as input and converted into standard data as an output (SOC/SOH/RUL) by the hidden layer (Figure 2).

*Figure 2. ANN with input, output and hidden layer*

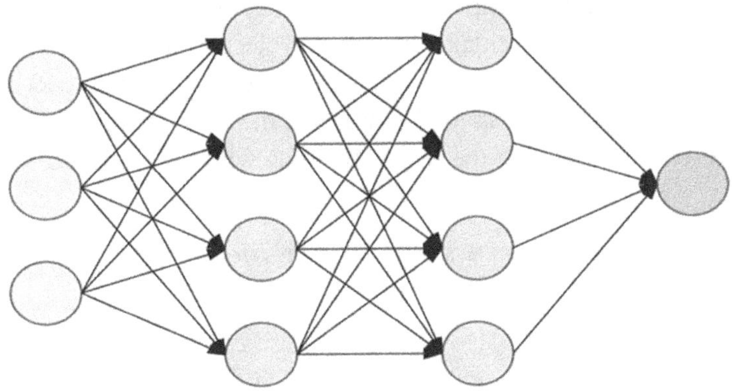


ANN is considered an adaptive system because it can change its shape based on a given different structure, thereby capturing the information flow of the learning phase. Chandran et al. explained that the ANN method can form a nonlinear map to show a complex nonlinear model [Chandran, 2021]. There are many ANN methods available, among them, for the estimation of SOC, Ali. et. al., have chosen Multi-Layer-Perceptron (MLP) which can determine the ages of the batteries [Ali Gharbani, 2019]. Boulakhbar et al. had developed an artificial neural network model to predict the individual daily load profiles of electric vehicles. They trained and tested an artificial neural network (ANN) model with 12 connected electric vehicles (PEVs) and reached very accurate conclusions with < 5% error. The prediction of SOC by ANN also gives the value at different temperatures. Wei et.al predicted the state and lifetime of a battery with only a 10% error at 250C & 17% error at 200 °C [Boulakhbar, 2022]. Li et.al described two types of ANNs called feed forward neural networks (FFNNs) and recurrent neural networks (RNNs). These are used to predict the RUL of the battery [Li, 2019]. Charkhgard et.al described that FFNN is extended to include feedback connections with ANN and extended KF. They estimated SOC at room temperature with 2% of a root mean square error (RMSE) value [Charkhgard, 2018].

## Linear Regression (LR) Algorithm

LR algorithm is applied when the output is a continuous variable. In contrast, the rating algorithm has a pass/fail output, good/average/bad, etc. [Venkatesan, 2021; Koohfar, 2023; Wei, 2023; Ma, 2022; Reis, 2022; Ali, 2022]. By LR, the SOC, SOH, RUL, voltage, and capacity of a lithium-ion can be predicted and estimated in a statistical method. Koohfar et.al. [Koohfar, 2023] used LR as a linear model that combines the nine battery descriptors used to predict the RUL of lithium iron phosphate/graphite cells after 100 charge/discharge cycles. In this model, the inputs are power cycle count, voltage, current flow, and capacitance, predicting RUL (output) with a typical error of 9.1%. Figure 3 represents the RUL of a LIBs by the linear regression (LR), by comparing the real RUL value with the predicted RUL value.

*Figure 3. RUL prediction statistic by LR in EVs (Li-ion battery)*

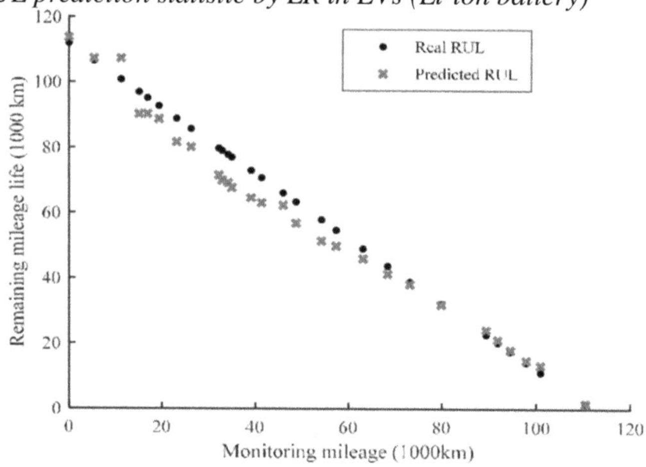


LR simply fitting a straight line (one input dimension) or a hyper plane (multiple input dimensions) to the data is probably the simplest model.

## Gaussian Process of Regression

Gaussian process of regression (GPR) is a nonparametric, Bayesian approach to regression that is making waves in the area of machine learning [Atefeh Daemi, 2019; Ali, 2022; Lombardo, 2022]. This is a stochastic method that delivers a probability distribution of possible predictions

$P(y) = N (\mu (x), \sigma^2 (x))$

Where $p(y) = N$ is a normal distribution with modified mean $\mu(x)$ and variance $\sigma^2 (x)$ derived from the covariance of the training data. GPR has various advantages, Alagar et. al., stated that GPR can provide predictive uncertainty measurement and it works well on small data sets. The GPR provides SOC prediction with 0.8% accuracy and is superior to support vector machines and neural networks [Su, 2022; Zhang, 2020].

The RUL of EV, LIBs can be easily predicted by the GPR, with the help of Kalman filters, which can determine the driving mileage of an EV. For example, Zhang et al. [Zhang, 2020] showed that accurate RUL estimates can be obtained by taking the full spectrum of EIS and combining it with Gaussian process regression and automatic relevance algorithms. There they identified two specific frequencies: 17 Hz and 2 Hz. Figure 4 is the sample of GPR value of a battery, it determines the capacity of a battery by calculating the no cycles performed.

*Figure 4. GPR detection of a battery*

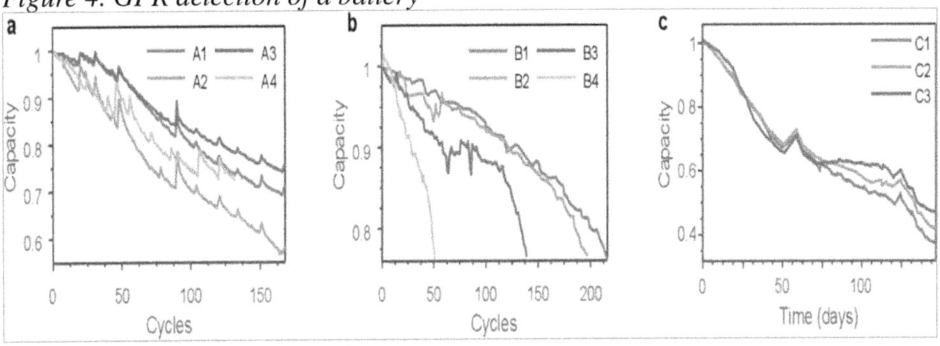


## Close-Loop Optimization-Bayesian Optimization

With the help of Bayesian optimization, CLO quickly identifies high-performance charging protocols and provides early prediction. This is done experimentally by adding 100-cycle data (lithium-ion batteries), especially electrochemical experimental data. Battery cycle life is predicted by the ML model sent to the BO algorithm to test the following protocols: This process is repeated to predict battery capacity [Chen, 2023].The combined the datasets in ML driven for RUL estimation with a BO algorithm. In addition, closed-loop optimization has significantly reduced the number of experiments required in the parameter space. They allowed this with 244 different loading protocols and studied 16 vs. 500 days [Jalem, 2018]. It also paves the way for significant reductions in time consumption by reducing the number of experiments required for analysis and creating new types of batteries [Meng, 2023]. Figure 5, illustrates a BO-CLO and Loop test data is taken from the battery (by adding 100 cyclic battery data) via a closed loop system (specified as input).

*Figure 5. BMS by Bayesian optimization in closed loop system*

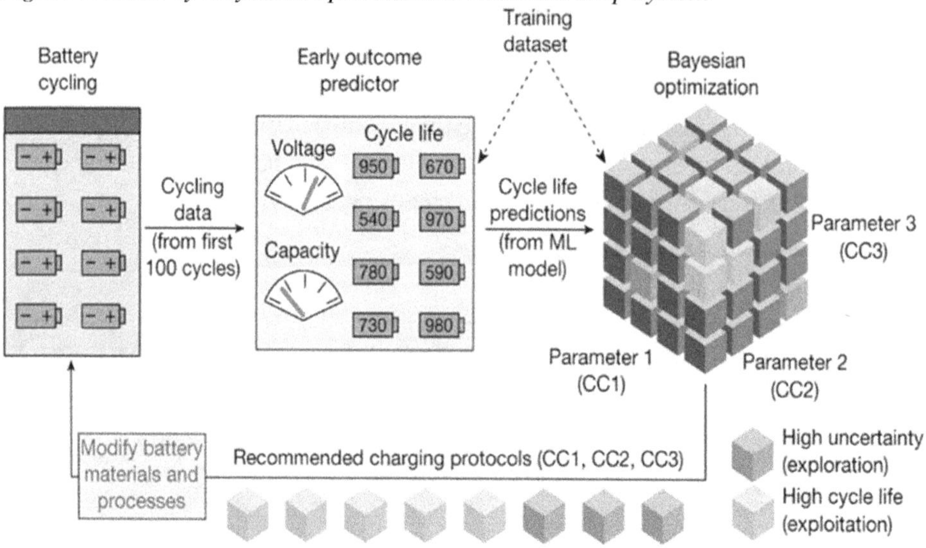


Bayesian optimization method is used for almost all battery development, including designing the chemical and electrochemical properties of batteries, determining battery size and shape, better manufacturing, discovering charge and discharge cycles, and aging batteries and storage systems. You can accelerate the Energy storage device with advanced technology. Chao, 2020; Wang, 2021

## Support Vector Machines (SVMs)

SVM was originally developed to solve logistic / classification problems and kernel-based functions. The SVM method is used to predict both the SOH and RUL of lithium-ion batteries [Chao, 2020; Wang, 2021]. By the combination of the dual Kalman filter (DKF) and the SVM method, the SOH is estimated online, which demonstrates that the minimum variance estimates of the battery aging state, as well as the SVM model and extreme ML model are used to predict the remaining lifetime of energy LIBs [Vasta,2023]. The battery data in this reference study is from a dynamic configuration using terminal voltage, current, and ambient temperature (100 Ah cells are obtained) [Ren, 2023; Chen, 2018]

The advantages of SVM (Figure 6) are low generalization error with a brief description, small sample size, non-linearity, and fewer computational problems with large dimensions. Vasta et.al. [Vasta,2023] is helpful for easy prediction as it explains that the SVM method can partition the dataset space in multiple regions using the best possible hyper plane to minimize the errors associated with classifying the dataset. In the current SVM study, many scientists defined three properties of the slurry in the SVM model as descriptors of the model, and there are no restrictions in terms of study parameters.

*Figure 6. ML sample of SVM statistic prediction*

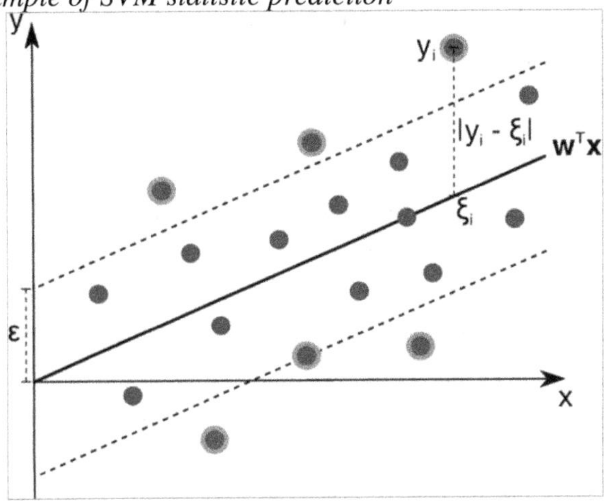


## Support Vector Regression (SVR)

SVR is a form of SVM designed for regression problems a form of regression in SVM. SVR can solve classification and regression problems of nonlinear systems in LIBs [Chen, 2018]. SVR was applied to integrate the appropriate training dataset to improve stability. However, this procedure also increases the computational cost, which is the biggest drawback of SVR [Liu, 2020]. Another kernel and Kalman filter are used to estimate the SOC and SOH of lithium-ion batteries. By creating an SVR paired with a dual filter, they were able to estimate the SOC with high accuracy with less than 1% error [Zhao, 2018]. Ref. [Wang, 2019; Wang, 2023] showed that SVR is used to model SOFC anode electrical conductivity. In this case, the inputs to the SVR model are the operating temperature and copper content. The output of the SVR model is electrical conductivity. In addition, the trained SVR shows high simulation accuracy in the test results (e.g., the mean absolute error expressed as a percentage is 1.05%).

## Random Forest Regression (RFR)

RFR is based on ensemble learning and contains a generalized set of classification trees. RFRs often choose to split each layer to minimize the distribution of the remaining training data as much as possible. RF is most often used to solve regression problems and classification problems. In particular, random forests are easiest to train with categorical data. The main advantages of RF are accuracy, ease of training, and resilience to outliers. Sometimes the functionality provided by RFR is discontinuous rather than fluid. Zhang and colleagues [Zang, 2015] demonstrated a tree method which is a successful application to predict the RUL of lithium-ion batteries, a random forest regression. The authors aimed to increase the flight time of unmanned aerial vehicles by focusing on batteries. The authors also found that in the random forest approach, the input is simply a change in battery voltage over time. This outperforms linear models, SVMs, and neural networks, with a typical prediction error of RUL of 3.3%. At the same time, it performs SVM with RFR to predict the state of LIBs. It has been reported that RFT can predict the state of lithium-ion batteries such as SOC, SOH, and RUL. Wang [Wang, 2023] was achieved high accuracy in SOH prediction; the RF model contained 500 decision trees, and provided a LIB with a root-mean-square error (MSE) of less than 1.3%.

## Relevance Vector Machine (RVM)

RVM is based on the Bayesian framework for obtaining an economical solution and is considered one of the most important potential methods of RUL estimation for LIBs. Hu et al. presented a sparse Bayesian learning method to estimate lithium-ion battery capacity and trained an RVM regression model. RVM is most likely used to predict the RUL of a LIBs [Hu, 2016]. RVM uses experimental data from multiple constant current discharges of a LIBs under constant temperature and constant load for prediction. This method uses three parameters to estimate the RUL. This model is called the empirical degradation model, but it cannot dynamically update. Liu et al. with the same data, they proposed an improved optimized RVM algorithm that improves the dynamic model update capability and predicts the RUL of the LIB with high accuracy [Liu, 2015].

## Recurrent Neural Network (RNN)

RNN (Figure 7) is a type of neural network that uses information transmitted in a closed loop. A neural network can be implemented recursively by simply passing the output of the network, or an intermediate state, as input [Yang, 2019]. RNN defines input and output as dependent variables based on time series. RNNs perform the same task for each element of a sequence. For example, the SOC for k1 could be the network input at time step k. This type of ML is suitable when short-term sequence dependencies are required, but it may not work well for the long-term dependencies found in batteries. For this type of RNN, there are challenges in the training process, such as errors "disappearing" or "exploding" during back propagation [Zhang, 2019]. Both types of RNN machine learning methods can estimate the SOC and SOH of lithium-ion batteries. Figure 7 represents the RNN machine learning to predict the SOH by proving different kinds of output into it and getting a single output (SOH).

*Figure 7. SOH by RNN*

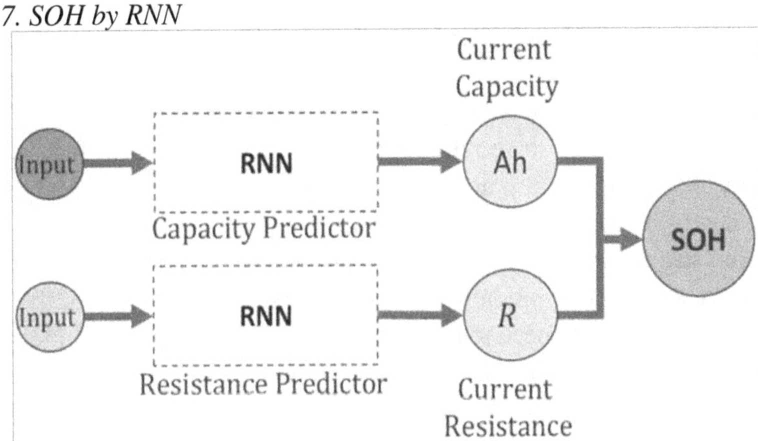


## Fuzzy Model (FM)

The FM is a unique type of ML prediction; it can easily predict the SOC and SOH of the battery. The authors state that the fuzzy logic method treats the measurement data of the nonlinear system model with the fuzzy theory to obtain the battery SOH [Siva Suriya Narayanan, 2023]. Zhang et.al. [Zhang, 2019] compared back-propagation artificial neural network (BPANN) with ANFIS for more accurate SOC estimation. Using the internal resistance, voltage, and current of the battery as the main input variables, it is possible to estimate the SOC of the battery. Xi et al. proposed a ML system implemented by a cybernetic, FNN, and a common controller network of cerebellar model for SOC estimation [Xi, 2022]. Zenati et.al evaluated the SOC/SOH of two different LIBs using the fuzzy logic method [Zenati, 2010]. In addition, the available power state was measured by the FM and an ANN in the Adaptive Neural Fuzzy Interference System (ANFIS).

## Kalman Filters (KL)

KF is used as the important sampling density function, which is purely a RUL prediction accuracy algorithm in LIBs. In another work, a dual filter consisting of a standard KF and an odorless KF were used to estimate the SOC and SOH of LIB [Karaboga, 2019; Lv, 2020]. The combination of an artificial neural network (ANN) with an extended KL yields the least false SOC value in battery prediction. The odorless KL and standard KL with ML support vector machine (SVM) only give a <0.5% error in SOC prediction. SVR is used to pair with the dual filter and it has achieved high accuracy estimation of SOC with an error of less than 1%.

## Future Outlook of ML in LIBs

ML in LIBs prediction brings greater advantages in the future. ML has the potential to overcome and solve the problem of battery evolution. It paves in the energy storage testing program and the algorithms are used to diagnose degradation mechanisms, increase life prediction accuracy, production to make advanced batteries, and state of prediction like SOC, SOH, and RUL. ML will open prospects to improve the accuracy of prediction. To develop a holistic model of the battery, the hybrid approach would need to achieve the best of both the short and long-term behavior of the battery. ML reports high uncertainty when additional first-principles simulations are run out of the database and the machine learning model is recycled. Thus, one can also develop a ML algorithm model for that particular farm, collecting default data, and fine-tuning with the on-site data to capture the specific characteristics of the farm.

# CONCLUSION

A wide range of machine learning (ML) approaches by AI are suitable for the estimation of SOC, SOH, and RUL of lithium-ion batteries to develop and create a better battery management system with quick identification, high performance, high charging protocol, with less degradation of batteries. It could highly aid the extent of the work on battery making by monitoring the data by ML approach. A combination of ML with BMS can lead to the production of next-generation batteries with better performance with less time consumption. The continuous development of ML applied in material science will become broader and have an ever-increasing effect on the efficacy of many research. Methods like ANN, FNN, RNN, SVM, SVR, GPR, BO, FIS, RVM, and RFR are immense in the BMS of the Li-ion battery. It could predict and estimate the SOC, SOH, SoAP, and RUL of the Li-ion battery with accuracy. In

SVM method of ML gives the LESS % of error, which could aid for the better BMS of Li-ion batteries. On the contrary, experimental testing is still essential, and the only way, to decipher which conditions cater to specific degradation paths. Its input is, therefore, essential to decipher the applicability of batteries for a given application. Machine getting to know can integrate fashions with one-of-a-kind time and period scales for one-of-a-kind forms of approach in batteries. Moreover, high-throughput experimentation, possibly guided via way of means of the initial system getting to know results, is the important thing to offer real lifestyles and awesome datasets on battery overall performance for the system getting to know. With the development of computational technology and mathematical algorithms, collectively with the decreased charges of records garage gadgets and high-throughput experiments, envision records-pushed systems getting to know to be a promising approach for superior battery modeling in the future. Therefore, the AI technique results in the chance of brand-new superior lithium-ion batteries, different electricity garage devices, different disciplines, and additionally in numerous discoveries along to broaden the wished algorithms as soon as a mobiliary became selected. However, the usage of AI in fabric studies nevertheless has sure short-comes.

## REFERENCES


Abakumov, A. M., Fedotov, S. S., Antipov, E. V., & Tarascon, J.-M. (2020). Solid state chemistry for developing better metal-ion batteries. *Nature Communications*, 11(1), 4976. DOI: 10.1038/s41467-020-18736-7 PMID: 33009387

Ali, O., Ishak, M. K., Ahmed, A. B., Mohd Salleh, M. F., Ooi, C. A., Akbar Jalaludin Khan, M. F., & Khan, I. (2022). On-line WSN SoC estimation using Gaussian Process Regression: An Adaptive Machine Learning Approach. *Alexandria Engineering Journal*, 61(12), 9831–9848. DOI: 10.1016/j.aej.2022.02.067

Ali, O., Khairi Ishak, M., Ahmed, A. B., Mohd Salleh, M. F., Ooi, C. A., Jalaludin Khan, M. F. A., & Khan, I. (2022). On-line WSN SoC estimation using Gaussian Process Regression: An Adaptive Machine Learning Approach. *Alexandria Engineering Journal*, 61(12), 9831–9848. DOI: 10.1016/j.aej.2022.02.067

Ali Gharbani, K., Hamed, F., Zhiya, M., & Zhongwu, C. (2019).. . *Journal of the Electrochemical Society*, 166(4), A605–A615. DOI: 10.1149/2.0411904jes

Azis, N., Joelianto, E., & Widyotriatmo, A. (2019). State of Charge (SoC) and State of Health (SoH). *Estimation of Lithium-Ion Battery Using Dual Extended Kalman Filter Based on Polynomial Battery Model.*, 2019, 88–93. DOI: 10.1109/ICA.2019.8916734

Bai, Y., Su, Y., Maisha Rahman, M., & Wang, Z. (2023). Prognostics of Lithium-Ion batteries using knowledge-constrained machine learning and Kalman filtering. *Reliability Engineering & System Safety*, 231, 108944. DOI: 10.1016/j.ress.2022.108944

Bai, Y. T., Wang, X. Y., Jin, X. B., Zhao, Z. Y., & Zhang, B. H. (2020, January 5). A Neuron-Based Kalman Filter with Nonlinear Autoregressive Model. *Sensors (Basel)*, 20(1), 299. DOI: 10.3390/s20010299 PMID: 31948060

Barrett, D. H., & Adiremi, H. (2020). Artificial intelligence and machine learning for targeted energy storage solutions. *Current Opinion in Electrochemistry*, 21, 160–166. DOI: 10.1016/j.coelec.2020.02.002

Bonfitto, A. (2020). A Method for the Combined Estimation of Battery State of Charge and State of Health Based on Artificial Neural Networks. *Energies*, 13(10), 2548. DOI: 10.3390/en13102548

Boujelbene, M., Goodarzi, M., & Ashraf Ali, M. (2023). Shigidi, I. M.T.A., Pashameah, R. A., Homod, R.Z., Alzahrani, E.; and Safaei, M. R. Machine-learning optimization of an innovative design of a Li-ion battery arrangement cooling system. *Journal of Energy Storage*, 58, 106331. DOI: 10.1016/j.est.2022.106331

Boulakhbar, M., Farag, M., Benabdelaziz, K., Kousksou, T., & Zazi, M. (2022). Benabdelaziz, K., Kousksou, T., and Zazi,M. A deep learning approach for prediction of electrical vehicle charging stations power demand in regulated electricity markets: The case of Morocco. *Cleaner Energy Systems*, 3, 100039. DOI: 10.1016/j.cles.2022.100039

Busu, C., & Busu, M. (2021). An Application of the Kalman Filter Recursive Algorithm to Estimate the Gaussian Errors by Minimizing the Symmetric Loss Function. *Symmetry*, 13(2), 240. DOI: 10.3390/sym13020240

Cao, R., Zhang, X., & Yang, H. (2023). Prediction of the Heat Generation Rate of Lithium-Ion Batteries Based on Three Machine Learning Algorithms. *Batteries*, 9(3), 165. DOI: 10.3390/batteries9030165

Chandran, V., Patil, C. K., Karthick, A., Ganeshaperumal, D., Rahim, R., & Ghosh, A. (2021). State of Charge Estimation of Lithium-Ion Battery for Electric Vehicles Using Machine Learning Algorithms. *World Electr. Veh. J.*, 12(1), 38. DOI: 10.3390/wevj12010038

Chao, D., Zhou, W., Xie, F., Ye, C., Li, H., Jaroniec, M., & Qiao, S.-Z. (2020). Roadmap for advanced aqueous batteries: From design of materials to applications. *Science Advances*, 6(21), 4098. DOI: 10.1126/sciadv.aba4098 PMID: 32494749

Charkhgard, H., Savelsbergh, M., & Talebian, M. (2018). A linear programming based algorithm to solve a class of optimization problems with a multi-linear objective function and affine constraints. *Computers & Operations Research*, 89, 17–30. DOI: 10.1016/j.cor.2017.07.015

Chen, C., Wei, J., & Li, Z. (2023). Remaining Useful Life Prediction for Lithium-Ion Batteries Based on a Hybrid Deep Learning Model. *Processes (Basel, Switzerland)*, 11(8), 2333. DOI: 10.3390/pr11082333

Christian, F., Wladislaw, W., Ziou, B., & Dirk, U. S. (2013).. . *J. Power Electron*, 13, 516–527. DOI: 10.6113/JPE.2013.13.4.516

Daemi, A., Kodamana, H., & Huang, B. (2019). Gaussian process modelling with Gaussian mixture likelihood. *Journal of Process Control*, 81, 209–220. DOI: 10.1016/j.jprocont.2019.06.007

Dan, W., Masood, A. A., Asad, A., Rishabh, C., Ali, M. R., & Sohail, M. (2023). A numerical investigation of a two-phase nanofluid flow with phase change materials in the thermal management of lithium batteries and use of machine learning in the optimization of the horizontal and vertical distances between batteries. *Case Studies in Thermal Engineering*, 41, 102582. DOI: 10.1016/j.csite.2022.102582

Duquesnoy, M., Liu, C., Dominguez, D.Z., Kumar, V., Ayerbe, E., & Franco, A.A. Machine learning-assisted multi-objective optimization of battery manufacturing from synthetic data generated by physics-based simulations, *Energy Storage Materials.*, vol. 56, p.50-61, https://doi.org/. DOI: 10.1016/j.csite.2022.102582

Entezari, A., Aslani, A., Zahedi, R., & Noorollahi, Y. (2023). Artificial intelligence and machine learning in energy systems: A bibliographic perspective. *Energy Strat. Rev*, 45, 101017. DOI: 10.1016/j.esr.2022.101017

Faraji-Niri, M., Rashid, M., Sansom, J., Sheikh, M., Widanage, D., & Marco, J. (2023). Accelerated state of health estimation of second life lithium-ion batteries via electrochemical impedance spectroscopy tests and machine learning techniques. *Journal of Energy Storage*, 58, 106295. DOI: 10.1016/j.est.2022.106295

Farmann, A., & Uwe Sauer, D. (2016). A comprehensive review of on-board State-of-Available-Power prediction techniques for lithium-ion batteries in electric vehicles. *Journal of Power Sources*, 329, 123–137. DOI: 10.1016/j.jpowsour.2016.08.031

Gabbar, H. A., Othman, A. M., & Abdussami, M. R. (2021). Review of Battery Management Systems (BMS) Development and Industrial Standards. *Technologies*, 9(2), 28. DOI: 10.3390/technologies9020028

Gao, K., Xu, J., Li, Z., Cai, Z., Jiang, D., & Zeng, A. (2022). A Novel Remaining Useful Life Prediction Method for Capacity Diving Lithium-Ion Batteries. *ACS Omega*, 7(30), 26701–26714. DOI: 10.1021/acsomega.2c03043 PMID: 35936419

Hannan, M. A., Lipu, M. S. H., Hussain, A., & Mohamed, A. (2017). A Review of Lithium-Ion Battery State of Charge Estimation and Management System in Electric Vehicle Applications: Challenges and Recommendations. *Renewable & Sustainable Energy Reviews*, 78, 834–854. DOI: 10.1016/j.rser.2017.05.001

He, W., Li, Z., Liu, T., Liu, Z., Guo, X., Du, J., Li, X., Sun, P., & Ming, W. (2023). Research progress and application of deep learning in remaining useful life, state of health and battery thermal management of lithium batteries. *Journal of Energy Storage*, 70, 107868. DOI: 10.1016/j.est.2023.107868

Hong, J., Zhang, H., & Xu, X. (2023). Thermal fault prognosis of lithium-ion batteries in real-world electric vehicles using self-attention mechanism networks. *Applied Thermal Engineering*, 226, 120304. DOI: 10.1016/j.applthermaleng.2023.120304

Hu, S., & Huang, C. (2023). Machine-Learning Approaches for the Discovery of Electrolyte Materials for Solid-State Lithium Batteries. *Batteries.*, 9(4), 228. DOI: 10.3390/batteries9040228

Hu, X., Jiang, J., Cao, D., & Egardt, B. (2016). Battery Health Prognosis for Electric Vehicles Using Sample Entropy and Sparse Bayesian Predictive Modeling. *IEEE Transactions on Industrial Electronics*, 63, 2645–2656. DOI: 10.1109/TIE.2015.2461523

Huang, S.-C., Tseng, K.-H., Liang, J.-W., Chang, C.-L., & Pecht, M. G. (2017). An Online SOC and SOH Estimation Model for Lithium-Ion Batteries. *Energies*, 10(4), 512. DOI: 10.3390/en10040512

Jalem, R., Kanamori, K., Takeuchi, I., Nakayama, M., Yamasaki, H., & Saito, T. (2018). Bayesian-Driven First-Principles Calculations for Accelerating Exploration of Fast Ion Conductors for Rechargeable Battery Application. *Scientific Reports*, 8(1), 5845. DOI: 10.1038/s41598-018-23852-y PMID: 29643423

Jiang, Y., & Song, W. (2023). Predicting the Cycle Life of Lithium-Ion Batteries Using Data-Driven Machine Learning Based on Discharge Voltage Curves. *Batteries*, 9(8), 413. DOI: 10.3390/batteries9080413

Karaboga, D., & Kaya, E. (2019). Adaptive network based fuzzy inference system (ANFIS) training approaches: A comprehensive survey. *Artificial Intelligence Review*, 52(4), 2263–2293. DOI: 10.1007/s10462-017-9610-2

Kashkooli, G. Ali & Fathiannasab, Hamed & Mao, Zhiyu & Chen, Zhongwei. (2019). Application of Artificial Intelligence to State-of-Charge and State-of-Health Estimation of Calendar-Aged Lithium-Ion Pouch Cells. Journal of The Electrochemical Society. 166. A605-A615. DOI: 10.1149/2.0411904jes

Khawaja, Y., Shankar, N., Qiqieh, I., Alzubi, J., Alzubi, O., Nallakaruppan, M. K., & Padmanaban, S. (2023). Battery management solutions for li-ion batteries based on artificial intelligence. *Ain Shams Engineering Journal*, 14(12), 102213. DOI: 10.1016/j.asej.2023.102213

Kilic, A., Oral, B., Eroglu, D., & Yildirim, R. (2023). Machine learning for beyond Li-ion batteries: Powering the research. *Journal of Energy Storage*, 73, 109057. DOI: 10.1016/j.est.2023.109057

Koohfar, S., Woldemariam, W., & Kumar, A. (2023). Prediction of Electric Vehicles Charging Demand: A Transformer-Based Deep Learning Approach. *Sustainability (Basel)*, 15(3), 2105. DOI: 10.3390/su15032105

Korkmaz, M. (2023). SoC estimation of lithium-ion batteries based on machine learning techniques: A filtered approach. *Journal of Energy Storage*, 72, 108268. DOI: 10.1016/j.est.2023.108268

Kosuru, V. S. R., & Kavasseri Venkitaraman, A. (2023). A Smart Battery Management System for Electric Vehicles Using Deep Learning-Based Sensor Fault Detection. *World Electr. Veh. J.*, 14(4), 101. DOI: 10.3390/wevj14040101

Li, A., Tian, H., & Li, K. (2023). Remaining useful life prediction of lithium-ion batteries using a spatial temporal network model based on capacity self-recovery effect. *Journal of Energy Storage*, 67, 107557. DOI: 10.1016/j.est.2023.107557

Li, C., Chen, Z., Cui, J., Wang, Y., & Zou, F. The lithium-ion battery state-of-charge estimation using random forest regression, *2014 Prognostics and System Health Management Conference (PHM-2014 Hunan)*, Zhangjiajie, China, 2014, pp. 336-339, DOI: 10.1109/PHM.2014.6988190

Li, W., Weng, J., Yuen, A. C. Y., Wang, W., Liu, H., Lee, E. W. M., Wang, J., Kook, S., & Yeoh, G. H. (2023). A., J., Chun Yin Yuen, A., Wang, W., Liu, H., Ming Lee, E.W., Wang, J., Kook, S., and Heng Yeoh, G. Machine learning assisted advanced battery thermal management system: A state-of-the-art review. *Journal of Energy Storage*, 60, 106688. DOI: 10.1016/j.est.2023.106688

Li, X., Yu, D., Søren Byg, V., & Ioan, S. D. (2023). The development of machine learning-based remaining useful life prediction for lithium-ion batteries. *Journal of Energy Chemistry*, 82, 103–121. DOI: 10.1016/j.jechem.2023.03.026

Li, X., Yuan, C., & Wang, Z. (2020). State of Health Estimation for Li-Ion Battery via Partial Incremental Capacity Analysis Based on Support Vector Regression. *Energy*, 203, 117852. DOI: 10.1016/j.energy.2020.117852

Li, Y., Liu, K., Foley, A. M., Zulke, A., Berecibar, M., Nanini-Maury, E., Van Mierlo, J., & Hoster, H. E. (2019).. . *Renewable & Sustainable Energy Reviews*, 113, 1–66.

Liu, D., Zhou, J., Pan, D., Peng, Y., & Peng, X. (2015). Lithium-ion battery remaining useful life estimation with an optimized Relevance Vector Machine algorithm with incremental learning. *Measurement*, 63, 143–151. DOI: 10.1016/j.measurement.2014.11.031

Liu, H., Li, Y., Luo, L., & Zhang, C. (2023). A Lithium-Ion Battery Capacity and RUL Prediction Fusion Method Based on Decomposition Strategy and GRU. *Batteries*, 9(6), 323. DOI: 10.3390/batteries9060323

Liu, Y., Liu, C., Liu, Y., Sun, F., Qiao, J., & Xu, T. (2023). Review on degradation mechanism and health state estimation methods of lithium-ion batteries. *Journal of Traffic and Transportation Engineering*, 10(4), 578–610. DOI: 10.1016/j.jtte.2023.06.001

Liu, Y., Yang, Z., Yu, Z., Liu, Z., Liu, D., Lin, H., Li, M., Ma, S., Avdeev, M., & Shi, S. (2023). Generative artificial intelligence and its applications in materials science: Current situation and future perspectives. *Journal of Materiomics*, 9(4), 798–816. DOI: 10.1016/j.jmat.2023.05.001

Liu, Z., Zhao, J., Wang, H., & Yang, C. (2020). A New Lithium-Ion Battery SOH Estimation Method Based on an Indirect Enhanced Health Indicator and Support Vector Regression in PHMs. *Energies*, 13(4), 830. DOI: 10.3390/en13040830

Lombardo, T., Duquesnoy, M., El-Bouysidy, H., Årén, F., Gallo-Bueno, A., Jørgensen, P. B., Bhowmik, A., Demortière, A., Ayerbe, E., Alcaide, F., Reynaud, M., Carrasco, J., Grimaud, A., Zhang, C., Vegge, T., Johansson, P., & Franco, A. A. (2022). Artificial Intelligence Applied to Battery Research: Hype or Reality? *Chemical Reviews*, 122(12), 10899–10969. DOI: 10.1021/acs.chemrev.1c00108 PMID: 34529918

Luo, Z., Yang, X., Wang, Y., Liu, W., Liu, S., Zhu, Y., Huang, Z., Zhang, H., Dou, S., Xu, J., Tian, J., Xu, K., Zhang, X., Hu, W., & Deng, Y. (2020). A Survey of Artificial Intelligence Techniques Applied in Energy Storage Materials R&D. *Frontiers in Energy Research*, 8, 116. https://www.frontiersin.org/articles/10.3389/fenrg.2020.00116. DOI: 10.3389/fenrg.2020.00116

Lv, J., Jiang, B., Wang, X., Liu, Y., & Fu, Y. (2020). Estimation of the State of Charge of Lithium Batteries Based on Adaptive Unscented Kalman Filter Algorithm. *Electronics (Basel)*, 9(9), 1425. DOI: 10.3390/electronics9091425

Ma, G., Xu, S., Jiang, B., Cheng, C., Yang, X., Shen, Y., Yang, T., Huang, Y., Ding, H., & Yuan, Y. (2022). Real-time personalized health status prediction of lithium-ion batteries using deep transfer learning. *Energy & Environmental Science*, 15(10), 4083–4094. DOI: 10.1039/D2EE01676A

Man- Fai. (2020). Ng., Jin, Z., Quingyu, Y., Gareth. J.C., and Zhiwei, Sheh. *Nature Machine Intelligence*, 2, 161–170.

Mehta, Y., Xu, R., Lim, B., Wu, J., & Gao, J. (2023). A Review for Green Energy Machine Learning and AI Services. *Energies*, 16(15), 5718. DOI: 10.3390/en16155718

Meng, H., Geng, M., & Han, T. (2023). Long short-term memory network with Bayesian optimization for health prognostics of lithium-ion batteries based on partial incremental capacity analysis. *Reliability Engineering & System Safety*, 236, 109288. DOI: 10.1016/j.ress.2023.109288

Milner, R. (2006). Turing, Computing and Communication. In Goldin, D., Smolka, S. A., & Wegner, P. (Eds.), *Interactive Computation*. Springer., DOI: 10.1007/3-540-34874-3_1

Muhammad, H. Z., Majad, M., Mohamad, A. H., Noman, M. K., Kamran, K., Syed Kumayl, R. M., & Filippo, S. (2023). Hybrid deep learning model for efficient state of charge estimation of Li-ion batteries in electric vehicles. *Energy*, 282, 128317. DOI: 10.1016/j.energy.2023.128317

Naya, M. Á., Sanjurjo, E., Rodríguez, A. J., & Cuadrado, J. (2023). Kalman filters based on multibody models: Linking simulation and real world. A comprehensive review. *Multibody System Dynamics*, 58(3-4), 479–521. DOI: 10.1007/s11044-023-09893-w

Olabi, A. G., Abdelghafar, A. A., Soudan, B., Alami, A. H., Semeraro, C., Al Radi, M., Al-Murisi, M., & Abdelkareem, M. A. (2024). Artificial neural network driven prognosis and estimation of Lithium-Ion battery states: Current insights and future perspectives. *Ain Shams Engineering Journal*, 15(2), 102429. DOI: 10.1016/j.asej.2023.102429

Payette, M., & Abdul-Nour, G. (2023). Machine Learning Applications for Reliability Engineering: A Review. *Sustainability (Basel)*, 15(7), 6270. DOI: 10.3390/su15076270

Qiao, W., Min, Y., Xue, C., Dirk, U. S., & Weihan, L. (2023). Transferable data-driven capacity estimation for lithium-ion batteries with deep learning: A case study from laboratory to field applications. *Applied Energy*, 350, 121747. DOI: 10.1016/j.apenergy.2023.121747

Rauf, H., Khalid, M., & Arshad, N. (2023). A novel smart feature selection strategy of lithium-ion battery degradation modelling for electric vehicles based on modern machine learning algorithms. *Journal of Energy Storage*, 68, 107577. DOI: 10.1016/j.est.2023.107577

Reis, M. S., & Jiang, B. (2022). Predicting the lifetime of Lithium–Ion batteries: Integrated feature extraction and modeling through sequential Unsupervised-Supervised Projections (USP). *Chemical Engineering Science*, 252, 117510. DOI: 10.1016/j.ces.2022.117510

Ren, Z., & Du, C. (2023). A review of machine learning state-of-charge and state-of-health estimation algorithms for lithium-ion batteries. *Energy Reports*, 9, 2993–3021. DOI: 10.1016/j.egyr.2023.01.108

Rimsha, Murawwat, S., Majid Gulzar, M., Alzahrani, A., Hafeez, G., Aslam Khan, F., and Abed, A.M. State of charge estimation and error analysis of lithium-ion batteries for electric vehicles using Kalman filter and deep neural network, *J. Energy Storage.*, vol.72, p.108039, https://doi.org/DOI: 10.1016/j.egyr.2023.01.108

Rundo, F., Conoci, S., Battiato, S., Pino, C., Villari, M., Genovese, A., Kollias, S., & Plataniotis, K. N. (2023). Editorial: Deep neural computing for advanced automotive system applications. *Frontiers of Computer Science*, 5, 1192413. DOI: 10.3389/fcomp.2023.1192413

Scarpelli, C., Gazzarri, J., Huria, T., Lutzemberger, G., & Ceraolo, M. (2023). Neural network for the estimation of LFP battery SOH cycled at different power levels. *Journal of Energy Storage*, 66, 107027. DOI: 10.1016/j.est.2023.107027

Sesidhar, D. V. S. R., Badachi, C., Robert, C., & Green, I. I. (2023). A review on data-driven SOC estimation with Li-Ion batteries: Implementation methods & future aspirations. *Journal of Energy Storage*, 72, 108420. DOI: 10.1016/j.est.2023.108420

Severson, K. A., Attia, P. M., Jin, N., Perkins, N., Jiang, B., Yang, Z., Chen, M. H., Aykol, M., Herring, P. K., Fraggedakis, D., Bazant, M. Z., Harris, S. J., Chueh, W. C., & Braatz, R. D. (2019). Data-driven prediction of battery cycle life before capacity degradation. *Nature Energy*, 4(5), 383–391. DOI: 10.1038/s41560-019-0356-8

Shi, D., Zhao, J., Eze, C., Wang, Z., Wang, J., Lian, Y., & Burke, A. F. (2023). Cloud-Based Artificial Intelligence Framework for Battery Management System. *Energies*, 16(11), 4403. DOI: 10.3390/en16114403

Shi, D., Zhao, J., Wang, Z., Zhao, H., Eze, C., Wang, J., Lian, Y., & Burke, A. F. (2023). Cloud-Based Deep Learning for Co-Estimation of Battery State of Charge and State of Health. *Energies*, 16(9), 3855. DOI: 10.3390/en16093855

Shi, E., Xia, F., Peng, D., Li, L., Wang, X., & Yu, B. (2019). Fei Xia., Daogang Peng., Liang Li., Xiaokang Wang., and Beili Yu. State-of-health estimation for lithium battery in electric vehicles based on improved unscented particle filter. *Journal of Renewable and Sustainable Energy*, 11(2), 024101. DOI: 10.1063/1.5065477

Shu, X., Shen, S., Shen, J., Zhang, Y., Li, G., Chen, Z., & Liu, Y. (2021). State of health prediction of lithium-ion batteries based on machine learning: Advances and perspectives. *iScience*, 24(11), 103265. DOI: 10.1016/j.isci.2021.103265 PMID: 34761185

Siva Suriya Narayanan, S., & Thangavel, S. (2023). A novel static model prediction method based on machine learning for Li-ion batteries operated at different temperatures. *Journal of Energy Storage*, 61, 106789. DOI: 10.1016/j.est.2023.106789

Song, K., Hu, D., Tong, Y., & Yue, X. (2023). Remaining life prediction of lithium-ion batteries based on health management: A review. *Journal of Energy Storage*, 57, 106193. DOI: 10.1016/j.est.2022.106193

Su, X., Sun, B., Wang, J., Zhang, W., Ma, S., He, X., & Ruan, H. (2022). Fast capacity estimation for lithium-ion battery based on online identification of low-frequency electrochemical impedance spectroscopy and Gaussian process regression. *Applied Energy*, 322, 119516. DOI: 10.1016/j.apenergy.2022.119516

Swarnkar, R., Ramachandran, H., Ali, S. H. M., & Jabbar, R. (2023). A Systematic Literature Review of State of Health and State of Charge Estimation Methods for Batteries Used in Electric Vehicle Applications. *World Electr. Veh. J.*, 14(9), 247. DOI: 10.3390/wevj14090247

Syed, S. A., & Bong, J. C. (2020).. . *Electronics (Basel)*, 9, 1–25.

Tianhangau, W. L. (2021).. . *Science*, 24, 1–33.

Tudoroiu, N., Zaheeruddin, M., Tudoroiu, R.-E., Radu, M. S., & Chammas, H. (2023). Investigations on Using Intelligent Learning Techniques for Anomaly Detection and Diagnosis in Sensors Signals in Li-Ion Battery—Case Study. *Inventions (Basel, Switzerland)*, 8(3), 74. DOI: 10.3390/inventions8030074

Vakharia, V., Shah, M., Nair, P., Borade, H., Sahlot, P., & Wankhede, V. (2023). Estimation of Lithium-ion Battery Discharge Capacity by Integrating Optimized Explainable-AI and Stacked LSTM Model. *Batteries.*, 9(2), 125. DOI: 10.3390/batteries9020125

Valencia, N., Fotouhi, A., Shateri, N., & Auger, D. (2023). Development of a Hybrid Adaptive Neuro-fuzzy Inference System with Coulomb-Counting State-of-Charge Estimator for Lithium–Sulphur Battery. *International Journal of Fuzzy Systems*, 25(2), 407–422. DOI: 10.1007/s40815-022-01403-y

Vasta, E., Scimone, T., Nobile, G., Eberhardt, O., Dugo, D., De Benedetti, M. M., Lanuzza, L., Scarcella, G., Patanè, L., Arena, P., & Cacciato, M. (2023). Models for Battery Health Assessment: A Comparative Evaluation. *Energies*, 16(2), 632. DOI: 10.3390/en16020632

Venkatesan, C., Chandra Shekhar, K. P., Alagar, K., Dharmarcy, G., Robbi, R., & Aritra, G. (2021).. . *World Electr. Veh. J.*, 12, 1–17.

Wang, B., Sun, Z., Jiang, X., Zeng, J., & Liu, R. Kalman Filter and Its Application in Data Assimilation. *Atmosphere,2023, vol.14, p.* 1319. https://doi.org/DOI: 10.3390/atmos14081319

Wang, G., Lyu, Z., & Li, X. (2023). An Optimized Random Forest Regression Model for Li-Ion Battery Prognostics and Health Management. *Batteries*, 9(6), 332. DOI: 10.3390/batteries9060332

Wang, Y., Ni, Y., Lu, S., Wang, J., & Zhang, X. (2019). Remaining Useful Life Prediction of Lithium-Ion Batteries Using Support Vector Regression Optimized by Artificial Bee colony. *IEEE Transactions on Vehicular Technology*, 68(10), 9543–9553. DOI: 10.1109/TVT.2019.2932605

Wang, Y., Zhang, X., Li, K., Zhao, G., & Chen, Z. (2023). Perspectives and challenges for future lithium-ion battery control and management. *eTransportation*, 18, 100260. DOI: 10.1016/j.etran.2023.100260

Wang, Z., Feng, G., Zhen, D., Gu, F., & Ball, A. (2021). A review on online state of charge and state of health estimation for lithium-ion batteries in electric vehicles. *Energy Reports*, 7, 2352–4847. DOI: 10.1016/j.egyr.2021.08.113

Wei, L., Tobias, P., & Chau, K. T. (2022). Overview of batteries and battery management for electric vehicles. *Energy Reports*, 8, 4058–4084. DOI: 10.1016/j.egyr.2022.03.016

Wei, X., Gang, X., Yumei, L., Feng, Z., Peng, Y., & Ben, L. (2023). Early prediction of lithium-ion battery cycle life based on voltage-capacity discharge curves. *Journal of Energy Storage*, 62, 106790. DOI: 10.1016/j.est.2023.106790

Wu, J., Kong, L., Cheng, Z., Yang, Y., & Zuo, H. (2022). RUL Prediction for Lithium Batteries Using a Novel Ensemble Learning Method. *Energy Reports*, 8, 313–326. DOI: 10.1016/j.egyr.2022.10.298

Xi, Z., Wang, R., Fu, Y., & Mi, C. (2022). Accurate and reliable state of charge estimation of lithium ion batteries using time-delayed recurrent neural networks through the identification of overexcited neurons. *Applied Energy*, 305, 117962. DOI: 10.1016/j.apenergy.2021.117962

Xing, Y., Ma, E. W. M., Tsui, K. L., & Pecht, M. Battery Management Systems in Electric and Hybrid Vehicles. *Energies,* 2011, vol.*4*, p.1840-1857. https://doi.org/ DOI: 10.3390/en4111840

Xu, X., Tang, S., Han, X., Lu, L., Wu, Y., Yu, C., Sun, X., Xie, J., Feng, X., & Ouyang, M. (2023). Fast capacity prediction of lithium-ion batteries using aging mechanism-informed bidirectional long short-term memory network. *Reliability Engineering & System Safety*, 234, 109185. DOI: 10.1016/j.ress.2023.109185

Yao, Z., Lum, Y., Johnston, A., Mejia-Mendoza, L. M., Zhou, X., Wen, Y., Aspuru-Guzik, A., Sargent, E. H., & Seh, Z. W. (2023). Machine learning for a sustainable energy future. *Nature Reviews. Materials*, 8(3), 202–215. DOI: 10.1038/s41578-022-00490-5 PMID: 36277083

Ye, X., He, Y., Zhang, M., Fournier-Viger, P., & Huang, J. Z. (2023). A novel correlation Gaussian process regression-based extreme learning machine. *Knowledge and Information Systems*, 65(5), 2017–2042. DOI: 10.1007/s10115-022-01803-4 PMID: 36683607

Yuan, C., Duan, W., Ding, Z., & Li, Y. (2022). Battery Life Prediction Based on a Hybrid Support Vector Regression Model. *Frontiers in Energy Research*, 10, •••. https://www.frontiersin.org/articles/10.3389/fenrg.2022.899804

Zazoum, B. (2023). Lithium-ion battery state of charge prediction based on machine learning approach. *Energy Reports*, 9, 1152–1158. DOI: 10.1016/j.egyr.2023.03.091

Zenati, A., Desprez, P., Razik, H., & Rael, S. (2010). *Impedance Measurements combined with the Fuzzy Logic methodology to assess the SOC and SOH of Lithium-ion Cells*. VPPC., DOI: 10.1109/VPPC.2010.5729069

Zhang, C., He, Y., Yuan, L., Xiang, S., & Wang, J. (2015). Prognostics of Lithium-Ion Batteries Based on Wavelet Denoising and DE-RVM. *Computational Intelligence and Neuroscience*, 2015, 8. DOI: 10.1155/2015/918305 PMID: 26413090

Zhang, S., Zhai, B., Guo, X., Wang, K., Peng, N., & Zhang, X. (2019). Synchronous estimation of state of health and remaining useful lifetime for lithium-ion battery using the incremental capacity and artificial neural networks. *Journal of Energy Storage*, 26, 100951. DOI: 10.1016/j.est.2019.100951

Zhang, Y., Tang, Q., & Zhang, Y. Identifying degradation patterns of lithium ion batteries from impedance spectroscopy using machine learning. *Nat Commun.*, 2020, vol. 11, p.1706 (2020). https://doi.org/DOI: 10.1016/j.egyr.2023.01.108

Zhao, Q., Qin, X., Zhao, H., & Feng, W. (2018). A Novel Prediction Method Based on the Support Vector Regression for the Remaining Useful Life of Lithium-Ion Batteries. *Microelectronics and Reliability*, 85, 99–108. DOI: 10.1016/j.microrel.2018.04.007

Zhou, L., Lai, X., Li, B., Yao, Y., Yuan, M., Weng, J., & Zheng, Y. (2023). State Estimation Models of Lithium-Ion Batteries for Battery Management System: Status, Challenges, and Future Trends. *Batteries*, 9(2), 131. DOI: 10.3390/batteries9020131

Zhu, G., Sun, T., Xu, Y., Zheng, Y., & Zhou, L. (2023). Identification of Internal Short-Circuit Faults in Lithium-Ion Batteries Based on a Multi-Machine Learning Fusion. *Batteries.*, 9(3), 154. DOI: 10.3390/batteries9030154

Ziyilluo, X. Y., Yingxue, W., Weidi, L., Silang, L., Yuankun, Z., Zihan, H., Hong, Z., Shuming, D., Jie, X., Jiachen, T., Kui, X., Xiowang, Z., Wenbin, H., & Yida, D. (2020)... *Frontiers in Energy Research*, 8, 1–12. DOI: 10.3389/fenrg.2020.00001

# Chapter 8
# Machine Learning for Safer Autonomous Vehicles:
## Tackling Traffic Detection and Collision in Smart Cities

**Bhupinder Singh**
https://orcid.org/0009-0006-4779-2553
*Sharda University, India*

**Christian Kaunert**
https://orcid.org/0000-0002-4493-2235
*Dublin City University, Ireland & University of South Wales, UK*

**Saurabh Chandra**
https://orcid.org/0000-0003-4172-9968
*Bennett University, India*

## ABSTRACT

*Machine learning is enhancing the transportation system and the robotic process automation and artificial intelligence are used in autos to provide intelligent automation (IA), which allows autonomous vehicles to undergo digital transformation. Smart automation has the power to completely replace human interaction, guaranteeing enhanced safety and intelligent vehicle movement. With a comparative study, this article analyzes current approaches that use IoT, AI, and machine learning in autonomous cars. It is critical to comprehend risk-reduction technology as the sector transitions from manual to automated processes. The study outlines the theoretical drawbacks and advantages of autonomous technology, highlighting artificial intel-*

DOI: 10.4018/979-8-3373-2530-9.ch008

*ligence's crucial role in vehicle management going forward. It makes recommendations for future lines of inquiry to further the advancement of autonomous car technology. This chapter focuses on the requirements for safety and the difficulties associated with autonomous cars, specifically with regard to object detection, cybersecurity and V2X privacy.*

## 1. INTRODUCTION AND RELEVANCE

The sharp rise in car ownership in smart cities has resulted in traffic jams, pollution, and interruptions to the flow of commodities. Daily traffic accidents result in an increasing number of fatalities and cases of lifelong disability each year (He et al., 2023). An Internet of Things (IoT)-based traffic management system (ITM) is used to identify accidents, manage traffic congestion, and guarantee safe data transmission in order to address these problems (Gu et al., 2023). Sensors are used by IoT-based ITM systems in autonomous cars and smart gadgets to recognize, gather, and transfer data. The transit system is getting better thanks to machine learning. In order to control traffic congestion and identify accidents, this project combines an Accident Alert Sound System (AALS) with an Adaptive Traffic Management system (ATM). Secure Early Traffic-Related EveNt Detection (SEE-TREND) is used to transmit traffic data securely (Zhang et al., 2023). To address possible problems in the transportation system, the design takes into account a number of eventualities (Hu et al., 2023). The suggested ATM model continually modifies traffic signal timing in response to predicted movements from surrounding intersections and traffic volume (Zhang et al., 2023). With gradually giving cars the all-clear, it cuts down on travel time and eases traffic congestion by promoting efficient traffic flow.

This study deeply dives into the efficient tools and frameworks that researchers and organizations created for AI and IoT-based autonomous cars (Sharifi et al., 2023). Also, the practical uses of autonomous electric cars in a variety of transportation modes and sectors, including manufacturing and supply chain management, are discussed, as well as their functioning and applicability. The precision of route selection is improved with the proposed ATM-ALTREND system (He et al., 2024). The model's quality is evaluated using the lowest limit accuracy level of the test. If the proposed model is able to reach the lower bound with the necessary degree of accuracy, it will show which paths are efficient while excluding less efficient channels of communication. To increase the set of vital paths for effective vehicle positioning, more routes are required if the lower bound is higher than the predicted accuracy rate. The functional design of the suggested vehicle position monitoring system module and sensors and camera equipment are used to collect data. ITM requires data preparation which includes methods for predicting missing values.

The processing technique is applied to the obtained data, and the training method is used to train the dataset. This procedure collects the exact position of the vehicle as well as traffic data (Zhang et al., 2023).

*Figure 1. Shows the landscapes of introduction split sections (Source- Original)*

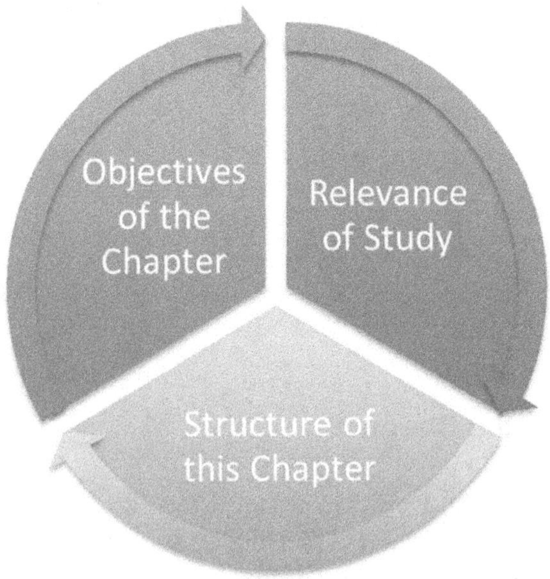


## 1.1 Objectives of the Chapter

This chapter has the following objectives to:

- Explore machine learning methods that enhance traffic control and lessen gridlock in metropolitan settings.
- Look at cutting-edge object detection methods for recognizing cars, people, and other obstructions.
- Examine AV safety-enhancing ML-based collision avoidance systems.

*Figure 2. Express the objectives of the chapter (Source- Original)*

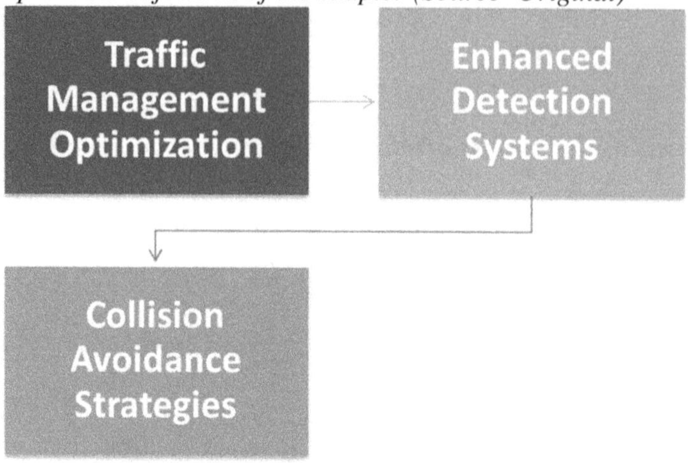


## 1.2 Structure of the Chapter

This chapter comprehensively explores the diverse arena of the Machine Learning for Safer Autonomous Vehicles: Tackling Traffic, Detection, and Collision in Smart Cities. Section 2 discusses the Traffic Management in Smart Cities. Section 3 explores the Safe Autonomous Driving: Relevance and Importance. Section 4 lays down the Machine Learning in Autonomous Vehicles. Section 5 expresses the Machine Learning for Traffic Congestion, Object Detection and Collision Avoidance. Section 6 highlights the Challenges, Concerns and Viable Solutions. Section 7 Conclude the Chapter with Future Scope.

*Figure 3. Share the flow of this chapter (Source- Original)*

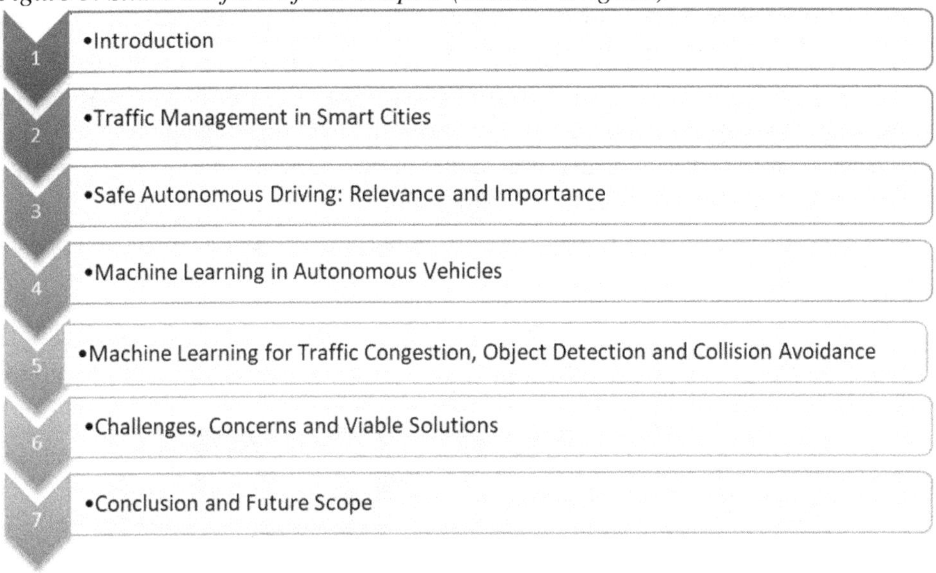


## 2. TRAFFIC MANAGEMENT IN SMART CITIES

Intelligent streets, cooperative transportation systems, and autonomous cars are just a few examples of the things that are now directly connected through the Internet of Things (IoT) for Information Technology Management (ITM) (feng et al., 2023). Improved data transfer and support for various low-bandwidth devices in high-capacity areas throughout the globe are made possible by this link. ITM systems are a frequently utilized strategy to handle traffic control issues. With reducing traffic, these technologies improve passenger transportation and logistics (Chi et al., 2023). The intelligent and sustainable development of IoT-based ITM Systems will be determined by the innovations embraced to improve quality of life. Smart city governance, which improves planning methods through strengthened laws, must be included in ITM projects. One of the main components of smart city management systems is creative social service policy.

IoT entails utilizing cutting-edge ITM technologies to establish wireless transmission links, intelligent networks, and physical item linkages to the internet (Cai et al., 2023). The connectivity between IoT-based cars is a revolutionary information sharing mechanism that facilitates ITM. To efficiently monitor and maintain traffic networks, IoT combines compute, sensor data processing, and data collecting. Every stage of autonomous mobility has its own traffic signal (Candela et al., 2023).

Electronic sensors are also used for vehicle tracking. Computerized traffic-control sensors are used to regulate traffic on the roads. An intelligent transportation system may be used to tackle problems like traffic congestion. Sensing and data fusion for smart cities provide a plethora of potential and uncharted research territory. While some of these prospects concentrate on sensing and data fusion technology, others are unique to smart cities. It is imperative that these issues be resolved quickly. The determining of the boundaries of information extraction from raw and primary data comes next, after a basic set of passive sensing properties has been discovered (Du et al., 2023).

*Figure 4. Displays the key genesis of traffic management in smart cities (source-original)*

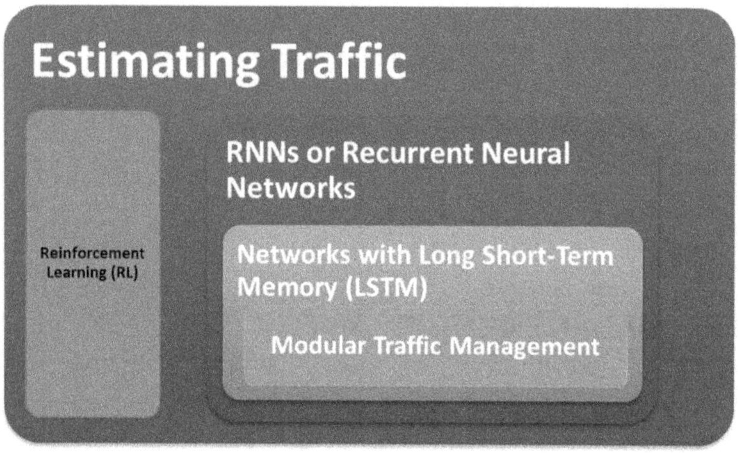


## 2.1 Estimating Traffic

Fixed size resolution data is commonly used to train object detection algorithms. Nevertheless, a lot of traffic signs are rather little, and it might get challenging to identify small signs when high-resolution photos are scaled to match the model's needed input size. Resized photos of large signboards are easily recorded however this may cause a problem with tiny signs being misidentified (ElSamadisy et al., 2024). The quick camera motion might distort the structure of tiny signs at very high speeds, like 100 km/h, making it difficult to see and identify them. It is still challenging to locate and identify every kind of traffic sign. Rather than providing scaled photographs as input to the model, this difficulty may be solved by employing high-resolution images.

## 2.2 RNNs or Recurrent Neural Networks

Predicting future network traffic characteristics from historical traffic measurements is the challenge of network traffic prediction. Numerous applications, including resource management, threat detection, and network monitoring, fall under this category. To solve the network traffic prediction problem, we suggest multiple RNN designs in this study: regular RNNs, Long Short-Term Memory (LSTM) networks, and Gated Recurrent Units (GRU). It assesses these models' performance on three major tasks as-distribution prediction, packet protocol prediction, and volume prediction (Chib & Singh, 2023).

## 2.3 Networks with Long Short-Term Memory (LSTM)

The upgraded recurrent neural network (RNN) is called Long Short-Term Memory (LSTM). LSTM is quite good at capturing long-term dependencies and is especially well-suited for jobs involving sequence prediction. Its uses include processing data sequences and doing time series analysis. The power of LSTM rests on its capacity to represent and retain sequential data, an essential skill for addressing intricate issues like speech recognition and machine translation (Gulino et al., 2024). This provides a thorough overview of LSTM, including topics such as its model, architecture, operational principles, and important function in a variety of applications. The goal of route optimization is to identify the AVs' most effective path, reducing both travel time and fuel consumption. For this, machine learning (ML) approaches like reinforcement learning (RL) and genetic algorithms (GAs) are frequently employed.

## 2.4 Reinforcement Learning (RL)

At metropolitan crossroads, ineffective and strict traffic signal control frequently leads to bottlenecks, delays, congestion, and environmental problems. The biggest challenges in urban traffic management are the intelligent regulation of traffic through smart signal management. Recent developments in machine learning, especially reinforcement learning (RL), present a viable way to deal with this problem (Pini et al., 2023). In order to tackle the complicated traffic signal management issue, where the state space might be large and the action space discrete, it uses neural networks as Q-function approximators (Q-networks). Real-time traffic data, such as vehicle placements, directions, and speeds, is used to define the state space. The action space includes several phases of traffic signals, which are essential for developing a sensible and workable control mechanism considering the unique spatiotemporal features of urban traffic.

## 2.5 Modular Traffic Management

The established area of interest in urban traffic management is traffic signal control. Traffic congestion can be relieved, traveler wait times can be cut, road network throughput can be increased, and vehicle emissions and fuel consumption can be decreased with the help of efficient traffic signal regulation. The spatial and temporal dynamics of urban traffic, however, present difficulties for traffic signal optimization at junctions (Chen et al., 2023). Urban traffic varies significantly between peak and off-peak hours in the time dimension. For example, in big cities like Beijing, peak hours (7:00–9:00 and 17:00–19:00) account for around 40% of daily traffic and it changes in urban transportation also take place in the spatial dimension (Pandharipande et al., 2023). This is to help traffic control systems learn and adjust to changing traffic circumstances; DRL blends reinforcement learning and deep learning. It has been demonstrated that using this strategy would lessen traffic jams and enhance overall traffic flow (Ashwin & Naveen Raj, 2023).

# 3. SAFE AUTONOMOUS DRIVING: RELEVANCE AND IMPORTANCE

As AVs are integrated into edge intelligence, blockchain smart contracts, Internet of Things (IoT) and vehicular networks, they will be able to fulfill user needs in a comprehensive way by exhibiting desirable qualities like self-execution, self-verification, immutability, data reliability and secrecy. The Autonomous vehicles (AVs) provide a possible answer by potentially mitigating traffic, accidents, pollution and economic and environmental problems. Their main advantages are that they can reduce accidents caused by human mistake which is the cause of a large number of collisions (Karimi et al., 2023). Up to 33% less injuries and fatalities may result from features like lane departure alerts and front collision prevention. AVs can increase mobility for a variety of groups, including the elderly and disabled in addition to conserving fuel and improving traffic conditions. Notwithstanding these benefits, there are technological obstacles and safety issues to overcome before reaching level 5 autonomy (Wang et al., 2023). Prominent tech giants such as Google, Tesla, Audi, BMW and Mercedes-Benz support on-road autonomous vehicle testing; yet, a current statistical analysis of the primary bottlenecks in AV design is still elusive. Understanding trust and safety concerns is essential to AVs being a more dependable and safer alternative for the general population and to a faster pace of commercialization.

The future of the automotive industry is now propelled by cutting-edge technology as Automotive Analytics. In this comprehensive guide, we'll explore the realm of Automotive Analytics and its transformative impact on the era of self-driving cars (Morooka et al., 2023). Automotive Analytics is at the forefront of a groundbreaking revolution. It promises safer roads and more efficient transportation, showcasing its clear benefits. This technology goes beyond just cars; it's about revolutionizing how we move and interact with our vehicles (Li et al., 2023).

## 4. MACHINE LEARNING IN AUTONOMOUS VEHICLES

Driverless cars (AVs) provide those who have never driven before or people with impairments with the ease and freedom to travel in style while doing things like reading, unwinding, or working from the passenger seat, which increases productivity (Yang et al., 2023). To evaluate their surroundings, AVs use a variety of sensors including GPS, LiDAR, odometry, radar, sonar and inertial estimation units. In order to select the best path directions, sophisticated control algorithms decode information about barriers and other markers from sensor data (Liu et al., 2023). The majority of AVs on the market today are outfitted with Level 2 and Level 3 automation, which denotes conditional driving automation (environmental detection) or partial automation which includes features like cruise control, lane departure warnings, collision detection and Advanced Driver Assistance Systems, or ADAS. Examples of Level 2 automation include Tesla's Autopilot and General Motors' Super Cruise, whereas Level 3 automation is designated for the 2019 Audi A8L. However, several projections suggest that the market will soon witness the release of Level 4 (high driving automation) and Level 5 (complete driving automation) autonomous vehicles (AVs), signifying a fast development in the AV sector.

*Figure 5. Showcase the levels of AVs (Source- Original)*

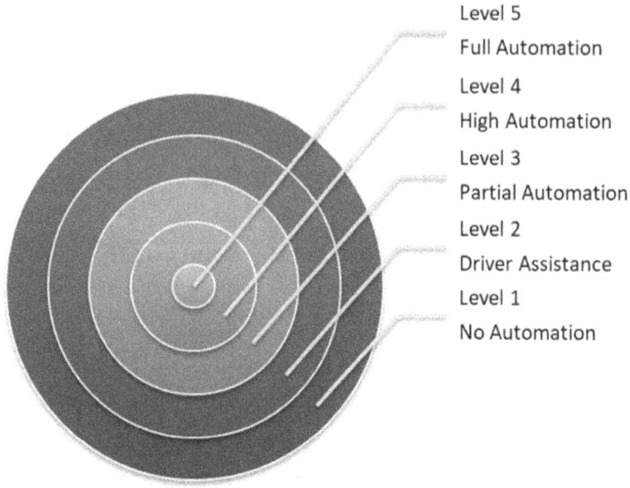


A key component of self-driving car technology is neural networks which are used to analyze driver behaviour. Facial recognition technology may identify the driver and confirm that they have permission to operate the car, improving security against theft or illegal usage (Wang et al., 2023). Utilizing occupancy recognition algorithms, the autonomous car system enhances the ride quality inside the vehicle by automatically modifying air conditioning and other elements according to the number and positioning of passengers. Deep learning frameworks like Caffe and Google TensorFlow use algorithms to train neural networks for tasks like image processing, which enables the car to understand and react to its surroundings. This technology is used in driving assistance. These algorithms play a crucial role in activities like lane detection, where the AI properly predicts the way ahead by determining the appropriate turning angles to avoid obstacles or stay in the lane. Neural networks are also very good at classifying objects (Evans et al., 2023). They use machines to tell between different objects, including automobiles, bikes, people, lampposts, and animals. The autonomous car may compute clearance and change lanes for better navigation by using visualization techniques to evaluate an object's proximity, speed, and direction of movement (Juyal et al., 2023).

## 5. MACHINE LEARNING FOR TRAFFIC CONGESTION, OBJECT DETECTION AND COLLISION AVOIDANCE

Autonomous driving systems have a hurdle when it comes to object misclassification; even little variations in picture pixels might result in mistakes. The improved and more comprehensive training of machine learning models reduces misclassifications and increases object perception accuracy. Diverse inputs regarding crucial factors enhance the dependability of data validation by mitigating reliance on certain information that might potentially distort outcomes (Zheng et al., 2023). Every sensor modality has advantages and disadvantages, such as cameras, radar, and LiDAR. Although cameras can recognize textures and colors with great fidelity, they are susceptible to changes in sunlight or fog. However, because they are active sensors, radar and LiDAR are better at estimating distance but may miss certain texture information (Zhao et al., 2023).

The growth of the transportation sector has both beneficial and difficult negative effects on society. Of these difficulties, the regularity of traffic accidents stands out as a major impediment to cities' stable development. The research on road safety analysis as well as proactive risk prevention and management are necessary to address the urgent state of road traffic safety. Through routine operations, traffic management departments have gathered a significant amount of accident data (Reda & Vasarhelyi, 2023). The finding and using the potential value contained in this data, as well as identifying the underlying laws and contributing causes to accidents, are the current essential study emphasis areas. In order to improve traffic safety big data, "the 13th Five-Year Plan for Road Traffic Safety" from 2017 placed a strong emphasis on the thorough collecting of traffic accident data foundation and theoretical analysis support for overall traffic safety improvement (Yadav et al., 2023). Using more than 60 accident data items from road traffic accident information system, a descriptive analysis based on conventional statistical methods was conducted which summarized the factors underlying road accidents by analyzing national standardized accident data.

*Figure 6. Conveys the diverse aspects of machine learning- traffic congestion, object detection and collision avoidance (Source- Original)*

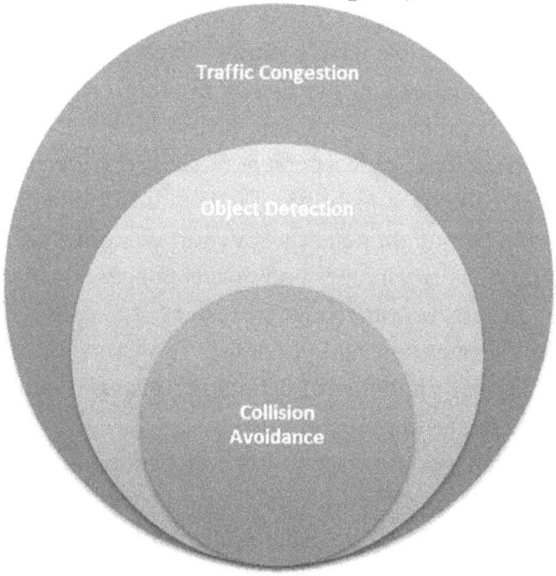


Using big data techniques for deep mining of hidden value information, data association and collision perspectives are investigated (Chen et al., 2023). In order to provide decision support for accident early warning and traffic safety management, techniques and algorithms are used to mine association rules among numerous components in traffic accidents. Visual analysis of accident data using human-computer interfaces that integrate machine and human cognition based on data interpretation. This method builds multiview association visualization analysis tools to improve people's comprehension of large amounts of complicated data (Gao et al., 2023). The whole usefulness of this data is still unrealized and is restricted to descriptive statistics of the four accident indicators, despite the fact that domestic traffic control agencies have gathered a substantial amount of original accident data utilizing standardized accident information gathering technologies (Voogd et al., 2023). The goal of the current study is to uncover the hidden value in traffic accident data and use cutting-edge technology for traffic safety to prevent and reduce accidents (Ghosh et al., 2023).

## 5.1 Integration of Sensors

The sensors track the position of the vehicle in relation to traffic flow, detecting it and its communication devices. IoT sensor devices are used by cars to send and share information, which helps to ease traffic and guarantee safe travel (Nie et al., 2023). The platform is made to prevent accidents and fatalities, notify users ahead of time of vehicle-related and dangerous driving scenarios, and handle data problems that drivers must identify in order to drive safely. It is imperative that drivers get information based on an extensive database of historically precise statistics, contingent upon the state of traffic.

*Figure 7. specifies the Variety of Fusion Sensors and Technologies for Protection of Peoples Live during Driving and Bolster Road Safety (Source- Original)*

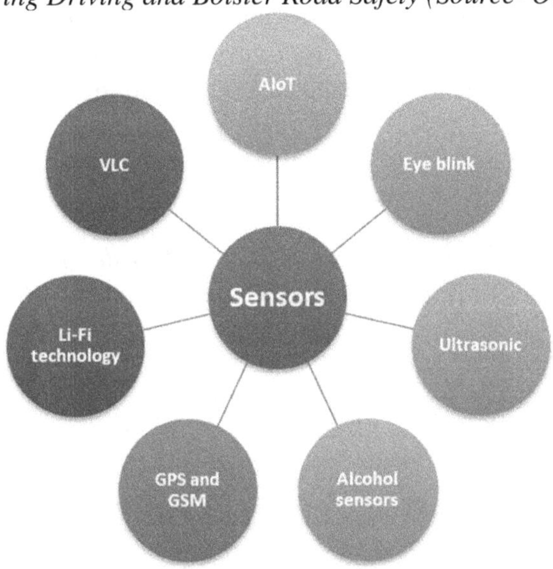


## 5.2 Camera Fusion and LiDAR

LiDAR, radar, cameras, and ultrasonic sensors are just a few of the sensors that autonomous cars use to map and identify their surroundings. Specifically, methods for sensor fusion have been developed for applications including path planning, localization, and object detection (Zhang et al., 2023). For instance, the detection of moving objects like cars and motorbikes is the main goal of traditional LiDAR and radar fusion. In this instance, object detection combines the width and length of vehicles acquired from LiDAR with velocity information from radar using Doppler data. It initially utilizes a calibration matrix acquired during sensor calibration to fuse data from a camera and a LiDAR sensor in order to estimate object distance information. Precisely taking into account the relative placements of the sensors is essential in sensor fusion techniques (Zhao et al., 2023). It uses the object recognition output from the camera along with distance data from the LiDAR to determine the distance of objects in the path of the vehicle after combining the sensor data. As a result, an accurate sensor fusion technique is required for object recognition in order to efficiently merge camera and LiDAR data (Giannaros et al., 2023).

## 5.3 Fusion of Radar and Camera

The ability of LiDAR sensors to classify objects is a limitation because it can depict situations in three dimensions, the stereovision based approach seems to be more appropriate for general object recognition among more modern techniques, while real-time performance is still a crucial concern. The cooperative combination of laser scanners and cameras, as demonstrated in is mostly restricted to the identification of vehicles and has difficulty identifying stationary objects like bicycles and humans.

*Figure 8. Illuminates the technologies in machine learning for traffic congestion, object detection and collision avoidance (Source- Original)*

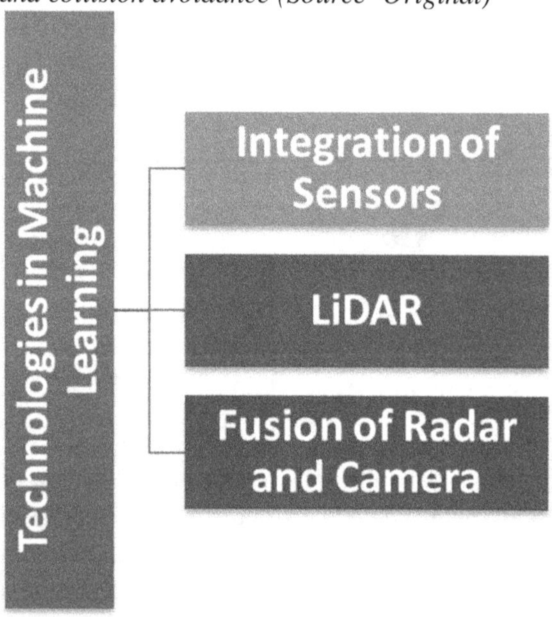

## 6. CHALLENGES AND CONCERNS

Smart cities use extensive infrastructures to keep an eye on a range of urban events in an effort to improve urban living conditions. However, because of their somewhat hazy connection to public goals, these infrastructures which frequently have a restricted emphasis, like traffic monitoring are expensive to install, need expert administration, and are not always welcomed by locals (Aksjonov & Kyrki, 2023). The intricacy of software-based infrastructures is increasing as a result of sensing technologies, possibly creating new opportunities for the provision of citizen services. This strategy may lower construction and management expenses, broaden the scope of services provided, and allay public mistrust about smart cities in general. There are some challenges and concerns (Ahmad et al., 2024).

*Figure 9. Highlights the challenges and concerns (Source- Original)*

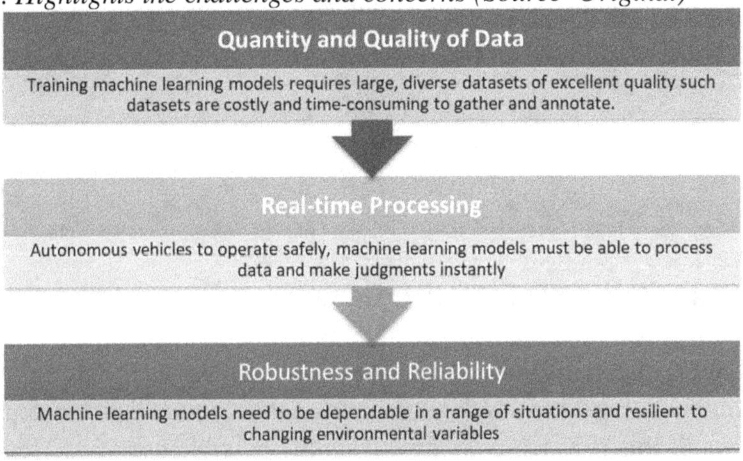


Machine learning with the use of LiDAR, radar, cameras, and ultrasonic sensors are just a few of the sensors that autonomous cars use to map and identify their surroundings (Razaei et al., 2024). Specifically, methods for sensor fusion have been developed for applications including path planning, localization, and object detection. For instance, the detection of moving objects like cars and motorbikes is the main goal of traditional LiDAR and radar fusion (Yuan et al., 2024). In this instance, object detection combines the width and length of vehicles acquired from LiDAR with velocity information from radar. However, their object categorization skills restrict object identification and tracking with many LiDAR sensors (Xiong & Huang, 2024). Because it can depict situations in three dimensions, the stereovision based approach seems to be more appropriate for general object recognition among more modern techniques, while real-time performance is still a crucial concern (Dhaif

& Abbadi, 2024). The cooperative combination of laser scanners and cameras, as demonstrated in is mostly restricted to the identification of vehicles and has difficulty identifying stationary objects like bicycles and humans (Rajendran et al., 2024).

*Figure 10. Specifies the viable solutions (Source- Original)*

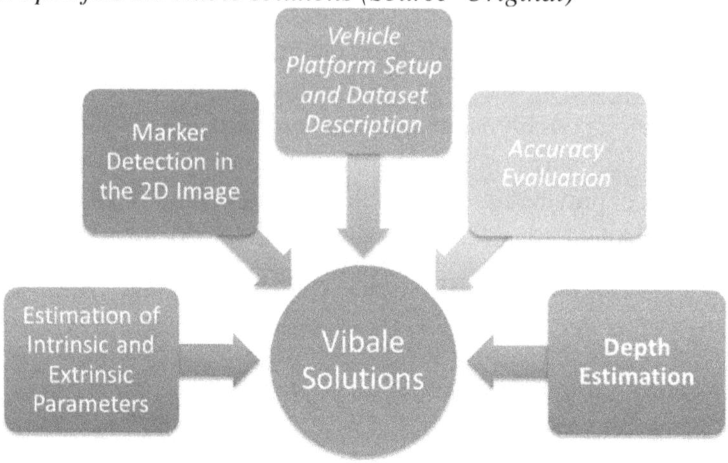


## 7. CONCLUSION AND FUTURE SCOPE

The study of autonomous vehicles' (AVs) operational and safety implications is becoming more important as they move from theory to real-world application. The purpose of this research is to investigate the possible use of AV sensor data to detect safety threats for nearby road users in real time, as well as to contribute to the continuous development of algorithms used by AVs in traversing crowded metropolitan environments. Real-time data on road user directions and trajectories is used to train a machine learning conflict prediction model that incorporates layers of the Isolation Forest; Convolutional Neural Network; Long Short-Term Memory (IF-CNN-LSTM) architecture. Three seconds into the future, this model forecasts the likelihood and seriousness of possible disputes. It looks at how well the trained model applies to new sets of data and environments, evaluating any possible accuracy trade-offs against the time and expense of retraining. The futuristic study detects and categorizes traffic disputes involving surrounding road users as well as conflicts involving AVs themselves using AV data gathered from many smart cities.

## REFERENCES


Ahmad, J., Zia, M. U., Naqvi, I. H., Chattha, J. N., Butt, F. A., Huang, T., & Xiang, W. (2024). Machine learning and blockchain technologies for cybersecurity in connected vehicles. *Wiley Interdisciplinary Reviews. Data Mining and Knowledge Discovery*, 14(1), e1515. DOI: 10.1002/widm.1515

Aksjonov, A., & Kyrki, V. (2023). A safety-critical decision-making and control framework combining machine-learning-based and rule-based algorithms. *SAE International Journal of Vehicle Dynamics, Stability, and NVH, 7*(10-07-03-0018), 287-299. DOI: 10.1002/widm.1515

Ashwin, S. H., & Naveen Raj, R. (2023). Deep reinforcement learning for autonomous vehicles: Lane keep and overtaking scenarios with collision avoidance. *International Journal of Information Technology : an Official Journal of Bharati Vidyapeeth's Institute of Computer Applications and Management*, 15(7), 3541–3553. DOI: 10.1007/s41870-023-01412-6

Cai, Y., Zhou, R., Wang, H., Sun, X., Chen, L., Li, Y., Liu, Q., & He, Y. (2023). Rule-constrained reinforcement learning control for autonomous vehicle left turn at unsignalized intersection. *IET Intelligent Transport Systems*, 17(11), 2143–2153. DOI: 10.1049/itr2.12336

Candela, E., Doustaly, O., Parada, L., Feng, F., Demiris, Y., & Angeloudis, P. (2023). Risk-aware controller for autonomous vehicles using model-based collision prediction and reinforcement learning. *Artificial Intelligence*, 320, 103923. DOI: 10.1016/j.artint.2023.103923

Chen, H., Yuan, K., Huang, Y., Guo, L., Wang, Y., & Chen, J. (2023). Feedback is all you need: From ChatGPT to autonomous driving. *Science China. Information Sciences*, 66(6), 1–3. DOI: 10.1007/s11432-023-3740-x

Chen, H., Zhang, Y., Bhatti, U. A., & Huang, M. (2023). Safe decision controller for autonomous drivingbased on deep reinforcement learning innondeterministic environment. *Sensors (Basel)*, 23(3), 1198. DOI: 10.3390/s23031198 PMID: 36772238

Chib, P. S., & Singh, P. (2023). Recent advancements in end-to-end autonomous driving using deep learning: A survey. *IEEE Transactions on Intelligent Vehicles.*

Cui, J., Yuan, L., He, L., Xiao, W., Ran, T., & Zhang, J. (2023). Multi-input autonomous driving based on deep reinforcement learning with double bias experience replay. *IEEE Sensors Journal*, 23(11), 11253–11261. DOI: 10.1109/JSEN.2023.3237206

Dhaif, Z. S., & El Abbadi, N. K. (2024). A Review of Machine Learning Techniques Utilised in Self-Driving Cars. *Iraqi Journal For Computer Science and Mathematics*, 5(1), 205–219. DOI: 10.52866/ijcsm.2024.05.01.015

Du, Y., Chen, J., Zhao, C., Liao, F., & Zhu, M. (2023). A hierarchical framework for improving ride comfort of autonomous vehicles via deep reinforcement learning with external knowledge. *Computer-Aided Civil and Infrastructure Engineering*, 38(8), 1059–1078. DOI: 10.1111/mice.12934

ElSamadisy, O., Shi, T., Smirnov, I., & Abdulhai, B. (2024). Safe, efficient, and comfortable reinforcement-learning-based car-following for AVs with an analytic safety guarantee and dynamic target speed. *Transportation Research Record: Journal of the Transportation Research Board*, 2678(1), 643–661. DOI: 10.1177/03611981231171899

Evans, B. D., Jordaan, H. W., & Engelbrecht, H. A. (2023). Safe reinforcement learning for high-speed autonomous racing. *Cognitive Robotics*, 3, 107–126. DOI: 10.1016/j.cogr.2023.04.002

Feng, S., Sun, H., Yan, X., Zhu, H., Zou, Z., Shen, S., & Liu, H. X. (2023). Dense reinforcement learning for safety validation of autonomous vehicles. *Nature*, 615(7953), 620–627. DOI: 10.1038/s41586-023-05732-2 PMID: 36949337

Gao, L., Zhou, R., & Zhang, K. (2023). Scenario generation for autonomous vehicles with deep-learning-based heterogeneous driver models: Implementation and verification. *Sensors (Basel)*, 23(9), 4570. DOI: 10.3390/s23094570 PMID: 37177774

Ghosh, S., Zaboli, A., Hong, J., & Kwon, J. (2023). An integrated approach of threat analysis for autonomous vehicles perception system. *IEEE Access : Practical Innovations, Open Solutions*, 11, 14752–14777. DOI: 10.1109/ACCESS.2023.3243906

Giannaros, A., Karras, A., Theodorakopoulos, L., Karras, C., Kranias, P., Schizas, N., Kalogeratos, G., & Tsolis, D. (2023). Autonomous vehicles: Sophisticated attacks, safety issues, challenges, open topics, blockchain, and future directions. *Journal of Cybersecurity and Privacy*, 3(3), 493–543. DOI: 10.3390/jcp3030025

Gu, Z., Gao, L., Ma, H., Li, S. E., Zheng, S., Jing, W., & Chen, J. (2023). Safe-state enhancement method for autonomous driving via direct hierarchical reinforcement learning. *IEEE Transactions on Intelligent Transportation Systems*, 24(9), 9966–9983. DOI: 10.1109/TITS.2023.3271642

Gulino, C., Fu, J., Luo, W., Tucker, G., Bronstein, E., Lu, Y., & Sapp, B. (2024). Waymax: An accelerated, data-driven simulator for large-scale autonomous driving research. *Advances in Neural Information Processing Systems*, •••, 36.

He, X., Huang, W., & Lv, C. (2024). Toward Trustworthy Decision-Making for Autonomous Vehicles: A Robust Reinforcement Learning Approach with Safety Guarantees. *Engineering (Beijing)*, 33, 77–89. DOI: 10.1016/j.eng.2023.10.005

He, X., Wu, J., Huang, Z., Hu, Z., Wang, J., Sangiovanni-Vincentelli, A., & Lv, C. (2023). Fear-neuro-inspired reinforcement learning for safe autonomous driving. *IEEE Transactions on Pattern Analysis and Machine Intelligence*. PMID: 37801378

Hu, Y., Fu, J., & Wen, G. (2023). Safe reinforcement learning for model-reference trajectory tracking of uncertain autonomous vehicles with model-based acceleration. *IEEE Transactions on Intelligent Vehicles*, 8(3), 2332–2344. DOI: 10.1109/TIV.2022.3233592

In *Sustainable Disposal Methods of Food Wastes in Hospitality Operations* (pp. 176-192). IGI Global. DOI: 10.1109/TIV.2022.3233592

Juyal, A., Sharma, S., & Matta, P. (2023, March). Object Classification Using A rtificial I ntelligence Technique sin Autonomous Vehicles. In *2023 3rd International conference on Artificial Intelligence and Signal Processing (AISP)* (pp. 1-6). IEEE.

Karimi, S., Karimi, A., & Vahidi, A. (2023). Level-$ K $ Reasoning, Deep Reinforcement Learning, and Monte Carlo Decision Process for Fast and Safe Automated Lane Change and Speed Management. *IEEE Transactions on Intelligent Vehicles*, 8(6), 3556–3571. DOI: 10.1109/TIV.2023.3265311

Li, J., Liu, X., Zhu, B., Jiao, J., Tomizuka, M., Tang, C., & Zhan, W. (2023). Guided online distillation: Promoting safe reinforcement learning by offline demonstration. *arXiv preprint arXiv:2309.09408.*

Liu, Z., Guo, Z., Lin, H., Yao, Y., Zhu, J., Cen, Z., . . . Zhao, D. (2023). Datasets and benchmarks for offline safe reinforcement learning. *arXiv preprint arXiv:2306.09303.*

Mohanty, A., Rahamathunnisa, U., Sudhakar, K., & Sathiyaraj, R. (2024). Age of Computational AI for Autonomous Vehicles. *Artificial Intelligence for Autonomous Vehicles*, 25-54. DOI: 10.3390/make5030041

Morooka, F. E., Junior, A. M., Sigahi, T. F., Pinto, J. D. S., Rampasso, I. S., & Anholon, R. (2023). Deep learning and autonomous vehicles: Strategic themes, applications, and research agenda using SciMAT and content-centric analysis, a systematic review. *Machine Learning and Knowledge Extraction*, 5(3), 763–781. DOI: 10.3390/make5030041

Nie, X., Liang, Y., & Ohkura, K. (2023). Autonomous highway driving using reinforcement learning with safety check system based on Time-To-Collision. *Artificial Life and Robotics*, 28(1), 158–165. DOI: 10.1007/s10015-022-00846-8

Pandharipande, A., Cheng, C. H., Dauwels, J., Gurbuz, S. Z., Ibanez-Guzman, J., Li, G., Piazzoni, A., Wang, P., & Santra, A. (2023). Sensing and machine learning for automotive perception: A review. *IEEE Sensors Journal*, 23(11), 11097–11115. DOI: 10.1109/JSEN.2023.3262134

Pini, S., Perone, C. S., Ahuja, A., Ferreira, A. S. R., Niendorf, M., & Zagoruyko, S. (2023, May). Safe real-world autonomous driving by learning to predict and plan with a mixture of experts. In *2023 IEEE International Conference on Robotics and Automation (ICRA)* (pp. 10069-10075). IEEE. DOI: 10.1109/ICRA48891.2023.10160992

Rajendran, S., Sabharwal, M., Hu, Y. C., & Balusamy, B. (Eds.). (2024). *Artificial Intelligence for Autonomous Vehicles: The Future of Driverless Technology*. John Wiley & Sons. DOI: 10.1002/9781119847656

Reda, A., & Vásárhelyi, J. (2023). Design and implementation of reinforcement learning for automated driving compared to classical mpc control. *Designs*, 7(1), 18. DOI: 10.3390/designs7010018

Rezaei, S., Masoud, N., & Khojandi, A. (2024). GAAD: GAN-enabled autoencoder for real-time sensor anomaly detection and recovery in autonomous driving. *IEEE Sensors Journal*, 24(7), 11734–11742. DOI: 10.1109/JSEN.2024.3361460

Sharifi, I., Yildirim, M., & Fallah, S. (2023). Towards Safe Autonomous Driving Policies using a Neuro-Symbolic Deep Reinforcement Learning Approach. *arXiv preprint arXiv:2307.01316.*

Voogd, K. L., Allamaa, J. P., Alonso-Mora, J., & Son, T. D. (2023). Reinforcement learning from simulation to real world autonomous driving using digital twin. *IFAC-PapersOnLine*, 56(2), 1510–1515. DOI: 10.1016/j.ifacol.2023.10.1846

Wang, X., Zhang, J., Hou, D., & Cheng, Y. (2023). Autonomous driving based on approximate safe action. *IEEE Transactions on Intelligent Transportation Systems*, 24(12), 14320–14328. DOI: 10.1109/TITS.2023.3292253

Wang, Z., Liu, X., & Wu, Z. (2023). Design of Unsignalized Roundabouts Driving Policy of Autonomous Vehicles Using Deep Reinforcement Learning. *World Electric Vehicle Journal*, 14(2), 52. DOI: 10.3390/wevj14020052

Xiong, N., Du, Y., & Huang, L. (2024). Provably safe reinforcement learning with step-wise violation constraints. *Advances in Neural Information Processing Systems*, •••, 36.

Yadav, P., Mishra, A., & Kim, S. (2023). A comprehensive survey on multi-agent reinforcement learning for connected and automated vehicles. *Sensors (Basel)*, 23(10), 4710. DOI: 10.3390/s23104710 PMID: 37430623

Yang, Y., Jiang, Y., Liu, Y., Chen, J., & Li, S. E. (2023). Model-free safe reinforcement learning through neural barrier certificate. *IEEE Robotics and Automation Letters*, 8(3), 1295–1302. DOI: 10.1109/LRA.2023.3238656

Yuan, K., Huang, Y., Yang, S., Wu, M., Cao, D., Chen, Q., & Chen, H. (2024). Evolutionary Decision-Making and Planning for Autonomous Driving: A Hybrid Augmented Intelligence Framework. *IEEE Transactions on Intelligent Transportation Systems*, 25(7), 7339–7351. DOI: 10.1109/TITS.2023.3349198

Zhang, E., Zhang, R., & Masoud, N. (2023). Predictive trajectory planning for autonomous vehicles at intersections using reinforcement learning. *Transportation Research Part C, Emerging Technologies*, 149, 104063. DOI: 10.1016/j.trc.2023.104063

Zhang, L., Zhang, Q., Shen, L., Yuan, B., Wang, X., & Tao, D. (2023, June). Evaluating model-free reinforcement learning toward safety-critical tasks. *Proceedings of the AAAI Conference on Artificial Intelligence*, 37(12), 15313–15321. DOI: 10.1609/aaai.v37i12.26786 PMID: 38464961

Zhang, Y., Liang, X., Li, D., Ge, S. S., Gao, B., Chen, H., & Lee, T. H. (2023). Adaptive safe reinforcement learning with full-state constraints and constrained adaptation for autonomous vehicles. *IEEE Transactions on Cybernetics*. PMID: 37363853

Zhang, Z., Han, S., Wang, J., & Miao, F. (2023, May). Spatial-temporal-aware safe multi-agent reinforcement learning of connected autonomous vehicles in challenging scenarios. In *2023 IEEE International Conference on Robotics and Automation (ICRA)* (pp. 5574-5580). IEEE. DOI: 10.1109/ICRA48891.2023.10161216

Zhao, J., Zhao, W., Deng, B., Wang, Z., Zhang, F., Zheng, W., & Burke, A. F. (2023). Autonomous driving system: A comprehensive survey. *Expert Systems with Applications*, •••, 122836.

Zhao, W., He, T., Chen, R., Wei, T., & Liu, C. (2023). State-wise safe reinforcement learning: A survey. *arXiv preprint arXiv:2302.03122*. DOI: 10.24963/ijcai.2023/763

Zheng, H., Chen, C., Li, S., Zheng, S., Li, S. E., Xu, Q., & Wang, J. (2023). Learning-based safe control for robot and autonomous vehicle using efficient safety certificate. *IEEE Open Journal of Intelligent Transportation Systems*, 4, 419–430. DOI: 10.1109/OJITS.2023.3280573

# Chapter 9
# Integrating Artificial Intelligence and Machine Learning for Sustainable Practices in the Legal Sector:
## A Study From a Global Perspective

**Tanaya Das**
https://orcid.org/0000-0001-9196-9738
*JIS University, India*

**Souraneel Mandal**
https://orcid.org/0009-0004-5181-8993
*Ghani Khan Choudhury Institute of Engineering and Technology, India*

**Bidisha Bhabani**
https://orcid.org/0000-0003-4261-1849
*JIS University, India*

## ABSTRACT

*Sustainability is an emerging need in all service sectors of society. The legal sector, traditionally perceived as a traditional industry, is increasingly recognizing the importance of sustainability in practices and operations. The emergence of Artificial Intelligence based techniques provides new opportunities for enhancing access to justice, enhancing efficiency, and streamline workflows. However, the conventional legal system has some constraints and limitations that can impact its effectiveness and ability to provide justice. Hence, this chapter analyzes Artificial Intelligence*

DOI: 10.4018/979-8-3373-2530-9.ch009

*and Machine Learning as a solution to the challenges. With the help of thorough investigations, this chapter provides a comprehensive study on the worldwide use of Artificial Intelligence-based applications fostering sustainable practices within the legal industry to improve society. By integrating Artificial Intelligence and Machine Learning, the legal sector can move towards a more sustainable and efficient future, ensuring faster service delivery by legal professionals.*

## 1. INTRODUCTION

The primary objective of any research endeavor is to lead to the development of potential solutions to some of the challenges faced by society. The continuous process of improving various sectors through research and technology has the potential to bring about significant advancements and positive changes. Healthcare (Ali, 2023), Education (Rismanchian and et al., 2023), Transportation (Iyer, 2021), Environment (Verma,2024), etc., demonstrate how research and technology can drive innovation and progress in these sectors, thereby making them more efficient, sustainable, and accessible for everyone.

*Figure 1. Multivariate applications of artificial intelligence*

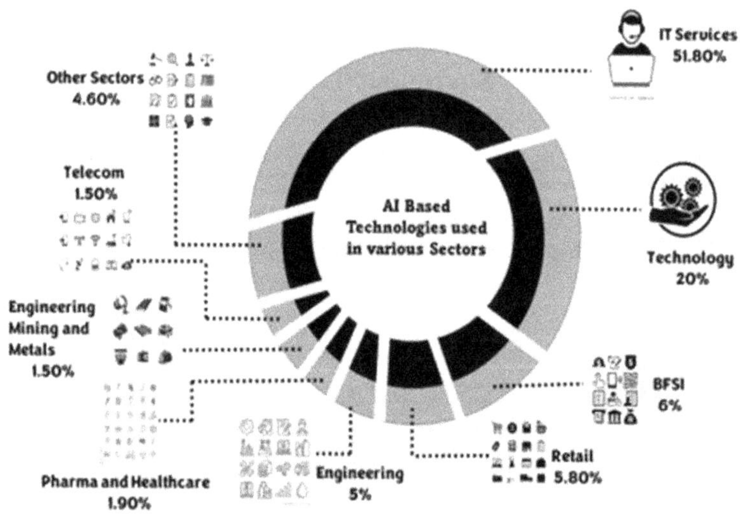


The data shown by (Tprestianni, 2024), illustrates the utilization of Artificial Intelligence equipped technologies in different service industries, demonstrating the growing integration of practices across these sectors to improve sustainability as shown in Figure1. Indeed, it is increasingly emerging as a potent instrument for promoting sustainability in many service industries, therefore facilitating the more effective utilization of resources in society.

The legal system is one of the important parameters for the growth of any society. It provides the framework for protecting property rights, enforcing contracts, resolving disputes, protecting human rights, and promoting innovation and entrepreneurship. For this purpose, laws may be enacted to maintain the balance by protecting the interest of marginalized sections to live freely, as well as facilitate the normal functioning of wealthy sections of society. The legal industry has experienced a profound transformation in recent years, driven by the exponential growth of data and the rapid advancements in artificial intelligence and machine learning technologies (Wright, 2020). The abundance of data, coupled with increased computing power and more effective algorithms, has enabled the automation of numerous tasks that were once exclusively performed by human legal professionals (Becerra, 2018). According to Global Legal Analytics Market (Sackman et. al, 1996) the topmost players are Wolters Kluwer (Netherlands), Thomson Reuters (Canada), Mind Crest (US), United Lex Corporation (US), LexisNexis (US), Premonition (US), Analytics Consulting (US), The Bureau of National Affairs (BNA) (US), IBM Corporation (US). In India the elite law firm Cyril Amarchand Mangaldas has made the first move to use the advantage of artificial intelligence and legal analytics by partnering with Toronto-headquartered Kira Systems. It provides services such as contract search, analytics, and knowledge management. Legal firms can significantly reduce manual labor and resource consumption, such as paper and energy, traditionally associated with legal processes. This transition aligns with sustainable practices by optimizing workflows, minimizing errors, and enhancing precision in legal documentation, thereby reducing waste and environmental impact.

However, the legal sector faces numerous challenges due to the large number of unsettled legal cases, inadequate technological infrastructure, time-consuming nature of legal cases by the legal professionals, etc. This chapter investigates the integration of Artificial Intelligence and Machine Learning technologies as a solution to these challenges, promoting sustainable practices within the legal industry for a better society. The authors provide a comprehensive study, examining existing applications of Artificial Intelligence and Machine Learning in legal industry around the globe and discussing the relationship of AI-based legal applications and sustainability, emphasizing how these technologies can contribute to long-term ecological, social, and economic goals. This chapter is discussed in six sections. Section1 addressed the use of Artificial Intelligence and Machine Learning for the purpose of sustainable practices in various sectors including the legal sector. Section 2 focused on a literature review of the emerging role of Artificial Intelligence based techniques in the legal industry from two perspectives. Section 3 addressed the sustainable practices and challenges observed in traditional legal practice. Sections 4 provide an analysis on the use of Artificial Intelligence based tools in the legal field for sustainable practice. With the help of some case studies, it demonstrates the implementation of Artificial based legal tools to provide faster legal services by legal professionals. Section 5 highlights the role of Artificial Intelligence based tools in streamlining legal research, acceptance of paperless work ensuring the alignment with environmental and societal objectives. The core purpose of this chapter is to promote an interdisciplinary research approach of bridging law and technology via Artificial Intelligence for sustainable legal practices. Also, it focused on the way these Artificial Intelligence based legal applications could support sustainable development by contributing to long-term ecological, social, and economic goals.

## 2. LITERATURE REVIEW

The legal industry has witnessed a significant transformation in recent years. Researchers have explored Artificial Intelligence based techniques to automate repetitive legal tasks, such as legal text classification, document summarization, contract review, etc. These applications within the legal domain have potential to contribute to the achievement of sustainable development goals (Goh & Vinuesa, 2021).

(Zhang et al., 2023) discussed innovative tools have the potential to revolutionize various aspects of legal practice. The tools are effective from improving the efficiency of delivery services by legal professionals and law firms to democratizing legal services accessible to the public.

Recently, Legal Analytics has emerged as an important arena of Legal Research. Legal Analytics (Mandal et al., 2022) aims to combine digitized legal data and Machine Intelligence to understand, manage and improve legal services and outcomes. With the help of Artificial Intelligence based techniques like Natural Language Processing, Machine Learning, etc. the legal professionals are delivering services like legal discovery (Efthimiadis et al., 2008), legal research (Bhat et al.,2020), document summarization (Ghosh et al., 2022), drafting (Geng et al., 2022), etc.

Legal professionals thoroughly examine and organize major information in a systematic way. Previously, they used to manually examine and arrange raw legal data in a specific way to generate the arguments from it. It involves some analytical and legal logical reasoning skills of a lawyer which leads to a conclusion for that particular case. In legal profession, the need for efficient and effective knowledge capturing has become increasingly paramount. The legal domain is a complex and information-rich field, with a vast amount of data available in structured and unstructured forms. In recent years, the increasing availability of legal information in electronic form has sparked a growing interest in the application of machine learning and deep learning techniques for legal document analysis and processing (Bansal et al., 2019; Katz et al., 2023). The conclusion of any legal case can be drawn when all of the aforementioned factors have been considered and completely examined. Legal case analysis can be conducted with the help of a knowledge base (Das et al.,2020). Early knowledge-based systems were predominantly noted as expert systems which were used as experts to assist the decision-making process. The efficiency of these expert systems was measured by their problem-solving capability which determines its sustainability in the long run. In legal domain, to capture and manage the vast knowledge effectively is crucial for sustainable legal practice. (Zakaria et al., 2014). Ontology has emerged as another crucial discipline in improving information organization, management, and understanding (Ding & Foo, 2002). Approaches for developing ontologies that can effectively capture and represent the knowledge within the legal domain. The techniques and approaches for developing ontologies that can effectively capture and represent the knowledge within the legal domain was explained in (Das et. al, 2022). Nowadays, Large Language Models (LLMs) (Veres, 2022) are advanced Artificial Intelligence models designed to understand and generate human-like text based on the input they receive. These models are trained in vast amounts of text data and use Deep Learning techniques to generate coherent and contextually relevant responses. The use of Artificial Intelligence based legal applications facilitates paperless documentation leading to sustainable resource utilization worldwide (Hasan et.al, 2023) and reduced environmental impact.

From the overall literatures it has been found that as the legal landscape evolves, the integration of Artificial Intelligence and Machine Learning has emerged as a transformative force, offering unprecedented opportunities to enhance sustainability within legal practice. While significant progress has been made in the application of Artificial Intelligence and Machine Learning to the legal domain, there are still numerous challenges and open problems that need to be addressed. Also, some research studies illustrate how these technologies align with sustainable practices by optimizing operations, reducing errors, and enhancing accuracy in legal paperwork, therefore reducing waste and environmental effect. Furthermore, the worldwide implementation of Artificial Intelligence based solutions illustrate the scalability of the technologies in creating more efficient and ecologically sustainable legal ecosystems elaborated in subsequent sections of this chapter.

## 3. SUSTAINABLE PRACTICES IN THE LEGAL SECTOR

The legal industry can play a vital role in promoting sustainability through its advisory and advocacy functions. Through the utilization of legal knowledge and skills, professionals in the legal sector have the ability to make valuable contributions to the wider sustainability movement, so facilitating beneficial transformations within their area of impact. One key aspect of sustainable practice in the legal profession is the adoption of paperless workflows (Gupta, A., 2017). By transitioning to digital document management and communication, law firms can significantly deliver quick service.

## 3.1. Understanding Sustainability

Sustainability, a term that has gained increasing popularity in recent decades, encompasses a multifaceted and complex concept that encompasses the ability to meet the needs of the present without compromising the ability of future generations to meet their own needs. The term "sustainability" has been discussed in terms of three interconnected pillars: environmental, social, and economic sustainability (Thompson, 2021). Economic sustainability, meanwhile, is concerned with the long-term viability of economic systems and the ability to maintain economic growth and prosperity without compromising environmental or social well-being (Nieto, 1997; Özşen et al., 2022). The concept of sustainability has been widely adopted and promoted in various sectors, from business and industry to government and academia (Ginting, 2020; Danis et al., 2022). Businesses, for example, are increasingly embracing sustainability principles in their operations, seeking to reduce their environmental impact, improve their social responsibility, and ensure the long-term viability of their enterprises (Fayomi et al., 2021; Danis et al., 2022). Similarly, educational sectors are integrating sustainability into their curricula, research, and campus operations, recognizing the critical role they play in shaping the knowledge and values of future generations (Özşen et al., 2022).

Sustainable development is now globally accepted as a supreme long-term goal of humanity, and the sustainable utilization of natural resources is essential for sustainable development. The technical definition of sustainability is "the ability of a natural resource system to produce a socially optimum level of output that is necessary to meet the needs and aspirations of the people dependent on the system perpetually without any detrimental effects on the resource system itself and the physical environment, and with no imposition of significantly greater risks on future generations" (Nallathiga, 2003).

## 3.2. Challenges in Traditional Legal Practice

The conventional legal system refers to the system of laws, courts, and legal processes that are used in many countries around the world. This system is usually based on a written constitution or set of laws, which defines the powers and responsibilities of the government and its various subsidiaries (Suganda et al., 2020) . In this system, disputes are resolved through a formal legal process, which involves a trial in a court of law. The trial is presided over by a judge, who is responsible for interpreting and applying the law over the facts and figures of the case. The parties to the dispute are typically represented by attorneys, who present evidence and arguments on their behalf. However, the conventional legal system has some constraints and limitations that can impact its effectiveness and ability to provide justice. The high legal fees, court costs, etc., create barriers for individuals to afford legal professionals. Another constraint is the length and time-consuming legal process where the cases sometimes take years to solve. There is a steady rise in the number of pending cases due to the recruitment of a smaller number of legal professionals. The prolonged process and the lack of available numbers of legal professionals make it difficult to perform detailed case analysis and to extract the important context of their cases.

## 4. ARTIFICIAL INTELLIGENCE AND MACHINE LEARNING AS ENABLERS OF TRADITIONAL LEGAL PRACTICE

The significance of technology in problem-solving depends on its ability to provide innovative solutions and streamline processes, making them more efficient. The tools and techniques used for data analysis, automation, simulation, etc. have proven to be a good solution to solve many business problems. The legal system is adapting to cutting-edge tools to speed up the working process of the conventional legal system. The provisions of legal services rendered by legal professionals are gradually depending on the use of digital technologies. Legal services expect to benefit greatly from these cutting-edge technologies like Natural Language Processing, Machine Learning, etc. Legal practitioners usually rely on various investigative findings and evidence to take decisions based on alternative outcomes of the inquiry made. Applications of Artificial Intelligence to legal services (Dragoni et al., 2020) are changing the approach of a lawyer to analyze and solve the cases.

### 4.1. Case Studies of Integrating Artificial Intelligence and Machine Learning in Legal Practice

Case studies on the integration of Artificial Intelligence and Machine Learning in legal practice demonstrate the practical applications of technologies in transforming traditional legal services. The legal industry is undergoing a transformation driven by technology and data analytics, impacting various traditional practices. Legal research (Slorach et al., 2017) remains the foundation of legal work, but with advancements of natural language based in contract analysis (Dobrovolska, 2020), lawyers can now review and manage contractual obligations, reducing human error efficiently.

Ensuring adherence to laws and regulations is critical, making compliance and risk management (Makowicz, 2023) a key focus area, particularly as businesses navigate complex legal landscapes. Document review and due diligence have become more streamlined through automation, allowing for faster and more accurate processing of large volumes of information. This shift towards automation of legal processes has paved the way for predictive analytics, where data is used to forecast legal outcomes and optimize decision-making. Additionally, the emergence of legal chatbot for assisting routine legal queries, enhancing client engagement and operational efficiency. Together, these advancements are reshaping the legal profession, making it more efficient, data-driven, and client-focused. Figure 2 depicts the various case studies of Artificial Intelligence based legal applications to deliver legal services by professionals.

*Figure 2. Case studies of legal services using artificial intelligence and machine learning*

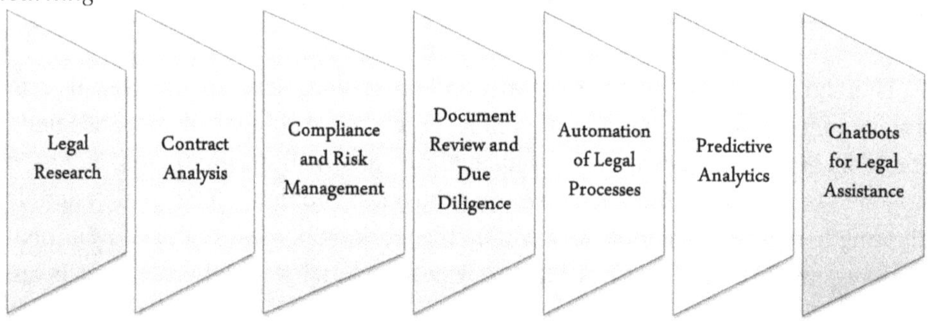


## 4.2. Legal Research

### 4.2.1. What is Legal Research?

Legal research is the process of identifying and retrieving information necessary to support legal decision-making. It involves finding legal precedents, statutes, case law, and other relevant materials to address specific legal questions or issues. It helps in drafting legal documents, representing clients effectively, and staying updated with legal developments.

### 4.2.2. Traditional Legal Research Methods

The practice of legal research has long been rooted in traditional methodologies, but these approaches are increasingly facing scrutiny and criticism. The conventional approach to legal research sometimes depends significantly on text materials, such as law books, periodicals, journals, etc., which can be time-consuming and expensive.

In India, the conventional legal system has some constraints and limitations that can impact its effectiveness and ability to provide justice. The high legal fees, court costs, etc., create barriers for individuals to afford legal professionals. Another constraint is the length and time-consuming legal process where the cases sometimes take years to solve. Nowadays, the overloading state of the legal profession (India, P. T., 2023) can be traced by recruitment of a smaller number of legal professionals at various courts. As a result, there is a steady rise in the number of pending cases. The accessibility of legal documents has changed from the traditional methods. In the past, individuals were required to attend courts in order to gather case-related records physically. The documents are now available digitally as a result of digitization. Online databases provide public access to electronic versions of cases and judgements.

### 4.2.3. Shift to Digital Legal Research

The Rise of Platforms Like Westlaw, LexisNexis, and Hein Online databases have revolutionized legal research by providing comprehensive, searchable collections of legal information, including case law, statutes, and legal commentary. Online Databases Revolutionized Legal Research Digital databases offer faster and more efficient access to a vast array of legal resources, transforming how legal research is conducted. A lawyer can get various case references and citation material by searching websites. In India, legal search engines such as Indlaw, Indian Kanoon, and Manupatra has been developed to assist legal practitioners in India. The case information is available in digital format.

### 4.2.4. Role of Artificial Intelligence in Legal Research

Artificial Intelligence based techniques involve the use of computer systems to perform tasks that typically require human intelligence, such as understanding natural language and making decisions. Artificial Intelligence based tools like Westlaw Edge, Casetext, and ROSS Intelligence offer advanced research capabilities, such as context-aware search and legal prediction. These tools can analyse large datasets, identify patterns, and provide insights that are not apparent through traditional research methods. Artificial Intelligence based tools such as Natural Language

Processing understand (Mandal et al., 2023) and interpret complex legal language, enhancing the ability to find and analyse relevant information.

## 4.3. Contract Analysis

### 4.3.1. What is Contract Analysis?

Contract analysis in the legal sector is a critical function that involves the review, interpretation, and management of contracts to ensure compliance, mitigate risks, and support business objectives. This process is becoming increasingly automated with the advent of legal technology, but the core principles remain essential to legal practice. It complies with relevant laws and regulations. Legal professionals ensure that the contract adheres to industry standards, corporate policies, and legal requirements.

### 4.3.2. Traditional Approach of Legal Professionals in Contract Analysis

Legal professionals provide crucial advice during contract analysis. They guide their clients on potential risks, negotiation strategies, and legal implications of various contract terms. This advisory role is vital in ensuring that contracts are fair, enforceable, and aligned with the client's best interests. They use their understanding of the contract to support their client's position in negotiations, mediation, or litigation. Thorough contract analysis can prevent disputes, but when they do occur, it provides a solid basis for resolving them.

### 4.3.3 Challenges and Limitations

Contracts typically follow a structured format that includes definitions, scope, obligations, warranties, indemnities, and termination clauses. Understanding this structure is essential for efficient analysis. Legal professionals manually start by ensuring that the contract's structure is logical and that all necessary elements are present. Legal professionals must accurately interpret these terms to ensure that they reflect the intended meaning and do not lead to ambiguity. Certain clauses are crucial in any contract, such as confidentiality, indemnification, and dispute resolution clauses. Legal professionals make a lot of effort to manually evaluate these terms in order to protect the client's interests and guarantee enforcement.

### 4.3.4 Role of Artificial Intelligence in Contract Analysis

Artificial Intelligence and Machine Learning are increasingly used in contract analysis to automate the review process. These technologies can scan contracts to identify standard clauses, detect anomalies, and suggest revisions. Use of Natural Language Based concepts understand and interpret the language in contracts. It allows for the extraction of key information, such as party names, dates, and payment terms, and can even analyse the sentiment behind contract language.

## 4.4. Compliance and Risk Management

### 4.4.1. What is Compliance and Risk Management?

Compliance and risk management are critical functions within the legal sector, as they ensure that law firms and legal departments operate within the bounds of the law and manage the risks associated with their activities.

### 4.4.2 Traditional Approach of Legal Professionals in Compliance and Risk Management

Law firms and legal departments must ensure that they comply with all applicable local, national, and international regulations. This includes staying up to date with changes in legislation, understanding the implications of these changes, and adopting practices accordingly. Continuous training for legal professionals is essential to ensure they understand the regulatory landscape. Legal professionals are bound by strict ethical codes, such as those established by bar associations or legal societies.

### 4.4.3 Role of Artificial Intelligence in Compliance and Risk Management

As artificial intelligence continues to transform various industries, its impact on risk management and compliance in the legal sector has become increasingly significant (Golbin et al., 2020; Al-Shabandar et al., 2019). AI-powered systems can influence decisions ranging from hiring and credit approvals to criminal sentencing and information dissemination by social media platforms. Machine learning and Artificial Intelligence based techniques are revolutionizing financial risk control, providing solutions for fraud detection, compliance monitoring, and the reduction of model risk. However, the successful implementation of these technologies requires suitable data management policies, transparency, and the development of necessary skillsets within organizations.

## 4.4. Document Review and Due Diligence

### 4.4.1. What is Document Review and Due Diligence?

These are essential processes in various professional fields, particularly in legal, financial, and business sectors. These processes ensure that transactions, agreements, and operations are conducted with a comprehensive understanding of the associated risks, liabilities, and opportunities. The process of meticulously examining documents to ensure they meet specific criteria for accuracy, completeness, and compliance. This process is essential in various stages of legal and business operations, including litigation, compliance audits, and transactional due diligence.

### 4.4.2. Scope of Document Review and Due Diligence in Legal Sector

Document analysis and due diligence are relevant in many service sectors such as finance, commerce, environmental, etc. Likewise, in legal proceedings, document review is vital for identifying relevant information, ensuring compliance, and building a case. Due diligence helps in assessing the legal standing and potential liabilities of entities involved. The document review refers to the comprehensive examination and analysis of documents to ensure they are complete, accurate, and comply with legal and regulatory standards. This process is crucial in legal proceedings, compliance audits, business transactions and operations including litigation, compliance audits, and transactional due diligence.

### 4.4.3. Role of Artificial Intelligence in Document Review and Due Diligence

The use of big data using Artificial Intelligence and machine learning in document review and due diligence is expected to increase, providing more efficient and accurate analysis. These technologies can automate routine tasks, identify patterns, and extract relevant information from large volumes of data. Tools like SharePoint and Documentum help in organizing and managing documents. AI tools like Kira Systems and eBrevia use machine learning to automate the identification and extraction of relevant information from documents. Optimal Character Recognition (OCR) technology converts scanned documents into editable and searchable text, aiding in document review. Similarly, tools like QuickBooks and Xero facilitate financial due diligence by providing detailed financial reports and analysis. Westlaw, LexisNexis, and Bloomberg Law provide access to legal documents, case law, and regulatory information. Virtual data rooms like Intralinks and Merrill Datasite provide secure platforms for sharing and reviewing documents during due diligence.

## 4.5. Predictive Analytics

### 4.5.1. What are Predictive Analytics?

Predictive analytics is the branch of data analytics that focuses on making predictions about future outcomes based on historical data and statistical algorithms. It utilizes a variety of techniques, including data mining, machine learning, and artificial intelligence, to analyze current and historical facts to make predictions about future or otherwise unknown events. The core objective of predictive analytics is to go beyond knowing what has happened to provide a best assessment of what will happen in the future.

### 4.5.2. Scope of Predictive Analytics in the Legal Sector

Predictive analytics is a rapidly growing field that has been successfully applied across numerous sectors, including finance, healthcare, retail, and marketing. Likewise, legal sector, traditionally seen as conservative and slow to adopt new technologies, is increasingly recognizing the value of predictive analytics. Legal professionals deal with vast amounts of data daily, including case files, legal documents, contracts, and court records. By applying predictive analytics, legal practitioners can gain insights that were previously inaccessible, leading to better decision-making, improved client outcomes, and increased efficiency in legal processes. A range of machine learning methods, including classification and regression, are employed to forecast the outcome of a case.

### 4.5.3. Role of Artificial Intelligence in Predictive Analytics in Legal

Big data analytics can provide deeper insights into legal trends, patterns, and outcomes, allowing for more accurate and reliable predictions. In the legal sector, data sources include court records, legal documents, contracts, case law databases, and client information. Additionally, external data sources such as financial records, social media data, and news articles can provide valuable context for legal predictions. The challenge will be in managing and analysing the vast amounts of data generated in the legal sector. It has the potential to impact international law by providing insights into global legal trends, predicting the outcomes of international disputes, and assisting in the interpretation of international treaties. Several machine learning models are commonly used in legal analytics such as decision trees, support vector machines, neural network, natural language processing, etc. As predictive analytics becomes more prevalent in the legal sector, there will be a growing need for legal professionals to be trained in data analytics and technology at Law schools.

## 4.6. Use of Chatbots in Legal Assistance

### 4.6.1. Chatbot: Basic Introduction

Chatbots are applications designed to emulate human conversation through text or voice. At their core, chatbots use Artificial Intelligence based conversations to interpret and respond to user inputs. Chatbots are operated on rule-based systems, following predefined scripts to handle user queries. Chatbots was first introduced in 1960s with the creation of program ELIZA for mimicking a psychotherapist's responses. It was operated on a set of pre-programmed rules and lacked the ability to learn from interactions. In 1990, it brought advancements with ALICE, a more complex chatbot that used AIML (Artificial Intelligence Markup Language) to engage in more sophisticated dialogues. In recent years, the rise of deep learning and neural networks has enhanced chatbot capabilities, allowing them to understand context, manage complex conversations, and learn from user interactions.

### 4.6.2. Scope of Chatbot in Providing Legal Assistance

Nowadays, chatbots are useful to provide legal assistance as they address several challenges within the legal industry. Legal services are often expensive and difficult for common people. Chatbots offer a solution by providing immediate, cost-effective assistance that makes legal help more accessible. For individuals who may not have the means to consult a lawyer directly, chatbots can offer preliminary legal advice, information on legal procedures, and guidance on documentation. Moreover, chatbots can enhance the efficiency of legal practices by automating routine tasks. For example, they can handle common queries, assist in document preparation, and manage case-related schedules, thus allowing legal professionals to focus on more complex and nuanced aspects of their work. The functionality of legal chatbots is primarily based on natural language processing (NLP) and machine learning (ML). By accessing up-to-date legal information and managing documents efficiently, chatbots can provide accurate legal advice and streamline administrative tasks. The rise of chatbots has revolutionized customer interactions across various industries, and the legal domain is no exception (Khennouche et al., 2023). Developing a legal chatbot to provide legal assistance, however, presents unique challenges that need to be addressed. (Radziwill & Benton, 2017). One of the primary hurdles is ensuring the accuracy and reliability of the chatbot's responses. (Xu et al., 2021). Legal matters often involve complex and nuanced issues, requiring a deep understanding of the law and the ability to interpret and apply it correctly (Wollny et al., 2021) (Khennouche et al., 2023). Integrating the chatbot with comprehensive knowledge bases and fine-tuning its natural language processing capabilities are crucial steps to overcome this challenge.

### 4.6.3. Role of Artificial Intelligence Based Techniques in Developing Legal Chatbot

Natural Language Processing (NLP) plays a pivotal role in enabling legal chatbots to understand and process legal language. NLP involves several sub-tasks, including tokenization (breaking down text into words or phrases), part-of-speech tagging (identifying the grammatical role of each word), and named entity recognition (identifying key legal terms and entities). These techniques allow chatbots to accurately interpret user queries, recognize legal terminology, and provide relevant responses. For instance, NLP can help a chatbot differentiate between terms like "plaintiff" and "defendant," ensuring that the advice provided is contextually appropriate.

Machine learning algorithms are integral to enhancing the capabilities of legal chatbots. Classification algorithms, for example, can categorize user queries into predefined classes, such as contract-related questions or family law inquiries. Recommendation systems, another type of ML algorithm, can suggest relevant legal information or documents based on user inputs and interaction history.

## 4.7 Categories of Legal Chatbots

### 4.7.1. Chatbots for Legal Advice

Chatbots designed for legal advice provide users with general information and guidance on a range of legal issues. These chatbots can address common queries about legal processes, rights, and responsibilities. For instance, a legal advice chatbot might assist users in understanding the basics of contract law, explain the steps involved in filing a complaint, or provide information on consumer rights.

### 4.7.2. Chatbots for Document Preparation

Legal chatbots that focus on document preparation assist users in creating and managing legal documents. These chatbots often provide templates for common legal forms, such as wills, contracts, and power of attorney documents. Users can interact with the chatbot to answer questions and provide relevant information, which the chatbot uses to generate customized documents.

### 4.7.3. Chatbots for Case Management

Case management chatbots are designed to assist with the administrative aspects of managing legal cases. These chatbots can handle tasks such as scheduling appointments, sending reminders, and tracking important deadlines. For example, a case management chatbot might notify clients of upcoming court dates, remind them of document submission deadlines, or schedule meetings with legal professionals.

### 4.7.4. Chatbots for Legal Research

Legal research chatbots assist users in finding and navigating legal information and resources. These chatbots can help users search for case law, statutes, regulations, and legal articles relevant to their queries. By querying legal databases and using NLP techniques to interpret user inputs, these chatbots can provide users with accurate and relevant research results. For example, a legal research chatbot might help a user find recent case law on a specific legal issue or identify applicable statutes for a legal argument. This assistance can be particularly valuable for individuals who may not be familiar with legal research techniques or who need help accessing specialized legal resources.

### 4.7.5. Chatbots for Client Interaction

Chatbots designed for client interaction focus on enhancing communication between clients and legal professionals. These chatbots can handle a variety of tasks, such as answering client inquiries, providing information about legal services, and offering updates on case status. By providing immediate and accurate responses to client questions, these chatbots help improve the overall client experience and ensure that clients have access to the information they need.

The above-mentioned categories of various legal chatbots, to address various aspects of the legal industry, require both general and specialized needs. Every category of legal chatbot is specifically engineered to carry out particular functions, providing customized services that span from delivering legal counsel to overseeing case management. Below is a detailed exploration of 16 different types of legal chatbots, their names, and the specific roles they fulfill within the legal domain explained in Figure 3.

*Figure 3. Various legal chatbots used for different legal domains*

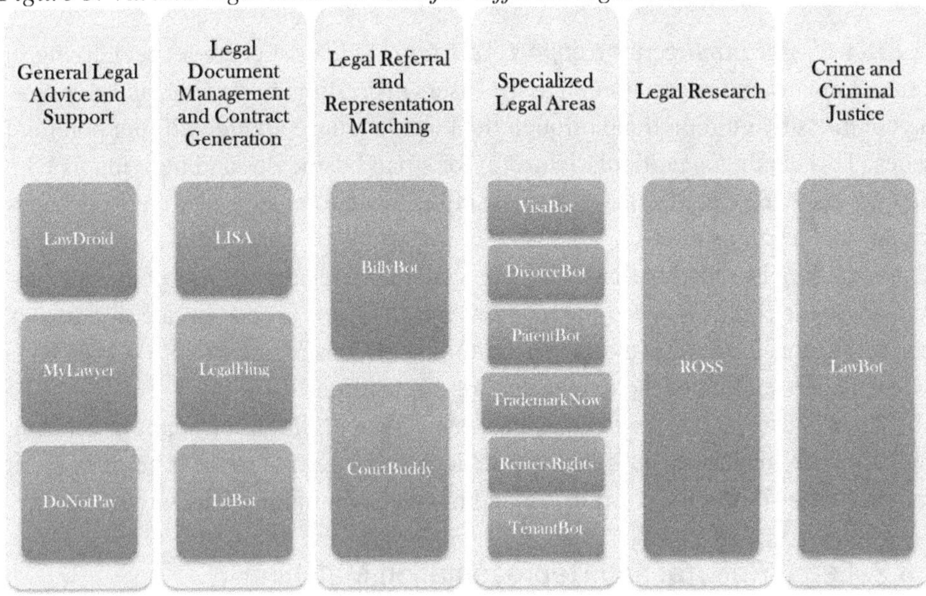


## 4.8. General Legal Advice and Support

***LawDroid*** is versatile chatbot designed to offer general legal advice to users. It provides information on a wide range of legal topics, from understanding basic legal rights to navigating more complex legal issues like contract disputes or property law. LawDroid uses natural language processing to interpret user queries and provide relevant legal guidance, making it accessible to individuals who may not have a legal background. Its primary function is to act as a first point of contact for users seeking legal information, helping them understand their situation and guiding them on the appropriate steps to take.

***MyLawyer*** offers personalized legal advice based on user queries. It asks users questions about their legal situation and provides tailored advice on how to proceed. It covers a broad range of legal topics, from employment law to personal injury claims. It also provides information on potential legal strategies and the likely outcomes of different courses of action. By offering customized legal advice, MyLawyer helps users make informed decisions about their legal matters.

***DoNotPay*** is often dubbed as "robot lawyer," that assists users in resolving disputes, particularly those involving consumer rights. Originally developed to help users contest parking tickets, has expanded its capabilities to include helping users fight bank fees, obtain refunds, and navigate small claims court.

### 4.8.1. Legal Document Management and Contract Generation

***LISA (Legal Intelligence Support Assistant)*** is a legal chatbot specializing in contract review and negotiation. It assists users in drafting, reviewing, and negotiating contracts by guiding them through the legal language and identifying potential issues. This chatbot is particularly useful for small businesses and individuals who may not have easy access to legal counsel but need to ensure that their contracts are fair and legally sound.

***LegalFling*** is a chatbot that focuses on generating legally binding contracts, particularly in the context of personal relationships. It allows users to create agreements that define consent and boundaries in relationships, ensuring that both parties have a clear understanding of their rights and responsibilities.

***LitBot*** is designed to assist legal professionals with litigation support, offering tools for case management, document review, and legal research. It helps lawyers organize case files, track court dates, and manage communication with clients.

### 4.8.2. Legal Referral and Representation Matching

***BillyBot*** is designed to assist users in finding the right legal professional for their needs. It acts as a legal referral service, asking users questions about their legal issues and then matching them with an appropriate lawyer or law firm. It can also provide information on legal services and offer insights into what users can expect when working with a lawyer.

***CourtBuddy*** is a chatbot that matches users with legal professionals based on their specific needs and budget. It helps users find attorneys for various legal issues, such as family law, criminal defense, or civil litigation. It offers flexible payment options, including flat fees and payment plans, making legal services more affordable and accessible. By connecting users with the right lawyer, ensures that individuals can get the legal representation they need without the usual barriers of cost and complexity.

### 4.8.3. Specialized Legal Areas

***VisaBot*** is a chatbot that provides legal assistance related to immigration processes. It helps users navigate the complexities of visa applications, green card processes, and citizenship requirements. It guides users through the necessary steps, providing information on required documents, application procedures, and eligibility criteria.

***DivorceBot*** specializes in family law, particularly in guiding users through the divorce process. It provides information on divorce laws, child custody arrangements, alimony, and division of assets. DivorceBot helps users understand their rights and responsibilities during a divorce, offering advice on how to negotiate settlements and navigate the legal system.

***PatentBot*** specializes in intellectual property law, particularly in helping users file patents. It guides inventors and businesses through the patent application process, offering advice on the necessary documentation, filing procedures, and legal requirements.

***TrademarkNow*** is a legal chatbot that assists users with trademark registration and protection. It guides users through the process of conducting trademark searches, filing trademark applications, and managing trademark portfolios.

***RentersRights*** is a legal chatbot dedicated to assisting tenants with housing-related legal issues. It provides information on tenant rights, lease agreements, eviction processes, and dispute resolution with landlords. It helps tenants understand their legal protections and what steps they can take if their rights are being violated.

***TenantBot*** is a legal chatbot that focuses on resolving disputes between landlords and tenants. It provides guidance on handling issues such as lease violations, rent increases, maintenance problems, and eviction proceedings.

### 4.8.4. Legal Research

***ROSS*** is an Artificial Intelligence powered legal research assistant designed to help legal professionals find relevant case law, statutes, and legal articles. ROSS uses natural language processing to understand complex legal queries and retrieve the most pertinent information from vast legal databases. It is particularly useful for lawyers who need to quickly access legal precedents and other resources to build strong legal arguments. ROSS enhances the efficiency of legal research, allowing lawyers to focus on case strategy and analysis rather than spending hours sifting through legal texts.

### 4.8.5 Crime and Criminal Justice

***LawBot*** is a chatbot designed to assist users in understanding their legal rights in criminal matters. It provides guidance on what actions to take if someone is a victim of a crime or accused of a crime. It explains the legal processes involved, from reporting a crime to navigating the criminal justice system. It also offers advice on what to expect during police interactions, court proceedings, and sentencing.

### 4.8.6. Automation of Legal Process

In the ever-evolving landscape of the legal industry, the concept of automating legal processes has gained significant traction in recent years. The above mentioned some case studies globally, the rise of artificial intelligence and other advanced technologies has transformed the way legal services are delivered, offering new opportunities to streamline workflows, enhance efficiency, and improve access to justice. One of the primary requirements behind the automation of legal processes is the recognition that many routine tasks performed by lawyers can be automated, so that they may utilize their time and resources to focus on more complex and strategic matters (Gravett, 2020; Davis, 2020). This includes tasks such as document review, contract analysis, and case prediction, which can be carried out more quickly, accurately, and cost-effectively with the help of Artificial Intelligence tools. The automation of legal processes has the potential to address long-standing challenges within the legal industry, such as the high cost of legal services and the limited accessibility of the justice system.

Figure. 4 depicts specific Artificial Intelligence techniques employed in different countries for the purpose of conducting Legal Research and Analytics. The paradigm has transitioned towards automated technologies.

*Figure 4. Globally used legal assistance tools*

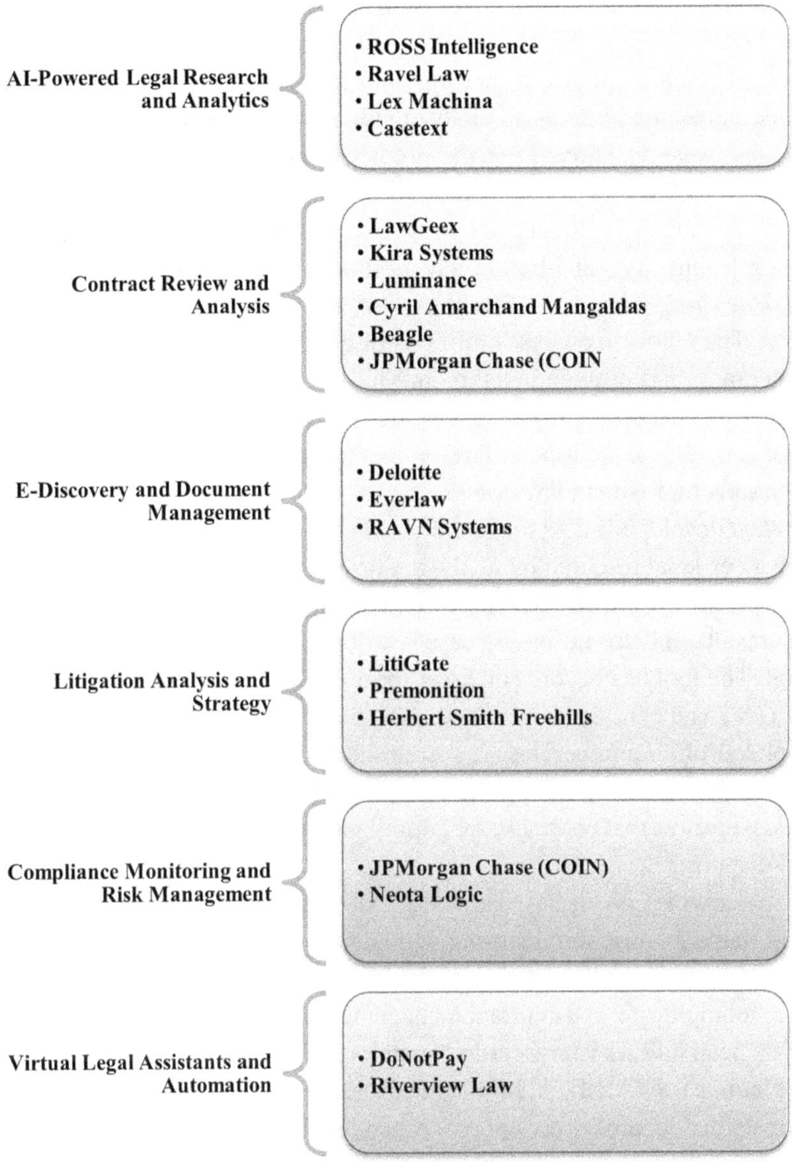


***ROSS Intelligence*** (Ross, T. J., 2007) is Artificial Intelligence powered legal research platform developed in United States that utilizes natural language processing (NLP) to assist lawyers in finding relevant legal precedents and case law efficiently. The system can understand questions in natural language, provide answers, and suggest relevant documents, making legal research faster and more accurate. Legal professionals have reported significant reductions in research time, enabling them to focus more on client work and case strategy.

***Ravel Law***, (Adams, W. H., 2020) acquired by LexisNexis, developed an AI-driven legal research platform that provides visualizations and insights into case law. It uses machine learning to analyze judicial opinions and identify patterns in how judges make decisions, offering predictive analytics for case outcomes. The platform allows lawyers to anticipate how a judge might rule on a case, providing a strategic advantage in litigation. It also streamlines legal research by highlighting the most relevant cases and trends, saving time and improving accuracy.

***Lex Machina*** (Markou, C., 2019) uses AI and ML to provide legal analytics for litigation. The platform analyses millions of court cases to identify trends, predict case outcomes, and provide insights into judges, lawyers, and parties involved in litigation. It can make data-driven decisions, improve case strategy, and better understand the competitive landscape. The tool has been particularly useful in intellectual property and employment law cases.

***Casetext*** developed an AI tool called CARA (Case Analysis Research Assistant) that enhances legal research by analysing briefs and suggesting relevant case law. The AI system uses deep learning to understand the context and provide highly relevant results. It helps in finding case law that traditional research methods might overlook. The tool has become an asset for quickly developing legal arguments.

***LawGeex*** is a contract review and analysis platform that automates the review and approval of contracts. The AI system compares contracts against predefined criteria and legal standards, highlighting discrepancies and suggesting necessary changes. It ensures that contracts are compliant and free of errors, reducing the risk of legal disputes.

***Kira Systems*** is Canada based law firm that offers an AI-powered contract review platform that uses machine learning to identify, extract, and analyse key clauses from contracts and legal documents. The platform is designed to assist with due diligence, compliance, and contract management by automating the review process. One of its head quarter is present in Bangalore, India.

***Luminance*** uses Artificial Intelligence and Machine Learning based techniques to automate the document review process in legal due diligence, contract analysis, and regulatory compliance. The platform can quickly analyse and categorize large volumes of documents, identifying key information and potential risks.

***Cyril Amarchand Mangaldas*** is one of India's leading law firms, Cyril Amarchand Mangaldas, implemented Kira systems to assist in contract review and due diligence processes. Kira uses machine learning to analyse contracts and identify relevant clauses and potential risks. The firm reported a significant reduction in the time required for contract review, with improved accuracy in identifying critical issues.

***Beagle*** is an AI tool that assists with contract analysis by quickly reading and analysing contracts to highlight key terms, clauses, and potential risks. It uses natural language processing to understand the context of legal language and provide insights. It has enabled legal teams to speed up contract review processes, allowing for quicker decision-making.

***JPMorgan Chase***, United States implemented an AI program called COIN (Contract Intelligence) to review and interpret commercial loan agreements. The AI system uses machine learning algorithms to analyse legal documents, extracting key data points and identifying potential risks.

***Deloitte***, a global professional services firm, uses AI in its e-discovery services. Their AI tools sift through vast amounts of electronic data during the discovery phase of litigation, identifying relevant documents, patterns, and key information. It has drastically reduced the time and costs associated with manual document review and increases accuracy in identifying pertinent information, helping legal teams build stronger cases.

***Everlaw*** uses AI to enhance the e-discovery process, leveraging predictive coding and machine learning to categorize and prioritize documents. The platform assists legal teams in reviewing large datasets, identifying relevant documents, and generating reports. It also helps reduce legal costs and improves the efficiency of litigation preparation.

***RAVN Systems***, United Kingdom acquired by iManage, developed AI solutions for automating document management and review. Their AI tools are used for contract analysis, due diligence, and compliance monitoring, extracting relevant data from unstructured documents. Law firms and corporate legal departments using RAVN have seen substantial improvements in document management efficiency.

***LitiGate***, Israel is an AI-powered platform that assists litigators by analysing case law, legal arguments, and judges' decisions to predict the success of litigation strategies. It uses NLP to break down complex legal arguments and suggest counterarguments. It helps legal teams develop stronger, more persuasive arguments by providing data-driven insights. It also reduces the time spent on manual analysis, allowing lawyers to focus on case strategy and client interaction.

***Premonition*** uses Artificial Intelligence to analyse court data and provide insights into the performance of attorneys, law firms, and judges. The platform helps clients choose legal representation based on success rates, providing data-driven recommendations. Premonition has disrupted traditional methods of selecting legal counsel by providing transparency into the performance of legal professionals. This has empowered clients to make more informed decisions and improve their chances of winning cases.

***Herbert Smith Freehills*** has integrated AI tools into its dispute resolution practice, using machine learning algorithms to analyse litigation data, predict outcomes, and assist in strategy development. The predictive capabilities also help in making informed decisions about whether to pursue or settle a case.

***Neota Logic*** provides AI-driven expert systems that automate complex legal processes, such as compliance checks, risk assessments, and legal diagnostics. The platform allows law firms to create custom applications that can provide legal advice based on predefined rules and algorithms. They have also enhanced access to legal advice by enabling self-service options for clients.

***Riverview Law***, acquired by Ernst & Young, United States, uses virtual assistants powered by AI to handle routine legal tasks such as contract management, compliance monitoring, and legal research. The AI assistants interact with clients and provide real-time legal support. The use of virtual assistants has streamlined legal operations, reduced costs, and improved client satisfaction. Table 1 presents a summary of the category of the legal applications deployed globally as discussed above.

*Table 1. Summary of artificial intelligence based tools used globally and its uses*

| *Category* | *Tool/Platform* | *Location* | *Key Points* | *Uses* |
|---|---|---|---|---|
| **AI-Powered Legal Research and Analytics** | **ROSS Intelligence** | United States | AI-based legal research tool. | Assists lawyers in finding relevant case law. |
| | **Ravel Law** | United States | Offers legal research with analytics. | Identifies patterns in case law. |
| | **Lex Machina** | United States | Legal analytics platform. | Helps predict litigation outcomes. |
| | **Casetext** | United States | AI-assisted legal research. | Provides case law and legal briefs. |
| **Contract Review and Analysis** | **LawGeex** | Israel | AI for contract review. | Ensures contract compliance. |
| | **Kira Systems** | Canada | AI-driven contract analysis. | Speeds up due diligence processes. |
| | **Luminance** | United Kingdom | AI document review platform. | Enhances document analysis in M&A. |
| | **Cyril Amarchand Mangaldas** | India | AI in contract review. | Provides legal contract analysis in India. |
| | **Beagle** | Canada | AI contract analysis tool. | Identifies contract risks and clauses. |
| | **JPMorgan Chase (COIN)** | United States | AI for contract analysis. | Reviews financial contracts for compliance. |

continued on following page

*Table 1. Continued*

| *Category* | *Tool/Platform* | *Location* | *Key Points* | *Uses* |
|---|---|---|---|---|
| **E-Discovery and Document Management** | **Deloitte** | Global | AI in e-discovery. | Facilitates legal document discovery. |
| | **Everlaw** | United States | AI for e-discovery and review. | Streamlines legal discovery processes. |
| | **RAVN Systems** | United Kingdom | AI for document management. | Manages legal documents and contracts. |
| **Litigation Analysis and Strategy** | **LitiGate** | Israel | AI litigation analysis tool. | Analyzes case strengths and weaknesses. |
| | **Premonition** | United States | AI-powered litigation analytics. | Provides insights into litigation strategies. |
| | **Herbert Smith Freehills** | United Kingdom, Australia, Global | AI in dispute resolution. | Supports legal strategy and dispute resolution. |
| **Compliance Monitoring and Risk Management** | **JPMorgan Chase (COIN)** | United States | AI for compliance monitoring. | Monitors compliance in financial contracts. |
| | **Neota Logic** | United States | Expert systems for compliance. | Automates compliance and risk management tasks. |
| **Virtual Legal Assistants and Automation** | **DoNotPay** | United States | AI legal assistance. | Automates small claims and legal services. |
| | **Riverview Law** | United Kingdom | Virtual legal assistants. | Provides automated legal support. |

# 5. USE OF ARTIFICIAL INTELLIGENCE BASED LEGAL APPLICATIONS BRIDGING ECOLOGICAL, ECONOMIC AND SOCIAL SUSTAINABILITY

*Figure 5. Legal applications and sustainability*

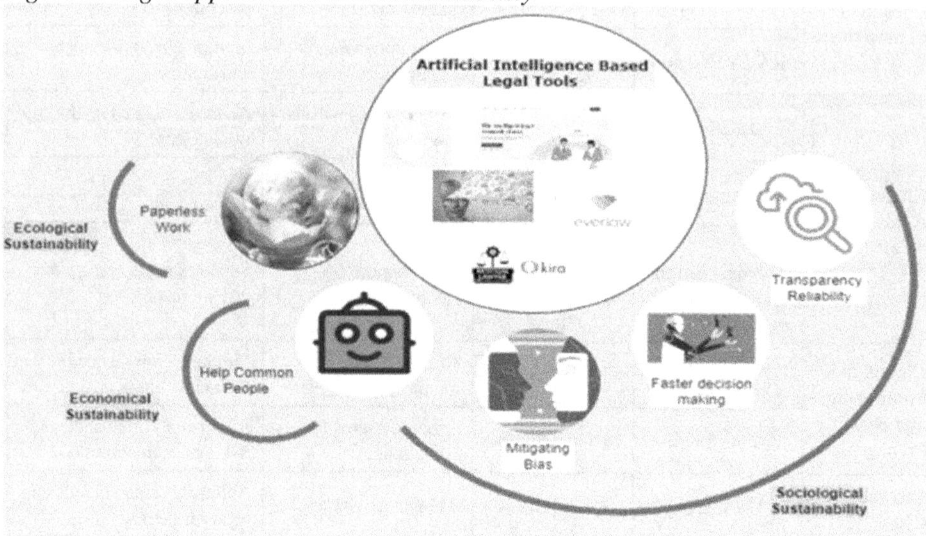


Implementation of Artificial Intelligence based applications in the legal sector significantly assist in achieving some of the sustainable objectives. Artificial Intelligence driven legal frameworks might enhance transparency, trustworthiness, and efficiency across various fields, hence supporting sustainable ecological, social, and economic goals (Napolitano, G.,2024). Figure 5 illustrates the association between legal applications and sustainability.

## 5.1. Ecological Sustainability

The incorporation of Artificial Intelligence in legal process significantly promotes ecological sustainability by minimizing dependence on physical resources such as paper and energy consuming manual operations. Legal hard copy documents are numerous, and printing each one is a labor-intensive operation that consumes significant time. Consequently, AI-based legal applications may facilitate document management and legal research, reducing the necessity for large printing and storage. By automating repeated tasks, these systems minimize the energy consumption related to prolonged human engagement in administrative duties. After the COVID-19 pandemic, Artificial Intelligence based remote legal consultations and virtual court proceedings reduced travel related carbon-emissions of the people. The transition to digitization in the legal industry corresponds with eco-friendly practices, fostering a more sustainable and environmentally friendly legal system.

## 5.2. Economy Sustainability

The use of various types of chatbots in legal services as mentioned above extensively promote economic sustainability by reducing the cost of accessing legal assistance and making it more affordable for common people (Ho, J.-H., and et.al, 2020). By providing immediate and automated support, chatbots eliminate the need for expensive initial consultations and help streamline routine legal tasks, such as document review and procedural guidance. This efficiency not only saves costs for people but also enables legal system to optimize their resources, hence reducing overhead expenses. Moreover, by reducing the financial barriers to legal services, chatbots assure that economically deprived communities can access essential legal information, promoting a more inclusive and sustainable legal framework. For example, ***Sophia*** (Sophia chatbot, 2023) anonymously assists survivors of domestic violence in collecting potential evidence, offers access to resources and support, and continually adapts to fulfil the requirements of survivors worldwide. Automation of common legal tasks such as providing preliminary advice, guiding on documentation, and offering information on legal procedures, these applications reduce dependency on expensive legal consultations.

## 5.3. Social Sustainability

Some legal Artificial Intelligence based applications are playing an important role in promoting social sustainability by addressing key issues such as bias, decision-making speed, transparency, and reliability in the legal system. As discussed above, there are many pending cases which need fast decision so that the accused may get the punishment within stipulated time. These technologies reduce bias by utilizing data-driven algorithms, which assist in removing subjective human preconceptions and ensuring equitable results. It facilitates expedited decision-making by automating repetitive tasks, optimizing legal research, and offering immediate access to case precedents, so considerably diminishing the time necessary for legal procedures. Legal applications enhance transparency through analysing extensive legal data and delivering clear, well-documented reasoning behind decisions, so encouraging trust in the system. Collectively, these innovations enhance social sustainability by facilitating access to justice, ensuring fairness, and strengthening public trust in the judicial system.

## CONCLUSION

Applications of Artificial Intelligence and machine learning have the potential to implement sustainable practices in legal industry. The emergence of Large Language Models enhances the efficiency of legal professionals, deepens their expertise and provides more services to their clients. While the legal profession has traditionally been slow to adopt technological advancements, the current trends of using Artificial Intelligence based legal tools show a promising future. However, the successful integration of Artificial Intelligence and Machine Learning based applications in the legal sector necessitates multidisciplinary research, which involves the collaboration of experts from the multidisciplinary fields to confront the challenges. As the legal landscape continues to evolve, the strategic deployment of Artificial Intelligence based tools will be crucial in enhancing the sustainability of legal practices worldwide. Legal applications are driving transformative changes that support ecological, economic, and social sustainability. These applications lead to reduce environmental impact by minimizing paper usage, reducing carbon emissions due to virtual interaction for court proceedings. Economically, these applications help to reduce the expenses of the individuals and organizations by making legal services accessible and affordable. The legal sector can provide positive changes, improve decisions, deliver more equitable and accessible justice systems to society.

## REFERENCES

Adams, W. H. (2012, January 24). *Ravel chronology*. De Gruyter. https://www.degruyter.com/document/doi/10.12987/9780300170122-016/html

Al-Shabandar, R., Lightbody, G., Browne, F., Liu, J., Wang, H., & Zheng, H. (2019, October 17). The Application of Artificial Intelligence in Financial Compliance Management. DOI: 10.1145/3358331.3358339

Ali, R. (2023). *AI Usage in Healthcare*. DOI: 10.31219/osf.io/b36y5

Bansal, N., Sharma, A., & Singh, R K. (2019, January 1). A Review on the Application of Deep Learning in Legal Domain. Springer Science+Business Media, 374-381. DOI: 10.1007/978-3-030-19823-7_31

Becerra, S. D. (2018, January 1). The Rise of Artificial Intelligence in the Legal Field: Where We Are and Where We Are Going., 11(1), 27-52. https://digitalcommons.pepperdine.edu/cgi/viewcontent.cgi?article=1169&context=jbel

Bhat, P. I. (2020). Thinking process in legal research. *Idea and Methods of Legal Research*, 32–53. DOI: 10.1093/oso/9780199493098.003.0002

Danis, M., Acar, A Z., & Arslan, A. (2022, January 1). Is the Use of Green Certification Strategic or Not?. Gdynia Maritime University, 16(2), 203-209. DOI: 10.12716/1001.16.02.01

Das, T., Roy, A., & Majumdar, A. K. (2020). A study on legal knowledge base creation using artificial intelligence and ontology. Innovative Data Communication Technologies and Application, 647–653. DOI: 10.1007/978-3-030-38040-3_73

Das, T., Sil, R., Roy, A., & Majumdar, A. K. (2022). UML-based modelling for legal rules using natural language processing. *Lecture Notes in Electrical Engineering*, 481–492. DOI: 10.1007/978-981-16-8542-2_39

Davis, A. E. (2020, January 1). The Future of Law Firms (and Lawyers) in the Age of Artificial Intelligence. Fundação Getúlio Vargas, Escola de Direito, 16(1). https://doi.org/DOI: 10.1590/2317-6172201945

Ding, Y., & Foo, S. (2002, April 1). Ontology research and development. Part 1 - a review of ontology generation. *Journal of Information Science*, 28(2), 123–136. DOI: 10.1177/016555150202800204

Dobrovolska, N. V. (2020). Administrative contract: Analysis of the normative definition. *Legal Position*, (3), 28–34. DOI: 10.32836/2521-6473.2020-3.5

Dragoni, M., Villata, S., Rizzi, W., & Governatori, G. (2016, December). Combining NLP approaches for rule extraction from legal documents. In *1st Workshop on Mining and Reasoning with Legal texts (MIREL 2016)*.

Efthimiadis, E. N., & Hotchkiss, M. A. (2008). Legal discovery: Does domain expertise matter? *Proceedings of the American Society for Information Science and Technology*, 45(1), 1–2. DOI: 10.1002/meet.2008.1450450125

Fayomi, G. U., Mini, S. E., Fayomi, O., Odunlami, A., & Oyeleke, O. (2021, April 1). Sustainability and Clean Technology: A Technological Perspective. *IOP Conference Series. Materials Science and Engineering*, 1107(1), 012076–012076. DOI: 10.1088/1757-899X/1107/1/012076

Geng, B. (2022a). Legal text mining and analysis based on Artificial Intelligence. *International Journal of Artificial Intelligence Tools*, 31(04), 2240006. Advance online publication. DOI: 10.1142/S0218213022400061

Ghosh, S., Dutta, M., & Das, T. (2022). Indian legal text summarization: A text normalization-based approach. *2022 IEEE 19th India Council International Conference (INDICON)*. DOI: 10.1109/INDICON56171.2022.10039891

Ginting, P. (2020, January 1). Sustainable Growth and Development. DOI: 10.1142/S0218213022400061

Goh, H.-H., & Vinuesa, R. (2021b). Regulating artificial-intelligence applications to achieve the Sustainable Development Goals. *Discover Sustainability*, 2(1), 52. Advance online publication. DOI: 10.1007/s43621-021-00064-5 PMID: 35425914

Golbin, I., Rao, A S., Hadjarian, A., & Krittman, D. (2020, December 10). Responsible AI: A Primer for the Legal Community. DOI: 10.1142/S0218213022400061

Gravett, W. (2020, June 15). Is the Dawn of the Robot Lawyer upon us? The Fourth Industrial Revolution and the Future of Lawyers. *Potchefstroom Electronic Law Journal*, 23, 1–37. DOI: 10.17159/1727-3781/2020/v23i0a6794

Gupta, A., Khanna, V. S., & Wilkins, D. B. (2017). Overview of legal practice in India and the Indian Legal Profession. *The Indian Legal Profession in the Age of Globalization*, 40–66. DOI: 10.1142/S0218213022400061

Hasan, Md. T., Shamael, M. N., Akter, A., Islam, R., Mukta, Md. S. H., & Islam, S. (2023). An Artificial Intelligence-based Framework to Achieve the Sustainable Development Goals in the Context of Bangladesh. In arXiv (Cornell University). Cornell University. https://doi.org//arxiv.2304.11703DOI: 10.48550

Ho, J.-H., Lee, G.-G., & Lu, M.-T. (2020). Exploring the implementation of a legal AI bot for Sustainable Development in Legal Advisory institutions. *Sustainability (Basel)*, 12(15), 5991. DOI: 10.3390/su12155991

India, P. T. of. (2023, February 9). *Nearly 5 crore pending cases in courts, over 69,000 in Supreme Court*. NDTV.com. https://www.ndtv.com/india-news/nearly-5-crore-pending-cases-in-courts-over-69-000-in-supreme-court-3768720

Iyer, L. S. (2021). AI enabled applications towards Intelligent Transportation. *Transportation Engineering*, 5, 100083. DOI: 10.1016/j.treng.2021.100083

Katz, D., Hartung, D., Gerlach, L., Jana, A., & Bommarito, M. J. (2023, January 1). Natural Language Processing in the Legal Domain. Cornell University. https://doi.org//arxiv.2302.12039DOI: 10.48550

Khennouche, F., Elmir, Y., Djebari, N., Himeur, Y., & Amira, A. (2023, January 1). Revolutionizing Customer Interactions: Insights and Challenges in Deploying ChatGPT and Generative Chatbots for FAQs. Cornell University. https://doi.org//arxiv.2311.09976DOI: 10.48550

Makowicz, B. (2023). Governance und compliance-management. *Risk, Fraud &amp. Compliance*, (4), 7. Advance online publication. DOI: 10.37307/j.1867-8394.2023.04.07

Mandal, S., & Das, T. (2023). N-gram-based legal parameters retrieval: The state-of-the-art and future research trends of Indian judiciary. *Lecture Notes in Networks and Systems*, 703–711. DOI: 10.37307/j.1867-8394.2023.04.07

Mandal, S., Saha, S., & Das, T. (2022). An approach to extract major parameters of legal documents using text analytics. *Lecture Notes in Networks and Systems*, 331–338. DOI: 10.37307/j.1867-8394.2023.04.07

Markou, C., & Deakin, S. F. (2019). Ex Machina Lex: The limits of legal computability. SSRN *Electronic Journal*. DOI: 10.2139/ssrn.3407856

Nallathiga, R. (2003, April 1). Production System Planning for Natural Resource Conservation in a Micro-Watershed. *Electronic Green Journal*, 1(18). Advance online publication. DOI: 10.5070/G311810507

Napolitano, G. (2024). Artificial Intelligence to advance sustainability: A review of progress. *Artificial Intelligence, Finance, and Sustainability*, 85–109. DOI: 10.5070/G311810507

Nieto, C. C. (1997, January 1). Toward a Holistic Approach to the Ideal of Sustainability. *Techné: Research in Philosophy and Technology*, 2(2), 79–83. DOI: 10.5840/techne19972227

Özşen, T., Uslu, B., & Aypay, A. (2022, October 18). Strategy adaptation for sustainable quality management in universities: a systematic literature review. Springer Science+Business Media, 29(4), 447-469. DOI: 10.5070/G311810507

Radziwill, N., & Benton, M. C. (2017, January 1). Evaluating Quality of Chatbots and Intelligent Conversational Agents. Cornell University. https://doi.org//arxiv.1704.04579DOI: 10.48550

Rismanchian, S., & Doroudi, S. (2023). *Four Interactions between AI and Education: Broadening Our Perspective on What AI Can Offer Education*. DOI: 10.1007/978-3-031-36336-8_1

Ross, T. J. (2007). Book review. *Artificial Intelligence*, 171(18), 1114–1115. DOI: 10.1016/j.artint.2007.10.003

Sackman, S., & Coltman, M. (1996). Legal aspects of a global securities market. *The Future for the Global Securities Market*, 19–30. DOI: 10.5070/G311810507

Slorach, S., Embley, J., Goodchild, P., & Shephard, C. (2017). *8. legal research. Legal Systems &amp*. Skills., DOI: 10.1093/he/9780198785903.003.0008

*Sophia chatbot*. The Innovation in Politics Institute. (2023, July 24). https://innovationinpolitics.eu/showroom/project/sophia-chatbot/#:~:text=Sophia%20is%20a%20digital%20chatbot,the%20needs%20of%20survivors%20globally

Suganda, A., & Siregar, M. A. (2020). The meaning and development of state emergency laws based on constitution in the Indonesian legal system. *Proceedings of the 2nd International Conference of Law, Government and Social Justice (ICOLGAS 2020)*. DOI: 10.2991/assehr.k.201209.336

Thompson, P. B., & Norris, P. E. (2021). What is sustainability? *Sustainability*. Advance online publication. DOI: 10.1093/wentk/9780190883249.003.0001

Tprestianni. (2024, March 1). *131 AI statistics and Trends for 2024*. National University. https://www.nu.edu/blog/ai-statistics-trends/

Veres, C. (2022). Large language models are not models of natural language: They are corpus models. *IEEE Access : Practical Innovations, Open Solutions*, 10, 61970–61979. DOI: 10.1109/ACCESS.2022.3182505

Verma, Dr. P. (2024). Tackling of environment by artificial intelligence. *Artificial Intelligence and Emerging Technologies*, 21–27. DOI: 10.1109/ACCESS.2022.3182505

Wollny, S., Schneider, J., Boulay, B. D., Weidlich, J., Rittberger, M., & Drachsler, H. (2021, July 15). Are We There Yet? - A Systematic Literature Review on Chatbots in Education. *Frontiers of Medicine*, 4, 654924. Advance online publication. DOI: 10.3389/frai.2021.654924 PMID: 34337392

Wright, S A. (2020, December 10). AI in the Law: Towards Assessing Ethical Risks. DOI: 10.1109/ACCESS.2022.3182505

Xu, L., Sanders, L., Li, K., & Chow, J. (2021, November 29). Chatbot for Health Care and Oncology Applications Using Artificial Intelligence and Machine Learning: Systematic Review. *JMIR Cancer*, 7(4), e27850–e27850. DOI: 10.2196/27850 PMID: 34847056

Zakaria, H., Hassan, R., Othman, R M., Asmuni, H., & Shah, Z A. (2014, September 1). A study of lightweight ontology for herb domain. DOI: 10.2196/27850 PMID: 34847056

Zhang, D., Schilder, F., Conrad, J. G., Makrehchi, M., von Rickenbach, D., & Moulinier, I. (2023). Making a computational attorney. *Proceedings of the 2023 SIAM International Conference on Data Mining (SDM)*, 965–968. DOI: 10.1137/1.9781611977653.ch111

# Chapter 10
# AI for Cyber-Security in E-Health Ensuring Security and Privacy of Patient Data and Information:
## Legal Landscape and Futuristic Approach in Smart Healthcare

**Bhupinder Singh**
https://orcid.org/0009-0006-4779-2553
*Sharda University, India*

**Saurabh Chandra**
https://orcid.org/0000-0003-4172-9968
*Bennett University, India*

**Christian Kaunert**
https://orcid.org/0000-0002-4493-2235
*Dublin City University, Ireland*

**Santosh Kumar**
https://orcid.org/0009-0002-3115-6772
*Sharda University, India*

**Anjali Raghav**
https://orcid.org/0009-0004-0248-7956
*Sharda University, India*

**Saloni Mishra**
https://orcid.org/0009-0007-4900-2292
*Manav Rachna University, India*

## ABSTRACT

*This digital transformation brings forth significant challenges related to cyber-security, particularly in safeguarding the security and privacy of patient data and information. Artificial intelligence has great promise in the healthcare industry because of its capacity to mimic human cognitive processes and carry out activities that traditionally needed human intellect. There are various artificial intelligence*

DOI: 10.4018/979-8-3373-2530-9.ch010

*(AI) techniques, such as computer vision, natural language processing and machine learning algorithms which enable healthcare systems to immediately produce actionable insights, analyze large datasets and reveal complex patterns. With employing these capabilities, healthcare practitioners may improve clinical judgment, optimize treatment strategies and effectively manage resources, all of which lead to better patient outcomes and a more efficient healthcare system. This chapter focuses on the intersection of AI, cyber-security, and E-Health, examining the current legal landscape and proposing a futuristic approach for securing smart healthcare systems.*

## 1. INTRODUCTION AND BACKGROUND

The delivery, organization and optimization of medical services are undergoing major changes in the healthcare industry in this era of fast technological innovation. The incorporation of cutting-edge technology is primarily driving this change, with artificial intelligence (AI) emerging as a revolutionary force that has the potential to completely transform the healthcare industry. AI is becoming more and more important as healthcare professionals and organizations strive to provide more accurate diagnoses, customize treatment programs to each patient's requirements, and expedite administrative procedures (Algarni, 2019).

The prevalence of Internet of Things (IoT) applications stands out as a prominent contemporary trend as the multitude of interconnected devices is not only yielding substantial business profits but also carrying out numerous automated tasks in various daily human endeavors. Within the arena of healthcare service provision, the significance of IoT capabilities cannot be overstated with their integration increasingly being referred to as the Internet of Medical Things (IoMT). These nodes involved in IoMT networks generate, collect and exchange vast amounts of highly private and sensitive data. The complexity and diversity of the technology give rise to numerous security vulnerabilities. The complexity introduced by IoMT systems results in new risks that are not easily accommodated by existing risk management frameworks. The current cyber-security risk assessment methods and approaches employed by various organizations may not adequately address the inherent risks associated with IoMT (Ikharo et al., 2021).

With the healthcare sector going through a digital revolution, new cyber-security issues have emerged. The major participants in the healthcare industry are depending more and more on a wider variety of technology such as public cloud services and mobile apps. Although the advantages are clear as new cyber-security risks are brought about by the computer environment's increasing complexity. The significant potential risks are posed by security events involving sensitive health data and ransom-ware assaults on vital life functions. The adoption of Electronic Medical

Records (EMRs) by healthcare organizations can offer numerous advantages to physicians, patients and healthcare services. Though, the apprehensions regarding the privacy and security of patient information contribute to a relatively low adoption rate of EMRs by several health institutions. The effective safeguarding a vast amount of sensitive health data stored at various locations in diverse formats poses a significant challenge for EMRs.

*Figure 1. Shows the dimensions of introduction section (Source- Original)*

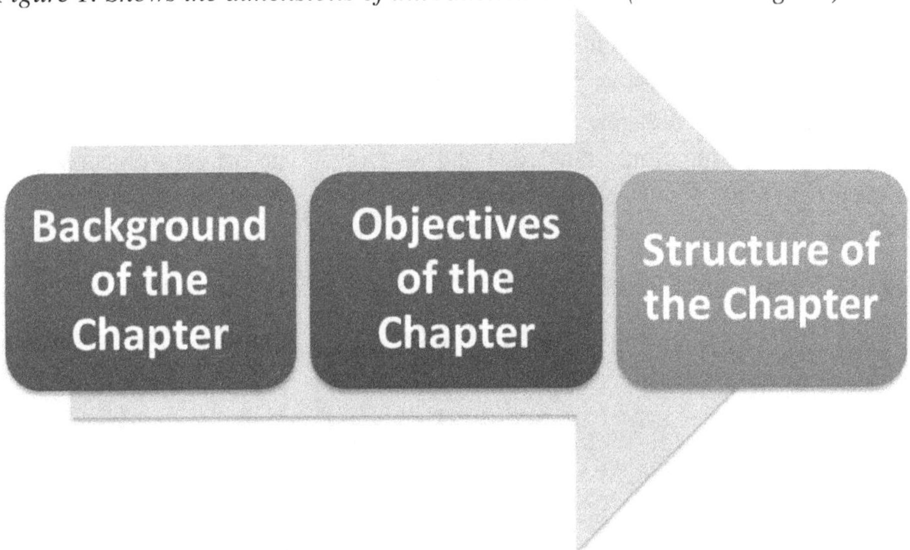


## 1.1 Background of the Chapter

The increasing adoption of E-Health systems has revolutionized healthcare delivery, but it also exposes sensitive patient information to cyber threats. The widespread implementation of e-healthcare hinges on its reliability and the trust patients place in the security of their communications and the safeguarding of their sensitive data. For the businesses in this sector, the expansion of electronic connected devices within the healthcare economy relies on maintaining low transaction costs while ensuring the effective and efficient transfer of data with acceptable risks (Thuemmler & Bai, 2017). So, implementing robust security measures incurs additional process costs and the management of risks is an indirect cost borne by builders of e-health systems. AI has the potential to significantly accelerate the drug discovery process. Molecular structures may be analyzed and predictions about the efficacy and possible adverse effects of medications can be formed by using machine learning algorithms. The development of novel cures and treatments might proceed more quickly and economically as a result of this expedited drug candidate screening procedure (Tyagi et al., 2023).

## 1.2 Objectives of the Chapter

Healthcare comprises a range of services provided to the patient's aimed at enhancing their physical, mental and emotional well-being. Typically, these services are administered within hospitals following various procedures (Yeng et al., 2022). The notion of e-health is expansive and according to the World Health Organization (WHO), it is characterized as "the cost-effective and secure utilization of ICT to support health and health-related domains, encompassing healthcare, health surveillance, health education, knowledge and research." The primary objectives of this chapter are to:

*Figure 2. Illuminates the objectives of the chapter (Source- Original)*

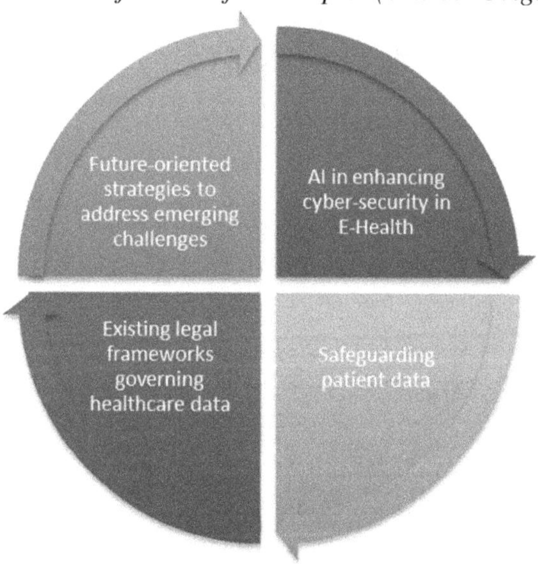


## 1.3 Structure of the Chapter

This chapter comprehensively explores the various dimensions of the Artificial Intelligence for Cyber-Security in E-Health Ensuring Security and Privacy of Patient's Data and Information along with the Analysis of Legal Landscape and Futuristic

Approach in Smart Healthcare. Section 2 elaborates the AI for Cyber-Security in E-Health. Section 3 explores the Privacy Protection and Ensuring Safety of Patient's Data: Legal Landscape. Section 4 lays down the AI-Based Cyber-security Solutions. Section 5 discusses the Blockchain Technology and Machine Learning for Ensuring Security and Privacy of Patient's Data and Information. Section 6 specifies the Challenges and Considerations. And finally, Section 7 Conclude the Chapter with Future Scope.

*Figure 3. Showcasing the structure of the chapter (Source- Original)*

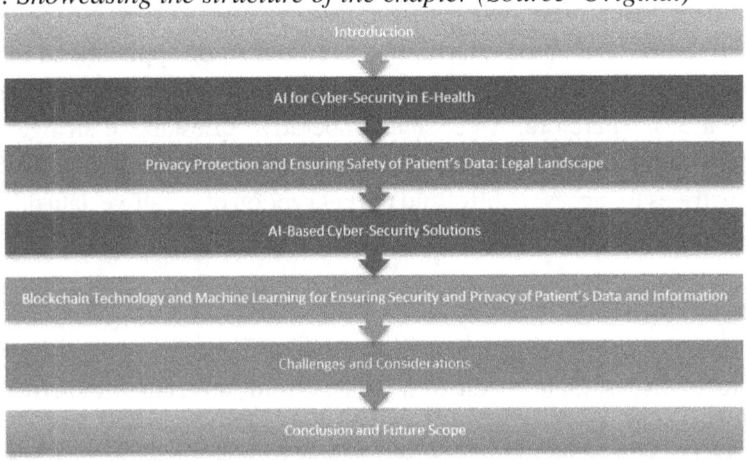


## 2. AI FOR CYBER-SECURITY IN E-HEALTH

Artificial intelligence (AI) is becoming more and more important in the healthcare industry. It helps physicians diagnose patients, manages medical duties and helps in the development of novel medications. Artificial intelligence methods such as machine learning and deep learning can analyze large amounts of medical data, spot trends, and forecast possible results. AI for example can help physicians diagnose patients more quickly and accurately by helping them to spot problems in medical imaging. Artificial intelligence has demonstrated significant potential in the field of medical imaging particularly in the processing of images like X-rays, CT scans and MRIs (Kalinaki et al., 2023).

Artificial intelligence algorithms may be used to find patterns, detect irregularities and assist radiologists in the diagnosis of illnesses including cancer, heart problems, and neurological issues. This technological development might improve the speed and accuracy of diagnosis while lowering the possibility of human mistake. Each development in technology or other fields leads to the inevitable emergence of vulnerabilities (Ameen et al., 2023). Every weakness becomes a possible avenue for bad actors to take advantage of and there are significant technological advancements that have been made in recent years including the migration of manual processes to online platforms, the broad availability of data and applications via public platforms and the rise of new technologies like artificial intelligence and the internet of things. The swift advancement of technology, particularly in the healthcare industry has drawn in parties looking to take advantage of weaknesses putting healthcare institutions in serious danger (Awotunde et al., 2021). The vital and sensitive nature of healthcare data which must always be available increases the hazards even more. The unavailability of data or interruptions in the use of applications can create significant gaps in critical processes, such as ordering medicines for patients in fragile situations. Therefore, it becomes imperative to establish stringent norms and standards, including robust multifactor authentication, meticulously designed approval matrices for access control and the encryption of sensitive data during both storage and transmission (Munyolo, 2021).

## 2.1 AI in E-Health

The actuators, sensors and medical equipment are all part of the interactive network that powers e-health applications. E-health systems are becoming more vulnerable to cyber-security events because of a number of factors which include the type of data generated, the amount of information shared, the patient identity management, the variety of protocols that communicating nodes use and the device's limited resources (Taimoor & Rehman, 2021). The variety of traits are present in healthcare information systems and if they are made available for Internet access even if they were not built for it as they are vulnerable to cyber-attacks. The security features are not supported by a lot of antiquated information systems and apps. They are subject to various security flaws and breaches when linked to open environments. There are various applications of AI in E-Health, including predictive analytics, diagnostic support and personalized medicine which highlighting the benefits and potential security concerns associated with these technologies (Lehto et al., 2022).

## 2.2 Applications of E-Healthcare

Digital medical records, telemedicine, tele-care services, and healthcare networks and processes are the key areas where e-health is used. These days the smart healthcare services are essential to improving the patient experience as a whole. These services entail the alteration of vital sign data so that information may be analyzed, and judgments can be made with confidence. The decision support software and the possibility of real-time data exchange enable practitioners to make more linked judgments, while end users are becoming more involved in the healthcare system (Khalid et al., 2023). AI models have proven to be adept at analyzing vast amounts of patient data such as symptoms, medical histories and genetic information, in the field of illness diagnosis and prediction. It helps to detect diseases more precisely and effectively. Machine learning algorithms are particularly good at seeing complex patterns that human doctors would find difficult to recognize, which translates into early detection and increased accuracy. AI can predict the probability of particular diseases based on genetic markers and risk factors, allowing for preemptive therapies (AbdulRaheem et al., 2023).

## 2.3 Cyber-Security in Healthcare

There has never been a more important time for cyber-security in medical and healthcare. The data theft, identity theft and ransom assaults can affect a variety of organizations, including health departments, community and aged care providers, diagnostic service providers, research and academic institutes, healthcare consultancies and primary healthcare clinics (Isichei et al., 2023). Staff training is an important but frequently disregarded activity that should be done in conjunction with the implementation of strong authentication methods in security measures to reduce the probability of breaches. If such precautions are neglected, a company runs the danger of being the subject of cyber-security news. The cybercriminals target the healthcare industry, which makes it particularly vulnerable and potentially weakens the company's supply chain. Health organizations maintain a wide network in which significant volumes of data are continuously shared, and they depend on a variety of outside providers and services.

Medical facilities may now offer patient care, access shared data and interact with patients and staff via linked devices thanks to technological improvements. These powers have certain inherent hazards. Working with a trustworthy, knowledgeable partner who is aware of compliance, these risks can be greatly reduced. Cyber-security is essential since the healthcare industry has emerged as a top target for malevolent hackers. The social security numbers, bank account information and contact details are all protected since fraudsters take advantage of holes in healthcare systems (Marengo, 2023).

*Figure 4. Displays the AI for cyber-security in E-Health (Source- Original)*

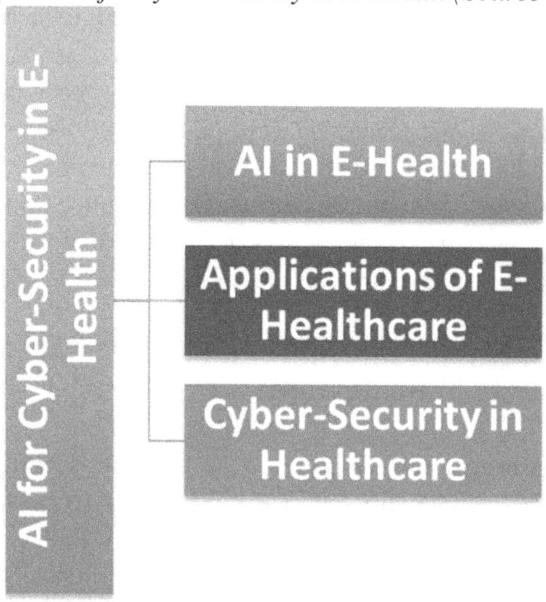


## 3. PRIVACY PROTECTION AND ENSURING SAFETY OF PATIENT'S DATA: LEGAL LANDSCAPE

The getting of patient's approval requires above all guaranteeing data protection. This may be accomplished by carefully illustrating the permission, authentication and data flow procedures for a range of operations, including data transfer, processing, storage and collecting. The unauthorized access such as data collection, usage, access, storage and sharing are directly associated with risks to data privacy. These acts might endanger personal information and jeopardize privacy, especially when it comes to healthcare information, which is extremely sensitive and valuable. Thus, it is essential to put in place suitable security and protection measures via legal framework (Estrela, 2023).

The laws pertaining to data privacy and protection are in place to guarantee the safe handling of patient's personal information. To emphasize the goals and characteristics of these laws, to investigate how these laws offer security characteristics at different levels of the proposed healthcare architecture, a comparative study is carried out. In terms of legal issues, human rights and social norms, the adoption of IoT data privacy legislation is crucial (Affia et al., 2023). So, generally in order to maintain core privacy objectives including accountability, proportionality, justice and purpose fulfillment, IoT data privacy laws are required. To accomplish these aims, cooperation between public and private entities is crucial. Law enforcement organizations from the US, EU and other top nations are working together to create a unified platform for resolving privacy concerns pertaining to healthcare data and improving the efficacy of the current legal system. The ensuring of user awareness and control over IoT healthcare devices and services is crucial for a successful legal framework. Its adequacy is increased by alignment with existing international data privacy frameworks (Jiang, 2021).

## 3.1 HIPAA and Other Regulatory Frameworks

The analysis of Health Insurance Portability and Accountability Act (HIPAA) and other relevant regulations governing the protection of patient data are significant. Also, the evaluating their adequacy in addressing the challenges posed by AI and evolving cyber threats is required for patient's privacy. The US government enacted HIPAA to establish the security and privacy standards for healthcare data pertaining to American citizens. HIPAA comprises distinct rule sets addressing security and privacy concerns (Sanchez-Iborra & Skarmeta, 2022). The privacy rules are designed to safeguard health data, ensuring its protection against unauthorized disclosure. The security rules aim to secure individuals' health information through the adoption of advanced technologies, facilitating more efficient means of patient care. These HIPAA security and privacy rules are applicable to both healthcare and non-healthcare organizations engaged in storing, transmitting, and processing healthcare data of US citizens through any means (Martínez et al., 2023).

## 3.2 International Perspectives

The large-scale healthcare data integration is difficult particularly when it comes to security and privacy. Within data centers, patient information is processed at different security levels. Although HIPAA certification is held by many US firms, it does not ensure patient record security since HIPAA prioritizes the establishment of security standards above guaranteeing their diligent application (Jagatheesaperumal et al., 2022). The sending of large datasets from different places puts additional strain on storage and processing resources. The big changing databases are difficult to manage with traditional security methods. The lack of specific standards in current healthcare data protection legislation exacerbates the security demands brought about by the introduction of cloud healthcare technologies (Vyas & Bhargava, 2021).

When it comes to data governance, the first step in managing healthcare data properly should be to address the governance of that data. This is especially true when the healthcare sector is shifting toward a value-based business model (Kumar et al., 2023). This calls for a consistent data format that incorporates many security standards. The current diversity of data collected in the healthcare sector need a thorough governance approach. The necessity of appropriate data governance is further highlighted by the lack of regulations for the standardization and normalization of healthcare data.

## 4. AI-BASED CYBER-SECURITY CONCERNS AND SOLUTIONS

The term persistent data describes the information that is vulnerable to theft and is kept in several locations inside healthcare systems, such as sensors and actuators. The sensors and actuators in the healthcare industry retain event logs in their memory, which include the most recent readings, configuration changes, and connection histories (Rajamäki & Hummelholm, 2022). As a result of non-encrypted data storage and generally inadequate security measures, attackers can take advantage of these weaknesses to steal data. Because IoHT servers have all of the patient's bio-data and a thorough history, they are especially appealing targets for hackers looking to steal healthcare data (Sharma & Singh, 2022). The digital transformation in the healthcare sector has brought about numerous advantages, but it has also introduced a range of cyber-security challenges. There are some of the concerns associated with implementing cyber-security. With comprehending these concerns and finding solutions, healthcare organizations can proactively strengthen their cyber-security defenses which ensuring the security and privacy of both patient data and critical medical operations (Qiu et al., 2018). There are some concerns in healthcare cyber-security as-

**Human Error and Insider Threats:** Even a simple mistake such as an employee unintentionally sending patient data to the wrong email address can result in significant breaches. Also, the malicious insider threats may exploit their access for personal gain. The occurrence of a hospital employee selling patient data to identity thieves serves as a poignant reminder of the risks associated with both human fallibility and malicious intent.

**Resource Constraints and Budget Limitations:** The smaller healthcare providers often struggle with limited budgets and resources allocated for cyber-security initiatives. This predicament can lead to delayed updates, inadequate training for staff, and a lack of investment in advanced cyber-security tools. These challenges render them attractive targets for cybercriminals seeking vulnerabilities to exploit (Noura, 2019).

**Device Vulnerabilities in Medicine:** The Medtronic insulin pump breach brought attention to the vulnerabilities present in medical equipment. The researchers found that the gadget may be controlled remotely which might lead to the administration of inaccurate insulin dosages. This brought attention to the security issues surrounding Internet of Things (IoT) devices in the healthcare industry and highlighted worries about patient safety (Nyangaresi et al., 2022).

These privacy concerns arise from the accessibility and availability of personal healthcare information on the Internet. But there is an expectation for transparency in the privacy framework for Internet of Healthcare Things (IoHT) systems and services which ensuring that updated information is accessible to patients to safeguard their data. Healthcare systems gather data primarily from sensing devices, transmitting it through intermediate devices to the management layer (Kitchin, 2016). Throughout this process, various protocols and encoding schemes are employed to facilitate reliable data communication. The vulnerabilities in different components of the healthcare system can be identified using search engines aiding attackers in locating connected vulnerable devices on the Internet. Similarly, a vast dataset containing millions of records with user healthcare information can be exchanged seamlessly and rapidly leaving little to no consistent trace (Kumar et al., 2022).

The healthcare industry is increasingly adopting privacy-preserving analytics by leveraging IoT devices for monitoring and transmitting vital signs to healthcare clouds. The need arises to process and analyse data in an ad-hoc decentralized manner. The performing resource-intensive operations while ensuring privacy preservation pose a significant challenge. With the rising popularity of new healthcare data analytics approaches, there is a necessity for a review of healthcare data privacy laws. New legislation should be drafted to explicitly outline all processes associated with the utilization of patient's private data (Razzaq et al., 2017).

## 5. BLOCKCHAIN TECHNOLOGY AND MACHINE LEARNING FOR ENSURING SECURITY AND PRIVACY OF PATIENT'S DATA AND INFORMATION

The concept of privacy of patient's in environments that are open and untrust-worthy, maintaining privacy is of utmost importance as the disclosure of a medical patients' data could have severe repercussions on their life (Soni et al., 2022). The confidentiality of data must be rigorously upheld. In e-health settings, privacy encompasses the concept of anonymity, ensuring that inappropriate users such as insurance providers, researchers and management staff cannot identify patients (Solangi et al., 2018). However, healthcare professionals like physicians, nurses and cashiers may have access to certain information for the purpose of treatment and billing. The confidentiality is designed to ensure that only authorized entities can access the data. So, given that various users may require access to data in e-health systems, proper authorizations must be established to safeguard the private information of patients (Ksibi et al., 2023).

Blockchain is a revolutionary technology that has made crypto-currency transactions easier by removing the need for management or a central authority to approve transactions. Instead, transactions are authorized based on principles of transparency and trust (Nowrozy et al., 2023). The complete anonymity and privacy are also given top priority by the Blockchain Network when identifying users during transactions. Since its conception, research has been conducted on Blockchain Technology looking at different ways to improve access control systems in comparison to traditional systems (Wahab et al., 2022). Blockchain has shown itself to be extremely dependable in a number of industries recently, including banking, healthcare, smart homes, information storage management and security. Blockchain functions as a decentralized database for information and data (Pandey et al., 2021). The key characteristic of blockchain is its distributed nature where each node within the technology possesses a copy of the information or data. To alter this data, a system must obtain consensus from all nodes, convincing them of the need for manipulation and updates (Sriram & Subrahmanian, 2020). Blockchain operates through a unique network, where each node within the authentication communication network can directly exchange data and information with other nodes. There is no centralized database or system in blockchain that governs the exchange of information and data across the network (Suleski et al., 2023).

## 5.1 Patient's Information and Use of Blockchain Technology

The smart healthcare industry has made great strides in effectively providing medical treatment while protecting patient privacy and giving medical professionals access to reliable and up-to-date information in real time. Though, because there are many parties involved in the Smart Healthcare space, the main concerns center on patient data security and privacy (Zala et al., 2024; Asad, 2023). There are difficulties in guaranteeing physicians get correct and timely data particularly when the pertinent issue is outside the purview of on-site medical services. To guarantee proper patient care in the future smart health, a medical facility needs strong data security and confidentiality (Keshta & Odeh, 2021). The method of exchanging medical data is sending it to other hospitals without maintaining confidentiality. This isn't the best way because patient care is based on the core premise of medical information privacy (Algatus, 2022). This framework takes a different task by consulting specialists at other hospitals to ascertain the best course of treatment for patients. There are two levels to this strategy as Blockchain technology is used for data transfer at the first layer and Machine learning techniques are used in the second layer to examine blocks that include patient information (Ahouanmenou et al., 2023).

## 5.2 Machine Learning and Patient's Privacy of Data

Patient records are securely placed within a block of the blockchain, and these blocks are transmitted to other medical centers (Khatun et al., 2023). Each treatment center has the ability to suggest the recommended treatment to attach it to the blockchain and disseminate it to all nodes and treatment centers. Upon receiving patient data, each medical center utilizes data mining methods to predict the appropriate treatment (Hussien et al., 2021). The innovation lies in the secure and confidential transmission of medical data between medical centers using blockchain technology. Since sensitive information might leak during transmission due to interception, it is imperative to ensure the security of medical data and its transmission inside smart cities (Mateus-Coelho & Cruz-Cunha, 2023; Mendelson, 2017). When medical data is transferred, there is a chance that it may be manipulated without authorization which might interfere with treatment or, in extreme situations, endanger the lives of the patients. Transmitting patient records to other medical facilities using the Internet of Things (IoT) and blockchain is an innovative strategy in smart cities. Using this approach enables every medical facility to review patient records and take its doctors' opinions into consideration (Mariettou et al., 2023).

# 6. CHALLENGES AND CONSIDERATIONS

E-healthcare holds the potential to offer efficient and economical services to patients in underserved areas. It brings along a series of challenges that, if unaddressed, may hinder its success (Alamri et al., 2022).

**Technical Reliability:** This pertains to the safety of the device and its capability to gather and transmit data accurately without disruptions or malfunctions. So, given that patients will be utilizing the device, it is anticipated that technical oversight and assurance will be provided by vendors or healthcare providers (Vulpe et al., 2021).

**Outdated Infrastructure:** Many hospitals still use paper-based records and have antiquated electronic equipment. The construction of new work procedures and substantial expenses are associated with the implementation of an e-health system (Alamri et al., 2022).

**Scalability:** The significant amount of data will be generated as a result of the real-time connectivity and the large number of continuously linked devices. The sufficient computing power and storage capacity will be essential (Vulpe et al., 2021).

**Inadequately Competent Stakeholders:** The major obstacle to the effective deployment of an e-health system is the lack of competent users. The e-health system's users include patients, maintainers, developers and health professionals. These individuals especially those in poorer nations may have less education or less ICT abilities (Nyakina & Taher, 2023).

**Legal Considerations:** The handling of legal issues and managing the vast array of rules and regulations connected to this phenomena is unquestionably is the key variables impacting the deployment and progress of e-health (Van kessel et al., 2023). The inability to comply with government-approved laws, the lack of support for national and international standards, the absence of appropriate existing laws pertaining to personal rights and the preservation of patients' privacy, the need to establish a legal framework for its management in healthcare and the need to develop a framework for transmitting and unifying heterogeneous data are just a few of the legal challenges surrounding electronic health systems in many countries (Fitzek & Choi, 2023).

*Figure 5. Specifies the challenges and considerations (Source- Original)*

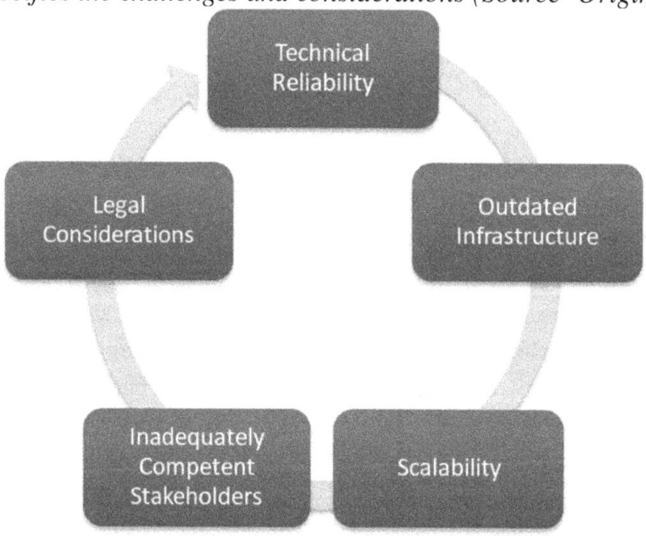

## 7. CONCLUSION AND FUTURE SCOPE

The ensuring of security of patient data has become a major duty as although cutting-edge healthcare apps and technology are essential for patient care, hackers frequently target them. The hackers are deliberately compromising medical records and after gaining illegal access, hackers may use ransom-ware to encrypt information or shut down important services and demand a certain fee to unlock them. The hospital organizations in the time-sensitive healthcare industry are frequently forced to pay the ransom in the hopes that the money would eventually be recovered. Although less often, network-connected devices can also be taken over and used to deliver the wrong prescription or alter a machine's operation. To protect all data, cyber-security safeguards must be put in place in the healthcare industry. Because data is gathered and accessed from a variety of sources, the healthcare business has particularly broad and constantly changing security obligations. There are numerous sources, such as lab and hospital records, insurance information, fitness applications, trackers, devices, health portals and more which share and provide patient data. This sensitive and varied data may be efficiently protected with the use of cyber-security technologies.

## REFERENCES


AbdulRaheem. M., Awotunde, J. B., Chakraborty, C., Adeniyi, E. A., Oladipo, I. D., & Bhoi, A. K. (2023). Security and privacy concerns in smart healthcare system. In *Implementation of Smart Healthcare Systems using AI, IoT, and Blockchain* (pp. 243-273). Academic Press.

Affia, A. A. O., Finch, H., Jung, W., Samori, I. A., Potter, L., & Palmer, X. L. (2023). IoT Health Devices: Exploring Security Risks in the Connected Landscape. *IoT*, 4(2), 150–182. DOI: 10.3390/iot4020009

Ahouanmenou, S., Van Looy, A., & Poels, G. (2023). Information security and privacy in hospitals: A literature mapping and review of research gaps. *Informatics for Health & Social Care*, 48(1), 30–46. DOI: 10.1080/17538157.2022.2049274 PMID: 35300555

Alamri, B., Crowley, K., & Richardson, I. (2022). Cybersecurity Risk Management Framework for Blockchain Identity Management Systems in Health IoT. *Sensors (Basel)*, 23(1), 218. DOI: 10.3390/s23010218 PMID: 36616816

Algarni, A. (2019). A survey and classification of security and privacy research in smart healthcare systems. *IEEE Access : Practical Innovations, Open Solutions*, 7, 101879–101894. DOI: 10.1109/ACCESS.2019.2930962

Algatus, W. A. (2022). *Propose an architecture for e-health within smart cities* (Master's thesis, Altınbaş Üniversitesi/Lisansüstü Eğitim Enstitüsü).

Ameen, A. H., Mohammed, M. A., & Rashid, A. N. (2023). Dimensions of artificial intelligence techniques, blockchain, and cyber security in the Internet of medical things: Opportunities, challenges, and future directions. *Journal of Intelligent Systems*, 32(1), 20220267. DOI: 10.1515/jisys-2022-0267

Asad, M. (2023). Security Management in Cloud Computing for healthcare. *Data*.

Awotunde, J. B., Jimoh, R. G., Folorunso, S. O., Adeniyi, E. A., Abiodun, K. M., & Banjo, O. O. (2021). Privacy and security concerns in IoT-based healthcare systems. In *The Fusion of Internet of Things, Artificial Intelligence, and Cloud Computing in Health Care* (pp. 105–134). Springer International Publishing. DOI: 10.1007/978-3-030-75220-0_6

Estrela, V. V. (2023). Intelligent. *Health Care Systems*.

Fitzek, S., & Choi, K. E. A. (2023). Potential Impact and Challenges of Implementing Artificial Intelligence in the Romanian Healthcare System. *Postmodernism Problems*, 13(2), 148–192. DOI: 10.2196/27850 PMID: 34847056

Hassanaly, P., & Dufour, J. C. (2021). Analysis of the regulatory, legal, and medical conditions for the prescription of mobile health applications in the United States, the European Union, and France. *Medical Devices: Evidence and Research*, 389-409. DOI: 10.2196/27850 PMID: 34847056

Hussien, H. M., Yasin, S. M., Udzir, N. I., Ninggal, M. I. H., & Salman, S. (2021). Blockchain technology in the healthcare industry: Trends and opportunities. *Journal of Industrial Information Integration*, 22, 100217. DOI: 10.1016/j.jii.2021.100217

Ikharo, B., Obiagwu, A., Obasi, C., Hussein, S. U., & Akah, P. (2021, July). Security for Internet-of-Things Enabled E-Health using Blockchain and Artificial Intelligence: A Novel Integration Framework. In *2021 1st International Conference on Multidisciplinary Engineering and Applied Science (ICMEAS)* (pp. 1-4). IEEE. DOI: 10.1109/ICMEAS52683.2021.9692368

Isichei, J. C., Khorsandroo, S., & Desai, S. (2023). Cybersecurity and privacy in smart bioprinting. *Bioprinting (Amsterdam, Netherlands)*, •••, 00321.

Jagatheesaperumal, S. K., Mishra, P., Moustafa, N., & Chauhan, R. (2022). A holistic survey on the use of emerging technologies to provision secure healthcare solutions. *Computers & Electrical Engineering*, 99, 107691. DOI: 10.1016/j.compeleceng.2022.107691

Jiang, L. (2021). IoT Sensors for Smart Health Devices and Data security in Healthcare. DOI: 10.1016/j.compeleceng.2022.107691

Kalinaki, K., Fahadi, M., Alli, A. A., Shafik, W., Yasin, M., & Mutwalibi, N. (2023). Artificial Intelligence of Internet of Medical Things (AIoMT) in Smart Cities: A Review of Cybersecurity for Smart Healthcare. *Handbook of Security and Privacy of AI-Enabled Healthcare Systems and Internet of Medical Things*, 271-292.

Keshta, I., & Odeh, A. (2021). Security and privacy of electronic health records: Concerns and challenges. *Egyptian Informatics Journal*, 22(2), 177–183. DOI: 10.1016/j.eij.2020.07.003

Khalid, N., Qayyum, A., Bilal, M., Al-Fuqaha, A., & Qadir, J. (2023). Privacy-preserving artificial intelligence in healthcare: Techniques and applications. *Computers in Biology and Medicine*, 158, 106848. DOI: 10.1016/j.compbiomed.2023.106848 PMID: 37044052

Khatun, M. A., Memon, S. F., Eising, C., & Dhirani, L. L. (2023). Machine Learning for Healthcare-IoT Security: A Review and Risk Mitigation. *IEEE Access : Practical Innovations, Open Solutions*, 11, 145869–145896. DOI: 10.1109/ACCESS.2023.3346320

Kitchin, R. (2016). Getting smarter about smart cities: Improving data privacy and data security. DOI: 10.1016/j.compeleceng.2022.107691

Ksibi, S., Jaidi, F., & Bouhoula, A. (2023). A comprehensive study of security and cyber-security risk management within e-Health systems: Synthesis, analysis and a novel quantified approach. *Mobile Networks and Applications*, 28(1), 107–127. DOI: 10.1007/s11036-022-02042-1

Kumar, A., Jain, R., Gupta, M., & Islam, S. M. (Eds.). (2023). *6G-Enabled IoT and AI for Smart Healthcare: Challenges, Impact, and Analysis*. CRC Press. DOI: 10.1201/9781003321668

Kumar, P., Singh, A., & Sengupta, A. (2022). Securing Cyber-Resilience in Healthcare Sector. In *Cyber Security in Intelligent Computing and Communications* (pp. 211–226). Springer Singapore. DOI: 10.1007/978-981-16-8012-0_17

Lehto, M., Neittaanmäki, P., Pöyhönen, J., & Hummelholm, A. (2022). Cyber Security in Healthcare Systems. In *Cyber Security: Critical Infrastructure Protection* (pp. 183–215). Springer International Publishing. DOI: 10.1007/978-3-030-91293-2_8

Marengo, A. (2023). The Future of AI in IoT: Emerging Trends in Intelligent Data Analysis and Privacy Protection. DOI: 10.1109/ACCESS.2023.3338170

Mariettou, S., Koutsojannis, C., & Triantafillou, V. (2023). Security Systems in Greek Health Care Institutions: a Scoping Review Towards an Effective Benchmarking Approach. DOI: 10.1109/ACCESS.2023.3338170

Martínez, A. L., Pérez, M. G., & Ruiz-Martínez, A. (2023). A Comprehensive Model for Securing Sensitive Patient Data in a Clinical Scenario. *IEEE Access : Practical Innovations, Open Solutions*, 11, 137083–137098. DOI: 10.1109/ACCESS.2023.3338170

Mateus-Coelho, N., & Cruz-Cunha, M. (Eds.). (2023). *Exploring Cyber Criminals and Data Privacy Measures*. IGI Global. DOI: 10.4018/978-1-6684-8422-7

Mendelson, D. (2017). Legal protections for personal health information in the age of Big Data—a proposal for regulatory framework. DOI: 10.1109/ACCESS.2023.3338170

Munyolo, G. N. O. (2021). *Cyber-security in E-health: a Critical Analysis of the Regulatory Framework in Kenya* (Doctoral dissertation, University of Nairobi).

Noura, M. (2019). *Efficient and secure cryptographic solutions for medical data* (Doctoral dissertation, Université Bourgogne Franche-Comté).

Nowrozy, R., Ahmed, K., Wang, H., & Mcintosh, T. (2023, July). Towards a universal privacy model for electronic health record systems: An ontology and machine learning approach. [). MDPI.]. *Informatics (MDPI)*, 10(3), 60. DOI: 10.3390/informatics10030060

Nyakina, J. N., & Taher, B. H.Judith Nyakanga NyakinaBahaa Hussein Taher. (2023). A survey of healthcare sector digitization strategies: Vulnerabilities, countermeasures and opportunities. *World Journal of Advanced Engineering Technology and Sciences*, 8(1), 282–301. DOI: 10.30574/wjaets.2023.8.1.0050

Nyangaresi, V. O., Abduljabbar, Z. A., Mutlaq, K. A. A., Hussain, M. A., & Hussien, Z. A. (2022). Forward and Backward Key Secrecy Preservation Scheme for Medical Internet of Things. In *Human-Centric Smart Computing* [Singapore: Springer Nature Singapore.]. *Proceedings of ICHCSC*, 2022, 15–29.

Pandey, M., Agarwal, R., Shukla, S. K., & Verma, N. K. (2021). Security of healthcare data using blockchains: A survey. *arXiv preprint arXiv:2103.12326*. DOI: 10.1201/9781003133179-9

Pandey, M., Agarwal, R., Shukla, S. K., & Verma, N. K. (2021). 9 Security of Healthcare Data Using Blockchains. *Blockchain in Digital Healthcare*.Ahmad, I., Asghar, Z., Kumar, T., Li, G., Manzoor, A., Mikhaylov, K., & Harjula, E. (2022). Emerging technologies for next generation remote health care and assisted living. *IEEE Access : Practical Innovations, Open Solutions*, 10, 56094–56132.

Qiu, J., Liang, X., Shetty, S., & Bowden, D. (2018, September). *Towards secure and smart healthcare in smart cities using blockchain. In 2018 IEEE international smart cities conference (ISC2)*. IEEE.

Rajamäki, J., & Hummelholm, A. (2022). Ethical Resilience Management Framework for Critical Healthcare Information Infrastructure.

Razzaq, M. A., Gill, S. H., Qureshi, M. A., & Ullah, S. (2017). Security issues in the Internet of Things (IoT): A comprehensive study. *International Journal of Advanced Computer Science and Applications*, 8(6).

Sanchez-Iborra, R., & Skarmeta, A. (2022). Securing the hyperconnected healthcare ecosystem. In *AI and IoT for Sustainable Development in Emerging Countries: Challenges and Opportunities* (pp. 455–471). Springer International Publishing. DOI: 10.1007/978-3-030-90618-4_22

Sharma, A., & Singh, B. (2022). Measuring Impact of E-commerce on Small Scale Business: A Systematic Review. *Journal of Corporate Governance and International Business Law*, 5(1).

Solangi, Z. A., Solangi, Y. A., & Chandio, S., bin Hamzah, M. S., & Shah, A. (2018, May). The future of data privacy and security concerns in Internet of Things. In *2018 IEEE International Conference on Innovative Research and Development (ICIRD)* (pp. 1-4). IEEE. DOI: 10.1109/ICIRD.2018.8376320

Soni, P., Pradhan, J., Pal, A. K., & Islam, S. H. (2022). Cybersecurity attack-resilience authentication mechanism for intelligent healthcare system. *IEEE Transactions on Industrial Informatics*, 19(1), 830–840. DOI: 10.1109/TII.2022.3179429

Sriram, R. D., & Subrahmanian, E. (2020). Transforming health care through digital revolutions. *Journal of the Indian Institute of Science*, 100(4), 753–772. DOI: 10.1007/s41745-020-00195-0 PMID: 33132546

Suleski, T., Ahmed, M., Yang, W., & Wang, E. (2023). A review of multi-factor authentication in the Internet of Healthcare Things. *Digital Health*, 9, 20552076231177144. DOI: 10.1177/20552076231177144 PMID: 37252257

Taimoor, N., & Rehman, S. (2021). Reliable and resilient AI and IoT-based personalised healthcare services: A survey. *IEEE Access : Practical Innovations, Open Solutions*, 10, 535–563. DOI: 10.1109/ACCESS.2021.3137364

Thuemmler, C., & Bai, C. (2017). Health 4.0: Application of industry 4.0 design principles in future asthma management. *Health 4.0: How virtualization and big data are revolutionizing healthcare*, 23-37. DOI: 10.1109/ACCESS.2021.3137364

Tyagi, A. K., Hemamalini, V., & Soni, G. (2023). Digital Health Communication With Artificial Intelligence-Based Cyber Security. In *AI-Based Digital Health Communication for Securing Assistive Systems* (pp. 178–213). IGI Global. DOI: 10.4018/978-1-6684-8938-3.ch009

van Kessel, R., Haig, M., & Mossialos, E. (2023). Strengthening cybersecurity for patient data protection in Europe. *Journal of Medical Internet Research*, 25(1), e48824. DOI: 10.2196/48824 PMID: 37616048

Vulpe, A., Crăciunescu, R., Drăgulinescu, A. M., Kyriazakos, S., Paikan, A., & Ziafati, P. (2021). Enabling security services in socially assistive robot scenarios for healthcare applications. *Sensors (Basel)*, 21(20), 6912. DOI: 10.3390/s21206912 PMID: 34696125

Vyas, S., & Bhargava, D. (2021). Smart Health Systems: Emerging Trends. DOI: 10.1109/ACCESS.2021.3137364

Wahab, F., Zhao, Y., Javeed, D., Al-Adhaileh, M. H., Almaaytah, S. A., Khan, W., Saeed, M. S., & Kumar Shah, R. (2022). An AI-driven hybrid framework for intrusion detection in IoT-enabled E-health. *Computational Intelligence and Neuroscience*, 2022, 2022. DOI: 10.1155/2022/6096289 PMID: 36045979

Yeng, P. K., Fauzi, M. A., Sun, L., & Yang, B. (2022). Assessing the legal aspects of information security requirements for health care in 3 countries: Scoping review and framework development. *JMIR Human Factors*, 9(2), e30050. DOI: 10.2196/30050 PMID: 35612891

Zala, K., Thakkar, H. K., Dholakia, N., Shukla, M., & Thumar, D. (2024). Designing an Attribute-Based Encryption Scheme with an Enhanced Anonymity Model for Privacy Protection in E-Health. *SN Computer Science*, 5(2), 203. DOI: 10.1007/s42979-023-02541-2

# Chapter 11
# Empowering Celiac Disease Management:
## Integrating AI Technology With Research Insights

**Anoop Johny**
*Manipal School of Life Sciences, India*

## ABSTRACT

*Celiac disease, a chronic autoimmune disorder triggered by gluten ingestion, poses significant challenges in diagnosis, management, and adherence to a strict gluten-free diet. This paper presents an innovative approach to address these challenges by integrating artificial intelligence (AI) technology with comprehensive research insights. The AI-enabled tool developed herein aims to enhance early detection, personalized treatment recommendations, dietary management, and patient education. By leveraging machine learning algorithms, natural language processing techniques, and data analytics, the tool assists healthcare professionals in optimizing patient care and improving outcomes. This article elucidates the rationale, methodology, and potential impact of integrating AI into celiac disease management, highlighting the interdisciplinary collaboration between medical research, technology development, and healthcare delivery.*

## 1. INTRODUCTION

Celiac disease (CD) is an autoimmune disorder that is systemic in nature and is induced as a result of gluten intake in genetically predisposed individuals, more commonly in the HLA-DQ2 or the HLA-DQ8 haplotypes predominantly seen in many patients. CD accounts for about 1% of the population worldwide but is

DOI: 10.4018/979-8-3373-2530-9.ch011

largely undiagnosed worldwide. The most common presentations are diarrhea and mal-absorption, but other clinical manifestations include anemia, osteoporosis, and abnormal liver tests, which can be appreciated in both children and adults. Admittedly, AI has gone a step further to improve endoscopic imaging with regard to the diagnosis of Crohn's disease. The coupling of machine learning with wireless capsule endoscopy (WCE) and esophagogastroduodenoscopy (EGD) images enhances both the sensitivity and the specificity of diagnosis. Ciaccio et al. (2010) successfully achieved 80% sensitivity and 96% specificity when applying quantitative markers to WCE images to screen for celiac disease (CD) and report small bowel involvement without extensive manual examination. Zhou et al. (2017) reported those who trained GoogLeNet based CNN with WCE images to be able to achieve 100% sensitivity and specificity, besides introducing an evaluation confidence (EC) measure of disease severity to be used in diagnosis and treatment. Modified CNN mimicking human visual perception, proposed by Wang et al. (2019), achieved a detection accuracy of subtle changes in villi morphology of as much as 95.9% being the result of the study. The above clearly show how promising AI is in bringing a huge difference in the analysis of endoscopic images.

*Figure 1. Crystal structure of HLA-DQ2 complexed with deamidated gliadin peptide RCSB PDB - 1S9V: Crystal structure of HLA-DQ2 complexed with deamidated gliadin peptide. (n.d.). Retrieved May 10, 2024, from https://www.rcsb.org/structure/1S9V.*

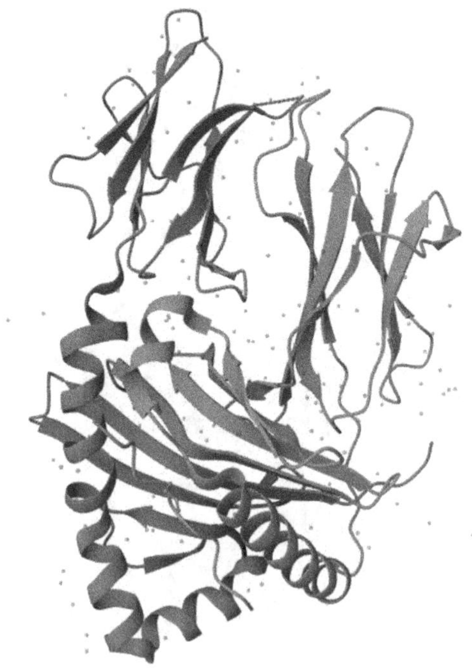

Gluten, which is protein not in the gluten complex found in wheat, rye, and barley, causes different levels of damage to the small intestine and different levels of response in serum autoantibody. Gluten prevalence-case differs from countries to countries across the global map, from 0.3% entry into Germany, to 2.4% entry into Finland. Shown in the Figure 1 crystallography is an HLA-DQ2 peptide complexed with deamidated gliadin, illustrating a complex immune response in celiac disease. It thus probably triggers T cell activation at gliadin (Figure 1). It is another place of importance on the globe such as North Africa, the Middle East, and northwestern India, where wheat is a staple food in the diet. In most cases, the increase is attributed to changes in dietary habits associated with westernization, changes in wheat productivity, and increased awareness of diseases (Fasano, 2001).

*Figure 2. Bel502-DQ8-glia-alpha1 complex RCSB PDB - 5KS9: Bel502-DQ8-glia-alpha1 complex. (n.d.). Retrieved May 10, 2024, from https://www.rcsb.org/structure/5KS9*

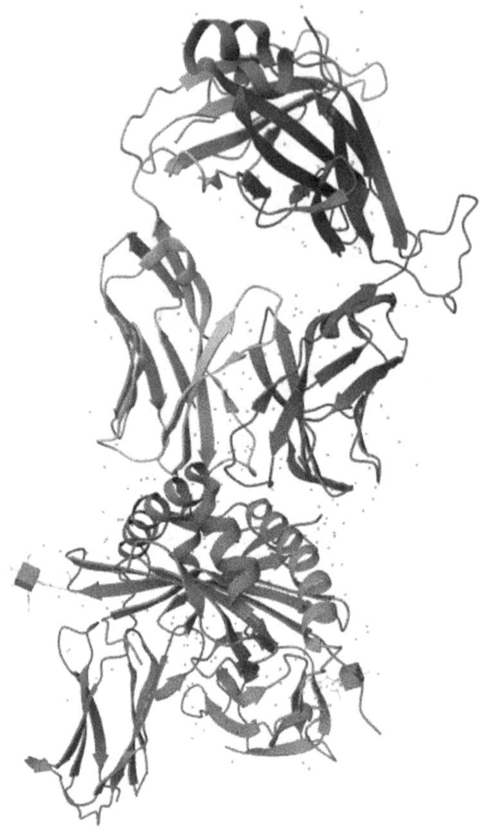

Celiac disease is 1.5 to 2 times higher in women as well as closely associated with diseases such as type 1 diabetes, hashimoto thyroiditis, Down syndrome, Turner's syndrome, and IgA deficiency (Fasano, 2001). The Bel502-DQ8-glia-alpha1 complex (Figure 2) shows hepatic components interacting with DQ8 accounting for association with celiac disease and antigen presentation route.

*Table 1. Serum tests for the diagnosis of celiac disease (Husby et al., 2012).*

| Test | Sensitivity (Range) % | Specificity (Range) % | Notes |
|---|---|---|---|
| IgA anti-tTG antibodies | >95.0 (73.9–100) | >95.0 (77.8–100) | Recommended as first-level screening test |
| IgG anti-tTG antibodies | Widely variable (12.6–99.3) | Widely variable (86.3–100) | Useful in patients with IgA deficiency |
| IgA antiendomysial antibodies | >90.0 (82.6–100) | >90.0 (80.1–98.6) | Useful in patients with an uncertain diagnosis |
| IgG DGP | 91.0 (82.6–97.0) | 98.2 (94.7–100) | Useful in patients with IgA deficiency and young children |
| HLA-DQ2 or HLA-DQ8 | >90.0 (86.0–96.9) | 54.0 (12.0–68.0) | High negative predictive value |

Patients (90%) possess the HLA-DQ2 haplotype (DQA10501/DQB10201), which is present in about a third of the population, while 5% have HLA-DQ8 (DQA10301/DQB10302). Patients have one gene encoding DQ2 diagnosis conducted serologic testing, as in Table 1 it involves accuracy and tests. IgA anti-tTG is useful for first-line tests as it has a high level of sensitivity and specificity. Alternatively, IgG antibodies for tTG and IgG-DGP can be used. Haplotypes allow antigen-presenting cells to bind deaminated gluten peptides and elicit immune responses. However, DQ2 and DQ8 alone are insufficient to generate the disease: At least 39 non-HLA genes encoding immune and inflammatory responses have been implicated in its development (Fasano, 2001). Celiac disease, caused by gluten exposure, alteration of intestinal permeability, recognition by HLA, and immune responses involving the self-antigens such as transglutaminase, results in enteropathy.

## 2. THE PRECIPITATING FACTOR: TESTING FOR TOXICITY

### 2.1 In Vivo and In Vitro Methods

*Figure 3. HMW glutenin subunits (HMW-GS), Large proteins often with repetitive sequences rich in Gln, Gly, and Pro.(RCSB PDB - 5KS9: Bel502-DQ8-Glia-Alpha1 Complex, n.d.)*

Historically, the great in vivo methods based on clinical symptoms like steatorrhea and mucosal damage have involved feeding trials and intestinal biopsies. HMW glutenin subunits (GS-HMW) have repetitive Gln-Gly-Pro motifs influencing gluten immunogenicity and elasticity (Figure 3). Gluten challenges were performed with massive doses in the range of 10-100 g and brought down to as low as 1 g by oral techniques. Important indicators of damage included villus height, villus-to-crypt depth ratio, and intraepithelial lymphocyte (IEL) counts (Wieser & Koehler, 2008). In vitro methods transformed toxicity testing, especially peptide studies requiring minimal gluten (about 1 mg). Organ culture of gut tissue from CD patients remains effective for evaluating enzyme activity and structural changes. T-cell lines and clones from CD patients are used to assess immune responses, with tests like T-cell proliferation and cytokine production (e.g., IFN-γ, IL-4). However, antigenic responses observed in vitro often fail to correlate with in vivo toxicity. Additional vitro assays include fetal rat or chicken intestinal organ culture, leukocyte migration inhibition, macrophage procoagulant activity, and K562 cell agglutination tests. Despite advancements, in vivo testing remains essential for comprehensive CD toxicity evaluation.

## 3. CELIAC DISEASE POPULATION AND SUSCEPTIBILITY

### 3.1 In General Population

In the past few decades, Celiac disease (CD) has appeared as one of the most common hereditary diseases. Previously limited mostly within the geographical boundaries of Europe-prevalence rates have been reported ranging between 1% and 2%-studies have shown comparably similar rates within the United States (0.75%) and Australia. (Elli et al., 2015). However, global prevalence is not well defined with differences in sample size, screening methods, and geographic factors (Mustalahti et al., 2010). The range of prevalence in Europe is also influenced by diagnostic criteria and awareness. Diagnosis usually follows the presence of complaints suggestive of CD (Lionetti & Catassi, 2011). The "iceberg model" illustrates the many undiagnosed celiac disease cases, often with atypical or no symptoms. A U.S. multicenter study found a 0.75% prevalence (1 in 133 healthy individuals), similar to rates in Europe and Australia. These findings fuel debate over whether variations reflect underdiagnosis or actual disease variability. The significant number of undetected cases, particularly among asymptomatic individuals, poses a challenge to accurately determining CD prevalence, with most cases remaining "submerged" and unidentified (Lionetti & Catassi, 2011). Celiac disease has been found to affect about 0.75% of the total population in the surveyed US centers, according to previous evaluations done in Australia and Europe. Thus, it can be concluded that celiac disease is a common ailment worldwide, affecting almost 0.75% of the general population, or may reach 4.5% in high-risk populations. It's not limited to developed countries. A multicenter study carried out in the United States revealed a prevalence rate of 1 in 133 among healthy persons, which translates to 0.75% of the general population, despite the uncertainty in particular places (Cataldo & Montalto, 2007). This number supports research from Australia and Europe, emphasizing the fact that celiac disease is very common. Celiac disease is present in 0.75% of the general population worldwide and can reach 4.5% in high-risk groups. The affliction of celiac disease is not exclusive to developed countries.

## 3.2 Susceptibility

A significant portion of the total genetic predisposition to celiac disease, around 35%, is attributed to the presence of certain genes encoding MHC class II proteins, namely human leukocyte antigen (HLA) DQ2 and HLA-DQ8. HLA-DQ2 is expressed by over 90% of people with celiac disease, whereas HLA-DQ8 is expressed in the remaining instances (Dieli-Crimi et al., 2015; Trynka et al., 2010). While these HLA risk genes are present in about 30% of the general population, only 1% to 3% of people actually get celiac disease. This suggests that although HLA plays a major role, the disease cannot be entirely caused by it. Research on monozygotic twins provides more evidence for the involvement of several genetic variables in the susceptibility to celiac disease. 39 non-HLA genetic loci have been linked to celiac disease in recent years by genome-wide association studies (GWAS) (Dubois et al., 2010). MYO9B, one of these genes on chromosome 19, may be related to an individual's ability to adapt to a gluten-free diet. Antigen-presenting cells (APCs) express the HLA-DQ2 and HLA-DQ8 molecules, which are essential for the immune response (Freeman et al., 2011). In the intestinal mucosa, gluten peptides induce the activation of specific T-lymphocytes, which trigger the production of cytokines. Tissue transglutaminase 2 (tTG2) modifies gluten peptides by converting the glutamines to glutamic acid and amplifying the immune response typical of celiac disease (CD). Many environmental factors have been mentioned that are associated with the occurrence of CD, such as the pattern of infant feeding and the early viral infections, such as those caused by rotavirus. It was shown in a prospective study that frequent rotavirus-infected children are exposed to an increased risk of CD autoimmunity. Gluten is composed of glutenin and prolamines (the gliadins in wheat, secalins in rye, and hordeins in barley). According to research by Catassi et al., persons with CD may experience apparent small intestine damage from as little as 50 mg of gluten per day (Troncone & Jabri, 2011). Other elements that may impact the intestinal environment and perhaps exacerbate CD include the type of milk fed and the length of time breastfed.

## 3.3 Celiac Disease Pathophysiology

The immunological (tissue transglutaminase, tTG), genetic (HLA-DQ2 and HLA-DQ8), and environmental (gluten) variables that are important in the development of celiac disease are distinct from one another. The absence of a trustworthy animal model has been a significant obstacle in CD research, despite the possibility that an Irish setter dog could become gluten-sensitive. On the other hand, developments in human immunology and gut biology are opening up new directions for future research.

*Table 2. Adults can be serologically screened for celiac disease in the general population, with confirmation obtained through duodenal biopsy (Caio et al., 2019).*

| Study | Antibody Test | Number of Cases | Age (Years) | Country | Celiac Disease (CD) Prevalence | Additional Information |
|---|---|---|---|---|---|---|
| Corazza et al., 1997 (Bach, 2018) | EmA (Anti-Endomysium Antibodies) | 2,237 | 20–87 | Italy | 0.18% | One of the earliest population-based studies on CD, focusing on the prevalence in Italy using EmA as the primary test. |
| Ivarsson et al., 1999 (Corazza et al., 1997) | EmA (Anti-Endomysium Antibodies) | 1,894 | 25–74 | Sweden | 0.53% | This Swedish study emphasized a higher prevalence of CD in Northern Europe. The study helped to raise awareness of CD's underdiagnosis. |
| Riestra et al., 2000 (Ivarsson et al., 1999) | EmA (Anti-Endomysium Antibodies) | 1,170 | 14–89 | Spain | 0.26% | Conducted in Spain, this study highlighted that CD is present in populations outside Northern Europe, though at a slightly lower rate. |
| Volta et al., 2001 (Riestra et al., 2000) | EmA (Anti-Endomysium Antibodies) | 3,483 | 14–65 | Italy | 0.57% | This study showed an increased prevalence of CD in Italy compared to earlier research and helped establish EmA testing for diagnosis. |
| Mustalahti et al., 2010 (Volta et al., 2001) | Anti-tTG (Anti-Tissue Transglutaminase), EmA | 6,403 | 30–93 | Finland | 2.5% | One of the largest studies on CD, finding the highest prevalence in Finland, potentially due to genetic and environmental factors. |

continued on following page

*Table 2. Continued*

| Study | Antibody Test | Number of Cases | Age (Years) | Country | Celiac Disease (CD) Prevalence | Additional Information |
|---|---|---|---|---|---|---|
| Rubio-Tapia et al., 2012 (Mustalahti et al., 2010) | Anti-tTG (Anti-Tissue Transglutaminase), EmA | 7,798 | 23–66 | USA | 0.71% | This study found a moderate prevalence of CD in the US, highlighting the importance of serological screening for better detection. |
| Singh et al., 2016 (Fasano et al., 2003) | Anti-tTG (Anti-Tissue Transglutaminase), EmA | 43,955 | Not specified | Asia | 0.5% | A large-scale study in Asia showing a prevalence similar to that of Europe and the US, though CD is still under-recognized in many Asian countries. |

Table 2 depicts adult screening for celiac disease (CD) with blood tests with duodenal biopsy confirmation. The hygiene hypothesis suggests that less exposure to microbes due to improved living conditions in developed countries during the past 40 years might contribute to an increasing rate of autoimmune diseases. This theory is being revisited in light of new evidence indicating the role of the gut microbiome in the regulation of immune tolerance and autoimmunity. Regardless of microbes, skewed reactivity by T helper 1 and 2 cells or deficiencies in the adaptive immunity are recognized as the most important players in autoimmune diseases including celiac disease (Verdu et al., 2015). With a familial recurrence rate of 10-15% and a high concordance (75-80%) among monozygotic twins, celiac disease exhibits a significant genetic component (Lundin & Wijmenga, 2015). As for most autoimmune diseases, the heritability of celiac disease (CD) is highly dependent on HLA class II heterodimers, especially DQ2 and DQ8. Homozygous for HLA-DQ2, infants with one first-degree relative affected by the same condition face 25-30% risk increase. However, CD will develop in only about 3% of persons having HLA-DQ2 or HLA-DQ8 although they are found in 25-35% of the general population because there are further genetic factors. Mendelian genome-wide association studies have identified more than 100 different non-HLA genes as being linked to CD, but each of them adds only a small contribution to the hereditary risk profile (Lundin & Wijmenga, 2015).

## 4. IMMUNOLOGICAL STUDY

Gluten, a component of the human diet for over 10,000 years, contains non-digestible immunogenic peptides. These peptides, especially gliadins with high proline and glutamine content, resist complete breakdown by intestinal enzymes, contributing to their immunogenicity and association with celiac disease. Partial digestion of gluten produces peptides that trigger immune responses, such as increased intestinal permeability, similar to reactions caused by harmful microbes. An example is gliadin, which increases intestinal permeability. This leads to the release of zonulin, which deconsolidates tight junctions within intestinal cells to allow such substances to pass more easily. Such is paracellular transport (Hollon et al., 2015). This effect occurs regardless of whether the individual has celiac disease or not. In experiments with C57BL/6 mice, gliadin was shown to increase gut mucosa permeability through a mechanism dependent on the myeloid differentiation primary response 88 (MyD88) protein. Additionally, specific motifs in alpha-gliadin can bind to chemokine receptor 3, triggering zonulin release and further disrupting tight junctions. Genetic studies have also found associations between certain tight junction genes and celiac disease, supporting the role of the paracellular pathway in gluten trafficking to the lamina propria (Dieli-Crimi et al., 2015). There is strong evidence that gluten can also cross the intestinal barrier via the transcellular pathway, particularly when tolerance to gluten is lost. In celiac disease patients, the transferrin receptor CD71, which is typically found on the basolateral side of enterocytes, becomes overexpressed on the luminal side during the acute phase of the disease. Transcellular transport involves the movement of substances through the cells themselves. This leads to the retrotranscytosis (movement from the apical to the basal side) of gliadin peptides complexed with secretory IgA. This process protects gliadin fragments from degradation in lysosomes and facilitates their entry into the lamina propria, perpetuating inflammation initiated by the paracellular passage of these peptides. Due to their resistance, gluten immunogenic peptides (GIP) can cross the compromised epithelial lining, enter the bloodstream, and eventually be excreted in the urine (Loeff et al., 2012). The intestinal barrier has tight junctions, which are regulated by zonulin. Gliadin increases zonulin by activating MyD88 pathway and chemokine receptor 3, disrupting junctions. In celiac disease, overexpression of CD71 enhances the transport of gliadin. Secreted IgA binds gliadin into complexes, inhibiting its degradation and allowing access to the epithelium. Innate immune-related cytokines (IL15, interferon-alpha) prime dendritic cells and intraepithelial lymphocytes, which are crucial for the development of the disease in celiac patients. According to recent research, certain gliadin peptides can promote the proliferation of enterocytes that is dependent on IL-15 and epithelial growth factor (Kim et al., 2015). There are associated structural changes and immune activation following the ingestion of gluten, as it acts via alpha-amylase/trypsin inhibitors. These latter substances trigger the Toll-like receptor 4-MD2-CD14 complex. Cell maturation markers and proinflammatory cytokines are increased in CD cells. Gliadin may cause the release of zonulin, which diminishes the epithelial barrier and allows exposure to toxic peptides. Such processes lead, in particular, to the stimulation of IL-8 and neutrophils. Gliadin attracts neutrophils through the fMet-Leu-Phe receptor 1, according to our findings. The immune response in CD is determined by the interaction of gluten peptides with the T cells restricted by the HLA-DQ2/8 molecules (Stamnaes & Sollid, 2015). The way celiac disease is caused includes the removal of gluten by the enzyme named transglutaminase 2 (TG2). More IL-15 stimulates the innate immune system, thereby bettering the actions of CD4+ T cells in adaptive responses. Gluten presentation by HLA class II antigen-presenting cells (e.g., DCs, macrophages, B cells, enterocytes) activates CD4+ T cells, leading to their recirculation in the lamina propria. Upon exposure to gluten, such T cells become active through proliferation and production of proinflammatory cytokines, metalloproteinases, and keratinocyte growth factor. Crypt hyperplasia and partial villous blunting are due to the loss of intestinal epithelial cell by the action of intraepithelial lymphocyte (IELs) (Pagliari et al., 2015). In active celiac disease, there is an excess of enterocyte-derived interleukin-15, which activates the CD3+ intraepithelial lymphocytes to express NK receptors, such as CD94 and NKG2D. Hyperplastic crypts are thought to be a consequence of stem cells that cannot repair the damage to continuous autoimmune attacks. Immature progenitor cell expansion and inhibition of Hedgehog signaling explain recent findings associating hyperplastic crypts with an immature progenitor cell population. Thus, these findings clarify the molecular basis of the histopathology of CD and the absence of enteropathy in models of CD in mice (Ju et al., 2015). Celiac Disease-like enteropathy is not displayed in immune-deficient mice, ruling out the possibility that the rapid destruction of enterocytes by CD4+ T cells is almost the cause of Celiac Disease pathogenesis; rather, a defect might lie in stem cells associated with predisposition to disease. Celiac Disease is closely associated with a number of other diseases like properly genetic disorders Down syndrome, Turner syndrome, and Williams syndrome, as well as autoimmune and neurological disorders. Type 1 diabetes is closely studied among them. Ludvigsson's study revealed that type 1 diabetes amplifies the risk of developing celiac disease by 5-to10-fold in children (Akirov & Pinhas-Hamiel, 2015). The HLA genes common in type 1 diabetes patients increase their risk of celiac disease, with 75% experiencing intestinal complications and 5-10% carrying celiac disease-related antibodies, and their prevalence ranging from 1-19%. The gluten exposure heightens the risk of these conditions for genetically predisposed infants. Graves disease and Hashimoto's thyroiditis are thyroid disorders that affect 2-5% of patients, often after/before gluten enteropathy. Selenium malabsorption for crucial thyroid functions, linking thyroid and gastrointestinal issues. This monitors the growth, development, and screening of diseases and is essential for follow-up positive cases (Stazi & Trinti, 2010).

## 5. TOXIC CEREALS, TOXIC PROTEINS, TOXIC PEPTIDES

Understanding the CD toxicity associated with cereals has evolved significantly over the years. While the classical features of CD were described more than a century ago, it was not until 1950 that wheat's toxicity was established. Subsequent research indicated that rye and barley were also harmful, whereas corn, rice, and buckwheat were not. The toxicity of oats remains controversial; early studies suggested oats could cause malabsorption, but more recent comprehensive studies have shown that pure oats are generally well-tolerated by CD patients. However, some studies reported adverse effects in a small number of patients, highlighting the need for further research (Wieser & Koehler, 2008). Cereal storage proteins are further categorized into prolamins and glutelins according to solubility, and then into HMW, MMW, and LMW with respect to molecular weights. HMW proteins (e.g., in wheat- HMW-GS, in rye- HMW-secals) are generally rich in Gln, Gly, and Pro. MMW proteins (e.g., ω-gliadins in wheat and C-hordeins in barley) contain Gln, Pro, and Phenylalanine (Phe). LMW proteins (e.g., α/β-gliadins in wheat or avenins in oats) are also rich in Gln and Pro and have the potential to be toxic in celiac disease (CD). Toxic peptides, including PSQQ and QQQP from α/β-gliadins, are resistant to degradation and stimulate CD by activating T cells and damaging the intestines. Specific peptides are cardinal in the pathogenesis of CD.

## 6. EPIDEMIOLOGY IN GENERAL POPULATION

Celiac disease was once considered a rare childhood disorder, primarily affecting white Caucasian children, a view still held in some European countries that classify it as rare. However, it is now recognized as one of the most common chronic diseases worldwide. Many cases go undiagnosed due to atypical symptoms, with detection relying on sensitive serological tests like serum IgA anti-transglutaminase and anti-endomysial antibodies. Prevalence ranges from 0.75-1% in Europe and is higher in isolated communities. Studies show similar rates in North America (e.g., 1:133 prevalence in a study of 4,126 individuals), as well as in countries with European-descended populations like Australia, New Zealand, and Argentina. Celiac disease is also becoming more prevalent in developing regions such as North Africa, the Middle East, and India, contributing to childhood morbidity and mortality. In the

Saharawi population, the prevalence is 5.6%, linked to genetic factors like HLA-DQ2 and -DQ8 genotypes and high gluten consumption (Shahbazkhani et al., 2003). Middle East has significant history of celiac disease, being the region where ancient grains were first domesticated. Figure 4 X-ray crystallography reveals novel HLA-B8E76C N-termini

*Figure 4. Structural insights into HLA-B8E76C: Novel N-Terminal features revealed by X-Ray crystallography*

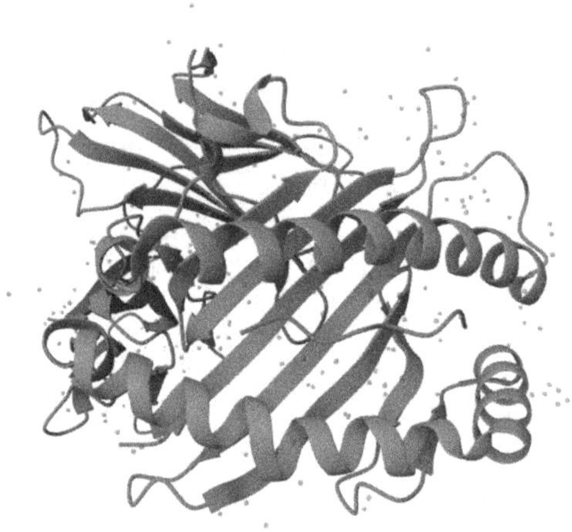

# 7.APPLICATIONS OF ARTIFICIAL INTELLIGENCE IN CELIAC DISEASE MANAGEMENT

## 7.1 Endoscopic Image Analysis

Machines like AI are promising for analyzing endoscopic photographs for the diagnosis of Crohn's disease. The use of WCE and EGD images in training machine-learning models has proved to enhance the possibility to diagnosis with sensitivity and specificity:

- Ciaccio et al. (2010) used WCE images and achieved 80% sensitivity and 96% specificity. Their method applied quantitative markers to screen for CD and assess small bowel involvement, thus minimizing the manual image analysis.

- Zhou et al. (2017) trained a CNN (GoogLeNet) on WCE images measuring 100% sensitivity and specificity. Their model presents an evaluation confidence (EC) that quantifies the severity of disease as an additional tool during diagnosis and treatment decisions (Zhou et al., 2017).
- Wang et al. (2019) modified a CNN in such a way that input features are obtained as similar to a human eye. They achieved a 95.9 percent accuracy in fine detection of subtle changes in villous morphology.

## 7.2 Deep Learning for the Diagnosis of Celiac Disease

Although they are proven to be very useful, because of limited public datasets, convolutional neural networks (CNN) have the potential to bring about significant changes in the way images can be interpreted and understood in terms of celiac disease (CD) diagnosis. Unfortunately, the only available CD-related endoscopic image dataset today contains only 1,661 image patches (128×128 pixels). In (Wimmer, Hegenbart, et al., 2017), Shallow and deep neural architecture comparison revealed the performance of the small networks with pre-training and data augmentation over imaging diagnostic. Networks having a medium-to-large filter size were instead performing better than having greater number of parameters. Pretraining of CNN on networks like ImageNet improved feature extraction and fine-tuned and even fully adapted all these networks. It needs larger datasets for the reason that full adaptation has more risk for overfitting as small dataset size caused. Improvement was in the data augmentation techniques such as flipping, cropping, and affine/projective transformations up to almost doubles the performance of the method with the highest impact when combining affine and projective transformations (Wimmer, Uhl, et al., 2017). The most improvement was recorded when both comprehensive affine and projective transformations were used at once.

## 7.3 Electronic Medical Records Analysis

AI models analyzing electronic medical records (EMR) show potential for enhancing CD detection and risk assessment. Tenorio et al. (2011) developed a web-based clinical decision support system using EMR data, achieving 80% accuracy with 270 classifiers across five ML techniques, aiding primary care diagnosis. Chen et al. (2016) created an automated system that outperformed ICD-9 coding, with an AUROC of 0.94, improving CD identification in large datasets (Chen et al., 2016). Ludvigsson et al. (2013) used natural language processing (NLP) to screen high-risk individuals, achieving 72.9% sensitivity compared to 17.1% for ICD-9 algorithms. These advancements highlight AI's role in mining healthcare data, improving CD case finding, screening, and early intervention for better outcomes.

## 7.4 Histopathology

AI has shown a lot of potential in automating and improving the histopathological diagnosis of CD. Syed et al. (2019) developed a CNN model to distinguish between healthy and diseased duodenal tissues with an accuracy of 93.4% while achieving a 2.4% false-negative rate. Their model, integrated with CNN and deconvolutional network, automatically identified micro-features association with CD status where epithelial secretory cells were among the examples. This could lead to the standardization of CD diagnoses across settings so that variability is reduced and the accuracy of diagnosis is improved as well, especially with subtle or atypical cases (Syed et al., 2019). All in all, the applications of AI within CD management show great promise for making diagnosis, monitoring, and treatment processes much better. Image analysis and EMR processing, biomarker development, and genetics-based AI all have a chance to transfom CD care.

## 7.5 AI-Driven Diagnosis and Management

Recent advancements in artificial intelligence (AI) have opened new avenues for improving the diagnosis and management of celiac disease (CD). This section explores specific AI applications that show promise in enhancing CD care.

1. **Enhanced Diagnostic Accuracy Through Image Analysis:** AI-powered image analysis has shown significant potential in improving CD diagnosis. Convolutional Neural Networks (CNNs) have been particularly effective in analyzing endoscopic imagery. For instance, Wimmer et al. (2016b) demonstrated that CNN transfer learning could achieve high accuracy in automated CD diagnosis. Their study using pre-trained CNNs (AlexNet, VGG-f, and VGG-16) achieved classification accuracies between 90.5% and 95.3% (Wimmer et al., 2016).
2. **Advanced Feature Extraction for Improved Classification:** Various feature extraction methods have been employed to enhance CD classification. Gadermayr et al. (2016a) combined computer-aided texture analysis with expert knowledge, achieving a sensitivity of 98.5% and specificity of 99.1% in CD diagnosis. This hybrid approach demonstrates the potential of integrating AI with human expertise.
3. **Video Capsule Endoscopy Analysis:** AI has also been applied to video capsule endoscopy for CD diagnosis. Zhou et al. (2017) used a deep learning method based on GoogLeNet to analyze video capsule endoscopy images, achieving 100% sensitivity and specificity. This suggests that AI could potentially enhance the diagnostic yield of video capsule endoscopy in CD (Zhou et al., 2017).

4. **Scale-Invariant Feature Analysis:** Scale-invariant features have shown promise in CD diagnosis. Gadermayr et al. (2016a) used multifractal spectrum features and SIFT Fisher vectors, achieving an accuracy of 98.1%. When incorporating human knowledge, the accuracy increased to 98.9%, highlighting the potential of combining AI with clinical expertise.
5. **Addressing Image Quality Issues:** AI techniques have been developed to address challenges related to image quality in endoscopic CD diagnosis. Gadermayr et al. (2014a) proposed degradation adaptive texture classification to handle varying image quality, which is crucial for real-world application of AI in CD diagnosis (Gadermayr et al., 2014).
6. **Multimodal Data Integration:** AI systems show potential in integrating various data types for CD management. While not explicitly mentioned in the provided paper, the review suggests that combining endoscopic imagery with other clinical data could enhance diagnostic accuracy and patient management.

## 7.6 Challenges and Future Directions

Despite these promising developments, several challenges remain:

1. **Data Variability:** As noted by Hegenbart et al. (2015), there is significant variability in the databases used for AI studies in CD, making direct comparisons challenging (Hegenbart et al., 2015).
2. **Clinical Validation:** Many of the AI techniques described have been validated on retrospective datasets. Future research should focus on prospective clinical trials to validate these tools in real-world settings.
3. **Differential Diagnosis:** As mentioned in the paper, AI systems need to differentiate CD from other causes of villous atrophy, such as giardiasis, Helicobacter pylori infection, and other conditions that can mimic CD endoscopically (Gadermayr et al., 2014).
4. **Integration with Clinical Workflow:** Future research should focus on seamlessly integrating AI tools into existing clinical workflows to maximize their practical impact.

# 8. COMPUTER-AIDED DIAGNOSIS OF COELIAC DISEASE

## 8.1 Overview of AI Techniques Used

Several AI approaches have been applied to celiac disease diagnosis:

- **Convolutional Neural Networks (CNNs):** CNNs have emerged as a powerful tool for image classification tasks. Studies have utilized various CNN architectures such as AlexNet, VGGNet, and GoogLeNet for analyzing endoscopic images.
- **Support Vector Machines (SVMs):** While not as prevalent as CNNs, SVMs have also been employed, often in combination with CNNs or other feature extraction methods(Gadermayr et al., 2018).
- **Transfer Learning:** This technique, which involves adapting pre-trained networks to the specific task of celiac disease diagnosis, has shown promise in improving performance, especially when working with limited datasets.

## 8.2 Performance Comparison with Traditional Methods

AI-based methods have generally outperformed traditional feature extraction techniques in the classification of celiac disease from endoscopic images:

- **Accuracy:** Wimmer et al. reported an accuracy of 90.5% using CNNs on a dataset of 1,661 image patches (Wimmer et al., 2016), while Zhou et al. achieved 100% sensitivity and specificity using GoogLeNet on video capsule endoscopy images.
- **Feature Learning:** Unlike traditional methods that rely on hand-crafted features, AI algorithms can automatically learn relevant features from the data, potentially capturing subtle patterns that might be missed by conventional approaches (Seguí et al., 2016).
- **Scalability:** AI methods have shown the ability to handle larger datasets more effectively, with performance often improving as more data becomes available.

## 8.3 Advantages of AI Approaches

Automated Feature Extraction: AI algorithms, particularly deep learning models, can automatically learn relevant features from raw image data, reducing the need for manual feature engineering (Seguí et al., 2016).

- **High Accuracy:** Several studies have reported high accuracy rates, sometimes surpassing human experts in controlled settings.
- **Consistency:** AI systems can provide consistent results, potentially reducing inter-observer variability in diagnosis.
- **Speed:** Once trained, AI models can analyze images rapidly, potentially enabling real-time analysis during endoscopic procedures.

## 8.4 Limitations and Challenges

Despite the promising results, several challenges remain:

- **Data Requirements:** Deep learning models often require large datasets for optimal performance, which can be challenging to obtain in medical settings.
- **Generalizability:** Models trained on data from one institution or using a specific endoscopy system may not perform as well on data from other sources.
- **Interpretability:** The 'black box' nature of deep learning models can make it difficult to understand how decisions are made, which is crucial in medical applications.
- **Validation:** Most studies to date have been retrospective. Prospective studies and clinical trials are needed to validate the performance of AI systems in real-world settings.

## 8.5 XGBoost for Celiac Disease prediction

Combining XGBoost with Particle Swarm Optimization (PSO) offers an efficient approach for feature selection and eliminating redundant records, enhancing disease prediction accuracy and providing actionable insights for clinicians (Tapkire & Arun, 2023). The very way by which the approach explains has evident versatility for application concerning the features of other medical conditions, in addition to celiac disease (CD). As with the earlier, the MetaCognitive Neural Networks (McNN) dynamically evaluate learning performances to better decision-making by discriminating redundant and novel information. When combined with the PBL classifier, this enhances generalization and classification performance, as demonstrated in depression prediction. In order to forecast heart disease, developed a hybrid method called HRFLM that combines Random Forest and Linear Methods. After examining KNN and CNN algorithms, (Dahiwade et al., 2019) came to the conclusion that CNN performs better than KNN in patient classification, with an accuracy rate of 84%. Furthermore, methods such as SVM and fuzzy C-means have been used to predict Parkinson's disease with accuracy rates ranging from 72% to 92%. Additional developments include deep artificial neural networks, which utilized to predict chronic kidney disease with 97% accuracy, and data mining techniques like Support Vector Machines and Decision Trees for the prediction of breast cancer recurrence, with SVM turning out to be the most accurate. The application of neural networks, decision trees, and random forests in the prediction of diabetes was also highlighted by (Zou et al., 2018). With an accuracy of 80.84%, random forests have emphasized the increasing impact of machine learning in predictive healthcare, whether for diagnosis, treatment, or efficiency. The power of combining XGBoost with Particle

Swarm Optimization (PSO) can further enhance disease prediction through optimal feature selection, duplicate data elimination, and actionable understandings crafted for informed medical decision-making. These models can generalize beyond CD scenarios to other diseases (Tapkire & Arun, 2023). AI does not just predict CD but also changes the way food is formulated for susceptible individuals. Traditional food reformulation is a lengthy and laborious process filled with trials and sensory evaluations. However, this can be streamlined using AI by analyzing large volumes of data regarding ingredients and foods along with patient needs to generate tailor-made food composition in lesser time (Tapkire & Arun, 2023). A hybrid machine learning and mechanistic model created by uses sensory data to forecast the ideal components and processing circumstances for food products. A similar strategy was used by to create probiotic formulations to re-establish a balanced, healthy microbiota.

## 9. FUTURE DIRECTIONS

The future of AI in celiac disease diagnosis looks promising, with several potential developments on the horizon:

- **Integration with Clinical Workflows:** Efforts are underway to seamlessly integrate AI tools into existing endoscopy systems and clinical workflows.
- **Multimodal AI:** Combining image analysis with other data sources, such as patient history and serological tests, could improve diagnostic accuracy.
- **Explainable AI:** Developing more interpretable AI models could increase trust and adoption among clinicians.
- **AI-Assisted Biopsy Guidance:** AI could potentially guide endoscopists to the most appropriate biopsy sites, improving diagnostic yield (Wimmer, Hegenbart, et al., 2017).

In conclusion, AI technologies, particularly deep learning approaches, show great promise in enhancing the computer-aided diagnosis of celiac disease from endoscopic images. While challenges remain, ongoing research and technological advancements are likely to further improve the accuracy, efficiency, and clinical utility of these tools in the coming years.

## 10. CONCLUSION

In order to enhance care of celiac disease (CD), more research and randomized clinical trials are required as the condition is still controversial and complex. There are still a lot of unanswered problems regarding CD, such as the real relationships it has with other illnesses and how environmental variables affect its pathogenesis. It's still unclear if nursing provides long-term protection against CD or just postpones the disease's development. This is because the topic of breastfeeding and CD are related issues. Improvements in non-invasive diagnostic testing, which might make use of artificial intelligence (AI) to provide more precise and effective diagnoses, could do away with the necessity for endoscopy, particularly in patients who are younger. Through the reduction of problems and improvement of social and physical well-being, more efficacious therapeutic methods have the potential to improve quality of life.Many patients are still unidentified with CD, even though diagnoses have increased significantly over the past 30 years (Hujoel et al., 2018). Intestinal biopsies and serology should always be part of the diagnostic process for adults; genetic testing should only be used in certain circumstances. A gluten-free diet (GFD) is still the main treatment for CD, and it involves a lot of patient education, motivation, and follow-up. Treatment response is frequently delayed, particularly in individuals who are identified later in life. A review of the original diagnosis, examination of alternative diagnoses, assessment of GFD adherence, and serologic and histological assessments to monitor disease should be prompted by persistent or recurrent symptoms.

## REFERENCES


*Active Machine learning for formulation of precision probiotics—ScienceDirect*. (n.d.). Retrieved September 17, 2024, from https://www.sciencedirect.com/science/article/pii/S0378517322001223

Akirov, A., & Pinhas-Hamiel, O. (2015). Co-occurrence of type 1 diabetes mellitus and celiac disease. *World Journal of Diabetes*, 6(5), 707–714. DOI: 10.4239/wjd.v6.i5.707 PMID: 26069719


Akirov, A., & Pinhas-Hamiel, O. (2015). Co-occurrence of type 1 diabetes mellitus and celiac disease. *World Journal of Diabetes*, 6(5), 707–714. DOI: 10.4239/wjd.v6.i5.707 PMID: 26069719


Al-Bluwi, G. S. M., AlNababteh, A. H., Östlundh, L., Al-Shamsi, S., & Al-Rifai, R. H. (2021). Prevalence of Celiac Disease in Patients With Turner Syndrome: Systematic Review and Meta-Analysis. *Frontiers in Medicine*, 8, 674896. DOI: 10.3389/fmed.2021.674896 PMID: 34222285

Bach, J.-F. (2018). The hygiene hypothesis in autoimmunity: The role of pathogens and commensals. *Nature Reviews. Immunology*, 18(2), 105–120. DOI: 10.1038/nri.2017.111 PMID: 29034905


Bach, J.-F. (2018). The hygiene hypothesis in autoimmunity: The role of pathogens and commensals. *Nature Reviews. Immunology*, 18(2), 105–120. DOI: 10.1038/nri.2017.111 PMID: 29034905


Bank, R. P. D. (n.d.). *RCSB PDB - 8E13: Structures of HLA-B8E76C loaded with long peptides reveal novel features at the N-terminus of the groove*. Retrieved June 13, 2024, from https://www.rcsb.org/structure/8E13

Bao, F., Yu, L., Babu, S., Wang, T., Hoffenberg, E. J., Rewers, M., & Eisenbarth, G. S. (1999). One third of HLA DQ2 homozygous patients with type 1 diabetes express celiac disease-associated transglutaminase autoantibodies. *Journal of Autoimmunity*, 13(1), 143–148. DOI: 10.1006/jaut.1999.0303 PMID: 10441179

Barker, J. M., & Liu, E. (2008). Celiac disease: Pathophysiology, clinical manifestations, and associated autoimmune conditions. *Advances in Pediatrics*, 55(1), 349–365. DOI: 10.1016/j.yapd.2008.07.001 PMID: 19048738

Caetano Dos Santos, F. L., Michalek, I. M., Laurila, K., Kaukinen, K., Hyttinen, J., & Lindfors, K. (2019). Automatic classification of IgA endomysial antibody test for celiac disease: A new method deploying machine learning. *Scientific Reports*, 9(1), 9217. DOI: 10.1038/s41598-019-45679-x PMID: 31239486

Caio, G., Volta, U., Sapone, A., Leffler, D. A., De Giorgio, R., Catassi, C., & Fasano, A. (2019). Celiac disease: A comprehensive current review. *BMC Medicine 2019 17:1, 17*(1), 1–20. DOI: 10.1038/s41598-019-45679-x PMID: 31239486

Caio, G., Volta, U., Sapone, A., Leffler, D. A., De Giorgio, R., Catassi, C., & Fasano, A. (2019). Celiac disease: A comprehensive current review. *BMC Medicine 2019 17:1, 17*(1), 1–20. DOI: 10.1038/s41598-019-45679-x PMID: 31239486

Cataldo, F., & Montalto, G. (2007). Celiac disease in the developing countries: A new and challenging public health problem. *World Journal of Gastroenterology*, 13(15), 2153–2159. DOI: 10.3748/wjg.v13.i15.2153 PMID: 17465493

Cataldo, F., & Montalto, G. (2007). Celiac disease in the developing countries: A new and challenging public health problem. *World Journal of Gastroenterology*, 13(15), 2153–2159. DOI: 10.3748/wjg.v13.i15.2153 PMID: 17465493

Catassi, C., Fabiani, E., Rätsch, I. M., Coppa, G. V., Giorgi, P. L., Pierdomenico, R., Alessandrini, S., Iwanejko, G., Domenici, R., Mei, E., Miano, A., Marani, M., Bottaro, G., Spina, M., Dotti, M., Montanelli, A., Barbato, M., Viola, F., Lazzari, R., & Ventura, A. (1996). The coeliac iceberg in Italy. A multicentre antigliadin antibodies screening for coeliac disease in school-age subjects. *Acta Paediatrica (Oslo, Norway: 1992). Supplement, 412*, 29–35. DOI: 10.1038/s41598-019-45679-x PMID: 31239486

Catassi, C., Kryszak, D., Bhatti, B., Sturgeon, C., Helzlsouer, K., Clipp, S. L., Gelfond, D., Puppa, E., Sferruzza, A., & Fasano, A. (2010). Natural history of celiac disease autoimmunity in a USA cohort followed since 1974. *Annals of Medicine*, 42(7), 530–538. DOI: 10.3109/07853890.2010.514285 PMID: 20868314

Ch'ng, C. L., Jones, M. K., & Kingham, J. G. C. (2007). Celiac disease and autoimmune thyroid disease. *Clinical Medicine & Research*, 5(3), 184–192. DOI: 10.3121/cmr.2007.738 PMID: 18056028

Chen, W., Huang, Y., Boyle, B., & Lin, S. (2016). The utility of including pathology reports in improving the computational identification of patients. *Journal of Pathology Informatics*, 7(1), 46. DOI: 10.4103/2153-3539.194838 PMID: 27994938

Chen, W., Huang, Y., Boyle, B., & Lin, S. (2016). The utility of including pathology reports in improving the computational identification of patients. *Journal of Pathology Informatics*, 7(1), 46. DOI: 10.4103/2153-3539.194838 PMID: 27994938

Choung, R. S., Khaleghi Rostamkolaei, S., Ju, J. M., Marietta, E. V., Van Dyke, C. T., Rajasekaran, J. J., Jayaraman, V., Wang, T., Bei, K., Rajasekaran, K. E., Krishna, K., Krishnamurthy, H. K., & Murray, J. A. (2019). Synthetic Neoepitopes of the Transglutaminase-Deamidated Gliadin Complex as Biomarkers for Diagnosing and Monitoring Celiac Disease. *Gastroenterology*, 156(3), 582–591.e1. DOI: 10.1053/j.gastro.2018.10.025 PMID: 30342033

Ciaccio, E. J., Tennyson, C. A., Bhagat, G., Lewis, S. K., & Green, P. H. (2010). Classification of videocapsule endoscopy image patterns: Comparative analysis between patients with celiac disease and normal individuals. *Biomedical Engineering Online*, 9(1), 44. DOI: 10.1186/1475-925X-9-44 PMID: 20815911

Cinova, J., Palová-Jelínková, L., Smythies, L. E., Cerná, M., Pecharová, B., Dvorák, M., Fruhauf, P., Tlaskalová-Hogenová, H., Smith, P. D., & Tucková, L. (2007). Gliadin peptides activate blood monocytes from patients with celiac disease. *Journal of Clinical Immunology*, 27(2), 201–209. DOI: 10.1007/s10875-006-9061-z PMID: 17260166

Clemente, M. G., De Virgiliis, S., Kang, J. S., Macatagney, R., Musu, M. P., Di Pierro, M. R., Drago, S., Congia, M., & Fasano, A. (2003). Early effects of gliadin on enterocyte intracellular signalling involved in intestinal barrier function. *Gut*, 52(2), 218–223. DOI: 10.1136/gut.52.2.218 PMID: 12524403

Corazza, G. R., Andreani, M. L., Biagi, F., Corrao, G., Pretolani, S., Giulianelli, G., Ghironzi, G., & Gasbarrini, G. (1997). The smaller size of the "coeliac iceberg" in adults. *Scandinavian Journal of Gastroenterology*, 32(9), 917–919. DOI: 10.3109/00365529709011202 PMID: 9299671

Corazza, G. R., Andreani, M. L., Biagi, F., Corrao, G., Pretolani, S., Giulianelli, G., Ghironzi, G., & Gasbarrini, G. (1997). The smaller size of the "coeliac iceberg" in adults. *Scandinavian Journal of Gastroenterology*, 32(9), 917–919. DOI: 10.3109/00365529709011202 PMID: 9299671

Dahiwade, D., Patle, G., & Meshram, E. (2019). *Designing Disease Prediction Model Using Machine Learning Approach*. 2019 3rd International Conference on Computing Methodologies and Communication (ICCMC). DOI: 10.1109/ICCMC.2019.8819782

*Detection of gluten immunogenic peptides in the urine of patients with coeliac disease reveals transgressions in the gluten-free diet and incomplete mucosal healing—PubMed*. (n.d.). Retrieved September 21, 2024, from https://pubmed.ncbi.nlm.nih.gov/26608460/

Dieli-Crimi, R., Cénit, M. C., & Núñez, C. (2015). The genetics of celiac disease: A comprehensive review of clinical implications. *Journal of Autoimmunity*, 64, 26–41. DOI: 10.1016/j.jaut.2015.07.003 PMID: 26194613

Dieli-Crimi, R., Cénit, M. C., & Núñez, C. (2015). The genetics of celiac disease: A comprehensive review of clinical implications. *Journal of Autoimmunity*, 64, 26–41. DOI: 10.1016/j.jaut.2015.07.003 PMID: 26194613

Dubois, P. C. A., Trynka, G., Franke, L., Hunt, K. A., Romanos, J., Curtotti, A., Zhernakova, A., Heap, G. A. R., Adány, R., Aromaa, A., Bardella, M. T., van den Berg, L. H., Bockett, N. A., de la Concha, E. G., Dema, B., Fehrmann, R. S. N., Fernández-Arquero, M., Fiatal, S., Grandone, E., & van Heel, D. A. (2010). Multiple common variants for celiac disease influencing immune gene expression. *Nature Genetics*, 42(4), 295–302. DOI: 10.1038/ng.543 PMID: 20190752

Dubois, P. C. A., Trynka, G., Franke, L., Hunt, K. A., Romanos, J., Curtotti, A., Zhernakova, A., Heap, G. A. R., Adány, R., Aromaa, A., Bardella, M. T., van den Berg, L. H., Bockett, N. A., de la Concha, E. G., Dema, B., Fehrmann, R. S. N., Fernández-Arquero, M., Fiatal, S., Grandone, E., & van Heel, D. A. (2010). Multiple common variants for celiac disease influencing immune gene expression. *Nature Genetics*, 42(4), 295–302. DOI: 10.1038/ng.543 PMID: 20190752

Elli, L., Branchi, F., Tomba, C., Villalta, D., Norsa, L., Ferretti, F., Roncoroni, L., & Bardella, M. T. (2015). Diagnosis of gluten related disorders: Celiac disease, wheat allergy and non-celiac gluten sensitivity. *World Journal of Gastroenterology*, 21(23), 7110–7119. DOI: 10.3748/wjg.v21.i23.7110 PMID: 26109797

Elli, L., Branchi, F., Tomba, C., Villalta, D., Norsa, L., Ferretti, F., Roncoroni, L., & Bardella, M. T. (2015). Diagnosis of gluten related disorders: Celiac disease, wheat allergy and non-celiac gluten sensitivity. *World Journal of Gastroenterology*, 21(23), 7110–7119. DOI: 10.3748/wjg.v21.i23.7110 PMID: 26109797

Fasano, A. (2001). Celiac Disease: The Past, the Present, the Future. *Pediatrics*, 107(4), 768–770. DOI: 10.1542/peds.107.4.768 PMID: 11335755

Fasano, A. (2001). Celiac Disease: The Past, the Present, the Future. *Pediatrics*, 107(4), 768–770. DOI: 10.1542/peds.107.4.768 PMID: 11335755

Fasano, A., Berti, I., Gerarduzzi, T., Not, T., Colletti, R. B., Drago, S., Elitsur, Y., Green, P. H. R., Guandalini, S., Hill, I. D., Pietzak, M., Ventura, A., Thorpe, M., Kryszak, D., Fornaroli, F., Wasserman, S. S., Murray, J. A., & Horvath, K. (2003). Prevalence of celiac disease in at-risk and not-at-risk groups in the United States: A large multicenter study. *Archives of Internal Medicine*, 163(3), 286–292. DOI: 10.1001/archinte.163.3.286 PMID: 12578508

Fasano, A., Berti, I., Gerarduzzi, T., Not, T., Colletti, R. B., Drago, S., Elitsur, Y., Green, P. H. R., Guandalini, S., Hill, I. D., Pietzak, M., Ventura, A., Thorpe, M., Kryszak, D., Fornaroli, F., Wasserman, S. S., Murray, J. A., & Horvath, K. (2003). Prevalence of celiac disease in at-risk and not-at-risk groups in the United States: A large multicenter study. *Archives of Internal Medicine*, 163(3), 286–292. DOI: 10.1001/archinte.163.3.286 PMID: 12578508

Freeman, H. J., Chopra, A., Clandinin, M. T., & Thomson, A. B. (2011). Recent advances in celiac disease. *World Journal of Gastroenterology*, 17(18), 2259–2272. DOI: 10.3748/wjg.v17.i18.2259 PMID: 21633592

Freeman, H. J., Chopra, A., Clandinin, M. T., & Thomson, A. B. (2011). Recent advances in celiac disease. *World Journal of Gastroenterology*, 17(18), 2259–2272. DOI: 10.3748/wjg.v17.i18.2259 PMID: 21633592

Gadermayr, M., Uhl, A., & Vécsei, A. (2014). *Degradation Adaptive Texture Classification: A Case Study in Celiac Disease Diagnosis Brings New Insight.* DOI: 10.3748/wjg.v17.i18.2259 PMID: 21633592

Gadermayr, M., Uhl, A., & Vécsei, A. (2014). *Degradation Adaptive Texture Classification: A Case Study in Celiac Disease Diagnosis Brings New Insight.* DOI: 10.3748/wjg.v17.i18.2259 PMID: 21633592

Gadermayr, M., Wimmer, G., Kogler, H., Vécsei, A., Merhof, D., & Uhl, A. (2018). Automated classification of celiac disease during upper endoscopy: Status quo and quo vadis. *Computers in Biology and Medicine*, 102, 221–226. DOI: 10.1016/j.compbiomed.2018.04.020 PMID: 29739614

Gadermayr, M., Wimmer, G., Kogler, H., Vécsei, A., Merhof, D., & Uhl, A. (2018). Automated classification of celiac disease during upper endoscopy: Status quo and quo vadis. *Computers in Biology and Medicine*, 102, 221–226. DOI: 10.1016/j.compbiomed.2018.04.020 PMID: 29739614

Hegenbart, S., Uhl, A., & Vécsei, A. (2015). Survey on computer aided decision support for diagnosis of celiac disease. *Computers in Biology and Medicine*, 65, 348–358. DOI: 10.1016/j.compbiomed.2015.02.007 PMID: 25770906

Hollon, J., Puppa, E. L., Greenwald, B., Goldberg, E., Guerrerio, A., & Fasano, A. (2015). Effect of gliadin on permeability of intestinal biopsy explants from celiac disease patients and patients with non-celiac gluten sensitivity. *Nutrients*, 7(3), 1565–1576. DOI: 10.3390/nu7031565 PMID: 25734566

Hollon, J., Puppa, E. L., Greenwald, B., Goldberg, E., Guerrerio, A., & Fasano, A. (2015). Effect of gliadin on permeability of intestinal biopsy explants from celiac disease patients and patients with non-celiac gluten sensitivity. *Nutrients*, 7(3), 1565–1576. DOI: 10.3390/nu7031565 PMID: 25734566

Hüe, S., Mention, J.-J., Monteiro, R. C., Zhang, S., Cellier, C., Schmitz, J., Verkarre, V., Fodil, N., Bahram, S., Cerf-Bensussan, N., & Caillat-Zucman, S. (2004). A direct role for NKG2D/MICA interaction in villous atrophy during celiac disease. *Immunity*, 21(3), 367–377. DOI: 10.1016/j.immuni.2004.06.018 PMID: 15357948

Hujoel, I. A., Van Dyke, C. T., Brantner, T., Larson, J., King, K. S., Sharma, A., Murray, J. A., & Rubio-Tapia, A. (2018). Natural history and clinical detection of undiagnosed coeliac disease in a North American community. *Alimentary Pharmacology & Therapeutics*, 47(10), 1358–1366. DOI: 10.1111/apt.14625 PMID: 29577349

Hujoel, I. A., Van Dyke, C. T., Brantner, T., Larson, J., King, K. S., Sharma, A., Murray, J. A., & Rubio-Tapia, A. (2018). Natural history and clinical detection of undiagnosed coeliac disease in a North American community. *Alimentary Pharmacology & Therapeutics*, 47(10), 1358–1366. DOI: 10.1111/apt.14625 PMID: 29577349

Hummel, M., Bonifacio, E., Naserke, H. E., & Ziegler, A. G. (2002). Elimination of dietary gluten does not reduce titers of type 1 diabetes-associated autoantibodies in high-risk subjects. *Diabetes Care*, 25(7), 1111–1116. DOI: 10.2337/diacare.25.7.1111 PMID: 12087006

*Interactions within the MHC contribute to the genetic architecture of celiac disease—PMC*. (n.d.). Retrieved July 30, 2024, from https://www.ncbi.nlm.nih.gov/pmc/articles/PMC5345796/

Ivarsson, A., Persson, L. A., Juto, P., Peltonen, M., Suhr, O., & Hernell, O. (1999). High prevalence of undiagnosed coeliac disease in adults: A Swedish population-based study. *Journal of Internal Medicine*, 245(1), 63–68. DOI: 10.1046/j.1365-2796.1999.00403.x PMID: 10095818

Ivarsson, A., Persson, L. A., Juto, P., Peltonen, M., Suhr, O., & Hernell, O. (1999). High prevalence of undiagnosed coeliac disease in adults: A Swedish population-based study. *Journal of Internal Medicine*, 245(1), 63–68. DOI: 10.1046/j.1365-2796.1999.00403.x PMID: 10095818

Ju, J. M., Marietta, E. V., & Murray, J. A. (2015). Generating Transgenic Mouse Models for Studying Celiac Disease. In Ryan, A. W. (Ed.), *Celiac Disease: Methods and Protocols* (pp. 23–33). Springer., DOI: 10.1007/978-1-4939-2839-2_3

Junker, Y., Zeissig, S., Kim, S.-J., Barisani, D., Wieser, H., Leffler, D. A., Zevallos, V., Libermann, T. A., Dillon, S., Freitag, T. L., Kelly, C. P., & Schuppan, D. (2012). Wheat amylase trypsin inhibitors drive intestinal inflammation via activation of toll-like receptor 4. *The Journal of Experimental Medicine*, 209(13), 2395–2408. DOI: 10.1084/jem.20102660 PMID: 23209313

Kim, S. M., Mayassi, T., & Jabri, B. (2015). Innate immunity: Actuating the gears of celiac disease pathogenesis. *Best Practice & Research. Clinical Gastroenterology*, 29(3), 425–435. DOI: 10.1016/j.bpg.2015.05.001 PMID: 26060107

Kim, S. M., Mayassi, T., & Jabri, B. (2015). Innate immunity: Actuating the gears of celiac disease pathogenesis. *Best Practice & Research. Clinical Gastroenterology*, 29(3), 425–435. DOI: 10.1016/j.bpg.2015.05.001 PMID: 26060107

Lionetti, E., Castellaneta, S., Francavilla, R., Pulvirenti, A., Tonutti, E., Amarri, S., Barbato, M., Barbera, C., Barera, G., Bellantoni, A., Castellano, E., Guariso, G., Limongelli, M. G., Pellegrino, S., Polloni, C., Ughi, C., Zuin, G., Fasano, A., & Catassi, C. (2014). Introduction of gluten, HLA status, and the risk of celiac disease in children. *The New England Journal of Medicine*, 371(14), 1295–1303. DOI: 10.1056/NEJMoa1400697 PMID: 25271602

Lionetti, E., & Catassi, C. (2011). New clues in celiac disease epidemiology, pathogenesis, clinical manifestations, and treatment. *International Reviews of Immunology*, 30(4), 219–231. DOI: 10.3109/08830185.2011.602443 PMID: 21787227

Lionetti, E., & Catassi, C. (2011). New clues in celiac disease epidemiology, pathogenesis, clinical manifestations, and treatment. *International Reviews of Immunology*, 30(4), 219–231. DOI: 10.3109/08830185.2011.602443 PMID: 21787227

Loeff, T., Araya, M., & Pérez-Bravo, F. (2012). Frequency of MYO9B polymorphisms in celiac patients and controls. *Revista Española de Enfermedades Digestivas*, 104(11), 566–571. DOI: 10.4321/S1130-01082012001100003 PMID: 23368647

Loeff, T., Araya, M., & Pérez-Bravo, F. (2012). Frequency of MYO9B polymorphisms in celiac patients and controls. *Revista Española de Enfermedades Digestivas*, 104(11), 566–571. DOI: 10.4321/S1130-01082012001100003 PMID: 23368647

Ludvigsson, J. F., Ludvigsson, J., Ekbom, A., & Montgomery, S. M. (2006). Celiac disease and risk of subsequent type 1 diabetes: A general population cohort study of children and adolescents. *Diabetes Care*, 29(11), 2483–2488. DOI: 10.2337/dc06-0794 PMID: 17065689

Ludvigsson, J. F., Pathak, J., Murphy, S., Durski, M., Kirsch, P. S., Chute, C. G., Ryu, E., & Murray, J. A. (2013). Use of computerized algorithm to identify individuals in need of testing for celiac disease. *Journal of the American Medical Informatics Association : JAMIA*, 20(e2), e306–e310. DOI: 10.1136/amiajnl-2013-001924 PMID: 23956016

Lundin, K. E. A., & Wijmenga, C. (2015). Coeliac disease and autoimmune disease-genetic overlap and screening. *Nature Reviews. Gastroenterology & Hepatology*, 12(9), 507–515. DOI: 10.1038/nrgastro.2015.136 PMID: 26303674

Lundin, K. E. A., & Wijmenga, C. (2015). Coeliac disease and autoimmune disease-genetic overlap and screening. *Nature Reviews. Gastroenterology & Hepatology*, 12(9), 507–515. DOI: 10.1038/nrgastro.2015.136 PMID: 26303674

Malekzadeh, R., Sachdev, A., & Fahid Ali, A. (2005). Coeliac disease in developing countries: Middle East, India and North Africa. *Best Practice & Research. Clinical Gastroenterology*, 19(3), 351–358. DOI: 10.1016/j.bpg.2005.01.004 PMID: 15925841

Matysiak-Budnik, T., Moura, I. C., Arcos-Fajardo, M., Lebreton, C., Ménard, S., Candalh, C., Ben-Khalifa, K., Dugave, C., Tamouza, H., van Niel, G., Bouhnik, Y., Lamarque, D., Chaussade, S., Malamut, G., Cellier, C., Cerf-Bensussan, N., Monteiro, R. C., & Heyman, M. (2008). Secretory IgA mediates retrotranscytosis of intact gliadin peptides via the transferrin receptor in celiac disease. *The Journal of Experimental Medicine*, 205(1), 143–154. DOI: 10.1084/jem.20071204 PMID: 18166587

Mazzilli, M. C., Ferrante, P., Mariani, P., Martone, E., Petronzelli, F., Triglione, P., & Bonamico, M. (1992). A study of Italian pediatric celiac disease patients confirms that the primary HLA association is to the DQ(alpha 1*0501, beta 1*0201) heterodimer. *Human Immunology*, 33(2), 133–139. DOI: 10.1016/0198-8859(92)90064-T PMID: 1563982

Mohan, S., Thirumalai, C., & Srivastava, G. (2019). Effective Heart Disease Prediction Using Hybrid Machine Learning Techniques. *IEEE Access, 7*, 81542–81554. IEEE Access. DOI: 10.3109/07853890.2010.505931 PMID: 21070098

Mustalahti, K., Catassi, C., Reunanen, A., Fabiani, E., Heier, M., McMillan, S., Murray, L., Metzger, M.-H., Gasparin, M., Bravi, E., Mäki, M., & Coeliac, E. U. (2010). The prevalence of celiac disease in Europe: Results of a centralized, international mass screening project. *Annals of Medicine*, 42(8), 587–595. DOI: 10.3109/07853890.2010.505931 PMID: 21070098

Mustalahti, K., Catassi, C., Reunanen, A., Fabiani, E., Heier, M., McMillan, S., Murray, L., Metzger, M.-H., Gasparin, M., Bravi, E., Mäki, M., & Coeliac, E. U. (2010). The prevalence of celiac disease in Europe: Results of a centralized, international mass screening project. *Annals of Medicine*, 42(8), 587–595. DOI: 10.3109/07853890.2010.505931 PMID: 21070098

Norris, J. M., Barriga, K., Klingensmith, G., Hoffman, M., Eisenbarth, G. S., Erlich, H. A., & Rewers, M. (2003). Timing of initial cereal exposure in infancy and risk of islet autoimmunity. *Journal of the American Medical Association*, 290(13), 1713–1720. DOI: 10.1001/jama.290.13.1713 PMID: 14519705

Okada, H., Kuhn, C., Feillet, H., & Bach, J.-F. (2010). The "hygiene hypothesis" for autoimmune and allergic diseases: An update. *Clinical and Experimental Immunology*, 160(1), 1–9. DOI: 10.1111/j.1365-2249.2010.04139.x PMID: 20415844

Pagliari, D., Urgesi, R., Frosali, S., Riccioni, M. E., Newton, E. E., Landolfi, R., Pandolfi, F., & Cianci, R. (2015). The Interaction among Microbiota, Immunity, and Genetic and Dietary Factors Is the Condicio Sine Qua Non Celiac Disease Can Develop. *Journal of Immunology Research*, 123653, 1–10. Advance online publication. DOI: 10.1155/2015/123653 PMID: 26090475

Pagliari, D., Urgesi, R., Frosali, S., Riccioni, M. E., Newton, E. E., Landolfi, R., Pandolfi, F., & Cianci, R. (2015). The Interaction among Microbiota, Immunity, and Genetic and Dietary Factors Is the Condicio Sine Qua Non Celiac Disease Can Develop. *Journal of Immunology Research*, 123653, 1–10. Advance online publication. DOI: 10.1155/2015/123653 PMID: 26090475

Pande, A. A. (2024). Predicting Kidney Disease Using Deep. *Neural Networks*. Advance online publication. DOI: 10.5281/ZENODO.10597492

*(PDF) Computer-aided texture analysis combined with experts' knowledge: Improving endoscopic celiac disease diagnosis*. (n.d.). Retrieved July 31, 2024, from https://www.researchgate.net/publication/306105255_Computer-aided_texture_analysis_combined_with_experts%27_knowledge_Improving_endoscopic_celiac_disease_diagnosis

Qiao, S.-W., Sollid, L. M., & Blumberg, R. S. (2009). Antigen presentation in celiac disease. *Current Opinion in Immunology*, 21(1), 111–117. DOI: 10.1016/j.coi.2009.03.004 PMID: 19342211

Ráki, M., Schjetne, K. W., Stamnaes, J., Molberg, Ø., Jahnsen, F. L., Issekutz, T. B., Bogen, B., & Sollid, L. M. (2007). Surface expression of transglutaminase 2 by dendritic cells and its potential role for uptake and presentation of gluten peptides to T cells. *Scandinavian Journal of Immunology*, 65(3), 213–220. DOI: 10.1111/j.1365-3083.2006.01881.x PMID: 17309775

Rewers, M. (2005). Epidemiology of celiac disease: What are the prevalence, incidence, and progression of celiac disease? *Gastroenterology*, 128(4, Suppl 1), S47–S51. DOI: 10.1053/j.gastro.2005.02.030 PMID: 15825126

Rewers, M. (2005). Epidemiology of celiac disease: What are the prevalence, incidence, and progression of celiac disease? *Gastroenterology*, 128(4, Suppl 1), S47–S51. DOI: 10.1053/j.gastro.2005.02.030 PMID: 15825126

Riestra, S., Fernández, E., Rodrigo, L., Garcia, S., & Ocio, G.S. Riestra, E. Fernández, L. Rodrig. (2000). Prevalence of Coeliac disease in the general population of northern Spain. Strategies of serologic screening. *Scandinavian Journal of Gastroenterology*, 35(4), 398–402. DOI: 10.1080/003655200750023967 PMID: 10831263

Seguí, S., Drozdzal, M., Pascual, G., Radeva, P., Malagelada, C., Azpiroz, F., & Vitrià, J. (2016). Generic feature learning for wireless capsule endoscopy analysis. *Computers in Biology and Medicine*, 79, 163–172. DOI: 10.1016/j.compbiomed.2016.10.011 PMID: 27810622

Shahbazkhani, B., Malekzadeh, R., Sotoudeh, M., Moghadam, K. F., Farhadi, M., Ansari, R., Elahyfar, A., & Rostami, K. (2003). High prevalence of coeliac disease in apparently healthy Iranian blood donors. *European Journal of Gastroenterology & Hepatology*, 15(5), 475–478. DOI: 10.1097/00042737-200305000-00003 PMID: 12702902

Singh, P., Arora, S., Singh, A., Strand, T. A., & Makharia, G. K. (2016). Prevalence of celiac disease in Asia: A systematic review and meta-analysis. *Journal of Gastroenterology and Hepatology*, 31(6), 1095–1101. DOI: 10.1111/jgh.13270 PMID: 26678020

Sollid, L. M., Markussen, G., Ek, J., Gjerde, H., Vartdal, F., & Thorsby, E. (1989). Evidence for a primary association of celiac disease to a particular HLA-DQ alpha/beta heterodimer. *The Journal of Experimental Medicine*, 169(1), 345–350. DOI: 10.1084/jem.169.1.345 PMID: 2909659

Stamnaes, J., & Sollid, L. M. (2015). Celiac disease: Autoimmunity in response to food antigen. *Seminars in Immunology*, 27(5), 343–352. DOI: 10.1016/j.smim.2015.11.001 PMID: 26603490

Stazi, A. V., & Trinti, B. (2010). Selenium status and over-expression of interleukin-15 in celiac disease and autoimmune thyroid diseases. *Annali dell'Istituto Superiore di Sanita*, 46(4), 389–399. DOI: 10.4415/ANN_10_04_06 PMID: 21169670

Syed, S., Al-Boni, M., Khan, M. N., Sadiq, K., Iqbal, N. T., Moskaluk, C. A., Kelly, P., Amadi, B., Ali, S. A., Moore, S. R., & Brown, D. E. (2019). Assessment of Machine Learning Detection of Environmental Enteropathy and Celiac Disease in Children. *JAMA Network Open*, 2(6), e195822. DOI: 10.1001/jamanetworkopen.2019.5822 PMID: 31199451

Tang, F., Chen, Z., Ciszewski, C., Setty, M., Solus, J., Tretiakova, M., Ebert, E., Han, J., Lin, A., Guandalini, S., Groh, V., Spies, T., Green, P., & Jabri, B. (2009). Cytosolic PLA2 is required for CTL-mediated immunopathology of celiac disease via NKG2D and IL-15. *The Journal of Experimental Medicine*, 206(3), 707–719. DOI: 10.1084/jem.20071887 PMID: 19237603

Tapkire, M. D., & Arun, V. (2023). Application of artificial intelligence to corelate food formulations to disease risk prediction: A comprehensive review. *Journal of Food Science and Technology*, 60(9), 2350–2357. DOI: 10.1007/s13197-022-05550-w PMID: 37424577

Troncone, R., & Jabri, B. (2011). Coeliac disease and gluten sensitivity. *Journal of Internal Medicine*, 269(6), 582–590. DOI: 10.1111/j.1365-2796.2011.02385.x PMID: 21481018

Trynka, G., Wijmenga, C., & van Heel, D. A. (2010). A genetic perspective on coeliac disease. *Trends in Molecular Medicine*, 16(11), 537–550. DOI: 10.1016/j.molmed.2010.09.003 PMID: 20947431

Verdu, E. F., Galipeau, H. J., & Jabri, B. (2015). Novel players in coeliac disease pathogenesis: Role of the gut microbiota. *Nature Reviews. Gastroenterology & Hepatology*, 12(9), 497–506. DOI: 10.1038/nrgastro.2015.90 PMID: 26055247

Volta, U., Bellentani, S., Bianchi, F. B., Brandi, G., De Franceschi, L., Miglioli, L., Granito, A., Balli, F., & Tiribelli, C. (2001). High prevalence of celiac disease in Italian general population. *Digestive Diseases and Sciences*, 46(7), 1500–1505. DOI: 10.1023/A:1010648122797 PMID: 11478502

Wieser, H., & Koehler, P. (2008). The Biochemical Basis of Celiac Disease. *Cereal Chemistry*, 85(1), 1–13. DOI: 10.1094/CCHEM-85-1-0001

Wimmer, G., Hegenbart, S., Vécsei, A., & Uhl, A. (2017). Convolutional Neural Network Architectures for the Automated Diagnosis of Celiac Disease. In *Lecture Notes in Computer Science* (Vol. 10170, p. 113). DOI: 10.1007/978-3-319-54057-3_10

Wimmer, G., Uhl, A., & Vecsei, A. (2017). Evaluation of domain specific data augmentation techniques for the classification of celiac disease using endoscopic imagery. *2017 IEEE 19th International Workshop on Multimedia Signal Processing (MMSP)*, 1–6. DOI: 10.1109/MMSP.2017.8122221

Wimmer, G., Vécsei, A., & Uhl, A. (2016). *CNN transfer learning for the automated diagnosis of celiac disease.*, DOI: 10.1109/IPTA.2016.7821020

Wolters, V. M., Verbeek, W. H. M., Zhernakova, A., Onland-Moret, C., Schreurs, M. W. J., Monsuur, A. J., Verduijn, W., Wijmenga, C., & Mulder, C. J. J. (2007). The MYO9B gene is a strong risk factor for developing refractory celiac disease. *Clinical Gastroenterology and Hepatology: The Official Clinical Practice Journal of the American Gastroenterological Association, 5*(12), 1399–1405, 1405.e1-2. DOI: 10.1109/IPTA.2016.7821020

Xiang, Z., Fung, K., & Ng, K. (2019). Food Product Design: A Hybrid Machine Learning and Mechanistic Modeling Approach. *Industrial & Engineering Chemistry Research*, 58(36), 16743–16752. Advance online publication. DOI: 10.1021/acs.iecr.9b02462

Zhou, T., Han, G., Li, B. N., Lin, Z., Ciaccio, E. J., Green, P. H., & Qin, J. (2017). Quantitative analysis of patients with celiac disease by video capsule endoscopy: A deep learning method. *Computers in Biology and Medicine*, 85, 1–6. DOI: 10.1016/j.compbiomed.2017.03.031 PMID: 28412572

Zou, Q., Qu, K., Luo, Y., Yin, D., Ju, Y., & Tang, H. (2018). Predicting Diabetes Mellitus With Machine Learning Techniques. *Frontiers in Genetics*, 9, 515. Advance online publication. DOI: 10.3389/fgene.2018.00515 PMID: 30459809

# Chapter 12
# Decoding New Languages:
## Leveraging Artificial Intelligence for Language Understanding

**Yabit Alas**
*Universiti Brunei Darussalam, Brunei*

**Muhammad Anshari**
https://orcid.org/0000-0002-8160-6682
*Universiti Brunei Darussalam, Brunei*

## ABSTRACT

*The emergence of artificial intelligence (AI) has transformed the field of learning a language by providing innovative methods to enhance the learning process and attain proficiency in languages. This systematic review examines how artificial intelligence (AI) affects language learning. The chapter explores the ways in which AI can help to overcome challenges in learning, enhance language proficiency, and improve the development of language skills. The analysis highlights the advantages of AI-driven tools like language learning platforms, chatbots, and speech recognition systems. These technologies provide personalised feedback, flexible learning options, and engaging experiences. It explores the advantages of AI-driven language learning, such as enhanced student engagement, improved pronunciation, and enhanced vocabulary learning. The study also explores the challenges and limitations related to utilising AI in learning languages.*

DOI: 10.4018/979-8-3373-2530-9.ch012

## INTRODUCTION

Artificial intelligence (AI) has recently revolutionized the way we learn new languages. Chatbots that provide prompt language practice and personalised language learning platform are just examples of the many ways artificial intelligence is helping students improve their language abilities. The ability of AI to offer personalised feedback and recommendations to learners is a critical component that is revolutionising the field of language learning (Anshari et al., 2023; Syafrudin et al., 2024).

AI can optimise the learning process and resolve individual deficiencies by customising lessons and exercises through an analysis of a student's language proficiency and learning style (Molenaar, 2022). In addition, AI-powered language learning platforms are capable of monitoring a student's progress in real time, which enables the development of more effective and targeted learning strategies (Peng et al., 2022).

The use of artificial intelligence (AI) to personalise language learning experiences through the integration of machine learning algorithms into widely used applications like Babbel and Duolingo. Students benefit from an improved learning experience and more efficient language acquisition as a result of this degree of customisation. The use of AI allows language learners to be more adaptable and proactive in their approach to learning a new language, resulting in more rapid and persistent improvement (Liua et al., 2021).

AI integration into language learning applications is a significant step because it has the potential to transform language instruction by making it more engaging and approachable for learners of all ability levels (Anshari, 2020). It is generally accepted that integrating AI into language education would improve the standard of instruction for learners. AI enables language learning software to customise their lessons and practise exercises to match the unique requirements of every student (Chen et al., 2024).

The consequence is that students learn a language within a shorter amount of time since they are actively interested and enthusiastic throughout the entire process of learning language (Anshari et al., 2024). Language education has many varieties of new and effective learning experiences. This indicates well for the future of the subject. This chapter discusses the diverse methods by which AI is being employed in language learning and its prospective influence on the future of language education. The introduction in Section 1 offers a comprehensive examination of the significance of personalised learning in the field of language education. Section 2 reviews the research that is available on the role of AI in language learning, emphasising the key investigations and conclusions. Section 3 describes the methodology, as findings and discussions in Section 4. Section 5 concludes with the key findings.

## LITERATURE REVIEW

In reviewing the literature on AI's impact on language acquisition, several studies have highlighted the possible advantages of incorporating AI into language classrooms. For example, research has demonstrated that AI can personalise learning experiences for students by providing them with feedback and support according to their unique learning style and needs. AI also helps with language learning by providing interesting and engaging experiences that get students attention about practicing and eventually mastering the language. The study highlights an important role of AI in learning new language.

### AI and Language Learning Platform

The use of AI in language learning apps such as Duolingo and Babbel and how these platforms incorporate machine learning algorithms to personalise lessons for individual users. These language learning apps utilise AI to track users' progress and provide personalised feedback, making the learning experience more efficient and effective (Li, 2020). Through the use of machine learning algorithms, these apps are able to adapt to each user's learning style and pace, ultimately improving the overall learning outcome. As AI continues to advance, the possibilities for enhancing language education through technology are endless (Kolhar & Alameen, 2021; Anshari et al., 2022).

One potential future application of AI in language learning could be the development of virtual language tutors that can provide real-time feedback and support to users (Fitria, 2021). These virtual tutors could use natural language processing algorithms to understand and respond to users' questions and challenges in real-time, creating a more interactive and engaging learning experience. Additionally, AI could be used to create personalised lesson plans based on each user's specific goals and learning preferences, further enhancing the effectiveness of language learning apps (Anshari et al., 2021a). The integration of AI into language education has the potential to revolutionise the way we learn new languages, making it more accessible and efficient for users of all levels.

By analysing data on users' progress and performance, AI could also provide valuable insights and recommendations for improvement, helping users track their language learning journey and stay motivated. With the ability to adapt to individual learning styles and paces, AI-powered language education platforms could cater to a wider range of learners and provide a more customised and effective learning experience (Aini et al., 2023). As AI continues to advance and evolve, the possibilities for its integration into language education are endless, promising a future where mastering a new language is easier and more enjoyable than ever before.

For example, AI could analyse a user's pronunciation and grammar mistakes in real-time during language practice sessions, offering instant feedback and corrections. Additionally, AI could personalise lesson plans based on a user's progress and areas of weakness, creating a tailored learning experience that maximises efficiency and results (Anshari et al., 2021). However, a detailed counterexample could be the potential limitations of AI in understanding and teaching more nuanced aspects of language, such as cultural context and idiomatic expressions (Niu et al., 2022).

While AI can provide valuable support in language learning, it may not fully replace the need for human interaction and guidance in certain areas. This optimistic view could be a scenario where AI language education platforms struggle to accurately assess regional accents or dialects, leading to incorrect feedback and frustration for users. Furthermore, the reliance on AI for personalised lesson plans may overlook important cultural nuances and individual learning preferences, resulting in a one-size-fits-all approach that hinders rather than enhances language learning (Zubani et al., 2022).

## Chatbot

The role of chatbots in providing instant feedback and conversation practice for language learners, including their ability to simulate real-life conversations in multiple languages, However, the limitations of chatbots in understanding the subtleties of human emotions and context can also hinder the learning experience. For example, a chatbot may not be able to pick up on sarcasm or humour in a conversation, leading to misunderstandings and misinterpretations (Haristiani, 2019).

Additionally, the repetitive and formulaic responses of chatbots may not provide the dynamic and engaging practice that learners need to truly improve their language skills. In order to truly enhance language learning, a balance between AI technology and human interaction may be necessary to provide a more comprehensive and effective learning experience (Kim et al., 2019).

Chatbot technology can be a valuable tool for language learners, offering instant feedback and personalised practice. However, it is important to acknowledge its limitations and supplement it with opportunities for authentic communication with native speakers or language teachers. By combining the efficiency of AI technology with the emotional intelligence and cultural awareness of human interaction, language learners can receive a well-rounded education that caters to their individual needs and preferences (Kuddus, 2022). This combination could be crucial in realising the full potential of language learning in the digital era. For example, a language learner may use AI technology like language learning apps to practice vocabulary and grammar exercises, receiving immediate feedback on their progress (Rahman et al., 2017). However, to improve their conversational skills and cultural understanding, they could also participate in language exchange programmes or take conversational classes with native speakers or teachers. By combining both AI technology and human interaction, the learner can develop a more comprehensive understanding of the language and ultimately achieve fluency.

## METHODOLOGY

The study utilised qualitative secondary data from academic journals, books, and online resources to analyse the effectiveness of AI in language learning. Additionally, the study involved interviews with language learners and educators to collect firsthand experiences and opinions on the subject. The findings suggest that while AI can be a valuable tool for language practice, it is crucial to consider its limitations and potential drawbacks in order to create a more holistic and effective language learning experience. Furthermore, the study also explored the various types of AI technology currently being used in language learning, such as chatbots, language translation tools, and speech recognition software. These technologies have shown promise in providing personalised feedback, practice opportunities, and cultural immersion for language learners. However, concerns were raised about the potential for AI to replace human interaction and the importance of maintaining a balance between technology and traditional teaching methods. Overall, the research highlights the need for further investigation and development of AI in language learning to ensure its optimal use and integration into educational settings.

## DISCUSSION

This section discusses the potential, challenges, and future trends in the use of AI in language learning. The discussion emphasises the importance of thoughtful and intentional use of AI in language learning to maximise its potential benefits while addressing its limitations. Figure 1 shows the role of AI in language learning from several perspectives: first, language learning tools, language practice, language learning resources, and language learning strategies.

### Potentials

AI in language education offers numerous benefits and potential. Some of these potentials include personalised learning experiences tailored to individual students' needs, increased engagement through interactive and adaptive technology, and access to a wide range of resources and tools for language practice. Additionally, AI has the potential to provide immediate feedback to students, allowing for continuous improvement and progress in language skills. Using AI in language education can enhance teaching efficiency and prepare students for success in a globalised world. For instance, an AI-driven language learning platform can analyse a student's progress and tailor lesson plans to address their strengths and weaknesses. The platform could also utilise interactive exercises and games to keep students engaged and motivated to practice their language skills regularly.

One major potential is the development of personalised and adaptive learning systems. AI algorithms can analyse a learner's progress, strengths, weaknesses, and learning styles to tailor the content, pace, and methods accordingly. This personalised approach could significantly enhance the effectiveness and efficiency of language acquisition compared to traditional one-size-fits-all methods. Additionally, AI-powered tutoring systems could provide real-time feedback, corrections, and guidance, mimicking the experience of having a personal language tutor.

AI-based speech recognition and natural language processing (NLP) technologies could enable more immersive and interactive language learning experiences. Learners could practice conversational skills with AI agents that can understand and respond in the target language, providing a realistic simulation of real-world conversations. Moreover, NLP techniques could analyse a learner's spoken and written language production, providing targeted feedback on grammar, pronunciation, and idiomatic usage.

Intelligent language translation tools powered by AI could also enhance language learning. Rather than direct word-for-word translations, AI systems could provide contextual and idiomatic translations, helping learners understand nuances and cultural contexts. Additionally, AI-based language environments could be created where learners are surrounded by the target language in various multimedia formats for vocabulary learning and comprehension.

Furthermore, AI could potentially unlock new frontiers in language learning accessibility. AI-powered tools could be adapted for learners with varying abilities, learning styles, and disabilities, ensuring inclusive and equitable access to language education. Automated language tutors could also make high-quality language instruction available to learners in remote or underserved areas, bridging geographical and socioeconomic barriers.

Finally, the potential of AI in language learning is vast, spanning personalisation, immersion, accessibility, and innovation. As AI technologies continue to advance, their integration into language education could lead to more effective, engaging, and inclusive learning experiences, fostering cross-cultural understanding and communication in an increasingly globalised world.

*Figure 1. AI and learning new language*

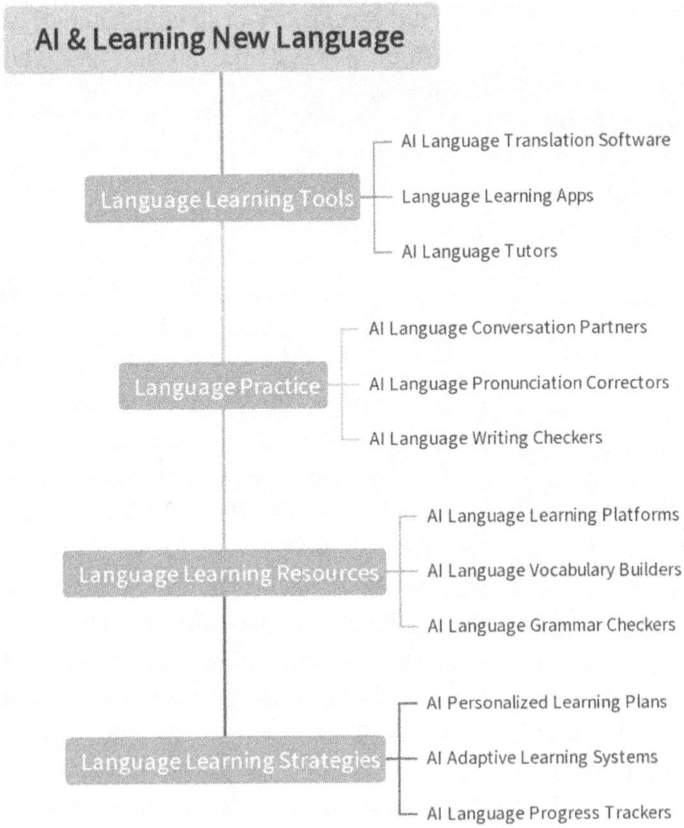


## Challenges

While AI can provide immediate feedback and personalised lesson plans, it may not be able to fully replace the human element of teaching, such as building rapport with students and providing emotional support. Additionally, some students may prefer traditional teaching methods and find AI-driven platforms impersonal or less effective for their learning style. Challenges and limitations associated with the use of AI in language learning, such as concerns about data privacy, the need for human interaction in mastering communication skills, and the risk of over-reliance on technology.

A significant challenge lies in the complexity of natural language and the nuances involved in language acquisition. AI systems, despite their advancements, may struggle to fully capture the intricacies of language, including idioms, cultural references, and contextual meanings. This could lead to inaccuracies or oversimplifications in language instruction, hindering the learner's ability to develop true fluency and natural communication skills.

Another challenge lies in the availability and quality of the data used to train AI language models. Many AI systems rely on large datasets of language samples, but these datasets may not always be representative of diverse linguistic contexts, dialects, and variations. Consequently, the AI-powered language learning tools may exhibit biases or lack the ability to cater to learners from different cultural and linguistic backgrounds effectively.

Ensuring the ethical and responsible development of AI language learning tools is also a significant challenge. There are concerns about privacy and data security, as these tools may require collecting and processing personal language data from learners. Additionally, there is a risk of perpetuating stereotypes or propagating harmful biases if the AI systems are not designed and trained with care.

Furthermore, the integration of AI into language education may raise concerns about the potential displacement of human language instructors and the erosion of the human element in language learning. While AI can augment and support language instruction, it may not be able to fully replicate the nuanced feedback, cultural insights, and interpersonal connections that human instructors can provide.

Lastly, the rapid pace of technological advancements in AI poses challenges in keeping language learning tools up-to-date and relevant. As new AI techniques and language models emerge, there may be a need for continuous updating and adaptation to ensure that the tools remain effective and aligned with the latest developments in the field.

## Future Research Directions

Upcoming trends in AI-driven language education involve improvements like integrating sentiment analysis for chatbots and enhancing speech recognition for virtual tutors. One promising area for future research is the development of multimodal AI systems for language learning. These systems would integrate various modalities, such as speech recognition, natural language processing, computer vision, and virtual reality, to create immersive and interactive language learning environments. By combining these technologies, learners could engage in simulated real-world scenarios, practice conversational skills with AI agents, and receive real-time feedback on their language production, all while being exposed to authentic cultural and contextual cues.

Another direction for future research could be to explore transfer learning and cross-lingual language models. These approaches aim to leverage knowledge from one language to facilitate the learning of another, potentially accelerating the language acquisition process. By developing AI models that can effectively transfer linguistic knowledge across languages, learners could benefit from a more efficient and personalised learning experience, building upon their existing language skills.

Researchers could also investigate the integration of AI-powered language learning tools with educational technologies, such as adaptive learning platforms, gamification, and virtual classrooms. By combining the strengths of AI and educational technology, learners could benefit from personalised learning paths, engaging and gamified learning experiences, and seamless integration of AI-driven feedback and support within their existing learning environments.

Finally, as AI language learning tools become more prevalent, it will be crucial to conduct research on their ethical implications, fairness, and accessibility. Future studies could explore ways to mitigate biases in AI language models, ensure data privacy and security, and promote inclusive and equitable access to AI-powered language learning resources, particularly for underrepresented and marginalised communities.

## CONCLUSION

Artificial intelligence development affects all kinds of aspects, including learning new language competencies. AI development is continuously evolving to adapt to the diverse needs of language learners. With the integration of personalised learning algorithms, AI can provide tailored language lessons that cater to the specific strengths and weaknesses of each individual. This customised approach has the potential to significantly improve the overall language acquisition process and make learning more efficient and enjoyable for learners of all levels. One advantage of AI is its capacity to offer immediate feedback to learners, enabling more productive and efficient practice sessions. However, the potential for AI to replace human teachers and the need for proper training and support for educators to integrate AI into their teaching practices must be addressed. Looking ahead, future trends in AI for language learning may include more advanced natural language processing capabilities, increased personalisation of learning experiences, and a greater emphasis on collaborative learning through AI-driven platforms.

## REFERENCES


Aini, D. N., Setiawan, S., Syafi'ul Anam, R. M., & Ibad, W. (2023, September). Artificial Intelligence Learning Platform for Promoting Speaking Competence: A Suggested Scaffolding for Autonomous Learning in Pesantren. In *Proceedings of the 4th International Conference on English Language Teaching (ICON-ELT 2023)* (Vol. 780, p. 131). Springer Nature. DOI: 10.2991/978-2-38476-120-3_13

Anshari, M. (2020, March). Workforce mapping of fourth industrial revolution: Optimization to identity. [). IOP Publishing.]. *Journal of Physics: Conference Series*, 1477(7), 072023. DOI: 10.1088/1742-6596/1477/7/072023

Anshari, M., Almunawar, M. N., Masri, M., & Hrdy, M. (2021a). Financial technology with AI-enabled and ethical challenges. *Society*, 58(3), 189–195. DOI: 10.1007/s12115-021-00592-w

Anshari, M., Fithriyah, M., Polak, P., & Razzaq, A. (2021). Islamic FinTech and artificial intelligence (AI) for assessing creditworthiness. In *Artificial Intelligence and Islamic Finance* (pp. 48–60). Routledge. DOI: 10.4324/9781003171638-4

Anshari, M., Hamdan, M., Ahmad, N., & Ali, E. (2024). Public service delivery, artificial intelligence and the sustainable development goals: trends, evidence and complexities. *Journal of Science and Technology Policy Management*. DOI: 10.4324/9781003171638-4

Anshari, M., Syafrudin, M., & Fitriyani, N. L. (2022). Fourth industrial revolution between knowledge management and digital humanities. *Information (Basel)*, 13(6), 292. DOI: 10.3390/info13060292

Anshari, M., Syafrudin, M., Tan, A., Fitriyani, N. L., & Alas, Y. (2023). Optimisation of knowledge management (KM) with machine learning (ML) Enabled. *Information (Basel)*, 14(1), 35. DOI: 10.3390/info14010035

Chen, W., Shen, Z., Pan, Y., Tan, K., & Wang, C. (2024). Applying Machine Learning Algorithm to Optimize Personalized Education Recommendation System. *Journal of Theory and Practice of Engineering Science*, 4(01), 101–108.

Fitria, T. N. (2021, December). Artificial intelligence (AI) in education: Using AI tools for teaching and learning process. In *Prosiding Seminar Nasional & Call for Paper STIE AAS* (pp. 134-147).

Haristiani, N. (2019, November). Artificial Intelligence (AI) chatbot as language learning medium: An inquiry. [). IOP Publishing.]. *Journal of Physics: Conference Series*, 1387(1), 012020. DOI: 10.1088/1742-6596/1387/1/012020

Kim, N. Y., Cha, Y., & Kim, H. S. (2019). Future English learning: Chatbots and artificial intelligence. *Multimedia-Assisted Language Learning, 22*(3). DOI: 10.1088/1742-6596/1387/1/012020

Kolhar, M., & Alameen, A. (2021). Artificial Intelligence Based Language Translation Platform. *Intelligent Automation & Soft Computing*, 28(1), 1–9. DOI: 10.32604/iasc.2021.014995

Kuddus, K. (2022). Artificial intelligence in language learning: Practices and prospects. *Advanced Analytics and Deep Learning Models*, 1-17. DOI: 10.1088/1742-6596/1387/1/012020

Li, R. (2020, November). Using artificial intelligence in learning English as a foreign language: an examination of IELTS LIULISHUO as an online platform. In *Conference Proceedings. Innovation in Language Learning 2020*. DOI: 10.32629/jher.v1i2.178

Liua, Y., Salehb, S., & Huang, J. (2021). Artificial intelligence in promoting teaching and learning transformation in schools. *Artificial Intelligence*, 15(3).

Molenaar, I. (2022). Towards hybrid human-AI learning technologies. *European Journal of Education*, 57(4), 632–645. DOI: 10.1111/ejed.12527

Niu, S. J., Luo, J., Niemi, H., Li, X., & Lu, Y. (2022). Teachers' and students' views of using an AI-aided educational platform for supporting teaching and learning at Chinese schools. *Education Sciences*, 12(12), 858. DOI: 10.3390/educsci12120858

Peng, T., Luo, Y., & Liu, Y. (2022). Ai-based equipment optimization of the design on intelligent education curriculum system. *Wireless Communications and Mobile Computing*, 2022, 2022. DOI: 10.1155/2022/3614883

Rahman, A. M., Al Mamun, A., & Islam, A. (2017, December). *Programming challenges of chatbot: Current and future prospective. In 2017 IEEE region 10 humanitarian technology conference (R10-HTC)*. IEEE.

Syafrudin, M., Alfian, G., Fitriyani, N. L., & Anshari, M. (2024). Applied Artificial Intelligence for Sustainability. *Sustainability (Basel)*, 16(6), 2469. DOI: 10.3390/su16062469

Zubani, M., Sigalini, L., Serina, I., Putelli, L., Gerevini, A. E., & Chiari, M. (2022). A performance comparison of different cloud-based natural language understanding services for an Italian e-learning platform. *Future Internet*, 14(2), 62. DOI: 10.3390/fi14020062

# Chapter 13
# Overviewing Biases in Generative AI-Powered Models in the Arabic Language:
## AI Fairness for Sustainable Future

**Mussa Saidi Abubakari**
https://orcid.org/0000-0003-3782-281X
*Sultan Hassanal Bolkiah Institute of Education, Universiti Brunei Darussalam, Brunei*

## ABSTRACT

*Natural Language Processing (NLP) is an emerging field often integrated into Artificial Intelligence (AI) technologies. NLP has significantly advanced, leading to the widespread use of generative AI-powered (Gen-AI) models across various domains. However, while Gen-AI systems have been successfully implemented in several languages, AI-based language models still face considerable challenges and shortcomings, including generating biases in sensitive languages like Arabic. Therefore, the primary objective of this chapter is to provide an overview of the biases in Gen-AI-powered models in the context of the Arabic language, exploring the sources of these biases, their implications, and potential strategies for mitigation. The biases in Gen-AI-powered models underscore the need for ongoing research and development to create more equitable and accurate AI systems. By understanding the origins and implications of these biases and implementing effective mitigation strategies, we can work towards AI models that better serve diverse linguistic communities.*

DOI: 10.4018/979-8-3373-2530-9.ch013

## INTRODUCTION

Natural Language Processing (NLP) is an emerging field often integrated into Artificial Intelligence (AI) technologies. In recent years, NLP has significantly advanced, leading to the widespread use of generative AI-powered (GenAI) models across various domains, and foreign language learning is no exception. GenAI-based models, particularly chatbots like Claude, Gemini, ChatGPT, and others, have emerged as potentially valuable tools in language learning, especially in acquiring a foreign or second language (Omar et al., 2024; Sulaeman et al., 2023; Vo & Nguyen, 2024). These technologies employ NLP to examine, understand, and respond to human languages (Aljanabi, 2024; Shafik, 2024; Yassine & Gammoudi, 2023), creating interactive and personalised learning experiences. That is, these GenAI-powered platforms can adapt to individual learner needs and preferences, including providing customised feedback, lesson plans, and learning materials based on proficiency level and learning style (İnci Kavak et al., 2024; Omar et al., 2024; Vo & Nguyen, 2024). Further, thanks to features such as personalised activities, feedback, and diverse learning materials that help maintain student interest and involvement (Abubakari, Shafik, et al., 2024; Omar et al., 2024), GenAI chatbots can offer interactive opportunities that make language learning and acquisition more engaging and enjoyable (Fitrianto et al., 2024; Standen et al., 2020; Sulaeman et al., 2023). All these showcase the potential of GenAI-based systems to enhance the process of learning or acquiring languages, both foreign and native.

Moreover, GenAI-based models align well with and support Second Language Acquisition (SLA) principles by delivering comprehensible input tailored to individual language skills and simulating real-life language use through interactive exercises (Omar et al., 2024; Young & Shishido, 2023). Thus, by offering more interactive and engaging learning experiences by tailoring activities and feedback to individual needs (Abolkasim & Shtewi, 2023; Muttaqin, 2023; Omar et al., 2024), they address the limitations of conventional language instruction methods, which often rely heavily on rote learning and repetitive exercises (O. Ali et al., 2024; Omar et al., 2024). Nevertheless, while GenAI systems have been successfully implemented in several languages and predominantly English, AI-based language models still face considerable challenges and shortcomings, including generating biases in sensitive and complicated languages such as Arabic (A. Ahmed et al., 2022; Aljanabi, 2024). The unique and complex characteristics of the Arabic language, such as its rich morphology and complex syntax (H. Al-Khalifa et al., 2024; Aljanabi, 2024), pose significant challenges for AI-powered systems, leading to grave biases. These biases are not merely technical issues but also include cultural and linguistic aspects that can lead to profound ethical and moral implications.

Biases that arise from different aspects can lead to unintended consequences, such as reinforcing stereotypes or providing inaccurate information. Thus, it is essential to critically evaluate and ensure the accuracy and reliability of AI-generated content, particularly in languages other than English, because studies have highlighted that AI models are primarily and predominantly trained on English data, which can impact their performance in other languages like Arabic (Nasayreh et al., 2024; Sallam et al., 2024). For example, a study comparing ChatGPT's performance in English and Arabic revealed lower accuracy in answering medical-associated questions in Arabic compared to the counterpart language (Sallam et al., 2024). Besides that, unlike English, where few standard forms predominate, Arabic is characterised by both Modern Standard Arabic (MSA) and a plethora of regional dialects. These dialects vary not only by country but also by region within the same country, often diverging significantly from MSA, which is typically used in formal writing and media (Sallam & Mousa, 2024). Consequently, AI models that are predominantly trained on MSA are ill-equipped to handle the nuances of regional dialects, resulting in biased responses that fail to resonate with native speakers of different Arabic dialects (Mohideen, 2024; Slim & Melouah, 2024).

Therefore, biases existing in AI-powered models for the Arabic language stem from linguistic complexities, training data limitations, and cultural misinterpretations (Abolkasim & Shtewi, 2023; Alshammari et al., 2024; Sallam et al., 2024). These biases and shortcomings have significant implications for user trust, education, and cultural and ethical nuances and considerations. Addressing these biases requires a multidisciplinary approach involving collaboration between researchers, developers, and policymakers. The biases in GenAI-powered models, particularly in the Arabic language, underscore the need for ongoing research and development to create more equitable and accurate AI systems. By understanding the origins and implications of these biases and implementing effective mitigation strategies, we can work towards AI models that better serve diverse linguistic communities. The proposed mitigation strategies, which will be discussed in detail in the chapter, hold the potential to significantly improve the fairness and accuracy of AI-powered systems in the Arabic language context, instilling a sense of hope and optimism for the future of ethical AI in this context.

## Chapter Objectives and Structure

Artificial Intelligence (AI) has revolutionised the way we interact with digital technologies, mainly through the development of Generative AI. The GenAI-powered models are designed to simulate human interaction and provide users with information in different formats and assistance. However, as these models become more sophisticated, concerns about inherent biases, especially in non-English languages like Arabic, have come to the forefront. Thus, this chapter aspires to overview the biases present in GenAI-powered models when processing the Arabic language, drawing on recent research findings. That is, the chapter, based on the exploration of relevant and current literature, overviews the biases in AI-powered models in the context of Arabic language learning, focusing on understanding and addressing AI biases in this unique and sensitive language.

The chapter's organisation, with its significant contribution to the field, commences with an introduction to the topic and its significance in the first section, followed by background information on GenAI systems and the unique features of the Arabic language. It will then delve into the concept of biases in AI-powered models, exploring their types, manifestations, and importance. Specific sources of AI bias in the Arabic language context will be examined in the next section, along with case studies and examples to illustrate these issues. The chapter will proceed to discuss strategies for addressing and mitigating AI biases, including improvements in data collection, algorithm development, and cultural sensitivity. Ethical and regulatory considerations will be explored, followed by an examination of future directions and research opportunities in the field. The chapter then concludes by summarising key points and reflecting on the future of AI in Arabic language learning.

## GENAI MODELS SIGNIFICANCE AND THE ARABIC LANGUAGE

### GenAI and NLP in Linguistic Domains

GenAI and NLP are closely connected AI disciplines that are transforming the science of linguistics and are becoming more and more essential in a wide range of linguistic applications, including language comprehension, production, translation, and more. As these technologies progress, they are not just improving computational linguistics but also transforming established linguistic approaches. Literature pinpoints that the use of GenAI models has significantly transformed language comprehension and production activities in several languages. These technologies have shown remarkable proficiency, while there are still difficulties in handling languages with little resources. A recent study conducted by Ahuja et al. (2023) has compared GenAI models, such as GPT-4, with other models in 70 different languages. The study has shown that these models have great promise but also identified areas that need rigorous work, especially in multilingual contexts (Ahuja et al., 2023). Moreover, the incorporation of GenAI into multilingual NLP tasks exhibits the potential to tackle linguistic variety, but there is still a need for substantial improvement in the models' performance in less widely spoken languages (Keezhatta, 2019). The following are some of the roles, applications, or significance of GenAI and NLP in linguistic domains (that is, in processing, understanding, and generating human-like natural languages):

- **Cross-Linguistic Applications:** The capability of generative models to handle multiple languages, including low-resource languages, underscores their significance in promoting linguistic diversity and inclusivity (Babaali et al., 2024; Bella et al., 2024). This is particularly crucial in global communication and preserving linguistic heritage. However, the effective integration of these models into multilingual NLP tasks requires continuous refinement to overcome existing limitations (Bhat et al., 2023; Keezhatta, 2019). Additionally, cognitive models in linguistics, such as predictive processing, are being scaled to handle more complex linguistic phenomena, further enhancing our understanding of language processing across different linguistic contexts (Jackendoff, 2007; Lenci & Padó, 2022).
- **Linguistic Pedagogy (Educational) Applications:** In linguistic educational settings, Generative AI tools have made significant strides by facilitating personalised learning experiences. They are now employed in generating natural language text for educational purposes, crafting exercises, explaining code, and more, thus transforming teaching methodologies (Pérez-Núñez, 2023; Zastudil et al., 2023). The rapid adoption of these technologies in education highlights both their potential and the challenges they pose, such as ensuring alignment with educational goals and ethical standards (Abubakari, Shafik, et al., 2024; Abubakari, Zakaria, et al., 2024; Z. E. Ahmed et al., 2024; Zastudil et al., 2023). Thus, the implementation of GenAI in foreign language instruction showcases its versatility and impact on linguistic pedagogy.
- **Language Generation and Active Inference:** The application of generative models in language generation is pivotal in understanding linguistic processing from a cognitive perspective. These models simulate language comprehension and production, mimicking neural processes involved in real-time dialogues (Feng & Shi, 2021). Such models highlight the emergence of neurophysiological patterns like theta-gamma coupling during belief updating, which is essential for processing linguistic inputs (Friston et al., 2020). Additionally, predictive processing frameworks are being scaled to accommodate more complex linguistic structures, providing deeper insights into how language is processed cognitively (Michel, 2023).
- **Advancement in Computational Linguistics:** GenAI and NLP have been instrumental in shifting computational linguistics from rule-based systems to data-driven approaches. This shift has facilitated breakthroughs in understanding and processing natural languages, mainly through the adoption of deep learning models. These models have injected new life into both AI en-

gineering and linguistic research, bridging the gap between theoretical and applied linguistics (Deng & Liu, 2018; Feng & Shi, 2021). Thus, as research continues to evolve, these technologies are poised to drive further advancements in how we understand and utilise language computationally.

## Arabic Language Features and GenAI Models Challenges

Because of its profound historical significance and diversified cultural diversity, the Arabic language has posed a distinctive challenge and difficulties to GenAI-driven chatbots, leading them to have a number of biases and challenges when responding to users. The language presents a challenging phenomenon for GenAI designers and engineers working in the subject of linguistics due to its complex structure, which encompasses a wide variety of regional speech patterns and varied writing systems (Awadallah et al., 2022; Babaali et al., 2024). In contrast to English, Arabic has distinguished features entailing the presence of both Modern Standard Arabic (MSA) and a number of regional dialects or colloquial varieties. These dialects demonstrate variances not just across nations but also within areas, often diverging significantly from MSA, which is widely prevalent in official writing and media. These linguistic variants are present in both countries and regions. As a direct result of this and the fact that GenAI models are predominantly trained on Modern MSA, they are not adequately equipped to comprehend the nuances of regional dialects (Almurayh, 2021). Consequently, this condition results in skewed responses that do not connect with native speakers of the different Arabic dialects (Sallam & Mousa, 2024).

Furthermore, constraints placed on the available training data make this issue much more challenging to solve. When it comes to Arabic, there is limited availability of datasets that have been well-curated, particularly those that include a wide variety of dialects and cultural environments (Alruqi & Alzahrani, 2023). In other words, there are significant biases in the responses provided by GenAI-based chatbots because of the restricted availability of data. That is because the AI models are, by default, forced to rely on datasets that are insufficient and not representative of the population (Yassine & Gammoudi, 2023). The ending result of this situation is the presence of GenAI-based chatbots that struggle to provide responses that are precise or contextually relevant. As a result, these models often resort to using multiple examples of the same sentence or generate responses that are clunky or nonsensical to the users. Not only does this separation make the users' experiences more difficult, but it also weakens the validity of GenAI technology in nations where Arabic is the primary language. On top of that, the lack of diverse training data that encompasses the various cultural contexts within the Arabic-speaking world can substantially lead to GenAI models' inability to interpret and respond accurately to culturally specific queries, which can result in responses that are either inappropriate or irrelevant (Khoshafah, 2023; Zhu et al., 2024). That is because the cultural nuances and contextual understanding surrounding the Arabic language are crucial to consider during the model's training.

In general, the Arabic language, with its deep-rooted history and intricate linguistic structure, presents unique challenges for Generative AI models like Chat-GPT. The complexity of Arabic, driven by its rich morphology, diverse dialects, and unique script, significantly affects the ability of language models to perform various tasks, such as generating a contextual output or translation as requested by a user. The following are some of the intrinsic characteristics of the Arabic language that pose challenges to GenAI models, supported by recent research findings.

a. **Morphological (Grammar and Syntax) Richness:** Arabic's morphology is notably complex, with a single root capable of generating a multitude of word forms through various patterns of affixation. This morphological complexity results in a vast array of word forms, making it challenging for models to generalise effectively across different forms (Antoun et al., 2020; Ouali & El Garouani, 2024). Research has revealed that GenAI models like ChatGPT have faced limitations in understanding and applying Arabic grammar and syntax. For instance, they have difficulty differentiating between "*Hamzat al-Wasl*" and "*Hamzat al-Qat'a*", two types of *hamza* (glottal stop) in Arabic, in addition to struggling to parse Arabic sentences accurately, even simple ones (Abolkasim & Shtewi, 2023). Recent studies have emphasised the need for large, diverse corpora to train models that can effectively capture these variations (A. R. Ali et al., 2023).
b. **Complex Script and Diacritics:** Arabic's script is inherently complex, with letters that change shape depending on their position in a word and the presence of diacritics that alter pronunciation (Mujahid et al., 2023). Diacritics (or small markings added to letters, play a crucial role in indicating pronunciation and meaning in Arabic), often omitted in everyday writing, create ambiguity in text processing (Alshammari et al., 2024; Yassine & Gammoudi, 2023), making tasks like text generation and recognition more challenging. Further, a study (Abolkasim & Shtewi, 2023) observed that ChatGPT struggled to translate Arabic idioms to English and vice versa accurately. It tended to translate idioms literally, failing to capture the intended meaning. For instance, it could translate the Arabic equivalent of "a friend in need is a friend indeed" into English, but not the other way around. Recent advancements in character-level models have shown promise in improving speech recognition and text generation for Arabic (Azim et al., 2023), but challenges remain.

c. **Gender-Specific Language and Wording Order:** Arabic's gender-specific nature, where nouns, verbs, and adjectives change based on the gender of the subject, adds complexity to generative tasks. This complexity is particularly evident in machine translation and text generation, where the correct gender must be accurately reflected. Addressing this requires models that are explicitly trained to handle gender-specific nuances, as demonstrated by recent advancements in gender-rewriting tasks (Alrowili & Shanker, 2022). Moreover, unlike other languages with a fixed word order, Arabic allows for flexibility in sentence structure. This flexibility, coupled with the language's pro-drop nature (omission of pronouns), presents difficulties for syntactic parsers and analysers (Ouali & El Garouani, 2024).
d. **Diglossia and Dialectal Variations:** The Arabic language is characterised by diglossia, where Modern Standard Arabic (MSA) coexists with various regional dialects. MSA is used in formal contexts, while dialects are prevalent in everyday communication (Farghaly & Shaalan, 2009). This diglossia introduces variability that complicates the training of models capable of understanding and generating text across these different forms (Sallam & Mousa, 2024). Research has shown that current models struggle particularly with dialectal Arabic due to the scarcity of resources and training data for these variants (Kadaoui et al., 2023).

## CONCEPTUALISING BIASES IN GENAI-POWERED LANGUAGE MODELS

### Categories, Sources, and Manifestations of Biases in GenAI Models

Generative AI models in large language systems like Gemini, Claude, and ChatGPT generally exhibit various forms of biases that can impact their outputs and the broader societal implications of their use. These biases arise from various aspects, such as the training data, model architecture, and the design choices made during model development. The following are some categories (and manifestations) of biases (see also Figure 1) commonly observed in generative AI models (like Claude and ChatGPT) when dealing with, besides English, the Arabic language and other non-Engling languages:

*Figure 1. Some categories and sources of GenAI biases*

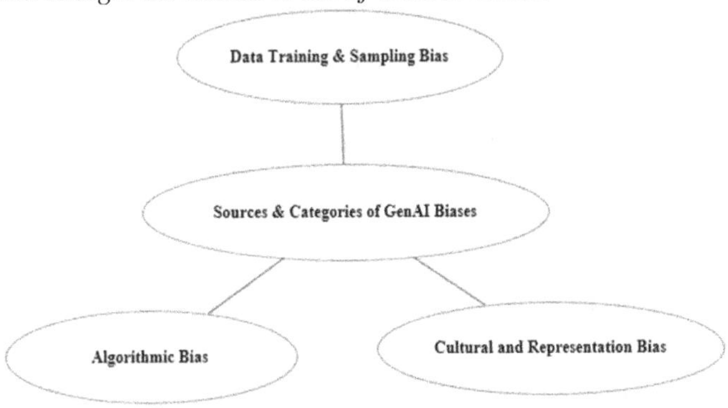


- **Data Training and Sampling Bias:** The primary source of bias in generative AI models stems from the training data, and literature shows that English dominates the datasets used for training, resulting in insufficient representation of other languages like Arabic. This imbalance leads to models that are less effective and more biased when processing non-English text. Studies show that for Arabic, generative models often underperform compared to state-of-the-art models in specific tasks due to limited training data and poor adaptation strategies (Abdelali et al., 2023). Thus, these biases stem from the datasets used to train the model, where the data may reflect societal inequalities or stereotypical associations. That is, Sampling bias occurs during the data collection or training process, where the data sampled does not adequately cover the linguistic diversity of the target language, leading to biased model outputs. For example, when a GenAI model is trained only on specific datasets, aspects, or texts, it can overrepresent certain demographics in specific occupations, reinforcing stereotypes (Sun et al., 2024). Generative text models, like GPT-3, often reflect gender and racial biases present in their training data, leading to outputs that can reinforce negative stereotypes. This was highlighted in a study where models trained on real human conversations were found to exhibit unbalanced gender and ethnicity references, leading to biased dialogue generation (Smith & Williams, 2021). In the context of the Arabic language, data bias often manifests in the underrepresentation of particular dialects or regional variations. Arabic is a highly diverse language with multiple dialects spoken across different countries, yet many AI models are predominantly trained on an MSA standard. This bias results in models that may struggle to understand or generate text in other dialects, which are widely spoken but less represented in training datasets (El-Shangiti et al., 2024; Slim & Melouah, 2024). For instance, in the Arabic language, if a model's training data is primarily sourced from online newspapers or academic publications, it might develop a bias towards formal language and ignore colloquial or regional dialects. This results in generative models that produce text that feels overly formal or detached from everyday conversational Arabic.

- **Algorithmic Bias:** Algorithmic bias is introduced by the model's underlying architecture or the algorithms used, which might inadvertently prioritise certain linguistic or cultural features over others. Even if the training data were perfectly balanced, the model's architecture might still introduce biases due to how it processes and prioritises information. A common issue in NLP-GenAI models is that they might rely heavily on superficial features, such as the presence of specific words, rather than understanding the deeper context (Abubakari, 2024a; Mutawa, 2024). For example, models trained for natural language inference have been shown to classify inputs based on biased subsets of data, leading to superficial generalisations rather than proper understanding (Asael et al., 2022). In Arabic NLP, algorithmic bias can occur when models are optimised using techniques that favour the syntactic structures of English, resulting in poor handling of the more complex morphology and syntax found in Arabic. For example, Arabic's rich inflectional system and root-based morphology can lead to incorrect tokenisation or parsing by models not explicitly designed for the language's intricacies (Abdelali et al., 2022; H. Al-Khalifa et al., 2024).
- **Cultural and Representation Bias:** Cultural bias in generative AI models refers to the overemphasis on the cultural norms and values of the dominant culture in the training data, leading to outputs that may be inappropriate or insensitive in other cultural contexts. This bias occurs when certain cultural or social groups are underrepresented or misrepresented in the model's training data, leading to outputs that do not accurately reflect the diversity of the language or culture (Zhu et al., 2024). A clear example of cultural bias is seen in generative models trained predominantly on Western-centric datasets. When applied to Arabic, these models might generate content that reflects Western values, idioms, or references, which may not align with or might even be offensive to Arabic-speaking users (Aljanabi, 2024; Yassine & Gammoudi, 2023). This is particularly problematic in the generation of culturally sensitive content (Kuck, 2023), such as religious or family-oriented topics. Additionally, cultural bias can manifest in the form of language models that fail to recognise the importance of specific cultural practices or traditions in the Arab world. For instance, models might generate text that overlooks key cultural holidays or misrepresents traditional customs, leading to outputs that

feel inauthentic or disconnected from the users' lived experiences (Abdelali et al., 2022). Another representation bias is evident in generative text models that produce Arabic content with a skewed focus on topics prevalent in the media, such as politics or religion while underrepresenting everyday social issues or the arts (S. Al-Khalifa et al., 2023). This bias can lead to a narrow portrayal of Arabic culture, reinforcing stereotypes rather than showcasing the full breadth of the language's expressive capacity.

## The Negative Consequences of Biases in GenAI-based Language Models

GenAI-driven language models, such as ChatGPT, Gemini, and Claude, have significantly revolutionised language processing, demonstrating impressive performance in natural language understanding and generation. However, the presence of noticeable biases within these models can lead to negative consequences, mainly when applied to languages other than English, such as Arabic. The following highlights the detrimental consequences for users of Arabic as a non-English language and the broader implications for the deployment of these AI systems.

- **Exacerbated Inequalities and Discrimination:** GenAI models trained on biased data can perpetuate existing inequalities and discrimination in society. This is particularly concerning in healthcare, where inaccurate or culturally insensitive responses can have severe consequences for patients (Sulaeman et al., 2023). For example, suppose an AI model is trained on data that associates certain health conditions with specific ethnic groups. In that case, it may provide inaccurate or biased information to users from those groups. Further, the lower performance of GenAI models in specific languages, particularly under-resourced dialects, can limit speakers and learners of those languages' access to information and technology (Abdelali et al., 2023; Sallam et al., 2024). This can exacerbate existing social and economic disparities (Ferrara, 2023b). For instance, when AI-powered translation services are less accurate for particular languages like Arabic, it can limit the ability of Arabic learners or speakers to access information and participate in online communities, especially considering most individuals are less competent in using digital technologies (Abubakari et al., 2023a; Abubakari & Kalinaki, 2024; Hawamdeh & Abdelhafid, 2024), underscoring the cruciality of fostering and cultivating digital competencies in all groups of people and cultures (Abubakari et al., 2023b; Abubakari, 2024b; Vuorikari et al., 2022).
- **Misinformation and Harm to Learning:** Errors in grammar, vocabulary, and cultural understanding can mislead users and hinder the learning pro-

cess (Sulaeman et al., 2023). This is particularly relevant in education, where students may rely on AI models for language learning or academic writing. Inaccurate information provided by biased AI models can negatively impact student learning and reinforce harmful stereotypes (Ferrara, 2023a; Kuck, 2023). Moreover, GenAI-based models still struggle with cultural nuances and context-specific meanings in non-English languages. This situation can result in outputs that are either irrelevant or offensive in the target language. For instance, the formality levels in the generated text can vary significantly across languages, with models often producing overly formal or informal text in languages like Arabic, which may not align with the intended context (Ersoy et al., 2023).

- **Reinforcement of Societal Biases:** The biases present in training data can lead to the reinforcement of harmful stereotypes and societal biases in AI outputs. In multilingual settings, this issue is exacerbated when models trained on biased English data are applied to other languages. This can have severe implications, such as perpetuating negative stereotypes in Arabic language outputs (H. Al-Khalifa et al., 2024), which could impact public perception and exacerbate existing social inequalities (Capraro et al., 2024; Mei et al., 2023). More specifically, when an AI model is trained on a dataset of Arabic text that reflects negative stereotypes about certain religious or ethnic groups. In that case, the model's output might reinforce those harmful stereotypes, leading to discrimination or prejudice against those groups (S. Al-Khalifa et al., 2023; Koubaa et al., 2023). Thus, biased GenAI models can create barriers to effective communication and understanding between speakers of different languages and cultures. This can have negative consequences for intercultural relations, business, and cultural exchange. For example, mistranslations or culturally insensitive responses generated by AI models can lead to misunderstandings and conflicts in social settings.
- **Limited Adoption and Loss of Trust in GenAI:** If AI models consistently provide inaccurate, biased, or culturally insensitive information, it can erode trust in AI technology as a whole. This can hinder the development and adoption of AI applications, even in areas where AI has the potential to be beneficial. For example, people may be less likely to trust AI-powered medical diagnoses or legal advice if they believe that the AI systems are biased against their language or cultural background (Sallam et al., 2024). Therefore, when GenAI models exhibit biases in languages like Arabic, trust in these technologies can be eroded, especially among marginalised communities already facing existing societal biases (Koubaa et al., 2023). This lack of trust can result in the further exclusion of these communities from technological advancements and benefits.

## Significance and Implications of Addressing Biases for Fair and Ethical AI

Addressing GenAI model biases, particularly in the linguistic field, is crucial to establishing fair, ethical, and trustworthy AI systems. These GenAI language models' biases may perpetuate and exacerbate the existing social inequalities, misrepresenting or marginalising some populations and undermining artificial intelligence technologies. The implications of addressing the biases found in GenAI language systems extend beyond the technical aspects of AI, such as improving AI performance and robustness; addressing these biases also affects the moral and ethical aspects of AI technology, including user confidence and trust in AI, social equality, and AI deployment regulations. Thus, by tackling these preconceptions, we may ensure that GenAI technologies promote fairness and impartiality in all societies. In the following outline (see also Figure 2), we highlight the significance and implications of addressing the biases arising from GenAI systems like ChatGPT when dealing with various languages like Arabic.

*Figure 2. Some implications and significance of addressing GenAI biases*

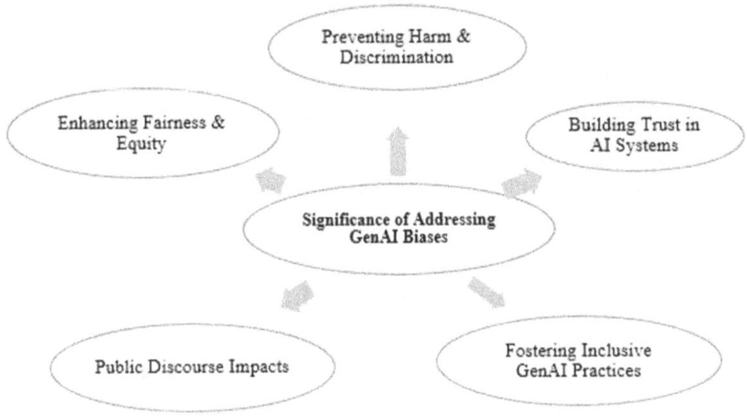


— **Preventing Harm and Discrimination:** Biased AI models can lead to discriminatory practices, mainly when used in sensitive areas like healthcare, criminal justice, and employment. These biases can exacerbate existing inequalities and lead to unjust outcomes. For example, in healthcare, NLP models used for psychiatric evaluations have been found to contain biases related to religion, race, gender, and nationality, which could worsen health disparities if not adequately addressed (Straw & Callison-Burch, 2020). Moreover, another study directly addressed the potential for social bias in GenAI models when dealing with Arabic and topics related to regions, gender, or colour (Billah Nagoudi et al., 2023). The study underscores the importance of recognising the sensitive nature of these attributes and avoiding discriminatory language.

— **Building Trust in AI Systems:** Trust is a fundamental component of user adoption of AI technologies. If users perceive AI systems as biased or unfair, they are less likely to trust and use these technologies. A survey on fairness and bias in GenAI systems highlights the importance of transparency and accountability in AI to build trust among users (Ferrara, 2023a). Recent studies have consistently raised concerns about ethical implications, the spread of misinformation, and the potential misuse of GenAI systems like ChatGPT in the context of the Arabic language (S. Al-Khalifa et al., 2023; Lakhani & Khan, 2023). Thus, mitigating biases, especially in systems that generate content or make decisions impacting people's lives, is essential for fostering user confidence.

— **Enhancing Fairness and Equity:** GenAI models characterised by NLP technology can influence many aspects of daily life, from hiring decisions to medical diagnoses. If these models are biased, they can perpetuate unfair outcomes that disproportionately affect underrepresented or marginalised groups. For instance, studies have shown that GPT-based language models exhibited gender biases when translating gender-neutral sentences from languages like Turkish into English, where roles such as “doctor” and “nurse” were automatically gendered based on societal stereotypes (Caliskan, 2023). Therefore, addressing such biases is crucial to ensure that AI systems do not reinforce these stereotypes.

— **Social Perception and Public Discourse Impacts:** GenAI language models, particularly those involved in content generation or translation, have a significant influence on public perception and discourse. Biases in these models can shape narratives and reinforce harmful stereotypes. For instance, research has shown that biased AI-generated articles can influence readers' perceptions of different nationalities, potentially leading to a shift in public opinion based on skewed information (Narayanan Venkit et al., 2023). Therefore, addressing these biases is critical to maintaining the integrity of public discourse.

— **Fostering Inclusive GenAI Practices:** Addressing biases in GenAI models in linguistic domains encourages the inclusion of diverse perspectives in AI development, ensuring that GenAI's benefits are equitably distributed across different social and cultural groups. The push for diversity in AI, as discussed in research on the ethical alignment of prominent models, highlights the importance of including varied cultural and social perspectives in the development process to avoid reinforcing societal inequities (Yi et al., 2023).

## CASE STUDIES OF BIASES IN GENAI MODELS

Several studies have been conducted to demonstrate the strengths and weaknesses of various GenAI-based language models in processing and generating texts in different languages, including Arabic. Some researchers have compared the results of different GenAI systems within one study, while others have analysed one GenAI system in the Arabic language. Some of the recent case studies analysing the capabilities of GenAI models in the context of Arabic are provided as follows:

1. **Study 1: Arabic Parsing Capabilities of Claude and ChatGPT:** In a recent investigation, some researchers (Aljanabi, 2024) assessed the Arabic parsing capabilities of two Gen-AI tools, ChatGPT and Claude. The investigation focused much on determining the effectiveness of these two Gen-AI systems in accurately analysing Arabic sentences and highlighting the challenges presented by the Arabic language's complex morphology, inflectional nature, and syntactic ambiguity. These challenges were shown to hinder the development of NLP technologies. Using a systematic approach, three proficient evaluators analysed the parsing results of both programs using a detailed rubric that included different areas of Arabic grammar. The results showed that Claude (72.9% accuracy) was more accurate than ChatGPT (33.3% accuracy) overall, especially when it came to dealing with complex morphology and more superficial syntactic connections. This finding was factual even though both tools had trouble with idiomatic phrases and unclear constructions. The researchers suggested the vitality of incorporating specialised knowledge from specific domains, using transfer learning techniques, and investigating ensemble approaches to enhance Arabic parsing systems based on AIs. The researchers also emphasised the need for regular reassessment of these AI-based tools as they progress.
2. **Study 2: ChatGPT's Potential as a Tool to Improve Arabic Learning Online:** Other researchers (Abolkasim & Shtewi, 2023) looked at ChatGPT's potential as a tool to improve online learning in another research. The authors carried out two experiments to assess ChatGPT's efficacy in Arabic and English. The first experiment tested ChatGPT's efficacy as a tool for learning Arabic, focusing on academic writing, grammar, and syntax. In order to evaluate ChatGPT's performance and test its understanding, the researchers—native Arabic speakers—posed questions on various facets of the language. One exciting discovery was that, in spite of acknowledged difficulties with Arabic grammar and syntax, ChatGPT

showed accurate translation capabilities between Arabic and English. The experiment did, however, also highlight ChatGPT's inadequacies in producing trustworthy academic writing in Arabic that complied with scientific paper requirements. The emphasis of the second experiment was on ChatGPT's abilities to write academic papers and find references in English. ChatGPT was fed with several research paper components by the researchers, such as a literature review and an academic article detailing ChatGPT's strengths and weaknesses in online learning. Specifically, ChatGPT demonstrated difficulty in accurately translating Arabic idioms into English and vice versa. While it could sometimes provide correct equivalents for Arabic idioms in English, it often resorted to word-for-word translations when asked to do the opposite, resulting in nonsensical or inaccurate phrases. Moreover, beyond strict grammatical rules, the study noted that ChatGPT's Arabic output often lacks the natural phrasing and flow of human-written Arabic. This suggests that while ChatGPT might grasp basic grammatical structures, it struggles with the nuances and stylistic conventions of the language, particularly in formal or academic writing. Overall, both tests demonstrated ChatGPT's shortcomings in producing accurate and thorough academic writing in both Arabic and English. Experiment 1 indicated that ChatGPT has the potential to be a valuable tool for Arabic learners, especially when it comes to translation. Still, it also emphasised the need for prudence and further work (Abolkasim & Shtewi, 2023). This finding was further supported by Experiment 2, which highlighted ChatGPT's limitations in generating thorough reference lists and high-calibre academic writing, even when done in English.

3. **Study 3: ChatGPT's Accuracy in Arabic-English Translation:** In another study, a researcher explored the use of ChatGPT as a tool for Arabic-English translation (Khoshafah, 2023). The author argues that while ChatGPT offers promising potential for cross-cultural communication, it is essential to evaluate its accuracy. Through a comparative analysis of ChatGPT translations with human translations across various text genres, the study revealed ChatGPT's strengths in translating more straightforward content and its severe limitations in handling the complexities of specialised domains like legal, scientific, or literary texts. The article concludes that while ChatGPT is a valuable tool, users should exercise caution, especially with specialised texts, and human intervention remains necessary to ensure translation accuracy.
4. **Study 4: Google Machine vs. ChatGPT Translation Comparative Analysis:** Another study investigated the potential of Gen-AI models like ChatGPT to improve machine translation (AlAfnan, 2024). The researcher compared Arabic-English and English-Arabic translations produced by ChatGPT and Google Translate, benchmarking them against professionally translated speeches of the Jordanian King delivered on different occasions. The results from analyses

revealed that while ChatGPT generates more accurate and natural-sounding translations than Google Translate, both tools still fell short of human translators in terms of accurately conveying nuanced meaning, textual adequacy, and style. The study has highlighted the irreplaceable role of human expertise in achieving high-quality translations, particularly for complex or culturally sensitive texts. Despite their limitations, GenAI language models like ChatGPT show promise in enhancing machine translation, especially as their contextual understanding and natural language processing abilities continue to improve.

## STRATEGIES FOR MITIGATING GENAI BIASES IN THE ARABIC CONTEXT

Multiple strategies must be intentionally implemented to reduce the impact of biases in GenAI-based language models. These strategies include but are not limited to enhancing training data, generating more effective assessment metrics, and incorporating ethical norms and practical technical guidelines into the design and building process of GenAI models. Using recent literature, we present, in the following, some of the key strategies to mitigate or at least minimise the biases of GenAI systems when dealing with sensitive and complicated languages like Arabic:

- **Incorporating Diverse and Comprehensive Arabic Datasets:** Among the significant challenges in Arabic AI-based chatbots is the reliance on datasets primarily from a single dialect or lacking representation from diverse Arabic-speaking communities (Nasayreh et al., 2024; Slim & Melouah, 2024). Thus, the development and utilisation of diverse and comprehensive datasets are crucial in mitigating GenAI biases. These datasets must include a wide range of Arabic dialects and cultural contexts to ensure that GenAI models are trained on data that is representative of the entire Arabic-speaking population. Further, ensuring that the training data for language models is diverse and representative of various religious groups can help reduce biases. This approach includes carefully curating datasets to include positive and neutral contexts related to different groups and faiths (Zekun et al., 2023).
- **Developing and Implementing Advanced NLP Techniques:** In addition to improving datasets, the application of advanced NLP techniques is vital. Recent advancements in transformer-based models and transfer learning offer promising avenues for enhancing the performance of Arabic chatbots. Models such as AraBERT and AraElectra have demonstrated their potential to provide more accurate and contextually appropriate responses, addressing some of the biases inherent in earlier AI models (Alruqi & Alzahrani, 2023;

Alshammari et al., 2024; Antoun et al., 2020). These advanced models can be fine-tuned to understand better and generate responses in various Arabic dialects, thereby reducing the likelihood of biased outputs. Moreover, developing robust frameworks for detecting and correcting biases in language models is crucial (Ferrara, 2023b). This includes using stereotype detection datasets and implementing debiasing algorithms to minimise the impact of biased outputs (Barikeri et al., 2021).

- **Developing Culturally Sensitive GenAI Models:** Arabic, like many languages, carries cultural nuances that can significantly influence the interpretation or generation of texts. For example, specific phrases or expressions might have different meanings or connotations in various Arabic-speaking cultures (Yassine & Gammoudi, 2023). Hence, beyond the development of diverse datasets and the application of advanced NLP techniques, another critical strategy for mitigating bias in Arabic chatbots is the implementation of culturally context-aware AI systems. Traditionally, GenAI chatbots often rely on a surface-level understanding of language, which can lead to misinterpretations, especially in a linguistically rich environment like Arabic. Context-aware AI systems, however, when designed intentionally, can understand and maintain the context of a conversation over time. This approach allows a GenAI chatbot to provide responses that are not only grammatically correct but also contextually appropriate, taking into account the nuances of ongoing dialogue. Implementing such AI systems requires sophisticated algorithms that can track the conversation's history and dynamically adjust responses based on the evolving context. Further, to mitigate the risk of misinterpretations or culturally insensitive outputs, it is crucial to incorporate cultural awareness and sensitivity into the design and training processes of Arabic AI models. That can be achieved by engaging with cultural experts, linguists, and native speakers from diverse backgrounds to provide insights, annotations, and feedback throughout the development lifecycle. These approaches not only reduce the likelihood of biased or irrelevant responses but also enhance the overall user experience, making interactions with the chatbot more fluid and human-like (Alhassan et al., 2022).
- **AI Ethical and Technical Collaborative Efforts:** Given the increasing use of AI in various domains, establishing ethical guidelines and regulations for AI development and deployment in the context of the Arabic language is crucial (S. Al-Khalifa et al., 2023). These guidelines should address issues like data privacy, algorithmic transparency, fairness, and accountability to ensure that Arabic-AI processing systems are used responsibly and do not perpetuate existing biases or create new forms of harm. In order to achieve this ethical approach, developers and AI designers should adopt a proactive approach

to ethical considerations, incorporating checks and balances throughout the development lifecycle. That could include regular audits of the chatbot's decision-making processes, the implementation of bias detection tools, and the involvement of diverse stakeholders in the design and testing phases. By embedding ethical considerations into the fabric of AI development, we can work towards minimising bias and ensuring that Arabic chatbots serve the best interests of their users (Ferrara, 2023b, 2023a). Moreover, collaborative efforts among linguists, AI researchers, and cultural experts are essential to creating these datasets and continuously updating them to reflect changes in language use and cultural practices (Touma et al., 2023). Involving interdisciplinary teams, including ethicists, linguists, and AI researchers, can help create more balanced and fair language models (Kolisko & Anderson, 2023).

- **Continuous Human Evaluation and Feedback:** Continuous evaluation and feedback mechanisms are essential for the ongoing improvement of Arabic chatbots. Regular assessments of chatbot performance, utilising both automated metrics and human evaluations, can help identify and correct biases (Billah Nagoudi et al., 2023; Fabiyi, 2024; Touma et al., 2023). User feedback should be actively sought and integrated into the development process, ensuring that the chatbot evolves to meet the needs of its users. This iterative approach not only helps in mitigating existing biases but also in adapting the chatbot to new challenges and contexts as they arise (Alsheddi & Alhenaki, 2022).

## CONCLUSION, FUTURE DIRECTIONS AND RESEARCH

This chapter has provided, using the latest empirical research on GenAI-based systems, an overview of the biases existing in language-based AI models, together with the mitigation strategies. When looking forward to the future of GenAI-driven chatbots for the Arabic language, it is evidenced by the current literature that cultural sensitivity and technical expertise are equally important on the path to eradicating prejudice. There are two sides to GenAI: on the one hand, GenAI-driven chatbots might completely change the way people in the Arab world get their hands on information, services, and education. However, these GenAI technologies run the danger of adding to preexisting biases and prejudices and fostering new kinds of digital exclusion if they fail to take into account the specific cultural and linguistic features of Arabic. Consequently, a solid grasp of the Arabic language and its speakers is essential for the creation of GenAI models, which process the Arabic language. In achieving the goal of creating AI tools that are really representative and inclusive, it is necessary to go deeper than superficial solutions and have substantive conversations with communities, linguists, and cultural academics.

Future developments in Gen-AI research, especially in NLP and deep learning, will likely determine the fate of the Arabic language, along with other languages in cyberspace, along with community interactions. With the development of increasingly advanced AI models, the dialectal variances and cultural background of Arabic will become less of a challenge. Nevertheless, progress in technology cannot be relied upon in isolation. Consistent investigation into the moral and societal effects of GenAI must coexist with these developments. Part of this process is looking at how GenAI might be used to combat prejudice and advance equality and inclusion. The future of Arabic-based GenAI chatbots depends on our ability to coordinate AI research with larger social objectives so that they benefit the communities they are designed to assist. Therefore, a middle ground between technical innovations and cultural and social responsibilities is necessary for Arabic-based GenAI language chatbots to progress and mitigate both internal and external biases. There is a chance to build GenAI-driven chatbots that are socially responsible, culturally aware, and technologically competent if academics, developers, and lawmakers work together to tackle the problems of GenAI biases in various languages. These GenAI-based chatbots might be used as examples for various languages and areas, showing how AI-driven technologies can be used to bring people from diverse backgrounds together and encourage understanding. Our shared capacity to identify and combat AI systems' inherent biases and prejudices is crucial to the achievement of the sustainable goal of creating a world where technology genuinely caters to, irrespective of their language or cultural background, the needs of all humans.

# REFERENCES


Abdelali, A., Durrani, N., Dalvi, F., & Sajjad, H. (2022). Post-hoc analysis of Arabic transformer models. *Proceedings of the Fifth BlackboxNLP Workshop on Analyzing and Interpreting Neural Networks for NLP*, 91–103. DOI: 10.18653/v1/2022.blackboxnlp-1.8

Abdelali, A., Mubarak, H., Chowdhury, S. A., Hasanain, M., Mousi, B., Boughorbel, S., El Kheir, Y., Izham, D., Dalvi, F., Hawasly, M., Nazar, N., Elshahawy, Y., Ali, A., Durrani, N., Milic-Frayling, N., & Alam, F. (2023). LAraBench: Benchmarking Arabic AI with Large Language Models. *Proceedings Ofthe 18th Conference Ofthe European Chapter Ofthe Association for Computational Linguistics, 1*, 487–520. http://arxiv.org/abs/2305.14982

Abolkasim, E., & Shtewi, A. (2023). Analyzing the Efficacy of ChatGPT for Online Learning: An Experimental Study. *AlQalam Journal of Medical and Applied Sciences*, 6(2), 617–625. DOI: 10.5281/zenodo.10005016

Abubakari, M. S. (2024a). Overviewing the Maze of Research Integrity and False Positives Within AI-Enabled Detectors. In Mutawa, A. (Ed.), *Impacts of Generative AI on the Future of Research and Education* (pp. 335–366). IGI Global., DOI: 10.4018/979-8-3693-0884-4.ch013

Abubakari, M. S. (2024b). The digital frontier within Islamic education: Research gaps overview in digital competence. *Journal of Computing Research and Innovation*, 9(2), 317–331. DOI: 10.24191/jcrinn.v9i2.435

Abubakari, M. S., & Kalinaki, K. (2024). Digital Competence in Islamic Education for Lifelong Learning: Preliminary Analysis Using DigComp 2.1 Framework. In Hawamdeh, M. M. K., & Abdelhafid, F. (Eds.), *Embracing Technological Advancements for Lifelong Learning* (pp. 1–31). IGI Global., DOI: 10.4018/979-8-3693-1410-4.ch001

Abubakari, M. S., Shafik, W., & Hidayatullah, A. F. (2024). Evaluating the Potential of Artificial Intelligence in Islamic Religious Education: A SWOT Analysis Overview. In *AI-Enhanced Teaching Methods* (pp. 216–239). IGI Global. DOI: 10.4018/979-8-3693-2728-9.ch010

Abubakari, M. S., Zakaria, G. A. N., & Musa, J. (2024). Perceived compatibility and students' intention to adopt digital technologies in Islamic education institutions. *Cogent Education*, 11(1), 2430869. DOI: 10.1080/2331186X.2024.2430869

Abubakari, M. S., Zakaria, G. A. N., Musa, J., & Kalinaki, K. (2023a). Assessing Digital Competence in Higher Education: A Gender Analysis of DigComp 2.1 Framework in Uganda. *SAGA: Journal of Technology and Information System*, 1(4), 114–120. DOI: 10.58905/saga.v1i4.210

Abubakari, M. S., Zakaria, G. A. N., Musa, J., & Kalinaki, K. (2023b). Validating the Digital Competence (Dig-Comp 2.1) Framework in Higher Education Using Confirmatory Factor Analysis: Non-Western Perspective. *Canadian Journal of Educational and Social Studies*, 3(6), 15–26. DOI: 10.53103/cjess.v6i1.184

Ahmed, A., Ali, N., Alzubaidi, M., Zaghouani, W., Abd-alrazaq, A., & Househ, M. (2022). Arabic chatbot technologies: A scoping review. *Computer Methods and Programs in Biomedicine Update*, 2(April), 100057. DOI: 10.1016/j.cmpbup.2022.100057

Ahmed, Z. E., Hassan, A. A., & Saeed, R. A. (2024). *AI-Enhanced Teaching Methods* (Ahmed, Z. E., Hassan, A. A., & Saeed, R. A., Eds.). IGI Global., DOI: 10.4018/979-8-3693-2728-9

Ahuja, K., Diddee, H., Hada, R., Ochieng, M., Ramesh, K., Jain, P., Nambi, A., Ganu, T., Segal, S., Ahmed, M., Bali, K., & Sitaram, S. (2023). MEGA: Multilingual Evaluation of Generative AI. *Proceedings of the 2023 Conference on Empirical Methods in Natural Language Processing*, 4232–4267. DOI: 10.18653/v1/2023.emnlp-main.258

Al-Khalifa, H., Al-Khalefah, K., & Haroon, H. (2024). Error Analysis of Pretrained Language Models (PLMs) in English-to-Arabic Machine Translation. *Human-Centric Intelligent Systems*, 4(2), 206–219. DOI: 10.1007/s44230-024-00061-7

Al-Khalifa, S., Alhumaidhi, F., Alotaibi, H., & Al-Khalifa, H. S. (2023). ChatGPT across Arabic Twitter: A Study of Topics, Sentiments, and Sarcasm. *Data*, 8(11), 171. DOI: 10.3390/data8110171

AlAfnan, M. A. (2024). Large Language Models as Computational Linguistics Tools: A Comparative Analysis of ChatGPT and Google Machine Translations. *Journal of Artificial Intelligence and Technology*. DOI: 10.3390/data8110171

Alhassan, N. A., Saad Albarrak, A., Bhatia, S., & Agarwal, P. (2022). A Novel Framework for Arabic Dialect Chatbot Using Machine Learning. *Computational Intelligence and Neuroscience*, 2022, 1–11. DOI: 10.1155/2022/1844051 PMID: 35310584

Ali, A. R., Siddiqui, M. A., Algunaibet, R., & Ali, H. R. (2023). A Large and Diverse Arabic Corpus for Language Modeling. *Procedia Computer Science*, 225, 12–21. DOI: 10.1016/j.procs.2023.09.086

Ali, O., Murray, P. A., Momin, M., Dwivedi, Y. K., & Malik, T. (2024). The effects of artificial intelligence applications in educational settings: Challenges and strategies. *Technological Forecasting and Social Change*, 199, 123076. DOI: 10.1016/j.techfore.2023.123076

Aljanabi, M. (2024). Assessing the Arabic Parsing Capabilities of ChatGPT and Cloude: An Expert-Based Comparative Study. *Mesopotamian Journal of Arabic Language Studies*, 2024(2024), 16–23. DOI: 10.58496/MJALS/2024/002

Almurayh, A. (2021). The Challenges of Using Arabic Chatbot in Saudi Universities. *International Journal of Computational Science*, 48(1), 190–201. https://www.semanticscholar.org/paper/f56ba4e0912b1906df9fad255bf39e829f80e1ab

Alrowili, S., & Shanker, V. (2022). Generative Approach for Gender-Rewriting Task with ArabicT5. *Proceedings of the Seventh Arabic Natural Language Processing Workshop (WANLP)*, 491–495. DOI: 10.18653/v1/2022.wanlp-1.55

Alruqi, T. N., & Alzahrani, S. M. (2023). Evaluation of an Arabic Chatbot Based on Extractive Question-Answering Transfer Learning and Language Transformers. *AI*, 4(3), 667–691. DOI: 10.3390/ai4030035

Alshammari, H., El-Sayed, A., & Elleithy, K. (2024). AI-Generated Text Detector for Arabic Language Using Encoder-Based Transformer Architecture. *Big Data and Cognitive Computing*, 8(3), 32. DOI: 10.3390/bdcc8030032

Alsheddi, A. S., & Alhenaki, L. S. (2022). English and Arabic Chatbots: A Systematic Literature Review. *International Journal of Advanced Computer Science and Applications*, 13(8). Advance online publication. DOI: 10.14569/IJACSA.2022.0130876

Antoun, W., Baly, F., & Hajj, H. (2020). *AraBERT: Transformer-based Model for Arabic Language Understanding*. https://doi.org//arXiv.2003.00104DOI: 10.48550

Asael, D., Ziegler, Z., & Belinkov, Y. (2022). A Generative Approach for Mitigating Structural Biases in Natural Language Inference. *Proceedings of the 11th Joint Conference on Lexical and Computational Semantics*, 186–199. DOI: 10.18653/v1/2022.starsem-1.16

Awadallah, M. S., de Arriba-Pérez, F., Costa-Montenegro, E., Kholief, M., & El-Bendary, N. (2022). Investigation of Local Interpretable Model-Agnostic Explanations (LIME) Framework with Multi-Dialect Arabic Text Sentiment Classification. *2022 32nd International Conference on Computer Theory and Applications (ICCTA)*, 116–121. DOI: 10.1109/ICCTA58027.2022.10206274

Azim, M. A., Hussein, W., & Badr, N. L. (2023). Using Character-Level Sequence-to-Sequence Model for Word Level Text Generation to Enhance Arabic Speech Recognition. *IEEE Access : Practical Innovations, Open Solutions*, 11, 91173–91183. DOI: 10.1109/ACCESS.2023.3302257

Babaali, B., Salem, M., & Alharbe, N. R. (2024). Breaking language barriers with ChatGPT: Enhancing low-resource machine translation between algerian arabic and MSA. *International Journal of Information Technology : an Official Journal of Bharati Vidyapeeth's Institute of Computer Applications and Management*. Advance online publication. DOI: 10.1007/s41870-024-01926-7

Barikeri, S., Lauscher, A., Vulić, I., & Glavaš, G. (2021). RedditBias: A Real-World Resource for Bias Evaluation and Debiasing of Conversational Language Models. *Proceedings of the 59th Annual Meeting of the Association for Computational Linguistics and the 11th International Joint Conference on Natural Language Processing(*Volume 1*: Long Papers)*, 1941–1955. DOI: 10.18653/v1/2021.acl-long.151

Bella, G., Helm, P., Koch, G., & Giunchiglia, F. (2024). Tackling Language Modelling Bias in Support of Linguistic Diversity. *The 2024 ACM Conference on Fairness, Accountability, and Transparency*, 562–572. DOI: 10.1145/3630106.3658925

Bhat, S., Varma, V., & Pedanekar, N. (2023). Generative Models For Indic Languages: Evaluating Content Generation Capabilities. *Proceedings of the Conference Recent Advances in Natural Language Processing - Large Language Models for Natural Language Processings*, 187–195. DOI: 10.26615/978-954-452-092-2_021

Billah Nagoudi, E. M., Abdul-Mageed, M., Elmadany, A., Inciarte, A., & Islam Khondaker, M. T. (2023). JASMINE: Arabic GPT Models for Few-Shot Learning. *Proceedings of the 2023 Conference on Empirical Methods in Natural Language Processing*, 16721–16744. DOI: 10.18653/v1/2023.emnlp-main.1040

Caliskan, A. (2023). Artificial Intelligence, Bias, and Ethics. *Proceedings of the Thirty-Second International Joint Conference on Artificial Intelligence*, 7007–7013. DOI: 10.24963/ijcai.2023/799

Capraro, V., Lentsch, A., Acemoglu, D., Akgun, S., Akhmedova, A., Bilancini, E., Bonnefon, J.-F., Brañas-Garza, P., Butera, L., Douglas, K. M., Everett, J. A. C., Gigerenzer, G., Greenhow, C., Hashimoto, D. A., Holt-Lunstad, J., Jetten, J., Johnson, S., Kunz, W. H., Longoni, C., & Viale, R. (2024). The impact of generative artificial intelligence on socioeconomic inequalities and policy making. *PNAS Nexus*, 3(6), pgae191. Advance online publication. DOI: 10.1093/pnasnexus/pgae191 PMID: 38864006

Deng, L., & Liu, Y. (2018). *Deep Learning in Natural Language Processing* (Deng, L., & Liu, Y., Eds.). Springer Singapore., DOI: 10.1007/978-981-10-5209-5

El-Shangiti, A. O., Alwajih, F., & Abdul-Mageed, M. (2024). *Arabic Automatic Story Generation with Large Language Models.* http://arxiv.org/abs/2407.07551 DOI: 10.18653/v1/2024.arabicnlp-1.13

Ersoy, A., Vizcarra, G., Mayeesha, T., & Muller, B. (2023). *What Languages are Generative Language Models the Most Formal? Analyzing Formality Distribution across Languages. Findings of the Association for Computational Linguistics.* EMNLP., DOI: 10.18653/v1/2023.findings-emnlp.175

Fabiyi, S. D. (2024). What can ChatGPT not do in education? Evaluating its effectiveness in assessing educational learning outcomes. *Innovations in Education and Teaching International*, 00(00), 1–15. DOI: 10.1080/14703297.2024.2333395

Farghaly, A., & Shaalan, K. (2009). Arabic Natural Language Processing. *ACM Transactions on Asian Language Information Processing*, 8(4), 1–22. DOI: 10.1145/1644879.1644881

Feng, H., & Shi, F. (2021). Deep Learning in Natural Language Processing. *Natural Language Engineering*, 27(3), 373–375. DOI: 10.1017/S1351324919000597

Ferrara, E. (2023a). Fairness and Bias in Artificial Intelligence: A Brief Survey of Sources, Impacts, and Mitigation Strategies. *Sci*, 6(1), 3. DOI: 10.3390/sci6010003

Ferrara, E. (2023b). Should ChatGPT be biased? Challenges and risks of bias in large language models. *First Monday*, 28(11). Advance online publication. DOI: 10.5210/fm.v28i11.13346

Fitrianto, I., Setyawan, C. E., & Saleh, M. (2024). Utilizing Artificial Intelligence for Personalized Arabic Language Learning Plans. *International Journal of Post Axial: Futuristic Teaching and Learning*, 2(1), 132–142. DOI: 10.59944/postaxial.v2i1.273

Friston, K. J., Parr, T., Yufik, Y., Sajid, N., Price, C. J., & Holmes, E. (2020). Generative models, linguistic communication and active inference. *Neuroscience and Biobehavioral Reviews*, 118, 42–64. DOI: 10.1016/j.neubiorev.2020.07.005 PMID: 32687883

Hawamdeh, M. M. K., & Abdelhafid, F. (2024). *Embracing Technological Advancements for Lifelong Learning* (Hawamdeh, M. M. K., & Abdelhafid, F., Eds.). IGI Global., DOI: 10.4018/979-8-3693-1410-4

İnci Kavak, V., Evis, D., & Ekinci, A. (2024). The Use of ChatGPT in Language Education. *Experimental and Applied Medical Science*, 5(2), 72–82. DOI: 10.46871/eams.1461578

Jackendoff, R. (2007). Linguistics in Cognitive Science: The state of the art. *Linguistic Review*, 24(4). Advance online publication. DOI: 10.1515/TLR.2007.014

Kadaoui, K., Magdy, S. M., Waheed, A., Khondaker, M. T. I., El-Shangiti, A. O., Nagoudi, E. M. B., & Abdul-Mageed, M. (2023). *TARJAMAT: Evaluation of Bard and ChatGPT on Machine Translation of Ten Arabic Varieties.* DOI: 10.1515/TLR.2007.014

Keezhatta, M. S. (2019). Understanding EFL Linguistic Models through Relationship between Natural Language Processing and Artificial Intelligence Applications. *Arab World English Journal*, 10(4), 251–262. DOI: 10.24093/awej/vol10no4.19

Khoshafah, F. (2023). ChatGPT for Arabic-English Translation: Evaluating the Accuracy ChatGPT for Arabic-English Translation: Evaluating the Accuracy. *Research Square.* DOI: 10.21203/rs.3.rs-2814154/v2

Kolisko, S., & Anderson, C. J. (2023). Exploring Social Biases of Large Language Models in a College Artificial Intelligence Course. *Proceedings of the AAAI Conference on Artificial Intelligence*, 37(13), 15825–15833. DOI: 10.1609/aaai.v37i13.26879

Koubaa, A., Boulila, W., Ghouti, L., Alzahem, A., & Latif, S. (2023). Exploring ChatGPT Capabilities and Limitations: A Survey. *IEEE Access : Practical Innovations, Open Solutions*, 11(October), 118698–118721. DOI: 10.1109/ACCESS.2023.3326474

Kuck, K. (2023). Generative Artificial Intelligence: A Double-Edged Sword. *2023 World Engineering Education Forum - Global Engineering Deans Council (WEEF-GEDC)*, 1–10. DOI: 10.1109/WEEF-GEDC59520.2023.10343638

Lakhani, M., & Khan, H. M. A. (2023). Fighting Disinformation in the Palestine Conflict: The Role of Generative AI and Islamic Values. *Al Misbah Research Journal, 3*(4), 02–13. https://zenodo.org/records/11265514

Lenci, A., & Padó, S. (2022). Editorial: Perspectives for natural language processing between AI, linguistics and cognitive science. *Frontiers in Artificial Intelligence*, 5, 1059998. Advance online publication. DOI: 10.3389/frai.2022.1059998 PMID: 36406471

Mei, K., Fereidooni, S., & Caliskan, A. (2023). Bias Against 93 Stigmatized Groups in Masked Language Models and Downstream Sentiment Classification Tasks. *2023 ACM Conference on Fairness, Accountability, and Transparency*, 1699–1710. DOI: 10.1145/3593013.3594109

Michel, C. (2023). Scaling up Predictive Processing to language with Construction Grammar. *Philosophical Psychology*, 36(3), 553–579. DOI: 10.1080/09515089.2022.2050198

Mohideen, H. L. M.H. L. M. Mohideen. (2024). Exploring the Opportunities of Implementing Artificial Intelligence (AI) Technology for Teaching Arabic to Non-Native Speakers: A Theoretical Approach. *JOURNAL OF DIGITAL LEARNING AND DISTANCE EDUCATION*, 2(10), 760–767. DOI: 10.56778/jdlde.v2i9.225

Mujahid, M., Kanwal, K., Rustam, F., Aljedaani, W., & Ashraf, I. (2023). Arabic ChatGPT Tweets Classification Using RoBERTa and BERT Ensemble Model. *ACM Transactions on Asian and Low-Resource Language Information Processing*, 22(8), 1–23. DOI: 10.1145/3605889

Mutawa, A. (2024). *Impacts of Generative AI on the Future of Research and Education* (Mutawa, A., Ed.). IGI Global., DOI: 10.4018/979-8-3693-0884-4

Muttaqin, Z. (2023). Implementation of Islamic Education Learning with Artificial Intelligence (CHATGPT). *The 6th ICIS (2023): Islamic Thought and the Digital Challenge: Exploring the Future of Education, Business, Law, and Society*, 1–9. DOI: 10.1145/3605889

Narayanan Venkit, P., Gautam, S., Panchanadikar, R., Huang, T.-H., & Wilson, S. (2023). Unmasking Nationality Bias: A Study of Human Perception of Nationalities in AI-Generated Articles. *Proceedings of the 2023 AAAI/ACM Conference on AI, Ethics, and Society*, 554–565. DOI: 10.1145/3600211.3604667

Nasayreh, A., Al Mamlook, R. E., Samara, G., Gharaibeh, H., Aljaidi, M., Alzu'bi, D., Al-Daoud, E., & Abualigah, L. (2024). Arabic Sentiment Analysis for ChatGPT Using Machine Learning Classification Algorithms: A Hyperparameter Optimization Technique. *ACM Transactions on Asian and Low-Resource Language Information Processing*, 23(3), 1–19. DOI: 10.1145/3638285

Omar, H., Owida, H. A., Abuowaida, S., Alshdaifat, N., Alazaidah, R., Elsoud, E., & Batyha, R. (2024). ChatGPT: A new AI tool for English language teaching and learning among Jordanian students. *Kurdish Studies*, 12(1), 3628–3637. DOI: 10.58262/ks.v12i1.257

Ouali, S., & El Garouani, S. (2024). Arabic Chatbots Challenges and Solutions: A Systematic Literature Review. *Iraqi Journal for Computer Science and Mathematics*, 5(3), 128–169. DOI: 10.52866/ijcsm.2024.05.03.007

Pérez-Núñez, A. (2023). Exploring the Potential of Generative AI (ChatGPT) for Foreign Language Instruction: Applications and Challenges. *Hispania*, 106(3), 355–362. DOI: 10.1353/hpn.2023.a906568

Sallam, M., Al-Mahzoum, K., Ahmad Almutawaa, R., Ahmad Alhashash, J., Abdullah Dashti, R., Raed AlSafy, D., Abdullah Almutairi, R., & Barakat, M. (2024). *The Performance of OpenAI ChatGPT-4 and Google Gemini in Virology Multiple-Choice Questions: A Comparative Analysis of English and Arabic Responses*. DOI: 10.21203/rs.3.rs-4220786/v1

Sallam, M., & Mousa, D. (2024). Evaluating ChatGPT performance in Arabic dialects: A comparative study showing defects in responding to Jordanian and Tunisian general health prompts. *Mesopotamian Journal of Artificial Intelligence in Healthcare*, 2024, 1–7. DOI: 10.58496/MJAIH/2024/001

Shafik, W. (2024). Introduction to ChatGPT. In A. J. Obaid, B. Bhushan, M. S., & S. S. Rajest (Eds.), *Advanced Applications of Generative AI and Natural Language Processing Models* (pp. 1–25). IGI Global. DOI: 10.4018/979-8-3693-0502-7.ch001

Slim, A., & Melouah, A. (2024). Low Resource Arabic Dialects Transformer Neural Machine Translation Improvement through Incremental Transfer of Shared Linguistic Features. *Arabian Journal for Science and Engineering*, 49(9), 12393–12409. Advance online publication. DOI: 10.1007/s13369-023-08543-9

Smith, E. M., & Williams, A. (2021). *Hi, my name is Martha: Using names to measure and mitigate bias in generative dialogue models*. https://doi.org//arXiv.2109.03300DOI: 10.48550

Standen, P. J., Brown, D. J., Taheri, M., Galvez Trigo, M. J., Boulton, H., Burton, A., Hallewell, M. J., Lathe, J. G., Shopland, N., Blanco Gonzalez, M. A., Kwiatkowska, G. M., Milli, E., Cobello, S., Mazzucato, A., Traversi, M., & Hortal, E. (2020). An evaluation of an adaptive learning system based on multimodal affect recognition for learners with intellectual disabilities. *British Journal of Educational Technology*, 51(5), 1748–1765. DOI: 10.1111/bjet.13010

Straw, I., & Callison-Burch, C. (2020). Artificial Intelligence in mental health and the biases of language based models. *PLoS One*, 15(12), e0240376. DOI: 10.1371/journal.pone.0240376 PMID: 33332380

Sulaeman, I., Syuhadak, S., & Sulaeman, I. (2023). ChatGPT as a New Frontier in Arabic Education Technology. *Al-Arabi: Journal of Teaching Arabic as a Foreign Language*, 7(1), 83–105. DOI: 10.17977/um056v7i1p83-105

Sun, L., Wei, M., Sun, Y., Suh, Y. J., Shen, L., & Yang, S. (2024). Smiling women pitching down: Auditing representational and presentational gender biases in image-generative AI. *Journal of Computer-Mediated Communication*, 29(1), zmad045. Advance online publication. DOI: 10.1093/jcmc/zmad045

Touma, R., Hajj, H., El-Hajj, W., & Shaban, K. (2023). Automated Generation of Human-readable Natural Arabic Text from RDF Data. *ACM Transactions on Asian and Low-Resource Language Information Processing*, 22(4), 1–13. DOI: 10.1145/3582262

Vo, T. K. A., & Nguyen, H. (2024). Generative Artificial Intelligence and ChatGPT in Language Learning: EFL Students' Perceptions of Technology Acceptance. *Journal of University Teaching & Learning Practice*, 21(06). Advance online publication. DOI: 10.53761/fr1rkj58

Vuorikari, R., Kluzer, S., & Punie, Y. (2022). *DigComp 2.2, The Digital Competence Framework for Citizens - with new examples of knowledge, skills and attitudes*. Publications Office of the European Union., DOI: 10.2760/115376

Yassine, S., & Gammoudi, M. M. (2023). Trends and Challenges of Arabic Chatbots : Literature Review. *Jordanian Journal of Computers and Information Technology*, 09(03), 261–286.

Yi, X., Yao, J., Wang, X., & Xie, X. (2023). Unpacking the Ethical Value Alignment in Big Models. *Journal of Computer Research and Development*, 60(9), 1926–1945. DOI: 10.7544/issn1000-1239.202330553

Young, J. C., & Shishido, M. (2023). Investigating OpenAI's ChatGPT Potentials in Generating Chatbot's Dialogue for English as a Foreign Language Learning. *International Journal of Advanced Computer Science and Applications*, 14(6). Advance online publication. DOI: 10.14569/IJACSA.2023.0140607

Zastudil, C., Rogalska, M., Kapp, C., Vaughn, J., & MacNeil, S. (2023). Generative AI in Computing Education: Perspectives of Students and Instructors. *2023 IEEE Frontiers in Education Conference (FIE)*, 1–9. DOI: 10.1109/FIE58773.2023.10343467

Zekun, W., Bulathwela, S., & Koshiyama, A. S. (2023). *Towards Auditing Large Language Models: Improving Text-based Stereotype Detection*. http://arxiv.org/abs/2311.14126

Zhu, L., Mou, W., Lai, Y., Lin, J., & Luo, P. (2024). Language and cultural bias in AI: Comparing the performance of large language models developed in different countries on Traditional Chinese Medicine highlights the need for localized models. *Journal of Translational Medicine*, 22(1), 319. DOI: 10.1186/s12967-024-05128-4 PMID: 38553705

# Chapter 14
# Supporting Consumer Protection in the Phase of Green Washing:
## Endorsing Sustainable Development With Judicial Perspectives

**Bhupinder Singh**
https://orcid.org/0009-0006-4779-2553
*Sharda University, India*

**Christian Kaunert**
https://orcid.org/0000-0002-4493-2235
*Dublin City University, Ireland*

**Tarun Kumar Kaushik**
https://orcid.org/0000-0002-3279-8307
*Sharda University, India*

**Hind Hammouch**
https://orcid.org/0000-0002-5897-1649
*University Sidi Mohamed Ben Abdellah, Morocco*

**Laeeq Razzak Janjua**
https://orcid.org/0000-0002-1948-5859
*WSB University, Poland*

DOI: 10.4018/979-8-3373-2530-9.ch014

## ABSTRACT

*Since many consumers are worried about the ecological footprint of their purchasing decisions today, "green-washing" has only emerged as an even more pronounced phenomenon. It is nothing but just a misleading which defames the original initiative of making our environment sustainable. Consumer Protection Consumer protection laws and regulations are created to guarantee the rights of consumers in a market, as well provide access to transparency. It shows that fighting greenwashing calls for all stakeholders, from policy makers to companies and civil society organizations. The reliance of industry on voluntary measures to report performance means that transparency is a function of media campaigns, third-party certification and similar levels in accountability. The analytical angle of judicial enforcement is applied and ridicule out the rest as to base-case strategy that requires some legal reform in conjunction with existing consumer protection on which focus has been made under this chapter, conversely green washing mitigation.*

## 1. INTRODUCTION

In recent years, there has been a significant surge in global environmental consciousness, leading customers to seek out products or services that align with their sustainability and social responsibility principles. This alteration has resulted in an expanding market of commitments centered around environmental friendliness and sustainability. However, alongside this positive development, a highly concerning practice emerged: Greenwashing. Greenwashing refers to the deceptive practice employed by companies to mislead consumers about the true environmental effects of their products or services. This is typically done through the use of exaggerated promises that are often disguised using complex terminology. These deceptive marketing tactics undermine genuine attempts by responsible businesses to conduct themselves ethically (Apostu et al., 2023). Greenwashing poses a direct menace to all endeavors aimed at safeguarding consumers. Greenwashing is a strategic action that certain firms do to limit their market share and attract a specific group of purchasers who are growing more discriminating and demanding transparency in the items they purchase. This behaviour of perpetuates the loop of consumer suspicion towards corporations who view sustainability as a mere means of generating profit, hence impeding the success of genuinely sustainable businesses. Therefore, it is crucial that consumer protection mechanisms are rigorously implemented. The consumer protection laws are established to prevent individuals from unfair practices or fraudulent activities in trade. The purpose of this is to safeguard consumers by ensuring that they possess the requisite information to exercise their discretion in all circumstances. Moreover, in situations when misstatements may be promptly addressed, such as in cases of greenwashing claims, the implementation of these rules by users serves as a means to prevent deceptive advertisements. However, like any legislation, the effectiveness of these restrictions depends on their implementation and the ability of legal systems to interpret them while considering the nuances of environmental marketing. This article argues for the importance of adopting a comprehensive consumer-centric approach to address the problems associated with greenwashing. It suggests that firms should be cautious when making environmental claims and that a legal perspective is necessary to evaluate such claims. Courts should not only assess the veracity of claims, but also take into account the context in which those claims are made and the implications they have for consumers. Implementing a systemic approach theoretical framework will enhance the judiciary's ability to effectively accomplish its existing goals, which include safeguarding consumers from fraudulent activities and promoting sustainability. Although society is making progress towards sustainability, it is crucial to have a robust consumer protection framework to combat misleading techniques such as greenwashing. By upholding the principles of fairness and collaborating with all parties involved, utilizing legal expertise and effort, we may establish a revered marketplace where integrity retains its significance, so making a positive impact towards a more enduring world.

## 2. EFFECTS OF GREENWASHING ON CONSUMER CONFIDENCE AND THE INTEGRITY OF THE MARKET

Greenwashing undermines customer trust and market credibility by raising skepticism about the authenticity of sustainability assertions. The study focuses on analyzing the current legal frameworks in different jurisdictions, namely the Consumer Protection Act in the Indian context and the Guidelines for Prevention and Regulation of Greenwashing by the Central Consumer Protection Authority. These instruments aim to curb misleading environmental claims. The chapter highlights the need for "enhanced implementation of existing regulations and more explicit guidelines regarding environmental assertions." The argument proposes that courts should adopt a more comprehensive approach when determining whether greenwashing can be legally challenged. This would involve taking into account elements such as consumer comprehension and the overall scope or context of an advertisement, rather than solely relying on literal interpretations. Ultimately, the primary aim of consumer protection law is to protect customers from substandard and deceptive tactics. An increasing wave of greenwashing has emerged as corporations increasingly prioritize incorporating sustainability into their marketing strategies, leading customers to doubt the honesty around alternative products. Research indicates that consumers who have experienced greenwashing are less inclined to trust the brand and may exhibit caution towards future claims made by corporations. This skepticism may lead them to shift their preference from specific brands to all sustainable items. The absence of trust not only diminishes the significance of our purchasing choices, but also weakens the potential influence of genuine sustainability efforts. However, it not only causes consumer attitude to become unstable, but also weakens the trustworthiness of markets. Companies that engage in this form of systematic deception contribute to the ongoing perpetuation of an uneven playing field that favors unsustainable systems, placing truly sustainable enterprises at a disadvantage as they strive to catch up and remain competitive (Mondal et al., 2023). Resource misallocation occurs when consumers unknowingly support companies that do not follow sustainable policies. Consumer trust is crucial for their active involvement in the market and ultimately determines the long-term sustainability of the green trend. The enhancement of environmental assertions and regulatory actions fosters scientific precision and honesty in consumer markets, thereby augmenting market transparency. This not only aids in rebuilding consumer trust in these chemicals but also has the potential to advance overall inter-product sustainability (Gunay et al., 2023).

*Figure 1. Shows the effects of greenwashing on consumer confidence and the integrity of the market (Source- Original)*

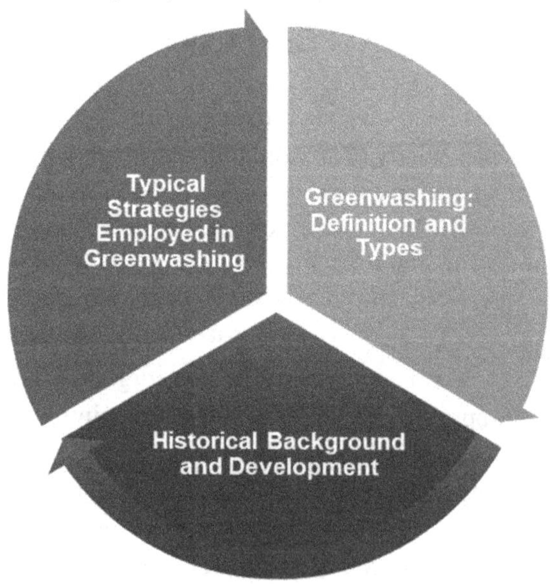

## 2.1 Greenwashing: Definition and Types

Greenwashing refers to the act of making false or deceptive statements regarding the environmental advantages of a product, service, technology, or enterprise. This kind of marketing, characterized by cynicism, aims to promote the perception of being environmentally conscious. However, it frequently conceals nefarious environmental actions instead. In 1986, environmentalist Jay Westerveld created the phrase "greenwashing" to criticize hotels that claimed to be environmentally friendly by encouraging guests to reuse towels, but were actually harming local surroundings through their expansion and other activities (Ye & Dela, 2023). Greenwashing encompasses a wide range of strategies and techniques aimed at deceiving consumers. Indefinite statements are a prevalent kind of communication used by businesses. However, instead of relying on concrete evidence or factual information, they often use ambiguous terms such as "eco-friendly" or "natural". Hidden trade-offs refer to situations where a product is claimed to be sustainable based on one feature, yet this one aspect may actually decrease the overall sustainability of the product more than it improves it. For instance, a car manufacturer may promote the fuel efficiency of its vehicles without disclosing the environmental impact of the manufacturing process. If your branding is well-executed and you possess appropriate visuals to remind an impartial reader of the increased vulnerability of dolphins (despite their previous state of well-being), it is not feasible to utilize the tumultuous ocean for sustainable kelp farming. An often cited counterfeit example involves incorporating foliage and other organic elements (even animals) into marketing materials just to create the illusion of being an environmentally conscious corporation, yet lacking any substantive commitment to sustainability in their operations. Greenwashing can undermine genuine sustainability initiatives by eroding customer confidence and creating market misunderstanding (Houssam et al., 2023).

## 2.2 Historical Background and Development

The concept of greenwashing has a long history, which mirrors the evolving views towards environmental responsibility and aligns with the growth of consumer awareness. The phrase "greenwashing" gained popularity in the 1980s, a period characterized by increasing environmental consciousness and consumer engagement in environmentally friendly practices (D'Angelo et al., 2023). Whether justified or not, environmental stewardship emerged as a brand attribute as public consciousness regarding environmental issues increased. Regrettably, the absence of stringent rules or mandated guidelines pertaining to this significant matter has resulted in many corporations adopting false labels, exploiting the popular trend of environmental consciousness. Has eco branding become excessively unrestrained?

This created an opportunity for unrestricted promotion, and as uncontrolled eco-friendly claims became more widespread (Short 65), various forms of deceptive environmental marketing practices also increased: from absolutely meaningless sustainability statements to deliberately crafted nature imagery that falsely imply environmental benefits. As high-profile instances of greenwashing continue to emerge and consumer awareness of digital transparency increases, there has been a corresponding rise in overall skepticism towards environmental claims. Meanwhile, customers have an additional means to exert pressure on businesses, which is via gaining a deeper understanding of a company's environmental practices through various channels of communication that involve taking action. In response, states have enacted their own laws and regulations to govern green claims. The citation is from Vasilescu et al. in 2023. The EU has enacted a similar regulation through the Unfair Commercial Practices Directive to make false promotion of environmentally friendly items illegal. Nevertheless, greenwashing remains a prominent issue, as an increasing number of corporations recognize the lucrative prospects in offering sustainable products. It is crucial to monitor changes in public knowledge regarding the regulation and policy clarification of greenwashing tactics in product naming rights, as well as the promotion of sustainability messaging (Cai & Le, 2023).

## 2.3 Typical Strategies Employed in Greenwashing

Greenwashing employs many strategies to mislead others into believing that items and services has ecologically friendly qualities. The utilization of ambiguous, insignificant, and unsubstantiated terminology is an ancient strategy, without a doubt. To ensure credibility, it is advisable to refrain from using phrases such as eco-friendly, natural, or green without providing supporting information to substantiate these assertions (Chen et al., 2023). Slagging refers to the act of belittling a political adversary, while greenwashing involves establishing deceptive impressions of environmental accountability, for as by utilizing visuals of nature reserves or wildlife (Barna et al., 2023). Greenwashes enhance their public image by selectively disclosing positive aspects of their operations while neatly omitting less favorable elements. This has created an illusion of greater sustainability than they actually possess. Other corporations employ rudimentary greenwashing strategies, such as marketing a limited selection of expensive yet ostentatiously “green” products or engaging in a solitary tree-planting initiative that falsely presents them as really environmentally conscious. However, these could potentially distract from more significant inquiries regarding the environmental sustainability of a corporation that primarily focuses on energy production. Labels that imply a product is environmentally friendly might deceive consumers by creating the perception of positive environmental impact, even without providing concrete data to support this claim. A clothing business may choose to withhold the complete disclosure of the extensive environmental consequences resulting from its production method, opting instead to label a collection as "conscious" or "sustainable". By employing deceptive strategies, greenwashers aim to get advantages from being linked to a supposedly eco-friendly sector, even when they do not bear the burdens or follow the environmental practices connected with it.

## 3. LEGISLATION SAFEGUARDING CONSUMER RIGHTS AND ADDRESSING DECEPTIVE ENVIRONMENTAL MARKETING PRACTICES, KNOWN AS GREENWASHING

Anti-consumer protection laws are a collection of regulations designed to safeguard the rights and welfare of consumers in the numerous activities conducted by industries. These are intended to enhance transparency regarding a novel product, ensuring customer safety and providing support for purchase decisions. Regulating greenwashing, which pertains to misleading representations of environmentally-friendly products or services, is crucial for safeguarding customers from false marketing claims. Consumer protection laws play a vital role in this endeavor.

*Figure 2. Stipulates the consumer protection laws and greenwashing (Source-Original)*

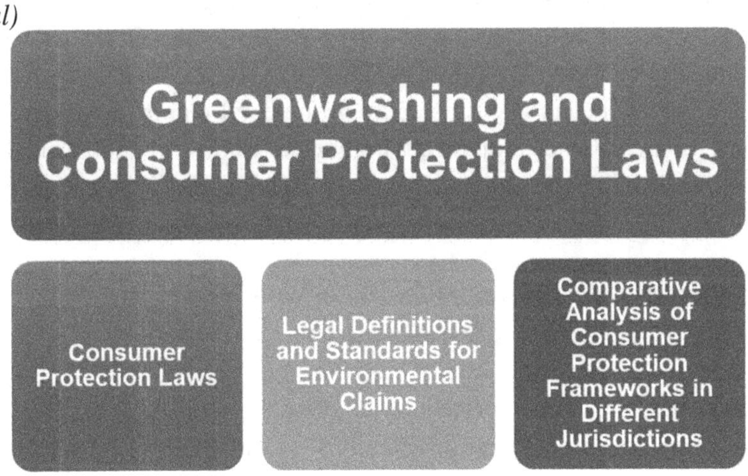

## 3.1 Overview of Consumer Protection Laws

In numerous jurisdictions, including India consumer protection laws specifically outlaw such fake or deceptive advertisements. For example, the 2019 Consumer Protection Act grants powers to the Central Consumer Protection Authority (CCPA) exercised by it in relation to misrepresentation including greenwashing. Guidelines defining greenwashing and environmental advertising claims were recommended with particular stress on substantiating evidence in California by the CCPA (California Consumer Protection Act). Broadly speaking, different countries around the world have established Consumer Protection legal frameworks for combating Greenwashing. The green economy, in order to enhance their competitiveness and resilience The European Union, too, has created guidelines on environmental claims in order to keep these factual and verifiable. In conclusion, consumer protection laws play a significant role in the fight against greenwashing and are necessary to create an environment where consumers can trust environmentally friendly claims from businesses which enable sustainable practices while protecting their rights (Huang & He, 2023).

## 3.2 Legal Definitions and Standards for Environmental Claims

Laws around the world define and create standards for environmental claims, with an intention to prevent businesses from misleading consumers by providing false facts or information-literally "greenwashing" (Liu et al., 2023). In the U.S., for example, the Federal Trade Commission (FTC) has created their own set of Green Guides advising marketers about using environmental claims in advertising and marketing. The Green Guides call for environmental claims to be substantiated, they must not be misleading and should have competent rigorously scientific evidence (Dzwigol et al., 2023).

## 3.3 Comparative Analysis of Consumer Protection Frameworks in Different Jurisdictions

Comparison of consumer protection frameworks concerning environmental claim also shows how much other jurisdictions, especially the USA, Australia and India differ. In the U.S., environmental claims are regulated by Federal Trade Commission (FTC) through Green Guides that help marketers avoid making misleading and deceptive advertising (Li et al., 2023). And the FTC announced that any environmental claim must be clear, direct and truthful. It would require companies to provide real substantiation for the claims they are making so that consumers were not mislead as to how green their products really were. Misleading or deceptive conduct in Australia is subject to extremely severe regulations enforced by the Australian Consumer Law (ACL). It is against the law for businesses to make false or misleading claims about their products under the ACL (Hutajulu et al., 2024). The Australian Government Regulatory and Consumer Commission (ACCC) strictly monitors the enforcement of these regulations, providing guidance on what would count as a permissible environmental claim while stressing that all claims made should be transparent and substantiated. In India, Central Consumer Protection Authority has been empowered by the Consumer Protection Act of 2019 to regulate misleading advertisements including those about environmental claims as it will also violate Rule 20. The CCPA has issued guidelines to reduce greenwashing and require companies for substantiating their claims & sharing relevant details with consumers (Wang et al., 2023).

## 4. JUDICIAL INTERPRETATION AND ENFORCEMENT

The judiciary, through its decisions, provides the enforcement machiner4y for consumer protection laws and challenges of green washing. With respect to the interpretation and enforcement of consumer protection statutes, courts play a key role in holding businesses accountable for making false environmental claims. That means that courts can help clarify what definitions and standards for environmental marketing should be so companies know when they might engage in deceptive practices. In a growing number of jurisdictions, courts are starting to accept that understanding how consumers perceive greenwashing allegations is crucial. With exercising judicial review, they create case law that strengthens the precedent for honest and transparent environmental advertising. Also, the courts can make things easier for consumers to get their grievances redressed by allowing individuals and collective grievance as regards a deceptive practice committed by companies. For the marketplace to be more just, it is precocious that by protecting consumption rights and punishing violators; these acts are put forward through courts. In the context of environmental claims, it is an activist judiciary that plays a pivotal role in melding consumer protection law so as to combat what many consider to be one of today's most common forms or deception of greenwashing.

### 4.1 Role of the Judiciary in Consumer Protection

One of the key players in enforcing consumer protection laws and checking greenwashing-related issues is the judiciary. If that is the ultimate goal, it would seem to require some font of interpretation and application - in this case courts - because enforcing consumer protection statutes depends on having a way to hold businesses accountable for deceptive environmental claims. Courts can clarify the definitions and standards for environmental marketing through judicial interpretation, thereby illustrating what qualifies as deceptive practices Courts are now starting to acknowledge the significance of how a reasonable consumer would perceive claims when ruling on greenwashing lawsuits. In the United States, cases like Dorris v. Danone Waters of America provide an interesting survey about how judges analyse whether potentially misleading terms - such as "carbon neutral"-would actually deceive a reasonable consumer. This judicial oversight helps to set a legal precedent that sends the message about accountability and truth in green marketing. In fact, the judiciary can also help in consumer redress by permitting consumers (individuals and groups) to file a lawsuit against those organizations that indulge in misleading activities. This holds consumers rights higher and simultaneously offers punishment to the violators, making it a fairer market place. All in all, the judiciary would play a pivotal role to construct of consumerism safe zone - notably for addressing one of perennial issue that is greenwashing.

## 4.2 Judicial Challenges in Adjudicating Greenwashing Claims

Resolving claims of greenwashing is an Ut challenge for the judiciary. A major challenge is the fact that environmental claims are some of the hardest cases to explain-the language and scientific data involved can often be complex or difficult for judge a jury member to understand. These can result in inconsistent judgements, as the courts may find it difficult to decide on whether a claim is misleading or not lest they have evidence to prove such a fact (Chaaben et al., 2024). A further difficultly is the changing nature of marketing practices and consumer expectations. The judiciary will need to implement a similar evolution of standing and other doctrines as companies adapt advertising strategies, so that new iterations of greenwashing are effectively handled. It involves teaching judges about the latest trends and norms in environmental marketing. Another problem is that it places the burden of proof with consumers who must show that a company has made deceptive claims. For the average consumer (whether that be a private individual or even an attorney without resources to do extensive research) this is no simple task (Garbis et al., 2023).

## 4.3 Advertising Practices

Many legitimate claims, in turn, may go unchallenged and consumer protection laws become less effective. Additionally, as jurisdictions continue to regulate CAM and IMS differently, it also can lead to challenges during the adjudication process. In the third leg of this scenario, even if everyone agrees that greenwashing is a marketing practice no one should be engaged in and say they oppose it, when we get down to specifics like what constitutes deceptive advertising practices or not can still leave both consumers and retailers scratching their heads. Because of this inconsistency, the judiciary is less likely to set clear legal standards - and therefore more difficult it will be for consumer protection laws to really defeat greenwashing (Nugroho et al., 2023).

*Figure 3. Specifies the judicial interpretation and enforcement (Source- Original)*

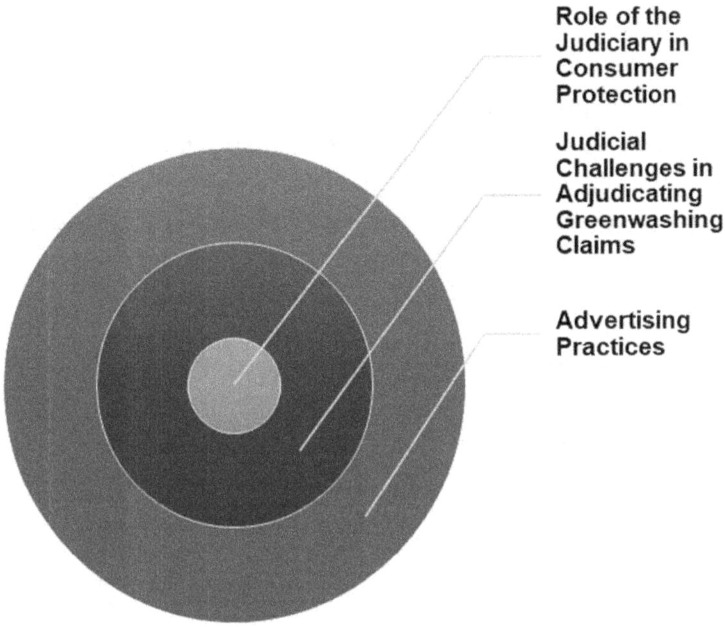


## 5. REGULATORY MEASURES AND ENFORCEMENT MECHANISMS

Regulatory Bodies to Prevent Greenwashing with a focus on how branding affects the earth, regulatory bodies have been crucial in regulating consumer protection laws when it comes to environmental claims (Ma et al., 2023). Some jurisdictions assign these organizations responsibility for upholding established standards and ensuring that businesses do not act in a materially misleading way - those to which the U.S. Chamber refers as "forces of labour ad misgovernment". For example, it is the Federal Trade Commission (FTC) in United States doing anti-deceptive advertising control enforcement, including environmental claims. The Green Guides published by the FTC outlined exactly how companies should make environmental marketing i.e. eco-marketing, a field that bared a strong resemblance to greenwashing so as not to deceive consumers. Also similar in that Environmental Protection Agency (EPA) uses technology to ensure regulation compliance and keep businesses from lying about the impact their operations have environmentally. Central Consumer Protection Authority (CCPA) under the Consumer Protection Act 2019, deals with such issues within India. Inconveniently, it is armed with the power to control advertising that is either fundamentally or materially misleading e.g. greenwashing- and having regard to consumer rights. The CCPA can release regulations aimed at stopping businesses from engaging in greenwashing, making companies prove their environmental statements. Consumer protection laws in Australia are administered by the Australian Competition and Consumer Commission (ACCC), which includes provisions relating to false or misleading representations as to environmental benefits. The ACCC also closely enforces compliance and can take action against companies who have engaged in misleading conduct. IMHO, these agencies are important long-term steps to keep market-place clean & consumers off perceiving fake-green claims by businesses more seriously.

## 5.1 Enforcement Mechanisms and Penalties

Without enforcement mechanisms in place to ensure laws are abided by and greenwashing is challenged, consumer protection will always fall short. Regulatory bodies have used a suite of tools to implement rules and fine firms they find using deceptive practices. INVESTIGATIONS AND INSPECTIONS: Regulatory agencies create their own enforcement mechanisms such as conducting audits or reviews of a company's marketing practices to ultimately determine if such guidelines are being adhered too (Simmou et al., 2023). This is a proactive approach that helps the regulators in flagging out possible violations before they turn into more serious issues. Penalties for non-compliance are levied based on a scale that corresponds to the seriousness of the offense. This includes monetary penalties, which act as a deterrent against deceptive advertising. As one example, the FTC has the right to levy hefty fines against companies who fail to meet regulatory standards around advertising guidelines and practices but in India which mandate something similar are armed with powers of penalties levied for misleading advertisements which have prejudiced consumer interests. On top of the financial ramifications, regulators can issue injunctions to halt further misleading advertising. This can mean requiring the company to undo its false claims, or even that it stops marketing certain ways altogether. Second, public accountability mechanisms (e.g., the publication of violators and issuance of enforcement press releases) serve to increase compliance by raising reputational costs for engaging in greenwashing. The net result is a potent enforcement regime comprising investigations, sanctions and transparency mechanisms which to the undoubted benefit of consumers facilitates true environmental responsibility on the market.

## 5.2 Effectiveness of Current Regulatory Frameworks

However, the ability of existing regulations to curb greenwashing and protect consumers naturally depends on where they are located. It is a work in progress, with some guidelines and enforcement mechanisms put into place but many problems left ahead. The FTC, EPA, CCPA and ACCC are regulatory bodies that attains power in ensuring legal compliance of consumer protection laws; including environmental claims. The FTCs Green Guides and the proposed greenwashing regulations in CCPA are some of these guidelines which have been issued by authorities to make clear what counts as deceptive environmental marketing (Purnamawati et al., 2023).

Companies are being held accountable using enforcement tools, such as investigations of companies and employees; civil penalties for violations; injunctions to stop fraudulent conduct in the future; a broad range of relief against companies that perpetrate fraud by repeated misstatements or omissions about material information affecting publicly traded company securities public accountability measures (e.g., denying wrongdoers access to U.S. capital markets); cost-effective investor protection aids like valid class and derivative action procedures (Sarwar et al., 2023). The process of international cooperation and harmonization is underway to set common specifications that will help in establishing uniform standards so the burden on businesses across borders can be minimized.

## 5.3 International Cooperation and Harmonization of Standards

Greenwashing represents a serious challenge and compliance with the standards of international cooperation, as well as effective consumer protection worldwide (Agrawal et al., 2024). Environmental claims should, therefore, be truthful and based on substantiated standards - as cross-border operations increasingly make the development of harmonised regulatory frameworks and standards necessary. The United Nations Economic Commission for Europe (UNECE) and the Organisation for Economic Co-operation and Development (OECD), among others, are key players in regulatory cooperation that help develop common standards. The UNECE calls for an integrated approach to technical regulations and standardization policies in support of international trade, ensuring consumer protection, environmental safety. The Directive calls upon member states to see that best practices in regulatory harmonization are adhered to, and this can have the benefit of increased transparency/accountability with regard to environmental claims (Hao & Fu, 2023). In a similar vein, the OECD supports international Regulatory Cooperation (IRC) as one of the generic tools referred to above that provides for interoperability and allows countries to collaborate in regulatory issues including environmental standards. The maintenance of only one public record makes harmonization-related compliance costs less for businesses, and reduces the risk that they may deliberately mislead stakeholders (for example through quoting cherry-picked performance metrics) - a problem known as greenwashing. Incentivizing countries to enact standards is beneficial in bolstering trust between consumers and businesses, as countries can exercise global influence on how claims will need to be substantiated (Kulakov et al., 2023). Global collaborations and the standardization of practices are essential to enhance a level playing field on the international market where consumers may buy with confidence safe in the knowledge that what they purchase is indeed eco-friendly.

## 6. PROMOTING SUSTAINABLE DEVELOPMENT THROUGH LEGAL MECHANISMS

Sustainable development is a fuzzy concept that has been variously defined, but never in terms of the law. We can nonetheless aggregate the following key components from extant legal frameworks and academic discourse: Children and upland women planting trees for the future 5 Sustainability pillar Intergenerational equity: The idea that Development should not come at a cost or compromise of needs present populations to meet their own modest developments long term Interventions our Future is in good hands sustainable development balances the requirements current generations one day its someone else problem now it must be yours too (Zhang et al., 2023). Conservation of Natural Resources are a necessity: For the needs of all future generations, it is imperative that natural resources like air, water and soil be kept safe from contamination as per sustainable development idea. A balanced and comprehensive approach will focus on the need to balance economic, social and environmental factors in decision-making. When an activity raises threats of harm to human health or the environment, precautionary measures should be taken even if some cause and effect relationships are not fully established scientifically (Obeidat et al., 2023).

### 6.1 Intersection of Consumer Protection and Environmental Law

Consumer protection law is different from environmental regulation in the field of sustainable development (Jayaraman et al., 2023). Consumer protection laws are designed to prevent unfair, deceptive or fraudulent practices in the marketplace and environmental law protects natural resources for both present as well as future generations. This is where the two areas of law meet, and where it matters for greenwashing - or baseless allegations about environmental benefits associated with a product. By invoking consumer protection laws, they can keep the companies responsible for such fraud to be answerable and ensure that there is full disclosure thus helping a common man make well informed decisions which would further strengths legitimate sustainability projects. In contrast, environmental law establishes the legal structure for controlling any activity that effects our environment like laws on air quality control, nuisance and waste management. Environmental law helps to advance sustainable development overall by making sure that businesses remain within environmental standards.

## 6.2 Legal Instruments Promoting Sustainability

These legal instruments on sustainability cover regulations, rules and frameworks crafted to incorporate the environmental component in several sectors. These are instruments which ensure that we go for economic development only at the cost of no ecological integrity or use any natural resource beyond their capacity. The EIA is one of the most important legal documents for developers and demands that they conduct a comprehensive analysis of their project's environmental consequences before moving forward. It has been vastly improved by year-on-year amendments; however, enforcement sometimes remains weak because often there are insufficient human resources to see this procedure through according to best practices dictated in legislation or policies. In this way, decision-makers are required to factor in environmental considerations at an early stage of development and encourage sustainable practices. Another framework is the Polluter Pays Principle which means that those who cause environmental damage or pollution should bear the costs of it. This will drive businesses to adopt sounder technologies and practices because if they don't it could cost them economically. In addition, international treaties like the Paris Agreement impose legally binding obligations on nations to curb their emissions and work towards sustainable living. Above all, they suggest that countries should work together on environmental problems in a global perspective to building sustainable management. In addition, incorporation of artificial intelligence (AI) either in environmental monitoring and compliance serves as a useful instrument for the new era to promote regulatory efficiency. The technology can be deployed to detect the routine violations and would optimize the distribution of resources thereby making enforcement effective on-ground. These laws taken together give a broad structure which emphasizes that ecological concerns be at the core of economic /developmental prospects and mechanism to bring about sustainability (Elshaer et al., 2023).

## 6.3 Role of Corporate Social Responsibility (CSR) and Environmental Governance

The sustainability of these regulations includes legal instruments, which are rules and frameworks developed to integrate the environmental aspect into various sectors. These are tools to make sure that we grow only at the expense of ecological integrity and not use more than nature can afford. The EIA is one of the environments clears meant for developers and requires them to incorporate full environmental study into their projects before getting permissions. That has been much ameliorated by the amendments over years; however, enforcement sometimes remains poor in practice as there are often not enough people working to follow this process properly by what is required of them with legislation or policy. Thus, this forces decisionmakers to integrate environmental considerations from the very beginning of development and thus promote sustainable behaviour. The Polluter Pays Principle (PPP) another framework that states those causing damage to the environment should pay for it. And it will push business to adopt more sane technologies and practices because if they do not, then the price might be economical. Moreover, renowned international agreements like Paris Agreement also place enforceable demands on countries to cut down their emission and propound long term living. Most importantly, they indicate that countries work with each other to address environmental issues in the context of global sustainable governance. Furthermore, use of artificial intelligence (AI) in environmental monitoring and compliance is a valuable tool that the new era can utilize to enhance regulatory effectiveness. The technology can be used to identify the frequent violations and would rationalize resources for better enforcement in the ground on a real-time basis. In combination with each other these laws together form a broad framework for enforcing ecological perspective to be central in economic /developmental perspectives and procedural net of promoting sustainability.

## 7. CHALLENGES AND OPPORTUNITIES

Both obstacles and opportunities manifest in such terms amidst battle cry for consumer protection regarding greenwashing. A key challenge centres around the increasing difficulty of understanding what companies mean when they refer to environmentally related terms - and it seems very little is actually spelt out in hard standards or definitions. Such ambiguity can deceive customers looking for real sustainable products, while undermining the work of valid environmental initiatives in general. Consumers often also bear the burden of proof, which can be an expensive and difficult process to challenge such assertions or for that matter find out what scientific data if any provided is actually true. Yet, to the same extent these are problems they are solutions as well in relation to consumer protection. Today, consumers are developing a greater appetite for awareness around the sustainability issues which can help ignite demand towards more transparency and accountability from businesses. Businesses will be more encouraged to do act genuinely sustainable if that is what consumer behaviour dictates in order not to lose their foothold in the market. Finally, through the creation of robust regulatory frameworks and guidance to detail what constitutes misleading environmental claims - giving consumers some teeth in enforcement so they can make informed decisions as well. In addition to this, the growing number of third-party certification programs and eco-labels also provide consumers with a trusted means of recognizing products which are genuinely sustainable. All Together Now By engaging with these opportunities, stakeholders can work together to confront greenwashing and build a consumer protection ecosystem in which meaningful sustainability is the priority (Mihai & Ulman, 2023).

## 7.1 Challenges in Combating Greenwashing

Greenwashing is a serious problem to solve, as it threatens the credibility of corporate businesses and hampers sustainable development efforts. One of the main challenges is that most environmental claims are a bit vague. Not to mention that there are many companies out used the term too much away from its real meaning by throwing terms like "eco-friendly", or "natural" and not having a true definition behind it. But, because of that murkiness consumers do not know when practices with true environmental benefits and those which have only the appearance of being green are indistinguishable from one another feeding doubt in all environmentally friendly claims. One of those challenges is the consumer burden of proof. Many have a requirement that the consumer must prove that they were misled, and this is often very difficult for an individual without access to scientific research or legal forensic resources. Is compounded by a cumbersome legal framework; the difference in laws and standards between nations opens up gaps where shady operators can partake in greenwashing without reprisal. At the same time, the pace and complexity of marketing tactics are changing which makes enforcement efforts challenging. Given businesses are ever evolving their strategies to skirt the existing norms, regulators need well Prompt mechanisms. Indeed, this has led to a dynamic environment that can easily challenge enforcement agencies without the necessary resources or expertise to keep up with state-of-the-art greenwashing techniques. Consumer awareness of their rights and the availability to seek redress in almost all states under Australian Consumer Law for environmental claims that are unsubstantiated can often be low. This knowledge gap can deter consumers from pursuing companies that participate in greenwashing - creating something of a vicious cycle. Tackling these challenges needs a broad solution framed around clearer regulations, better consumer education and robust enforcement mechanisms.

## 7.2 Opportunities for Strengthening Legal Frameworks

However, this notwithstanding, there exist significant scope to enhance policy frameworks via legally. There is a potential opportunity in the creation of more robust regulatory or standards framework around environmental claims. A concerted effort for defining terms such sustainably or eco-friendly can eliminate the risk factor and provide consumers with all the knowledge they need to make an informed decision. In addition, the proliferation of standing independent third-party certification programs offers a chance to build consumer confidence. They serve as trustworthy ways for consumers to recognize products that adhere to specific established environmental requirements and decrease the chances of greenwashing. Businesses; Penalizing only companies that do not participate in such certification programs would promote an atmosphere of transparency and ownership. Secondly, the use of technology and data tools would increase tracking as well as ensure compliance with environmental claims. These are sophisticated tools and they enable the regulators to zero-in far more accurately on deceptive marketing practices than otherwise done, which then assures that best-of-the-breed advertisement standards enforced by the system. This move toward greater technological integration ultimately serves as a way to modernize enforcement operations altogether and make regulatory frameworks more effective. On top of that, international participation and standard harmonization can make environmental claims implemented more uniformly cross-borders. Countries might work together to harmonize regulatory practices, reducing the cost of compliance for businesses and increasing consumer protection worldwide. This ultimately creates a more informed and assertive consumer base that in turn can ask businesses for increased transparency. The better the consumer knows about existing sustainability issues, the more willing they are to call out and demand for real sustainable solutions leading businesses towards marketing strategies that portray them as responsible. Overall, while fighting greenwashing remains difficult, there are plenty of openings to enhance the legal system. Stakeholders in the industry should keep leaning into clearer legislation, independent certifications, technological innovation, global collaboration and consumer education to cultivate a fairer marketplace for sustainable products - one that respects sustainability first & foremost as well as protects consumers.

## 8. ENHANCING LEGAL AND REGULATORY FRAMEWORKS

Strengthening legal and regulatory frameworks is essential to effectively combating greenwashing and achieving sustainable development. The definition of environmental claims is given and characteristics are set for a well-defined legal framework under which the businesses might seek to make them. One way of doing this might be to set out rules that specify when environmental marketing is misleading. These standards should be developed by regulatory bodies in collaboration with stakeholders such as consumer advocacy organizations, environmental groups and industry representatives. For example, defining words like "sustainable," "green" and even eco-friendly can remove ambiguity about their true meanings that will surely help better inform the consumer. Further, all existing laws such as the Consumer Protection Act should be amended to add clear provisions dealing with greenwashing. This would also involve requiring tougher sanctions for organizations practicing dark patterns and ensuring that the enforcement mechanisms are strong. They should also have adequate resources and powers for active monitoring compliance from regulatory bodies. Policy makers can foster an environment that discourages greenwashing and fosters genuine sustainability efforts by supplementing the legal frameworks to govern environmental claims. In addition, there is a need for international collaboration to standardize protocols across boundaries Since many businesses are now operating on a much more global basis, having standardised regulations could significantly lower the costs of compliance and help to create an equal footing. It allows countries to collectively learn from one another and work together in developing holistic measures against greenwashing.

### 8.1 Strengthening Judicial Capacity and Resources

A strong judicial increase in terms of capacity and resource is key to give bite to consumer protection laws which make up the lexicon that step on greenwashed feet. Courts are crucial for interpreting the legal framework and enforcing it, but their performance significantly depends on resources being allocated to them. This includes training judges and legal professionals in the field of environmental law as well as consumer protection. This training will help to better understand the intricate matter of greenwashing and provide tools for council officers when assessing potentially deceptive environmental clams. Additionally, ensuring access to legal resources - like expert witnesses and scientific data- strengthens the judiciary's potential for adequately addressing greenwashing cases. How to better evaluate environmental claims and the harms caused by false marketing is a topic that courts need more information on in order to do their job properly. This might include setting up special environmental courts or tribunals specializing in greenwash and sustainability issues. Moreover, the public deserves to be better informed on what the law says about protecting them against greenwashing. By understanding consumer rights and the instruments that backs them up, people can become a part of making misleading claims an exception rather than it being rule. The enhanced scrutiny could in turn result in a continuing stream of cases before the courts, illustrating the need for judicial control to help tackle greenwashing.

## 8.2 Encouraging Corporate Transparency and Accountability

Promoting corporate transparency and accountability is an integral part of enhancing sustainable development, as well a taking action against greenwash errors. Business is obliged to disclose the facts about its environments performance and Environmental claims must be true, not misleading and can easily verified. This can occur through the adoption of strong reporting frameworks that demand full and accurate disclosure by companies in relation to their environmental footprint, sustainability programs and rigorous verification methods for all alleged quantifications. Adopt independent third-party certification programs and eco-labelling initiatives By giving consumers trustworthy information on the environmental performance of goods and services, these programmes can set apart truly sustainable offerings from greenwashing. Participation in these programs can also help companies signal that transparency and accountability are paramount to their reputations, establishing consumer trust. In addition, businesses need to be incentivized with stakeholder dialogs on consumers, environmentalists and regulators. In seeking feedback from multiple sectors, companies are able to determine the concerns of consumers and ensure best practices for their sustainability objectives. This co-operative model could facilitate the establishment of well-recognised and effective industry standards, including those that foster transparency and accountability. In brief, upgrading legal and regulatory frameworks; building judicial capacity to process these kinds of cases quickly (both in the US as well as over time worldwide); incentivizing good behaviour among corporations would all be important strategies for advancing consumer protection globally when it comes greenwashing efforts. At the same time, we can begin working together to build a marketplace that centres true sustainability, guarantees consumer rights and breeds more responsible business behaviour by tackling these key areas in tandem.

## 9. CONCLUSION AND FUTURE SCOPE

It is evident that looking at existing legal frameworks, a few conclusions can be made on the effectiveness of objectives to tackle greenwashing. Regulatory bodies like the FTC, EPA and ACCC have authority oversea enforcement of consumer protection laws but inconsistency in these regulations across borders contributes to differing interpretations about what constitutes deceptive marketing practices. Consumers are often the ones who need to prove that an ad is false but they don't always have resources to do it. A number of important strategies come to the fore when considering how courts can be made more oracular. Improving legal and regulatory frameworks, including creating transparent, precise environmental claim requirements that have penalties for not following them is an essential first step. The Codependent Creation of Standards in which regulatory bodies build a consensus on the use of vocabulary such as "sustainable" or "eco-friendly", which would once again provide consumers with clearer options. In the second place, for consumers consumption laws to be enforced better there is a need to improve judicial ability and resources. Judges should have to go through specific training on environmental and consumer protection law, including access to expert witnesses and scientific data. Dedicated environmental courts or tribunals would help improve the judicial capacity to hear cases on greenwashing. Thirdly, to promote sustainable development it is essential that business transparency and accountability are encouraged. Companies need to be transparent in their claims about environmental stewardship and the extent of supply chains are on a sustainable footing. Such information may be realized through independent 3rd party certification schemes and eco-labelling initiatives that can improve the reliability of the promise, distinguishing between actual sustainable from those engaging greenwash recycling transactions. International cooperation and harmonization of standards are also important in that they foster global stakeholders to devise a more uniform view or approach related to environmental claims. By sharing regulatory best practices across borders, the world can lower business compliance costs and raise global consumer protection standards. Finally, preventing greenwashing and encouraging sustainable development require an effort on the part of all concerned-regulators including the judiciary or businesses or us constituents. A level playing field that gives priority to the real and not just greener businesses, which respects consumer rights, punishes companies who lie about their environmental performance; all this can be done with better legal frameworks in place complemented by judicial capacity building, corporate transparency through disclosures and international cooperation. The judiciary in particular are crucial to the meaningful interpretation and enforcement of consumer protection laws, by holding business accountable for their marketing practices and enabling consumers make informed choices that help deliver real environmental benefits.

Combating greenwashing and promoting sustainable development must be a multi-faceted approach. One of the viable solutions which spring to mind is developing transparent, detailed and enforceable environmental claims guidelines. Authorities also need to define 'eco-friendly' and other loose terms like accuracy as opposed to vague blurbs in order that companies cannot mislead the general public. The process should be transparent and involve stakeholders, who include consumer groups, environmentalist organizations as well the industry. Implementation of enforced rules is also a key to this. These regulatory agencies need to be well-resourced and have a depth of expertise that will enable them to catch those companies greenwashing. There need to be severe consequences that prevent businesses from conducting fraudulent marketing of this kind, and they can only really come in the form of crippling fines or lawsuits. Similarly, independent third-party certification programs and eco-labels can help inform consumers what the environmental impact is of products/ services; they also serve a function to reduce unscrupulous greenwashing. In the future, legislation and regulation to combat greenwashing will invariably need to sharpen further up. New and complex marketing techniques, increased concern over the environment all raise legal issues to be handled by appropriate laws. This will help towards an international alignment and conformity to environmental claims by borders, in so enhancing that the cost of compliance for businesses compared with more effective global consumer protection systems.

## REFERENCES


Agrawal, R., Agrawal, S., Samadhiya, A., Kumar, A., Luthra, S., & Jain, V. (2024). Adoption of green finance and green innovation for achieving circularity: An exploratory review and future directions. *Geoscience Frontiers*, 15(4), 101669. DOI: 10.1016/j.gsf.2023.101669

Apostu, S. A., Gigauri, I., Panait, M., & Martín-Cervantes, P. A. (2023). Is Europe on the way to sustainable development? Compatibility of green environment, economic growth, and circular economy issues. *International Journal of Environmental Research and Public Health*, 20(2), 1078. DOI: 10.3390/ijerph20021078 PMID: 36673838

Arsawan, I. W. E., Koval, V., Suhartanto, D., Hariyanti, N. K. D., Polishchuk, N., & Bondar, V. (2024). Circular economy practices in SMEs: Aligning model of green economic incentives and environmental commitment. *International Journal of Productivity and Performance Management*, 73(3), 775–793. DOI: 10.1108/IJPPM-03-2022-0144

Barna, C., Zbuchea, A., & Stănescu, S. M. (2023). Social economy enterprises contributing to the circular economy and the green transition in Romania. *CIRIEC-España, revista de economía pública, social y cooperativa*, (107), 47-69. DOI: 10.1108/IJPPM-03-2022-0144

Cai, L., & Le, T. T. (2023). Natural resources and financial development: Role of corporate social responsibility on green economic growth in Vietnam. *Resources Policy*, 81, 103279. DOI: 10.1016/j.resourpol.2022.103279

Chaaben, N., Elleuch, Z., Hamdi, B., & Kahouli, B. (2024). Green economy performance and sustainable development achievement: Empirical evidence from Saudi Arabia. *Environment, Development and Sustainability*, 26(1), 549–564. DOI: 10.1007/s10668-022-02722-8 PMID: 36320556

Chen, D., Hu, H., & Chang, C. P. (2023). Green finance, environment regulation, and industrial green transformation for corporate social responsibility. *Corporate Social Responsibility and Environmental Management*, 30(5), 2166–2181. DOI: 10.1002/csr.2476

D'Angelo, V., Cappa, F., & Peruffo, E. (2023). Green manufacturing for sustainable development: The positive effects of green activities, green investments, and non-green products on economic performance. *Business Strategy and the Environment*, 32(4), 1900–1913. DOI: 10.1002/bse.3226

Dzwigol, H., Kwilinski, A., Lyulyov, O., & Pimonenko, T. (2023). The role of environmental regulations, renewable energy, and energy efficiency in finding the path to green economic growth. *Energies*, 16(7), 3090. DOI: 10.3390/en16073090

Elshaer, I. A., Azazz, A. M., & Fayyad, S. (2023). Green management and sustainable performance of small-and medium-sized hospitality businesses: Moderating the role of an employee's pro-environmental behaviour. *International Journal of Environmental Research and Public Health*, 20(3), 2244. DOI: 10.3390/ijerph20032244 PMID: 36767609

Garbis, Z., McCarthy, E., Orttung, R. W., Poelzer, G., Shaiman, M., & Tafrate, J. (2023). Governing the green economy in the Arctic. *Climatic Change*, 176(4), 33. DOI: 10.1007/s10584-023-03506-3

Gunay, S., Kurtishi-Kastrati, S., & Krsteska, K. (2023). Regional green economy and community impact on global sustainability. *Journal of Enterprising Communities: People and Places in the Global Economy*, 17(6), 1118–1134. DOI: 10.1108/JEC-03-2022-0040

Hao, X., Fu, W., & Albitar, K. (2023). Innovation with ecological sustainability: Does corporate environmental responsibility matter in green innovation? *Journal of Economic Analysis*, 2(3), 21–42. DOI: 10.58567/jea02030002

Houssam, N., Ibrahiem, D. M., Sucharita, S., El-Aasar, K. M., Esily, R. R., & Sethi, N. (2023). Assessing the role of green economy on sustainable development in developing countries. *Heliyon*, 9(6), e17306. DOI: 10.1016/j.heliyon.2023.e17306 PMID: 37389081

Huang, W., & He, J. (2023). Impact of energy intensity, green economy, and natural resources development to achieve sustainable economic growth in Asian countries. *Resources Policy*, 84, 103726. DOI: 10.1016/j.resourpol.2023.103726

Hutajulu, H., Tahir, U., Utami, E. Y., Harsono, I., & Yuniarti, T. (2024). Green Growth Strategy and Environmental Policy Integration in Sustainable Economic Development: A Review of Bibliometric Analysis. *West Science Social and Humanities Studies*, 2(03), 474–482. DOI: 10.58812/wsshs.v2i03.761

Jayaraman, K., Jayashree, S., & Dorasamy, M. (2023). The effects of green innovations in organizations: Influence of stakeholders. *Sustainability (Basel)*, 15(2), 1133. DOI: 10.3390/su15021133

Kulakov, O., Popova, O., Popova, S., & Tomashevskaya, E. (2023). Investments in green business and corporate governance by Ukraine's cooperation with the European Union. [). IOP Publishing.]. *IOP Conference Series. Earth and Environmental Science*, 1126(1), 012011. DOI: 10.1088/1755-1315/1126/1/012011

Li, W., Bhutto, M. Y., Waris, I., & Hu, T. (2023). The nexus between environmental corporate social responsibility, green intellectual capital and green innovation towards business sustainability: An empirical analysis of Chinese automobile manufacturing firms. *International Journal of Environmental Research and Public Health*, 20(3), 1851. DOI: 10.3390/ijerph20031851 PMID: 36767217

Liu, R., Yue, Z., Ijaz, A., Lutfi, A., & Mao, J. (2023). Sustainable business performance: Examining the role of green HRM practices, green innovation and responsible leadership through the lens of pro-environmental behavior. *Sustainability (Basel)*, 15(9), 7317. DOI: 10.3390/su15097317

Ma, M., Zhu, X., Liu, M., & Huang, X. (2023). Combining the role of green finance and environmental sustainability on green economic growth: Evidence from G-20 economies. *Renewable Energy*, 207, 128–136. DOI: 10.1016/j.renene.2023.02.046

Mihai, F. C., & Ulman, S. R. (2023). Circular economy in Green Deal strategies. In *Sustainable and circular management of resources and waste towards a Green Deal* (pp. 49–63). Elsevier. DOI: 10.1016/B978-0-323-95278-1.00029-2

Mondal, S., Singh, S., & Gupta, H. (2023). Assessing enablers of green entrepreneurship in circular economy: An integrated approach. *Journal of Cleaner Production*, 388, 135999. DOI: 10.1016/j.jclepro.2023.135999

Nugroho, L. D., Melati, S. R., Wahyuliana, I., Pawestri, A., & Kurniawan, L. F. (2023, May). Legal Policy of Implementation Green Economy In the Tourism Sector To Realize Sustainable Tourism And Environment. [). IOP Publishing.]. *IOP Conference Series. Earth and Environmental Science*, 1181(1), 012018. DOI: 10.1088/1755-1315/1181/1/012018

Obeidat, S. M., Abdalla, S., & Al Bakri, A. A. K. (2023). Integrating green human resource management and circular economy to enhance sustainable performance: An empirical study from the Qatari service sector. *Employee Relations*, 45(2), 535–563. DOI: 10.1108/ER-01-2022-0041

Purnamawati, I. G. A., Yuniarta, G. A., & Jie, F. (2023). Strengthening the role of corporate social responsibility in the dimensions of sustainable village economic development. *Heliyon*, 9(4), e15115. DOI: 10.1016/j.heliyon.2023.e15115 PMID: 37095962

Sarfraz, M., Ozturk, I., Yoo, S., Raza, M. A., & Han, H. (2023). Toward a new understanding of environmental and financial performance through corporate social responsibility, green innovation, and sustainable development. *Humanities & Social Sciences Communications*, 10(1), 1–17. DOI: 10.1057/s41599-023-01799-4

Sarwar, H., Aftab, J., Ishaq, M. I., & Atif, M. (2023). Achieving business competitiveness through corporate social responsibility and dynamic capabilities: An empirical evidence from emerging economy. *Journal of Cleaner Production*, 386, 135820. DOI: 10.1016/j.jclepro.2022.135820

Simmou, W., Govindan, K., Sameer, I., Hussainey, K., & Simmou, S. (2023). Doing good to be green and live clean!-Linking corporate social responsibility strategy, green innovation, and environmental performance: Evidence from Maldivian and Moroccan small and medium-sized enterprises. *Journal of Cleaner Production*, 384, 135265. DOI: 10.1016/j.jclepro.2022.135265

Vasilescu, M. D., Dimian, G. C., & Gradinaru, G. I. (2023). Green entrepreneurship in challenging times: A quantitative approach for European countries. *Economic research-. Ekonomska Istrazivanja*, 36(1), 1828–1847. DOI: 10.1080/1331677X.2022.2093767

Wang, W., Zhang, D., Wang, H., Zhu, Q., & Morabbi Heravi, H. (2023). How do businesses achieve sustainable success and gain a competitive advantage in the green era? *Kybernetes*, 52(9), 3241–3260. DOI: 10.1108/K-07-2021-0614

Ye, J., & Dela, E. (2023). The effect of green investment and green financing on sustainable business performance of foreign chemical industries operating in Indonesia: The mediating role of corporate social responsibility. *Sustainability (Basel)*, 15(14), 11218. DOI: 10.3390/su151411218

Zhang, L., Xu, M., Chen, H., Li, Y., & Chen, S. (2023). Globalization, green economy and environmental challenges: State of the art review for practical implications. Front. *Financial and Trade Globalization. Greener Technologies and Energy Transition*, 16648714, 133.

# Chapter 15
# Deep Learning-Driven Smart Fashion Recommender for Modern Shoppers

**K. Tamilarasi**
*Vellore Institute of Technology, Chennai, India*

**K. Arthi**
*SRM Institute of Science and Technology, India*

**Dhanalakshmi Teekaraman**
https://orcid.org/0000-0001-8039-3120
*Jerusalem College of Engineering, India*

**B. Bharathi**
https://orcid.org/0009-0001-1068-996X
*R.M.K. Engineering College, India*

**T. Chandrasekar**
https://orcid.org/0000-0003-3591-2205
*Kalasalingam Academy of Research and Education, India*

**S. Nalini**
https://orcid.org/0000-0003-2393-5848
*SRM Institute of Science and Technology, India*

## ABSTRACT

*In today's world, everyone is busy with daily routines, making it hard to focus on attire. Busy schedules make shopping in stores increasingly outdated, and technology has rapidly advanced online shopping. Artificial intelligence creates virtual shopping experiences on e-commerce websites, allowing everything to be done with a single click. The proposed system can understand user input, whether an image or text, and recommend related products. Users have individual logins with a personalized wardrobe feature to track styles they've tried. A new "Recommendation" feature helps users quickly choose from available options, with an added comment feature for feedback. Users can also edit and delete their wardrobe collection. A chatbot is*

DOI: 10.4018/979-8-3373-2530-9.ch015

*available to guide users and answer queries anytime, enhancing convenience and user experience.*

## 1.INTRODUCTION

The fashion industry is a continually evolving field where trends shift quickly, making it difficult for customers to sort through the plethora of online apparel selections. As a result, fashion recommendation engines have become indispensable resources for improving the e-commerce experience. These systems make use of cutting-edge technology, such deep learning, to deliver users tailored outfit recommendations that suit their individual interests and tastes. The topic of fashion advice has undergone a significant change thanks in large part to deep learning techniques. The remarkable capacity of the ResNet-50 convolutional neural network, or CNN, to extract rich and discriminative information from images has made it a popular choice among the many deep learning designs. Fashion recommendation systems can accurately evaluate and comprehend visual attributes of clothing goods, such as colour, texture, pattern, and style, by utilizing ResNet-50.

The Fashion Recommendation System (FRS), which uses ResNet-50 as its primary technology, is introduced in this section. We will examine how ResNet-50 is used to analyse and encode fashion photos in the upcoming sections. This will result in a strong feature representation that serves as the basis for customized outfit suggestions. Additionally, we will investigate the idea of content-based recommendation, which uses the feature representations that ResNet-50 collected to offer clothing items that closely correspond to users' visual preferences.

We will also talk about the FRS's flexibility and ongoing development thanks to machine learning techniques. In the e-commerce fashion industry, this flexibility guarantees that the system stays current with shifting fashion trends as well as user preferences, which eventually leads to better user engagement, higher conversion rates, and higher customer happiness.

Fashion recommendation systems have the potential to revolutionize online shopping by utilizing ResNet-50 technology and sophisticated suggestion methodologies. This might lead to a more efficient, personalized, and delightful online buying experience for customers. By giving consumers personalized and eye-catching recommendations, ResNet-50 and profound deep learning are altering the fashion business. This investigation seeks to shed light on this process.

## 2.LITERATURE SURVEY

The existing work that is currently being done can both provide visual explanations and record the user's choices for features that are visible. The Dual-direction Two-Layer Adaptive Attention Reviews Models and the Review-driven Visual Attention Model are the algorithms that are employed by Q.Wu et. al (2020). Based on the product image and historical assessment, a Visual & Textual Jointly Enhanced Interpretable (VTJEI) framework has been presented for fashion recommendations. By combining textual and visual information, the VTJEI can offer recommendations and explanations that are both more accurate and visually appealing. Record the user's apparent and hidden preferences for the intended product and, by underlining specific terms, offer textual explanations. Receive a customized picture representation based on the user's preferences gleaned from past reviews. By emphasizing certain areas, the combined improvement of textual and visual information is not only accomplished but also gives a visual explanation. Finally, our model's superiority on Top-N suggestions is verified through numerous tests conducted on real datasets. Additionally, a labeled dataset is constructed for a quantitative assessment of our explanations, both visible and invisible. The outcome demonstrates that the system can offer recommendations that are more accurate in both textual and visual explanations.

Jing et. al (2022) proposed a tripartite graph standardized latent low-rank representational method (TGRLLR) for fashion compatible prediction to improve fashion compatibility prediction. By breaking down the initial feature matrix in both the row and column directions, the latent low-rank representations were considered in TGRLLR to address the issue of insufficient observations and learn more low-dimensional and efficient representations. To produce more useful representations, various regularization algorithms have been simultaneously used to encode the geometrical forms of outfits, the high-order interactions among items, and the hierarchical correlations among attributes. Comprehensive tests carried out on an actual dataset show how effective our suggested approach is when compared to the most advanced technique, and the clothing's quality provides both written and visual explanations. We validated our model's superiority on Top-N suggestions through extensive trials on real datasets. The outcome demonstrates that recommendations made in both written and visual explanations were more correct.

Using an innovative Attentive Attribute-Aware Fashionable Knowledge Graphic (A3-FKG) to create the relationship between different clothes with both outfit- and item-level qualities, the task of customized outfit preference prediction is carried out by H.Zhan et. al (2022). To also capture the user's desire, a two-level attention method is developed: The user's fine-grained preferences are captured via a specific to users' relation-aware attention layer and concentrating on distinct connections to learn clothing representation. The user's latent heterogeneous interests are characterized by the target-aware attentive layer, which uses behavior sequences to learn user representation. Comprehensive tests on a fashion outfit dataset show notable gains over existing approaches, confirming the superiority of our suggested strategy.

Y. Ding et. al (2022) proposed a unique Cognitive Content-level Translation-based Recommender (ACTR) architecture that predicts the intent-specific transition probability and the immediate user intent of each transition simultaneously. The three basic domain-specific relationships—match, replace, and others—between nearby items that users interacted with have been specifically used to describe instant intent. A variety of content-level elements have been added to the item-level transition modelling with several sub-transitions to better utilize the features of the fashion domain and address the item transition sparsity issue. To further efficiently combine various content-level transitions, an attention technique is being further developed. This was the first study to explicitly state the instantaneous, implicit user activities during online fashion shopping, which improves the suggestion performance and increases the connection of fashion goods. The efficiency of the suggested strategy in sequential fashion advice is demonstrated by extensive research on two real-world fashionable commerce datasets.

To forecast consumer feedback based on online evaluations of fashion products, an aspect-based fashionable recommendation model that uses attention mechanism (AFRAM) was suggested by W. Li et. Al (2020) in this study. By using two parallel channels of convolution neural network models (the CNN), networks of short- and long-term memory (LSTM), and attention processes, this model may gather latent aspect characteristics about persons and items separately. User reviews are processed by one method, while item reviews are handled by the other. To obtain local aspect attributes and global aspect features, respectively, CNN and LSTM are connected to an attention mechanism on each path. These features are then integrated via a mutual operation module. The mutual actions on both pathways have the potential to improve the AFRAM model's generalization. To forecast users' ratings, the features that were taken from the two pathways are combined even more. AFRAM was trained and tested using actual customer evaluations and ratings that were gathered from two well-known company websites. The experiment's outcomes show that, when compared to multiple cutting-edge fashion recommenders, AFRAM performs better in predicting client ratings.

The kind of clothing, hair color, and accessories that are taken from a human body are examples of soft biometrics qualities that are valuable for tracking and identifying individuals. Researchers continue to have difficulties in semantically segmenting these qualities from photos due to the wide range of garment designs, layering, forms, and colors. A framework for garment segmentation called EPYNET has been presented by A. De Souza Inácio et. al (2020) as a solution to these problems. The

EfficientNet model serves as the foundation for EPYNET, which is built upon the Single Shots multiBox Detectors (SSD) as well as the Feature Pyramid Networks (FPN). To improve segmentation accuracy, the framework also incorporates noise reduction and data augmentation approaches. A recently proposed dataset called UTFPR-SBD3 has 4,500 manually annotated photos categorized into 18 kinds of objects, in addition to the backdrop. In contrast to publicly accessible datasets that exhibit unbalanced class distributions, and the UTFPR-SBD3 features a minimum of 100 occurrences per class, hence reducing the challenge of training deep learning models. The challenge of comparing disparate datasets for apparel segmentation led to the introduction of a new dataset imbalance metric. Such a metric allows one to identify classes with little items, classes with an excessively high or low number of instances, and the impact of the background. The usefulness of EPYNET is demonstrated by experimental results on UTFPR-SBD3, where it outperforms the state-of-the-art techniques for apparel segmentation on public datasets. These findings lead us to conclude that the suggested method has a wide range of practical applications in the actual world, including image description, clothing selection, soft biometrics, and people surveillance.

These days, recommendation engines are a must, particularly for online retailers. Lately, most recommendation algorithms that are employed in numerous fields have drawn notice and have been emphasizing apparel and fashion. Ü. Turkut et. al (2020) proposed an online recommendation system using a Convolutional Neural Network, also called deep learning. The CNN architecture's classes of various patterns have been established based on the interests of users and designers. The deep learning system makes recommendations for patterns that take textile product color compatibility into account. 12000 photos from our own patterns' dataset were used to train and evaluate the suggested model. Tests conducted on pattern datasets demonstrate the efficacy of our suggested methodology.

There aren't many systems that have been developed to do the job of proposing clothing that someone currently has, i.e., from their personal wardrobe. The latter problem has been addressed in this study by M. Jain et. al (2020), which also conducted an in-depth investigation of the many Machine Learning methods that can be applied to complete the assignment. The recommender system deviates from the conventional method in that it requires the recommendations to be made from the user's own wardrobe. In addition, the paper provides a thorough explanation of the outcomes of the tests that were carried out and identifies the optimal strategy along with suitable rationale.

X.Liu et. al (2021) proposed a revolutionary fashion collocation framework called Neural Graph Filtering, which uses a graph neural network to simulate a flexible set of fashion products. Each garment's visual embeddings have been regarded as a node in a graph, and the edge connecting nodes represents the inter-garment link. This framework is independent of the ordering of the inputs and outputs and supports a range of input and output numbers by using symmetric computations on the edge vectors. Furthermore, to facilitate the aggregation of significantly divergent styles—which are naturally unbalanced in the training set—a style classifier supplemented with focus loss has been added. The Amazon Fashion database has been rearranged using thoroughly thought-out evaluation criteria to enable an extensive investigation on varied fashion collocation. Three widely used benchmarks—the Polyvore data set, the Polyvore-D data set, and the restructured Amazon Fashion dataset—have been used to assess the suggested methodology. According to extensive experimental results, this methodology performs over 10% better on the conventional Area Under the Receiver Operating Curve (AUC) metric than state-of-the-art methods. More significantly, in the real-life perception survey, 82.5% of consumers preferred the diversified style recommendations above other options.

M.Ahsan et. al (2020) critically examined the potential for wearables and other smart apparel to generate Big Data, with particular attention on applications in sports, fashion, and healthcare. Modern data analytics frameworks and techniques for health monitoring are also covered in the paper. A unique data analytics system that can make accurate decisions in both routine and urgent medical scenarios is then suggested. The unique framework that is being presented identifies and examines the sources of Big Data derived from the human body. It also covers data collecting, communication, storage, analytics, and decision-making processes that utilise Artificial Intelligence (AI) algorithms.

AI systems can provide highly tailored fashion recommendations by utilizing user preferences, measurements of the body, and style selections. The seamless integration of several input modalities, including as text, photos, and sketches, facilitates the easy communication of design concepts between designers and consumers. The main findings by Z. Guo et. al (2023) demonstrated the revolutionary potential of improved personalization as well as seamless multimodal interfaces, enabling customers and designers to collaborate on the creation of distinctive and customized designs. Within the fashion sector, this paradigm change encourages a higher degree of engagement and inventiveness. Accepting this development opens up previously unheard-of possibilities for companies, consumers, and designers and ushers in a new phase of inventiveness and originality in the fashion industry.

Fashion brands are using social media more and more for marketing communications, thus it's important to analyze and get fashion knowledge about them scientifically. Social brands are making investments in them as a result. They can comprehend the preferences of the customer in this way. Data analysis on social media is being significantly impacted by this trend as well. Because of its capacity for automated learning, deep learning (DL) techniques have shown to be successful in resolving this problem. Nevertheless, there is still a dearth of systematic research on the use of deep learning (DL) by researchers to analyze fashion expertise from social media information. Thus, this work describes DL-based methods for fashion-related social media data. M. Mameli et. al (2022) presented an overview of the fashion industry dataset and the deep learning techniques used to analyze it, with the goal of assisting upcoming scholars who may be interested in this area. Specifically, five tasks will be taken into consideration: Fashion Classification, Clothes Production, Automatic Fashion Information Extraction, Clothes Landmark Recognition, Clothes Parse and Product Retrieval, and Clothes Detection. Thus, the goal of this study is to highlight the various ways that deep learning techniques are applied in the fashion industry. Nevertheless, only Deep Learning techniques have been examined in this review, leaving out other approaches. This decision was made because Deep Learning techniques outperform other methods in terms of precision and time, especially considering the enormous quantity of fashion online information that has been gathered.

To enhance fashion recognition, a Fashion Attribute Recognition Net (FARNet) built on a multi-task learning structure has been presented in this research by Huang et. al (2021). FARNet predicts three different kinds of garment qualities at once rather than one at a time. After training, the network uses the noisy labels to produce correct labels using the input photos. According to experimental results, this strategy performs noticeably better than current ones. We describe Asian fashion patterns and street styles according to predicted labels as well as image clusters using latent feature vectors by applying the trained algorithm to the RichWear dataset.

R.Koshy et. al (2021) suggested a system that functions as a customized fashion consultant. To do this, "Pocket Fashionista," a personalized fashion advisor, is launched. It offers users advice for the best outfits and color combinations depending on their complexion, ensuring that they look wonderful and are comfortable about their physical appearance. To better grasp how the suggested outfits and combinations of colors look on them, users can also picture these suggested outfits on themselves. The user is also given seasonal recommendations based on weather data. As a result, the system will assist sales representatives, merchants, and e-commerce websites in understanding customer demand in real time.

By gaining an understanding of users' dynamic preferences over items through sequential user-item interactions, Sequential Recommender System (SRS) proposed by S. Wang et. al (2022) seek to forecast the next item that a user may find interesting. Most SRSs in use today simply model a user's primary preference for an item's functionality, ignoring the user's auxiliary visual preference for an item's appearance and style. In this research, we propose modeling users' visual preferences to bridge this gap and enhance sequential recommendation performance. To learn a user's primary preference, visual preference, and the relationships between them simultaneously, a connected Double-chain Preferences learning Net (DPN) was developed.

In DPN, a user's primary preference is modeled using the item IDs as the input in one chain, while their visual preference is modeled using the item appearance images in a different chain. Lastly, a meticulous integration of the two preference kinds is done with a module for attention for the next element prediction. Comprehensive tests on several real-world transaction datasets demonstrate our suggested DPN's superiority over the representative and cutting-edge SRSs.

Neural Outfit Recommendation (The NOR) is a unique neural network framework that concurrently generates abstractive comments and outfit recommendations. The two components of NOR are comment generating and outfit matching. Lin et. al (2018) suggested a CNN (Convolutional Neural Network) using a mutual attention strategy to extract visual information for outfit matching. Next, a rating score for the corresponding prediction is generated by decoding the visual information. A cross-modality attention system combined with a controlled recurrent neural network, or RNN, was employed for abstractive comment creation, turning visual data into a succinct statement. The two components are trained together using an end-to-end backward propagation paradigm and a multi-task learning framework. Comprehensive tests on a real-world dataset gathered from the field as well as an existing dataset demonstrate that NOR significantly outperforms state-of-the-art baselines in outfit recommendation. The generated comments might be thought of as justifications for the outcomes of the recommendations.

B. Wu et. al (2022) was to increase suggestion quality using fine-grained modeling for product features. The visual as well as functional aspects of a product, or its look and functionality, were initially separated out as distinct features. One realization is that, for products in the visually aware domain (clothing, for example), the visual feature is critical, while for products in the visually non-conscious domain (office products, for example), the functional characteristic is more significant. To integrate the two aspects and estimate user preferences on items, a novel probabilistic model was developed and dubbed Visual & Functional Probabilistic Matrix Factoring (VFPMF). However, parameter learning from indirect input presents an efficiency hurdle when using such an expressive model. A computationally effective learning system based on alternate least squares was developed to overcome the technological difficulty. Moreover, an online algorithm updating process is given, which helps to clarify how to modify our approach for real-world recommendation scenarios where a constant flow of data is present. Comprehensive tests on four real-world datasets show that our approach works well for both online and offline protocols.

A Personalized Attention Networks (PAN) for fashion advice was presented in this research by H. Zhan et. al (2021). A user encoder as well as an item encoder, and a choice predictor make up the essential parts of PAN. An attention net was created to include the learned user representations into its encoder component, thereby simulating the diverse interests of users. More precisely, a sequence of user-aware channel-level as well as a spatial-level sub-module make up the attention module. Additionally, a unique ranking system with a user-specific loss is suggested to pique the curiosity of various people wearing the same outfit. A novel online severe negative mining technique that is aware of the user is offered to improve the effectiveness and efficiency of the training.

H. Zhang et. al (2020) offered a novel approach to clothing matching by taking item in-between compatibility into account. Unlike how the visual characteristics of the clothing items were used, the basic features of the textual descriptions were limited to title lines. More specifically, feature embeddings of title sentences were performed using a long-short term memory, or LSTM, network. Siamese LSTMs were utilized to generate feature embeddings for item pairs of candidates and queries. These embeddings were then incorporated into a style-compatible space that was identified by a compatibility matrix. Three substantial clothing item sets that were gathered from Polyvore, Taobao, and Amazon, respectively, were used to test our approach.

L. Zhong et. al (2021) used a fashion dataset to test transfer-learning enabled object detection on fashion detection. To be more precise, the process involves first compressing data used for testing and training into the ".tfrecord" file type and then uploading both the data and the bounding box labels to Google Cloud Storage. Google's Deep Learning open-source applications programming interface (API), Tensorflow Object Detection, is used in the training process after the pre-trained model as well as training parameter have been configured. Lastly, our model obtains good prediction accuracy on the Color-Fashion Dataset under specific conditions. Additionally, this study uses Android Studio to visualize the work using a lightweight framework on the Android OS.

## 3. PROPOSED SYSTEM

Shopping plays a vital role in everyone's day-to-day lives. From purchasing everyday requirements to buying products for personal satisfaction, there is trade occurring in one or the other form. Purchasing all these items is what is being done when all that people require is to buy products that they like. When there is a wide variety of options to select from, more than half of the people go for the immediate choices that they are encountered with. This is because people often find it difficult to devote time to understanding their likes and dislikes and proceed with purchasing. This may be due to the packed work schedule or that the people are unaware of the styling options that suit them. This may even seem to be a setback in how presentable one looks. However, with the advancements in technology, things have been modified to understand the mindset of users and provide them with the correct styling options that they are looking for.

The scope of the research work is to address the above-mentioned issue. At present there are various number of software programs that have been developed and in development that makes shopping a fair and easy choice with technological information. However, they don't provide an effective and interactive way of recommendations to choose from. The proposed system overcomes the drawbacks of a typical shopping scenario into a modernized case where things get done spontaneously with much ease.

The main objective is to provide the users with a better alternative to usual shopping scenario by developing an exclusive web application that addresses the features like Recommendations as requested by the user through an image or textual input, Wardrobe options with Category management and Product management where a personalized wardrobe collection is maintained as preferred by the user. For the recommendations, a Deep Learning (DL) based algorithm called RESNET50 is used. The application also has a chatbot to answer their queries through active interaction.

The proposed system facilitates the development of the application with the core functionalities of a Recommendations as requested by the user through an image or textual input using RESNET50, a Deep Learning algorithm, Wardrobe options with Category management and Product management where a personalized wardrobe collection is maintained as preferred by the user. The algorithm has got its roots in Convolutional Neural Network, where the data present in the dataset undergoes iterations as many number of times, until an optimized output is obtained. Additionally, the application also has observable contributions in the field of Machine Learning, Natural Language Processing and Artificial Intelligence. Furthermore, the application has an easy-to-use interface that facilitates smooth navigation over different available pages in the application.

The proposed system provides a well-defined algorithm logic that provides suitable recommendations that align well with the requests made by the user. The application allows creation of a personalized wardrobe setup which keeps varying as per the preference of the user. The system also has a comment section where the user can keep tabs on the products which they prefer by adding a comment to them. The comments added using this feature is subjected to that user only. This prevents the chances of other users accessing the platform from getting influenced by the common public reviews.

## System Architecture

There are three primary components to the suggested system:

- Pre-processing of images
- Recommendation engine
- Web application

The architecture diagram as shown in Figure 5 defines the fundamental structures of a software system and the discipline of creating such structures and the structured solution of the proposed idea. The admin will permit the user to enter the website if he/she is an authorized user. Once on the home page, the user can choose for which page they wish to navigate. The user provides the input either in text or image form which will be processed with the entries stored in the database and the relevant recommendations will be provided as output. The user can also add their preferred options into a wardrobe and create a personalized collection. The user can add comments to the options making it easier for them to review it later for future purposes. The user will also be provided with chatbot and language options to enable interactive conversations.

*Figure 1. System architecture diagram*

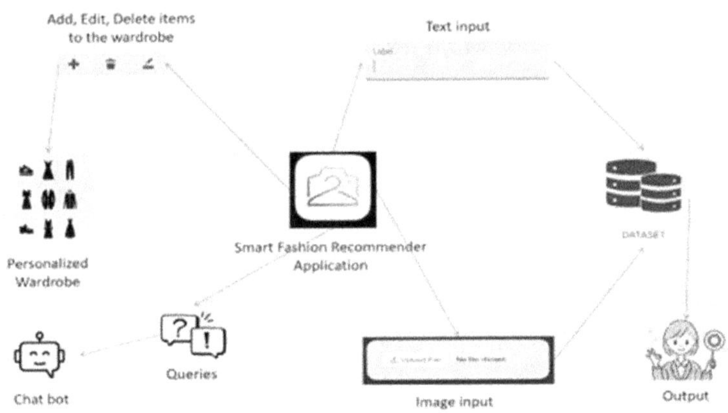


## Dataset

As of 2024, 44,441 photos were taken from Kaggle's Fashion product make up this dataset (Figure 2). For a total of 100 objects, we chose 10 pictures from each of the 10 categories in the Fashion-MNIST dataset. We made the decision to use most of the photos that did not feature people carrying bags, shoes, or clothing when choosing which ones to use. We took this decision because we eliminated characteristics that would have produced a dataset that resembled the Fashion-MNIST dataset. We used the following procedures to transform the RBG photos into images resembling those in the Fashion-MNIST dataset: Adjust the shortest side by 28 pixels, center crop, convert to one channel of grayscale, normalize into [0–1], and then change the white backdrop to black in accordance with Fashion-MNIST.

*Figure 2. Fashion product images*

The pictures shown in Figure 3 are from the Product Images Dataset on Kaggle Fashion. After the inventory has been classified and embedded using neural networks, recommendations are generated based on the output. Figure displays an example of inventory data.

*Figure 3. Product images dataset on Kaggle*

## Image Preprocessing

In the overall scheme of ResNet-50, picture preprocessing refers to getting images ready for use according to this deep learning architecture as shown in Figure 4. Important processes include scaling photos to a predetermined size (e.g., 224x224 pixel), performing random changes to data augmentation, mean subtraction, normalizing pixel values (usually in the range of [0, 1] or standardised), and consistent preparation during inference and training stages. By following these procedures, the model's capacity to analyse images efficiently, increase training stability, and adapt well to new data is ensured.

*Figure 4. Working of convolutional neural networks*

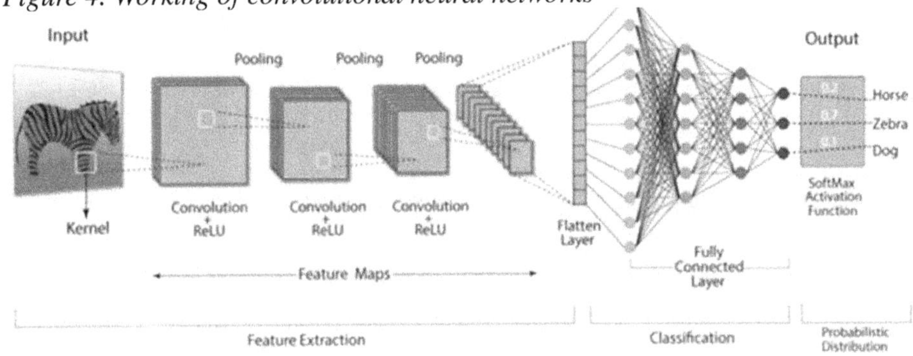


Pre-processing the image involves the following steps:

- *View the picture:* The user-provided image is used as input and is kept on the server in a temporary folder.
- *Resize the picture:* The generated image is adjusted to match the input size (224 x 224) that the model was trained with.
- *Segmentation:* To improve feature extraction, the stored image is transformed from RGB into BGV at this stage.
- *Flatten:* In this phase, the image's 2D matrix is transformed into a vector after preprocessing the saved

## Recommendations

*Figure 5. Browsing an image (User input)*

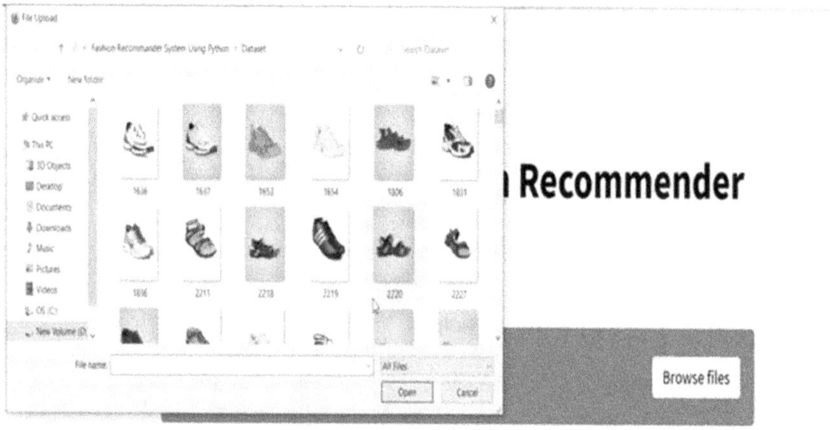


The user makes requests by providing textual details or uploading an actual image as shown in Figure 5. The application responds to the user's input by analyzing, processing and identifying the relevant solutions stored in the database and provides them as suitable recommendations for the user's input as shown in Figure 6 and Figure 7. A pre-trained Convolutional Neural Network (CNN) based model for image classification called RESNET50 is used. ResNet stands for Residual Network and is a specific type of CNN.

*Figure 6. Uploading fashion item of user's interest*

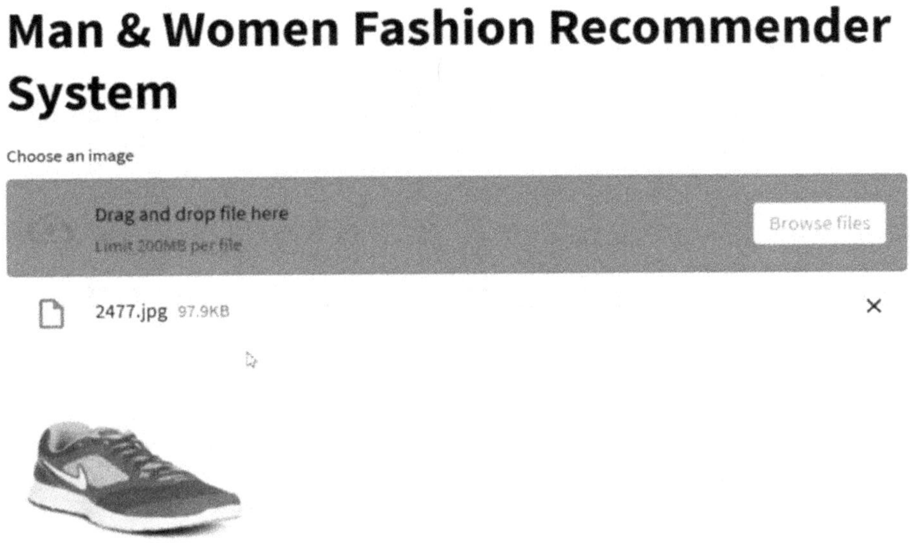


*Figure 7. Recommendations for the user's interest*

## Product Management

Each category has got a variety of different items with varying brands, color options and cost details. All the items are stored into separate fields based on what category they belong to. The system makes use of dataset downloaded from open-source community software that serves as storehouse of numerous datasets.

*Figure 8. Uploading fashion item of user's interest*

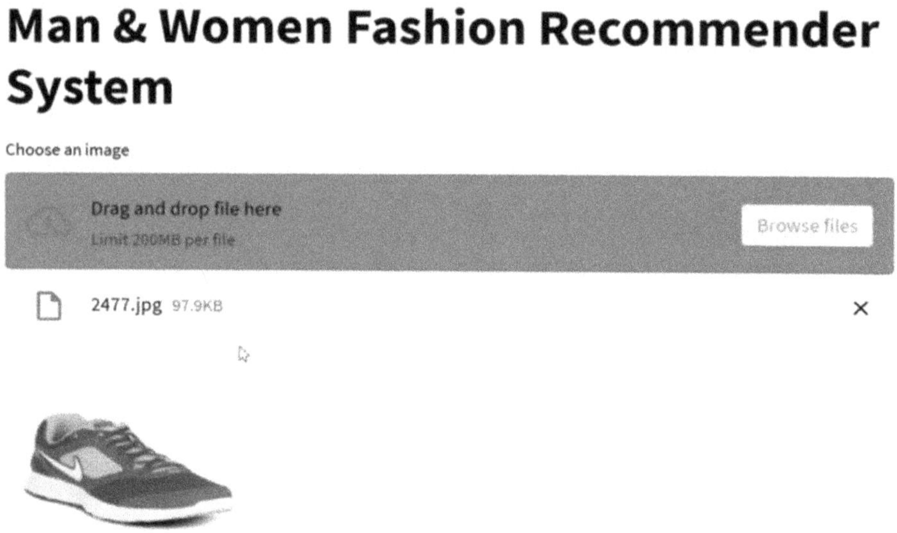


## Dataset Preparation

Data is collected from open-source database community. It is then downloaded to the local machine and used in the RESNET50 model after careful import and processing. It should be ensured that all are image specific data because the bottom-line classification takes place based on the images of the fashion wear. There should be no redundant copies of a single entry. Also, none of the entries in the dataset should be left null. Every entry should be unique and distinguishable from one another. All the images should be of uniform dimension that is 224x224 pixels of width and height respectively, and the images should be present in Red Green Blue (RGB) color format.

## Feature Identification

Once the images are identified to be in a uniform trend, it is processed by the RESNET50 model. The input passes through each layer of the total available layers, i.e., 50. After processing the input image uploaded in the user's input field, it is observed that each image generates about 2048 feature vectors that are equivalent to a single feature vector of a single input. Likewise, a dataset having 'N' entries is said to produce 'N' feature vectors for 'N' distinct images stored in the dataset.

## Effective Query and Response

At any point of time, if the user finds it difficult to navigate through the different available features of the application, queries can be asked using the chatbot which provides corresponding responses. The chatbot is fed with a predefined set of inputs and the relevant outputs which are stored in the IBM cloud DB2 and Postgresql databases. The set of questions and answers are connected into a dialog that establishes a meaningful interaction like speaking to a human being.

## ResNet-50

It is a pre-trained Convolutional Neural Network that is 50 layers deep. It's a type of Artificial Neural Network (ANN) that uses residual blocks to form networks as shown in Figure 9. ResNet-50 is made up of the following:

- 48 convolutional layers
- 1 MaxPool layer
- 1 average pool layer
- 1 convolution layer of 64 feature maps with filter size $7 \times 7$
- 4 bottleneck layers

*Figure 9. Workflow of RESNET50 algorithm*

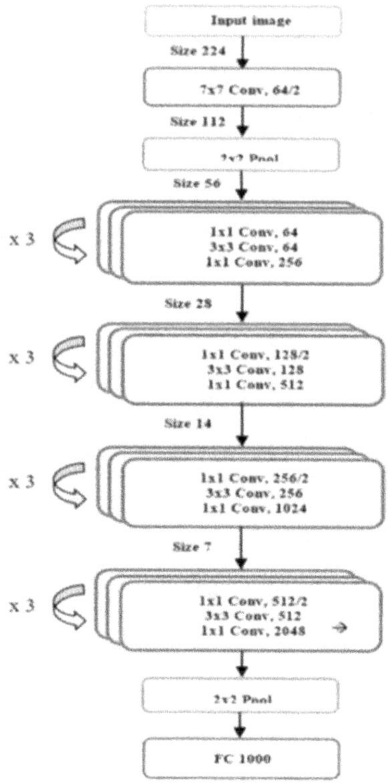


*Table 1. Layer function description of RESNET50*

| LAYER | FUNCTION |
|---|---|
| Convolutional layer | Backbone of ResNet-50<br>Allow the information to bypass one or more layers<br>Mitigate the vanishing gradient problem<br>Enable the training of very deep networks |
| MaxPool layer | Performs max pooling, a down-sampling operation that reduces the spatial dimensions of the input feature maps<br>Helps the network to be spatially invariant to small translations and distortions in the input data<br>Reduces the computational load and the number of parameters while retaining important features |
| Average Pool Layer | Performs average pooling, another down-sampling operation that computes the average value of each feature map<br>Used in the final layers of a CNN to reduce spatial dimensions further and produce a condensed representation of the features<br>Helps in achieving spatial invariance and reducing the risk of overfitting |

continued on following page

*Table 1. Continued*

| LAYER | FUNCTION |
|---|---|
| Convolution layer of 64 feature maps with filter size 7x7 | First layer of the network |
| Bottleneck layers | Consists of three convolutional layers: 1x1, 3x3, and 1x1<br>Computationally efficient and allows the model to learn both shallow and deep features effectively |

The confusion matrix for Product Fashion Dataset as shown in Figure 10.

*Figure 10. Confusion matrix of fashion dataset*

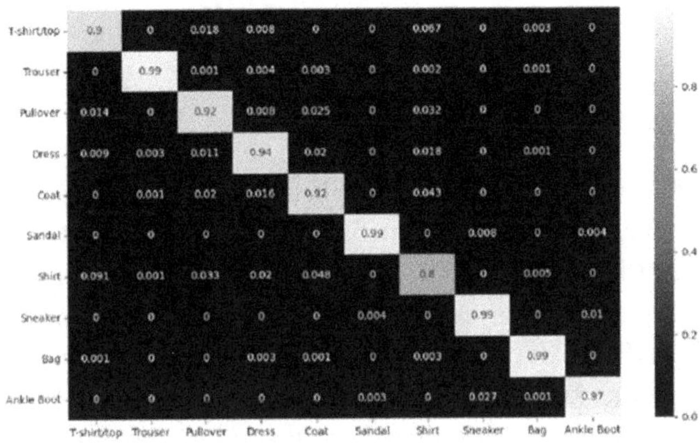


Figure 11 shows that the Resnet-50 has an area under the Receiver's operating characteristics (ROC) curve of 0.998, indicating great performance. AUC, or area under the ROC curve, is a scalar value that falls between 0 and 1 and represents the ROC curve analysis. The overall performance of the program is better the closer the AUC score is to 1.

*Figure 11. AUC curve for fashion dataset*

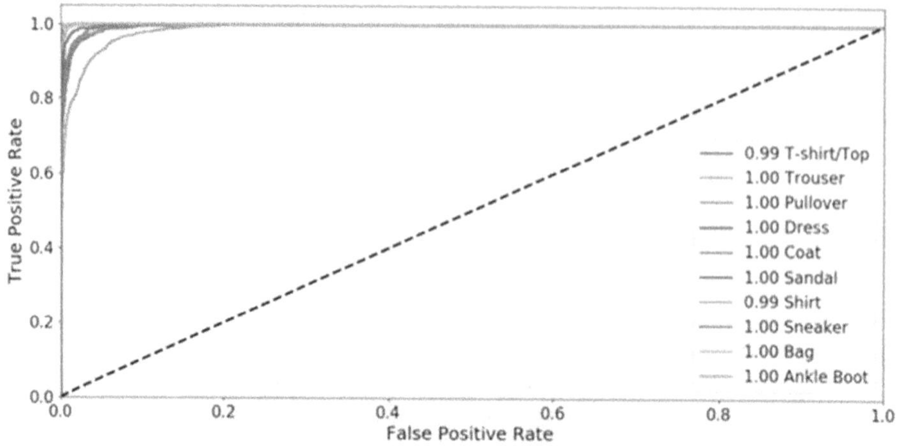


The Smart Fashion Recommender Application gets input from the user in the form of image which is of uniform dimension that is 224x224 pixels of height and width. It is then verified with the various entries present in the trained dataset. The input image undergoes a 50-layer processing under the Convolutional Neural Network model RESNET50. It carefully explores the input image for peculiar features which will be used for comparison with the pre-existing data in the dataset. After computation, the image is identified as feature vectors. The model performance is being tested on various testing procedures with zero compromises. It is observed that the model shows a performance accuracy of 95.5%. Finally, the input image is supported with relevant recommendations from the trained model.

## 4. CONCLUSION

The proposed system allows the users to get precise recommendations and better understand their fashion choices. It aids the user by providing recommendations and wardrobe options which upgrades the shopping process to the next level. The application helps users to understand their genre of styling from the various available options. The application is well developed with advanced routing and navigation that provides a friendly user interface to the end user. For further improvements, a Virtual try-on option can be enabled which is a smart way of trying on clothing and fashion wear, so that the user might get a better understanding whether the product will be a right fit or not. Like the "Recommendations" feature for eatables, this Virtual try-on option will be an initiative for developing a smart application. Furthermore, day-to-day updates on current trends in the market can be visualized in the news/blog page. The introduction of audio option in the chatbot (voice bot) and search options will be an added improvement to the application making it more user friendly.

## REFERENCES


Ahsan, M., Hon, S. T., & Albarbar, A. (2020). Development of novel big data analytics framework for smart clothing. *IEEE Access : Practical Innovations, Open Solutions*, 8, 146376–146394. DOI: 10.1109/ACCESS.2020.3015152

De Souza Inácio, A., & Lopes, H. S. (2020). EPYNET: Efficient pyramidal network for clothing segmentation. *IEEE Access : Practical Innovations, Open Solutions*, 8, 187882–187892. DOI: 10.1109/ACCESS.2020.3030859

Dhanalakshmi, R., Kalpana, A. V., Umamageswaran, J., & Kumar, B. P. "Health Information Broadcast Distributed Pattern Association based on Estimated Volume," *2023 Third International Conference on Artificial Intelligence and Smart Energy (ICAIS)*, Coimbatore, India, 2023, pp. 1326-1330. DOI: 10.1109/ICAIS56108.2023.10073672

Ding, Y., Ma, Y., Wong, W. K., & Chua, T. S. (2022). Modeling instant user intent and content-level transition for sequential fashion recommendation. *IEEE Transactions on Multimedia*, 24, 2687–2700. DOI: 10.1109/TMM.2021.3088281

Guo, Z., Zhu, Z., Li, Y., Cao, S., Chen, H., & Wang, G. (2023). AI assisted fashion design: A review. *IEEE Access : Practical Innovations, Open Solutions*, 11, 88403–88415. DOI: 10.1109/ACCESS.2023.3306235

Huang, F. H., Lu, H. M., & Hsu, Y. W. (2021). From street photos to fashion trends: Leveraging user-provided noisy labels for fashion understanding. *IEEE Access : Practical Innovations, Open Solutions*, 9, 49189–49205. DOI: 10.1109/ACCESS.2021.3069245

Jain, M., Singh, S., Chandrasekaran, K., Rathnamma, M. V., & Venkata Ramana, V. (2020) Machine learning models with optimization for clothing recommendation from personal wardrobe 3rd International Conference on Emerging Technologies in Computer Engineering: Machine Learning and Internet of Things (ICETCE), Jaipur, India, Vol. 2020, pp. 1–6. DOI: DOI: 10.1109/ICETCE48199.2020.9091777

Jing, P., Zhang, J., Nie, L., Ye, S., Liu, J., & Su, Y. (2022). Tripartite graph regularized latent low-rank representation for fashion compatibility prediction. *IEEE Transactions on Multimedia*, 24, 1277–1287. DOI: 10.1109/TMM.2021.3062736

Kalpana, A. V., Geetha, A. V., Jagadeesh, M. S., & Shobana, J. (2024). Secure 3D: Secure and Energy Efficient Localization in 3D Environment using Wireless Sensor Networks. *Wireless Personal Communications*, 136(3), 1375–1402. DOI: 10.1007/s11277-024-11290-1

Kalpana, V, Venkataramanan & Charulatha, G. & Geetha, G. (2023) A.V. & An intelligent voice-recognition wheelchair system for disabled persons, 668-672 DOI: . DOI: 10.1007/s11277-024-11290-1

Koshy, R., Gharat, A., Wagh, T., & Sonawane, S. (2021) A Complexion based Outfit color recommender using Neural Networks International Conference on Advances in Electrical, Computing, Communication and Sustainable Technologies (ICAECT), Bhilai, India, Vol. 2021, pp. 1–7. DOI: DOI: 10.1109/ICAECT49130.2021.9392418

Li, W., & Xu, B. (2020). Aspect-based fashion recommendation with attention mechanism. *IEEE Access : Practical Innovations, Open Solutions*, 8, 141814–141823. DOI: 10.1109/ACCESS.2020.3013639

Lin, Y., Ren, P., Chen, Z., Ren, Z., & Ma, J. (2018). *Rijke. Maarten.* Explainable Fashion Recommendation with Joint Outfit Matching and Comment Generation.

Liu, X., Sun, Y., Liu, Z., & Lin, D. (2021). Learning diverse fashion collocation by neural graph filtering. *IEEE Transactions on Multimedia*, 23, 2894–2901. DOI: 10.1109/TMM.2020.3018021

Mameli, M., Paolanti, M., Pietrini, R., Pazzaglia, G., Frontoni, E., & Zingaretti, P. (2022). Deep learning approaches for fashion knowledge extraction from social media: A review. *IEEE Access : Practical Innovations, Open Solutions*, 10, 1545–1576. DOI: 10.1109/ACCESS.2021.3137893

Praveen Kumar, B., Kalpana, A. V., & Nalini, S. (2023). Gated Attention Based Deep Learning Model for Analyzing the Influence of Social Media on Education. *Journal of Experimental & Theoretical Artificial Intelligence*, •••, 1–15. DOI: 10.1080/0952813X.2023.2188262

Sarala, B., Sumathy, G., Kalpana, A. V., & Jasmine Hephzipah, J. J. (2023) Glioma brain tumor detection using dual convolutional neural networks and histogram density segmentation algorithm. Biomedical Signal Processing and Control, 85, 104859, ISSN 1746-8094 DOI: DOI: 10.1016/j.bspc.2023.104859

Turkut, U., Tuncer, A., Savran, H., & Yılmaz, S. (2020) An online recommendation system using deep learning for textile products International Congress on Human-Computer Interaction, Optimization and Robotic Applications (HORA), Ankara, Turkey, Vol. 2020, pp. 1–4. DOI: DOI: 10.1109/HORA49412.2020.9152875

Wang, S., Yang, C., Qu, T., Yang, K., & Wan, W. (2022). Learning users' visual preferences for improving recommendations. *IEEE Access : Practical Innovations, Open Solutions*, 10, 2929–2940. DOI: 10.1109/ACCESS.2022.3140215

Wu, B., He, X., Chen, Y., Nie, L., Zheng, K., & Ye, Y. (2022). Modeling product's visual and functional characteristics for recommender systems. *IEEE Transactions on Knowledge and Data Engineering*, 34(3), 1330–1343. DOI: 10.1109/TKDE.2020.2991793

Wu, Q., Zhao, P., & Cui, Z. (2020). Visual and textual jointly enhanced interpretable fashion recommendation. *IEEE Access : Practical Innovations, Open Solutions*, 8, 68736–68746. DOI: 10.1109/ACCESS.2020.2978272

Zhan, H., & Lin, J. Anchorage, AK, USA (2021), pp. 2663–2667. DOI: DOI: 10.1109/ICIP42928.2021.9506344

Zhan, H., Lin, J., Ak, K. E., Shi, B., Duan, L. Y., & Kot, A. C. (2022). A^3A^3-FKG: Attentive attribute-aware fashion knowledge graph for outfit preference prediction. *IEEE Transactions on Multimedia*, 24, 819–831. DOI: 10.1109/TMM.2021.3059514

Zhang, H., Huang, W., Liu, L., & Chow, T. W. S. (2020). Learning to match clothing from textual feature-based compatible relationships. *IEEE Transactions on Industrial Informatics*, 16(11), 6750–6759. DOI: 10.1109/TII.2019.2924725

Zhong, L. (2020) Edge-based fashion detection by transfer learning 5th International Conference on Mechanical, Control and Computer Engineering (ICMCCE), Harbin, China, Vol. 2020, pp. 2132–2136. DOI: DOI: 10.1109/ICMCCE51767.2020.00464

# Compilation of References


*(PDF) Computer-aided texture analysis combined with experts' knowledge: Improving endoscopic celiac disease diagnosis*. (n.d.). Retrieved July 31, 2024, from https://www.researchgate.net/publication/306105255_Computer-aided_texture_analysis_combined_with_experts%27_knowledge_Improving_endoscopic_celiac_disease_diagnosis

Abakumov, A. M., Fedotov, S. S., Antipov, E. V., & Tarascon, J.-M. (2020). Solid state chemistry for developing better metal-ion batteries. *Nature Communications*, 11(1), 4976. DOI: 10.1038/s41467-020-18736-7 PMID: 33009387

Abbasi, T., & Abbasi, S. A. (2010). Biomass energy and the environmental impacts associated with its production and utilization. *Renewable & Sustainable Energy Reviews*, 14(3), 919–937. DOI: 10.1016/j.rser.2009.11.006

Abdelali, A., Durrani, N., Dalvi, F., & Sajjad, H. (2022). Post-hoc analysis of Arabic transformer models. *Proceedings of the Fifth BlackboxNLP Workshop on Analyzing and Interpreting Neural Networks for NLP*, 91–103. DOI: 10.18653/v1/2022.blackboxnlp-1.8

Abdelali, A., Mubarak, H., Chowdhury, S. A., Hasanain, M., Mousi, B., Boughorbel, S., El Kheir, Y., Izham, D., Dalvi, F., Hawasly, M., Nazar, N., Elshahawy, Y., Ali, A., Durrani, N., Milic-Frayling, N., & Alam, F. (2023). LAraBench: Benchmarking Arabic AI with Large Language Models. *Proceedings Ofthe 18th Conference Ofthe European Chapter Ofthe Association for Computational Linguistics, 1*, 487–520. http://arxiv.org/abs/2305.14982

Abdelgayed, T. S., Morsi, W. G., & Sidhu, T. S. (2018). Fault detection and classification based on co-training of semi supervised machine learning. *IEEE Transactions on Industrial Electronics*, 65(2), 1595–1606. DOI: 10.1109/TIE.2017.2726961

Abdelli, K., Griesser, H., & Pachnicke, S. (2022). A machine learning-basedframework for predictive maintenance of semiconductor laser for optical communication. *Journal of Lightwave Technology*, 40(14), 4698–4708. DOI: 10.1109/JLT.2022.3163579

AbdulRaheem. M., Awotunde, J. B., Chakraborty, C., Adeniyi, E. A., Oladipo, I. D., & Bhoi, A. K. (2023). Security and privacy concerns in smart healthcare system. In *Implementation of Smart Healthcare Systems using AI, IoT, and Blockchain* (pp. 243-273). Academic Press.

Abolkasim, E., & Shtewi, A. (2023). Analyzing the Efficacy of ChatGPT for Online Learning: An Experimental Study. *AlQalam Journal of Medical and Applied Sciences*, 6(2), 617–625. DOI: 10.5281/zenodo.10005016

Abubakari, M. S., Shafik, W., & Hidayatullah, A. F. (2024). Evaluating the Potential of Artificial Intelligence in Islamic Religious Education: A SWOT Analysis Overview. In *AI-Enhanced Teaching Methods* (pp. 216–239). IGI Global. DOI: 10.4018/979-8-3693-2728-9.ch010

Abubakari, M. S. (2024a). Overviewing the Maze of Research Integrity and False Positives Within AI-Enabled Detectors. In Mutawa, A. (Ed.), *Impacts of Generative AI on the Future of Research and Education* (pp. 335–366). IGI Global., DOI: 10.4018/979-8-3693-0884-4.ch013

Abubakari, M. S. (2024b). The digital frontier within Islamic education: Research gaps overview in digital competence. *Journal of Computing Research and Innovation*, 9(2), 317–331. DOI: 10.24191/jcrinn.v9i2.435

Abubakari, M. S., & Kalinaki, K. (2024). Digital Competence in Islamic Education for Lifelong Learning: Preliminary Analysis Using DigComp 2.1 Framework. In Hawamdeh, M. M. K., & Abdelhafid, F. (Eds.), *Embracing Technological Advancements for Lifelong Learning* (pp. 1–31). IGI Global., DOI: 10.4018/979-8-3693-1410-4.ch001

Abubakari, M. S., Zakaria, G. A. N., & Musa, J. (2024). Perceived compatibility and students' intention to adopt digital technologies in Islamic education institutions. *Cogent Education*, 11(1), 2430869. DOI: 10.1080/2331186X.2024.2430869

Abubakari, M. S., Zakaria, G. A. N., Musa, J., & Kalinaki, K. (2023a). Assessing Digital Competence in Higher Education: A Gender Analysis of DigComp 2.1 Framework in Uganda. *SAGA: Journal of Technology and Information System*, 1(4), 114–120. DOI: 10.58905/saga.v1i4.210

Abubakari, M. S., Zakaria, G. A. N., Musa, J., & Kalinaki, K. (2023b). Validating the Digital Competence (Dig-Comp 2.1) Framework in Higher Education Using Confirmatory Factor Analysis: Non-Western Perspective. *Canadian Journal of Educational and Social Studies*, 3(6), 15–26. DOI: 10.53103/cjess.v6i1.184

*Active Machine learning for formulation of precision probiotics—ScienceDirect.* (n.d.). Retrieved September 17, 2024, from https://www.sciencedirect.com/science/article/pii/S0378517322001223

Adams, W. H. (2012, January 24). *Ravel chronology*. De Gruyter. https://www.degruyter.com/document/doi/10.12987/9780300170122-016/html

Adinugroho, W. C., Krisnawati, H., Imanuddin, R., Siregar, C. A., Weston, C. J., & Volkova, L. (2023). Developing biomass allometric equations for small trees in mixed-species forests of tropical rainforest ecozone. *Trees, Forests and People*, 13, 100425. DOI: 10.1016/j.tfp.2023.100425

Affia, A. A. O., Finch, H., Jung, W., Samori, I. A., Potter, L., & Palmer, X. L. (2023). IoT Health Devices: Exploring Security Risks in the Connected Landscape. *IoT*, 4(2), 150–182. DOI: 10.3390/iot4020009

Agrawal, R., Agrawal, S., Samadhiya, A., Kumar, A., Luthra, S., & Jain, V. (2024). Adoption of green finance and green innovation for achieving circularity: An exploratory review and future directions. *Geoscience Frontiers*, 15(4), 101669. DOI: 10.1016/j.gsf.2023.101669

Ahmad, J., Zia, M. U., Naqvi, I. H., Chattha, J. N., Butt, F. A., Huang, T., & Xiang, W. (2024). Machine learning and blockchain technologies for cybersecurity in connected vehicles. *Wiley Interdisciplinary Reviews. Data Mining and Knowledge Discovery*, 14(1), e1515. DOI: 10.1002/widm.1515

Ahmed, A., Ali, N., Alzubaidi, M., Zaghouani, W., Abd-alrazaq, A., & Househ, M. (2022). Arabic chatbot technologies: A scoping review. *Computer Methods and Programs in Biomedicine Update*, 2(April), 100057. DOI: 10.1016/j.cmpbup.2022.100057

Ahmed, Z. E., Hassan, A. A., & Saeed, R. A. (2024). *AI-Enhanced Teaching Methods* (Ahmed, Z. E., Hassan, A. A., & Saeed, R. A., Eds.). IGI Global., DOI: 10.4018/979-8-3693-2728-9

Ahouanmenou, S., Van Looy, A., & Poels, G. (2023). Information security and privacy in hospitals: A literature mapping and review of research gaps. *Informatics for Health & Social Care*, 48(1), 30–46. DOI: 10.1080/17538157.2022.2049274 PMID: 35300555

Ahsan, M., Hon, S. T., & Albarbar, A. (2020). Development of novel big data analytics framework for smart clothing. *IEEE Access : Practical Innovations, Open Solutions*, 8, 146376–146394. DOI: 10.1109/ACCESS.2020.3015152

Ahuja, K., Diddee, H., Hada, R., Ochieng, M., Ramesh, K., Jain, P., Nambi, A., Ganu, T., Segal, S., Ahmed, M., Bali, K., & Sitaram, S. (2023). MEGA: Multilingual Evaluation of Generative AI. *Proceedings of the 2023 Conference on Empirical Methods in Natural Language Processing*, 4232–4267. DOI: 10.18653/v1/2023.emnlp-main.258

Aini, D. N., Setiawan, S., Syafi'ul Anam, R. M., & Ibad, W. (2023, September). Artificial Intelligence Learning Platform for Promoting Speaking Competence: A Suggested Scaffolding for Autonomous Learning in Pesantren. In *Proceedings of the 4th International Conference on English Language Teaching (ICON-ELT 2023)* (Vol. 780, p. 131). Springer Nature. DOI: 10.2991/978-2-38476-120-3_13

Akinyele, D. O., & Rayudu, R. K. (2014). Review of energy storage technologies for sustainable power networks. *Sustainable Energy Technologies and Assessments*, 8, 74–91. DOI: 10.1016/j.seta.2014.07.004

Akirov, A., & Pinhas-Hamiel, O. (2015). Co-occurrence of type 1 diabetes mellitus and celiac disease. *World Journal of Diabetes*, 6(5), 707–714. DOI: 10.4239/wjd.v6.i5.707 PMID: 26069719

Alamri, B., Crowley, K., & Richardson, I. (2022). Cybersecurity Risk Management Framework for Blockchain Identity Management Systems in Health IoT. *Sensors (Basel)*, 23(1), 218. DOI: 10.3390/s23010218 PMID: 36616816

Al-Bluwi, G. S. M., AlNababteh, A. H., Östlundh, L., Al-Shamsi, S., & Al-Rifai, R. H. (2021). Prevalence of Celiac Disease in Patients With Turner Syndrome: Systematic Review and Meta-Analysis. *Frontiers in Medicine*, 8, 674896. DOI: 10.3389/fmed.2021.674896 PMID: 34222285

Algarni, A. (2019). A survey and classification of security and privacy research in smart healthcare systems. *IEEE Access : Practical Innovations, Open Solutions*, 7, 101879–101894. DOI: 10.1109/ACCESS.2019.2930962

Algatus, W. A. (2022). *Propose an architecture for e-health within smart cities* (Master's thesis, Altınbaş Üniversitesi/Lisansüstü Eğitim Enstitüsü).

Alhassan, N. A., Saad Albarrak, A., Bhatia, S., & Agarwal, P. (2022). A Novel Framework for Arabic Dialect Chatbot Using Machine Learning. *Computational Intelligence and Neuroscience*, 2022, 1–11. DOI: 10.1155/2022/1844051 PMID: 35310584

Ali Gharbani, K., Hamed, F., Zhiya, M., & Zhongwu, C. (2019).. . *Journal of the Electrochemical Society*, 166(4), A605–A615. DOI: 10.1149/2.0411904jes

Ali, A. R., Siddiqui, M. A., Algunaibet, R., & Ali, H. R. (2023). A Large and Diverse Arabic Corpus for Language Modeling. *Procedia Computer Science*, 225, 12–21. DOI: 10.1016/j.procs.2023.09.086

Ali, M., Sharma, A., Joy, T., & Halim, M. (2024). A Comprehensive Review of Integrated Energy Management for Future Smart Energy System. *Control Systems and Optimization Letters*, 43--51.

Ali, O., Ishak, M. K., Ahmed, A. B., Mohd Salleh, M. F., Ooi, C. A., Akbar Jalaludin Khan, M. F., & Khan, I. (2022). On-line WSN SoC estimation using Gaussian Process Regression: An Adaptive Machine Learning Approach. *Alexandria Engineering Journal*, 61(12), 9831–9848. DOI: 10.1016/j.aej.2022.02.067

Ali, O., Murray, P. A., Momin, M., Dwivedi, Y. K., & Malik, T. (2024). The effects of artificial intelligence applications in educational settings: Challenges and strategies. *Technological Forecasting and Social Change*, 199, 123076. DOI: 10.1016/j.techfore.2023.123076

Ali, R. (2023). *AI Usage in Healthcare*. DOI: 10.31219/osf.io/b36y5

Ali, R., Marriam, L., Muhammad, A., Muhammad Sajid, I., Li, J., & Ijaz, A. (2024). SAARC super smart grid: Navigating the future - unleashing the power of an energy-efficient integration of renewable energy resources in the saarc region. *Computers & Electrical Engineering*, •••, 109405.

Ali, W., Ulasyar, A., Mehmood, M. U., Khattak, A., Imran, K., Zad, H. S., & Nisar, S. (2021). Hierarchical Control of Microgrid Using IoT and Machine Learning Based Islanding Detection. *IEEE Access : Practical Innovations, Open Solutions*, 9, 103019–103031. DOI: 10.1109/ACCESS.2021.3098163

Aljanabi, M. (2024). Assessing the Arabic Parsing Capabilities of ChatGPT and Cloude: An Expert-Based Comparative Study. *Mesopotamian Journal of Arabic Language Studies*, 2024(2024), 16–23. DOI: 10.58496/MJALS/2024/002

Al-Khalifa, H., Al-Khalefah, K., & Haroon, H. (2024). Error Analysis of Pretrained Language Models (PLMs) in English-to-Arabic Machine Translation. *Human-Centric Intelligent Systems*, 4(2), 206–219. DOI: 10.1007/s44230-024-00061-7

Al-Khalifa, S., Alhumaidhi, F., Alotaibi, H., & Al-Khalifa, H. S. (2023). ChatGPT across Arabic Twitter: A Study of Topics, Sentiments, and Sarcasm. *Data*, 8(11), 171. DOI: 10.3390/data8110171

AlMahamid, F., & Grolinger, K. (2021). Reinforcement Learning Algorithms: An Overview and Classification. *IEEE Canadian Conference on Electrical and Computer Engineering* (CCECE), 1-7. DOI: 10.1109/CCECE53047.2021.9569056

Almurayh, A. (2021). The Challenges of Using Arabic Chatbot in Saudi Universities. *International Journal of Computational Science*, 48(1), 190–201. https://www.semanticscholar.org/paper/f56ba4e0912b1906df9fad255bf39e829f80e1ab

Alpízar-Castillo, J., Linders, K., Slaifstein, D., Ramírez-Elizondo, L., & Bauer, P. (2024). Economic Opportunities of Power Curtailment and Peak Shaving on Residential PV-BESS Systems. *In 2024 20th International Conference on the European Energy Market (EEM) (pp. 1-6). IEEE.*

Alrowili, S., & Shanker, V. (2022). Generative Approach for Gender-Rewriting Task with ArabicT5. *Proceedings of the Seventh Arabic Natural Language Processing Workshop (WANLP)*, 491–495. DOI: 10.18653/v1/2022.wanlp-1.55

Alruqi, T. N., & Alzahrani, S. M. (2023). Evaluation of an Arabic Chatbot Based on Extractive Question-Answering Transfer Learning and Language Transformers. *AI*, 4(3), 667–691. DOI: 10.3390/ai4030035

Al-Saffar, M., & Musilek, P. (2021). Distributed Optimization for Distribution Grids with Stochastic DER Using Multi-Agent Deep Reinforcement Learning. *IEEE Access : Practical Innovations, Open Solutions*, 9, 63059–63072. DOI: 10.1109/ACCESS.2021.3075247

Al-Shabandar, R., Lightbody, G., Browne, F., Liu, J., Wang, H., & Zheng, H. (2019, October 17). The Application of Artificial Intelligence in Financial Compliance Management. DOI: 10.1145/3358331.3358339

Alshammari, H., El-Sayed, A., & Elleithy, K. (2024). AI-Generated Text Detector for Arabic Language Using Encoder-Based Transformer Architecture. *Big Data and Cognitive Computing*, 8(3), 32. DOI: 10.3390/bdcc8030032

Alshboul, O., Alzubaidi, M. A., Mamlook, R. E. A., Almasabha, G., Almuflih, A. S., & Shehadeh, A. (2022). Forecasting liquidated damages via machine learning-based modified regression models for highway construction projects. *Sustainability (Basel)*, 14(10), 5835. DOI: 10.3390/su14105835

Alsheddi, A. S., & Alhenaki, L. S. (2022). English and Arabic Chatbots: A Systematic Literature Review. *International Journal of Advanced Computer Science and Applications*, 13(8). Advance online publication. DOI: 10.14569/IJACSA.2022.0130876

Altman, N. (1992). *An Introduction to Kernel and Nearest-Neighbor Nonparametric Regression*. The Amerian Statitician. DOI: 10.1080/00031305.1992.10475879

Amaya-Tejera, N., Gamarra, M., Vélez, J. I., & Zurek, E. (2024). A distance-based kernel for classification via Support Vector Machines. *Frontiers in Artificial Intelligence*, 7, 1287875. DOI: 10.3389/frai.2024.1287875 PMID: 38469159

Ameen, A. H., Mohammed, M. A., & Rashid, A. N. (2023). Dimensions of artificial intelligence techniques, blockchain, and cyber security in the Internet of medical things: Opportunities, challenges, and future directions. *Journal of Intelligent Systems*, 32(1), 20220267. DOI: 10.1515/jisys-2022-0267

Amrut Hnath, N., & Gupta, T. (2018), research study on unsupervised machine learning algorithms for early fault detection in predictive maintenance, 2018 *5th International Conference on Industrial Engineering and Applications (ICIEA)*, Singapore, pp. 355-361, DOI: 10.1109/IEA.2018.8387124

Anitha, K., Verchot, L. V., Joseph, S., Herold, M., Manuri, S., & Avitabile, V. (2015). A review of forest and tree plantation biomass equations in Indonesia. *Annals of Forest Science*, 72(8), 981–997. DOI: 10.1007/s13595-015-0507-4

Anshari, M. (2020, March). Workforce mapping of fourth industrial revolution: Optimization to identity. [). IOP Publishing.]. *Journal of Physics: Conference Series*, 1477(7), 072023. DOI: 10.1088/1742-6596/1477/7/072023

Anshari, M., Almunawar, M. N., Masri, M., & Hrdy, M. (2021a). Financial technology with AI-enabled and ethical challenges. *Society*, 58(3), 189–195. DOI: 10.1007/s12115-021-00592-w

Anshari, M., Fithriyah, M., Polak, P., & Razzaq, A. (2021). Islamic FinTech and artificial intelligence (AI) for assessing creditworthiness. In *Artificial Intelligence and Islamic Finance* (pp. 48–60). Routledge. DOI: 10.4324/9781003171638-4

Anshari, M., Syafrudin, M., & Fitriyani, N. L. (2022). Fourth industrial revolution between knowledge management and digital humanities. *Information (Basel)*, 13(6), 292. DOI: 10.3390/info13060292

Anshari, M., Syafrudin, M., Tan, A., Fitriyani, N. L., & Alas, Y. (2023). Optimisation of knowledge management (KM) with machine learning (ML) Enabled. *Information (Basel)*, 14(1), 35. DOI: 10.3390/info14010035

Apajalahti, E. L., Lovio, R., & Heiskanen, E. (2015). From demand side management (DSM) to energy efficiency services: A Finnish case study. *Energy Policy*, 81, 76–85. DOI: 10.1016/j.enpol.2015.02.013

Apostu, S. A., Gigauri, I., Panait, M., & Martín-Cervantes, P. A. (2023). Is Europe on the way to sustainable development? Compatibility of green environment, economic growth, and circular economy issues. *International Journal of Environmental Research and Public Health*, 20(2), 1078. DOI: 10.3390/ijerph20021078 PMID: 36673838

Araujo, E. C. G., Sanquetta, C. R., Dalla Corte, A. P., Pelissari, A. L., Orso, G. A., & Silva, T. C. (2023). Global review and state-of-the-art of biomass and carbon stock in the Amazon. *Journal of Environmental Management*, 331, 117251. DOI: 10.1016/j.jenvman.2023.117251 PMID: 36657202

Arsawan, I. W. E., Koval, V., Suhartanto, D., Hariyanti, N. K. D., Polishchuk, N., & Bondar, V. (2024). Circular economy practices in SMEs: Aligning model of green economic incentives and environmental commitment. *International Journal of Productivity and Performance Management*, 73(3), 775–793. DOI: 10.1108/IJPPM-03-2022-0144

Asad, M. (2023). Security Management in Cloud Computing for healthcare. *Data*.

Asael, D., Ziegler, Z., & Belinkov, Y. (2022). A Generative Approach for Mitigating Structural Biases in Natural Language Inference. *Proceedings of the 11th Joint Conference on Lexical and Computational Semantics*, 186–199. DOI: 10.18653/v1/2022.starsem-1.16

Ashwin, S. H., & Naveen Raj, R. (2023). Deep reinforcement learning for autonomous vehicles: Lane keep and overtaking scenarios with collision avoidance. *International Journal of Information Technology : an Official Journal of Bharati Vidyapeeth's Institute of Computer Applications and Management*, 15(7), 3541–3553. DOI: 10.1007/s41870-023-01412-6

ATLAS Renewable Energy. (2024, febrero 15). *ATLAS Renewable Energy*. Retrieved from La IA y su impacto en las energías renovables: https://es.atlasrenewableenergy.com/la-ia-y-su-impacto-en-las-energias-renovables/

Awadallah, M. S., de Arriba-Pérez, F., Costa-Montenegro, E., Kholief, M., & El-Bendary, N. (2022). Investigation of Local Interpretable Model-Agnostic Explanations (LIME) Framework with Multi-Dialect Arabic Text Sentiment Classification. *2022 32nd International Conference on Computer Theory and Applications (ICCTA)*, 116–121. DOI: 10.1109/ICCTA58027.2022.10206274

Awotunde, J. B., Jimoh, R. G., Folorunso, S. O., Adeniyi, E. A., Abiodun, K. M., & Banjo, O. O. (2021). Privacy and security concerns in IoT-based healthcare systems. In *The Fusion of Internet of Things, Artificial Intelligence, and Cloud Computing in Health Care* (pp. 105–134). Springer International Publishing. DOI: 10.1007/978-3-030-75220-0_6

Ayaz Ali, K., & Muhammad, Z. (2021). Energy, performance and cost efficient cloud datacentres: A survey. *Computer Science Review*, 100390.

Azim, M. A., Hussein, W., & Badr, N. L. (2023). Using Character-Level Sequence-to-Sequence Model for Word Level Text Generation to Enhance Arabic Speech Recognition. *IEEE Access : Practical Innovations, Open Solutions*, 11, 91173–91183. DOI: 10.1109/ACCESS.2023.3302257

Azis, N., Joelianto, E., & Widyotriatmo, A. (2019). State of Charge (SoC) and State of Health (SoH). *Estimation of Lithium-Ion Battery Using Dual Extended Kalman Filter Based on Polynomial Battery Model.*, 2019, 88–93. DOI: 10.1109/ICA.2019.8916734

Babaali, B., Salem, M., & Alharbe, N. R. (2024). Breaking language barriers with ChatGPT: Enhancing low-resource machine translation between algerian arabic and MSA. *International Journal of Information Technology : an Official Journal of Bharati Vidyapeeth's Institute of Computer Applications and Management*. Advance online publication. DOI: 10.1007/s41870-024-01926-7

Bach, J.-F. (2018). The hygiene hypothesis in autoimmunity: The role of pathogens and commensals. *Nature Reviews. Immunology*, 18(2), 105–120. DOI: 10.1038/nri.2017.111 PMID: 29034905

Badmos, O., Kopp, A., Bernthaler, T., & Schneider, G. (2020). Image-based defect detection in lithium-ion battery electrode using convolutional neural networks. *Journal of Intelligent Manufacturing*, 31(4), 885–897. DOI: 10.1007/s10845-019-01484-x

Bai, Y. T., Wang, X. Y., Jin, X. B., Zhao, Z. Y., & Zhang, B. H. (2020, January 5). A Neuron-Based Kalman Filter with Nonlinear Autoregressive Model. *Sensors (Basel)*, 20(1), 299. DOI: 10.3390/s20010299 PMID: 31948060

Bai, Y., Su, Y., Maisha Rahman, M., & Wang, Z. (2023). Prognostics of Lithium-Ion batteries using knowledge-constrained machine learning and Kalman filtering. *Reliability Engineering & System Safety*, 231, 108944. DOI: 10.1016/j.ress.2022.108944

Bank, R. P. D. (n.d.). *RCSB PDB - 8E13: Structures of HLA-B8E76C loaded with long peptides reveal novel features at the N-terminus of the groove*. Retrieved June 13, 2024, from https://www.rcsb.org/structure/8E13

Bansal, N., Sharma, A., & Singh, R K. (2019, January 1). A Review on the Application of Deep Learning in Legal Domain. Springer Science+Business Media, 374-381. DOI: 10.1007/978-3-030-19823-7_31

Bao, F., Yu, L., Babu, S., Wang, T., Hoffenberg, E. J., Rewers, M., & Eisenbarth, G. S. (1999). One third of HLA DQ2 homozygous patients with type 1 diabetes express celiac disease-associated transglutaminase autoantibodies. *Journal of Autoimmunity*, 13(1), 143–148. DOI: 10.1006/jaut.1999.0303 PMID: 10441179

Barikeri, S., Lauscher, A., Vulić, I., & Glavaš, G. (2021). RedditBias: A Real-World Resource for Bias Evaluation and Debiasing of Conversational Language Models. *Proceedings of the 59th Annual Meeting of the Association for Computational Linguistics and the 11th International Joint Conference on Natural Language Processing(*Volume 1*: Long Papers)*, 1941–1955. DOI: 10.18653/v1/2021.acl-long.151

Barja-Martinez, S., Aragués-Peñalba, M., Munné-Collado, Í., Lloret-Gallego, P., Bullich-Massague, E., & Villafafila-Robles, R. (2021). Artificial intelligence techniques for enabling Big Data services in distribution networks: A review. *Renewable & Sustainable Energy Reviews*, 150, 111459. DOI: 10.1016/j.rser.2021.111459

Barker, J. M., & Liu, E. (2008). Celiac disease: Pathophysiology, clinical manifestations, and associated autoimmune conditions. *Advances in Pediatrics*, 55(1), 349–365. DOI: 10.1016/j.yapd.2008.07.001 PMID: 19048738

Barrett, C. (2019). Are the EU GDPR and the California CCPA becoming the de facto global standards for data privacy and protection? *Scitech Lawyer*, 15(3), 24–29.

Barrett, D. H., & Adiremi, H. (2020). Artificial intelligence and machine learning for targeted energy storage solutions. *Current Opinion in Electrochemistry*, 21, 160–166. DOI: 10.1016/j.coelec.2020.02.002

Battaglia, P. W., Hamrick, J. B., Bapst, V., Sanchez-Gonzalez, A., Zambaldi, V., Malinowski, M., Tacchetti, A., Raposo, D., Santoro, A., & Faulkner, R. (2018). Relational inductive biases, deep learning, and graph networks. *arXiv preprint arXiv:1806.01261*.

Becerra, S. D. (2018, January 1). The Rise of Artificial Intelligence in the Legal Field: Where We Are and Where We Are Going., 11(1), 27-52. https://digitalcommons.pepperdine.edu/cgi/viewcontent.cgi?article=1169&context=jbel

Bella, G., Helm, P., Koch, G., & Giunchiglia, F. (2024). Tackling Language Modelling Bias in Support of Linguistic Diversity. *The 2024 ACM Conference on Fairness, Accountability, and Transparency*, 562–572. DOI: 10.1145/3630106.3658925

Benhammou, A., Tedjini, H., Guettaf, Y., & Hartani Mohamed, A. (2023). Impact of artificial intelligence in renewable energy management of hybrid systems. In *Physical Sciences Forum* (p. 5). MDPI.

Bhat, P. I. (2020). Thinking process in legal research. *Idea and Methods of Legal Research*, 32–53. DOI: 10.1093/oso/9780199493098.003.0002

Bhatia, N. K., El-hag, A. H., & Shaban, K. B. (2020). Machine learning-based regression and classification models for oil assessment of power transformers. In 2020 IEEE International conference on informatics, IOT, and enabling technologies (ICIOT). IEEE, pp. 400–403. DOI: 10.1109/ICIoT48696.2020.9089647

Bhat, S., Varma, V., & Pedanekar, N. (2023). Generative Models For Indic Languages: Evaluating Content Generation Capabilities. *Proceedings of the Conference Recent Advances in Natural Language Processing - Large Language Models for Natural Language Processings*, 187–195. DOI: 10.26615/978-954-452-092-2_021

Bibi, A., Zhang, X., & Umar, M. (2021). The imperativeness of biomass energy consumption to the environmental sustainability of the United States revisited. *Environmental and Ecological Statistics*, 28(4), 821–841. DOI: 10.1007/s10651-021-00500-9

Billah Nagoudi, E. M., Abdul-Mageed, M., Elmadany, A., Inciarte, A., & Islam Khondaker, M. T. (2023). JASMINE: Arabic GPT Models for Few-Shot Learning. *Proceedings of the 2023 Conference on Empirical Methods in Natural Language Processing*, 16721–16744. DOI: 10.18653/v1/2023.emnlp-main.1040

Bobrowski, R., Winczek, M., Zięba-Kulawik, K., & Wężyk, P. (2023). Best practices to use the iPad Pro LiDAR for some procedures of data acquisition in the urban forest. *Urban Forestry & Urban Greening*, 79, 127815. Advance online publication. DOI: 10.1016/j.ufug.2022.127815

Bonet, B., Haslum, P., Hickmott, S., & Thiébaux, S. (2008). Directed unfolding of petri nets. In *Transactions on Petri Nets and Other Models of Concurrency I* (pp. 172–198). Springer. DOI: 10.1007/978-3-540-89287-8_11

Bonfitto, A. (2020). A Method for the Combined Estimation of Battery State of Charge and State of Health Based on Artificial Neural Networks. *Energies*, 13(10), 2548. DOI: 10.3390/en13102548

Boujelbene, M., Goodarzi, M., & Ashraf Ali, M. (2023). Shigidi, I. M.T.A., Pashameah, R. A., Homod, R.Z., Alzahrani, E.; and Safaei, M. R. Machine-learning optimization of an innovative design of a Li-ion battery arrangement cooling system. *Journal of Energy Storage*, 58, 106331. DOI: 10.1016/j.est.2022.106331

Boulakhbar, M., Farag, M., Benabdelaziz, K., Kousksou, T., & Zazi, M. (2022). Benabdelaziz, K., Kousksou, T., and Zazi,M. A deep learning approach for prediction of electrical vehicle charging stations power demand in regulated electricity markets: The case of Morocco. *Cleaner Energy Systems*, 3, 100039. DOI: 10.1016/j.cles.2022.100039

Buchelt, A., Adrowitzer, A., Kieseberg, P., Gollob, C., Nothdurft, A., Eresheim, S., Tschiatschek, S., Stampfer, K., & Holzinger, A. (2024). Exploring artificial intelligence for applications of drones in forest ecology and management. *Forest Ecology and Management*, 551, 121530. DOI: 10.1016/j.foreco.2023.121530

Bui, Q. T., Pham, Q. T., Pham, V. M., Tran, V. T., Nguyen, D. H., Nguyen, Q. H., Nguyen, H. D., Do, N. T., & Vu, V. M. (2024). Hybrid machine learning models for aboveground biomass estimations. *Ecological Informatics*, 79, 102421. DOI: 10.1016/j.ecoinf.2023.102421

Buiskikh, D., Zakeri, B., Syri, S., & Kauranen, P. (2018). Economic feasibility of flow batteries in grid-scale applications. *In 2018 15th International Conference on the European Energy Market (EEM)* (pp. 1-5). *IEEE.*

Bui, V. H., Hussain, A., & Kim, H. M. (2019). Q- learning-based operation strategy for community battery energy storage system (CBESS) in microgrid system. *Energies*, 12(9), 1789. Advance online publication. DOI: 10.3390/en12091789

Burggr¨, A. F. (2021). Machine learning-based prediction of missing components for assembly–a case study at an engineer-to-order manufacturer. *IEEE Access : Practical Innovations, Open Solutions*, 9, 105926–105938. DOI: 10.1109/ACCESS.2021.3075620

Busu, C., & Busu, M. (2021). An Application of the Kalman Filter Recursive Algorithm to Estimate the Gaussian Errors by Minimizing the Symmetric Loss Function. *Symmetry*, 13(2), 240. DOI: 10.3390/sym13020240

Butte, S., Prashanth, A., & Patil, S. (2018). *Machine learning based predictive maintenance strategy: A super learning approach with deep neural networks. In 2018. IEEE workshop on microelectronics and electron devices (WMED)*. IEEE.

Caetano Dos Santos, F. L., Michalek, I. M., Laurila, K., Kaukinen, K., Hyttinen, J., & Lindfors, K. (2019). Automatic classification of IgA endomysial antibody test for celiac disease: A new method deploying machine learning. *Scientific Reports*, 9(1), 9217. DOI: 10.1038/s41598-019-45679-x PMID: 31239486

Cai, L., & Le, T. T. (2023). Natural resources and financial development: Role of corporate social responsibility on green economic growth in Vietnam. *Resources Policy*, 81, 103279. DOI: 10.1016/j.resourpol.2022.103279

Cai, Y., Zhou, R., Wang, H., Sun, X., Chen, L., Li, Y., Liu, Q., & He, Y. (2023). Rule-constrained reinforcement learning control for autonomous vehicle left turn at unsignalized intersection. *IET Intelligent Transport Systems*, 17(11), 2143–2153. DOI: 10.1049/itr2.12336

Calabrese, M., Cimmino, M., Manfrin, M., Fiume, F., Kapetis, D., Mengoni, M., Ceccacci, S., Frontoni, E., & Paolanti, M. Carrotta, a., et al. (2019). An event based machine learning framework for predictive maintenance in industry 4.0. In international design engineering technical conferences and computers and information in engineering conference, Volume 59292. American Society of Mechanical Engineers, p. v009t12a037.

Caliskan, A. (2023). Artificial Intelligence, Bias, and Ethics. *Proceedings of the Thirty-Second International Joint Conference on Artificial Intelligence*, 7007–7013. DOI: 10.24963/ijcai.2023/799

Candela, E., Doustaly, O., Parada, L., Feng, F., Demiris, Y., & Angeloudis, P. (2023). Risk-aware controller for autonomous vehicles using model-based collision prediction and reinforcement learning. *Artificial Intelligence*, 320, 103923. DOI: 10.1016/j.artint.2023.103923

Cao, D., Zeng, K., Wang, J., Sharma, P. K., Ma, X., Liu, Y., & Zhou, S. (2021). BERT-based deep spatial-temporal network for taxi demand prediction. *IEEE Transactions on Intelligent Transportation Systems*, 23(7), 9442–9454. DOI: 10.1109/TITS.2021.3122114

Cao, R., Zhang, X., & Yang, H. (2023). Prediction of the Heat Generation Rate of Lithium-Ion Batteries Based on Three Machine Learning Algorithms. *Batteries*, 9(3), 165. DOI: 10.3390/batteries9030165

Capraro, V., Lentsch, A., Acemoglu, D., Akgun, S., Akhmedova, A., Bilancini, E., Bonnefon, J.-F., Brañas-Garza, P., Butera, L., Douglas, K. M., Everett, J. A. C., Gigerenzer, G., Greenhow, C., Hashimoto, D. A., Holt-Lunstad, J., Jetten, J., Johnson, S., Kunz, W. H., Longoni, C., & Viale, R. (2024). The impact of generative artificial intelligence on socioeconomic inequalities and policy making. *PNAS Nexus*, 3(6), pgae191. Advance online publication. DOI: 10.1093/pnasnexus/pgae191 PMID: 38864006

Cataldo, F., & Montalto, G. (2007). Celiac disease in the developing countries: A new and challenging public health problem. *World Journal of Gastroenterology*, 13(15), 2153–2159. DOI: 10.3748/wjg.v13.i15.2153 PMID: 17465493

Catassi, C., Kryszak, D., Bhatti, B., Sturgeon, C., Helzlsouer, K., Clipp, S. L., Gelfond, D., Puppa, E., Sferruzza, A., & Fasano, A. (2010). Natural history of celiac disease autoimmunity in a USA cohort followed since 1974. *Annals of Medicine*, 42(7), 530–538. DOI: 10.3109/07853890.2010.514285 PMID: 20868314

Ceci, M., Corizzo, R., Fumarola, F., Ianni, M., Malerba, D., Maria, G., . . . Rashkovska, A. (2015). *Big data techniques for supporting accurate predictions of energy production from renewable sources*. Proceedings of the 19th international database engineering \& applications symposium.

Ch'ng, C. L., Jones, M. K., & Kingham, J. G. C. (2007). Celiac disease and autoimmune thyroid disease. *Clinical Medicine & Research*, 5(3), 184–192. DOI: 10.3121/cmr.2007.738 PMID: 18056028

Chaaben, N., Elleuch, Z., Hamdi, B., & Kahouli, B. (2024). Green economy performance and sustainable development achievement: Empirical evidence from Saudi Arabia. *Environment, Development and Sustainability*, 26(1), 549–564. DOI: 10.1007/s10668-022-02722-8 PMID: 36320556

Chandran, V., Patil, C. K., Karthick, A., Ganeshaperumal, D., Rahim, R., & Ghosh, A. (2021). State of Charge Estimation of Lithium-Ion Battery for Electric Vehicles Using Machine Learning Algorithms. *World Electr. Veh. J.*, 12(1), 38. DOI: 10.3390/wevj12010038

Chao, D., Zhou, W., Xie, F., Ye, C., Li, H., Jaroniec, M., & Qiao, S.-Z. (2020). Roadmap for advanced aqueous batteries: From design of materials to applications. *Science Advances*, 6(21), 4098. DOI: 10.1126/sciadv.aba4098 PMID: 32494749

Charkhgard, H., Savelsbergh, M., & Talebian, M. (2018). A linear programming based algorithm to solve a class of optimization problems with a multi-linear objective function and affine constraints. *Computers & Operations Research*, 89, 17–30. DOI: 10.1016/j.cor.2017.07.015

Chazhoor, A., Mounika, Y., Sarobin, M. V. R., Sanjana, M., & Yasashvini, R. (2020). Predictive maintenance using machine learning based classification models. *IOP Conference Series. Materials Science and Engineering*, 954(1), 012001. DOI: 10.1088/1757-899X/954/1/012001

Chen, C., Wei, J., & Li, Z. (2023). Remaining Useful Life Prediction for Lithium-Ion Batteries Based on a Hybrid Deep Learning Model. *Processes (Basel, Switzerland)*, 11(8), 2333. DOI: 10.3390/pr11082333

Chen, D., Hu, H., & Chang, C. P. (2023). Green finance, environment regulation, and industrial green transformation for corporate social responsibility. *Corporate Social Responsibility and Environmental Management*, 30(5), 2166–2181. DOI: 10.1002/csr.2476

Cheng, C., Yuhan, H., Marimuthu, K., & Priyan Malarvizhi, K. (2021). Artificial intelligence on economic evaluation of energy efficiency and renewable energy technologies. *Sustainable Energy Technologies and Assessments*, 47, 101358. DOI: 10.1016/j.seta.2021.101358

Cheng, M., Zhang, X., Ran, A., Wei, G., & Sun, H. (2023). Optimal dispatch approach for second-life batteries considering degradation with online SoH estimation. *Renewable & Sustainable Energy Reviews*, 173, 113053. DOI: 10.1016/j.rser.2022.113053

Chen, H., Yuan, K., Huang, Y., Guo, L., Wang, Y., & Chen, J. (2023). Feedback is all you need: From ChatGPT to autonomous driving. *Science China. Information Sciences*, 66(6), 1–3. DOI: 10.1007/s11432-023-3740-x

Chen, H., Zhang, Y., Bhatti, U. A., & Huang, M. (2023). Safe decision controller for autonomous drivingbased on deep reinforcement learning innondeterministic environment. *Sensors (Basel)*, 23(3), 1198. DOI: 10.3390/s23031198 PMID: 36772238

Chen, W., Huang, Y., Boyle, B., & Lin, S. (2016). The utility of including pathology reports in improving the computational identification of patients. *Journal of Pathology Informatics*, 7(1), 46. DOI: 10.4103/2153-3539.194838 PMID: 27994938

Chen, W., Shen, Z., Pan, Y., Tan, K., & Wang, C. (2024). Applying Machine Learning Algorithm to Optimize Personalized Education Recommendation System. *Journal of Theory and Practice of Engineering Science*, 4(01), 101–108.

Chen, Z., Ting, D., Newbury, R., & Chen, C. (2021). Semantic segmentation for partially occluded apple trees based on deep learning. *Computers and Electronics in Agriculture*, 181, 105952. DOI: 10.1016/j.compag.2020.105952

Chen, Z., Wu, M., Zhao, R., Guretno, F., Yan, R., & Li, X. (2020). Machine remaining useful life prediction via an attention-based deep learning approach. *IEEE Transactions on Industrial Electronics*, 68(3), 2521–2531. DOI: 10.1109/TIE.2020.2972443

Chen, Z., Xiong, R., Lu, J., & Li, X. (2018). Temperature rise prediction of lithium-ion battery suffering external short circuit for all-climate electric vehicles application. *Applied Energy*, 213, 375–383. DOI: 10.1016/j.apenergy.2018.01.068

Chettibi, N., Mellit, A., Sulligoi, G., & Pavan, A. M. (2018). Adaptive Neural Network-Based Control of a Hybrid AC/DC Microgrid. *IEEE Transactions on Smart Grid*, 9, 1667–1679.

Chib, P. S., & Singh, P. (2023). Recent advancements in end-to-end autonomous driving using deep learning: A survey. *IEEE Transactions on Intelligent Vehicles*.

Choung, R. S., Khaleghi Rostamkolaei, S., Ju, J. M., Marietta, E. V., Van Dyke, C. T., Rajasekaran, J. J., Jayaraman, V., Wang, T., Bei, K., Rajasekaran, K. E., Krishna, K., Krishnamurthy, H. K., & Murray, J. A. (2019). Synthetic Neoepitopes of the Transglutaminase-Deamidated Gliadin Complex as Biomarkers for Diagnosing and Monitoring Celiac Disease. *Gastroenterology*, 156(3), 582–591.e1. DOI: 10.1053/j.gastro.2018.10.025 PMID: 30342033

Chowdary, V. T., Joel, M. R., Ebenezer, V., Edwin, B., Thanka, R., & Jeyaraj, A. (2022, March). A novel approach for effective crop production using machine learning. In *2022 International Conference on Electronics and Renewable Systems (ICEARS)* (pp. 1143–1147). IEEE. DOI: 10.1109/ICEARS53579.2022.9751798

Christian, F., Wladislaw, W., Ziou, B., & Dirk, U. S. (2013).. . *J. Power Electron*, 13, 516–527. DOI: 10.6113/JPE.2013.13.4.516

Ciaccio, E. J., Tennyson, C. A., Bhagat, G., Lewis, S. K., & Green, P. H. (2010). Classification of videocapsule endoscopy image patterns: Comparative analysis between patients with celiac disease and normal individuals. *Biomedical Engineering Online*, 9(1), 44. DOI: 10.1186/1475-925X-9-44 PMID: 20815911

Cinova, J., Palová-Jelínková, L., Smythies, L. E., Cerná, M., Pecharová, B., Dvorák, M., Fruhauf, P., Tlaskalová-Hogenová, H., Smith, P. D., & Tucková, L. (2007). Gliadin peptides activate blood monocytes from patients with celiac disease. *Journal of Clinical Immunology*, 27(2), 201–209. DOI: 10.1007/s10875-006-9061-z PMID: 17260166

Clark, A., Fox, C., & Lappin, S. (Eds.). (2010). *The Handbook of Computational Linguistics and Natural Language Processing* (1re éd.). Wiley. DOI: 10.1002/9781444324044

Clemente, M. G., De Virgiliis, S., Kang, J. S., Macatagney, R., Musu, M. P., Di Pierro, M. R., Drago, S., Congia, M., & Fasano, A. (2003). Early effects of gliadin on enterocyte intracellular signalling involved in intestinal barrier function. *Gut*, 52(2), 218–223. DOI: 10.1136/gut.52.2.218 PMID: 12524403

Corazza, G. R., Andreani, M. L., Biagi, F., Corrao, G., Pretolani, S., Giulianelli, G., Ghironzi, G., & Gasbarrini, G. (1997). The smaller size of the "coeliac iceberg" in adults. *Scandinavian Journal of Gastroenterology*, 32(9), 917–919. DOI: 10.3109/00365529709011202 PMID: 9299671

Cui, J., Yuan, L., He, L., Xiao, W., Ran, T., & Zhang, J. (2023). Multi-input autonomous driving based on deep reinforcement learning with double bias experience replay. *IEEE Sensors Journal*, 23(11), 11253–11261. DOI: 10.1109/JSEN.2023.3237206

D.C. M., E.A., P., G.G., V., & A.G., R. (2022). *Introduction to Linear Regression Analysis, 6e Solutions Manual.* John Wiley & Sons.

D'Angelo, V., Cappa, F., & Peruffo, E. (2023). Green manufacturing for sustainable development: The positive effects of green activities, green investments, and non-green products on economic performance. *Business Strategy and the Environment*, 32(4), 1900–1913. DOI: 10.1002/bse.3226

Daemi, A., Kodamana, H., & Huang, B. (2019). Gaussian process modelling with Gaussian mixture likelihood. *Journal of Process Control*, 81, 209–220. DOI: 10.1016/j.jprocont.2019.06.007

Dahiwade, D., Patle, G., & Meshram, E. (2019). *Designing Disease Prediction Model Using Machine Learning Approach.* 2019 3rd International Conference on Computing Methodologies and Communication (ICCMC). DOI: 10.1109/ICCMC.2019.8819782

Danis, M., Acar, A Z., & Arslan, A. (2022, January 1). Is the Use of Green Certification Strategic or Not?. Gdynia Maritime University, 16(2), 203-209. DOI: 10.12716/1001.16.02.01

Dan, W., Masood, A. A., Asad, A., Rishabh, C., Ali, M. R., & Sohail, M. (2023). A numerical investigation of a two-phase nanofluid flow with phase change materials in the thermal management of lithium batteries and use of machine learning in the optimization of the horizontal and vertical distances between batteries. *Case Studies in Thermal Engineering*, 41, 102582. DOI: 10.1016/j.csite.2022.102582

Darmawan, A., Asyhari, T., & Dunggio, I. Salmahaminati, & Aziz, M. (2023). Energy harvesting from tropical biomasses in Wallacea region: scenarios, technologies, and perspectives. In Biomass Conversion and Biorefinery. Springer Science and Business Media Deutschland GmbH. DOI: 10.1007/s13399-023-04223-8

Das, A., & Rad, P. (2020). Opportunities and challenges in explainable artificial intelligence (XAI): A survey. *arXiv preprint arXiv:2006.11371.*

Das, T., Roy, A., & Majumdar, A. K. (2020). A study on legal knowledge base creation using artificial intelligence and ontology. Innovative Data Communication Technologies and Application, 647–653. DOI: 10.1007/978-3-030-38040-3_73

Das, T., Sil, R., Roy, A., & Majumdar, A. K. (2022). UML-based modelling for legal rules using natural language processing. *Lecture Notes in Electrical Engineering*, 481–492. DOI: 10.1007/978-981-16-8542-2_39

Davis, A. E. (2020, January 1). The Future of Law Firms (and Lawyers) in the Age of Artificial Intelligence. Fundação Getúlio Vargas, Escola de Direito, 16(1). https://doi.org/DOI: 10.1590/2317-6172201945

De Souza Inácio, A., & Lopes, H. S. (2020). EPYNET: Efficient pyramidal network for clothing segmentation. *IEEE Access : Practical Innovations, Open Solutions*, 8, 187882–187892. DOI: 10.1109/ACCESS.2020.3030859

Debusschere, V., Lefieux, V., Mallet, P., & Roche, N. (2022). *Artificial Intelligence Serving Electrical Networks* [PhD Thesis, Think Smartgrids Scientific Council]. https://hal.science/hal-04050749/document

Deng, L., & Yu, D. (2014), Deep Learning: Methods and Applications, Foundations and Trends® in *Signal Processing:* Vol. 7: No. 3–4, pp 197-387. DOI: 10.1561/2000000039

Deng, C., Ji, X., Rainey, C., Zhang, J., & Lu, W. (2020). Integrating machine learning with human knowledge. *IScience*. https://doi.org/. isci.2020.101656. DOI: 10.1016/j

Deng, L., & Liu, Y. (2018). *Deep Learning in Natural Language Processing* (Deng, L., & Liu, Y., Eds.). Springer Singapore., DOI: 10.1007/978-981-10-5209-5

Derrick, M. (2024, septiembre 06). *ENERGY DIGITAL.* Retrieved from https://energydigital.com/top10/top-10-uses-of-ai-in-energy

*Detection of gluten immunogenic peptides in the urine of patients with coeliac disease reveals transgressions in the gluten-free diet and incomplete mucosal healing—PubMed.* (n.d.). Retrieved September 21, 2024, from https://pubmed.ncbi.nlm.nih.gov/26608460/

Dhaif, Z. S., & El Abbadi, N. K. (2024). A Review of Machine Learning Techniques Utilised in Self-Driving Cars. *Iraqi Journal For Computer Science and Mathematics*, 5(1), 205–219. DOI: 10.52866/ijcsm.2024.05.01.015

Dhanalakshmi, R., Kalpana, A. V., Umamageswaran, J., & Kumar, B. P. "Health Information Broadcast Distributed Pattern Association based on Estimated Volume," *2023 Third International Conference on Artificial Intelligence and Smart Energy (ICAIS)*, Coimbatore, India, 2023, pp. 1326-1330. DOI: 10.1109/ICAIS56108.2023.10073672

Dhananjay, k., HD, M., S, B., & Bansal, R. (2020). Forecasting of solar and wind power using LSTM RNN for load frequency control in isolated microgrid. *International Journal of Modelling and Simulation*, 311-323.

Diario El Peruano. (2024, marzo 05). Retrieved from https://elperuano.pe/noticia/237398-enel-inicia-generacion-de-energia-solar-en-sur-del-peru

Díaz, J. (2024, junio 09). *El confidencial.* Retrieved from China deja atrás al resto del mundo con la megaplanta solar más grande del planeta: https://www.elconfidencial.com/tecnologia/novaceno/2024-06-08/planta-solar-mas-grande-del-planeta_3898655/

Dieli-Crimi, R., Cénit, M. C., & Núñez, C. (2015). The genetics of celiac disease: A comprehensive review of clinical implications. *Journal of Autoimmunity*, 64, 26–41. DOI: 10.1016/j.jaut.2015.07.003 PMID: 26194613

Dileep, G. J. R. E. (2020). A survey on smart grid technologies and applications. *Renewable Energy*, 146, 2589–2625. DOI: 10.1016/j.renene.2019.08.092

Ding, Y., & Foo, S. (2002, April 1). Ontology research and development. Part 1 - a review of ontology generation. *Journal of Information Science*, 28(2), 123–136. DOI: 10.1177/016555150202800204

Ding, Y., Ma, Y., Wong, W. K., & Chua, T. S. (2022). Modeling instant user intent and content-level transition for sequential fashion recommendation. *IEEE Transactions on Multimedia*, 24, 2687–2700. DOI: 10.1109/TMM.2021.3088281

Dirisu, J. O., Salawu, E. Y., Ekpe, I. C., Udoye, N. E., Falodun, O. E., Oyedepo, S. O., Ajayi, O. O., & Kale, S. A. (2023). Promoting the use of bioenergy in developing nations: A CDM route to sustainable development. *Frontiers in Energy Research*, 11, 1184348. DOI: 10.3389/fenrg.2023.1184348

Dobrovolska, N. V. (2020). Administrative contract: Analysis of the normative definition. *Legal Position*, (3), 28–34. DOI: 10.32836/2521-6473.2020-3.5

Dobson, I., Carreras, B. A., Lynch, V. E., & Newman, D. E. (2007). Complex systems analysis of series of blackouts : Cascading failure, critical points, and self-organization. *Chaos (Woodbury, N.Y.)*, 17(2), 026103. Advance online publication. DOI: 10.1063/1.2737822 PMID: 17614690

Dolev, S., Florissi, P., Gudes, E., Sharma, S., & Singer, I. (2017). A survey on geographically distributed big-data processing using MapReduce. *IEEE Transactions on Big Data*, 5(1), 60–80. DOI: 10.1109/TBDATA.2017.2723473

Dong, L., Wesseloo, J., Potvin, Y., & Li, X. (2016). Discrimination of mine seismic events and blasts using the Fisher classifier, naive Bayesian classifier and logistic regression. *Rock Mechanics and Rock Engineering*, 49(1), 183–211. DOI: 10.1007/s00603-015-0733-y

Dong, R., Du, J., Liu, Y., Heidari, A. A., & Chen, H. (2023). An enhanced deep deterministic policy gradient algorithm for intelligent control of robotic arms. *Frontiers in Neuroinformatics*, 17, 1096053. DOI: 10.3389/fninf.2023.1096053 PMID: 36756212

Dragoni, M., Villata, S., Rizzi, W., & Governatori, G. (2016, December). Combining NLP approaches for rule extraction from legal documents. In *1st Workshop on Mining and Reasoning with Legal texts (MIREL 2016).*

Drakaki, M., Karnavas, Y. L., Tziafettas, I. A., Linardos, V., and Tzionas, p. (2022). Machine learning and deep learning based methods toward industry 4.0 predictive maintenance in induction motors: state of the art survey. Journal of industrial engineering and management (JIEM), 15 (1), 31–57.

Duan, J., Shi, D., Diao, R., Li, H., Wang, Z., Zhang, B., Bian, D., & Yi, Z. (2019). Deep-reinforcement-learning-based autonomous voltage control for power grid operations. *IEEE Transactions on Power Systems*, 35(1), 814–817. DOI: 10.1109/TPWRS.2019.2941134

Duan, J., Yi, Z., Shi, D., Lin, C., Lu, X., & Wang, Z. (2019). Reinforcement-Learning-Based Optimal Control of Hybrid Energy Storage Systems in Hybrid AC–DC Microgrids. *IEEE Transactions on Industrial Informatics*, 15(9), 5355–5364. DOI: 10.1109/TII.2019.2896618

Dubois, P. C. A., Trynka, G., Franke, L., Hunt, K. A., Romanos, J., Curtotti, A., Zhernakova, A., Heap, G. A. R., Adány, R., Aromaa, A., Bardella, M. T., van den Berg, L. H., Bockett, N. A., de la Concha, E. G., Dema, B., Fehrmann, R. S. N., Fernández-Arquero, M., Fiatal, S., Grandone, E., & van Heel, D. A. (2010). Multiple common variants for celiac disease influencing immune gene expression. *Nature Genetics*, 42(4), 295–302. DOI: 10.1038/ng.543 PMID: 20190752

Du, Y., Chen, J., Zhao, C., Liao, F., & Zhu, M. (2023). A hierarchical framework for improving ride comfort of autonomous vehicles via deep reinforcement learning with external knowledge. *Computer-Aided Civil and Infrastructure Engineering*, 38(8), 1059–1078. DOI: 10.1111/mice.12934

Dzwigol, H., Kwilinski, A., Lyulyov, O., & Pimonenko, T. (2023). The role of environmental regulations, renewable energy, and energy efficiency in finding the path to green economic growth. *Energies*, 16(7), 3090. DOI: 10.3390/en16073090

Efthimiadis, E. N., & Hotchkiss, M. A. (2008). Legal discovery: Does domain expertise matter? *Proceedings of the American Society for Information Science and Technology*, 45(1), 1–2. DOI: 10.1002/meet.2008.1450450125

Elli, L., Branchi, F., Tomba, C., Villalta, D., Norsa, L., Ferretti, F., Roncoroni, L., & Bardella, M. T. (2015). Diagnosis of gluten related disorders: Celiac disease, wheat allergy and non-celiac gluten sensitivity. *World Journal of Gastroenterology*, 21(23), 7110–7119. DOI: 10.3748/wjg.v21.i23.7110 PMID: 26109797

ElSamadisy, O., Shi, T., Smirnov, I., & Abdulhai, B. (2024). Safe, efficient, and comfortable reinforcement-learning-based car-following for AVs with an analytic safety guarantee and dynamic target speed. *Transportation Research Record: Journal of the Transportation Research Board*, 2678(1), 643–661. DOI: 10.1177/03611981231171899

Elshaer, I. A., Azazz, A. M., & Fayyad, S. (2023). Green management and sustainable performance of small-and medium-sized hospitality businesses: Moderating the role of an employee's pro-environmental behaviour. *International Journal of Environmental Research and Public Health*, 20(3), 2244. DOI: 10.3390/ijerph20032244 PMID: 36767609

El-Shangiti, A. O., Alwajih, F., & Abdul-Mageed, M. (2024). *Arabic Automatic Story Generation with Large Language Models*. http://arxiv.org/abs/2407.07551 DOI: 10.18653/v1/2024.arabicnlp-1.13

Entezari, A., Aslani, A., Zahedi, R., & Noorollahi, Y. (2023). Artificial intelligence and machine learning in energy systems: A bibliographic perspective. *Energy Strat. Rev*, 45, 101017. DOI: 10.1016/j.esr.2022.101017

Ersoy, A., Vizcarra, G., Mayeesha, T., & Muller, B. (2023). *What Languages are Generative Language Models the Most Formal? Analyzing Formality Distribution across Languages. Findings of the Association for Computational Linguistics*. EMNLP., DOI: 10.18653/v1/2023.findings-emnlp.175

Estrela, V. V. (2023). Intelligent. *Health Care Systems*.

Evans, B. D., Jordaan, H. W., & Engelbrecht, H. A. (2023). Safe reinforcement learning for high-speed autonomous racing. *Cognitive Robotics*, 3, 107–126. DOI: 10.1016/j.cogr.2023.04.002

Ewa, C., Joanicjusz, N., Lukasz, N., Hesham, S. R., Raed, M. A., & Rami, A. (2023). Arima models in solar radiation forecasting in different geographic locations. *Energies*, •••, 5029.

Fabiyi, S. D. (2024). What can ChatGPT not do in education? Evaluating its effectiveness in assessing educational learning outcomes. *Innovations in Education and Teaching International*, 00(00), 1–15. DOI: 10.1080/14703297.2024.2333395

Fan, Y., Feng, Z., Shen, C., Khan, T. U., Mannan, A., Gao, X., Chen, P., & Saeed, S. (2020). A trunk-based SLAM backend for smartphones with online SLAM in large-scale forest inventories. *ISPRS Journal of Photogrammetry and Remote Sensing*, 162, 41–49. DOI: 10.1016/j.isprsjprs.2020.02.006

Faraji-Niri, M., Rashid, M., Sansom, J., Sheikh, M., Widanage, D., & Marco, J. (2023). Accelerated state of health estimation of second life lithium-ion batteries via electrochemical impedance spectroscopy tests and machine learning techniques. *Journal of Energy Storage*, 58, 106295. DOI: 10.1016/j.est.2022.106295

Farghaly, A., & Shaalan, K. (2009). Arabic Natural Language Processing. *ACM Transactions on Asian Language Information Processing*, 8(4), 1–22. DOI: 10.1145/1644879.1644881

Farmann, A., & Uwe Sauer, D. (2016). A comprehensive review of on-board State-of-Available-Power prediction techniques for lithium-ion batteries in electric vehicles. *Journal of Power Sources*, 329, 123–137. DOI: 10.1016/j.jpowsour.2016.08.031

Fasano, A. (2001). Celiac Disease: The Past, the Present, the Future. *Pediatrics*, 107(4), 768–770. DOI: 10.1542/peds.107.4.768 PMID: 11335755

Fasano, A., Berti, I., Gerarduzzi, T., Not, T., Colletti, R. B., Drago, S., Elitsur, Y., Green, P. H. R., Guandalini, S., Hill, I. D., Pietzak, M., Ventura, A., Thorpe, M., Kryszak, D., Fornaroli, F., Wasserman, S. S., Murray, J. A., & Horvath, K. (2003). Prevalence of celiac disease in at-risk and not-at-risk groups in the United States: A large multicenter study. *Archives of Internal Medicine*, 163(3), 286–292. DOI: 10.1001/archinte.163.3.286 PMID: 12578508

Fasshauer, G. E., & McCourt, M. J. (2012). Stable evaluation of Gaussian radial basis function interpolants. *SIAM Journal on Scientific Computing*, 34(2), A737–A762. DOI: 10.1137/110824784

Fayomi, G. U., Mini, S. E., Fayomi, O., Odunlami, A., & Oyeleke, O. (2021, April 1). Sustainability and Clean Technology: A Technological Perspective. *IOP Conference Series. Materials Science and Engineering*, 1107(1), 012076–012076. DOI: 10.1088/1757-899X/1107/1/012076

Feng, H., & Shi, F. (2021). Deep Learning in Natural Language Processing. *Natural Language Engineering*, 27(3), 373–375. DOI: 10.1017/S1351324919000597

Feng, S., Sun, H., Yan, X., Zhu, H., Zou, Z., Shen, S., & Liu, H. X. (2023). Dense reinforcement learning for safety validation of autonomous vehicles. *Nature*, 615(7953), 620–627. DOI: 10.1038/s41586-023-05732-2 PMID: 36949337

Ferrara, E. (2023a). Fairness and Bias in Artificial Intelligence: A Brief Survey of Sources, Impacts, and Mitigation Strategies. *Sci*, 6(1), 3. DOI: 10.3390/sci6010003

Ferrara, E. (2023b). Should ChatGPT be biased? Challenges and risks of bias in large language models. *First Monday*, 28(11). Advance online publication. DOI: 10.5210/fm.v28i11.13346

Ferrer Márque, A., María-Tomé Gi, B., Pérez Díaz, S., & Vilallonga Ortiz, A. (2018, julio). Gestión eficiente de la energía en las organizaciones. https://www.ecoembes.com/sites/default/files/inline-files/administraciones-publicas/gestion-eficiente-energia-organizaciones-guia-completa.pdf, COEMBES, España.

Fitria, T. N. (2021, December). Artificial intelligence (AI) in education: Using AI tools for teaching and learning process. In *Prosiding Seminar Nasional & Call for Paper STIE AAS* (pp. 134-147).

Fitrianto, I., Setyawan, C. E., & Saleh, M. (2024). Utilizing Artificial Intelligence for Personalized Arabic Language Learning Plans. *International Journal of Post Axial: Futuristic Teaching and Learning*, 2(1), 132–142. DOI: 10.59944/postaxial.v2i1.273

Florian, E., Sgarbossa, F., & Zennaro, I. (2021). Machine learning-based predictive maintenance: A cost-oriented model for implementation. *International Journal of Production Economics*, 236, 108114. DOI: 10.1016/j.ijpe.2021.108114

Foiadelli, F., Longo, M., & Miraftabzadeh, S. (2018). Energy consumption prediction of electric vehicles based on big data approach. Proc. - 2018 *IEEE Int. Conf. Environ. Electr. Eng. 2018 IEEE Ind. Commer. Power Syst. Eur. EEEIC/I CPS Eur.* 2018. DOI: 10.1109/EEEIC.2018.8494573

Forootan, M. M., Larki, I., Zahedi, R., & Ahmadi, A. (2022). Machine Learning and Deep Learning in Energy Systems: A Review. *Sustainability (Basel)*, 14(8), 4832. DOI: 10.3390/su14084832

Forum, W. E. (2021, septiembre 06). *World Economic Forum.* Retrieved from https://www.weforum.org/agenda/2021/09/this-is-how-ai-will-accelerate-the-energy-transition/

Freeman, H. J., Chopra, A., Clandinin, M. T., & Thomson, A. B. (2011). Recent advances in celiac disease. *World Journal of Gastroenterology*, 17(18), 2259–2272. DOI: 10.3748/wjg.v17.i18.2259 PMID: 21633592

Friston, K. J., Parr, T., Yufik, Y., Sajid, N., Price, C. J., & Holmes, E. (2020). Generative models, linguistic communication and active inference. *Neuroscience and Biobehavioral Reviews*, 118, 42–64. DOI: 10.1016/j.neubiorev.2020.07.005 PMID: 32687883

Fu, H., Zhao, H., Jiang, J., Zhang, Y., Liu, G., Xiao, W., Du, S., Guo, W., & Liu, X. (2024). Automatic detection tree crown and height using Mask R-CNN based on unmanned aerial vehicles images for biomass mapping. *Forest Ecology and Management*, 555, 121712. DOI: 10.1016/j.foreco.2024.121712

Gabbar, H. A., Othman, A. M., & Abdussami, M. R. (2021). Review of Battery Management Systems (BMS) Development and Industrial Standards. *Technologies*, 9(2), 28. DOI: 10.3390/technologies9020028

Gadermayr, M., Wimmer, G., Kogler, H., Vécsei, A., Merhof, D., & Uhl, A. (2018). Automated classification of celiac disease during upper endoscopy: Status quo and quo vadis. *Computers in Biology and Medicine*, 102, 221–226. DOI: 10.1016/j.compbiomed.2018.04.020 PMID: 29739614

Gao, K., Xu, J., Li, Z., Cai, Z., Jiang, D., & Zeng, A. (2022). A Novel Remaining Useful Life Prediction Method for Capacity Diving Lithium-Ion Batteries. *ACS Omega*, 7(30), 26701–26714. DOI: 10.1021/acsomega.2c03043 PMID: 35936419

Gao, L., Zhou, R., & Zhang, K. (2023). Scenario generation for autonomous vehicles with deep-learning-based heterogeneous driver models: Implementation and verification. *Sensors (Basel)*, 23(9), 4570. DOI: 10.3390/s23094570 PMID: 37177774

Gao, T., & Lu, W. (2020). Physical model and machine learning enabled electrolyte channel design for fast charging. *J. Electrochem. Soc.* https://doi.org/DOI: 10.1149/1945-7111/aba096

Gao, T., Ying, L., Dai, M., Shen, G., Hu, P., & Shen, L. (2019). A comparative study of temperature-dependent interfacial heat transfer coefficient prediction methods for 22MnB5 steel in spray quenching process. *International Journal of Thermal Sciences*, 139, 36–60. Advance online publication. DOI: 10.1016/j.ijthermalsci.2018.12.041

Garbis, Z., McCarthy, E., Orttung, R. W., Poelzer, G., Shaiman, M., & Tafrate, J. (2023). Governing the green economy in the Arctic. *Climatic Change*, 176(4), 33. DOI: 10.1007/s10584-023-03506-3

Gautamee, H. (2024). *Solar and Wind Energy uptake to reach 5.4 TW from 2024 to 2023*, https://www.mercomindia.com/solar-and-wind-energy-from-2024-to-2033

Gayon-Lombardo, A., Mosser, L., Brandon, N. P., & Cooper, S. J. (2020). Pores for thought: Generative adversarial networks for stochastic reconstruction of 3D multi-phase electrode microstructures with periodic boundaries. *npj Computational Materials*, 6(1), 1–11. DOI: 10.1038/s41524-020-0340-7

Gené-Mola, J., Ferrer-Ferrer, M., Gregorio, E., Blok, P. M., Hemming, J., Morros, J. R., Rosell-Polo, J. R., Vilaplana, V., & Ruiz-Hidalgo, J. (2023). Looking behind occlusions: A study on amodal segmentation for robust on-tree apple fruit size estimation. *Computers and Electronics in Agriculture*, 209, 107854. DOI: 10.1016/j.compag.2023.107854

Geng, B. (2022a). Legal text mining and analysis based on Artificial Intelligence. *International Journal of Artificial Intelligence Tools*, 31(04), 2240006. Advance online publication. DOI: 10.1142/S0218213022400061

Ghosh, S., Dutta, M., & Das, T. (2022). Indian legal text summarization: A text normalization-based approach. *2022 IEEE 19th India Council International Conference (INDICON)*. DOI: 10.1109/INDICON56171.2022.10039891

Ghosh, S., Zaboli, A., Hong, J., & Kwon, J. (2023). An integrated approach of threat analysis for autonomous vehicles perception system. *IEEE Access : Practical Innovations, Open Solutions*, 11, 14752–14777. DOI: 10.1109/ACCESS.2023.3243906

Giannaros, A., Karras, A., Theodorakopoulos, L., Karras, C., Kranias, P., Schizas, N., Kalogeratos, G., & Tsolis, D. (2023). Autonomous vehicles: Sophisticated attacks, safety issues, challenges, open topics, blockchain, and future directions. *Journal of Cybersecurity and Privacy*, 3(3), 493–543. DOI: 10.3390/jcp3030025

Glavic, M., Fonteneau, R., & Ernst, D. (2017). Reinforcement learning for electric power system decision and control: Past considerations and perspectives. *IFAC-PapersOnLine*, 50(1), 6918–692. DOI: 10.1016/j.ifacol.2017.08.1217

Goh, H.-H., & Vinuesa, R. (2021b). Regulating artificial-intelligence applications to achieve the Sustainable Development Goals. *Discover Sustainability*, 2(1), 52. Advance online publication. DOI: 10.1007/s43621-021-00064-5 PMID: 35425914

Goodfellow, I., Bengio, Y., & Courville, A. (2016). *Deep Learning*. MIT Press.

Graves, A., & Schmidhuber, S. (2005). Framewise phoneme classification with bidirectional LSTM networks. *Proceedings.2005 IEEE International Joint Conference on Neural Networks,* 2005., pp. 2047--2052. DOI: 10.1109/IJCNN.2005.1556215

Gravett, W. (2020, June 15). Is the Dawn of the Robot Lawyer upon us? The Fourth Industrial Revolution and the Future of Lawyers. *Potchefstroom Electronic Law Journal*, 23, 1–37. DOI: 10.17159/1727-3781/2020/v23i0a6794

Gülci, S., Yurtseven, H., Akay, A. O., & Akgul, M. (2023). Measuring tree diameter using a LiDAR-equipped smartphone: A comparison of smartphone- and caliper-based DBH. *Environmental Monitoring and Assessment*, 195(6), 1–16. DOI: 10.1007/s10661-023-11366-8 PMID: 37191833

Gulino, C., Fu, J., Luo, W., Tucker, G., Bronstein, E., Lu, Y., & Sapp, B. (2024). Waymax: An accelerated, data-driven simulator for large-scale autonomous driving research. *Advances in Neural Information Processing Systems*, •••, 36.

Gunay, S., Kurtishi-Kastrati, S., & Krsteska, K. (2023). Regional green economy and community impact on global sustainability. *Journal of Enterprising Communities: People and Places in the Global Economy*, 17(6), 1118–1134. DOI: 10.1108/JEC-03-2022-0040

Gungor, V., Sahin, D., Kocak, T., Ergut, S., Buccella, C., Cecati, C., & Hancke, G. (2011). Smart grid technologies: Communication technologies and standards}. *IEEE Transactions on Industrial Informatics*, 7(4), 529–539. DOI: 10.1109/TII.2011.2166794

Guo, Z., Zhu, Z., Li, Y., Cao, S., Chen, H., & Wang, G. (2023). AI assisted fashion design: A review. *IEEE Access : Practical Innovations, Open Solutions*, 11, 88403–88415. DOI: 10.1109/ACCESS.2023.3306235

Gupta, V., Mishra, V. K., Singhal, P., & Kumar, A. (2022), An Overview of Supervised Machine Learning Algorithm, *2022 11th International Conference on System Modeling & Advancement in Research Trends (SMART)*, Moradabad, India, 2022, pp. 87-92, DOI: 10.1109/SMART55829.2022.10047618

Gu, Z., Gao, L., Ma, H., Li, S. E., Zheng, S., Jing, W., & Chen, J. (2023). Safe-state enhancement method for autonomous driving via direct hierarchical reinforcement learning. *IEEE Transactions on Intelligent Transportation Systems*, 24(9), 9966–9983. DOI: 10.1109/TITS.2023.3271642

Haider, S. N., Zhao, Q., & Li, X. (2020). Data driven battery anomaly detection based on shape-based clustering for the data centers class. *Journal of Energy Storage*, 29, 101479. DOI: 10.1016/j.est.2020.101479

Hák, T., Janoušková, S., & Moldan, B. (2016). Sustainable development goals: A need for relevant indicators. *Ecological Indicators*, 60, 565–573. DOI: 10.1016/j.ecolind.2015.08.003

Hannan, M. A., Hoque, M. M., Mohamed, A., & Ayob, A. (2017). Review of energy storage systems for electric vehicle applications: Issues and challenges. *Renewable & Sustainable Energy Reviews*, 69, 771–789. DOI: 10.1016/j.rser.2016.11.171

Hannan, M. A., Lipu, M. S. H., Hussain, A., & Mohamed, A. (2017). A Review of Lithium-Ion Battery State of Charge Estimation and Management System in Electric Vehicle Applications: Challenges and Recommendations. *Renewable & Sustainable Energy Reviews*, 78, 834–854. DOI: 10.1016/j.rser.2017.05.001

Hao, X., Fu, W., & Albitar, K. (2023). Innovation with ecological sustainability: Does corporate environmental responsibility matter in green innovation? *Journal of Economic Analysis*, 2(3), 21–42. DOI: 10.58567/jea02030002

Haristiani, N. (2019, November). Artificial Intelligence (AI) chatbot as language learning medium: An inquiry. [). IOP Publishing.]. *Journal of Physics: Conference Series*, 1387(1), 012020. DOI: 10.1088/1742-6596/1387/1/012020

Hasan, Md. T., Shamael, M. N., Akter, A., Islam, R., Mukta, Md. S. H., & Islam, S. (2023). An Artificial Intelligence-based Framework to Achieve the Sustainable Development Goals in the Context of Bangladesh. In arXiv (Cornell University). Cornell University. https://doi.org//arxiv.2304.11703DOI: 10.48550

Hassan, I. A., Ramadan, H. S., Saleh, M. A., & Hissel, D. (2021). Hydrogen storage technologies for stationary and mobile applications: Review, analysis and perspectives. *Renewable & Sustainable Energy Reviews*, 149, 111311. DOI: 10.1016/j.rser.2021.111311

Hegenbart, S., Uhl, A., & Vécsei, A. (2015). Survey on computer aided decision support for diagnosis of celiac disease. *Computers in Biology and Medicine*, 65, 348–358. DOI: 10.1016/j.compbiomed.2015.02.007 PMID: 25770906

He, W., Li, Z., Liu, T., Liu, Z., Guo, X., Du, J., Li, X., Sun, P., & Ming, W. (2023). Research progress and application of deep learning in remaining useful life, state of health and battery thermal management of lithium batteries. *Journal of Energy Storage*, 70, 107868. DOI: 10.1016/j.est.2023.107868

He, X., Huang, W., & Lv, C. (2024). Toward Trustworthy Decision-Making for Autonomous Vehicles: A Robust Reinforcement Learning Approach with Safety Guarantees. *Engineering (Beijing)*, 33, 77–89. DOI: 10.1016/j.eng.2023.10.005

He, X., Wu, J., Huang, Z., Hu, Z., Wang, J., Sangiovanni-Vincentelli, A., & Lv, C. (2023). Fear-neuro-inspired reinforcement learning for safe autonomous driving. *IEEE Transactions on Pattern Analysis and Machine Intelligence*. PMID: 37801378

Hill, C. A., Such, M. C., Chen, D., Gonzalez, J., & Grady, W. M. (2012). Battery Energy Storage for Enabling Integration of Distributed Solar Power Generation. *IEEE Transactions on Smart Grid*, 3(2), 850–857. DOI: 10.1109/TSG.2012.2190113

Hodge, B.-M., Brancucci Martinez-Anido, C., Wang, Q., Chartan, E., Florita, A., & Kiviluoma, J. (2018). The combined value of wind and solar power forecasting improvements and electricity storage. *Applied Energy*, 214, 1–15. DOI: 10.1016/j.apenergy.2017.12.120

Ho, J.-H., Lee, G.-G., & Lu, M.-T. (2020). Exploring the implementation of a legal AI bot for Sustainable Development in Legal Advisory institutions. *Sustainability (Basel)*, 12(15), 5991. DOI: 10.3390/su12155991

Hollon, J., Puppa, E. L., Greenwald, B., Goldberg, E., Guerrerio, A., & Fasano, A. (2015). Effect of gliadin on permeability of intestinal biopsy explants from celiac disease patients and patients with non-celiac gluten sensitivity. *Nutrients*, 7(3), 1565–1576. DOI: 10.3390/nu7031565 PMID: 25734566

Hong, J., Zhang, H., & Xu, X. (2023). Thermal fault prognosis of lithium-ion batteries in real-world electric vehicles using self-attention mechanism networks. *Applied Thermal Engineering*, 226, 120304. DOI: 10.1016/j.applthermaleng.2023.120304

Hongwen, he & Huang, Ruchen & Meng, Xiangfei & Zhao, Xuyang & Wang, Yong & Li, Menglin. (2022). A novel hierarchical predictive energy management strategy for plug-in hybrid electric bus combined with deep deterministic policy gradient. *Journal of Energy Storage*. 52. 104787. . DOI: 10.1016/j.est.2022.104787

Houssam, N., Ibrahiem, D. M., Sucharita, S., El-Aasar, K. M., Esily, R. R., & Sethi, N. (2023). Assessing the role of green economy on sustainable development in developing countries. *Heliyon*, 9(6), e17306. DOI: 10.1016/j.heliyon.2023.e17306 PMID: 37389081

Huang, F. H., Lu, H. M., & Hsu, Y. W. (2021). From street photos to fashion trends: Leveraging user-provided noisy labels for fashion understanding. *IEEE Access : Practical Innovations, Open Solutions*, 9, 49189–49205. DOI: 10.1109/ACCESS.2021.3069245

Huang, Q., Huang, R., & Hao, W., (2019). *Adaptive Power System Emergency Control using Deep Reinforcement Learning*, online. https://arxiv.org/abs/1903.03712

Huang, S.-C., Tseng, K.-H., Liang, J.-W., Chang, C.-L., & Pecht, M. G. (2017). An Online SOC and SOH Estimation Model for Lithium-Ion Batteries. *Energies*, 10(4), 512. DOI: 10.3390/en10040512

Huang, W., & He, J. (2023). Impact of energy intensity, green economy, and natural resources development to achieve sustainable economic growth in Asian countries. *Resources Policy*, 84, 103726. DOI: 10.1016/j.resourpol.2023.103726

Huang, X., Ye, Y., Xiong, L., Lau, R. Y. K., Jiang, N., & Wang, S. (2016). Time series k -means: A new k -means type smooth subspace clustering for time series data. *Information Sciences*, 367–368, 1–13. DOI: 10.1016/j.ins.2016.05.040

Hüe, S., Mention, J.-J., Monteiro, R. C., Zhang, S., Cellier, C., Schmitz, J., Verkarre, V., Fodil, N., Bahram, S., Cerf-Bensussan, N., & Caillat-Zucman, S. (2004). A direct role for NKG2D/MICA interaction in villous atrophy during celiac disease. *Immunity*, 21(3), 367–377. DOI: 10.1016/j.immuni.2004.06.018 PMID: 15357948

Hujoel, I. A., Van Dyke, C. T., Brantner, T., Larson, J., King, K. S., Sharma, A., Murray, J. A., & Rubio-Tapia, A. (2018). Natural history and clinical detection of undiagnosed coeliac disease in a North American community. *Alimentary Pharmacology & Therapeutics*, 47(10), 1358–1366. DOI: 10.1111/apt.14625 PMID: 29577349

Hummel, M., Bonifacio, E., Naserke, H. E., & Ziegler, A. G. (2002). Elimination of dietary gluten does not reduce titers of type 1 diabetes-associated autoantibodies in high-risk subjects. *Diabetes Care*, 25(7), 1111–1116. DOI: 10.2337/diacare.25.7.1111 PMID: 12087006

Hu, S., & Huang, C. (2023). Machine-Learning Approaches for the Discovery of Electrolyte Materials for Solid-State Lithium Batteries. *Batteries.*, 9(4), 228. DOI: 10.3390/batteries9040228

Hussain, A., Barua, B., Osman, A., Abozariba, R., & Taufiq Asyhari, A. (2021). Performance of MobileNetV3 Transfer Learning on Handheld Device-based Real-Time Tree Species Identification. 2021 26th International Conference on Automation and Computing: System Intelligence through Automation and Computing, ICAC 2021. DOI: 10.23919/ICAC50006.2021.9594222

Hussien, H. M., Yasin, S. M., Udzir, N. I., Ninggal, M. I. H., & Salman, S. (2021). Blockchain technology in the healthcare industry: Trends and opportunities. *Journal of Industrial Information Integration*, 22, 100217. DOI: 10.1016/j.jii.2021.100217

Hutajulu, H., Tahir, U., Utami, E. Y., Harsono, I., & Yuniarti, T. (2024). Green Growth Strategy and Environmental Policy Integration in Sustainable Economic Development: A Review of Bibliometric Analysis. *West Science Social and Humanities Studies*, 2(03), 474–482. DOI: 10.58812/wsshs.v2i03.761

Hu, W., Zheng, L., & Min, Y., (2017). Research on power system transient stability assessment based on deep learning of big data technique. *Power Syst Technol.*, 41(10), 3140–3146.

Hu, X., Jiang, J., Cao, D., & Egardt, B. (2016). Battery Health Prognosis for Electric Vehicles Using Sample Entropy and Sparse Bayesian Predictive Modeling. *IEEE Transactions on Industrial Electronics*, 63, 2645–2656. DOI: 10.1109/TIE.2015.2461523

Hu, Y., Fu, J., & Wen, G. (2023). Safe reinforcement learning for model-reference trajectory tracking of uncertain autonomous vehicles with model-based acceleration. *IEEE Transactions on Intelligent Vehicles*, 8(3), 2332–2344. DOI: 10.1109/TIV.2022.3233592

Iglhaut, J., Cabo, C., Puliti, S., Piermattei, L., O'Connor, J., & Rosette, J. (2019). Structure from Motion Photogrammetry in Forestry: A Review. *Current Forestry Reports*, 5(3), 155–168. DOI: 10.1007/s40725-019-00094-3

Ikharo, B., Obiagwu, A., Obasi, C., Hussein, S. U., & Akah, P. (2021, July). Security for Internet-of-Things Enabled E-Health using Blockchain and Artificial Intelligence: A Novel Integration Framework. In *2021 1st International Conference on Multidisciplinary Engineering and Applied Science (ICMEAS)* (pp. 1-4). IEEE. DOI: 10.1109/ICMEAS52683.2021.9692368

İnci Kavak, V., Evis, D., & Ekinci, A. (2024). The Use of ChatGPT in Language Education. *Experimental and Applied Medical Science*, 5(2), 72–82. DOI: 10.46871/eams.1461578

India, P. T. of. (2023, February 9). *Nearly 5 crore pending cases in courts, over 69,000 in Supreme Court*. NDTV.com. https://www.ndtv.com/india-news/nearly-5-crore-pending-cases-in-courts-over-69-000-in-supreme-court-3768720

*Interactions within the MHC contribute to the genetic architecture of celiac disease—PMC*. (n.d.). Retrieved July 30, 2024, from https://www.ncbi.nlm.nih.gov/pmc/articles/PMC5345796/

IRENA. (2023). WORLD ENERGY TRANSITIONS OUTLOOK 2023. https://h2chile.cl/wp-content/uploads/2024/01/2023_IRENA_World_energy_transitions_outlook_v1_2023.pdf, Abu Dhabi.

IRENA. I. R. (2020, agosto 20). *Renewable Energy Statistics2020*. Retrieved from The International Renewable Energy Agency, Abu Dhabi: https://www.irena.org/-/media/Files/IRENA/Agency/Publication/2020/Jul/IRENA_Renewable_Energy_Statistics_2020.pdf

IRENA. T. I. (2024, agosto 20). *Renewable capacity statistics2024.* Retrieved from The International Renewable Energy Agency (IRENA): https://www.irena.org/-/media/Files/IRENA/Agency/Publication/2024/Mar/IRENA_RE_Capacity_Statistics_2024.p

Isichei, J. C., Khorsandroo, S., & Desai, S. (2023). Cybersecurity and privacy in smart bioprinting. *Bioprinting (Amsterdam, Netherlands)*, •••, 00321.

Ivarsson, A., Persson, L. A., Juto, P., Peltonen, M., Suhr, O., & Hernell, O. (1999). High prevalence of undiagnosed coeliac disease in adults: A Swedish population-based study. *Journal of Internal Medicine*, 245(1), 63–68. DOI: 10.1046/j.1365-2796.1999.00403.x PMID: 10095818

Iyer, L. S. (2021). AI enabled applications towards Intelligent Transportation. *Transportation Engineering*, 5, 100083. DOI: 10.1016/j.treng.2021.100083

Jackendoff, R. (2007). Linguistics in Cognitive Science: The state of the art. *Linguistic Review*, 24(4). Advance online publication. DOI: 10.1515/TLR.2007.014

Jagatheesaperumal, S. K., Mishra, P., Moustafa, N., & Chauhan, R. (2022). A holistic survey on the use of emerging technologies to provision secure healthcare solutions. *Computers & Electrical Engineering*, 99, 107691. DOI: 10.1016/j.compeleceng.2022.107691

Jain, M., Singh, S., Chandrasekaran, K., Rathnamma, M. V., & Venkata Ramana, V. (2020) Machine learning models with optimization for clothing recommendation from personal wardrobe 3rd International Conference on Emerging Technologies in Computer Engineering: Machine Learning and Internet of Things (ICETCE), Jaipur, India, Vol. 2020, pp. 1–6. DOI: DOI: 10.1109/ICETCE48199.2020.9091777

Jalem, R., Kanamori, K., Takeuchi, I., Nakayama, M., Yamasaki, H., & Saito, T. (2018). Bayesian-Driven First-Principles Calculations for Accelerating Exploration of Fast Ion Conductors for Rechargeable Battery Application. *Scientific Reports*, 8(1), 5845. DOI: 10.1038/s41598-018-23852-y PMID: 29643423

James, S., Konidaris, G., & Rosman, B. (2017). An analysis of monte carlo tree search. *Proceedings of the AAAI Conference on Artificial Intelligence*, 31(1), DOI: 10.1609/aaai.v31i1.11028

Jayaraman, K., Jayashree, S., & Dorasamy, M. (2023). The effects of green innovations in organizations: Influence of stakeholders. *Sustainability (Basel)*, 15(2), 1133. DOI: 10.3390/su15021133

Jebali, F., Majumdar, A., Turck, C., Harabi, K.-E., Faye, M.-C., Muhr, E., Walder, J.-P., Bilousov, O., Michaud, A., Vianello, E., Hirtzlin, T., Andrieu, F., Bocquet, M., Collin, S., Querlioz, D., & Portal, J.-M. (2024). Powering AI at the edge : A robust, memristor-based binarized neural network with near-memory computing and miniaturized solar cell. *Nature Communications*, 15(1), 741. DOI: 10.1038/s41467-024-44766-6 PMID: 38272896

Jiang, Y., & Song, W. (2023). Predicting the Cycle Life of Lithium-Ion Batteries Using Data-Driven Machine Learning Based on Discharge Voltage Curves. *Batteries*, 9(8), 413. DOI: 10.3390/batteries9080413

Jing, P., Zhang, J., Nie, L., Ye, S., Liu, J., & Su, Y. (2022). Tripartite graph regularized latent low-rank representation for fashion compatibility prediction. *IEEE Transactions on Multimedia*, 24, 1277–1287. DOI: 10.1109/TMM.2021.3062736

Joel, M. R., Manikandan, G., & Bhuvaneswari, G. (2023, March). An analysis of security challenges in Internet of Things (IoT)-based smart homes. In *2023 Second International Conference on Electronics and Renewable Systems (ICEARS)* (pp. 490–497). IEEE. DOI: 10.1109/ICEARS56392.2023.10085106

Ju, J. M., Marietta, E. V., & Murray, J. A. (2015). Generating Transgenic Mouse Models for Studying Celiac Disease. In Ryan, A. W. (Ed.), *Celiac Disease: Methods and Protocols* (pp. 23–33). Springer., DOI: 10.1007/978-1-4939-2839-2_3

Jung-Pin, L., Yu-Ming, C., Chieh-Huang, C., & Ping-Feng, P. (2020). A survey of machine learning models in renewable energy predictions. *Applied Sciences (Basel, Switzerland)*, •••, 5975.

Junker, Y., Zeissig, S., Kim, S.-J., Barisani, D., Wieser, H., Leffler, D. A., Zevallos, V., Libermann, T. A., Dillon, S., Freitag, T. L., Kelly, C. P., & Schuppan, D. (2012). Wheat amylase trypsin inhibitors drive intestinal inflammation via activation of toll-like receptor 4. *The Journal of Experimental Medicine*, 209(13), 2395–2408. DOI: 10.1084/jem.20102660 PMID: 23209313

Jurjević, L., Liang, X., Gašparović, M., & Balenović, I. (2020). Is field-measured tree height as reliable as believed – Part II, A comparison study of tree height estimates from conventional field measurement and low-cost close-range remote sensing in a deciduous forest. *ISPRS Journal of Photogrammetry and Remote Sensing*, 169, 227–241. DOI: 10.1016/j.isprsjprs.2020.09.014

Juyal, A., Sharma, S., & Matta, P. (2023, March). Object Classification Using A rtificial I ntelligence Technique sin Autonomous Vehicles. In *2023 3rd International conference on Artificial Intelligence and Signal Processing (AISP)* (pp. 1-6). IEEE.

Kaile, Z., Chao, F., & Shanlin, Y. (2016). Big data driven smart energy management: From big data to big insights. *Renewable & Sustainable Energy Reviews*, •••, 215–225.

Kalinaki, K., Fahadi, M., Alli, A. A., Shafik, W., Yasin, M., & Mutwalibi, N. (2023). Artificial Intelligence of Internet of Medical Things (AIoMT) in Smart Cities: A Review of Cybersecurity for Smart Healthcare. *Handbook of Security and Privacy of AI-Enabled Healthcare Systems and Internet of Medical Things*, 271-292.

Kalpana, A. V., Geetha, A. V., Jagadeesh, M. S., & Shobana, J. (2024). Secure 3D: Secure and Energy Efficient Localization in 3D Environment using Wireless Sensor Networks. *Wireless Personal Communications*, 136(3), 1375–1402. DOI: 10.1007/s11277-024-11290-1

Karaboga, D., & Kaya, E. (2019). Adaptive network based fuzzy inference system (ANFIS) training approaches: A comprehensive survey. *Artificial Intelligence Review*, 52(4), 2263–2293. DOI: 10.1007/s10462-017-9610-2

Karimi, H., Beheshti, M. T. H., Ramezani, A., & Zareipour, H. (2021). Intelligent control of islanded AC microgrids based on adaptive neuro-fuzzy inference system. *International Journal of Electrical Power & Energy Systems*, 133, 107161. DOI: 10.1016/j.ijepes.2021.107161

Karimi, S., Karimi, A., & Vahidi, A. (2023). Level-$ K $ Reasoning, Deep Reinforcement Learning, and Monte Carlo Decision Process for Fast and Safe Automated Lane Change and Speed Management. *IEEE Transactions on Intelligent Vehicles*, 8(6), 3556–3571. DOI: 10.1109/TIV.2023.3265311

Kathirgamanathan, A., Mangina, E., & Finn, D. P. (2021). Development of a soft actor critic deep reinforcement learning approach for harnessing energy flexibility in a large office building. *Energy and AI*, 5, 100101. DOI: 10.1016/j.egyai.2021.100101

Kaur, J., & Ramkumar, K. R. (2022). The recent trends in cyber security: A review. *Journal of King Saud University. Computer and Information Sciences*, 34(8), 5766–5781. DOI: 10.1016/j.jksuci.2021.01.018

Keezhatta, M. S. (2019). Understanding EFL Linguistic Models through Relationship between Natural Language Processing and Artificial Intelligence Applications. *Arab World English Journal*, 10(4), 251–262. DOI: 10.24093/awej/vol10no4.19

Keshta, I., & Odeh, A. (2021). Security and privacy of electronic health records: Concerns and challenges. *Egyptian Informatics Journal*, 22(2), 177–183. DOI: 10.1016/j.eij.2020.07.003

Khalid, N., Qayyum, A., Bilal, M., Al-Fuqaha, A., & Qadir, J. (2023). Privacy-preserving artificial intelligence in healthcare: Techniques and applications. *Computers in Biology and Medicine*, 158, 106848. DOI: 10.1016/j.compbiomed.2023.106848 PMID: 37044052

Khanam, M., Mahboob, T., Imtiaz, W., Ghafoor, H., & Sehar, R. (2015). A Survey on Unsupervised Machine Learning Algorithms for Automation, Classification and Maintenance. *International Journal of Computer Applications*, 119(13), 34–39. DOI: 10.5120/21131-4058

Khatun, M. A., Memon, S. F., Eising, C., & Dhirani, L. L. (2023). Machine Learning for Healthcare-IoT Security: A Review and Risk Mitigation. *IEEE Access : Practical Innovations, Open Solutions*, 11, 145869–145896. DOI: 10.1109/ACCESS.2023.3346320

Khawaja, Y., Shankar, N., Qiqieh, I., Alzubi, J., Alzubi, O., Nallakaruppan, M. K., & Padmanaban, S. (2023). Battery management solutions for li-ion batteries based on artificial intelligence. *Ain Shams Engineering Journal*, 14(12), 102213. DOI: 10.1016/j.asej.2023.102213

Khoshafah, F. (2023). ChatGPT for Arabic-English Translation: Evaluating the Accuracy ChatGPT for Arabic-English Translation: Evaluating the Accuracy. *Research Square*. DOI: 10.21203/rs.3.rs-2814154/v2

Kilic, A., Oral, B., Eroglu, D., & Yildirim, R. (2023). Machine learning for beyond Li-ion batteries: Powering the research. *Journal of Energy Storage*, 73, 109057. DOI: 10.1016/j.est.2023.109057

Kim, S. M., Mayassi, T., & Jabri, B. (2015). Innate immunity: Actuating the gears of celiac disease pathogenesis. *Best Practice & Research. Clinical Gastroenterology*, 29(3), 425–435. DOI: 10.1016/j.bpg.2015.05.001 PMID: 26060107

Kim, S., Lee, S., & Cho, K. (2012). Design of high-performance unified circuit for linear and non-linear SVM classifications. J. *Journal of Semiconductor Technology and Science*, 12(2), 162–167. DOI: 10.5573/JSTS.2012.12.2.162

Kocer, M., Cengiz, C., Gezer, M., Gunes, D., Cinar, M., Alboyaci, B., & Onen, A. (2019). Assessment of Battery Storage Technologies for a Turkish Power Network. *Sustainability (Basel)*, 11(13), 3669. DOI: 10.3390/su11133669

Kofinas, P., Dounis, A. I., & Vouros, G. A. (2018a). Fuzzy Q-Learning for multi-agent decentralized energy management in microgrids. *Applied Energy*, 219, 53–67. DOI: 10.1016/j.apenergy.2018.03.017

Kofinas, P., Vouros, G., & Dounis, A. I. (2018b). Energy management in solar microgrid via reinforcement learning using fuzzy reward. *Advances in Building Energy Research*, 12(1), 97–115. DOI: 10.1080/17512549.2017.1314832

Kolambe, M. (2024). Forecasting the Future: A Comprehensive Review of Time Series Prediction Techniques. *Journal of Electrical Systems.*, 20(2s), 575–586. DOI: 10.52783/jes.1478

Kolhar, M., & Alameen, A. (2021). Artificial Intelligence Based Language Translation Platform. *Intelligent Automation & Soft Computing*, 28(1), 1–9. DOI: 10.32604/iasc.2021.014995

Kolisko, S., & Anderson, C. J. (2023). Exploring Social Biases of Large Language Models in a College Artificial Intelligence Course. *Proceedings of the AAAI Conference on Artificial Intelligence*, 37(13), 15825–15833. DOI: 10.1609/aaai.v37i13.26879

Koohfar, S., Woldemariam, W., & Kumar, A. (2023). Prediction of Electric Vehicles Charging Demand: A Transformer-Based Deep Learning Approach. *Sustainability (Basel)*, 15(3), 2105. DOI: 10.3390/su15032105

Korkmaz, M. (2023). SoC estimation of lithium-ion batteries based on machine learning techniques: A filtered approach. *Journal of Energy Storage*, 72, 108268. DOI: 10.1016/j.est.2023.108268

Koshy, R., Gharat, A., Wagh, T., & Sonawane, S. (2021) A Complexion based Outfit color recommender using Neural Networks International Conference on Advances in Electrical, Computing, Communication and Sustainable Technologies (ICAECT), Bhilai, India, Vol. 2021, pp. 1–7. DOI: DOI: 10.1109/ICAECT49130.2021.9392418

Kosuru, V. S. R., & Kavasseri Venkitaraman, A. (2023). A Smart Battery Management System for Electric Vehicles Using Deep Learning-Based Sensor Fault Detection. *World Electr. Veh. J.*, 14(4), 101. DOI: 10.3390/wevj14040101

Koubaa, A., Boulila, W., Ghouti, L., Alzahem, A., & Latif, S. (2023). Exploring ChatGPT Capabilities and Limitations: A Survey. *IEEE Access : Practical Innovations, Open Solutions*, 11(October), 118698–118721. DOI: 10.1109/ACCESS.2023.3326474

Ksibi, S., Jaidi, F., & Bouhoula, A. (2023). A comprehensive study of security and cyber-security risk management within e-Health systems: Synthesis, analysis and a novel quantified approach. *Mobile Networks and Applications*, 28(1), 107–127. DOI: 10.1007/s11036-022-02042-1

Kuck, K. (2023). Generative Artificial Intelligence: A Double-Edged Sword. *2023 World Engineering Education Forum - Global Engineering Deans Council (WEEF-GEDC)*, 1–10. DOI: 10.1109/WEEF-GEDC59520.2023.10343638

Kulakov, O., Popova, O., Popova, S., & Tomashevskaya, E. (2023). Investments in green business and corporate governance by Ukraine's cooperation with the European Union. [). IOP Publishing.]. *IOP Conference Series. Earth and Environmental Science*, 1126(1), 012011. DOI: 10.1088/1755-1315/1126/1/012011

Kumar, A., Jain, R., Gupta, M., & Islam, S. M. (Eds.). (2023). *6G-Enabled IoT and AI for Smart Healthcare: Challenges, Impact, and Analysis*. CRC Press. DOI: 10.1201/9781003321668

Kumar, N. M., Chand, A. A., Malvoni, M., Prasad, K. A., Mamun, K. A., Islam, F., & Chopra, S. S. (2020). Distributed energy resources and the application of AI, IOT, and blockchain in smart grids. *Energies*, 13(21), 5739. DOI: 10.3390/en13215739

Kumar, P., Singh, A., & Sengupta, A. (2022). Securing Cyber-Resilience in Healthcare Sector. In *Cyber Security in Intelligent Computing and Communications* (pp. 211–226). Springer Singapore. DOI: 10.1007/978-981-16-8012-0_17

Kurniawan, I. F., Aneiba, A., Hussain, A., Idrissi, M., Dunggio, I., & Asyhari, A. T. (2022). Large-scale Tree Detection through UAV-based Remote Sensing in Indonesia: Wallacea Case Study. Proceedings - 2022 8th International Conference on Information Management, ICIM 2022, 110–115. DOI: 10.1109/ICIM56520.2022.00027

Kwon, N., Ahn, Y., Son, B.-S., & Moon, H. (2021). Developing a machine learning based building repair time estimation model considering weight assigning methods. *Journal of Building Engineering*, 43, 102627. DOI: 10.1016/j.jobe.2021.102627

Lakhani, M., & Khan, H. M. A. (2023). Fighting Disinformation in the Palestine Conflict: The Role of Generative AI and Islamic Values. *Al Misbah Research Journal, 3*(4), 02–13. https://zenodo.org/records/11265514

Lakshmi, B. N., & Joel, M. R. (2023, March). IoT-based illness prediction system using machine learning. In *2023 Second International Conference on Electronics and Renewable Systems (ICEARS)* (pp. 1087–1091). IEEE. DOI: 10.1109/ICEARS56392.2023.10085553

Lasseter, R. H. (2002, January). Microgrids. In *2002 IEEE Power Engineering Society Winter Meeting. Conference Proceedings (Cat. No. 02CH37309)* (Vol. 1, pp. 305–308). IEEE. DOI: 10.1109/PESW.2002.985003

Le Guen, V. (2022). Deep learning for spatio-temporal forecasting—. *Applied Solar Energy*.

LeCun, Y., Bengio, Y., & Hinton, G. (2015). Deep learning. *Nature Publishing Group UK London*, 436--444.

LeCun, Y., Bengio, Y., & Hinton, G. (2015). Deep learning. *Nature*, 521(7553), 436–444. DOI: 10.1038/nature14539 PMID: 26017442

Lee, N. H., Kim, S. B., Sok, V., Kang, S. H., & Nam, S. R. (2019). A study on deep neural network-based DC offset removal for phase estimation in power systems. *Energies*, 12, 1–19.

Lee, S., & Choi, D. H. (2020). Energy management of smart home with home appliances, energy storage system and electric vehicle: A hierarchical deep reinforcement learning approach. *Sensors (Basel)*, 20(7), 2157. Advance online publication. DOI: 10.3390/s20072157 PMID: 32290345

Lehto, M., Neittaanmäki, P., Pöyhönen, J., & Hummelholm, A. (2022). Cyber Security in Healthcare Systems. In *Cyber Security: Critical Infrastructure Protection* (pp. 183–215). Springer International Publishing. DOI: 10.1007/978-3-030-91293-2_8

Lenci, A., & Padó, S. (2022). Editorial: Perspectives for natural language processing between AI, linguistics and cognitive science. *Frontiers in Artificial Intelligence*, 5, 1059998. Advance online publication. DOI: 10.3389/frai.2022.1059998 PMID: 36406471

Leonzio, G. (2019). Fluid dynamic study of anaerobic digester: Optimization of mixing and geometric configuration by using response surface methodology and factorial design. *Renewable Energy*, 136, 769–780. DOI: 10.1016/j.renene.2018.12.115

Li, C., Chen, Z., Cui, J., Wang, Y., & Zou, F. The lithium-ion battery state-of-charge estimation using random forest regression, *2014 Prognostics and System Health Management Conference (PHM-2014 Hunan)*, Zhangjiajie, China, 2014, pp. 336-339, DOI: 10.1109/PHM.2014.6988190

Li, J., Liu, X., Zhu, B., Jiao, J., Tomizuka, M., Tang, C., & Zhan, W. (2023). Guided online distillation: Promoting safe reinforcement learning by offline demonstration. *arXiv preprint arXiv:2309.09408.*

Li, A., Tian, H., & Li, K. (2023). Remaining useful life prediction of lithium-ion batteries using a spatial temporal network model based on capacity self-recovery effect. *Journal of Energy Storage*, 67, 107557. DOI: 10.1016/j.est.2023.107557

Lin, Y., Ren, P., Chen, Z., Ren, Z., & Ma, J. (2018). *Rijke. Maarten.* Explainable Fashion Recommendation with Joint Outfit Matching and Comment Generation.

Lionetti, E., Castellaneta, S., Francavilla, R., Pulvirenti, A., Tonutti, E., Amarri, S., Barbato, M., Barbera, C., Barera, G., Bellantoni, A., Castellano, E., Guariso, G., Limongelli, M. G., Pellegrino, S., Polloni, C., Ughi, C., Zuin, G., Fasano, A., & Catassi, C. (2014). Introduction of gluten, HLA status, and the risk of celiac disease in children. *The New England Journal of Medicine*, 371(14), 1295–1303. DOI: 10.1056/NEJMoa1400697 PMID: 25271602

Lionetti, E., & Catassi, C. (2011). New clues in celiac disease epidemiology, pathogenesis, clinical manifestations, and treatment. *International Reviews of Immunology*, 30(4), 219–231. DOI: 10.3109/08830185.2011.602443 PMID: 21787227

Li, Q., Qu, H., Liu, Z., Zhou, N., Sun, W., Sigg, S., & Li, J. (2019). AF-DCGAN: Amplitude feature deep convolutional GAN for fingerprint construction in indoor localization systems. *IEEE Transactions on Emerging Topics in Computational Intelligence*, 5(3), 468–480. DOI: 10.1109/TETCI.2019.2948058

Li, R. (2020, November). Using artificial intelligence in learning English as a foreign language: an examination of IELTS LIULISHUO as an online platform. In *Conference Proceedings. Innovation in Language Learning 2020*. DOI: 10.32629/jher.v1i2.178

Li, S., He, H., & Li, J. (2019). Big data driven lithium-ion battery modeling method based on SDAE-ELM algorithm and data pre-processing technology. *Applied Energy*, 242, 1259–1273. DOI: 10.1016/j.apenergy.2019.03.154

Li, S., Li, J., & Wang, H. (2019). Big data driven Lithium-ion battery modeling method: a cyber- physical system approach. Proc. - 2019 *IEEE Int. Conf. Ind. Cyber Phys. Syst. ICPS* 2019 161–166. DOI: 10.1109/ICPHYS.2019.8780152

Liu, Z., Guo, Z., Lin, H., Yao, Y., Zhu, J., Cen, Z., . . . Zhao, D. (2023). Datasets and benchmarks for offline safe reinforcement learning. *arXiv preprint arXiv:2306.09303*.

Liua, Y., Salehb, S., & Huang, J. (2021). Artificial intelligence in promoting teaching and learning transformation in schools. *Artificial Intelligence*, 15(3).

Liu, D., Zhou, J., Pan, D., Peng, Y., & Peng, X. (2015). Lithium-ion battery remaining useful life estimation with an optimized Relevance Vector Machine algorithm with incremental learning. *Measurement*, 63, 143–151. DOI: 10.1016/j.measurement.2014.11.031

Liu, D., Zhou, L., Pan, R., Chen, Z., & Bei, Z. (2021). Lithium-ion battery state-of-health online estimation based on multi-scale relevance vector machine. *Applied Energy*, 306, 118174.

Liu, H., Li, Y., Luo, L., & Zhang, C. (2023). A Lithium-Ion Battery Capacity and RUL Prediction Fusion Method Based on Decomposition Strategy and GRU. *Batteries*, 9(6), 323. DOI: 10.3390/batteries9060323

Liu, J., & Chen, Z. (2019). Remaining useful life prediction of lithium-ion batteries based on health indicator and Gaussian process regression model. *IEEE Access : Practical Innovations, Open Solutions*, 7, 39474–39484. DOI: 10.1109/ACCESS.2019.2905740

Liu, R., Yue, Z., Ijaz, A., Lutfi, A., & Mao, J. (2023). Sustainable business performance: Examining the role of green HRM practices, green innovation and responsible leadership through the lens of pro-environmental behavior. *Sustainability (Basel)*, 15(9), 7317. DOI: 10.3390/su15097317

Liu, X., Sun, Y., Liu, Z., & Lin, D. (2021). Learning diverse fashion collocation by neural graph filtering. *IEEE Transactions on Multimedia*, 23, 2894–2901. DOI: 10.1109/TMM.2020.3018021

Liu, Y., Liu, C., Liu, Y., Sun, F., Qiao, J., & Xu, T. (2023). Review on degradation mechanism and health state estimation methods of lithium-ion batteries. *Journal of Traffic and Transportation Engineering*, 10(4), 578–610. DOI: 10.1016/j.jtte.2023.06.001

Liu, Y., Yang, Z., Yu, Z., Liu, Z., Liu, D., Lin, H., Li, M., Ma, S., Avdeev, M., & Shi, S. (2023). Generative artificial intelligence and its applications in materials science: Current situation and future perspectives. *Journal of Materiomics*, 9(4), 798–816. DOI: 10.1016/j.jmat.2023.05.001

Liu, Z., Wu, K., Guo, J., Wang, Y., Deussen, O., & Cheng, Z. (2021). Single Image Tree Reconstruction via Adversarial Network. *Graphical Models*, 117, 101115. DOI: 10.1016/j.gmod.2021.101115

Liu, Z., Zhao, J., Wang, H., & Yang, C. (2020). A New Lithium-Ion Battery SOH Estimation Method Based on an Indirect Enhanced Health Indicator and Support Vector Regression in PHMs. *Energies*, 13(4), 830. DOI: 10.3390/en13040830

Li, W., Bhutto, M. Y., Waris, I., & Hu, T. (2023). The nexus between environmental corporate social responsibility, green intellectual capital and green innovation towards business sustainability: An empirical analysis of Chinese automobile manufacturing firms. *International Journal of Environmental Research and Public Health*, 20(3), 1851. DOI: 10.3390/ijerph20031851 PMID: 36767217

Li, W., Weng, J., Yuen, A. C. Y., Wang, W., Liu, H., Lee, E. W. M., Wang, J., Kook, S., & Yeoh, G. H. (2023). A., J., Chun Yin Yuen, A., Wang, W., Liu, H., Ming Lee, E.W., Wang, J., Kook, S., and Heng Yeoh, G. Machine learning assisted advanced battery thermal management system: A state-of-the-art review. *Journal of Energy Storage*, 60, 106688. DOI: 10.1016/j.est.2023.106688

Li, W., & Xu, B. (2020). Aspect-based fashion recommendation with attention mechanism. *IEEE Access : Practical Innovations, Open Solutions*, 8, 141814–141823. DOI: 10.1109/ACCESS.2020.3013639

Li, X., Yuan, C., & Wang, Z. (2020). State of Health Estimation for Li-Ion Battery via Partial Incremental Capacity Analysis Based on Support Vector Regression. *Energy*, 203, 117852. DOI: 10.1016/j.energy.2020.117852

Li, X., Yu, D., Søren Byg, V., & Ioan, S. D. (2023). The development of machine learning-based remaining useful life prediction for lithium-ion batteries. *Journal of Energy Chemistry*, 82, 103–121. DOI: 10.1016/j.jechem.2023.03.026

Li, X., Zhang, T., & Liu, Y. (2019). Detection of voltage anomalies in spacecraft storage batteries based on a deep belief network. [Switzerland]. *Sensors (Basel)*, 19(21), 1–21. DOI: 10.3390/s19214702 PMID: 31671886

Li, Y., Ding, Y., He, S., Hu, F., Duan, J., Wen, G., & Zhao, Y. (2024). Artificial intelligence-based methods for renewable power system operation. *Nature Reviews Electrical Engineering*, 163--179.

Li, Y., Liu, K., Foley, A. M., Zulke, A., Berecibar, M., Nanini-Maury, E., Van Mierlo, J., & Hoster, H. E. (2019)... *Renewable & Sustainable Energy Reviews*, 113, 1–66.

Loeff, T., Araya, M., & Pérez-Bravo, F. (2012). Frequency of MYO9B polymorphisms in celiac patients and controls. *Revista Española de Enfermedades Digestivas*, 104(11), 566–571. DOI: 10.4321/S1130-01082012001100003 PMID: 23368647

Lombardo, T., Duquesnoy, M., El-Bouysidy, H., Årén, F., Gallo-Bueno, A., Jørgensen, P. B., Bhowmik, A., Demortière, A., Ayerbe, E., Alcaide, F., Reynaud, M., Carrasco, J., Grimaud, A., Zhang, C., Vegge, T., Johansson, P., & Franco, A. A. (2022). Artificial Intelligence Applied to Battery Research: Hype or Reality? *Chemical Reviews*, 122(12), 10899–10969. DOI: 10.1021/acs.chemrev.1c00108 PMID: 34529918

Lopes, N., & Ribeiro, B. (2015). Deep Belief Networks (DBNs). In *Machine Learning for Adaptive Many-Core Machines - A Practical Approach. Studies in Big Data* (Vol. 7). Springer., DOI: 10.1007/978-3-319-06938-8_8

Lozoya Arandia, J., Vega Gómez, C., Coronado, A., Gonzalez Garcia, J., & Robles Dueñas, V. (2021). Green Energy HPC Data Centers to Improve Processing Cost Efficiency. *Latin American High Performance Computing Conference*, 91--105.

Luanna Maria, S. S., & Peng, W. (2021). Control strategy to smooth wind power output using battery energy storage system: A review, *Journal of Energy Storage*, Volume 35, 102252, ISSN 2352-152X, DOI: 10.1016/j.est.2021.102252

Lucu, M., Martinez-Laserna, E., Gandiaga, I., Liu, K., Camblong, H., Widanage, W. D., & Marco, J. (2020). Data-driven nonparametric Li-ion battery ageing model aiming at learning from real operation data - Part B: Cycling operation. *Journal of Energy Storage*, 101410, 101410. Advance online publication. DOI: 10.1016/j.est.2020.101410

Lu, D., Chen, Q., Wang, G., Liu, L., Li, G., & Moran, E. (2016). A survey of remote sensing-based aboveground biomass estimation methods in forest ecosystems. *International Journal of Digital Earth*, 9(1), 63–105. DOI: 10.1080/17538947.2014.990526

Ludvigsson, J. F., Ludvigsson, J., Ekbom, A., & Montgomery, S. M. (2006). Celiac disease and risk of subsequent type 1 diabetes: A general population cohort study of children and adolescents. *Diabetes Care*, 29(11), 2483–2488. DOI: 10.2337/dc06-0794 PMID: 17065689

Ludvigsson, J. F., Pathak, J., Murphy, S., Durski, M., Kirsch, P. S., Chute, C. G., Ryu, E., & Murray, J. A. (2013). Use of computerized algorithm to identify individuals in need of testing for celiac disease. *Journal of the American Medical Informatics Association : JAMIA*, 20(e2), e306–e310. DOI: 10.1136/amiajnl-2013-001924 PMID: 23956016

Lumnitz, S., Devisscher, T., Mayaud, J. R., Radic, V., Coops, N. C., & Griess, V. C. (2021). Mapping trees along urban street networks with deep learning and street-level imagery. *ISPRS Journal of Photogrammetry and Remote Sensing*, 175, 144–157. DOI: 10.1016/j.isprsjprs.2021.01.016

Lundin, K. E. A., & Wijmenga, C. (2015). Coeliac disease and autoimmune disease-genetic overlap and screening. *Nature Reviews. Gastroenterology & Hepatology*, 12(9), 507–515. DOI: 10.1038/nrgastro.2015.136 PMID: 26303674

Lund, J., & Toth, A. (2021). Direct utilization of geothermal energy 2020 worldwide review. *Geothermics*, 90, 101915. DOI: 10.1016/j.geothermics.2020.101915

Luo, X., Wang, J., Dooner, M., & Clarke, J. (2015). Overview of current development in electrical energy storage technologies and the application potential in power system operation. *Applied Energy*, 137, 511–536. DOI: 10.1016/j.apenergy.2014.09.081

Luo, Z., Yang, X., Wang, Y., Liu, W., Liu, S., Zhu, Y., Huang, Z., Zhang, H., Dou, S., Xu, J., Tian, J., Xu, K., Zhang, X., Hu, W., & Deng, Y. (2020). A Survey of Artificial Intelligence Techniques Applied in Energy Storage Materials R&D. *Frontiers in Energy Research*, 8, 116. https://www.frontiersin.org/articles/10.3389/fenrg.2020.00116. DOI: 10.3389/fenrg.2020.00116

Lv, J., Jiang, B., Wang, X., Liu, Y., & Fu, Y. (2020). Estimation of the State of Charge of Lithium Batteries Based on Adaptive Unscented Kalman Filter Algorithm. *Electronics (Basel)*, 9(9), 1425. DOI: 10.3390/electronics9091425

Ma, G., Xu, S., Jiang, B., Cheng, C., Yang, X., Shen, Y., Yang, T., Huang, Y., Ding, H., & Yuan, Y. (2022). Real-time personalized health status prediction of lithium-ion batteries using deep transfer learning. *Energy & Environmental Science*, 15(10), 4083–4094. DOI: 10.1039/D2EE01676A

Makowicz, B. (2023). Governance und compliance-management. *Risk, Fraud &amp. Compliance*, (4), 7. Advance online publication. DOI: 10.37307/j.1867-8394.2023.04.07

Ma, L., Xie, W., & Zhan, Y. (2019). Blister defect detection based on convolutional neural network for polymer lithium-ion battery. *Applied Sciences (Basel, Switzerland)*, 9(6), 1085. DOI: 10.3390/app9061085

Malekzadeh, R., Sachdev, A., & Fahid Ali, A. (2005). Coeliac disease in developing countries: Middle East, India and North Africa. *Best Practice & Research. Clinical Gastroenterology*, 19(3), 351–358. DOI: 10.1016/j.bpg.2005.01.004 PMID: 15925841

Ma, M., Zhu, X., Liu, M., & Huang, X. (2023). Combining the role of green finance and environmental sustainability on green economic growth: Evidence from G-20 economies. *Renewable Energy*, 207, 128–136. DOI: 10.1016/j.renene.2023.02.046

Mameli, M., Paolanti, M., Pietrini, R., Pazzaglia, G., Frontoni, E., & Zingaretti, P. (2022). Deep learning approaches for fashion knowledge extraction from social media: A review. *IEEE Access : Practical Innovations, Open Solutions*, 10, 1545–1576. DOI: 10.1109/ACCESS.2021.3137893

Man- Fai. (2020). Ng., Jin, Z., Quingyu, Y., Gareth. J.C., and Zhiwei, Sheh. *Nature Machine Intelligence*, 2, 161–170.

Manerba, D., Rinaldi, S., & Pasetti, M. (2018). A Virtual Power Plant Architecture for the Demand-Side Management of Smart Prosumers. *Applied Sciences (Basel, Switzerland)*, 8(3), 432. Advance online publication. DOI: 10.3390/app8030432

Marengo, A. (2023). The Future of AI in IoT: Emerging Trends in Intelligent Data Analysis and Privacy Protection. DOI: 10.1109/ACCESS.2023.3338170

Markou, C., & Deakin, S. F. (2019). Ex Machina Lex: The limits of legal computability. SSRN *Electronic Journal*. DOI: 10.2139/ssrn.3407856

Mateus-Coelho, N., & Cruz-Cunha, M. (Eds.). (2023). *Exploring Cyber Criminals and Data Privacy Measures*. IGI Global. DOI: 10.4018/978-1-6684-8422-7

Matysiak-Budnik, T., Moura, I. C., Arcos-Fajardo, M., Lebreton, C., Ménard, S., Candalh, C., Ben-Khalifa, K., Dugave, C., Tamouza, H., van Niel, G., Bouhnik, Y., Lamarque, D., Chaussade, S., Malamut, G., Cellier, C., Cerf-Bensussan, N., Monteiro, R. C., & Heyman, M. (2008). Secretory IgA mediates retrotranscytosis of intact gliadin peptides via the transferrin receptor in celiac disease. *The Journal of Experimental Medicine*, 205(1), 143–154. DOI: 10.1084/jem.20071204 PMID: 18166587

Mazzilli, M. C., Ferrante, P., Mariani, P., Martone, E., Petronzelli, F., Triglione, P., & Bonamico, M. (1992). A study of Italian pediatric celiac disease patients confirms that the primary HLA association is to the DQ(alpha 1*0501, beta 1*0201) heterodimer. *Human Immunology*, 33(2), 133–139. DOI: 10.1016/0198-8859(92)90064-T PMID: 1563982

Mbuwir, B. V., Kaffash, M., & Deconinck, G. (2018). Battery scheduling in a residential multi- carrier energy system using reinforcement learning. *2018 IEEE Int. Conf. Commun. Control. Comput. Technol. Smart Grids, SmartGridComm* 2018. DOI: 10.1109/SmartGridComm.2018.8587412

Megalingam, R. K., Darla, V. P., Nimmala, C. S. K., & Sankardas, K. S. (2022). Computer vision-based Measuring Method to Estimate the Diameter of the Coconut Tree Trunk. *2022 International Conference for Advancement in Technology, ICONAT 2022*. DOI: 10.1109/ICONAT53423.2022.9725999

Mehta, Y., Xu, R., Lim, B., Wu, J., & Gao, J. (2023). A Review for Green Energy Machine Learning and AI Services. *Energies*, 16(15), 5718. DOI: 10.3390/en16155718

Mei, K., Fereidooni, S., & Caliskan, A. (2023). Bias Against 93 Stigmatized Groups in Masked Language Models and Downstream Sentiment Classification Tasks. *2023 ACM Conference on Fairness, Accountability, and Transparency*, 1699–1710. DOI: 10.1145/3593013.3594109

Meng, H., Geng, M., & Han, T. (2023). Long short-term memory network with Bayesian optimization for health prognostics of lithium-ion batteries based on partial incremental capacity analysis. *Reliability Engineering & System Safety*, 236, 109288. DOI: 10.1016/j.ress.2023.109288

Michel, C. (2023). Scaling up Predictive Processing to language with Construction Grammar. *Philosophical Psychology*, 36(3), 553–579. DOI: 10.1080/09515089.2022.2050198

Mihai, F. C., & Ulman, S. R. (2023). Circular economy in Green Deal strategies. In *Sustainable and circular management of resources and waste towards a Green Deal* (pp. 49–63). Elsevier. DOI: 10.1016/B978-0-323-95278-1.00029-2

Milner, R. (2006). Turing, Computing and Communication. In Goldin, D., Smolka, S. A., & Wegner, P. (Eds.), *Interactive Computation*. Springer., DOI: 10.1007/3-540-34874-3_1

Ministerio para la Transición Ecológica y el Reto Demográfico. (2020). *La energía en España*.https://www.miteco.gob.es/content/dam/miteco/es/energia/files-1/balances/Balances/LibrosEnergia/Libro_Energia_Espana_2020.pdf: Ministerio para la Transición Ecológica y el Reto Demográfico, Madrid.

Miric, M., Pagani, M., & El Sawy, O. (2021). When and who do platform companies acquire? Understanding the role of acquisitions in the growth of platform companies. *Management Information Systems Quarterly*, 45(4), 2159–2174. DOI: 10.25300/MISQ/2022/16374

MM. S., Rabia Emhamed, A., Heba I, E., & Shimaa, B. (2022). Decision-making and optimal design of green energy system based on statistical methods and artificial neural network approaches. *Sustainable Cities and Society*, 104015. outlook, W. H. (2023, agosto 20). *World Hydropower outlook*. Retrieved from https://indd.adobe.com/view/4201016f-a51a-4f6f-998b-ec85219d1dfd

Mohamed, M. H., & Shaaban, S. (2013). Optimization of blade pitch angle of an axial turbine used for wave energy conversion. *Energy*, 56, 229–239. DOI: 10.1016/j.energy.2013.04.035

Mohan, S., Thirumalai, C., & Srivastava, G. (2019). Effective Heart Disease Prediction Using Hybrid Machine Learning Techniques. *IEEE Access, 7*, 81542–81554. IEEE Access. DOI: 10.3109/07853890.2010.505931 PMID: 21070098

Mohan, T. R., Roselyn, J. P., Uthra, R. A., Devaraj, D., & Umachandran, K. (2021). Intelligent machine learning based total productive maintenance approach for achieving zero downtime in industrial machinery. *Computers & Industrial Engineering*, 157, 107267. DOI: 10.1016/j.cie.2021.107267

Mohanty, A., Rahamathunnisa, U., Sudhakar, K., & Sathiyaraj, R. (2024). Age of Computational AI for Autonomous Vehicles. *Artificial Intelligence for Autonomous Vehicles*, 25-54. DOI: 10.3390/make5030041

Mohideen, H. L. M.H. L. M. Mohideen. (2024). Exploring the Opportunities of Implementing Artificial Intelligence (AI) Technology for Teaching Arabic to Non-Native Speakers: A Theoretical Approach. *JOURNAL OF DIGITAL LEARNING AND DISTANCE EDUCATION*, 2(10), 760–767. DOI: 10.56778/jdlde.v2i9.225

Molenaar, I. (2022). Towards hybrid human-AI learning technologies. *European Journal of Education*, 57(4), 632–645. DOI: 10.1111/ejed.12527

Molina, M. (2017). Energy Storage and Power Electronics Technologies: A Strong Combination to Empower the Transformation to the Smart Grid. *Proceedings of the IEEE*. PP. 1-29. DOI: 10.1109/JPROC.2017.2702627

Mondal, S., Singh, S., & Gupta, H. (2023). Assessing enablers of green entrepreneurship in circular economy: An integrated approach. *Journal of Cleaner Production*, 388, 135999. DOI: 10.1016/j.jclepro.2023.135999

Morcillo-Jimenez, R., Mesa, J., Gómez-Romero, J., Vila, M. A., & Martin-Bautista, M. J. (2024). Deep learning for prediction of energy consumption: An applied use case in an office building. *Applied Intelligence*, 54(7), 5813–5825. DOI: 10.1007/s10489-024-05451-9

Mosavi, A., Salimi, M., Faizollahzadeh Ardabili, S., Rabczuk, T., Shamshirband, S., & Varkonyi-Koczy, A. R. (2019). State of the art of machine learning models in energy systems, a systematic review. *Energies*, 12(7), 1301. DOI: 10.3390/en12071301

Muhammad, H. Z., Majad, M., Mohamad, A. H., Noman, M. K., Kamran, K., Syed Kumayl, R. M., & Filippo, S. (2023). Hybrid deep learning model for efficient state of charge estimation of Li-ion batteries in electric vehicles. *Energy*, 282, 128317. DOI: 10.1016/j.energy.2023.128317

Mujahid, M., Kanwal, K., Rustam, F., Aljedaani, W., & Ashraf, I. (2023). Arabic ChatGPT Tweets Classification Using RoBERTa and BERT Ensemble Model. *ACM Transactions on Asian and Low-Resource Language Information Processing*, 22(8), 1–23. DOI: 10.1145/3605889

Munyolo, G. N. O. (2021). *Cyber-security in E-health: a Critical Analysis of the Regulatory Framework in Kenya* (Doctoral dissertation, University of Nairobi).

Murnane, M., & Ghazel, A. (2017). *A closer look at state of charge (SOC) and state of health (SOH) estimation techniques for batteries. Analog devices.* https://www.analog.com/media/en/technical-documentation/technical-articles/acloser-look-at-state-of-charge-and-state-healthestimation- techniques.pdf

Mviri, F. (2022). Battery storage systems in electric power grid: A review. *Journal of Physics: Conference Series*, 2276(1), 012016. DOI: 10.1088/1742-6596/2276/1/012016

Nallathiga, R. (2003, April 1). Production System Planning for Natural Resource Conservation in a Micro-Watershed. *Electronic Green Journal*, 1(18). Advance online publication. DOI: 10.5070/G311810507

Narayanan Venkit, P., Gautam, S., Panchanadikar, R., Huang, T.-H., & Wilson, S. (2023). Unmasking Nationality Bias: A Study of Human Perception of Nationalities in AI-Generated Articles. *Proceedings of the 2023 AAAI/ACM Conference on AI, Ethics, and Society*, 554–565. DOI: 10.1145/3600211.3604667

Nasayreh, A., Al Mamlook, R. E., Samara, G., Gharaibeh, H., Aljaidi, M., Alzu'bi, D., Al-Daoud, E., & Abualigah, L. (2024). Arabic Sentiment Analysis for ChatGPT Using Machine Learning Classification Algorithms: A Hyperparameter Optimization Technique. *ACM Transactions on Asian and Low-Resource Language Information Processing*, 23(3), 1–19. DOI: 10.1145/3638285

Naskath, J., Sivakamasundari, G., & Begum, A. A. S. (2023). A study on different deep learning algorithms used in deep neural nets: MLP SOM and DBN. *Wireless Personal Communications*, 128(4), 2913–2936. DOI: 10.1007/s11277-022-10079-4 PMID: 36276226

Nations, U. (n.d.). Renewable energy – powering a safer future | United Nations. Retrieved February 23, 2024, from https://www.un.org/en/climatechange/raising-ambition/renewable-energy

Naya, M. Á., Sanjurjo, E., Rodríguez, A. J., & Cuadrado, J. (2023). Kalman filters based on multibody models: Linking simulation and real world. A comprehensive review. *Multibody System Dynamics*, 58(3-4), 479–521. DOI: 10.1007/s11044-023-09893-w

Nieto, C. C. (1997, January 1). Toward a Holistic Approach to the Ideal of Sustainability. *Techné: Research in Philosophy and Technology*, 2(2), 79–83. DOI: 10.5840/techne19972227

Nie, X., Liang, Y., & Ohkura, K. (2023). Autonomous highway driving using reinforcement learning with safety check system based on Time-To-Collision. *Artificial Life and Robotics*, 28(1), 158–165. DOI: 10.1007/s10015-022-00846-8

Niu, S. J., Luo, J., Niemi, H., Li, X., & Lu, Y. (2022). Teachers' and students' views of using an AI-aided educational platform for supporting teaching and learning at Chinese schools. *Education Sciences*, 12(12), 858. DOI: 10.3390/educsci12120858

Njoroge, P. C. (2013). A study of effectiveness of regulatory framework in construction industry in promoting sustainability (Doctoral dissertation).

Norris, J. M., Barriga, K., Klingensmith, G., Hoffman, M., Eisenbarth, G. S., Erlich, H. A., & Rewers, M. (2003). Timing of initial cereal exposure in infancy and risk of islet autoimmunity. *Journal of the American Medical Association*, 290(13), 1713–1720. DOI: 10.1001/jama.290.13.1713 PMID: 14519705

Noura, M. (2019). *Efficient and secure cryptographic solutions for medical data* (Doctoral dissertation, Université Bourgogne Franche-Comté).

Nowrozy, R., Ahmed, K., Wang, H., & Mcintosh, T. (2023, July). Towards a universal privacy model for electronic health record systems: An ontology and machine learning approach. [). MDPI.]. *Informatics (MDPI)*, 10(3), 60. DOI: 10.3390/informatics10030060

Nugroho, L. D., Melati, S. R., Wahyuliana, I., Pawestri, A., & Kurniawan, L. F. (2023, May). Legal Policy of Implementation Green Economy In the Tourism Sector To Realize Sustainable Tourism And Environment. [). IOP Publishing.]. *IOP Conference Series. Earth and Environmental Science*, 1181(1), 012018. DOI: 10.1088/1755-1315/1181/1/012018

Nyakina, J. N., & Taher, B. H.Judith Nyakanga NyakinaBahaa Hussein Taher. (2023). A survey of healthcare sector digitization strategies: Vulnerabilities, countermeasures and opportunities. *World Journal of Advanced Engineering Technology and Sciences*, 8(1), 282–301. DOI: 10.30574/wjaets.2023.8.1.0050

Nyangaresi, V. O., Abduljabbar, Z. A., Mutlaq, K. A. A., Hussain, M. A., & Hussien, Z. A. (2022). Forward and Backward Key Secrecy Preservation Scheme for Medical Internet of Things. In *Human-Centric Smart Computing* [Singapore: Springer Nature Singapore.]. *Proceedings of ICHCSC*, 2022, 15–29.

Obeidat, S. M., Abdalla, S., & Al Bakri, A. A. K. (2023). Integrating green human resource management and circular economy to enhance sustainable performance: An empirical study from the Qatari service sector. *Employee Relations*, 45(2), 535–563. DOI: 10.1108/ER-01-2022-0041

Oehmcke, S., Li, L., Trepekli, K., Revenga, J. C., Nord-Larsen, T., Gieseke, F., & Igel, C. (2024). Deep point cloud regression for above-ground forest biomass estimation from airborne LiDAR. *Remote Sensing of Environment*, 302, 113968. DOI: 10.1016/j.rse.2023.113968

Okada, H., Kuhn, C., Feillet, H., & Bach, J.-F. (2010). The "hygiene hypothesis" for autoimmune and allergic diseases: An update. *Clinical and Experimental Immunology*, 160(1), 1–9. DOI: 10.1111/j.1365-2249.2010.04139.x PMID: 20415844

Olabi, A. G., Abdelghafar, A. A., Soudan, B., Alami, A. H., Semeraro, C., Al Radi, M., Al-Murisi, M., & Abdelkareem, M. A. (2024). Artificial neural network driven prognosis and estimation of Lithium-Ion battery states: Current insights and future perspectives. *Ain Shams Engineering Journal*, 15(2), 102429. DOI: 10.1016/j.asej.2023.102429

Omar, H., Owida, H. A., Abuowaida, S., Alshdaifat, N., Alazaidah, R., Elsoud, E., & Batyha, R. (2024). ChatGPT: A new AI tool for English language teaching and learning among Jordanian students. *Kurdish Studies*, 12(1), 3628–3637. DOI: 10.58262/ks.v12i1.257

Ortiz, J. P., Valladolid, J. D., Garcia, C. L., Novillo, G., & Berrezueta, F. (2019). Analysis of machine learning techniques for the intelligent diagnosis of Ni-MH battery cells. *2018 IEEE Int. Autumn Meet. Power, Electron. Comput. ROPEC 2018*. DOI: 10.1109/ROPEC.2018.8661446

Ouali, S., & El Garouani, S. (2024). Arabic Chatbots Challenges and Solutions: A Systematic Literature Review. *Iraqi Journal for Computer Science and Mathematics*, 5(3), 128–169. DOI: 10.52866/ijcsm.2024.05.03.007

Pagliari, D., Urgesi, R., Frosali, S., Riccioni, M. E., Newton, E. E., Landolfi, R., Pandolfi, F., & Cianci, R. (2015). The Interaction among Microbiota, Immunity, and Genetic and Dietary Factors Is the Condicio Sine Qua Non Celiac Disease Can Develop. *Journal of Immunology Research*, 123653, 1–10. Advance online publication. DOI: 10.1155/2015/123653 PMID: 26090475

Pande, A. A. (2024). Predicting Kidney Disease Using Deep. *Neural Networks*. Advance online publication. DOI: 10.5281/ZENODO.10597492

Pandey, M., Agarwal, R., Shukla, S. K., & Verma, N. K. (2021). Security of healthcare data using blockchains: A survey. *arXiv preprint arXiv:2103.12326*. DOI: 10.1201/9781003133179-9

Pandey, M., Agarwal, R., Shukla, S. K., & Verma, N. K. (2021). 9 Security of Healthcare Data Using Blockchains. *Blockchain in Digital Healthcare*.Ahmad, I., Asghar, Z., Kumar, T., Li, G., Manzoor, A., Mikhaylov, K., & Harjula, E. (2022). Emerging technologies for next generation remote health care and assisted living. *IEEE Access : Practical Innovations, Open Solutions*, 10, 56094–56132.

Pandharipande, A., Cheng, C. H., Dauwels, J., Gurbuz, S. Z., Ibanez-Guzman, J., Li, G., Piazzoni, A., Wang, P., & Santra, A. (2023). Sensing and machine learning for automotive perception: A review. *IEEE Sensors Journal*, 23(11), 11097–11115. DOI: 10.1109/JSEN.2023.3262134

Parida, S., Dehuri, S., & Cho, S. B. (2014), Application of genetic algorithms and Gaussian Naïve Bayesian approach in pipeline for cognitive state classification, *IEEE International Advance Computing Conference (IACC),* Gurgaon, India, pp. 1237-1242, DOI: 10.1109/IAdCC.2014.6779504

Patil, M. A., Agade, P., Hariharan, K. S., Kolake, S. M., Song, T., Yeo, T., & Doo, S. (2015). A novel multistage Support Vector Machine based approach for Li ion battery remaining useful life estimation. *Applied Energy*, 159, 285–297. DOI: 10.1016/j.apenergy.2015.08.119

Payette, M., & Abdul-Nour, G. (2023). Machine Learning Applications for Reliability Engineering: A Review. *Sustainability (Basel)*, 15(7), 6270. DOI: 10.3390/su15076270

Pedretti, A., Santini, M., Scolimoski, J., de Queiroz, M. H. B., Toshioka, F., & Rocha, E., Junior. de P., Pauli Júnior, N. de, Yomura, M. T., Costa, C. H. da, Guerra, F. A., Mulinari, B. M., Grando, F. L., Mumbelli, J. D. C., Costa, C. I. A., Torres, G. L., & Ramos, M. P. (2021). Robotic Process Automation Extended with Artificial Intelligence Techniques in Power Distribution Utilities. *Brazilian Archives of Biology and Technology, 64*, e21210217. https://doi.org/DOI: 10.1590/1678-4324-75years-2021210217

Peng, T., Luo, Y., & Liu, Y. (2022). Ai-based equipment optimization of the design on intelligent education curriculum system. *Wireless Communications and Mobile Computing*, 2022, 2022. DOI: 10.1155/2022/3614883

Pérez-Núñez, A. (2023). Exploring the Potential of Generative AI (ChatGPT) for Foreign Language Instruction: Applications and Challenges. *Hispania*, 106(3), 355–362. DOI: 10.1353/hpn.2023.a906568

Pfenninger, S. (2024). Open code and data are not enough: understandability as design goal for energy system models. *Progress in Energy*, 033002.

Pini, S., Perone, C. S., Ahuja, A., Ferreira, A. S. R., Niendorf, M., & Zagoruyko, S. (2023, May). Safe real-world autonomous driving by learning to predict and plan with a mixture of experts. In *2023 IEEE International Conference on Robotics and Automation (ICRA)* (pp. 10069-10075). IEEE. DOI: 10.1109/ICRA48891.2023.10160992

Pisner, D. A., & Schnyer, D. M. (2020). Support vector machine. [Academic Press.]. *Machine Learning*, 101–121.

Prakash, K., Ali, M., Siddique, M. N. I., Chand, A. A., Kumar, N. M., Dong, D., & Pota, H. R. (2022). A review of battery energy storage systems for ancillary services in distribution grids: Current status, challenges and future directions. *Frontiers in Energy Research*, 10, 971704. DOI: 10.3389/fenrg.2022.971704

Prasad, S. (2023), *IEEFA projects exponential growth of battery storage assets in India,* https://www.downtoearth.org.in/renewable-energy/ieefa-projects-exponential -growth-of-battery-storage-assets-in-india-87343

Praveen Kumar, B., Kalpana, A. V., & Nalini, S. (2023). Gated Attention Based Deep Learning Model for Analyzing the Influence of Social Media on Education. *Journal of Experimental & Theoretical Artificial Intelligence*, •••, 1–15. DOI: 10.1080/0952813X.2023.2188262

Purnamawati, I. G. A., Yuniarta, G. A., & Jie, F. (2023). Strengthening the role of corporate social responsibility in the dimensions of sustainable village economic development. *Heliyon*, 9(4), e15115. DOI: 10.1016/j.heliyon.2023.e15115 PMID: 37095962

Putra, B. T. W., Ramadhani, N. J., Soedibyo, D. W., Marhaenanto, B., Indarto, I., & Yualianto, Y. (2021). The use of computer vision to estimate tree diameter and circumference in homogeneous and production forests using a non-contact method. *Forest Science and Technology*, 17(1), 32–38. DOI: 10.1080/21580103.2021.1873866

Qiang, W., & Zhongli, Z. (2011), Reinforcement learning model, algorithms and its application, *2011 International Conference on Mechatronic Science, Electric Engineering and Computer (MEC)*, Jilin, China, pp. 1143-1146, Doi: DOI: 10.1109/MEC.2011.6025669

Qiao, S.-W., Sollid, L. M., & Blumberg, R. S. (2009). Antigen presentation in celiac disease. *Current Opinion in Immunology*, 21(1), 111–117. DOI: 10.1016/j.coi.2009.03.004 PMID: 19342211

Qiao, W., Min, Y., Xue, C., Dirk, U. S., & Weihan, L. (2023). Transferable data-driven capacity estimation for lithium-ion batteries with deep learning: A case study from laboratory to field applications. *Applied Energy*, 350, 121747. DOI: 10.1016/j.apenergy.2023.121747

Qiu, J., Liang, X., Shetty, S., & Bowden, D. (2018, September). *Towards secure and smart healthcare in smart cities using blockchain. In 2018 IEEE international smart cities conference (ISC2)*. IEEE.

Qusay, H., Hsu, C.-Y., Kamilia, M., Sameer, A., Marek, J., Ahmad, T., & Bashar Mahmood, A. (2024). a). Enhancing smart grid integrated renewable distributed generation capacities: Implications for sustainable energy transformation. [Retrieved from Sustainable Energy Technologies and Assessments.]. *Sustainable Energy Technologies and Assessments*, •••, 103793.

Rahman, A. M., Al Mamun, A., & Islam, A. (2017, December). *Programming challenges of chatbot: Current and future prospective. In 2017 IEEE region 10 humanitarian technology conference (R10-HTC)*. IEEE.

Rajamäki, J., & Hummelholm, A. (2022). Ethical Resilience Management Framework for Critical Healthcare Information Infrastructure.

Rajendran, G., Vaithilingam, C. A., Misron, N., Naidu, K., & Ahmed, M. R. (2021). A comprehensive review on system architecture and international standards for electric vehicle charging stations. *Journal of Energy Storage*, 42, 103099. DOI: 10.1016/j.est.2021.103099

Rajendran, S., Sabharwal, M., Hu, Y. C., & Balusamy, B. (Eds.). (2024). *Artificial Intelligence for Autonomous Vehicles: The Future of Driverless Technology*. John Wiley & Sons. DOI: 10.1002/9781119847656

Rajesh, T., & Seetha, M. (2022). Optimization-Assisting Dual-Step Clustering of Time Series Data. [IJDST]. *International Journal of Distributed Systems and Technologies*, 13(1), 1–18. DOI: 10.4018/IJDST.313632

Ráki, M., Schjetne, K. W., Stamnaes, J., Molberg, Ø., Jahnsen, F. L., Issekutz, T. B., Bogen, B., & Sollid, L. M. (2007). Surface expression of transglutaminase 2 by dendritic cells and its potential role for uptake and presentation of gluten peptides to T cells. *Scandinavian Journal of Immunology*, 65(3), 213–220. DOI: 10.1111/j.1365-3083.2006.01881.x PMID: 17309775

Ram, J. P., Pillai, D. S., Ghias, A. M., & Rajasekar, N. (2020). Performance enhancement of solar PV systems applying P&O assisted Flower Pollination Algorithm (FPA). *Solar Energy*, 199, 214–229. DOI: 10.1016/j.solener.2020.02.019

Ramos, F. O., Pinheiro, A. L., Lima, R. N., Neto, M. M. B., Junior, W. A. S., & Bezerra, L. G. S. (2021). A Real Case Analysis of a Battery Energy Storage System for Energy Time Shift, Demand Management, and Reactive Control. *In Proceedings of the 2021 IEEE PES Innovative Smart Grid Technologies Conference* - Latin America (ISGT Latin America), Lima, Peru, 15–17 September 2021; pp. 1–5.

Rauf, H., Khalid, M., & Arshad, N. (2023). A novel smart feature selection strategy of lithium-ion battery degradation modelling for electric vehicles based on modern machine learning algorithms. *Journal of Energy Storage*, 68, 107577. DOI: 10.1016/j.est.2023.107577

Razzaq, M. A., Gill, S. H., Qureshi, M. A., & Ullah, S. (2017). Security issues in the Internet of Things (IoT): A comprehensive study. *International Journal of Advanced Computer Science and Applications*, 8(6).

Reda, A., & Vásárhelyi, J. (2023). Design and implementation of reinforcement learning for automated driving compared to classical mpc control. *Designs*, 7(1), 18. DOI: 10.3390/designs7010018

Reis, M. S., & Jiang, B. (2022). Predicting the lifetime of Lithium–Ion batteries: Integrated feature extraction and modeling through sequential Unsupervised-Supervised Projections (USP). *Chemical Engineering Science*, 252, 117510. DOI: 10.1016/j.ces.2022.117510

Rekioua, D. (2023). Energy storage systems for photovoltaic and wind systems: A review. *Energies*, 16(9), 3893. DOI: 10.3390/en16093893

Renewable Energy Directive. (n.d.). Retrieved June 20, 2024, from https://energy.ec.europa.eu/topics/renewable-energy/renewable-energy-directive-targets-and-rules/renewable-energy-directive_en

Ren, Y. (2021). Optimizing predictive maintenance with machine learning forreliability improvement. *ASCE-ASME Journal of Risk and Uncertainty in Engineering Systems, Part B. Mechanical Engineering*, 7(3), 030801. DOI: 10.1115/1.4049525

Ren, Z., & Du, C. (2023). A review of machine learning state-of-charge and state-of-health estimation algorithms for lithium-ion batteries. *Energy Reports*, 9, 2993–3021. DOI: 10.1016/j.egyr.2023.01.108

Research and Markets. (2024), *Global Battery Energy Storage System Market Forecast to 2029*: Increasing Opportunities in Rural Electrification Projects Worldwide and Rising Demand for Power Supply from Data Centers, https://www.globenewswire.com/news-release/2024/08/15/2930740/0/en/Global-Battery-Energy-Storage-System-Market-Forecast-to-2029-Increasing-Opportunities-in-Rural-Electrification-Projects-Worldwide-and-Rising-Demand-for-Power-Supply-from-Data-Cente.html

Rewers, M. (2005). Epidemiology of celiac disease: What are the prevalence, incidence, and progression of celiac disease? *Gastroenterology*, 128(4, Suppl 1), S47–S51. DOI: 10.1053/j.gastro.2005.02.030 PMID: 15825126

Rezaei, S., Masoud, N., & Khojandi, A. (2024). GAAD: GAN-enabled autoencoder for real-time sensor anomaly detection and recovery in autonomous driving. *IEEE Sensors Journal*, 24(7), 11734–11742. DOI: 10.1109/JSEN.2024.3361460

Ribeiro, M. T., Singh, S., & Guestrin, C. (n.d.). *Why Should I Trust You?* Explaining the Predictions of Any Classifier., DOI: 10.1145/2939672.2939778

Richard Evans, J. (2024, agosto 20). *DeepMind AI Reduces Google Data Centre Cooling Bill by 40%*. Retrieved from https://deepmind.google/discover/blog/deepmind-ai-reduces-google-data-centre-cooling-bill-by-40

Richardson, R. R., Osborne, M. A., & Howey, D. A. (2017). Gaussian process regression for forecasting battery state of health. *Journal of Power Sources*, 357, 209–219. Advance online publication. DOI: 10.1016/j.jpowsour.2017.05.004

Riestra, S., Fernández, E., Rodrigo, L., Garcia, S., & Ocio, G.S. Riestra, E. Fernández, L. Rodrig. (2000). Prevalence of Coeliac disease in the general population of northern Spain. Strategies of serologic screening. *Scandinavian Journal of Gastroenterology*, 35(4), 398–402. DOI: 10.1080/003655200750023967 PMID: 10831263

Rismanchian, S., & Doroudi, S. (2023). *Four Interactions between AI and Education: Broadening Our Perspective on What AI Can Offer Education*. DOI: 10.1007/978-3-031-36336-8_1

Roca, J. A. (2022, septiembre 29). *El periodico de la energía*. Retrieved from https://elperiodicodelaenergia.com/espana-debe-invertir-85-000-millones-al-ano-en-tecnologias-verdes-para-descarbonizar-su-economia-para-2050/

Rocchetta, R., Bellani, L., Compare, M., Zio, E., & Patelli, E. (2019). A reinforcement learning framework for optimal operation and maintenance of power grids. *Applied Energy*, 241, 291–301. DOI: 10.1016/j.apenergy.2019.03.027

Ross, T. J. (2007). Book review. *Artificial Intelligence*, 171(18), 1114–1115. DOI: 10.1016/j.artint.2007.10.003

Rundo, F., Conoci, S., Battiato, S., Pino, C., Villari, M., Genovese, A., Kollias, S., & Plataniotis, K. N. (2023). Editorial: Deep neural computing for advanced automotive system applications. *Frontiers of Computer Science*, 5, 1192413. DOI: 10.3389/fcomp.2023.1192413

Russell, S., & Norvig, P. (2021). Artificial Intelligence: A Modern Approach *(4th Edition).* California at Berkeley: Pearson.

Ryan, L., Dillon, J., La Monaca, S., Byrne, J., & O'Malley, M. (2016). Assessing the system and investor value of utility-scale solar PV. *Renewable & Sustainable Energy Reviews*, 64, 506–517. DOI: 10.1016/j.rser.2016.06.004

Sahinoglu, G. O., Pajovic, M., Shingle, Z., Wang, Y., Orlik, P. V., & Wada, T. (2017). Battery state-of-charge estimation based on regular/ recurrent Gaussian process regression. *IEEE Transactions on Industrial Electronics*, 65(5), 4311–4321. DOI: 10.1109/TIE.2017.2764869

Sainuddin, F. V., Chirakkal, S., Asok, S. V., & Putrevu, D. (2024). A comparative study on the efficacy of dual-pol and full-pol ASAR data in radiative transfer modeling for forest above-ground biomass estimation. *International Journal of Remote Sensing*, 45(3), 719–747. DOI: 10.1080/01431161.2024.2302952

Salehizadeh, M. R., & Soltaniyan, S. (2016). Application of fuzzy Q-learning for electricity market modeling by considering renewable power penetration. *Renewable & Sustainable Energy Reviews*, 56, 1172–1181. DOI: 10.1016/j.rser.2015.12.020

Salgado Reyes, N. (2023). Uso de la inteligencia artificial en la personalización de la experiencia del usuario en plataformas digitales. *Revista científico-profesional.*

Sallam, M., Al-Mahzoum, K., Ahmad Almutawaa, R., Ahmad Alhashash, J., Abdullah Dashti, R., Raed AlSafy, D., Abdullah Almutairi, R., & Barakat, M. (2024). *The Performance of OpenAI ChatGPT-4 and Google Gemini in Virology Multiple-Choice Questions: A Comparative Analysis of English and Arabic Responses*. DOI: 10.21203/rs.3.rs-4220786/v1

Sallam, M., & Mousa, D. (2024). Evaluating ChatGPT performance in Arabic dialects: A comparative study showing defects in responding to Jordanian and Tunisian general health prompts. *Mesopotamian Journal of Artificial Intelligence in Healthcare*, 2024, 1–7. DOI: 10.58496/MJAIH/2024/001

Salleh, M. N. M., Talpur, N., & Hussain, K. (2017). Adaptive neuro-fuzzy inference system: Overview, strengths, limitations, and solutions. In Data Mining and Big Data: 2nd International Conference, DMBD 2017, Fukuoka, Japan, July 27–August 1, 2017, *Springer International Publishing.Proceedings*, 2, 527–535.

Samuel, J. (2020). *Can Battery Storage Propel India's Energy Transition*https://science .thewire.in/economy/energy/can-battery-storage-propel-indias-energy-transition

Sanchez-Iborra, R., & Skarmeta, A. (2022). Securing the hyperconnected healthcare ecosystem. In *AI and IoT for Sustainable Development in Emerging Countries: Challenges and Opportunities* (pp. 455–471). Springer International Publishing. DOI: 10.1007/978-3-030-90618-4_22

Santos Valdés, L., & Garcia Sánchez, Z. (2023). SISTEMA DE GESTIÓN PARA LA OPERACIÓN DE LAS FUENTES RENOVABLES DE ENERGÍAS. *Operation Management System of Renewable Energy Sources).*

Sarala, B., Sumathy, G., Kalpana, A. V., & Jasmine Hephzipah, J. J. (2023) Glioma brain tumor detection using dual convolutional neural networks and histogram density segmentation algorithm. Biomedical Signal Processing and Control, 85, 104859, ISSN 1746-8094 DOI: DOI: 10.1016/j.bspc.2023.104859

Sarfraz, M., Ozturk, I., Yoo, S., Raza, M. A., & Han, H. (2023). Toward a new understanding of environmental and financial performance through corporate social responsibility, green innovation, and sustainable development. *Humanities & Social Sciences Communications*, 10(1), 1–17. DOI: 10.1057/s41599-023-01799-4

Sarker, I. H. (2021a). A Comprehensive Overview on Techniques, Taxonomy, Applications and Research Directions. *SN Computer Science*, 2(6), 420. DOI: 10.1007/s42979-021-00815-1 PMID: 34426802

Sarker, I. H. (2021b). Real-World Applications and Research Directions. *SN Computer Science*, 2(3), 160. DOI: 10.1007/s42979-021-00592-x PMID: 33778771

Sarwar, H., Aftab, J., Ishaq, M. I., & Atif, M. (2023). Achieving business competitiveness through corporate social responsibility and dynamic capabilities: An empirical evidence from emerging economy. *Journal of Cleaner Production*, 386, 135820. DOI: 10.1016/j.jclepro.2022.135820

Sathya, R., & Abraham, A. (2013). Comparison of Supervised and Unsupervised Learning Algorithms for Pattern Classification [IJARAI]. *International Journal of Advanced Research in Artificial Intelligence*, 2(2). Advance online publication. DOI: 10.14569/IJARAI.2013.020206

Scarpelli, C., Gazzarri, J., Huria, T., Lutzemberger, G., & Ceraolo, M. (2023). Neural network for the estimation of LFP battery SOH cycled at different power levels. *Journal of Energy Storage*, 66, 107027. DOI: 10.1016/j.est.2023.107027

Schiefer, F., Kattenborn, T., Frick, A., Frey, J., Schall, P., Koch, B., & Schmidtlein, S. (2020). Mapping forest tree species in high resolution UAV-based RGB-imagery by means of convolutional neural networks. *ISPRS Journal of Photogrammetry and Remote Sensing*, 170, 205–215. DOI: 10.1016/j.isprsjprs.2020.10.015

Seguí, S., Drozdzal, M., Pascual, G., Radeva, P., Malagelada, C., Azpiroz, F., & Vitrià, J. (2016). Generic feature learning for wireless capsule endoscopy analysis. *Computers in Biology and Medicine*, 79, 163–172. DOI: 10.1016/j.compbiomed.2016.10.011 PMID: 27810622

Selcuk, S. (2017). Predictive maintenance, its implementation and latest trends. *Proceedings of the Institution of Mechanical Engineers. Part B, Journal of Engineering Manufacture*, 231(9), 1670–1679. DOI: 10.1177/0954405415601640

Sesidhar, D. V. S. R., Badachi, C., Robert, C., & Green, I. I. (2023). A review on data-driven SOC estimation with Li-Ion batteries: Implementation methods & future aspirations. *Journal of Energy Storage*, 72, 108420. DOI: 10.1016/j.est.2023.108420

Severson, K. A., Attia, P. M., Jin, N., Perkins, N., Jiang, B., Yang, Z., Chen, M. H., Akyol, M., Herring, P. K., & Fraggedakis, D. (2019). Data- driven prediction of battery cycle life before capacity degradation. *Nature Energy*, 4(5), 383–391. Advance online publication. DOI: 10.1038/s41560-019-0356-8

Shafik, W. (2024). Introduction to ChatGPT. In A. J. Obaid, B. Bhushan, M. S., & S. S. Rajest (Eds.), *Advanced Applications of Generative AI and Natural Language Processing Models* (pp. 1–25). IGI Global. DOI: 10.4018/979-8-3693-0502-7.ch001

Shahabi, H., Shirzadi, A., Ronoud, S., Asadi, S., Pham, B. T., Mansouripour, F., & Bui, D. T. (2021). Flash flood susceptibility mapping using a novel deep learning model based on deep belief network, back propagation and genetic algorithm. *Geoscience Frontiers*, 12(3), 101100. DOI: 10.1016/j.gsf.2020.10.007

Shahbazkhani, B., Malekzadeh, R., Sotoudeh, M., Moghadam, K. F., Farhadi, M., Ansari, R., Elahyfar, A., & Rostami, K. (2003). High prevalence of coeliac disease in apparently healthy Iranian blood donors. *European Journal of Gastroenterology & Hepatology*, 15(5), 475–478. DOI: 10.1097/00042737-200305000-00003 PMID: 12702902

Shahinfar, S., Meek, P., & Falzon, G. (2020). "How many images do I need?" Understanding how sample size per class affects deep learning model performance metrics for balanced designs in autonomous wildlife monitoring. *Ecological Informatics*, 57, 101085. DOI: 10.1016/j.ecoinf.2020.101085

Sharifi, I., Yildirim, M., & Fallah, S. (2023). Towards Safe Autonomous Driving Policies using a Neuro-Symbolic Deep Reinforcement Learning Approach. *arXiv preprint arXiv:2307.01316.*

Sharma, A. (2019). *Analyzing Opportunities and Barriers of Using Solar PV and Battery Energy Storage System (BESS) on Apartments or new Residential Complex* (Doctoral dissertation, University of New South Wales Sydney).

Sharma, A. (2024)., *India launches National Electricity Plan to meet rising power demand. CNBCTV18.*https://www.cnbctv18.com/energy/india-launches-national-electricity-plan-to-meet-rising-power-demand-19492717.htm

Sharma, A., & Singh, B. (2022). Measuring Impact of E-commerce on Small Scale Business: A Systematic Review. *Journal of Corporate Governance and International Business Law*, 5(1).

Shead, S., & FORBES. (2019, febrero 27). *DeepMind and Google Train AI To Predict Energy Output Of Wind Farms*. Retrieved from (consultado 20/08/2024): https://www.forbes.com/sites/samshead/2019/02/27/deepmind-and-google-train-ai-to-predict-energy-output-of-wind-farms/

Shen, S., Sadoughi, M., Li, M., Wang, Z., & Hu, C. (2020a). Deep convolutional neural networks with ensemble learning and transfer learning for capacity estimation of lithium-ion batteries. *Applied Energy*, 114296, 114296. Advance online publication. DOI: 10.1016/j.apenergy.2019.114296

Shi, D., Zhao, J., Eze, C., Wang, Z., Wang, J., Lian, Y., & Burke, A. F. (2023). Cloud-Based Artificial Intelligence Framework for Battery Management System. *Energies*, 16(11), 4403. DOI: 10.3390/en16114403

Shi, D., Zhao, J., Wang, Z., Zhao, H., Eze, C., Wang, J., Lian, Y., & Burke, A. F. (2023). Cloud-Based Deep Learning for Co-Estimation of Battery State of Charge and State of Health. *Energies*, 16(9), 3855. DOI: 10.3390/en16093855

Shi, E., Xia, F., Peng, D., Li, L., Wang, X., & Yu, B. (2019). Fei Xia., Daogang Peng., Liang Li., Xiaokang Wang., and Beili Yu. State-of-health estimation for lithium battery in electric vehicles based on improved unscented particle filter. *Journal of Renewable and Sustainable Energy*, 11(2), 024101. DOI: 10.1063/1.5065477

Shi, F., & Liu, Z., and Li, e. (2017). Prediction of pipe performance with ensemble machine learning based approaches. *International conference on Sensing, Diagnostics, Prognostics, and Control (SDPC)*. IEEE, pp. 408–414. DOI: 10.1109/SDPC.2017.84

Shi, L., Liu, S., Shi, L., & Liu, S. (2017). *Methods of Estimating Forest Biomass: A Review*. Biomass Volume Estimation and Valorization for Energy., DOI: 10.5772/65733

Shu, X., Shen, S., Shen, J., Zhang, Y., Li, G., Chen, Z., & Liu, Y. (2021). State of health prediction of lithium-ion batteries based on machine learning: Advances and perspectives. *iScience*, 24(11), 103265. DOI: 10.1016/j.isci.2021.103265 PMID: 34761185

Simangunsong, B. C. H., Sitanggang, V. J., Manurung, E. G. T., Rahmadi, A., Moore, G. A., Aye, L., & Tambunan, A. H. (2017). Potential forest biomass resource as feedstock for bioenergy and its economic value in Indonesia. *Forest Policy and Economics*, 81, 10–17. DOI: 10.1016/j.forpol.2017.03.022

Simmou, W., Govindan, K., Sameer, I., Hussainey, K., & Simmou, S. (2023). Doing good to be green and live clean!-Linking corporate social responsibility strategy, green innovation, and environmental performance: Evidence from Maldivian and Moroccan small and medium-sized enterprises. *Journal of Cleaner Production*, 384, 135265. DOI: 10.1016/j.jclepro.2022.135265

Singh, A., Thakur, N., & Sharma, A. (2016). A review of supervised machine learning algorithms. 2016, *3rd International Conference on Computing for Sustainable Global Development (INDIACom)*, 1310-1315.

Singh, G., Appadurai, J. P., Perumal, V., Kavita, K., Chanil Kumar, T., Prasad, D., Azhagu Jaisudhan Pazhani, A., & Umamaheswari, K. (2022). Machine learning-based modelling and predictive maintenance of turning operation under cooling/lubrication for manufacturing systems. *Advances in Materials Science and Engineering*, 2022, 2022. DOI: 10.1155/2022/9289320

Singh, P., Arora, S., Singh, A., Strand, T. A., & Makharia, G. K. (2016). Prevalence of celiac disease in Asia: A systematic review and meta-analysis. *Journal of Gastroenterology and Hepatology*, 31(6), 1095–1101. DOI: 10.1111/jgh.13270 PMID: 26678020

Siva Suriya Narayanan, S., & Thangavel, S. (2023). A novel static model prediction method based on machine learning for Li-ion batteries operated at different temperatures. *Journal of Energy Storage*, 61, 106789. DOI: 10.1016/j.est.2023.106789

Skurikhin, A. N., Garrity, S. R., McDowell, N. G., & Cai, D. M. (2013). Automated tree crown detection and size estimation using multi-scale analysis of high-resolution satellite imagery. *Remote Sensing Letters*, 4(5), 465–474. DOI: 10.1080/2150704X.2012.749361

Slim, A., & Melouah, A. (2024). Low Resource Arabic Dialects Transformer Neural Machine Translation Improvement through Incremental Transfer of Shared Linguistic Features. *Arabian Journal for Science and Engineering*, 49(9), 12393–12409. Advance online publication. DOI: 10.1007/s13369-023-08543-9

Slorach, S., Embley, J., Goodchild, P., & Shephard, C. (2017). *8. legal research. Legal Systems &amp*. Skills., DOI: 10.1093/he/9780198785903.003.0008

Smith, O., Cattell, O., Farcot, E., O'Dea, R. D., & Hopcraft, K. I. (2022). The effect of renewable energy incorporation on power grid stability and resilience. *Science Advances*, 8(9), eabj6734. DOI: 10.1126/sciadv.abj6734 PMID: 35235363

Solangi, Z. A., Solangi, Y. A., & Chandio, S., bin Hamzah, M. S., & Shah, A. (2018, May). The future of data privacy and security concerns in Internet of Things. In *2018 IEEE International Conference on Innovative Research and Development (ICIRD)* (pp. 1-4). IEEE. DOI: 10.1109/ICIRD.2018.8376320

Soldani, D., & Illingworth, S. A. (2020). 5G AI-enabled automation. In *Wiley 5G Ref* (pp. 1–38). Wiley. DOI: 10.1002/9781119471509.w5GRef225

Sollid, L. M., Markussen, G., Ek, J., Gjerde, H., Vartdal, F., & Thorsby, E. (1989). Evidence for a primary association of celiac disease to a particular HLA-DQ alpha/beta heterodimer. *The Journal of Experimental Medicine*, 169(1), 345–350. DOI: 10.1084/jem.169.1.345 PMID: 2909659

Song, K., Hu, D., Tong, Y., & Yue, X. (2023). Remaining life prediction of lithium-ion batteries based on health management: A review. *Journal of Energy Storage*, 57, 106193. DOI: 10.1016/j.est.2022.106193

Song, Q., Albrecht, C. M., Xiong, Z., & Zhu, X. X. (2023). Biomass Estimation and Uncertainty Quantification From Tree Height. *IEEE Journal of Selected Topics in Applied Earth Observations and Remote Sensing*, 16, 4833–4845. DOI: 10.1109/JSTARS.2023.3271186

Soni, P., Pradhan, J., Pal, A. K., & Islam, S. H. (2022). Cybersecurity attack-resilience authentication mechanism for intelligent healthcare system. *IEEE Transactions on Industrial Informatics*, 19(1), 830–840. DOI: 10.1109/TII.2022.3179429

*Sophia chatbot*. The Innovation in Politics Institute. (2023, July 24). https://innovationinpolitics.eu/showroom/project/sophia-chatbot/#:~:text=Sophia%20is%20a%20digital%20chatbot,the%20needs%20of%20survivors%20globally

Sriram, K. P., Joel, M. R., Navaneethakrishnan, M., & Manonmani, S. P. (2023, March). Machine learning algorithms for predicting house prices in a smart city using its real-time data. In *2023 Second International Conference on Electronics and Renewable Systems (ICEARS)* (pp. 1064–1070). IEEE.

Sriram, R. D., & Subrahmanian, E. (2020). Transforming health care through digital revolutions. *Journal of the Indian Institute of Science*, 100(4), 753–772. DOI: 10.1007/s41745-020-00195-0 PMID: 33132546

Srivastava, N., Hinton, G., Krizhevsky, A., Sutskever, I., & Salakhutdinov, R. (2014). Dropout: A simple way to prevent neural networks from overfitting. *Journal of Machine Learning Research*, 15, 1929–1958.

Stadler, M., & Naslé, A. (2019). Planning and implementation of bankable micro-grids. *The Electricity Journal*, 32(5), 24–29. DOI: 10.1016/j.tej.2019.05.004

Stamnaes, J., & Sollid, L. M. (2015). Celiac disease: Autoimmunity in response to food antigen. *Seminars in Immunology*, 27(5), 343–352. DOI: 10.1016/j.smim.2015.11.001 PMID: 26603490

Standen, P. J., Brown, D. J., Taheri, M., Galvez Trigo, M. J., Boulton, H., Burton, A., Hallewell, M. J., Lathe, J. G., Shopland, N., Blanco Gonzalez, M. A., Kwiatkowska, G. M., Milli, E., Cobello, S., Mazzucato, A., Traversi, M., & Hortal, E. (2020). An evaluation of an adaptive learning system based on multimodal affect recognition for learners with intellectual disabilities. *British Journal of Educational Technology*, 51(5), 1748–1765. DOI: 10.1111/bjet.13010

Stas, S. M., Rutishauser, E., Chave, J., Anten, N. P. R., & Laumonier, Y. (2017). Estimating the aboveground biomass in an old secondary forest on limestone in the Moluccas, Indonesia: Comparing locally developed versus existing allometric models. *Forest Ecology and Management*, 389, 27–34. DOI: 10.1016/j.foreco.2016.12.010

Stazi, A. V., & Trinti, B. (2010). Selenium status and over-expression of interleukin-15 in celiac disease and autoimmune thyroid diseases. *Annali dell'Istituto Superiore di Sanita*, 46(4), 389–399. DOI: 10.4415/ANN_10_04_06 PMID: 21169670

Stecca, M., Elizondo, L. R., Soeiro, T. B., Bauer, P., & Palensky, P. (2020). A comprehensive review of the integration of battery energy storage systems into distribution networks. *IEEE Open Journal of the Industrial Electronics Society*, 1, 46–65. DOI: 10.1109/OJIES.2020.2981832

Stecuła, K., Wolniak, R., & Grebski, W. W. (2023). AI-driven urban energy solutions—From individuals to society: A review. *Energies*, 16(24), 7988. DOI: 10.3390/en16247988

Straw, I., & Callison-Burch, C. (2020). Artificial Intelligence in mental health and the biases of language based models. *PLoS One*, 15(12), e0240376. DOI: 10.1371/journal.pone.0240376 PMID: 33332380

Štrumbelj, E., & Kononenko, I. (2014). Explaining prediction models and individual predictions with feature contributions. *Knowledge and Information Systems*, 41(3), 647–665. DOI: 10.1007/s10115-013-0679-x

Suganda, A., & Siregar, M. A. (2020). The meaning and development of state emergency laws based on constitution in the Indonesian legal system. *Proceedings of the 2nd International Conference of Law, Government and Social Justice (ICOLGAS 2020)*. DOI: 10.2991/assehr.k.201209.336

Sulaeman, I., Syuhadak, S., & Sulaeman, I. (2023). ChatGPT as a New Frontier in Arabic Education Technology. *Al-Arabi: Journal of Teaching Arabic as a Foreign Language*, 7(1), 83–105. DOI: 10.17977/um056v7i1p83-105

Suleski, T., Ahmed, M., Yang, W., & Wang, E. (2023). A review of multi-factor authentication in the Internet of Healthcare Things. *Digital Health*, 9, 20552076231177144. DOI: 10.1177/20552076231177144 PMID: 37252257

Sun, L., Wei, M., Sun, Y., Suh, Y. J., Shen, L., & Yang, S. (2024). Smiling women pitching down: Auditing representational and presentational gender biases in image-generative AI. *Journal of Computer-Mediated Communication*, 29(1), zmad045. Advance online publication. DOI: 10.1093/jcmc/zmad045

Suresh, C., & Saini, R. P. (2020). Review on solar thermal energy storage technologies and their geometrical configurations. *International Journal of Energy Research*, 44(6), 4163–4195. DOI: 10.1002/er.5143

Sutton, R. S., & Barto, A. G. (1998). Reinforcement Learning: An Introduction. *IEEE Transactions on Neural Networks*, 9(5), 1054–1054. DOI: 10.1109/TNN.1998.712192

Su, X., Sun, B., Wang, J., Zhang, W., Ma, S., He, X., & Ruan, H. (2022). Fast capacity estimation for lithium-ion battery based on online identification of low-frequency electrochemical impedance spectroscopy and Gaussian process regression. *Applied Energy*, 322, 119516. DOI: 10.1016/j.apenergy.2022.119516

Swarnakar, P., & Singh, M. K. (2022). Local governance in just energy transition: Towards a community-centric framework. *Sustainability (Basel)*, 14(11), 6495. DOI: 10.3390/su14116495

Swarnkar, R., Ramachandran, H., Ali, S. H. M., & Jabbar, R. (2023). A Systematic Literature Review of State of Health and State of Charge Estimation Methods for Batteries Used in Electric Vehicle Applications. *World Electr. Veh. J.*, 14(9), 247. DOI: 10.3390/wevj14090247

Syafrudin, M., Alfian, G., Fitriyani, N. L., & Anshari, M. (2024). Applied Artificial Intelligence for Sustainability. *Sustainability (Basel)*, 16(6), 2469. DOI: 10.3390/su16062469

Syed, S. A., & Bong, J. C. (2020).. . *Electronics (Basel)*, 9, 1–25.

Syed, S., Al-Boni, M., Khan, M. N., Sadiq, K., Iqbal, N. T., Moskaluk, C. A., Kelly, P., Amadi, B., Ali, S. A., Moore, S. R., & Brown, D. E. (2019). Assessment of Machine Learning Detection of Environmental Enteropathy and Celiac Disease in Children. *JAMA Network Open*, 2(6), e195822. DOI: 10.1001/jamanetworkopen.2019.5822 PMID: 31199451

Taimoor, N., & Rehman, S. (2021). Reliable and resilient AI and IoT-based personalised healthcare services: A survey. *IEEE Access : Practical Innovations, Open Solutions*, 10, 535–563. DOI: 10.1109/ACCESS.2021.3137364

Takagishi, Y., Yamanaka, T., & Yamaue, T. (2019). Machine learning approaches for designing mesoscale structure of li-ion battery electrodes. *Batteries*, 5(3), 1–13. DOI: 10.3390/batteries5030054

Talluri, G., Lozito, G. M., Grasso, F., Iturrino Garcia, C., & Luchetta, A. (2021). Optimal Battery Energy Storage System Scheduling within Renewable Energy Communities. *Energies*, 14(24), 8480. DOI: 10.3390/en14248480

Tang, F., Chen, Z., Ciszewski, C., Setty, M., Solus, J., Tretiakova, M., Ebert, E., Han, J., Lin, A., Guandalini, S., Groh, V., Spies, T., Green, P., & Jabri, B. (2009). Cytosolic PLA2 is required for CTL-mediated immunopathology of celiac disease via NKG2D and IL-15. *The Journal of Experimental Medicine*, 206(3), 707–719. DOI: 10.1084/jem.20071887 PMID: 19237603

Tang, X., Yao, K., Liu, B., Hu, W., & Gao, F. (2018). Long-term battery voltage, power, and surface temperature prediction using a model- based extreme learning machine. *Energies*, 11(1), 86. Advance online publication. DOI: 10.3390/en11010086

Tapkire, M. D., & Arun, V. (2023). Application of artificial intelligence to corelate food formulations to disease risk prediction: A comprehensive review. *Journal of Food Science and Technology*, 60(9), 2350–2357. DOI: 10.1007/s13197-022-05550-w PMID: 37424577

Tatsumi, S., Yamaguchi, K., & Furuya, N. (2023). ForestScanner: A mobile application for measuring and mapping trees with LiDAR-equipped iPhone and iPad. *Methods in Ecology and Evolution*, 14(7), 1603–1609. DOI: 10.1111/2041-210X.13900

The International Energy Agency (IEA). (2023). Renewables 2023. https://www.iea.org/reports/renewables-2023

Thompson, P. B., & Norris, P. E. (2021). What is sustainability? *Sustainability*. Advance online publication. DOI: 10.1093/wentk/9780190883249.003.0001

Tianhangau, W. L. (2021).. . *Science*, 24, 1–33.

Touma, R., Hajj, H., El-Hajj, W., & Shaban, K. (2023). Automated Generation of Human-readable Natural Arabic Text from RDF Data. *ACM Transactions on Asian and Low-Resource Language Information Processing*, 22(4), 1–13. DOI: 10.1145/3582262

Tprestianni. (2024, March 1). *131 AI statistics and Trends for 2024*. National University. https://www.nu.edu/blog/ai-statistics-trends/

Tran, H., Woeste, K., Li, B., Verma, A., & Shao, G. (2023). Measuring tree stem diameters and straightness with depth-image computer vision. *Journal of Forestry Research*, 34(5), 1395–1405. DOI: 10.1007/s11676-023-01600-x

Troncone, R., & Jabri, B. (2011). Coeliac disease and gluten sensitivity. *Journal of Internal Medicine*, 269(6), 582–590. DOI: 10.1111/j.1365-2796.2011.02385.x PMID: 21481018

Trynka, G., Wijmenga, C., & van Heel, D. A. (2010). A genetic perspective on coeliac disease. *Trends in Molecular Medicine*, 16(11), 537–550. DOI: 10.1016/j.molmed.2010.09.003 PMID: 20947431

Tudoroiu, N., Zaheeruddin, M., Tudoroiu, R.-E., Radu, M. S., & Chammas, H. (2023). Investigations on Using Intelligent Learning Techniques for Anomaly Detection and Diagnosis in Sensors Signals in Li-Ion Battery—Case Study. *Inventions (Basel, Switzerland)*, 8(3), 74. DOI: 10.3390/inventions8030074

Turkut, U., Tuncer, A., Savran, H., & Yılmaz, S. (2020) An online recommendation system using deep learning for textile products International Congress on Human-Computer Interaction, Optimization and Robotic Applications (HORA), Ankara, Turkey, Vol. 2020, pp. 1–4. DOI: DOI: 10.1109/HORA49412.2020.9152875

Tyagi, A. K., Hemamalini, V., & Soni, G. (2023). Digital Health Communication With Artificial Intelligence-Based Cyber Security. In *AI-Based Digital Health Communication for Securing Assistive Systems* (pp. 178–213). IGI Global. DOI: 10.4018/978-1-6684-8938-3.ch009

Udo, W., Kwakye, J., Ekechukwu, D., & Ogundipe, O. (2024). Smart grid innovation: machine learning for real-time energy management and load balancing. *International Journal of Smart Grid Applications*, 405--423.

Ukey, N., Yang, Z., Li, B., Zhang, G., Hu, Y., & Zhang, W. (2023). Survey on exact knn queries over high-dimensional data space. *Sensors (Basel)*, 23(2), 629. DOI: 10.3390/s23020629 PMID: 36679422

Ustun, T. S. M., Suhail, H., Hannes, K., Bissan, G., & Ioannis, L. (2019). Data standardization for smart infrastructure in first-access electricity systems. *Proceedings of the IEEE*, 1790--1802. DOI: 10.1109/JPROC.2019.2929621

Vakharia, V., Shah, M., Nair, P., Borade, H., Sahlot, P., & Wankhede, V. (2023). Estimation of Lithium-ion Battery Discharge Capacity by Integrating Optimized Explainable-AI and Stacked LSTM Model. *Batteries.*, 9(2), 125. DOI: 10.3390/batteries9020125

Valencia, N., Fotouhi, A., Shateri, N., & Auger, D. (2023). Development of a Hybrid Adaptive Neuro-fuzzy Inference System with Coulomb-Counting State-of-Charge Estimator for Lithium–Sulphur Battery. *International Journal of Fuzzy Systems*, 25(2), 407–422. DOI: 10.1007/s40815-022-01403-y

Van Houdt, G., Mosquera, C., & Nápoles, G. (2020). A review on the long short-term memory model. *Artificial Intelligence Review*, 53(8), 5929–5955. DOI: 10.1007/s10462-020-09838-1

van Kessel, R., Haig, M., & Mossialos, E. (2023). Strengthening cybersecurity for patient data protection in Europe. *Journal of Medical Internet Research*, 25(1), e48824. DOI: 10.2196/48824 PMID: 37616048

Vasilescu, M. D., Dimian, G. C., & Gradinaru, G. I. (2023). Green entrepreneurship in challenging times: A quantitative approach for European countries. *Economic research-. Ekonomska Istrazivanja*, 36(1), 1828–1847. DOI: 10.1080/1331677X.2022.2093767

Vasta, E., Scimone, T., Nobile, G., Eberhardt, O., Dugo, D., De Benedetti, M. M., Lanuzza, L., Scarcella, G., Patanè, L., Arena, P., & Cacciato, M. (2023). Models for Battery Health Assessment: A Comparative Evaluation. *Energies*, 16(2), 632. DOI: 10.3390/en16020632

Velasquez-Camacho, L., Etxegarai, M., & de-Miguel, S. (2023). Implementing Deep Learning algorithms for urban tree detection and geolocation with high-resolution aerial, satellite, and ground-level images. *Computers, Environment and Urban Systems*, 105, 102025. DOI: 10.1016/j.compenvurbsys.2023.102025

Venkatesan, C., Chandra Shekhar, K. P., Alagar, K., Dharmarcy, G., Robbi, R., & Aritra, G. (2021).. . *World Electr. Veh. J.*, 12, 1–17.

Verdu, E. F., Galipeau, H. J., & Jabri, B. (2015). Novel players in coeliac disease pathogenesis: Role of the gut microbiota. *Nature Reviews. Gastroenterology & Hepatology*, 12(9), 497–506. DOI: 10.1038/nrgastro.2015.90 PMID: 26055247

Veres, C. (2022). Large language models are not models of natural language: They are corpus models. *IEEE Access : Practical Innovations, Open Solutions*, 10, 61970–61979. DOI: 10.1109/ACCESS.2022.3182505

Verwimp, E., Aljundi, R., Ben-David, S., Bethge, M., Cossu, A., Gepperth, A., & van de Ven, G. (2023). *Continual Learning: Applications and the Road Forward. ARXIV Transactions on Machine Learning Research*. TMLR.

Volta, U., Bellentani, S., Bianchi, F. B., Brandi, G., De Franceschi, L., Miglioli, L., Granito, A., Balli, F., & Tiribelli, C. (2001). High prevalence of celiac disease in Italian general population. *Digestive Diseases and Sciences*, 46(7), 1500–1505. DOI: 10.1023/A:1010648122797 PMID: 11478502

Von Stechow, C., McCollum, D., Riahi, K., Minx, J. C., Kriegler, E., Van Vuuren, D. P., Jewell, J., Robledo-Abad, C., Hertwich, E., Tavoni, M., Mirasgedis, S., Lah, O., Roy, J., Mulugetta, Y., Dubash, N. K., Bollen, J., Ürge-Vorsatz, D., & Edenhofer, O. (2015). Integrating global climate change mitigation goals with other sustainability objectives: A synthesis. *Annual Review of Environment and Resources*, 40(1), 363–394. DOI: 10.1146/annurev-environ-021113-095626

Voogd, K. L., Allamaa, J. P., Alonso-Mora, J., & Son, T. D. (2023). Reinforcement learning from simulation to real world autonomous driving using digital twin. *IFAC-PapersOnLine*, 56(2), 1510–1515. DOI: 10.1016/j.ifacol.2023.10.1846

Voss, W. G. (2021). The CCPA and the GDPR are not the same: Why you should understand both. *CPI Antitrust Chronicle*, 1(1), 7–12.

Vo, T. K. A., & Nguyen, H. (2024). Generative Artificial Intelligence and ChatGPT in Language Learning: EFL Students' Perceptions of Technology Acceptance. *Journal of University Teaching & Learning Practice*, 21(06). Advance online publication. DOI: 10.53761/fr1rkj58

Vulpe, A., Crăciunescu, R., Drăgulinescu, A. M., Kyriazakos, S., Paikan, A., & Ziafati, P. (2021). Enabling security services in socially assistive robot scenarios for healthcare applications. *Sensors (Basel)*, 21(20), 6912. DOI: 10.3390/s21206912 PMID: 34696125

Vuorikari, R., Kluzer, S., & Punie, Y. (2022). *DigComp 2.2, The Digital Competence Framework for Citizens - with new examples of knowledge, skills and attitudes*. Publications Office of the European Union., DOI: 10.2760/115376

Wahab, F., Zhao, Y., Javeed, D., Al-Adhaileh, M. H., Almaaytah, S. A., Khan, W., Saeed, M. S., & Kumar Shah, R. (2022). An AI-driven hybrid framework for intrusion detection in IoT-enabled E-health. *Computational Intelligence and Neuroscience*, 2022, 2022. DOI: 10.1155/2022/6096289 PMID: 36045979

Wang, B., Sun, Z., Jiang, X., Zeng, J., & Liu, R. Kalman Filter and Its Application in Data Assimilation. *Atmosphere,2023, vol.14, p.* 1319. https://doi.org/DOI: 10.3390/atmos14081319

Wang, J., & Shi, D. (2018, September). Cyber-attacks related to intelligent electronic devices and their countermeasures: A review. In *2018 53rd International Universities Power Engineering Conference (UPEC)* (pp. 1–6). IEEE. DOI: 10.1109/UPEC.2018.8542059

Wang, G., Lyu, Z., & Li, X. (2023). An Optimized Random Forest Regression Model for Li-Ion Battery Prognostics and Health Management. *Batteries*, 9(6), 332. DOI: 10.3390/batteries9060332

Wang, H., Lei, Z., Zhang, X., Zhou, B., & Peng, J. (2019). A review of deep learning for renewable energy forecasting. *Energy Conversion and Management*, 198, 111799. DOI: 10.1016/j.enconman.2019.111799

Wang, J., Liu, P., Hicks-Garner, J., Sherman, E., Soukiazian, S., Verbrugge, M., Tataria, H., Musser, J., & Finamore, P. (2011). Cycle-life model for graphite-LiFePO4 cells. *Journal of Power Sources*, 196(8), 3942–3948. DOI: 10.1016/j.jpowsour.2010.11.134

Wang, J., Lu, S., Wang, S. H., & Zhang, Y. D. (2022). A review on extreme learning machine. *Multimedia Tools and Applications*, 81(29), 41611–41660. DOI: 10.1007/s11042-021-11007-7

Wang, S., Yang, C., Qu, T., Yang, K., & Wan, W. (2022). Learning users' visual preferences for improving recommendations. *IEEE Access : Practical Innovations, Open Solutions*, 10, 2929–2940. DOI: 10.1109/ACCESS.2022.3140215

Wang, W., Zhang, D., Wang, H., Zhu, Q., & Morabbi Heravi, H. (2023). How do businesses achieve sustainable success and gain a competitive advantage in the green era? *Kybernetes*, 52(9), 3241–3260. DOI: 10.1108/K-07-2021-0614

Wang, X., Zhang, J., Hou, D., & Cheng, Y. (2023). Autonomous driving based on approximate safe action. *IEEE Transactions on Intelligent Transportation Systems*, 24(12), 14320–14328. DOI: 10.1109/TITS.2023.3292253

Wang, Y., Ni, Y., Lu, S., Wang, J., & Zhang, X. (2019). Remaining Useful Life Prediction of Lithium-Ion Batteries Using Support Vector Regression Optimized by Artificial Bee colony. *IEEE Transactions on Vehicular Technology*, 68(10), 9543–9553. DOI: 10.1109/TVT.2019.2932605

Wang, Y., Zhang, X., & Guo, Z. (2021). Estimation of tree height and aboveground biomass of coniferous forests in North China using stereo ZY-3, multispectral Sentinel-2, and DEM data. *Ecological Indicators*, 126, 107645. DOI: 10.1016/j.ecolind.2021.107645

Wang, Y., Zhang, X., Li, K., Zhao, G., & Chen, Z. (2023). Perspectives and challenges for future lithium-ion battery control and management. *eTransportation*, 18, 100260. DOI: 10.1016/j.etran.2023.100260

Wang, Z., Feng, G., Zhen, D., Gu, F., & Ball, A. (2021). A review on online state of charge and state of health estimation for lithium-ion batteries in electric vehicles. *Energy Reports*, 7, 2352–4847. DOI: 10.1016/j.egyr.2021.08.113

Wang, Z., Liu, X., & Wu, Z. (2023). Design of Unsignalized Roundabouts Driving Policy of Autonomous Vehicles Using Deep Reinforcement Learning. *World Electric Vehicle Journal*, 14(2), 52. DOI: 10.3390/wevj14020052

Watkins, C. J. C. H., & Dayan, P. (1992). Q-learning. *Machine Learning*, 8(3-4), 279–292. DOI: 10.1007/BF00992698

Wei, L., Tobias, P., & Chau, K. T. (2022). Overview of batteries and battery management for electric vehicles. *Energy Reports*, 8, 4058–4084. DOI: 10.1016/j.egyr.2022.03.016

Wei, X., Gang, X., Yumei, L., Feng, Z., Peng, Y., & Ben, L. (2023). Early prediction of lithium-ion battery cycle life based on voltage-capacity discharge curves. *Journal of Energy Storage*, 62, 106790. DOI: 10.1016/j.est.2023.106790

Wieser, H., & Koehler, P. (2008). The Biochemical Basis of Celiac Disease. *Cereal Chemistry*, 85(1), 1–13. DOI: 10.1094/CCHEM-85-1-0001

Wimmer, G., Hegenbart, S., Vécsei, A., & Uhl, A. (2017). Convolutional Neural Network Architectures for the Automated Diagnosis of Celiac Disease. In *Lecture Notes in Computer Science* (Vol. 10170, p. 113). DOI: 10.1007/978-3-319-54057-3_10

Wimmer, G., Uhl, A., & Vecsei, A. (2017). Evaluation of domain specific data augmentation techniques for the classification of celiac disease using endoscopic imagery. *2017 IEEE 19th International Workshop on Multimedia Signal Processing (MMSP)*, 1–6. DOI: 10.1109/MMSP.2017.8122221

Wimmer, G., Vécsei, A., & Uhl, A. (2016). *CNN transfer learning for the automated diagnosis of celiac disease*., DOI: 10.1109/IPTA.2016.7821020

WindESCO. (2024, octubre 1). Retrieved from AI Center Lightning Talk: AI-Driven Asset Health in Wind Energy: https://www.windesco.com/blog/ai-center-lightning-talk-ai-driven-asset-health-in-wind-energy

Wollny, S., Schneider, J., Boulay, B. D., Weidlich, J., Rittberger, M., & Drachsler, H. (2021, July 15). Are We There Yet? - A Systematic Literature Review on Chatbots in Education. *Frontiers of Medicine*, 4, 654924. Advance online publication. DOI: 10.3389/frai.2021.654924 PMID: 34337392

Woo, H., Kim, I., & Choi, B. (2021). Computer vision techniques in forest inventory assessment: Improving accuracy of tree diameter measurement using smartphone camera and photogrammetry. *Sensors and Materials*, 33(11), 3835–3845. DOI: 10.18494/SAM.2021.3605

World Bioenergy Association. (2022). GLOBAL BIOENERGY STATISTICS 2022 World Bioenergy Association. https://www.worldbioenergy.org/uploads/221223%20WBA%20GBS%202022.pdf

World Energy. (2024, april 15). *World Energy*. Retrieved from The Largest Photovoltaic Plant in the World in India, Bhadla Solar Park, Has 2,245 MW, 10 Million Solar Panels and Occupies an Area of 5 Thousand Hectares: https://www.world-energy.org/article/41570.html

Wu, B., Han, S., Shin, K. G., & Lu, W. (2018). Application of artificial neural networks in design of lithium-ion batteries. *Journal of Power Sources*, 395, 128–136. DOI: 10.1016/j.jpowsour.2018.05.040

Wu, B., He, X., Chen, Y., Nie, L., Zheng, K., & Ye, Y. (2022). Modeling product's visual and functional characteristics for recommender systems. *IEEE Transactions on Knowledge and Data Engineering*, 34(3), 1330–1343. DOI: 10.1109/TKDE.2020.2991793

Wu, J., Kong, L., Cheng, Z., Yang, Y., & Zuo, H. (2022). RUL Prediction for Lithium Batteries Using a Novel Ensemble Learning Method. *Energy Reports*, 8, 313–326. DOI: 10.1016/j.egyr.2022.10.298

Wu, N., & Wang, H. (2018). Deep learning adaptive dynamic programming for real time energy management and control strategy of micro-grid. *Journal of Cleaner Production*, 204, 1169–1177. DOI: 10.1016/j.jclepro.2018.09.052

Wu, Q., Zhao, P., & Cui, Z. (2020). Visual and textual jointly enhanced interpretable fashion recommendation. *IEEE Access : Practical Innovations, Open Solutions*, 8, 68736–68746. DOI: 10.1109/ACCESS.2020.2978272

Wu, W., Hasegawa, T., Ohashi, H., Hanasaki, N., Liu, J., Matsui, T., Fujimori, S., Masui, T., & Takahashi, K. (2019). Global advanced bioenergy potential under environmental protection policies and societal transformation measures. *Global Change Biology. Bioenergy*, 11(9), 1041–1055. DOI: 10.1111/gcbb.12614

Wu, Y., Tan, H., Peng, J., Zhang, H., & He, H. (2019). Deep reinforcement learning of energy management with continuous control strategy and traffic information for a series-parallel plug-in hybrid electric bus. *Applied Energy*, 247, 454–466. DOI: 10.1016/j.apenergy.2019.04.021

Xiang, Z., Fung, K., & Ng, K. (2019). Food Product Design: A Hybrid Machine Learning and Mechanistic Modeling Approach. *Industrial & Engineering Chemistry Research*, 58(36), 16743–16752. Advance online publication. DOI: 10.1021/acs.iecr.9b02462

Xi, L., Chen, J., Huang, Y., Xue, T., Zhang, T., & Zhang, Y. (2018). Smart generation control based on deep reinforcement learning with the ability of action self-optimization. *Sci Sin Inf*, 48(10), 1430–1449. DOI: 10.1360/N112018-00072

Xing, Y., Ma, E. W. M., Tsui, K. L., & Pecht, M. Battery Management Systems in Electric and Hybrid Vehicles. *Energies,* 2011, vol.*4*, p.1840-1857. https://doi.org/ DOI: 10.3390/en4111840

Xin, L., Haizhi, W., Yuanru, L., & Wanlin, L. (2021). A critical survey on renewable energy applications in the Philippines and China: Present challenges and perspectives. *Frontiers in Energy Research*, •••, 724892.

Xinmei, W., Aijun, X., & Tingting, Y. (2020). Passive Measurement Method of Tree Height and Crown Diameter Using a Smartphone. *IEEE Access : Practical Innovations, Open Solutions*, 8, 11669–11678. DOI: 10.1109/ACCESS.2020.2965216

Xiong, N., Du, Y., & Huang, L. (2024). Provably safe reinforcement learning with step-wise violation constraints. *Advances in Neural Information Processing Systems*, •••, 36.

Xiong, T., Bao, Y., Hu, Z., & Chiong, R. (2015). Forecasting interval time series using a fully complex-valued RBF neural network with DPSO and PSO algorithms. *Information Sciences*, 305, 77–92. DOI: 10.1016/j.ins.2015.01.029

Xi, Z., Wang, R., Fu, Y., & Mi, C. (2022). Accurate and reliable state of charge estimation of lithium ion batteries using time-delayed recurrent neural networks through the identification of overexcited neurons. *Applied Energy*, 305, 117962. DOI: 10.1016/j.apenergy.2021.117962

Xu, L., Sanders, L., Li, K., & Chow, J. (2021, November 29). Chatbot for Health Care and Oncology Applications Using Artificial Intelligence and Machine Learning: Systematic Review. *JMIR Cancer*, 7(4), e27850–e27850. DOI: 10.2196/27850 PMID: 34847056

Xu, X., Tang, S., Han, X., Lu, L., Wu, Y., Yu, C., Sun, X., Xie, J., Feng, X., & Ouyang, M. (2023). Fast capacity prediction of lithium-ion batteries using aging mechanism-informed bidirectional long short-term memory network. *Reliability Engineering & System Safety*, 234, 109185. DOI: 10.1016/j.ress.2023.109185

Yadav, P., Mishra, A., & Kim, S. (2023). A comprehensive survey on multi-agent reinforcement learning for connected and automated vehicles. *Sensors (Basel)*, 23(10), 4710. DOI: 10.3390/s23104710 PMID: 37430623

Yagang, Z., Zhiya, P., Hui, W., Jingchao, W., Zheng, Z., & Fei, W. (2023). Achieving wind power and photovoltaic power prediction: An intelligent prediction system based on a deep learning approach. *Energy*, •••, 129005.

Yang, C., Letourneau, S., Liu, J., Cheng, Q., & Yang, Y. (2017). Machine learning-based methods for TTF estimation with application to APU prognostics. *Applied Intelligence*, 46(1), 227–239. DOI: 10.1007/s10489-016-0829-4

Yang, C., Sun, Y., Ladubec, C., & Liu, Y. (2020). Developing machine learning based models for railway inspection. *Applied Sciences (Basel, Switzerland)*, 11(1), 13. DOI: 10.3390/app11010013

Yang, Y., Jiang, Y., Liu, Y., Chen, J., & Li, S. E. (2023). Model-free safe reinforcement learning through neural barrier certificate. *IEEE Robotics and Automation Letters*, 8(3), 1295–1302. DOI: 10.1109/LRA.2023.3238656

Yao, Z., Lum, Y., Johnston, A., Mejia-Mendoza, L. M., Zhou, X., Wen, Y., Aspuru-Guzik, A., Sargent, E. H., & Seh, Z. W. (2023). Machine learning for a sustainable energy future. *Nature Reviews. Materials*, 8(3), 202–215. DOI: 10.1038/s41578-022-00490-5 PMID: 36277083

Yassine, S., & Gammoudi, M. M. (2023). Trends and Challenges of Arabic Chatbots : Literature Review. *Jordanian Journal of Computers and Information Technology*, 09(03), 261–286.

Ye, J., & Dela, E. (2023). The effect of green investment and green financing on sustainable business performance of foreign chemical industries operating in Indonesia: The mediating role of corporate social responsibility. *Sustainability (Basel)*, 15(14), 11218. DOI: 10.3390/su151411218

Yeng, P. K., Fauzi, M. A., Sun, L., & Yang, B. (2022). Assessing the legal aspects of information security requirements for health care in 3 countries: Scoping review and framework development. *JMIR Human Factors*, 9(2), e30050. DOI: 10.2196/30050 PMID: 35612891

Ye, X., He, Y., Zhang, M., Fournier-Viger, P., & Huang, J. Z. (2023). A novel correlation Gaussian process regression-based extreme learning machine. *Knowledge and Information Systems*, 65(5), 2017–2042. DOI: 10.1007/s10115-022-01803-4 PMID: 36683607

Ying, L., Gao, T., Dai, M., & Hu, P. (2017). Investigation of interfacial heat transfer mechanism for 7075-T6 aluminum alloy in HFQ hot forming process. *Applied Thermal Engineering*, 118, 266–282. Advance online publication. DOI: 10.1016/j.applthermaleng.2017.02.107

Yi, X., Yao, J., Wang, X., & Xie, X. (2023). Unpacking the Ethical Value Alignment in Big Models. *Journal of Computer Research and Development*, 60(9), 1926–1945. DOI: 10.7544/issn1000-1239.202330553

Yoldas, Y., Goren, S., & Onen, A. (2020). Optimal Control of Microgrids with Multi-stage Mixed-integer Nonlinear Programming Guided Q -learning Algorithm. *Journal of Modern Power Systems and Clean Energy*, 8(6), 1151–1159. DOI: 10.35833/MPCE.2020.000506

Young, J. C., & Shishido, M. (2023). Investigating OpenAI's ChatGPT Potentials in Generating Chatbot's Dialogue for English as a Foreign Language Learning. *International Journal of Advanced Computer Science and Applications*, 14(6). Advance online publication. DOI: 10.14569/IJACSA.2023.0140607

Yuan, C., Duan, W., Ding, Z., & Li, Y. (2022). Battery Life Prediction Based on a Hybrid Support Vector Regression Model. *Frontiers in Energy Research*, 10, •••. https://www.frontiersin.org/articles/10.3389/fenrg.2022.899804

Yuan, G., Wang, H., Khazaei, E., & Khan, B. (2021). Collaborative advanced machine learning techniques in optimal energy management of hybrid AC/DC IoT-based microgrids. *Ad Hoc Networks*, 122, 102657. DOI: 10.1016/j.adhoc.2021.102657

Yuan, K., Huang, Y., Yang, S., Wu, M., Cao, D., Chen, Q., & Chen, H. (2024). Evolutionary Decision-Making and Planning for Autonomous Driving: A Hybrid Augmented Intelligence Framework. *IEEE Transactions on Intelligent Transportation Systems*, 25(7), 7339–7351. DOI: 10.1109/TITS.2023.3349198

Zagheni, E., & Weber, I. (2015). Demographic research with non-representative internet data. *International Journal of Manpower*, 36(1), 13–25. DOI: 10.1108/IJM-12-2014-0261

Zala, K., Thakkar, H. K., Dholakia, N., Shukla, M., & Thumar, D. (2024). Designing an Attribute-Based Encryption Scheme with an Enhanced Anonymity Model for Privacy Protection in E-Health. *SN Computer Science*, 5(2), 203. DOI: 10.1007/s42979-023-02541-2

Zastudil, C., Rogalska, M., Kapp, C., Vaughn, J., & MacNeil, S. (2023). Generative AI in Computing Education: Perspectives of Students and Instructors. *2023 IEEE Frontiers in Education Conference (FIE)*, 1–9. DOI: 10.1109/FIE58773.2023.10343467

Zazoum, B. (2023). Lithium-ion battery state of charge prediction based on machine learning approach. *Energy Reports*, 9, 1152–1158. DOI: 10.1016/j.egyr.2023.03.091

Zekun, W., Bulathwela, S., & Koshiyama, A. S. (2023). *Towards Auditing Large Language Models: Improving Text-based Stereotype Detection*. http://arxiv.org/abs/2311.14126

Zenati, A., Desprez, P., Razik, H., & Rael, S. (2010). *Impedance Measurements combined with the Fuzzy Logic methodology to assess the SOC and SOH of Lithium-ion Cells*. VPPC., DOI: 10.1109/VPPC.2010.5729069

Zenisek, J., Holzinger, F., & Affenzeller, M. (2019). Machine learning based concept drift detection for predictive maintenance. *Computers & Industrial Engineering*, 137, 106031. DOI: 10.1016/j.cie.2019.106031

Zhai, X., Chu, X., Chai, C. S., Jong, M. S. Y., Istenic, A., Spector, M., Liu, J.-B., Yuan, J., & Li, Y. (2021). A review of artificial intelligence (AI) in education from 2010 to 2020. *Complexity*, 2021(1), 8812542. DOI: 10.1155/2021/8812542

Zhan, H., & Lin, J. Anchorage, AK, USA (2021), pp. 2663–2667. DOI: DOI: 10.1109/ICIP42928.2021.9506344

Zhang, C., He, Y., Yuan, L., Xiang, S., & Wang, J. (2015). Prognostics of Lithium-Ion Batteries Based on Wavelet Denoising and DE-RVM. *Computational Intelligence and Neuroscience*, 2015, 8. DOI: 10.1155/2015/918305 PMID: 26413090

Zhang, D., Schilder, F., Conrad, J. G., Makrehchi, M., von Rickenbach, D., & Moulinier, I. (2023). Making a computational attorney. *Proceedings of the 2023 SIAM International Conference on Data Mining (SDM)*, 965–968. DOI: 10.1137/1.9781611977653.ch111

Zhang, E., Zhang, R., & Masoud, N. (2023). Predictive trajectory planning for autonomous vehicles at intersections using reinforcement learning. *Transportation Research Part C, Emerging Technologies*, 149, 104063. DOI: 10.1016/j.trc.2023.104063

Zhang, H., Huang, W., Liu, L., & Chow, T. W. S. (2020). Learning to match clothing from textual feature-based compatible relationships. *IEEE Transactions on Industrial Informatics*, 16(11), 6750–6759. DOI: 10.1109/TII.2019.2924725

Zhang, L., Xu, M., Chen, H., Li, Y., & Chen, S. (2023). Globalization, green economy and environmental challenges: State of the art review for practical implications. Front. *Financial and Trade Globalization. Greener Technologies and Energy Transition*, 16648714, 133.

Zhang, L., Zhang, Q., Shen, L., Yuan, B., Wang, X., & Tao, D. (2023, June). Evaluating model-free reinforcement learning toward safety-critical tasks. *Proceedings of the AAAI Conference on Artificial Intelligence*, 37(12), 15313–15321. DOI: 10.1609/aaai.v37i12.26786 PMID: 38464961

Zhang, S., Zhai, B., Guo, X., Wang, K., Peng, N., & Zhang, X. (2019). Synchronous estimation of state of health and remaining useful lifetime for lithium-ion battery using the incremental capacity and artificial neural networks. *Journal of Energy Storage*, 26, 100951. DOI: 10.1016/j.est.2019.100951

Zhang, Y., Liang, X., Li, D., Ge, S. S., Gao, B., Chen, H., & Lee, T. H. (2023). Adaptive safe reinforcement learning with full-state constraints and constrained adaptation for autonomous vehicles. *IEEE Transactions on Cybernetics*. PMID: 37363853

Zhang, Z. H., Zeng, S., & Jiang, D. J. (2022). Analysis and Improvement of the Q-iteration Method. [). IOP Publishing.]. *Journal of Physics: Conference Series*, 2147(1), 012005. DOI: 10.1088/1742-6596/2147/1/012005

Zhang, Z., Han, S., Wang, J., & Miao, F. (2023, May). Spatial-temporal-aware safe multi-agent reinforcement learning of connected autonomous vehicles in challenging scenarios. In *2023 IEEE International Conference on Robotics and Automation (ICRA)* (pp. 5574-5580). IEEE. DOI: 10.1109/ICRA48891.2023.10161216

Zhan, H., Lin, J., Ak, K. E., Shi, B., Duan, L. Y., & Kot, A. C. (2022). A^3A^3-FKG: Attentive attribute-aware fashion knowledge graph for outfit preference prediction. *IEEE Transactions on Multimedia*, 24, 819–831. DOI: 10.1109/TMM.2021.3059514

Zhao, W., He, T., Chen, R., Wei, T., & Liu, C. (2023). State-wise safe reinforcement learning: A survey. *arXiv preprint arXiv:2302.03122*. DOI: 10.24963/ijcai.2023/763

Zhao, J., Zhao, W., Deng, B., Wang, Z., Zhang, F., Zheng, W., & Burke, A. F. (2023). Autonomous driving system: A comprehensive survey. *Expert Systems with Applications*, •••, 122836.

Zhao, Q., Qin, X., Zhao, H., & Feng, W. (2018). A Novel Prediction Method Based on the Support Vector Regression for the Remaining Useful Life of Lithium-Ion Batteries. *Microelectronics and Reliability*, 85, 99–108. DOI: 10.1016/j.microrel.2018.04.007

Zhao, W., Zhang, H., Zheng, J., Dai, Y., Huang, L., Shang, W., & Liang, Y. (2021). A point prediction method based automatic machine learning for day-ahead power output of multi-region photovoltaic plants. *Energy*, 223, 120026. DOI: 10.1016/j.energy.2021.120026

Zheng, H., Chen, C., Li, S., Zheng, S., Li, S. E., Xu, Q., & Wang, J. (2023). Learning-based safe control for robot and autonomous vehicle using efficient safety certificate. *IEEE Open Journal of Intelligent Transportation Systems*, 4, 419–430. DOI: 10.1109/OJITS.2023.3280573

Zhong, L. (2020) Edge-based fashion detection by transfer learning 5th International Conference on Mechanical, Control and Computer Engineering (ICMCCE), Harbin, China, Vol. 2020, pp. 2132–2136. DOI: DOI: 10.1109/ICMCCE51767.2020.00464

Zhou, L., Lai, X., Li, B., Yao, Y., Yuan, M., Weng, J., & Zheng, Y. (2023). State Estimation Models of Lithium-Ion Batteries for Battery Management System: Status, Challenges, and Future Trends. *Batteries*, 9(2), 131. DOI: 10.3390/batteries9020131

Zhou, P., He, Z., Han, T., Li, X., Lai, X., Yan, L., Lv, T., Xie, J., & Zheng, Y. (2020). A rapid classification method of the retired LiCoxNiyMn1 x yO2 batteries for electric vehicles. *Energy Reports*, 6, 672–683. DOI: 10.1016/j.egyr.2020.03.013

Zhou, T., Han, G., Li, B. N., Lin, Z., Ciaccio, E. J., Green, P. H., & Qin, J. (2017). Quantitative analysis of patients with celiac disease by video capsule endoscopy: A deep learning method. *Computers in Biology and Medicine*, 85, 1–6. DOI: 10.1016/j.compbiomed.2017.03.031 PMID: 28412572

Zhou, X., Hsieh, S. J., Peng, B., & Hsieh, D. (2017). Cycle life estimation of lithium-ion polymer batteries using artificial neural network and support vector machine with time-resolved thermography. *Microelectronics and Reliability*, 79, 48–58. DOI: 10.1016/j.microrel.2017.10.013

Zhu, G., Sun, T., Xu, Y., Zheng, Y., & Zhou, L. (2023). Identification of Internal Short-Circuit Faults in Lithium-Ion Batteries Based on a Multi-Machine Learning Fusion. *Batteries.*, 9(3), 154. DOI: 10.3390/batteries9030154

Zhu, L., Mou, W., Lai, Y., Lin, J., & Luo, P. (2024). Language and cultural bias in AI: Comparing the performance of large language models developed in different countries on Traditional Chinese Medicine highlights the need for localized models. *Journal of Translational Medicine*, 22(1), 319. DOI: 10.1186/s12967-024-05128-4 PMID: 38553705

Zhu, S., Zhao, N., & Sha, J. (2019). Predicting battery life with early cyclic data by machine learning. *Energy Storage*, 1(6), 1–5. DOI: 10.1002/est2.98

Ziyilluo, X. Y., Yingxue, W., Weidi, L., Silang, L., Yuankun, Z., Zihan, H., Hong, Z., Shuming, D., Jie, X., Jiachen, T., Kui, X., Xiowang, Z., Wenbin, H., & Yida, D. (2020).. . *Frontiers in Energy Research*, 8, 1–12. DOI: 10.3389/fenrg.2020.00001

Zou, Q., Qu, K., Luo, Y., Yin, D., Ju, Y., & Tang, H. (2018). Predicting Diabetes Mellitus With Machine Learning Techniques. *Frontiers in Genetics*, 9, 515. Advance online publication. DOI: 10.3389/fgene.2018.00515 PMID: 30459809

Zubani, M., Sigalini, L., Serina, I., Putelli, L., Gerevini, A. E., & Chiari, M. (2022). A performance comparison of different cloud-based natural language understanding services for an Italian e-learning platform. *Future Internet*, 14(2), 62. DOI: 10.3390/fi14020062

# About the Contributors

**Muhammad Syafrudin** received the bachelor's degree from Universitas Islam Negeri Sunan Kalijaga at Yogyakarta, Yogyakarta, Indonesia, in 2013, and the Ph.D. degree from Dongguk University, Seoul, South Korea, in 2019. He has been an Assistant Professor with the Department of Artificial Intelligence, Sejong University, Seoul, since March 2022. Previously, he worked as an Assistant Professor with the Department of Industrial and Systems Engineering, Dongguk University, from 2019 to 2022. He is also an Instructor in a practical course on undergraduate topics in linear algebra, programming languages, databases, and big data systems. He has published numerous research articles in several international peer-reviewed journals, including Expert Systems with Applications, IEEE Access, Food Control, Sensors, and Mathematics. His research interests include industrial artificial intelligence (IAI), industrial analytics (IA), industrial informatics (II), the Industrial Internet of Things (IIoT), and industrial big data (IBD), ranging from theory to design and implementation. He is a Reviewer for well-known journals, such as Expert Systems with Applications, IEEE Transactions on Industrial Informatics, Computers & Industrial Engineering, and Algorithms. He has served as the guest editor for Scopus-and-Sciences Citation Index (SCI)-indexed journals.

**Norma Latif Fitriyani** has been an assistant professor at Sejong University, since March 2022. Norma Latif Fitriyani received the B.Eng. from the UIN Sunan Kalijaga in 2014, the Master of Information Management from the National Taiwan University of Science and Technology in 2016, and the Doctor of Engineering from Dongguk University in 2021. Norma Latif Fitriyani is also the director of the Data Driven Decisions Lab, focusing on the application of data mining and analysis, health informatics, machine learning, statistical learning, image processing, and artificial intelligence.

***

**Mussa S Abubakari** is a Postgraduate student at Sultan Hassanal Bolkiah Institute of Education, Universiti Brunei Darussalam. Before this, in 2022, he used to be an instructor in the Department of Physics and Mathematics at Kondoa Islamic Secondary School, Tanzania. Mr. Mussa obtained a Master's degree of Education in Electronics and Informatics Engineering at Yogyakarta State University, Indonesia, in July 2021. Moreover, he obtained his BSc. in Telecommunications Engineering at the University of Dodoma in June 2016. His academic and research interests include educational technology, technology-enhanced learning, technology acceptance, open and distance (online) learning, and digital competence, among others. He has over 13 journal articles published in internationally indexed journals and papers presented at international conferences.

**Yabit Alas** received his MA in Linguistics at the University of Hawaii at Manoa and PhD in Malay Language and Linguistics at University Kebangsaan Malaysia. He is currently the Director of the Language Centre, University Brunei Darussalam and Deputy Lead of ICE. He has held key positions in the University including Head of the Malay Language and Linguistics, Director of the Continuing Education Centre, and Dean of the Faculty of Arts and Social Sciences. He set up and became the first director of the Borneo Studies Network (BSN) (2014-2016), whose interest is to enhance research on Borneo as well as to promote various research institutions in Borneo. His main area of expertise is Comparative Linguistics, specifically among Austronesian Languages. He has been researching mostly the Dusunic Languages spoken in North Borneo. He has also been doing research on Malay languages especially Standard Malay and its relevance to globalisation. He is directly involved in the planning and implementation of the Malay language in Brunei as well as in Malaysia and Indonesia, as a member of the Language Council of Brunei, Indonesia and Malaysia (Mabbim). He has published in Malay and English. Examples include his co-edited volumes in English: Reflections in Borneo Rivers: Essays in Honour of Professor James T. Collins: Book I, Reflections in Southeast Asian Seas, Essays in Honour of Professor James T. Collins: Book II, and International Migration in Southeast Asia: Continuities and Discontinuities. Several of his recent publications also cover ICT and education.

**Bidisha Bhabani** is currently working as an Assistant Professor in the department of CSE at JIS University, Agarpara, Kolkata. She has 1 year of Industry experience and more than 10 years of teaching and research experience. She has 1 year of Industry experience and more than 10 years of teaching and research experience.

**Saurabh Chandra** is an accomplished legal scholar and currently serves as an Associate Professor & Assistant Dean at the School of Law, Bennett University, India. With a robust academic foundation, he earned his Bachelor of Arts and Bachelor of Laws (B.A. LL.B.) from the prestigious Aligarh Muslim University (A.M.U.). He further specialized in Business Laws, completing his Master of Laws (LL.M.) at the renowned National Law School of India University (NLSIU), Bangalore. Dr. Chandra's academic journey culminated in a Doctorate in Law (Ph.D.) from the esteemed National Law University (NLU) Delhi.Dr. Saurabh Chandra also holds a master's degree in Management with specialization in Human Resources in Management and another in Journalism and Mass Communication. With 16 years of teaching experience, he has established himself as an expert in Business Laws, with numerous publications to his credit. Dr. Saurabh Chandra is an expert in Business Laws, with a profound understanding of the intricate legal frameworks that govern the business world.Dr. Chandra brings a wealth of experience in Academic Administration, having successfully held various key administrative positions.

**G.Manikandan** received a B.E degree in Computer Science and Engineering from Madras University, M.E degree in Computer Science & Engineering from Sathyabama University, Post Graduate Diploma in Geo Spatial Information Technology from Periyar Maniammai University, the M.B.A degree in HR from Tamil Nadu Open University, Ph.D degree in Computer Science & Engineering at Sathyabama University. He is having more than 23 years of Valuable in-depth and extensive experience in Academics, Research & Development, and Administration. He is Currently working as a Professor in Department of Artificial intelligence and Data Science at RMK ENGINEERING COLLEGE RSM Nagar, Kavaraipettai, Gummidipoondi Taluk, Tiruvallur District, Tamil Nadu, India.. He completed the Post-doctoral Research in the topic of Enhanced AI Based machine learning model for an accurate segmentation and classification method & under the guidance of Dr. Bui Thanh Hung, Artificial Intelligence Laboratory, Faculty of Information Technology, Industrial University of Ho Chi Minh City VIETNAM. He is having more than seven patterns and one Copyright on different topics. He has published more than 36 Research papers in Scopus / SCI / WoS Journals and more than 32 Research papers presented in different National and International level Conferences. His area of interest includes Data mining, Spatial Databases, Geographic Information Systems and intelligent Transportation Systems, Artificial Intelligence, and Machine Learning.

**M. Robinson Joel** received the Doctorate Ph.D degree in Computer and Information Technology from the Manonmaniam Sundaranar University, Tirunelveli in March 2019. He completed his M.Tech and MCA from the same university year

2008 and 2002 respectively. He is currently working as an Associate Professor in the Department of Computer Science and Engineering at KCG College of Technology, Chennai. He has 16 years of teaching experience. He has published more than 50 papers in SCI/Scopus/IEEE Conference/Book Chapter / International Journals etc.

**Laeeq Razzak Janjua** is a finance professional working in a, compliance, and academia, whose journey is characterized by dedication, expertise, and a commitment to excellence. Mr. Janjua's academic prowess is reflected in his extensive body of work, which includes the publication of a book on corporate social responsibility as co-author and over 40 academic research papers. These contributions have solidified his reputation as a thought leader and a respected authority in his field, earning him recognition and acclaim from peers and scholars alike. Currently serving as a Compliance Officer at TMF Group, Mr. Janjua brings a wealth of experience and expertise to his role, where he navigates the complex landscape of regulatory requirements with precision and proficiency. In addition to his role at TMF Group, Mr. Janjua also serves as a lecturer at WSB University in Poland, where he imparts his knowledge and insights to the next generation of professionals. Prior to his current roles, Mr. Janjua amassed over 10 years of invaluable experience in the financial industry, having worked with esteemed institutions such as Citi Bank, MoneyGram Payment International, and BNP Paribas. Driven by a passion for excellence and a dedication to making a positive impact, Mr. Janjua continues to be a guiding force in the fields of compliance and academia. His unwavering commitment to integrity, coupled with his extensive knowledge and experience, positions him as a leader and a trailblazer in his field, shaping the future of compliance and corporate social responsibility.

**K.Thrisha** pursuing Ph. D under the guidance of Dr.R.Saratha, Professor, Department of Chemistry, Avinashilingam Institute for Home Science and Higher Education for Women. She is working in the Na-ion Batteries. She is availing the Savitribai Jyotirao Single Girl Child Fellowship granted by University Grants Commission (UGC).

**Christian Kaunert** is Professor of International Security at Dublin City University, Ireland. He is also Professor of Policing and Security, as well as Director of the International Centre for Policing and Security at the University of South Wales. In addition, he is Jean Monnet Chair, Director of the Jean Monnet Centre of Excellence and Director of the Jean Monnet Network on EU Counter-Terrorism (www.eucter.net).

**Souraneel Mandal** is actively engaged in research focused on addressing critical legal issues concerning gender-based violence and exploitation. Our work delves into various provisions of the Indian Penal Code (IPC), including IPC 304B (dowry death), IPC 498A (domestic violence), IPC 354A (sexual violence), IPC 370 & 370A (women trafficking), IPC 354D (stalking), IPC 354 & 364B (assault to outrage modesty), and IPC 326A (acid attack). Through our research, My aim is to support law enforcement and legal frameworks, contributing to creating a safer society for women and vulnerable individuals. Our mission is to help raise awareness, improve legal policies, and make the world a better place through his dedication to social justice.

**Saloni Mishra** is working in Manav Rachna University. She has completed her Ba. LLB. in 2023 with 9.19 CGPA and just after that she pursued LLM with scholarship in Criminal Law and completed it with 9.35 CGPA. during these years she got more interested in Research and done several Researches over Modern Trends of investigation and effect of digitalisation . Attended many conferences.

**IR. Kotteeswaran** is an accomplished researcher and Associate Professor at St. Joseph's College of Engineering in Chennai, India. He earned his Bachelor of Engineering in Instrumentation and Control from the University of Madras, Tamil Nadu, in 1999 and his Master of Engineering in Instrumentation and Control from the National Institute of Technical Teachers' Training and Research, Chandigarh, in 2003. Dr. Kotteeswaran completed his Ph.D. at Anna University, Chennai, in 2015, focusing on the optimization of multivariable PID controllers for coal gasifiers. With a robust academic background and extensive research experience, Dr. Kotteeswaran has published 23 research papers in reputed international journals. His areas of expertise encompass system identification, soft computing techniques, optimization algorithms, and multivariable systems.

**R. Saratha** M.Sc., M.Ed., M.Phil, Ph.D is a Professor in Chemistry, at Avinashilingam Institute for Home Science and Higher Education for Women, Bharathi Park Road, Coimbatore, Tamil Nadu. She has a teaching experience of 36 years and teaches General Chemistry (for UG) and Thermodynamics, Electrochemistry, Chemical Kinetics, Industrial Chemistry, Environmental Chemistry and Research Methodology (for PG). She is a recognized research guide and her areas of research specialization include Corrosion Inhibitors, Biodiesel studies, Electrochemical Energy Storage device; she has so far guided more than 50 students across M.Sc, M.Phil and Ph.D researches. At present she is working in the field of energy storage devices and is supervising 4 candidates in the field. She has completed one major project funded by DST to the tune of Rs. 30,39,600; published 2 books and 4 book chapters and more than 100 articles in various National/ International Journals and in conference proceedings. She has participated in more than 150 National/ International level Conferences, seminars, workshops and presented papers. She is a reviewer of 12 journals.

**Anjali Raghav** is a legal professional and accomplished academic, currently a Research Scholar at the Sharda School of Law, Sharda University, Greater Noida, India. With a solid educational foundation, she holds a Master in Law from Sharda School of Law, where she cultivated her expertise in Criminal Law, Intellectual Property Rights, Artificial Intelligence, Machine Learning, Blockchain Technology, Sustainable Energy, etc. Her three years of experience as a criminal practicing lawyer have equipped her with practical legal insights that she seamlessly integrates into her academic and editorial endeavors. She has a robust portfolio of publications in esteemed journals and books, reflecting her dedication to contributing to the body of knowledge in her fields of interest. Her research has been recognized on various platforms, as evidenced by her participation in national and international conferences, seminars, webinars, and symposiums. Also, in her academic and research pursuits, Anjali is a skilled editor, having successfully overseen the editorial process of several publications.

**R. Vinston Raja** is an Assistant Professor in the Department of Computational Intelligence in SRM Institute of Science and Technology with 15 years of teaching experience. He completed his PhD in the area of Deep Learning at Sathyabama Institute of Science and Technology. He also completed his M.Tech IT at Sathyabama University in 2012. Before becoming a Assistant professor, he worked as a Software Developer at Dexter Matrix Solution from 2007 to 2009. Dr. Raja's areas of interest are IOT with Wireless Sensor Networks, Robotics and Artificial Intelligence. He was awarded the Best Teacher Award in the academic year 2017-2018. He has experience in guiding student development projects and has presented many research papers at International and National Conferences. Additionally, he has published ten papers in International and National Journals and ten Anna University Curriculum textbooks.

**S. Nalini** currently working as an Assistant Professor in the Department of Computing Technologies, School of Computing, SRM Institute of Science and Technology, Kattankulathur, Chennai. She awarded Ph.D in Anna University, Chennai. She earned a Silver Medal for completing her M.E. (Computer Science and Engineering) at Vinayaka Missions University, Salem. She has published more papers in referred journals and international conference proceedings. She has supervised more than 30 undergraduate and 10 post graduate students. She has acted as co-investigator in many funding agencies like CSIR, DST, DRDO and organized many workshops, symposiums and technical events for the benefit of students, faculty members and research scholars. Her field of specialization includes Machine learning, Deep learning, Quantum Computing and Quantum Machine Learning.

**Elango Subramani** is currently serving as the Director at SHF Design Engineering Private Limited Company in India. Having accumulated more than 18+ years of extensive international experience and a vast amount of knowledge in the power sector. He is Currently pursuing a Doctor of Philosophy at Periyar University. He had earned a Bachelor of Engineering Degree in Electrical & Electronics Engineering from Anna University, followed by an MBA Degree in Project Management from Alagappa University. Completed a Post Graduate degree in Electrical Safety and Safety Management from Annamalai University. He Obtained Lean Six Sigma Black Belt certification and also received accreditation as Charted Engineer from the Institution of Engineers.

**Bhupinder Singh** working as Professor at Sharda University, India. Also, Honorary Professor in University of South Wales UK and Santo Tomas University Tunja, Colombia. His areas of publications as Smart Healthcare, Medicines, fuzzy logics, artificial intelligence, robotics, machine learning, deep learning, federated learning, IoT, PV Glasses, metaverse and many more. He has 3 books, 139 paper publications, 163 paper presentations in international/national conferences and seminars, participated in more than 40 workshops/FDP's/QIP's, 25 courses from international universities of repute, organized more than 59 events with international and national academicians and industry people's, editor-in-chief and co-editor in journals, developed new courses. He has given talks at international universities, resource person in international conferences such as in Nanyang Technological University Singapore, Tashkent State University of Law Uzbekistan; KIMEP University Kazakhstan, All'ah meh Tabatabi University Iran, the Iranian Association of International Criminal law, Iran and Hague Center for International Law and Investment, The Netherlands, Northumbria University Newcastle UK,

**T. Chandrasekar**, a distinguished professional with a Ph.D. in Management Studies from Anna University, Chennai, currently leads as the Head of Business Administration at Kalasalingam Academy of Research and Education, India. With a Six Sigma Black Belt certification from MSME, he brings over 18 years of teaching experience. Author of three impactful textbooks, he has 16 publications in Scopus indexed journals, holds a patent, and serves as a Reasoner for MoUs with MSME. His expertise spans Operation Management, Strategic Management, Human Resource Management, Marketing Management, Lean Six Sigma, Control System, and Digital Signal Processing. Formerly the Controller of Examinations at an autonomous institution, he exhibits administrative powers and a commitment to academic excellence.

**Dhanalakshmi Teekaraman** received her doctoral degree in 2020 from Anna University, Chennai. She received an Anna Centenary Research Fellowship during her research tenure. Her areas of expertise are Social Web Mining, Data Analytics, Fuzzy Logic, Recommendation Engine, and NLP. She has 17+ years of experience in the academic industry. She has more than 10 publications in international journals and conferences, in her credit. She has been a Reviewer of the Journal of Intelligent Fuzzy Systems since 2019, reviewing more than 10 articles and reviewing the Microsoft CMT conferences. She is a co-supervisor from the year 2023.

**Francois Yonga** obtained a diploma in technical and vocational education and training in 2011, specializing in electrical engineering, followed by a Master's degree in 2016, specializing in electronics, electrical engineering, and automation (EEA), from the University of Ngaoundéré, Cameroon. He obtained his PhD in the field of energy and the environment, in particular renewable energy. He is the Head of a Technical Secondary School Department and teaches in the Renewable Energy Department of the Faculty of Science at the University of Garoua (Cameroon). He has more than 15 years of teaching and research experience. He has published several research articles and contributed to books in various journals. His research interests include renewable energy, power quality optimization, artificial intelligence, data science and robotics, and power electronics. He is a reviewer for several peer-reviewed journals. He also works as a consultant for several local and international organizations.

# Index

## A



## B



## C

## D



## E



## F



## G



## J



## L

# M

## N



## P



## R



## S

## T



## U



## W

www.ingramcontent.com/pod-product-compliance
Lightning Source LLC
LaVergne TN
LVHW080614300926
849162LV00005B/1149